THE ROUGH GUIDE TO
LANGUEDOC
& ROUSSILLON

Written and researched by
Brian Catl

This edition u
Victoria Tr

**ROUGH
GUIDES**

Contents

Introduction to
Languedoc and Roussillon

Languedoc and Roussillon, down in the far south of France, offer a wide range of dramatically different experiences. The star of the show is undoubtedly the 240km Canal du Midi, one of seven UNESCO World Heritage Sites in the area, which in 2016 celebrated the 350th anniversary of the start of its construction. Then there are the major cities: Toulouse, capital of the new Occitanie region and HQ of Europe's aviation industry; and Montpellier, whose striking modern neighbourhoods and cutting-edge architecture sit in stark contrast to the narrow streets and tree-shaded squares of its delightful medieval old town. The region's wealth of delicious seafood, charming fishing villages and glorious beaches, meanwhile, comes courtesy of its 215km of coastline; and both here and inland, the Mediterranean climate provides the perfect conditions for producing some of the country's oldest and best-known wines.

In and around **Nîmes**, you'll find several examples of the finest **Roman remains** in existence, which are celebrated in the city's new Musée de la Romanité; while about 50km to the south lies **Port Camargue**, the largest pleasure-port in Europe and a magnet for watersports enthusiasts. In medieval times, the hills of **Aude** and **Ariège** offered the perfect hiding places for the **Cathar heretics**; their ruined vertiginous castles, including **Montségur**, still pierce the skyline, and are must-sees. Yet even away from the tourist hotspots, you'll encounter remote villages and wild landscapes that afford an invaluable window onto a vanishing European rural culture. Then factor in the more than twenty **ski** and **spa** resorts, six regional natural parks and huge network of **walking** and **cycling** routes – and you have a strong case for Languedoc and Roussillon together forming the most enticing and intriguing patch of the country.

ABOVE THE GRANDES CAUSSES **RIGHT** MONTPELLIER OLD TOWN

THE CANAL DU MIDI

In the 1660s a local tax-collector, **Paul Riquet**, dreamed of bringing prosperity back to Languedoc by building a **canal** to link it to the Mediterranean and the Atlantic. This mammoth undertaking was the most ambitious and complex civic engineering project since the time of the Romans. Although it bankrupted the visionary Riquet, who did not live to see its inauguration, by 1856 the canal was carrying one million passengers and more than 100,000 tonnes of freight per year. Struck down into sudden obsolescence by the invention of the steam engine, the canal system languished in disrepair for over a century, before being resurrected in the last few decades as a tourist attraction. The quintessential Languedoc experience is to **boat**, **walk** or **cycle** along Riquet's canal, travelling at an easy pace, the tree-lined banks providing shelter from the same sun that ripens up the region's famous grapes.

Yet while its charms are indisputable, the boundaries of **Languedoc** have never been easy to fix. It was at the end of the thirteenth century that agents of the King of France first spoke about the *patria lingue occitane,* the lands where the Occitan language (*langue d'Oc*) was spoken, when creating three administrative regions centred in Beaucaire, Carcassonne and Toulouse. Nowadays, that historical Languedoc is a hazy entity within Occitanie, the new super-region created in 2016. In defining Languedoc in this Guide we've avoided contemporary administrative boundaries in favour of its historical origins and the logistics of travel, so that the region butts up to neighbouring Provence at the Rhône, and stretches west and inland to include the medieval capital of Toulouse, as well as the lands around Foix in the south and Albi in the north. **Roussillon**, squashed in

between the eastern Pyrenees and the Corbières hills, is also characterized by a particular linguistic heritage, derived in this case from a long history as part of the Catalan confederacy centred in Barcelona. Both regions have distinct cultures, but share a common history of occupation and resistance – and of eventual submission to the modern France of Paris and the North.

Where to go

Toulouse, HQ of plane-builder Airbus, is the region's largest city and its most important cultural hub, with a collection of world-class museums and monuments, such as the Fondation Bemberg and the basilica of St-Sernin. To the north, the historic vineyards of **Gaillac** stretch east towards **Albi**, home to the UNESCO-listed Cité Episcopale and Toulouse-Lautrec museum. South of here, the hills and forests of the **Parc Naturel Régional du Haut Languedoc**, once the refuge of Protestant Huguenots, make for excellent hiking and cycling – check out the new Passa Païs trail – and are renowned for delicious charcuterie. Towards the Pyrenees, south of **Foix**, you'll find some of Europe's oldest and most enigmatic prehistoric caves. The mountains here offer skiing in winter and many outdoor activities in summer.

The **Canal du Midi** leads east from Toulouse towards the Mediterranean, passing beneath the walls of **Carcassonne**, the most impressive and intact of the Cathar fortresses. In this area are the ruins of several isolated Cathar castles, the most imposing being tragic **Montségur**, high on the *pog* (hill) above the village of the same name.

Nothing could contrast with this more than the **Camargue Gardoise**, the swampy delta of the Rhône, which forms Languedoc's northern frontier – home to white horses, flamingos and the bull ranches that fuel the region's passion for *tauromachie* (bull games). Just inland, the beauty of the sun-baked *garrigues* was well known to the Romans, whose monuments in and around **Nîmes**, including the famous **Pont du Gard** aqueduct, bear witness to the area's ancient glory. East of here, the genteel town of **Uzès** is noted for its truffles.

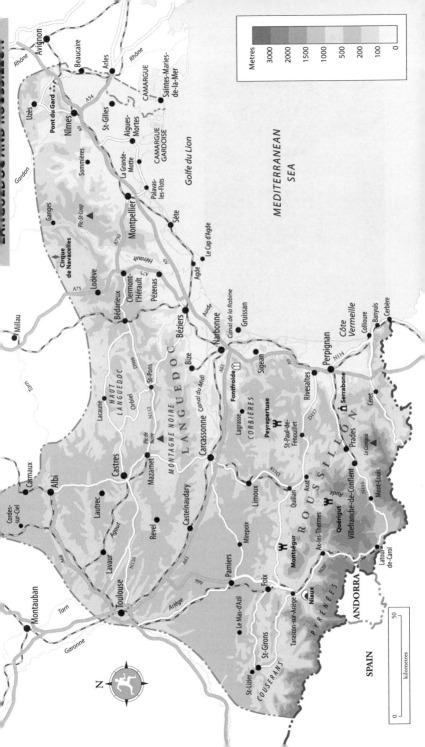

THE CATHARS

It's hard to imagine a more romantic episode of the Middle Ages. A peaceful people, living in a land of troubadours and poets, following the religion of their choosing, are declared **heretics** by a grasping and imperious papacy. This unleashes a series of brutal and drawn-out military campaigns, sanctified as **Crusades**, but that are in fact wars of aggressive colonialism waged by northern French nobles and churchmen on the locals. It's a story of knights and lords, martyrdoms, **Inquisition**, lost treasures, a proud but beleaguered nation and **castles** perched on rocky spurs, ending in the destruction of the **Cathar** faith, the suppression of Occitan culture and the subjugation of the people of Languedoc. The truth was far more complex than this popular and exaggerated Sir Walter Scott-ish version of events, but the story of the Cathars is a fascinating and exciting introduction to the region's history, long buried by the modern French state. For more on the Cathars, see Contexts (see p.314); you might even embark on our six-day Cathar itinerary (see p.19).

To the south, **Montpellier** is a lively city close to the sea, with some interesting modern architecture and a vibrant street-life sustained by the student population of its famous university, the third oldest in France. From here, the Hérault valley provides access to a rocky hinterland where you can visit the UNESCO-listed monastery and "devil's bridge" of **St-Guilhem-le-Désert**, or hike through the spectacular **Cirque de Navacelles**.

South of Montpellier, **Béziers**, the oldest town in the region, and **Narbonne**, once an important Roman capital, reside over an expanse of archetypal Midi landscape. Blue skies are set off against the red soil and the iridescent green of seemingly endless vineyards. Only the ports, **Agde** and **Sète**, justly famed for their seafood and maritime traditions, manage to shake off the pleasant torpor of the plains.

Further south, **Roussillon** (French Catalonia) snuggles in the foothills of the Pyrenees, a region whose vivid contrasts have inspired artists including the Fauvists and Picasso. The capital, **Perpignan**, once home to the kings of Majorca, makes an ideal jumping-off point for visiting the rocky coves of the Côte Vermeille, or ascending the river valleys into the heart of the Pyrénées-Orientales *département*. On the coast, **Collioure** is a beautifully set beach town, immune from the crass commercialism that characterizes the worst of the coastal resorts. Inland, **Céret**, noted for its cherries and artistic connections, makes a great introduction to the lively Catalan folk traditions with its annual festival of *sardanas* (Catalan dancing). The narrow-gauge **Train Jaune** winds upwards past **Le Canigó**, the mountain-symbol of the Catalan people and a Grand Site de France, and the evocative old garrison towns of **Villefranche** and **Mont-Louis** – both with UNESCO-listed Vauban fortifications.

Author picks

Our author travelled the length and breadth of Languedoc and Roussillon, combing coast and countryside, trying out the local activities and exploring its best hotels and restaurants. These are her personal highlights.

Room with a view The *Hôtel Mercure Albi Bastides* offers stunning views over the Garonne to the UNESCO-listed Cité Episcopale from its terrace and riverside rooms. See p.134.

Spectacular venue Perched on a rock next to the sea, Sète's open-air Théâtre de la Mer is an unforgettable place to enjoy a music concert in the summer months. See p.221.

Scenic trail Completed in 2013, the "Passa Païs" cycling and walking trail (*voie verte*) from Mazamet to Bédarieux is an excellent way to explore the Parc Naturel Régional du Haut Languedoc. See box, p.156.

Exquisite ices Savour home-made fruit- and flower-based ice creams and sorbets in the garden of *En Terre d'Abajou*, halfway up a mountain in the Bethmale valley. See p.119.

Luxury spa Treat yourself to some woad-based beauty treatments at the Terre de Pastel spa on the outskirts of Toulouse; the "Paranthèse" packages are the best value. See box, p.72.

Stunning seafood There's no better place to eat some of France's finest oysters than at the waterside farm-restaurant of third-generation producer Atelier & Co in the Bassin de Thau. See p.226.

Film-star beach Follow in the footsteps of Betty Blue and spend an afternoon sunning yourself (or enjoying a beachside drink) in front of the "stilt houses" at Gruissan-Plage. See p.249.

Local produce showcase St-Guilhem-le-Désert's excellent new Maison du Grand Site has a shop and a restaurant that both specialize in local produce; it also offers wine tastings – and what wine it is. See p.236.

> Our author recommendations don't end here. We've flagged up our favourite places – a perfectly sited hotel, an atmospheric café, a special restaurant – throughout the guide, highlighted with the ★ symbol.

FROM TOP THÉÂTRE DE LA MER, SÈTE (P.221); BASSIN DE THAU OYSTERS (P.225); GRUISSAN-PLAGE (P.249).

LANGUEDOC AND ROUSSILLON'S TOP WINE TYPES

Though the Greeks brought **wine** to Languedoc in the fifth century BC, production was developed and really established in the area by the Romans. Most of the oldest and best varieties, including Gaillac and Blanquette de Limoux, were first made by **medieval monks**, whose daily regime permitted them about half a litre each. Centuries later it had become France's drink of choice, with Languedoc producing most of the country's table wine (*vin de table*) come the late nineteenth century. By 1875, with vine-killing phylloxera ripping through France, the nation's vineyards were saved by replacing native stock with plants from the **United States** (raised from cuttings taken earlier from France) – the basis of the region's wine production today. Virtually every tourist office in the region has a brochure on local vintages and a list of **domaines** that can be visited for tasting. For a general introduction, consult ⓦcoteaux-languedoc.com and ⓦvinsduroussillon.com.

Gaillac ⓦwww.vins-gaillac.com. Established over a thousand years ago west of Albi; best known for its whites, but also excellent reds, rosés and sparkling Gaillacoise.
Corbières ⓦ20decorbieres.com. One of the great AOPs (*Appellation d'Origine Protégée*) of Languedoc, to the south of Narbonne, producing a variety of high-quality reds and whites.
Cabardès ⓦwww.aop-cabardes.fr. A tiny zone west of the Minervois, where Mediterranean and Atlantic grapes are combined for unique vintages.
Minervois ⓦleminervois.com. Located north of Carcassonne; famous for honey-tinted whites and fruity reds.
Picpoul de Pinet ⓦwww.picpoul-de-pinet.com. Produced near the Étang de Thau, this white wine is the locals' choice to accompany seafood.
Costières de Nîmes ⓦcostieres-nimes.org. Stretching from St-Gilles up past Beaucaire, these vineyards produce well-regarded reds, which are akin to those from the Rhône valley.
Blanquette de Limoux ⓦlimoux-aoc.com. A light, sparkling white, invented five centuries ago by monks near Limoux.
Côtes du Roussillon ⓦvinsduroussillon.com. Fruity and exciting reds from the *garrigues* and foothills of the Pyrenees.
Fitou ⓦfitouaoc.com. A recent AOP, founded in 1948, which boasts characteristics of the heavy, robust vintages of the Roussillon hills.
Muscat de Lunel ⓦmuscat-lunel.eu. A popular sweet white wine produced to the west of the Camargue Gardoise.

When to go

The **summer season** has both advantages and shortcomings. In July and August you can count on long **opening hours**, as well as the widest selection of hotels and restaurants, since many on the coast and in rural locations close in winter. Many of the region's **festivals** take place in the summer too. On the other hand, queues are longer and, especially in August when the French are on holiday, competition for accommodation is often fierce; you'll be forced to book ahead for hotels, particularly on the coast. **Traffic** is also increasingly problematic at this time; the coastal highways and byways are chock-a-block. So if you're thinking of a summer walking or cycling holiday, it's advisable to plan your journey along *voies vertes* (green routes), trails that usually follow disused railway lines.

The long **off-season**, from November through to Easter, sees many services shut down, including hotels and restaurants, and shorter museum and monument hours. The weather is frequently cold and grey (though a light layer of snow does at least make the Cathar ruins more romantic), while the Pyrenean **ski resorts** are, of course, at their busiest.

ABOVE RIGHT CIRQUE DE GAVARNIE

This can, however, be the best moment to visit urban centres like Toulouse and Montpellier, which spring to life at this time. Not only do theatre and opera seasons get underway, but the **bars** and **clubs** pack out thanks to their **student populations**. Christmas and Lent, meanwhile, breathe life into rural areas with an array of unique festivities.

The best time to go, though, is probably during the **shoulder seasons** – May, June, September and October – which offer a balance between tranquillity and action. In early June, a popular town like Cordes-sur-Ciel is likely to be quiet rather than overrun. With a bit of luck, the weather will be good, although prospective swimmers might find the water a little chilly. You'll avoid the worst of the high-season traffic and you should also more or less have your pick of accommodation, which will generally still be available at low-season prices.

AVERAGE TEMPERATURES AND RAINFALL

	Jan	March	May	July	Sept	Nov
TOULOUSE						
Ave temp (°C and °F)	4.6/40.3	8.2/46.8	14.9/58.8	21.1/70.0	18.1/64.6	8.3/46.9
Rainfall (mm)	47.1	51.6	78.7	45.5	58.4	52.4
MONTPELLIER						
Ave temp (°C and °F)	6.8/44.2	10.1/50.2	16.3/61.3	23.8/74.8	20.3/68.5	10.8/51.4
Rainfall (mm)	69.8	71.2	61.3	23.6	85.1	81.9
FOIX						
Ave temp (°C and °F)	4.4/39.9	8.5/47.3	14.3/57.7	20.6/69.1	17.8/64.0	8.4/47.1
Rainfall (mm)	51	59	83	49	68	61
PERPIGNAN						
Ave temp (°C and °F)	7.2/45.0	10.4/50.7	16.6/61.9	23.2/73.8	19.7/67.5	10.9/51.6
Rainfall (mm)	52.6	53.2	51.5	19.9	52.0	58.7

15

things not to miss

It's not possible to see everything that Languedoc and Roussillon have to offer in one trip – and we don't suggest you try. What follows, in no particular order, is a selective and subjective taste of the region's highlights: stunning landscapes, ancient traditions, gorgeous coastal spots and evocative historical sites. All entries are colour-coded by chapter and have a page reference to take you straight into the Guide, where you can find out more.

1 KAYAKING UNDER THE PONT DU GARD
Page 182
Kayaking down the Gardon river and under the lofty arches of this magnificent Roman aqueduct is great fun for all the family.

2 WATER-JOUSTING
Page 219
Invented centuries ago in Sète by soldiers training for the Crusades, this sport is a symbol of traditional Languedoc culture.

3 MUSÉE TOULOUSE-LAUTREC
Page 131
This Languedoc native revolutionized nineteenth-century art; the largest collection of his work is housed here in Albi's UNESCO-listed bishops' palace.

4 CORDES-SUR-CIEL
Page 138
Cruise the arts and crafts boutiques and soak up the medieval atmosphere – not forgetting the stunning views – in this hilltop Cathar town.

8

9

10

Itineraries

The following itineraries will take you right across the region, from tasting delicious charcuterie in the Montagne Noire and cassoulet in Castelnaudary to following in the footsteps of some of the twentieth century's most famou artists; going on the trail of the persecuted Cathars, meanwhile, you'll encounter spectacular hilltop castles and countless sobering tales.

GRAND FOODIE TOUR

To sample the region's main gastronomic highlights, taking in the *départements* of Tarn, Aude, Hérault and Gard, you'll need at least seven days. With a couple of bus changes to get from Lacaune-les-Bains to Castelanaudry and from Narbonne to Pézenas, this itinerary is easily doable by public transport.

❶ Lacaune-les-Bains Start by savouring some of this Montagne Noire spa town's celebrated charcuterie: superb salted and air-dried ham and sausages. **See p.151**

❷ Castelnaudary From Lacaune, head southeast to the Canal du Midi port where Languedoc's ubiquitous duck and bean dish, cassoulet, was invented; try some at *Le Tirou*. **See p.78**

❸ Narbonne There are many excellent covered markets in the southwest but Les Halles de Narbonne, east of Castelnaudary, is one of the best; check out the 66 stalls then have lunch in one of its restaurants. **See p.243**

❹ Pézenas Follow in Molière's footsteps around this well preserved Renaissance town, 59km northeast of Narbonne, before treating yourself to a "petit pâté" – a sweet, hot mutton pie – from Alary. **See p.228**

❺ Étang de Thau Seventy-five kilometres northeast of Narbonne, this lagoon produces some of France's best oysters; learn about them at the Musée de l'Étang de Thau in Bouzigues then sample a few at a waterside restaurant. **See p.226**

❻ St-Gilles Continue northeast to the gateway of the Camargue Gardoise, where you can tuck into an AOP bull meat steak or casserole (*gardiane de taureau*). **See p.188**

❼ Uzès From St-Gilles, head north to France's oldest duchy to try its famous black truffles fres from the ground. Wintertime is best, but you can find them in a variety of preserved product year-round. **See p.177**

ROUSSILLON'S ART TRAIL

Give yourself at least four days for this cultural trip, a more-or-less straight line up the Roussillon coast. These towns and villages are easily accessible by public transport.

❶ Banyuls-sur-Mer The best place to get a fee for Paris-trained Aristide Maillol's sculptures is in his hometown – a small seaside resort near the Spanish border where he lived his entire life; his former home is now a museum. **See p.307**

❷ Port-Vendres Eight kilometres northwest of Banyuls up the D114 coastal road, you can see some of the sites that inspired the watercolours of Charles Rennie Mackintosh, the Scottish architect, designer and artist, who spent some of his final years here. **See p.306**

ABOVE MARKET IN UZÈS; LASTOUF

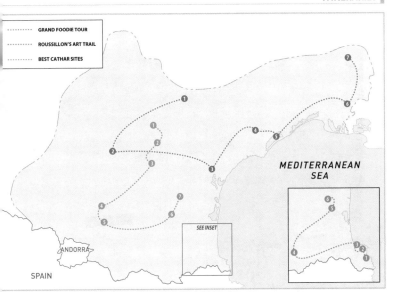

Collioure Walk or drive the 3km northwest to this charming seaside town that was frequented by the Fauvist artists Derain, Braques and Matisse, and their friend Picasso, in the early twentieth century; have a drink in *Les Templiers*, their favourite watering hole. **See p.304**

Céret Head inland along the D618 to the cherry capital of the southwest, where Picasso lived from 1911–12; you can see some of his works, along with those by his famous friends, in the Musée d'Art Moderne. **See p.297**

Cabestany Northeast of Céret is the small town of Cabestany, the supposed home of a distinctive twelfth-century sculptor, dubbed "The Master of Cabestany", whose work graces many of the region's churches. **See p.283**

Perpignan Named after a famous local seventeenth-century artist, the Musée Hyacinthe-Rigaud, just west of Cabestany, will be one of the best art museums in the region when it reopens in 2017. **See p.275**

BEST CATHAR SITES

To fully explore these historic sites, spread across the *départements* of Tarn, Aude and Ariège, you'll need a car; allow at least six days.

❶ Mazamet The best place to start is in Mazamet at the Musée du Catharisme, before heading uphill to the nearby medieval village of Hautpoul, whose ruined castle was besieged by Simon de Montfort in 1212. **See p.158**

❷ Lastours Drive south across the Montagne Noire for 30km to reach the four imposing ruined castles at Lastours, once the base of the Cathar bishop of Carcassès. **See p.159**

❸ Carcassonne Not far south, you'll hit the fairy-tale citadel of Carcassonne, once a seat of aristocratic Cathar supporter Raymond-Roger Trencavel. **See p.88**

❹ Montségur Further to the southeast lies the sinister-looking ruined castle at Montségur, the most emblematic of the Cathar sites, where more than two hundred followers were burned in 1244. **See p.103**

❺ Montaillou Head 40km south through remote territory to this ruined Cathar hamlet whose 250 inhabitants were arrested in 1308; their testimonies are recorded in *Montaillou, village occitan* by Emmanuel Le Roy Ladurie. **See p.105**

❻ Quéribus Next, head east for 80km to Quéribus, the last Cathar castle to fall in 1225 – undoubtedly due to its elevated, virtually impenetrable location. **See p.285**

❼ Villerouge-Termenès End your tour at this attractive, well-restored castle, north of Quéribus, where the last known Cathar monk was burnt alive in 1321; there's an excellent multimedia exhibition inside. **See p.252**

CAUNES-MINERVOIS

Basics

Getting there

Languedoc and Roussillon's major transport hub is Toulouse, home to the region's largest international airport and served by trains from England (via Paris or Lille) and Spain.

In general, the quickest and most cost-effective way of reaching Languedoc and Roussillon **from Britain** is by air, though from the southeast of England it's worth considering the Eurostar, which links with fast and efficient TGV services south from Lille and Paris.

From North America there are direct flights from over thirty major cities to Paris, from where you can either take an internal flight or transfer to France's excellent train network. Many people heading for France **from Australia, New Zealand and South Africa** travel via London, although there are scheduled flights to Paris from Sydney, Adelaide, Brisbane, Perth, Auckland, Johannesburg and Cape Town.

Airfares always depend on the **season**, with the highest being around mid-June to mid-September, when the weather is best; fares drop during the "shoulder" seasons – Easter to mid-June and mid-September through October – and you'll get the best prices during the low season, November to Easter (excluding Christmas and New Year). Note also that flying on weekends ordinarily adds to the round-trip fare.

Flights from the UK and Ireland

Several **low-cost airlines** offer scheduled flights into the region, or to hubs within easy striking distance of it. **Ryanair** (Ⓦryanair.com) flies from various airports in Ireland and Great Britain to Béziers, Carcassonne, Montpellier, Nîmes, Perpignan and Toulouse. **EasyJet** (Ⓦeasyjet.com) flies to Montpellier and Toulouse, while **Flybe** (Ⓦflybe .com) flies to Perpignan and Toulouse and **Jet2** (Ⓦjet2.com) from Manchester to Toulouse.

British Airways (Ⓦbritishairways.com) flies three times a day from London Heathrow to Toulouse,

and Aer Lingus (Ⓦaerlingus.com) has flights from Dublin to Toulouse, Montpellier and Perpignan.

Flights from the US, Canada, Australia, New Zealand and South Africa

To get to Languedoc and Roussillon from the major Anglophone countries, you can either fly to London and hook up with a **budget airline** or, better, fly to Paris and continue overland by renting a car or using France's excellent **rail** system (see p.24).

By train

The quickest way to get to Languedoc and Roussillon **by train** from the UK is on the **Eurostar** from London St Pancras and Ebbsfleet or Ashford International in Kent, through the Channel Tunnel, to Lille or Paris and then changing onto a fast TGV train to Toulouse (9hr 30min), Perpignan (9hr), Montpellier (7hr) or Nîmes (6hr 30min) – note that these times are for the total journey, starting in London. A standard return fare starts at around £120 to the region. Note that the France **Interrail** pass (see below) gives a discount on the Eurostar service called a "pass holder fare"; however, regular Eurostar tickets can work out cheaper.

Rail passes

There's a huge array of **rail passes** available, which may be worth considering if you're visiting

Languedoc and Roussillon as part of a longer pan-European journey. For details of local SNCF rail passes valid for journeys within France, see "Getting around" (see p.24).

Interrail pass

Interrail passes (W interrail.eu) are only available to European residents, and you will be asked to provide proof of residency before being allowed to purchase one. They come in over-26 and (cheaper) under-26 versions, and cover thirty European countries. There is a **One Country Pass** (so for France you would have the Interrail France Pass) which is available for three, four, six or eight days' travel within one month, and the **Interrail Global Pass**, which is available for five, seven, ten, fifteen, twenty-two or thirty days and gives unlimited travel in thirty countries – note that reservations (sometimes incurring a cost) will need to be made for high-speed services and overnight trains. The Global Pass includes a train trip from and to the holder's European country of residence. Both are available in 1st and 2nd class. Senior (over 60) and Family Passes are also available, with children under 4 travelling for free.

Eurail Pass

The **Eurail Pass**, which must be purchased before arrival in Europe (and cannot be purchased by European residents), is available as a Select Pass, which allows travel in France and up to four bordering countries, and the Global Pass, which allows travel in five or more countries from five t thirty days. There are also 1st and 2nd class passe and a Family Pass.

Details of prices for all these passes can be foun on the Eurail website (W eurail.com).

By car and ferry

If you don't want to drive far when you've reache France, you can take advantage of SNCF's **Aut Train**, which you can book through Voyages SNC (see opposite), putting your car on the train in Par and collecting it in Narbonne or Toulouse.

By car

It's a good nine hours' **drive** south from Calais on th north coast of France to Toulouse, but if you do war to drive, the quickest way across the Channel is v the Channel Tunnel (35min), on **Eurotunnel** (☎08443 35 35 35, W eurotunnel.com) daily shuttle Due to the frequency of the service, you don't hav to buy a ticket in advance (though it is advisable i mid-summer and during other school holidays), bu you must arrive at least thirty minutes befor departure; the target loading time is just ten minute

Fares are calculated per car, with up to nin passengers, and rates depend on the time of yea time of day and length of stay (the cheapest ticke is for a day-trip, followed by a five-day return); it cheaper to travel between 10pm and 6am, whil the highest fares are reserved for weeken departures and returns in July and August.

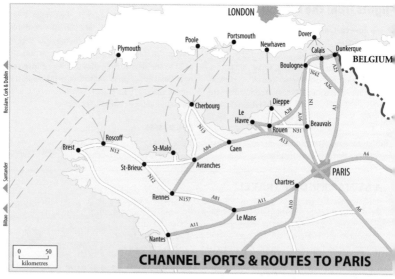

CHANNEL PORTS & ROUTES TO PARIS

By ferry

Alternatively, you can get to France by **ferry** from various ports along England's south coast to the north coast of France. If you're coming from the north of England or Scotland, consider an overnight ferry to Zeebrugge (Belgium) from Hull. From Ireland you can take a ferry direct from Rosslare (near Wexford) to either Cherbourg or Roscoff and from Dublin to Cherbourg.

Ferry **prices** are seasonal and, for motorists, depend on the size of your vehicle. Note that return prices are substantially cheaper than one-way fares, but generally need to be booked in advance. All ferry companies also offer foot passenger fares; accompanying bicycles can usually be carried free, at least in the low season. Check out the ferry company websites for **special deals** and also price comparison websites such as Eurodrive (☏0844 371 8021, Ⓦeurodrive.co.uk). Details of routes and companies are listed under Ferry Contacts (see below).

By bus

Eurolines runs regular bus-ferry services from London Victoria to around thirty French cities, including Toulouse, Nîmes, Montpellier and Perpignan. Prices are much lower than for the same journey by train; the journey time is roughly nineteen hours. Regional return fares from the rest of England and from Wales are available, as are student and youth discounts. **Tickets** can be bought directly from the company, from National Express agents and from most high-street travel agents.

Agents and specialist operators

Many airlines and discount travel websites offer you the opportunity to book your tickets **online**, cutting out the costs of agents and middlemen. Good deals can often be found through discount or auction sites, as well as through the **airlines'** own websites. There are also many tour operators offering **specialist tours** of Languedoc and Roussillon, such as walking, biking and boating.

SPECIALIST TOUR OPERATORS

Arblaster & Clarke Ⓦ winetours.co.uk. Luxury wine holidays.
Château de Quarante Ⓦ chateaudequarante.com. Gourmet accommodation in a private castle by night, chauffeur-driven custom tours by day. They also host cookery and painting courses.
Discover France Ⓦ discoverfrance.com. Cycling tours in Languedoc.
Exodus Ⓦ exodus.co.uk. Outdoor activity holidays including a cycling tour of the Canal du Midi and hiking in the Pyrenees.

French Cycling Holidays Ⓦ frenchcyclingholidays.com. Cycling specialists who run both leisure and sport cycling tours.
Inntravel Ⓦ inntravel.co.uk. Self-guided walking and cycling holidays.
Languedoc Nature Ⓦ languedoc-nature.com. Organizes a range of tours based on outdoor activities, history and gastronomy.
Martin Randall Travel Ⓦ martinrandall.com. Top-end art and architecture tours of the region.
Trésor Languedoc Tours Ⓦ tresor-languedoc.com. Bespoke day-trips and week-long cookery, pottery and regional discovery tours.
Unicorn Trails Ⓦ unicorntrails.com. Guided and self-guided riding holidays in Cathar country.
Vin en Vacances Ⓦ vinenvacances.com. Food and wine-themed tours and holidays.

RAIL CONTACTS

Eurostar UK ☏ 03432 186 186, France ☏ 0892 35 35 39, Ⓦ eurostar.com.
Rail Europe US ☏ 1 800 622 8600, Canada☏ 1 800 361 RAIL (7245), South Africa ☏ 271 1628 2319, Ⓦ raileurope.com. This is SNCF's international agent; you can book Eurostar, TGV and Eurail passes.
Voyages SNCF UK ☏ 0844 848 5848, France ☏ 36 35, Ⓦ voyages-sncf.com. SNCF's UK agent for Eurostar, TGV and Interrail.

BUS CONTACTS

Busabout UK ☏ 08450 267 576, Ⓦ busabout.com. Hop on/hop off bus travel in Europe.
Eurolines UK ☏ 08717 818 177, Ireland ☏ 01 83 66 111, Ⓦ eurolines.com.

FERRY CONTACTS

Brittany Ferries UK ☏ 0330 159 7000, Ⓦ brittany-ferries.co.uk. Poole to Cherbourg; Portsmouth to Le Havre, Caen, Cherbourg and St-Malo; Plymouth to Roscoff and Santander; Cork to Roscoff.
Condor Ferries UK ☏ 01202 207216, Ⓦ condorferries.co.uk. Portsmouth to Cherbourg and Poole to St-Malo via Guernsey.
DFDS UK ☏ 0871 574 7235, Ⓦ dfdsseaways.co.uk. Dover to Dunkerque and Calais; Newhaven to Dieppe.
Irish Ferries Ireland ☏ 0818 300 400, Ⓦ irishferries.com. Dublin to Cherbourg and Rosslare to Cherbourg and Roscoff.
P&O Ferries UK ☏ 0800 130 0030, Ⓦ poferries.com. Dover to Calais and Hull to Zeebrugge.

Getting around

France has the most extensive train network in western Europe, and rail is the best way of travelling between almost all the major towns within Languedoc and Roussillon. The nationally owned French train company, SNCF (Société Nationale des Chemins de Fer), runs fast modern trains. In rural areas where

branch lines have been closed, routes are covered by buses operated solely by SNCF or in partnership with independent companies. It's an integrated service, with buses timetabled to meet trains and the same ticket covering both.

Unfortunately, though, the private **bus** services that supplement the SNCF services are confusing and uncoordinated. Some areas, such as the coast or around larger centres like Toulouse, Albi and Castres, are quite well served, while the service in less populated regions, like the Corbières and parts of the Pyrenees and Haut Languedoc, is barely existent: often designed to carry the inhabitants of hamlets to and from weekly markets, they are not very useful for tourists. Weekends and holidays frequently have no service. We give details of train and bus services in each chapter of the Guide.

By rail

The SNCF has pioneered one of the most efficient, comfortable and user-friendly **railway systems** in the world. Its staff are, with few exceptions, courteous and helpful, and its trains – for the most part, fast, clean and frequent – continue, in spite of the closure of some rural lines, to cover much of Languedoc and Roussillon; a main rail corridor runs from Toulouse to Narbonne, where it joins the coastal line, linking Cerbère on the Spanish border and Beaucaire (Tarascon) at the Rhône, while spur lines run up major river valleys – including the Tarn, Ariège and Conflent. For **national train information**, see Ⓦ voyages-sncf.com.

Pride and joy of the system are the high-speed **TGVs** (*trains à grande vitesse*), capable of 300kmph, and their offspring Eurostar. There are several stations connected to the TGV in Languedoc and Roussillon, among them Nîmes (journey time from Paris around 3hr), Montpellier (3hr 30min), Narbonne (5hr), Béziers (4hr 20min), Perpignan (5hr 20min) and Toulouse (5hr 30min). A new section of high-speed track between Nîmes and Montpellier is expected to open in 2017. The TER (*Train Express Régional* Ⓦ ter.sncf.com/languedoc -roussillon) website is also useful and has a PDF of the regional rail network you can download. These trains are a bit slower than the TGVs and serve the regional stations.

For security reasons, most stations do not have **luggage lockers** (*consignes*); currently only Toulouse and Montpellier has any.

Leaflet timetables for particular lines are available free at stations. An *Autocar* symbol at the top of a column means it's an SNCF bus service, on which rail tickets and passes are valid.

Aside from the regular lines, there are a number of tourist-oriented railways, including the spectacular **Train Jaune** (see p.295) which winds its way up through the Pyrenees, and the *Train du Pays Cathare et du Fenouillèdes* which runs up into the Cathar heartland (see p.286).

Tickets

In person, it is easiest to use the automated ticket machines in the stations to **buy tickets** on the day, as they have instructions in English and are a good way to check fares and times – you can always press the red *annuler* button to cancel the transaction. All tickets – but not passes (see below) – must be **validated** in the orange machines at station platform entrances, and it is an offence not to follow the instruction *Compostez votre billet* ("Validate your ticket"). Seat reservations are necessary for the TGV, but not for the TER (regional trains).

French rail discounts and passes

SNCF offers a whole range of **discounted fares** and last-minute offers within France on standard rail prices. For travel on TGVs, the **cheapest** fare to look out for is Tarif Prem's, which must be bought ninety days before departure, followed by Tarif Loisir. Also, if there are four or more people travelling, enquire about the Pack Tribu, which offers a free ticket for every three tickets bought. The website lists all the latest deals and has a calendar showing when the cheapest fares are available. In addition, the SNCF has a budget service called **Ouigo** (Ⓦ ouigo.com) which has low-cost fares from Marne La Vallée near Paris to Nîmes and Montpellier. However, there is no buffet car and you can only take one cabin-size case and one piece of hand luggage.

Finally, a range of train **passes**, that give discounts (valid for a year) for young people up to the age of 27 (Carte Jeune), children under 12 (Carte Enfant) and the over 60s (Carte Senior), can be bought from main stations in France. However, due to the purchase price, they are only cost effective if you plan to be in the country for an extended period and intend doing a lot of travelling. For details of pan-European rail passes, see "Getting there" (see p.21).

By bus

The most convenient **bus services** are those that act as extensions of rail links by SNCF, which always run to and from the SNCF station and access areas ormerly served by rail. In addition to SNCF buses, private, municipal and *départemental* buses can be useful for mid- to long-distance journeys. In Toulouse, city buses can be used to access outlying villages, and in Montpellier the network goes as far out as the coast. Some *départements*, like the Hérault and the Tarn, have rural bus networks; their roadside stops usually have a copy of the schedule attached to the sign or shelter. Private operators cover much of rural Languedoc and Roussillon too – unfortunately, their routes miss some of the more interesting and less-inhabited areas, and the **timetable** is designed to suit working, market and school hours – all often dauntingly early. All buses are, generally speaking, cheaper and slower than trains.

Larger towns usually have a **gare routière** (bus station), often next to the *gare SNCF*. However, the private bus companies don't always work together and you'll frequently find them leaving from an array of different points (the local tourist office will usually help locate them).

By car

Driving in Languedoc and Roussillon can be a real pleasure, and gives you the freedom to explore parts of the region that would otherwise remain inaccessible, in particular the sparsely populated upland of Haut Languedoc, the Hérault and the Pyrenees. **Autoroutes** in the region run through the same corridors as the main rail lines, connecting Toulouse and Narbonne, and from here, running north and south along the Mediterranean coast. If you are in a hurry, it is well worth paying the toll for their use, as the free national routes, which also follow this corridor, tend to be heavily travelled by both local drivers and long-distance truckers. By *autoroute*, in good traffic conditions, you can reach Nîmes from Toulouse in two to three hours. Away from the main arteries, the older main roads or *routes nationales* (marked N9 or RN230, for example, on signs and maps) are generally uncongested and, passing through the centres of the towns along the way, make for a more scenic, if slower, drive than the *autoroutes*. Smaller *routes départementales* (marked D) should not be shunned. Although they are occasionally in relatively poor condition, you can often travel for kilometres across country, seeing few other cars, on broad and well-maintained roads.

Service stations (*aires de service*) are found at regular intervals on *autoroutes* while petrol stations (*stations-service*) are usually found on the edge of towns and cities. Petrol is known as *essence* and diesel is *gazole*. Prices are about the same as the UK but considerably more expensive than in North America. The cheapest petrol or diesel fuel can usually be found at out-of-town superstores or *hypermarchés*.

City driving

The most challenging part of driving in Languedoc and Roussillon is likely to be entering large cities for the first time: as a general rule of thumb you can usually reach the centre by following signs for the tourist office. That said, **parking** is likely to be problematic, so you may instead want to follow signs for the *gare SNCF*, which will have some pay parking and most likely be within walking distance of the centre. Most cities also have sufficient underground parking **garages**. Outside of the city cores, street parking is usually free, although it may mean spending a considerable time hunting around. Many hotels have garages for which there is usually a charge. In Toulouse's outlying metro stations, you can park for free for the day if you buy a metro ticket.

Of course, there are times when it is wiser not to drive: **congestion** is a major problem on the *Autoroute Méditerranéenne* in summer, particularly on the first and last few days of July and August, and the same goes for roads of all categories along the coast on summer weekends, when the going is frustratingly slow.

Breakdowns and insurance

All the major car manufacturers have **garages** in Languedoc and Roussillon, which can help if you run into mechanical difficulties. You can find them in the Yellow Pages (W pagesjaunes.fr) under "*Garages d'automobiles*". For breakdowns, look under "*Dépannages*". If you have an accident or break-in, you should report it to the local police (and keep a copy) in order to make an insurance claim. Many car insurance policies cover your car in Europe, but you're advised to take out extra cover for motor assistance in case your car breaks down. Check with your local automobile association before leaving home.

Traffic information and route planning

For up-to-the-minute **traffic information** regarding traffic jams and road works on *autoroutes* throughout France, consult the bilingual website W autoroutes.fr. Traffic information for other roads can be obtained from the *Bison Futé* website W www.bison-fute.gouv.fr.

For **route planning**, W viamichelin.com can provide you with point-to-point driving directions for itineraries throughout France.

Rules of the road

British, Irish, Australian, Canadian, New Zealand and US **driving licences** are valid in France, though an International Driver's Licence makes life easier if you get a police officer unwilling to peruse a document in English. Remember also that you have to be 18 years of age to drive in France, regardless of whether you hold a licence in your own country. If the vehicle is rented, its registration document (*carte grise*) and the insurance papers must be carried. GB stickers must, by law, be displayed, and a Green Card proving your liability insurance coverage, though not a legal requirement, might save some hassle. If your car is right-hand drive, you must have your headlight dip adjusted to the right before you go – it's a legal requirement – and as a courtesy change or paint them to yellow or stick on black glare deflectors. In case of breakdown, you should carry a warning triangle and reflective jackets for each occupant. It is prohibited to wear headphones or any earpiece; and radar detectors are banned.

Road laws and warnings

Priorité à droite – **give way** to traffic coming from your right. Keep a look-out for signs along the roadside with the yellow diamond on a white background that gives you right of way – until you see the same sign with an oblique black slash, which indicates vehicles emerging from the right have right of way. *Stop* signs mean stop completely; *Cédez le passage* means "Give way". Other signs warning of potential dangers are *déviation* (diversion), *gravillons* (loose chippings), *nids de poules* (potholes), *chaussée déformée* (uneven surface) and *virages* (bends).

Speed limits in France are: 130kmph (80mph) on *autoroutes*; 110kph (68mph) on dual carriageways; 90kmph (56mph) on other roads; and 50kmph (31mph) in towns. The town limit is constant, but in wet weather, and for drivers with less than two years' experience, the three road limits are 110kmph (68mph), 100kmph (62mph) and 80kmph (50mph) respectively. The legal blood **alcohol limit** while driving is 0.05 percent alcohol (0.02 percent for those who have been driving for less than three years), and random breath tests are common: if you are caught over the limit, your driving privileges may be immediately suspended.

Car rental

It's advisable to arrange your **car rental** in France before you leave and a good place to start is a price comparison website. You'll find the big firms – Hertz, Avis, Europcar and Budget – at airports and in most big cities, with addresses detailed throughout the Guide. Local firms can be cheaper but you need to check the small print and be sure of where the car can be returned to. It's normal to pay an indemnity against any damage to the car – they will take your credit card number. The cost of car rental includes the basic legally necessary car insurance.

North Americans and Australians in particular should be forewarned that it is very difficult to arrange the hire of a car with **automatic transmission**; if you can't drive a manual, you should try to book an automatic well in advance, possibly before you leave home, and be prepared to pay a much higher price for it.

Most rental companies will only deal with people **over 25** unless an extra insurance premium is paid (but you still must be over 18 and have driven for at least one year).

CAR RENTAL AGENCIES

Avis Ⓦ avis.com.
Budget Ⓦ budget.com.
Europcar Ⓦ europcar.com.
Europe by Car Ⓦ europebycar.com.
Hertz Ⓦ hertz.com.
Holiday Autos Ⓦ holidayautos.co.uk.
National Ⓦ nationalcar.com.
SIXT Ⓦ sixt.com.
Thrifty Ⓦ thrifty.com.

By moped or motorbike

Mopeds and scooters are relatively easy to find outside the mountainous areas everyone from young kids to grandmas seems to ride them, and although they're not built for any kind of long distance travel, they're ideal for shooting around town and nearby. Places that rent out bicycles (see opposite) will often also rent out mopeds. You need a valid licence and crash helmets are compulsory on all mopeds and motorbikes.

By hitching

If you're intent on **hitching**, you'll have to rely almost exclusively on car drivers, as lorries very rarely give lifts. Even so, it won't be easy. Looking as clean and respectable as possible makes a big difference, and hitching the less frequented D roads is much quicker. In mountain areas a rucksack and hiking gear will help procure a lift from fellow hikers.

Autoroutes are a special case. Hitching on the *autoroute* itself is strictly illegal, but you can make excellent time going from one service station to another and, if you get stuck, at least there's food, drink, shelter and washing facilities at most service stations. The Michelin 726 map shows all the rest stops, service stations, tollbooths (*péages*), exits and so on. The tollbooths are a second best (and legal) option; ordinary approach roads tend to be difficult and can easily lead to a fine. Check out Ⓦhitchwiki org/en/france for the latest information.

For long-distance rides, or for greater security, you might consider using **hitching organizations**, such as Bla Bla Car (Ⓦblablacar.fr) and Covoiturage Libre (Ⓦcovoiturage-libre.fr).

By taxi

Unlike in much of the world, **taxis** are not generally hailed on the street but rather at established taxi stands or booked by phone. If your French is not strong, your hotel or restaurant staff should assist if you need to call one.

All taxis are metered and function on the basis of mileage/time elapsed and time of day. Prices vary and there may be extra charges for luggage, airport service, waiting time and so on. For precise tariffs by region, see Ⓦtaxis-de-france.com/annuaire /region-occitanie.

By bicycle

Bicycles (*vélos*) have high status in France, and the French respect cyclists – both as traffic and, when you stop off at a restaurant or hotel, as customers. All *départements* are increasingly developing their *cyclotourisme* not only with city paths (Montpellier is one of France's best cities for cycling) but with comprehensive networks linking rural areas (frequently utilizing disused roadways and rail rights of way, known as *voies vertes*). The Via Rhôna (Ⓦviarhona .com), which follows the length of the Rhône river, has a newly opened section between Gallician In the Gard *département* and Palavas-les-Flots in Hérault. These days more and more cyclists are using **mountain bikes**, which the French call VTTs (*vélos tout terrain*), even for touring holidays, although it's much less effort, and much quicker, to cycle long distances and carry luggage on a traditionally styled touring or racing bike. Your primary concern using bicycle transport in this region will likely be the **traffic**, which on the narrow two-lane *routes nationales* is frequently heavy and extremely fast.

The Fédération Française de Cyclotourisme (Ⓦffct.org) is a further useful source of **information** on all things to do with cycling in France. As for **maps**, a minimum requirement is the IGN 1:100,000

CITY BIKE NETWORKS
Toulouse (Ⓦvelo.toulouse.fr), Perpignan (Ⓦwww.bip-perpignan.fr) and Montpellier (Vélomagg – Ⓦtam-voyages .com) all have **municipal bike networks**, designed for short-term hops within the city. Once you have subscribed (see the individual city listings) you pick up and drop off bikes at the automated stations that are peppered throughout each city. Charges are minimal, although there may be fines for overuse. If you are considering using these bike systems, sign up ahead of time by internet; typically you need to register a credit card to cover the fees.

series (see p.43) – the smallest scale that carries contours. The UK's national cyclists' association, Cycling UK (Ⓦcyclinguk.org), can suggest routes and supply advice for members, as well as running a particularly good insurance scheme.

Transporting your bike

The **train** network runs various services for cyclists, including bike parking at stations, which you can find out about on the SNCF website Ⓦsncf.com /en/services/sncf-velo. You can take your bike for free on the TERs but will need a reservation, costing up to €10, on the high-speed services.

Ferries usually take bikes for free. Non-budget airlines will usually let you take a bike as part of your baggage allowance for free. **Eurostar** allows you to take your bicycle on certain trains for £30 so long as it is less than 85cm long and can be folded and stored in a special bike bag. Otherwise it needs to be sent unaccompanied, with a guaranteed arrival of 24 hours; book through Eurodespatch (☎03448 225 822, ✉eurodespatch@eurostar.com).

Bike rental

Bikes – usually mountain bikes – are often available to **rent** from campsites, hostels and *gîtes d'étapes*, as well as from specialist cycle shops. The bikes are often not insured, however, and you will be presented with the bill for their replacement if they're stolen or damaged. Check whether your travel insurance policy covers you for this if you intend to rent a bike.

On foot

Long-distance **walkers** are well served in Languedoc and Roussillon by an extensive network of marked footpaths, including long-distance routes, known as *sentiers de grande randonnée* or, more commonly, **GRs** (see p.37). They're fully signposted and equipped with campsites and rest huts along the way. Some of the main routes in the region are the **GR10**, which runs the length of the Pyrenees, the **GRs 7** and **36**, which wind their way down from Haut Languedoc through the Corbières, and **GR653** which follows the medieval Arles–Jaca pilgrimage route (*le chemin de St-Jacques*) to Santiago in Spain. Other routes are composites, such as the "**Sentier Cathare**", which utilizes various GRs and ARs (local paths) to link Cathar sites between Perpignan and Foix.

The main **climbing** organization is the Club Alpin Français (☎01 53 72 87 00, ⊛ffcam.fr); most major towns in the region have a branch office.

Walking guides

Each path is described in a *Topoguide* (available in Britain from Stanfords; ⊛stanfords.co.uk), which gives a detailed account of the route (in French), including maps, campsites, *refuge* huts and sources of provisions. *Topoguides* are produced by the principal French walkers' organization, the Fédération Française de la Randonnée Pédestre (☎01 44 89 93 93, ⊛ffrandonnee.fr), and are widely available in bookshops. In addition, many tourist offices can provide **guides** to their local footpaths, especially in popular hiking areas, where they often share premises with professional mountain guides and hike leaders. The latter organize climbing and walking expeditions for all levels of experience.

By boat

Languedoc is home to one of France's most famous inland waterways, the **Canal du Midi**, which leads from Toulouse (where it hooks up with the River Garonne) to Agde and Sète, passing Carcassonne and Béziers en route. A spur, the **Canal de la Robine**, passes Narbonne before reaching the sea at Gruissan and Port-Nouvelle. From Sète, you can enter the **Canal du Rhône à Sète**, which heads east, passing St-Gilles and Beaucaire, until it reaches the Rhône. Subsidiary canals branch out through the flatlands of the Camargue Gardoise, and penetrate the extensive Rhône delta. For information on maximum dimensions, documentation, regulations and so forth check out the website of Voies Navigables de France (⊛vnf.fr), which has information on boating in Languedoc and Roussillon. In addition, you'll find detailed information on the Canal du Midi on p.81 and p.254.

Accommodation

Outside of summer, you can turn up in any town in Languedoc and Roussillon and find a room, or a place in a campsite. Booking a couple of nights in advance can be reassuring, however, and in high season it is often indispensible. The "Language" section at the back of the Guide (see p.332) should help you make a reservation, though many hoteliers and campsite managers – and almost all hostel managers – speak some English. In most towns you'll be able to get a double room for around €40–60, or a single for €35–50; as a general rule the areas around train stations have the highest density of cheap hotels. Note that many municipalities charge a hotel tax, calculated on top of the posted rate, ranging from €0.20 to €3 per night.

Some tourist offices offer a **booking service** but they cannot guarantee rooms at a particular price. A tourist office can provide lists of hotels and hostels as well as details of campsites and bed-and-breakfasts. With **campsites**, you can be more relaxed about finding an empty space, unless you're touring with a caravan or camper van or looking for a place on the Mediterranean coast or upper Ariège valley.

Hotels

Most French **hotels** are **graded** from one to five stars, with the ratings based on a variety of factors including room and lobby size, location, amenities and services. In the cheapest hotels, rooms usually have a sink (*lavabo*) in one corner; bathrooms and showers (*douches*) are almost invariably found on the landing. As you climb up the price scale amenities such as *en-suite* bathrooms, air conditioning and cable TV appear. Most hotels now have free wi-fi in rooms as well as a computer terminal in reception.

Breakfast is not normally included and can add upwards of €6 per person to a bill – though there is no obligation to take it and you will nearly always do better at a café. The cost of eating **dinner** in a hotel's restaurant can be a more important factor to bear in mind when picking a place to stay. Officially, it is

---

ACCOMMODATION PRICES

The prices quoted in the Guide are for the **cheapest available double room** in high season.

ACCOMMODATION ALTERNATIVES

Websites that list (shared or independent) accommodation in private properties.

Airbnb Ⓦairbnb.com.
CouchSurfing Ⓦcouchsurfing.com.

Housetrip Ⓦhousetrip.com.
Vacation Rentals by Owner Ⓦvrbo.com.

---

llegal for hotels to insist on your taking meals, but they even do in places heavily dependent on seasonal tourism. However, this is not always such a bad thing, and you can sometimes get a real bargain.

Single rooms are only marginally cheaper than doubles, so sharing always slashes costs. Most hotels willingly provide rooms with **extra beds**, for three or more people, at good discounts. Many have **family rooms** (*chambres familiales*) or connecting rooms (*chambres communicantes*).

Note that many family-run hotels are closed every year for two or three weeks sometime between May and September – where possible we've detailed this in the text. In addition, some hotels in smaller towns and villages close for one or two nights a week, usually Sunday or Monday – if in doubt, ring first to check.

Aparthotels

Aparthotels are increasingly popular in cities and resorts. They offer studios and apartments, ranging from two to four stars, sleeping two to six people, but also offer a breakfast service. The pick of the bunch are AppartCity (Ⓦappartcity.com), Lagrange (Ⓦlagrange-holidays.co.uk) and Odalys (Ⓦodalys -vacances.com). They are usually found near train stations in cities, but some also have accommodation in beach resorts; Lagrange has aparthotels in most of the main coastal resorts in this region, as well as in Montpellier and Toulouse.

Chain hotels

A very useful option, especially if it's late at night, are the **motel chains**. In contrast to the downtown hotels, which often offer doubtful value (worn-out mattresses, dust, noise, etc) you can count on a decent and reliable standard in the chains even if they are without much charm.

Among the cheapest is the **Hotel F1** chain (☎09 69 36 60 91, Ⓦhotelf1.com), well signposted on the outskirts of most big towns. They are characterless, but provide rooms for up to three people from €29. With a Visa, MasterCard or American Express credit card, you can let yourself into a room at any hour of the day or night. Other budget chains include **B&B** (☎02 98 33 75 29, Ⓦhotel-bb.com) and the slightly more comfortable **Première Classe** (☎08 92 23 48

14, Ⓦpremiereclasse.fr) and **Ibis Budget** (Ⓦibis .com). More upmarket but still affordable chains include **Campanile** (☎08 92 23 48 12, Ⓦcampanile .fr), where en-suite rooms with satellite TV and direct-dial phones cost from around €50.

Hotel federations

Aside from the chains, there are a number of **hotel federations** in France. The biggest of these is **Logis de France** (Ⓦlogishotels.com), an association of over three thousand hotels nationwide. They are usually family run and have good restaurants. **Hotels de Charme et de Caractère** (Ⓦhotels -charme.com) is the place to find charming hotels with character throughout the country. For luxury accommodation, usually with gourmet restaurants, check out **Châteaux & Hotels Collection** (Ⓦchateauxhotels.co.uk).

Hotel deals

If you're planning your trip in advance, contact local tourist offices before arrival; there are very often special accommodation **deals** on offer, especially outside high season.

Room prices can be cheaper at the last minute or by booking directly on the hotel website. However, it's a good idea to take a look at price comparison websites first.

Bed-and-breakfasts and rural accommodation

An excellent alternative to hotels are **chambres d'hôtes** (B&Bs) which are found in towns, villages and the countryside, and **fermes auberges** (farm B&Bs). Both options are good for getting to know locals and expats. It should be noted that *chambres d'hôtes* vary tremendously in style, amenities and price, ranging from rooms in rather nondescript townhouses to rural cottages to full-blown castles. The key is to research well ahead of time and reserve in advance during high season. Most of these establishments can provide an evening meal. These are called *table d'hôte* (although some places which provide meals do not have rooms). Meals must be booked a day in advance, and are usually in the €20–30 range. For this price you will be treated to excellent home cooking, featuring market-fresh ingredients; sometimes you will eat with the family and almost always with fellow tourists. For further information about B&B accommodation see ⓦfleursdesoleil.fr.

Gîtes de France (ⓦgites-de-france.fr) is a government-funded agency which promotes and manages a range of bed-and-breakfast and self-catering accommodation in France, the latter usually consisting of a self-contained country cottage, known as a *gîte rural* or *gîte de séjour*. The standard these days ranges from basic *gîtes d'étapes* used by walkers and cyclists up to luxury châteaux with pools. There are also *gîtes panda*, which adhere to eco-friendly principles and are usually found in national parks. For **rural bed-and-breakfast accommodation** contact Bienvenue à la Ferme (ⓦbienvenue-a-la-ferme.com) or Accueil Paysan (ⓦaccueil-paysan.com), which also list farms that sell fresh produce. Also, since this is wine country, many vineyards offer accommodation, from camping space up to top-end luxury; ask at tourist offices for details of **Vignoble & Découvertes** members in their area.

Renting a house

If you are planning to stay a week or more in any one place it might be worth considering **renting a house**, and there are many websites for agencies or for booking directly with owners (see box, p.29). If you're looking to save money, house-swapping is also an option; see ⓦhomeexchange .com. Otherwise, economical longer-term, self-catering options include *gîtes, aparthotels*, Airbnb and the *Clévacances* programme. For further information see ⓦclevacances.fr. Alternatively check local tourist office listings for *appartements* or *meublés*.

HOLIDAY RENTAL WEBSITES

ⓦ brittany-ferries.co.uk.
ⓦ cheznous.com.
ⓦ clevacances.com.
ⓦ french-country-cottages.co.uk.
ⓦ holidayfrancedirect.co.uk.
ⓦ homeaway.co.uk.
ⓦ oliverstravels.com.

Hostels

Generally less than €25 a night in high season for a dormitory bed, and usually with breakfast thrown in, **hostels** – *auberges de jeunesse* – are invaluable for single travellers on a budget. For hostels, **per-person prices** of dorm beds are given throughout the Guide. Many modern hostels now also offer rooms for couples, with en-suite showers, but they don't necessarily work out cheaper than hotels – particularly if you've had to pay a bus fare out to the edge of town to reach them. However, many hostels are beautifully sited, and they allow you to cut costs by preparing your own food in their kitchens, or eating in their cheap canteens.

There are three rival French **hostelling associations**: the main two are the Fédération Unie des Auberges de Jeunesse (FUAJ; ☎01 44 89 87 27, ⓦfuaj.org) and the Ligue Française pour les Auberges de Jeunesse (LFAJ; ☎01 44 16 78 78 ⓦauberges-de-jeunesse.com). Normally, to stay at FUAJ or LFAJ hostels, you must be a member of Hostelling International (HI) or the International Youth Hostel Federation (IYHF). If you don't join up before you leave home, you can purchase **membership card** on arrival in the French hostel for €11 (€7 for under-26). The third hostelling organization is Ethic Étapes (☎01 40 26 57 64 ⓦethic-etapes.fr), which has accommodation in Sommières and Narbonne; membership is not required.

Camping

Practically every village and town in France has at least one **campsite** to cater for the thousands of people who spend their holiday under canvas – camping is a very big deal in France. The cheapest – at around €5–10 per person per night – usually the *camping municipal*, run by the local municipality. In season or whenever they're officially open, they are always clean and have plenty of hot water; often they are situated in prime local positions. Even if camping isn't your thing, keep in mind that many sites rent mobile homes and bungalows, providing an affordable self-catering option and a good fall-back when local hotels are full up.

If you're planning to do a lot of camping, Camping Card International (CCI) is a good investment. The card serves as useful identification, covers you for third-party insurance when camping and gives up to 25 percent reductions at campsites listed on the CCI website (ⓦcampingcard-international.com). It is available in the UK from the Camping and Caravanning Club (☎024 7642 202 ⓦcampingandcaravanningclub.co.uk), who also book inspected camping sites in Europe and arrange ferry crossings.

Types of camping

On the coast around the beach towns, there are **superior categories** of campsite where you'll pay prices similar to those of a hotel for the facilities – bars, restaurants and sometimes swimming pools. These have rather more permanent status than the *campings municipaux*, with people often spending a whole holiday in the one base. If you plan to do the same, and particularly if you have a caravan, camper or a big tent, it's wise to book ahead. Inland, *camping à la ferme* – on somebody's farm – is another possibility (generally without facilities). Lists of sites are detailed on these websites: Ⓦ bienvenue a-la-ferme.com and Ⓦ accueil-paysan.com.

A number of companies in the UK specialize in **camping holidays** with well-equipped tents provided: try Canvas Holidays (☎ 0345 268 0827, Ⓦ canvasholidays.co.uk) or Eurocamp (☎ 01606 787125, Ⓦ eurocamp.co.uk).

Lastly, a word of caution: never **camp rough** (*camping sauvage*, as the French call it) on anyone's land without first asking permission, as you may well have to deal with an irate farmer and his dogs. On the other hand, a politely phrased request for permission will as often as not get positive results. Camping on public land is not officially permitted, but is widely practised. Check out Ⓦ lecamping sauvage.fr for advice.

Food and drink

Languedoc-Roussillon – a traditionally poor and marginalized region – isn't known for the elaborate haute cuisine which typifies French cookery in the popular imagination. The food of this overwhelmingly rural region tends to be simple, with small family restaurants serving classic peasant (*terroir*) dishes based on local produce for under €20 a head. As you cross the region, however, you'll find that the huge diversity of the landscape has contributed to a correspondingly wide range of local specialities – immediately obvious when you visit town and village produce markets – and in all but the most out-of-the-way hamlet you'll be able to find a more adventurous (and expensive) *gastronomique* restaurant. Due to its relative isolation Languedoc-Roussillon has also fared better than many regions in escaping the processed, boil-in-the-bag and ready-to-microwave **productions – known in France as** *mal-bouffe* **("bad grub") – of the global food industry.**

In the rarefied world of **haute cuisine**, the top chefs champion the best local produce but tend to create dishes infused with international flavours and influences from their travels. A tasting menu will usually set you back in excess of €80 but many gourmet places offer weekday lunchtime menus where you can sample culinary genius for less than €30.

Languedoc and Roussillon are also great places for **foreign cuisine**, in particular North African, Caribbean (known as *Antillais*) and Asiatic. Moroccan, Thai or Vietnamese restaurants are not necessarily cheap options but they are usually good value for money. You'll often come across Indian and Chinese restaurants in the larger towns and cities.

Vegetarians

On the whole, **vegetarians** can expect a somewhat lean time in Languedoc and Roussillon; *cuisine rurale* is relentlessly meat-based, and in some traditional farming villages even understanding the concept of vegetarianism can be a stretch. A few cities have specifically vegetarian restaurants (detailed in the text), but elsewhere you'll have to rely on crêperies and pizzerias, or hope you find a sympathetic restaurant willing to replace a meat dish on the *menu fixe* with an omelette. Remember the phrase "*Je suis végétarien(ne); il y a quelques plats sans viande?*" (I'm a vegetarian; are there any non-meat dishes?). However, things are slowly improving, with some restaurants actually offering specific vegetarian menus.

Vegans, however, should probably forget all about eating in French restaurants and stick to self-catering.

For a **food glossary**, see pp.336–340.

Regional terroir

In the east, Provençal influence is strong – especially in the use of the herbs that spring up throughout the *garrigues* – while the ranches of the **Camargue Gardoise** ensure bull meat's central role, whether as steak, in dried sausage form (*saucisson de taureau*) or the stew-like *Gardiane de taureau*. The bull meat, which has a stronger flavour than beef, has AOP (*Appellation d'Origine Protégée*; Ⓦ aoptaureaudecamargue.com) status, meaning its place of origin/production is protected. Camargue rice also has AOP status. Other local ingredients include truffles, gathered around **Uzès**, and olives. The fair climate favours fresh produce, including asparagus, peaches and apricots.

Fish and seafood abound in the coastal cuisine: in brothy *coquillages* (shellfish dishes), the garlicky *bourride* (fish soup) of Sète, or simply baked or barbecued. Tuna, anchovies and sardines dominate, while mussels and oysters are intensively farmed in the shallow *étangs*. Bouzigues, in the Bassin de Thau, is one of France's Sites Remarquables du Goût, a place noted for an exceptional product (in this case oysters). The transition to the cooler uplands is marked by an increase in sheep-based dishes (using both meat and cheese), along with fruits, such as figs. Tripe (*tripoux*) is another staple.

In Haut Languedoc, mountain and forest food, including wild mushrooms, add variety. The Cabardès, just north of Carcassonne, produces superb mutton. Northeast, in the Tarn, high-quality charcuterie, foie gras, land snails (*escargots*) and duck (*canard*) are hallmarks. Cassoulet, a local bean stew from Castelnaudary, has colonized the whole of Languedoc. Carcassonne and the Aude are home to excellent sweets, ranging from the rosemary-tinged honey of the Corbières to the nougat of Limoux and candied chestnuts, a traditional late-autumn treat.

Roussillonnais cuisine is Catalan- and Spanish-influenced – obvious in the prevalence of olive oil, and adaptations of tapas and paella. The dry and grilled pork sausages (*embutits* and *botifares*) are excellent, as is hearty pork-based *ollada* soup – a rural stand-by. Special occasions are celebrated with a *cargolada* – an elaborate dish of grilled land snails. Moving towards the coast, fruit reappears with the cherries of Céret, as well as almonds, peaches and pears. The coastal hills are covered in olive trees, while fishing has long been the mainstay of seaside villages like Collioure and Port-Vendres.

Breakfast and snacks

A croissant, *pain au chocolat*, or a sandwich in a bar or café, with hot chocolate or coffee, is generally the best **breakfast** you'll get – at a fraction of the cost charged by most hotels. Croissants are displayed on bar counters until around 9.30 or 10am. If you stand – cheaper than sitting down – you just help yourself to these with your coffee; the waiter keeps an eye on how many you've eaten and bills you accordingly. These days a French hotel breakfast is usually a buffet – cereal, yoghurt, cheese, meat, fruit, croissants, brioches, bread, jam, etc. – and of €6–12, and of varying quality; coffee increasingly comes out of a machine.

Lunch

At **lunchtime**, and sometimes in the evening, you may find cafés offering a *plat du jour* (chef's daily special) at between €9 and €14, or *formules*, a limited or no-choice menu. *Croques-monsieur* or *croques-madame* (variations on the toasted-cheese and ham sandwich) are sold at cafés, brasseries and many street stands, along with *frites* (potato fries), crêpes, *galettes* (wholewheat pancakes), *gauffre* (waffles), *glaces* (ice creams) and all kinds of fresh filled baguettes (these very filling sandwiches usually cost €3–5 to take away). For variety, there are Tunisian snacks like *brik à l'œuf* (a fried pastry with an egg inside), *merguez* (spicy North African sausage), Greek *souvlaki* (kebabs) and Middle Eastern falafel (deep-fried chickpea balls in flat bread with salad). Wine bars are good for platters of regional charcuterie and cheese, usually served with rustic bread (*pain de campagne*).

Crêpes, or pancakes with fillings, served up at ubiquitous crêperies, are popular lunchtime food. The savoury buckwheat variety (*galettes*) provide the main course; the sweet white-flour ones are dessert. **Pizzerias**, usually *au feu de bois* (wood-fire-baked), are also very common. They are somewhat better value than crêperies, but quality and quantity vary greatly – look before you leap into the nearest empty seats.

Picnics

Gallic culture is incredibly **picnic**-tolerant, and there's no problem in pulling off the road and spreading your blanket wherever you are. It's a very economical and pleasant way of dining, with the local outdoor market or supermarket able to provide everything you need from tomatoes and avocados to cheese and pâté. Cooked meat, prepared snacks, ready-made dishes and assorted salads can be bought at charcuteries (delicatessens), which you'll find everywhere – even in small villages, though the same things are cheaper at supermarket counters. You purchase by weight, or you can ask for *une tranche* (a slice), *une barquette* (a carton) or *une part* (a portion).

Tearooms

Salons de thé, which open from mid-morning to late evening, serve brunches, salads, quiches and so on, as well as gateaux, ice cream and a wide selection of teas. They tend to be a good deal pricier than cafés or brasseries – you're paying for the posh surroundings – and generally have a more male ambience and clientele. For cakes and astries to take away, you'll find impressive arrays at very boulangerie-pâtisserie.

Types of restaurant

here's no difference between **restaurants** (or auberges or relais as they sometimes call themselves) and **brasseries** in terms of quality or rice range. The distinction is that brasseries, which resemble cafés, serve quicker meals at most hours of the day, while restaurants tend to stick to the traditional meal times of noon to 2pm, and 7pm to 9.30pm or 10.30pm. In touristy areas in high season, and for all the more upmarket places, it's wise to make reservations – easily done on the same day. In small towns it may be impossible to get anything other than a bar sandwich after 10pm or even earlier; in major cities, town-centre brasseries will serve until 11pm or midnight and one or two may stay open all night.

When hunting for places to eat, avoid those that are half-empty at peak time, use your nose and regard long menus with suspicion. Don't forget that hotel restaurants are open to non-residents, and are often very good value and good quality, especially if it's a member of the Logis de France network. In many small towns and villages, you'll find the only restaurants are in hotels. Since restaurants change hands frequently and have their ups and downs, it's also worth asking locals for recommendations. This is the conversational equivalent of commenting on the weather in Britain and will usually elicit strong views and sound advice.

Wherever you are, look out for a **Bistro de Pays,** (bistrotdepays.com): a village café noted for offering simple dishes such as platters of local ham and cheese, and which often put on cultural events. Most are found in Roussillon.

Prices

Prices, and what you get for them, are posted outside. As you'd expect, eating out is more expensive in the bigger cities. Normally there's a choice between one or more menus fixes, where the number of courses has already been determined and the choice is limited, and choosing individually from the carte (menu). **Menus fixes** are normally the cheapest option. At the bottom end of the price range, they revolve around standard dishes such as steak and chips (steak frites), chicken and chips (poulet frites) and various concoctions involving innards. But further up the scale they can

be much the best-value way of sampling regional specialities, sometimes running to five or more courses. If you're simply not that hungry, just go for the plat du jour.

Going **à la carte** offers greater choice and, in the better restaurants, unlimited access to the chef's specialities – though you'll pay for the privilege. A simple and perfectly legitimate tactic is to have just one course instead of the expected three or four. You can share dishes or go for several starters – a useful strategy for vegetarians. There's no minimum charge.

In the French **sequence of courses**, any salad (sometimes vegetables, too) comes separate from the main dish, and cheese precedes a dessert. You will be offered coffee, which is always extra, to finish off the meal.

Wine (vin) or a **drink** (boisson) is occasionally included (compris) in the cost of a menu fixe. When ordering house wine (cuvée du patron), the cheapest option, ask for un quart (0.25 litre), un demi-litre (0.5 litre) or une carafe (1 litre). In the Guide the lowest price menu or the range of menus is given.

Children and dogs

The French are much better disposed towards **children** in restaurants than other nationalities, not simply by offering reduced-price children's menus but in creating an atmosphere – even in otherwise fairly snooty establishments – that positively welcomes kids; some even have in-house games and toys for them to occupy themselves with. It is regarded as self-evident that large family groups should be able to eat out together.

A rather murkier area is that of **dogs** in the dining room; it can be quite a shock in a provincial hotel to realize that the majority of your fellow diners are attempting to keep dogs concealed beneath their tables.

Drink

Wherever you can eat you can invariably drink, and vice versa. **Drinking** is done at a leisurely pace whether it's a prelude to food (apéritif or apéro), a sequel (digestif), or the accompaniment, and cafés are the standard places to do it. Every bar or café has to display its full price list, usually without the fifteen-percent service charge added, with the cheapest drinks at the bar (au comptoir), and progressively increasing prices for sitting at a table inside (la salle), or outside (la terrasse). If you are sitting outside, particularly in a touristy area, unpleasantness can be avoided by checking the price with the waiter when you put in your order. You pay when you leave, and it's perfectly acceptable to sit for hours over just one cup of coffee.

Wine

Wine is drunk at just about every meal or social occasion, be it red (*rouge*), white (*blanc*) or rosé. *Vin de table* or *vin ordinaire* – table wine – is generally drinkable and always cheap, although it may be disguised and priced up as the house wine, or *cuvée*. The price of AOP (*Appellation d'Origine Protégée*) wines can vary from €4 to around €15 a bottle, and that's the vineyard price. You can buy a decent bottle of wine for €5 in a supermarket and €10 and over will buy you something really nice. By the time restaurants have added their considerable mark-up, however, wine can constitute an alarming proportion of the bill.

The basic **wine terms** are: *brut*, very dry; *sec*, dry; *demi-sec*, sweet; *doux*, very sweet; *mousseux*, sparkling; *méthode champenoise*, mature and sparkling. A glass of wine is simply *un rouge*, *un rosé* or *un blanc*. You may have the choice of *un ballon* (round glass) or a smaller glass (*un verre*). *Un pichet* (a pitcher) is normally a quarter-litre. A glass of wine in a bar will cost around €3.

The best way to **buy bottles** of wine is directly from the producers (*vignerons*), either at vineyards, at Maisons or Syndicats du Vin (representing a group of wine-producers), or at Coopératifs Vinicoles (wine-producer co-ops). At all these places you can sample the wines first. It's best to make clear at the start how much you want to buy (if it's only one or two bottles) and you will not be popular if you drink several glasses and then leave without making a purchase. The most economical option is to buy *en vrac*, which you can also do at some wine shops (*caves*), taking an easily obtainable plastic five- or ten-litre container (usually sold on the premises) and getting it filled straight from the barrel. In cities, supermarkets are the best places to buy your wine, and their prices often beat those of the *vignerons*.

In Languedoc and Roussillon, some good **regional wines** can be found in the *vins de pays* category (also known as *vins d'Oc* in these parts). Quality wines are denoted by the *Appellation d'Origine Protégée* (AOP), which strictly controls quality and the amount of wine that a particular area may produce. Within each appellation there is enormous diversity generated by the different types of soil, the lie of the land, the type of grape

grown – there are over forty varieties grown Languedoc and Roussillon – the ability of the wir to age and the individual skills of the wine-grower.

There is a guide to wine tasting in Chapter (see box, p.141).

Beer

Familiar light Belgian and German brands, pl French brands from Alsace, account for most of th **beer** you'll find. Craft breweries are springing u across the region, some of which are listed in th Guide. Draught beer (*à la pression*) – usually Krone bourg – is the cheapest drink you can have next t coffee and wine; ask for *une pression* or *un den* (0.33 litre). A *demi* costs around €3. For a wid choice of draught and bottled beer you need to g to the special beer-drinking establishments English-style pubs found in most city centres ar resorts. A small bottle at one of these places w cost at least twice as much as a *demi* in a café. supermarkets, however, bottled or canned beer exceptionally cheap.

The hard stuff

Strong alcohol is consumed from as early as 5a as a pre-work fortifier, and then at any time throug the day according to circumstance, though th national reputation for drunkenness has lost muc of its truth. Brandies and the dozens of *eaux de v* (spirits) and liqueurs are always available. *Pastis* the generic name of aniseed drinks such as Pernc or Ricard and a favourite throughout Languedoc is served diluted with water and ice (*glaçons*). I very refreshing and not expensive. Mixed wit *crème de menthe* it's known as a *perroquet*. Amor less familiar names, try Poire William (pear brandy or Marc (a spirit distilled from grape pulp). Measure are generous, but they don't come cheap: the sam applies for imported spirits like whisky (*Scotch*). Tw drinks designed to stimulate the appetite – *u apéritif* – are Pineau (cognac and grape juice) ar Kir (white wine with a dash of Cassis – blackcurra liqueur – or with champagne instead of wine for Kir Royal). **Cocktails** are served at most late-nigl bars, clubs and music places, as well as at upmark hotel bars and at every seaside promenade caf they usually cost at least €7.

Soft drinks

On the **soft drink** front, you can buy cartons unsweetened fruit juice in supermarkets, althoug

n the cafés the bottled (sweetened) nectars such as
apricot (*jus d'abricot*) and blackcurrant (*cassis*) still
hold sway. You can also get fresh orange or lemon
juice (*orange/citron pressé*), at a price. A *citron pressé*
is a refreshing choice for the extremely thirsty on a
hot day – the lemon juice is served in the bottom of
a long ice-filled glass, with a jug of water and a
sugar bowl to sweeten it to your taste. Other drinks
to try are syrups (*sirops*) of mint, grenadine or other
flavours mixed with water. The standard fizzy drinks
of lemonade (*limonade*), Coke (*coca*) and so forth
are all available. Bottles of **mineral water** (*eau
minérale*) and spring water (*eau de source*) – either
sparkling (*gazeuse*) or still (*eau plate*) – abound,
from the big brand names to more obscure spa
products. But there's nothing wrong with the tap
water (*l'eau du robinet* or *une carafe d'eau*), which will
always be brought free to your table if you ask for it.

Hot drinks

Coffee is invariably espresso – small, black and very
strong. *Un café* or *un express* is the regular; *un crème*
is with milk; *un café américain* or *un grand crème* are
large cups. *Un déca* is decaffeinated, now widely
available. British and American-style coffee shops
are popping up in Toulouse and Montpellier.
Ordinary **tea** (*thé*) is Lipton's nine times out of ten,
and is normally served black, and you can usually
have a slice of lemon (*citron*) with it if you want; to
have milk with it, ask for *un peu de lait frais* (some
fresh milk). *Chocolat chaud* – **hot chocolate** –
unlike tea, lives up to the high standards of French
food and drink and can be had in any café. After
eating, **herbal teas** (*infusions* or *tisanes*), served in
every *salon de thé*, can be soothing. The more
common ones are *verveine* (verbena), *tilleul* (lime
blossom), *menthe* (mint) and *camomille* (camomile).

Tipping

With the general exception of the most expensive
places, bars and restaurants in France calculate the
service charge, or tip, and factor it into your bill.
When you see *"service compris"* or *"s.c."* on a menu,
you will be expected only to leave small change as
a sign of gratitude – perhaps €0.20 for a drink or up
to €2.50 for a meal. When you see *"service non
compris"*, *"s.n.c."* or *"servis en sus"* you should be
prepared to leave a gratuity of fifteen percent for
standard-quality service. It's worth remembering
that tipping less may penalize a waiter who will
share out tips with kitchen staff based on the total
he or she has billed.

The media

**English-language newspapers, such as
The Times and the International New York
Times, are on sale the day of publication
in the region's larger cities, including
Toulouse, Montpellier and Nîmes, and
sometimes the day after publication at
many resorts. Of the French daily papers,
Le Monde is the most intellectual; it is
widely respected, but somewhat austere,
while Libération, founded by Jean-Paul
Sartre in the 1960s, is moderately
left-wing, independent and more collo-
quial, with good, if choosy, coverage.
Rigorous left-wing criticism of the French
government comes from L'Humanité,
the Communist Party paper. The other
nationals are all firmly right-wing, with
Le Figaro being the most respected. The
top-selling national is L'Équipe, which
is dedicated to sports. Languedoc-
Roussillon's regional daily paper is the
Midi-Libre: for visitors, it's mainly of
interest for its listings. The regional daily
papers are La Dépêche, covering Aude,
Ariège, Tarn and Toulouse, and Midi-
Libre, covering the rest of the areas in
this Guide: for visitors, their main interest
is for listings.**

Newspapers and magazines

Weeklies, along the lines of *Newsweek/Time*,
include the wide-ranging and socialist-leaning *Le
Nouvel Observateur* and its right-wing counterpoint
L'Express. The best investigative journalism is to be
found in the weekly satirical paper *Le Canard
Enchaîné*, while *Charlie Hebdo* is a sort of *Private Eye*
equivalent. There is also *Paris-Match* for gossip
about stars and royal families.

Moral **censorship** of the press is rare. On the
newsstands you'll find pornography of every shade
alongside knitting patterns and DIY. You'll also find
French **comics** (*bandes dessinées*), which often
indulge such adult interests: wildly and wonderfully
illustrated, they are considered to be quite an art
form and whole museums are devoted to them.

Some of the huge numbers of homeless people
in France (*les sans-abri*), estimated at around 3.5
million, make a bit of money by selling magazines
on the streets which combine culture, humour and
self-help with social and political issues. Costing €2,
the best known of these is *L'Itinérant*.

Television

French TV has 26 terrestrial channels: five are public (France 2, France 3, France 4, France 5 and France Ô); the others are privately owned. Of these, **TF1** and **France 2** are the most popular channels, showing a broad mix of programmes. **Arte** is a joint Franco-German cultural venture that transmits simultaneously in French and German: offerings include highbrow programmes, daily documentaries, art criticism, serious French and German movies and complete operas. Subscription-only **Canal Plus** is the main movie channel, with repeats of foreign films usually shown at least once in the original language. **France 3** is strong on regional news and more heavyweight movies, including a fair number of undubbed foreign films, while **M6** shows a lot of US imports and programmes aimed at a younger market. The main French **news broadcasts** are at 8pm on France 2 and TF1. Most accommodation has BBC World and CNN on their TVs. The main French **music channel** is NRJ.

Festivals

It's hard to beat the experience of arriving in a small French village, expecting no more than a bed for the night, to discover the streets decked out with flags and streamers, a band playing in the square and the entire population out celebrating the feast of their patron saint. Apart from Bastille Day (July 14) and the Assumption of the Virgin Mary (August 15), there are many traditional folk festivals thriving in Languedoc and Roussillon. In the south, the Fête de la Saint-Jean (June 24), celebrated with a huge bonfire, is a big deal. Moreover, local and municipal governments have invested heavily in summer *fêtes* and free concert series, designed to bring visitors into the region's villages.

Celebrations of local patron saints are concentrated in summer months and are the occasion for fireworks, dancing and *pétanque* competitions. These are particularly colourful in the fishing ports of the Languedoc coast, where saints' effigies are paraded down to the sea and events include **water-borne jousting** competitions. In wine country, there are inevitably festivals coinciding with the grape harvest, and in other regions with that of the dominant local product. Throughout the

Languedocian plain – notably east from Béziers and in certain towns of the Pyrenees – *tauromachie* (see box, p.196), which involves Spanish-style *corrida* (**bullfights**) or indigenous *courses camarguaise* occurs regularly throughout the summer, and a other big holidays, such as Pentecost and the pre-Lenten carnival. The most important and interesting regional festivals are outlined at the beginning of each chapter of the Guide, but it worth consulting departmental tourist boards (see p.46) for specific and local events.

Sports and outdoor activities

Languedoc and Roussillon offer a wide range of sports, both to watch and take part in. The region has some top rugby teams and two football teams play in Ligue 1. In addition, you can partake in variety of outdoor activities, including hiking, cycling and skiing, and water-borne diversions such as rafting and sailing.

Football and rugby

Languedoc and Roussillon are not the best place in France for **football**, and the only two cities in the region with a team in the First Division (*Ligue 1*) are Montpellier and Toulouse, who tend respectively to hang around the middle and lower regions of the league. That said, Montpellier were Ligue champions in the 2011–2012 season and won the French cup in 1990.

Rugby is the field game of choice in the region and virtually every town of any size boasts a team. Top local teams are Stade Toulousain, Castres Olympique and Montpellier. Rugby originated in 1832, in England, and although it arrived in France (Le Havre) in the 1870s, it only really caught on in the south. Post-game camaraderie is a big part of the whole experience, and you'll find yourself caught up in the cheerful spirit of things whether you see a major team like Stade Toulousain in action, or a small-town match with local teams.

Tauromachie

Bulls have been raised in eastern Languedoc since time immemorial, and in the last centuries **tauromachie** – "the art of the bull" (see box, p.196)

has come to play an important role in the culture of the whole region. While the people of the Camargue see it as a measure of virility, Occitan patriots are attracted to it as a custom which has no equivalent in the north of France. To capture the authentic feel of southern French *tauromachie*, try to see one of the *courses camarguaises* that take place in the Camargue from March to November (see Chapter 4).

Pétanque

Once the preserve of sweatered old men in berets, **pétanque**, or *boules*, has recently seen a surge in popularity and a broadening of appeal to include more young people and women. The game is similar to English bowls. Two equally numbered teams (from one to three persons) find a space of hard, compact ground and throw a *cochonnet* (jack) a few metres (technically six to ten). A small circle is then marked on the ground to show the limit of the area in which the throwers must stand (hence *pétanque* from the Provençal *"pieds tanqués"* or *"feet together"*). They then proceed in turns to launch a total of three balls (two in a six-person match), each with the object of having their metal *boules* closest to the *cochonnet* at the end of the exchange. A point is gained for each ball that is closer than the nearest ball of the opposing team. The jack is then thrown again and play continues until one side scores thirteen. *Pétanque* matches invariably draw a crowd of onlookers, and you will not be considered rude if you stop to observe.

Hiking and walking

Walking is undoubtedly the way to get most out of a visit to the region. Well-marked and maintained **GR paths**, signposted with their distinctive yellow and red bars, span the region, punctuated by *gîtes*, *refuges* and campsites along the way. The highest concentration of paths (and the best hiking scenery) is found in the Pyrenees and its foothills, where you will find an extensive network of yellow- and red-marked GRP (*grandes randonnées du pays*) paths as well as HRP (*haute route des Pyrénées*) routes. In addition, local AR footpaths abound, and in virtually every village you'll find an information board with a map outlining local itineraries of varying length and difficulty. Even if you're spending only a few hours in a village, it's worth enquiring at the tourist office, which will almost certainly have a pamphlet outlining local walks.

Guides and refuges

A series of excellent *Topoguides* has been published for each *région* and *département*, by the Fédération Française de la Randonnée Pédestre (☎ 01 44 89 93 90, ⊛ ffrandonnee.fr). There are currently around forty guides available for Languedoc and Roussillon, whose routes include Cathar country and vineyards. You can get them in bookshops and at some tourist offices. Most tourist offices also give away free or cheap (under €5) guides to local walks and bike trails. If you're travelling with children or are looking for less challenging routes, try *Les Sentiers d'Emilie*, which details thirty easy walks in each *département*. All these guides are in French, but even non-French-speakers will be able to use them with the help of a pocket dictionary. For **mountain refuges**, the Club Alpin Français (⊛ ffcam.fr) has online information.

Cycling

After walking, **cycling** is the next best option, and the cities of the south have been remarkably quick to adapt to two-wheeled transport, particularly Toulouse, Perpignan and Montpellier. Around Montpellier, Agde and Narbonne, extensive networks of **cycle paths**, often using decommissioned roads, link the coastal villages and the cities. In the countryside disused rail lines, such as the Gijou Valley Trail (see box, p.151), have been set up as bicycle (VTT) routes, and canal towpaths make it possible to cross the region with ease. Traffic off the main roads is surprisingly light, but be warned that some of the narrow *routes nationales* often see heavy, fast traffic. That said, with the exception of the coastal plain you may find the biggest challenge to be the **hilliness** of the terrain.

Several of the ski resorts in the Ariège and in Roussillon open their pistes in summer to mountain bikers (check the web pages of the resorts in the chapters).

Horseriding

While **horseriding** is not practical as a means of transport, it is an excellent way of enjoying the countryside. Practically every town and many farms have equestrian centres where you can ride unaccompanied or with a guide on local trails. In the Pyrenees **mules** provide a more practical alternative. Local tourist offices can give you information on riding centres or you can contact the Fédération Française d'Équitation (☎ 02 54 94 46 00, ⊛ ffe.com). For mule-trekking, contact the

Fédération Nationale Ânes et Randonnées (☎06 95 26 29 96, ⓦane-et-rando.com).

Skiing

There are a number of **ski resorts** in the eastern Pyrenees, and although they cannot offer anything to compare with the great resorts of the French Alps, you will be able to find some decent downhill skiing between December and April. Cross-country skiing, or *ski de fond*, is also a possibility, and the broad massifs of the Cerdagne and Ariège are particularly well suited to it. The relatively low altitude of some resorts is partially offset by the extensive use of snow-making machines. The most important and better-known resorts, among them Font-Romeu and Formiguères, are detailed in the Guide, and the Ariège and Pyrénées-Orientales tourist offices (see p.46) also have information, with the DT Ariège website (ⓦariegepyrenees.com) often offering accommodation and lift-ticket deals. Alternatively, for winter sports (including snowshoeing) contact the Pyrénées Club de France (☎05 62 73 56 35, ⓦpyrenees-club.asso.fr).

Rafting, canoeing, pot-holing and climbing

While you are exploring the hilly uplands of Languedoc and Roussillon, you ought to sample the thrill of **rafting** down one of the region's many dramatic rivers. This sport has exploded in recent years, and you will scarcely pass a gorge that is not capped by a rafting outfit at its upper end. The biggest concentration is in the upper Hérault, south of Ganges, but good opportunities can be found on the Orbiel, west of Lamalou, and on the Ariège around Tarascon. More placid paddling can be done by **canoe**, notably on the calmer stretches of water of the Aude and Gardon, and at the Pont du Gard. **Pot-holing** and **climbing** are also popular throughout Languedoc and Roussillon – tourist offices can hook you up with local guides and operators.

Waterports

Most of the region's seaside towns are fully developed resorts, and have facilities for the whole gamut of **watersports**: in summer months you'll find everything from jet-skis and sailboards to houseboats and yachts for rent. If you are specifically looking for beachside activities, Le-Grau-du-Roi has the best range of facilities, with La Grande-Motte close second. There are a number of **scuba-diving** clubs in the beach towns of Roussillon, such as Cap d'Agde, Banyuls, Argelès-Plage, Sète and Port Camargue, which arrange outings and run certified basic diving courses.

Water jousting

Water-jousting (see box, p.219) is a coastal tradition, which pits boat-borne jousting teams against each other in an effort to unseat their opponents. It has its home in Sète, but is practised along the length of the coast.

Swimming

Swimming pools (*piscines*) are well signposted in most French towns and reasonably priced usually around €5 for a swim. Tourist offices have their addresses. You may be required to wear a bathing cap, whether you are male or female, so come prepared. Another common requirement is that all bathers wear lycra-style ("Speedo-type") bathing apparel only, with no "boxer"-style trunks or women's wear with flaps or panels allowed.

Shopping

It'll be hard not to be tempted to bring home a piece of Languedoc and Roussillon, particularly food and drink. One thing to check is your home country's rules regarding importation both in terms of quantity and types of foods allowed. Generally fresh meat, cheese and produce are a no-no, unless they are vacuum-sealed. Another excellent thing to shop for is antiques (see box opposite).

In general, the French country **market** experience is not to be missed. Villages typically hold a farmer's market weekly, larger towns twice weekly. Here you'll find fresh produce, baked goods, regional cheeses, sausages and meats, and a selection of ready-to-eat foods such as roast chicken, which makes putting together a picnic a pleasure. But even if you aren't buying, the ambience of these markets is something to be savoured – a vestige of "authenticity" which so many visitors seek out. The Saturday-morning market in Sommières is one such. Market days are detailed throughout the Guide.

TREASURE-HUNTING IN LANGUEDOC

Thanks to the healthy rural middle-class which characterized southern France throughout the twentieth century, the **flea markets** (*marchés aux puces*) of Languedoc are a perfect place to find rare and distinctive antiques (*brocanterie*). In recent years, holding informal local sales (usually on Sundays) has become a popular passion – locally referred to as *vide greniers*, or "attic-clearing." Even in the smallest hamlets, the pickings are excellent – far better than the typical North American flea market or British boot sale. Housewares, furniture and vintage clothing can be found, often at bargain prices (and it's always worth haggling).

Big cities like Toulouse have regular markets which often run on weekdays but the real gems (and prices) are found in **country towns**, particularly in the Hérault and Gard. A comprehensive and up-to-date directory of local markets and sales can be found at ⓦvide-greniers.org.

In Toulouse, look out for **violet**-based products; in Roussillon it's all about the ubiquitous stripy, colourful Catalan **fabrics**, which are used for home furnishings and espadrilles, but also **jewellery** made with the local garnets. St-Jean-de-Fos in the Hérault *département* is famous for its **pottery**.

Travelling with children

Children are generally welcome everywhere in France, including in most bars and restaurants. Especially in seaside towns, many restaurants have children's menus (*menu enfant*), while some will provide smaller portions of adult dishes on request. Most hotels charge by the room, with a small supplement for an additional bed or cot, while family-run places will usually babysit or offer a listening service while you eat or go out. Under-4s travel free on SNCF **trains and buses**, while 4–11s pay half-fare (see p.24 for other reductions). The SNCF also has a scheme called **Junior & Cie** where children aged 4–14 can be accompanied on a journey by a train-company employee for a fee. In many **museums**, under 18s go free while the Monuments Nationaux (ⓦmonuments-nationaux.fr) sites are free to European Union members aged under 26.

If you're travelling with a baby, be aware that most French **baby foods** have added sugar and salt, and the milk powders may be richer than your baby is accustomed to. Disposable **nappies/diapers** (*couches à jeter*) are available everywhere. Breast-feeding in public will generally raise few eyebrows, if done discreetly.

Most local tourist offices have details of specific **activities** for children – in particular, many resorts supervise "clubs" for children on the beach. Look out for resorts that have a **Famille Plus** label (ⓦfamilleplus.fr), which means they are geared towards families. Most **parks** have a children's play area. Something to be aware of is the difficulty of negotiating a child's **buggy** over the large cobbles that cover many of the older streets in town centres; if you don't have one already, consider purchasing a backpack-style carrier, which can be useful not only on trails, but also in towns.

Travel essentials

Costs

Because of the relatively low cost of accommodation and eating out, Languedoc and Roussillon are not expensive by northern European standards. For a reasonably comfortable existence, including a hotel room for two, a light restaurant lunch and a proper restaurant dinner plus moving around, café stops and museum visits, allow around €100 a day per person. But by counting the pennies, staying at cheap hostels (around €20 for bed and breakfast) or camping (from €10), and being strong-willed about extra cups of coffee and doses of culture, you could manage on €50 a day, including a cheap restaurant meal.

Accommodation and food

For two or more people, **hotel accommodation** is nearly always cheaper and better value than hostels, though hotel rates rise throughout the region in July and August, most dramatically in coastal resorts, and major tourist towns like Carcassonne. Many **restaurants** offer three-course menus for upwards of €20, though the lunchtime *menu de midi* is nearly always cheaper. **Wine** and **beer** are both very cheap in supermarkets, while buying wine from the barrel at village co-op cellars is even better value for money. The mark-up on wine in restaurants is high, though house wine in cheaper establishments is still very good value. **Drinks** in cafés and bars are what really make a hole in your pocket – remember that it's cheaper to drink at the bar than at a table. Also, given that a small bottle of water typically costs somewhere between €2.50 and €4, you can save considerably by ordering tap water – *une carafe d'eau* – which is always free.

Transport

French **trains** are good value, with many discounts available (see p.24 for details), though **buses** remain significantly cheaper (€1 to €1.60 for a journey). If you plan to do a lot of travelling, you can often buy ten bus journeys in advance, which saves money.

Attractions

Admission to **museums and monuments** can be pricey, though reduced admission is often available for those over 60 and under 18 (for which you'll need your passport as proof of age) and for students under 26. Many museums and monuments are free for children (the age bar for which may range from 12 to 18), and nearly always for kids under 4. Several towns operate a discount pass for their museums and monuments, which can be good value if you plan to visit a few.

Youth and student ID cards

Youth and student ID cards can soon pay for themselves in savings: full-time students are eligible for the International Student ID Card (ISIC; Ⓦ myisic .co.uk, or Ⓦ isic.org for other countries), which entitles the bearer to reduced air, rail and bus fares, and discounts at museums, theatres and other attractions. Those under 26 can buy the **International Youth Travel Card**, which carries the same benefits.

Crime and personal safety

Following the **terrorist attacks** in Paris in 2015 and Nice in 2016, France is generally on edge. People are advised to be vigilant and report any suspicious behaviour or unattended luggage to the nearest policeman. Expect to see machine-gun-toting soldiers patrolling the streets, stations and airports in major cities. You'll find that some museums, tourist sites, public buildings and department stores will want to look in your bag before letting you in. When travelling on a train, make sure your luggage is clearly labelled.

Theft and accidents

Petty theft is endemic in all the major cities and along the coast. Drivers, particularly with foreign number plates or in rental cars with Parisian registration, face a high risk of break-ins. Vehicles are rarely stolen, but car radios and luggage make tempting targets.

If you need to **report a theft**, go to the *ommissariat de police* (addresses are given in the Guide for the major cities), where they will fill out a *constat de vol*: you'll need to show your passport, and vehicle documents if relevant. If you have an **accident** while driving, you have to fill in and sign a *constat à l'amiable* (jointly agreed statement); car insurers are supposed to give you this with the policy. For **non-criminal driving offences** such as speeding, the police can impose an on-the-spot fine.

Police

The two main types of **police** that you are likely to come into contact with are the *Police Nationale*, who patrol cities and larger towns, and the *Gendarmerie Nationale*, who patrol the highways and rural areas. Some large cities also have a municipal force which often has jurisdiction only over traffic. In the Pyrenees, you may also come across specialized mountaineering sections of the police, who provide rescue services and guidance, and are unfailingly helpful, friendly and approachable.

Racism

Travellers of non-European origin, particularly those of African or Middle Eastern extraction, may encounter **racism**, such as hotels claiming to be booked up, police demanding to see papers and abuse. If you suffer a racial assault, you're likely to get a much more sympathetic hearing from your consulate than from the police. There are many anti-racism organizations which will offer support (though they may not have English-speakers). Mouvement Contre le Racisme et pour l'Amitié entre les Peuples (MRAP; Ⓦ mrap.fr) and SOS Racisme (Ⓦ sos-racisme.org) have offices in most big cities.

EMERGENCY NUMBERS

All these numbers are free.
Fire brigade (pompiers) ☎ 18
Medical emergencies ☎ 15
Police ☎ 17

Electricity

This is almost always 220V, using plugs with two round pins. If you haven't bought the appropriate adapter with you, you can buy one for around €10 from the electrical section of a department store. Before you plug in, check that the adapter (*adaptateur*) is of sufficient voltage and amperage for the appliance you plan on plugging in.

Entry requirements

Citizens of EU (European Union) countries can enter and travel freely within France with just a passport. Citizens of Australia, Canada, the United States and New Zealand, among other countries, can enter France and stay for up to ninety days without needing a visa. South African citizens require a visa. However, the situation can change and it is advisable to check with the French embassy or consulate in your own country before departure.

EU citizens (or other non-visa citizens) who stay longer than three months will need to register as a resident at the local *mairie,* for which you'll have to show your passport and proof of address.

FRENCH EMBASSIES AND CONSULATES OVERSEAS

Australia Canberra (embassy) **☎** 02 62 16 01 00; Sydney (consulate) **☎** 02 92 68 24 00, **Ⓦ** ambafrance-au.org.
Britain London (embassy) **☎** 020 7073 1200; Edinburgh (consulate) **☎** 0131 225 3377, **Ⓦ** ambafrance-uk.org.
Canada Ottawa (embassy) **☎** 613 789 1795, **Ⓦ** ambafrance-ca .org. See website for consulates.
Ireland Dublin **☎** 01 277 5000, **Ⓦ** ambafrance-ie.org.
New Zealand Wellington **☎** 04 384 2555, **Ⓦ** ambafrance-nz.org.
South Africa Pretoria (embassy) **☎** 012 425 1600, **Ⓦ** ambafrance-rsa.org; Johannesburg (consulate) **☎** 11 77 85 600, **Ⓦ** consulfrance-jhb.org; Cape Town (consulate) **☎** 21 48 85 080, **Ⓦ** consulfrance-lecap.org.
USA Washington (embassy) **☎** 202 944 6000, **Ⓦ** ambafrance-us .org. See website for consulates.

FOREIGN EMBASSIES IN FRANCE

Australia 4 rue Jean Rey, Paris **☎** 01 40 59 33 00, **Ⓦ** france .embassy.gov.au.
Canada 35 av Montaigne, Paris **☎** 01 44 43 29 00, **Ⓦ** canadainternational.gc.ca/france.
Ireland 12 av Foch, Paris **☎** 01 44 17 67 00, **Ⓦ** embassyof ireland.fr.
New Zealand 103 rue de Grenelle, Paris **☎** 01 45 01 43 43.
South Africa 59 quai d'Orsay, Paris **☎** 01 53 59 23 23, **Ⓦ** afriquesud.net.
United Kingdom 35 rue du Faubourg St Honoré, Paris **☎** 01 44 51 31 00, **Ⓦ** gov.uk/government/world/organisations/british -embassy-paris.
USA 2 av Gabriel, Paris **☎** 01 43 12 22 22, **Ⓦ** fr.usembassy.gov.

FOREIGN CONSULATES IN TOULOUSE

Canada 10 rue Jules de Resseguier, Toulouse **☎** 05 61 52 19 06, **Ⓦ** canadainternational.gc.ca/france.
USA 25 allées Jean-Jaurès, Toulouse **☎** 01 43 12 48 75, **Ⓦ** fr .usembassy.gov.

Health

With its gentle climate, easy pace of life and world-renowned **healthcare system**, France is one of the world's healthiest destinations. All **tap water** is safe to drink (except from taps labelled "*eau non potable*") and there are no nasty local maladies. No visitor requires any vaccinations. Languedoc and Roussillon will present you with few specific health risks, other than mosquito bites (especially on the coast and in the Camargue) or sunburn.

Pharmacies

For minor ailments, your immediate recourse should be to a **pharmacy**, marked by a flashing neon green cross. *Pharmacies* tend to be expensive, but well stocked and extremely efficient, and the pharmacist is well qualified to dispense advice as well as remedies. Opening hours are normally the same as shops (roughly 8/9am–noon & 2/3–6pm). Cities maintain a *pharmacie de garde* that stays open 24 hours according to a rota; addresses and hours are displayed in all pharmacy windows.

Doctors

For more **serious complaints**, pharmacists, tourist offices or police stations can direct you to a **doctor**, or you can always find one yourself by looking under "*Médecins généralistes*" in the *Yellow Pages* (*Pages Jaunes*). Many speak reasonably good English. Consultation fees, which you have to pay upfront, are €23 for a government-registered doctor (*un médecin conventionné*) – though fees are sometimes waived on an informal basis, partly to avoid paperwork. Non-registered doctors (*médecins non-conventionnés*), however, particularly special-ists, may charge considerably more.

Emergencies

In serious **emergencies** you should get to the nearest *Centre Hospitalier* (hospital), or call an **ambulance** (SAMU) on **☎** 15. In an accident or injury situation, the **fire service** (*les pompiers*) is usually fastest, and firemen and women are trained in first aid: call **☎** 18. Hospital phone numbers are given under "Directory" at the end of the main city accounts in the Guide.

Refunds

EU citizens are entitled to a refund (usually around seventy percent) of the standard fees of registered doctors and dentists. To apply for this refund, British citizens technically need a **European Health Insurance Card** (EHIC), which you can apply for online at Ⓦehic.org.uk. In practice, the card exists mainly to smooth the refund process rather than to guarantee it. If you don't have a card and need one, you can always apply for a "provisional replacement certificate". **Non-EU visitors**, including North Americans, should be sure to have their own adequate medical-insurance cover.

Prescriptions

French doctors are enthusiastic issuers of prescriptions (*ordonnances*), which can add considerably to the final cost of treatment. You will be given a **Statement of Treatment** (*feuille de soins*) with little stickers (*vignettes)* for each medicine prescribed, which you can use for insurance claims or – in the case of EU citizens – to be reimbursed on your return home under the terms of your EHIC (usually between 15 and 100 percent of the cost of prescription drugs and remedies). Similarly, if you're **treated at a hospital**, you'll have to pay upfront for outpatient treatment and then claim a refund later. If you are hospitalized, in-patients who are EU citizens can proffer their European Health Insurance Card to get 80 percent refund on bills. The other 20 percent,· and a daily hospital charge (*forfait journalier*) of €18, however, are non-refundable.

Insurance

Even though EU healthcare privileges apply in France, you'd do well to take out an **insurance policy** before travelling to cover against theft, loss and illness or injury. Most insurance companies charge an extra premium to include so-called **dangerous sports**, so if you plan to do any skiing, whitewater rafting, rock climbing or pot-holing make you sure you are covered.

If you need to make a claim on your insurance policy, you should keep **receipts** for medicines and medical treatment, and in the event you have anything stolen, you must obtain an **official statement from the police** (called a *constat de vol*).

Internet

Getting online in this part of France is usually easy. Most accommodation providers offer free **wi-fi** in rooms or in public spaces and also usually possess a computer in reception for public use. You'll also find free wi-fi in many tourist offices, train stations, public buildings, cafés and restaurants. Cybercafés do still exist; the tourist office should have details. Be mindful of security issues: try and use secure networks (password required) and make sure you log out of public computers.

Laundry

Laundries are common in French towns: some are listed in the "Directory" sections of the Guide, otherwise look in the phone book under "*Laveries Automatiques*". They are often unattended, so come pre-armed with small change. Machines are normally graded into 8kg, 12kg or 18kg wash sizes, and the smallest costs around €4 for a load plus €2 for drying. The advantage of staying in an aparthotel is that they usually have an on-site launderette. Hotel fees for laundering are normally extortionate.

LGBT travellers

France has a more liberal attitude towards **LGBT** people than most other European countries, with the legal **age of consent** being 15. In Languedoc, LGBT communities thrive in larger centres, such as oulouse and Montpellier, and some beach resorts, hough lesbian life is rather less upfront.

In general, the French consider sexuality to be a private matter and homophobic assaults are very are. On the whole, LGBT people tend to be discreet outside specific gay venues, parades and certain coastal resorts. **Montpellier**, traditionally politically eft-wing and socially liberal, is said to be the second gayest" city in France after Paris. **Toulouse** lso has a reputation for being a city with a vibrant ay and lesbian culture.

NFORMATION FOR LGBT TRAVELLERS

rc en Ciel Toulouse 81 rue St Roch **☎** 07 83 96 03 00, Ⓦ aectoulouse.fr. A local activist and community organization, which olds a public drop-in service on Saturday afternoons 2–5.30pm at 3 rue 'Aubuisson.

ay Provence Ⓦ gay-provence.com. This English-language website eatures a section on bars, restaurants and accommodation in the region.

ay Viking Ⓦ gayviking.com. Online French magazine featuring uides to Montpellier and Toulouse.

Hexagone Gay Ⓦ hexagonegay.com/region/languedoc roussillon80.html. National website with a section dedicated to gay life n the region.

Têtu Ⓦ tetu.com. France's mªin LGBT online magazine with news, avel and features.

Living and working in France

Jnemployment in France is high, and particularly o in traditionally depressed Languedoc and Roussillon, where it hovers around 14 percent. In he cities, bar work, club work, freelance translating, eaching English, software fixing, or working as an au pair are some of the most likely employment options, while in the countryside, it comes down to easonal fruit- or grape-picking (vendange), eaching English, busking or DIY odd-jobbing. Obviously, the better your French, the better your chances are of finding work.

An offbeat possibility if you want to discover rural ife is being a **working guest** on an organic farm, or anything from a week to a couple of months. The work may involve cheese making, market gardening, beekeeping, wine producing and building. For details of the scheme and a list of French addresses contact Willing Workers on Organic Farms (WWOOF) at Ⓦ wwoof.org.

Finally, if the region's splendid climate and aidback Mediterranean atmosphere tempt you to **buy a property or relocate**, you'll find a thriving expat community on hand to provide information and advice, with plenty of local businesses, services and cultural activities

catering to English speakers. As a starting point, see Ⓦ languedocsun.com, Ⓦ angloinfo.com /languedoc and Ⓦ frenchentree.com.

Maps

The best up-to-date **road maps** are the 1:100,000 maps of France produced by Michelin (Ⓦ via michelin.fr) or the Institut Géographique National (IGN; Ⓦ ign.fr). Both companies also issue good **regional maps** either as individual sheets or in one large spiral-bound "atlas routier"; Michelin's version is available in English as the France Tourist & Motoring Atlas (RRP £14.99).

If **walking or cycling**, it's worth investing in the more detailed IGN maps (see above). Their Carte de Randonnée series (1:25,000) is specifically designed for walkers, while the Carte de Promenade (1:100,000) is good for cyclists. For further details of walking guides, also see p.28.

Money

The French **currency** is the **euro** (€), with bank notes in denominations of 5, 10, 20, 50, 100, 200 and 500 euros, as well as coins of 1, 2, 5, 10, 20 and 50 cents and 1 and 2 euros.

By far the easiest way to access money in France is to use your credit or debit card to withdraw cash from an **ATM** (known as a distributeur or point d'argent); most machines give instructions in a variety of European languages. Note that there is often a transaction fee (although it's worth investigating credit cards that don't charge fees if you travel a lot), so it's more efficient to take out a sizeable sum each time rather than making lots of small withdrawals.

Credit and debit cards (although the latter should be a last resort due to high charges) are also widely accepted in shops, hotels and restaurants, although some smaller establishments don't accept them or levy a minimum purchase. Visa – called Carte Bleue in France – is almost universally recognized, followed by MasterCard. American Express is less widely accepted. Note that most French transactions require a PIN number: if your card is not a chip and PIN, explain that yours is a carte à piste and not a carte à puce.

If you prefer to take **traveller's cheques**, although these are now declining in use, the most widely recognized brand is American Express, which most banks and post offices will change. However these days, they are generally not accepted as payment in hotels, restaurants etc.

Prepaid cards, which are like a credit card loaded with a certain amount of euros, are a popular way to take money abroad.

Exchange

Rates and commission vary from bank to bank, so it's worth shopping around; the usual rate is a 1–2 percent commission on traveller's cheques and a flat rate charge on cash. Be wary of banks claiming to charge no commission – they merely adjust the exchange rate to their own advantage to compensate. Standard **banking hours** are Monday to Friday 9am to 4pm or 5pm. Some close at midday (noon/12.30pm–2/2.30pm); some are open on Saturday 9am to noon. All are closed on Sunday and public holidays. They will have a notice on the door if they do currency exchange. **Money exchange counters** (*bureaux de change*) open longer hours than the banks: you'll find them at all the airports in the region and at the train stations in Toulouse and Montpellier, with usually one or two in town centres as well.

Opening hours and public holidays

Basic **hours of business** are 8 or 9am to noon or 1pm, and 2pm or 3pm to 6 or 7pm. In big city centres, shops and other businesses stay open throughout the day, and in July and August most tourist offices and museums are open without

interruption. Otherwise almost everything closes for a couple of hours at midday, or even longer in the summer. Small food shops often don't reopen till halfway through the afternoon, closing around 7.30 or 8pm just before the evening meal. Supermarkets tend to stay open 9am to 9pm Monday to Saturday and some are open on Sunday mornings.

The standard **closing days** are Sunday and/or Monday, with shops taking turns to close with the neighbours; many food shops such as *boulangeries* (bakeries) that open on Sunday will do so in the morning only. In small towns you'll find everything except the odd *boulangerie* shut on both Sunday and Monday, while, even in cities, **restaurants and cafés** also often close on a Sunday or Monday.

Museums tend to open between 9 and 10am, close for lunch at noon until 2 or 3pm, and then run through to 5 or 6pm, although in the big cities they will stay open all day: **closing days** are usually Tuesday or Monday, sometimes both. Many state-owned museums have one day a week (often Sunday) when they're free or half-price. **Cathedrals** are almost always open all day every day, with charges only for the crypt, treasuries or cloister and little fuss about how you're dressed. **Church** opening hours are often more restricted; on Sunday mornings (or at other times which you'll see posted up on the door) you may have to attend a service to take a look. In small towns and villages, however, getting the key is not difficult – ask anyone nearby or seek out the priest, whose house is known as the *presbytère*.

Phones

The easiest option – though by no means the cheapest – is to use a **mobile phone**. France operates on the **European GSM standard**, and mobiles bought in the UK, Australia and New Zealand should work here, though US cellphones won't unless they're tri-band. If you plan to make a lot of calls you might consider buying a French mobile (*portable*) using pre-paid charge-up cards (*mobicartes*); inexpensive deals are always on offer from one of the big companies. Mobile phone **reception** is generally good throughout Languedoc and Roussillon although in isolated mountain valleys coverage may be poor and in summer months relays can become saturated. There are plenty of **public phone boxes** – you can usually use your credit card to pay.

Making calls

For **calls within France** – local or long-distance – simply dial all ten digits of the number. **Numbers**

CALLING CODES
CALLING FRANCE FROM OVERSEAS
International access code then 33 then ten-digit number (minus the initial 0).

CALLING OVERSEAS FROM FRANCE
Note that the initial zero is omitted from the area code when dialling the UK, Ireland, Australia and New Zealand from abroad.
US and Canada 00 + 1 + area code.
Australia 00 + 61 + area code.
New Zealand 00 + 64 + area code.
UK 00 + 44 + area code.
Ireland 00 + 353 + area code.
South Africa 00 + 27 + area code

beginning with ☎0800 are free numbers; local rate numbers begin ☎0801; most other numbers beginning with ☎08 are premium rate (price is indicated by law in the ad), and those beginning with ☎06 and ☎07 are mobile numbers.

For **international calls**, it's now cheap for UK and Irish travellers to make mobile phone calls from France to the UK and Ireland following the abolition of roaming charges (about €0.05/3p per minute to make a call and less than a penny to receive a call). Whether this will still be the case if and when the UK leaves the EU remains to be seen. Travellers from other countries should check with their own network provider about the cheapest way to make mobile phone calls while abroad.

Invariably, calls made from hotel room phones will be pricey. Increasingly, many people use the internet service **Skype** (☎skype.com) to stay in touch while they are away; it's free to call from and to computers and tablets but there is a charge to call mobiles and landlines.

Post

French **post offices** (*bureaux de poste* or *PTTs*) – look for bright yellow *La Poste* signs – are generally open Monday to Friday 9am–6pm and Saturday 9am–noon. In smaller towns and villages, however, offices may close earlier and for lunch. The cost of posting standard **letters** (20g or less) and postcards is €0.68 within France, €1 to EU countries, and €1.25 to North America, Australia, New Zealand and South Africa. **Stamps** (*timbres*) can also be bought from *tabacs*, often with less queuing. To post your letter on the street, look for the bright yellow postboxes.

Inside many post offices you will find a row of yellow *guichets automatiques* – automatic ticket machines – with instructions in English, where you can weigh packages and buy the appropriate stamps; sticky labels and tape are also dispensed. There's usually an employee on hand to help. If you're sending parcels abroad, you can check prices on the *guichet* or in various leaflets: small post offices don't often send foreign mail and may need reminding, for example, of the reductions for printed papers and books. See ☎laposte.fr for details on rates and services.

Poste restante
You can receive mail at the central post offices of most towns. It should be addressed (preferably with the surname first and in capitals) "**Poste Restante**", followed by the address of the post office you'd like it sent to. To collect your mail, which you must do within fifteen days, you need a passport or other ID and there will be a charge. You should ask for all your names to be checked, as filing systems are not brilliant. To receive a parcel or package, you'll also need to show the number that is given to the sender.

Time

France is **one hour ahead** of the UK, six hours ahead of Eastern Standard Time, and nine hours ahead of Pacific Standard Time. This also applies during daylight savings seasons, which are observed in France (as in most of Europe) from the end of March through to the end of October.

Toilets

Ask for *les toilettes* or look for signs for the WC (pronounced "vay say"); when reading the details of facilities outside hotels, don't confuse *lavabo*, which means wash basin, with lavatory. Usually found downstairs along with the phone, French **toilets** in bars are still often of the hole-in-the-ground squatting variety, and tend to lack toilet paper. Both bar and restaurant toilets are usually free, as are toilets in museums, though toilets in railway stations and department stores are commonly staffed by attendants who will expect a bit of spare change. Some have coin-operated locks, so always keep change handy for these and for the frequent Tardis-like public toilets found on the streets. These beige-coloured boxes have automatic doors that open when you insert coins and are cleaned automatically once you exit. Children under 10 aren't allowed in on their own.

Tourist information

Practically every town and many villages in Languedoc and Roussillon have a tourist office – usually an **Office du Tourisme** (**OT**) but sometimes a **Syndicat d'Initiative** (**SI**). For the practical purposes of visitors, there is little difference between them: SIs have wider responsibilities for encouraging business, while Offices du Tourisme deal exclusively with tourism; sometimes they share premises and call themselves an OTSI. In small villages where there is no OT or SI, the *mairie* (mayoral office), frequently located in the Hôtel de Ville (town hall), will offer a similar service.

From all these offices you can get specific local information, including listings of hotels and restaurants, leisure activities, car and bike rental, bus timetables, laundries and countless other things; many can also book accommodation for you. Most offices can provide a free town plan and will have maps and local walking guides on sale. In mountain regions they display daily meteorological information and often share premises with the local hiking and climbing organizations. In the larger cities you can usually also pick up free *What's On* guides.

REGIONAL AND DEPARTMENTAL TOURIST OFFICES

Comité Régional du Tourisme Languedoc-Roussillon Espace Capdeville – Le Millénaire II, 417 rue Samuel Morse, CS 79507, 34960 Montpellier Cedex 2 ✆ 04 67 22 98 09, 🖰 crtlr.org.

Comité Régional du Tourisme du Midi-Pyrénées 15 rue Rivals – CS 78543, BP 2166, 31685 Toulouse Cedex 6 ✆ 05 61 13 55 55, 🖰 tourisme-midi-pyrenees.com.

Agence de Développement Touristique d'Ariège-Pyrénées Maison du Tourisme, 2 bd du Sud, BP 30 143, 09000 Foix ✆ 05 61 02 30 70, 🖰 ariegepyrenees.com.

Agence de Développement Touristique de l'Aude, allée Raymond Courrière, 11855 Carcassonne Cedex 9 ✆ 04 68 11 66 00, 🖰 audetourisme.com.

Agence de Développement et de Réservation Touristiques du Gard 3 rue Cité Foulc, BP 122, 30010 Nîmes Cedex 4 ✆ 04 66 3 96 30, 🖰 tourismegard.com.

Comité Départemental du Tourisme Haute-Garonne 14 rue Bayard, CS 71509, 31015 Toulouse Cedex 6 ✆ 05 61 99 44 00, 🖰 tourisme.haute-garonne.com.

Agence de Développement Touristique de l'Hérault av des Moulins, 34184 Montpellier Cedex 4 ✆ 04 67 67 71 71, 🖰 herault-tourisme.com.

Agence de Développement Touristique des Pyrénées-Orientales 2 bd des Pyrénées, 66000 Perpignan ✆ 04 68 51 52 53 🖰 tourisme-pyreneesorientales.com.

Comité Départemental du Tourisme Tarn BP 225, 81006 Albi ✆ 05 63 77 32 10, 🖰 tourisme-tarn.com.

WEBSITES

TOURISM AND RECREATION

🖰 **plan-canal-du-midi.com** All you need to know about one of the world's greatest man-made waterways.

🖰 **destinationsuddefrance.com** The new Occitanie region's official tourist website, with links to activities, accommodation, gastronomy and culture.

🖰 **france.fr** The official website for tourism in France.

🖰 **france-beautiful-villages.org/en** The official site of the Plus Beaux Villages de France.

🖰 **grandsitedefrance.com** The place to find out all about the country's Grands Sites – places of outstanding national interest.

🖰 **languedoc.visite.org** A useful site for helping plan your stay.

🖰 **languedoc-wines.com** The place to look for information on regional wines.

🖰 **lespyrenees.net** Everything you need to organize your holiday in the mountains.

🖰 **little-france.com** Roussillonais weekly webzine with information on culture, tourism, art, politics and economy.

🖰 **monuments-nationaux.fr** Information on over two hundred national monuments and museums – many in Languedoc and Roussillon – including news on special events.

🖰 **pagesjaunes.fr** The complete French *Yellow Pages*, unbeatable for hunting down goods and services.

🖰 **www.pyrenees-online.fr** Information on accommodation, sights, recreational activities and regional specialities.

🖰 **viamichelin.com** Allows you to map out detailed point-to-point

---

LES PLUS BEAUX VILLAGES DE FRANCE

In 1982 an independent membership organization was set up to promote France's most beautiful villages. Now, **Les Plus Beaux Villages de France** has 155 members who fulfil its criteria of being in a rural location, have less than two thousand inhabitants and possess at least two natural heritage sites. Suitable candidates have to apply to become members and pay an annual fee if selected – but can expect up to a fifty per cent increase in tourism thanks to promotion via the organization's website (🖰 les-plus-beaux-villages-de-france.org). In this guide you'll find Camon (see p.107), Castelnou (see p.287), Lagrasse (see p.253), Lautrec (see p.144), Minerve (see p.256), Monestiés (see p.137), Olargues (see p.156), St-Guilhem-le-Désert (see p.236) and Villefranche-de-Conflent (see p.289).

LES GRANDS SITES DE FRANCE

The label of "**Grand Site de France**", a government initiative, is awarded to the country's most-visited natural sites which have a system in place to ensure their conservation. In Languedoc and Roussillon, the current sites who have successfully applied for this accreditation are the Massif du Canigó (see p.292), St-Guilhem-le-Désert – Gorges de l'Hérault (see p.236), Camargue Gardoise (see p.192) and Pont du Gard (see p.182). Sites working towards accreditation are the Cité de Carcassonne (see p.88); Cité de Minerve, Gorges de la Cesse et du Brian; Vallée du Salagou et Cirque de Mourèze (see p.231); Cirque de Navacelles (see p.234) and Gorges du Gardon (see p.184). For further information see ⓦ grandsitedefrance.com.

riving itineraries around France and Europe, and gives you complete trip information and driving directions, free.

ⓦ **whc.unesco.org/en/statesparties/FR** All you need to know about World Heritage Sites.

NEWS AND INFORMATION

ⓦ **angloinfo.com/languedoc** English-language expat website for classifieds and an online directory.

ⓦ **connexionfrance.com** English-language expat newspaper.

ⓦ **languedocsun.com** English-language online magazine for the region.

ⓦ **languedocliving.com** English-language news, features and event listings.

ⓦ **ladepeche.fr** French-language site of regional daily newspaper for Aude, Ariège, Tarn and Toulouse; with event listings.

ⓦ **lemonde.fr** The French-language version of one of France's most reputable daily newspapers. Includes national and international news, culture and sports.

ⓦ **midilibre.fr** French-language daily newspaper for Aude, Gard, Hérault and Pyrénées-Orientales; good travel features, including ski information, and listings.

ⓦ **radiofrance.fr** Radio France's official page has national and international news coverage, current affairs, as well as music, culture and the latest in French sports. French language only.

ⓦ **thelocal.fr** English-language web newspaper covering French and international news.

ARTS AND CULTURE

ⓦ **cathares.org** Everything you ever wanted to know about the Cathars. A French-only site featuring information on culture, history and historical sites, as well as regular updates on related events and exhibitions.

ⓦ **fraclr.org** French website about the region's contemporary art scene.

ⓦ **ladanse.com** Multilingual site with comprehensive information on French and international dance including news, links, and a database of artists and companies.

ⓦ **occitanet.free.fr** An English-language site dedicated to the Occitan language.

ⓦ **regionlrmp.fr/-Guide-des-festivals-30980-** The place to look for festivals throughout the new Occitanie region.

Travellers with disabilities

For wheelchair users, the haphazard parking habits of the French and stepped village streets can be serious obstacles, while public toilets with **disabled access** are few and far between. However, things are constantly improving thanks to the organization Tourisme et Handicap (ⓦ tourisme-handicaps.org); look out for the label on city and resort logos, accommodation providers and tourist sites.

Bus services are generally not wheelchair friendly; the **trains**, however, have improved considerably. The SNCF has a dedicated page for information about its services ⓦ accessibilite.sncf.com, which includes information about the accessibility of its stations, arranging assistance for boarding and getting off trains (need to book 48hr in advance on ☎ 0890 640 650) and arranging for an SNCF employee to accompany you on your journey. **Taxis** are obliged by law to carry you and to help you into the vehicle, also to carry guide dogs. The tourist office should be able to provide details of local taxi companies, including those that are wheelchair accessible.

CONTACTS FOR TRAVELLERS WITH DISABILITIES

APF (Association des Paralysés de France) ☎ 01 53 80 92 97, ⓦ apf.asso.fr. National organization providing reliable information on being disabled in France with a separate website for holidays ⓦ www.vacances-accessibles.apf.asso.fr, which includes information on travelling by public transport, accommodation and tours and activities.

Fédération Française Handisport ☎ 01 40 31 45 00, ⓦ handisport.org. Provides information on sports and leisure facilities for people with disabilities.

Toulouse and around

PLACE DU CAPITOLE, TOULOUSE

1

Toulouse and around

Midway between the cool shores of the Atlantic and the sun-baked Mediterranean coast, Toulouse and its surrounding area form the gateway to Languedoc. France's fourth-largest city – capital of the new Occitanie region – is a dynamo and undoubtedly the liveliest and most interesting place on the west side of the Rhône; in addition to being the European centre for aerospace engineering and boasting several notable museums, it has a vibrant cultural and café life, partly due to having the third-largest student population in the country.

Among the gently undulating wheat fields of the **Lauragais** region, heartland of Toulouse's traditional agricultural prosperity, are historic medieval towns like **Lavaur** and **Revel**. Scattered between these is an array of villages and castles whose ancient stones have witnessed both the success of the region's famous woad trade (see box, p.72), and the violence and terror of the Crusades and Wars of Religion. South of Revel is **Castelnaudary**, birthplace of the celebrated Languedocian dish, cassoulet; it is also the main inland port of the **Canal du Midi**, which flows east from Toulouse to Sète.

GETTING AROUND

By train Toulouse is the rail hub for this region. It is on the Narbonne–Bordeaux/Paris TGV line, with smaller TER lines going northeast to Albi and Castres and south to Foix from where it continues to Latour-de-Carol/Enveitg, which hooks up with the Train Jaune (see box, p.295). SNCF buses may run in lieu of trains on some of these lines; services are reduced on Sundays and holidays.

By bus In Haute Garonne, most lines have no Sunday service; holidays and school holiday periods often have little or no service (see timetables for regional routes a ⓦ cg31.fr/bus.asp). First buses leave around 7am to coincide with school journeys while services tend to end before 7pm. It costs €2.20 for a ticket from central Toulouse to another town in the *département*.

By bike This area has more than 1000km of cycle paths so getting around on two wheels is easy, whether you're heading into the hills or following the flat course of the Canal du Midi. The tourist offices have details of routes.

Toulouse

TOULOUSE, the capital of the old French province of Languedoc, became the capital of the newly created Occitanie region in 2016 following the restructuring of France's administrative regions. It's a lively and cosmopolitan place, thanks to its large student population and thriving aeronautics industry (Airbus has its HQ here), and has a distinct Mediterranean look – as the sun edges towards the horizon, the hallmark pink brick buildings soak up the soft light and glow with a muted luminescence (hence its

LA MONTAGNE NOIRE

Highlights

❶ Place du Capitole The square at the centre of Toulouse has been the heart of the city for eight hundred years; a bustling weekend market place, it is ideal for people-watching. **See p.55**

❷ Basilique St-Sernin Romanesque Toulouse's finest monument has been a stopping point for tourists and travellers since the twelfth century, as testified by the impressive gallery of relics in the crypt. **See p.57**

❸ Hôtels particuliers The ancient mansions of the city's woad lords evocatively recall Toulouse's rich past. **See box, p.59**

❹ Les Abattoirs This converted slaughterhouse is home to a world-class contemporary and modern art museum, the best in southwest France. **See p.61**

❺ La Montagne Noire The western arm of the massif is a France time has left behind, where half-forgotten villages punctuate verdant hills. **See p.75**

❻ Cassoulet Languedoc's emblematic dish is a treat for meat-lovers with a healthy appetite; try it at Castelnaudary, where it was invented. **See box, p.80**

HIGHLIGHTS ARE MARKED ON THE MAPS ON P.52 & P.54

1

traditional nickname, *La Ville Rose*). Aside from some fine medieval churches, interesting museums and Renaissance mansions, the city offers a vigorous nightlife and a good variety of restaurants. It also has a certain Catalan feel, thanks to its bilingual street signs and metro announcements in the Occitan language (although you won't hear it spoken in the street).

Toulouse's **old town**, straddling a curve in the River Garonne and hedged by a busy, roughly hexagon-shaped ring road (which marks the course of its former defensive walls), is where you'll find most of the city's points of interest. Its heart is the majestically broad **place du Capitole**, the town hall square near the northeastern edge, from which crooked streets radiate out, web-like, to a series of *places* (squares). East from place du Capitole is primarily a business district, where the city's offices, hotels and restaurants are concentrated. To the north, the area around the wonderful **Basilique St-Sernin**, with the nearby archeological museum, forms the university quarter, while south and west of the Capitole towards the river lies the bulk of medieval Toulouse

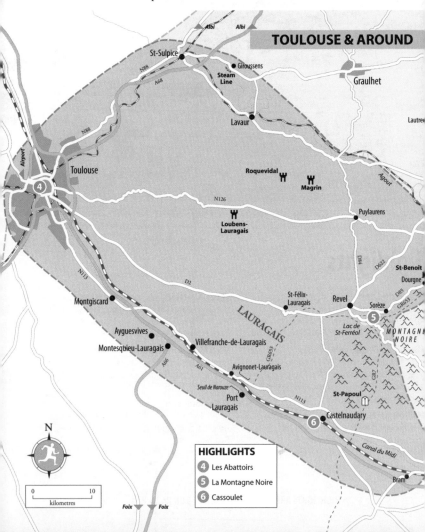

TOULOUSE & AROUND

HIGHLIGHTS

④ Les Abattoirs
⑤ La Montagne Noire
⑥ Cassoulet

N

0   10
kilometres

TOULOUSE FESTIVALS

Toulouse hosts a wealth of music, dance and art festivals that bring in top-notch names from around the world. For folk or traditional festivals, you're better off heading to the uplands of Languedoc or the Pyrenees to the south.

First weekend in Feb Fête de la Violette. Celebrates the violet (see box, p.55) via exhibitions relating to flower production, as well as a market and events.

Early April Carnaval de Toulouse Ⓦcarnaval detoulouse.fr. A pre-Lenten week of partying with parades, music and other events.

May International Art Festival Ⓦtoulouseartfestival.com. A free biannual festival where invited international artists create works for specific venues.

Mid-June Río Loco! Ⓦrio-loco.org. An annual festival celebrating world music, with a different theme each year; in 2016 it was "The Celtic World".

Late June Les Siestes Électroniques Ⓦwww .les-siestes-electroniques.com. Mainly free outdoor concerts of electronic and ambient music, featuring performers from around the world.

Early July Tangopostale Ⓦtangopostale .com. Carlos Gardel, one of the founders of tango, was born in Toulouse and this ten-day festival celebrates the dance form.

Mid-July to early Sept Toulouse Plages. Escape the city heat at three pop-up beaches: Prairie des Filtres, EDF Bazacle and Port Viguerie, complete with amenities and events.

Mid-July to early Aug Toulouse d'Été Ⓦtoulousedete.org. Eclectic programme of concerts held in atmospheric venues and featuring local musicians.

Sept Piano aux Jacobins Ⓦpianojacobins .com. Nightly recitals in the cloister of the Jacobins by internationally renowned pianists.

Late Sept Toulouse à Table Ⓦtoulouse atable.com. A weekend of culinary events and tastings.

– major sights here include the Dominicans' **Les Jacobins** complex, plus a number of noteworthy churches such as St-Pierre-des-Cuisines and Notre-Dame-de-la-Daurade. It's also home to most of the city's majestic Renaissance-era **hôtels particuliers** (private mansions), some of which, like the magnificent **Hôtel d'Assézat**, are now open as museums; most, though, are simply worth seeing for their striking and varied facades. The city's shopping district, focused on rue d'Alsace-Lorraine and rue St-Rome, stretches south to intersect with rue de Metz, south of which again, after the **cathedral**, a further series of *places* leads down to the formal gardens, the **Grand Rond** and **Jardin des Plantes** at the southeast corner of the old town. Beyond this, you'll find the town's canal port and a couple of small museums. Across the Garonne to the west, the neighbourhood of **St-Cyprien** is of interest for its stunningly renovated, cutting-edge modern art gallery, **Les Abattoirs**, while the only reason to visit the **suburbs** is to check out the three aeronautical attractions.

Brief history

Originally located a bit further upstream on the Garonne from the present city centre, Toulouse (then called Tolosa) was moved to the plain it currently occupies when the Romans took it over in 120 BC. Ruled after the decline of the Empire by Visigoths and Franks in turn, the town stagnated until the eleventh century, when the local **counts** (who were almost without exception named Raymond) began to encourage the nascent carpentry and leather industries. A century later a city council, or **Capitolo**, was set up to handle administration and justice and the wealthiest townsfolk – merchants and landholders – served as its members (the *capitouls*); the resulting convergence between their economic interests and political power allowed the city to flourish. Meanwhile, the counts – for all intents and purposes independent sovereigns – began to extend their influence over the other major families of the south, including the Trencavels (see p.89). By the late twelfth century they effectively controlled all of Languedoc, and adopted the surname of "St-Gilles", in honour of one of their favourite fiefs.

1

TOULOUSE

HIGHLIGHTS
1. Place du Capitole
2. Basilique St-Sernin
3. Hôtels particuliers

■ DRINKING AND NIGHTLIFE
Au Père Louis	8	La Luna Loca	2
Bar de la Lune	4	N5	9
Bar du Matin	11	Puerto Habana	10
Le Bikini	12	Le Purple	6
Le Cri de la Mouette	1	Le Shanghai	7
The Frog and Rosbif	5	Le Télégramme	3

0 — 200
metres

● SHOPPING
The Bookshop	2
Épicerie Bacquié	1
Graine de Pastel	3
Maison Pillon	4

● EATING
7 Place St-Sernin	2
Au Pois Gourmand	1
Bapz	17
Bibent	8
Le Café des Artistes	15
Chez Émile	13
Le Colombier	3
La Côte de Boeuf	12
Faim des Haricots	14
Le Florida	6
Le Genty Magre	16
L'Hémicycle	18
Les Jardins de l'Opéra	10
Le Louchebem	5
Michel Sarran	11
Sandyan	4
Saveurs Bio	9
Le Ver Luisant	7

■ ACCOMMODATION
		Cour des Consuls	15
Albert 1er	8	De France	11
Ambassadeurs	3	Des Beaux-Arts	14
Athénée	2	Garonne	16
Beauséjour	7	Grand Balcon	12
Camping Le Rupé		Lagrange City Toulouse	17
Castellane	9	Ours Blanc Victor Hugo	10
La Chartreuse	1	Royal Wilson	13
Le Clocher de Rodez	5	St-Sernin	6

Cathar influence

Both the counts and the city prospered until the r eign of Raymond VI, by which time **Cathar beliefs**, considered heretical by the Church, had taken firm root in the region (see p.315). Raymond may or may not have been a Cathar himself, but he was content to let his subjects choose their religious beliefs, thus provoking the ire of the papacy and providing the northern French aristocracy with a justification for war against him. When their knights stormed into Languedoc on a campaign of religious and political conquest – the **Albigensian Crusade** – Toulouse fell to forces led by the cruel Simon de Montfort. With the help of Catalan allies, Raymond recovered it in 1217, but it fell under the power of the French Crown in 1271. One of the consequences of the Catholic takeover early in the thirteenth century was the foundation of Toulouse's **university**, which thanks to the Dominican Order became the most important theological centre in France after Paris.

Woad and wars

Despite suffering grievously from a series of plagues, the city prospered with the booming **woad dye industry** in the 1400s (see box, p.72), and in the sixteenth century it became the official capital of Languedoc, although it later suffered – along with the whole of the South – as a result of the Wars of Religion, and as a consequence of the failed **revolt** against Cardinal Richelieu led by Henri de Montmorency (1595–1632), Governor of Languedoc. The Revolution of 1789, which the city fervently supported, heralded a new age of affluence as industry recovered and the Canal du Midi provided better market access for the agricultural hinterland. The good times were interrupted only by the Napoleonic Wars, during which the English general, Wellington, pursued the retreating Soult to the city in 1814; the French field marshal broke through the near encirclement, dealing the English a minor defeat before escaping.

The twentieth century and beyond

Occupied by the Germans during World War II when it was an important centre of the Resistance, Toulouse passed through the war more or less unscathed. Today, as well as for the **aerospace industry**, the city is known for its Oncopole cancer research centre and hospital. In 2012 Toulouse saw its darkest days in recent times when Islamic terrorist Mohammed Mera murdered eight people, including three soldiers and three Jewish children, in and around the city. In 2015, a new science museum, Quai des Savoirs, was opened, and the city as a whole has been undergoing a **€65 million facelift**, including improving the area around the station and access to the quays.

Place du Capitole and around

Place du Capitole, the sweeping plaza containing Toulouse's historical seat of government, the **Capitole**, forms the administrative and civic hub of the city. Apart from when it fills up with market stalls on Wednesday and Sunday mornings, the *place* is host to a constant surge of pedestrian traffic. Prettiest at sunset, when permeated by a

...ickwork, the square is best appreciated
...its western side – the perfect spot from
...metry and elegance of the building's

...nk holidays 10am–7pm • Free • ☏ 05 61 22 34 12
...-century administration of the city (see p.54), the
...e sixteenth century, although the frontage you see
...teenth. The main attraction inside is **La Salle des**
...great and the good from Toulouse's history via
...g from the nineteenth century. On the far side of the
palac... ...n is presided over by Viollet-le-Duc's (see box, p.94)
restored 1... ...ieval *donjon* – the only remnant of the original Capitole
and now the to... ...

Couvent des Jacobins

Rue Lakanal • Tues–Sun 10am–6pm • €4; church and chapelle de la Vierge free • ☏ 05 61 22 23 82, ⓦ jacobins.toulouse.fr • Metro
Capitole

The most colourful part of Toulouse's old town is found in the labyrinth of streets
radiating west and south from the place du Capitole, and dominated by the former
Dominican headquarters, known as the **Couvent des Jacobins**. Built in 1230, this
was the first-ever permanent convent of St Dominic's Order of Preachers (the
Dominicans), founded in the city in 1215 to combat the Cathar heresy. From its
humble beginnings the order quickly grew in power, soon taking charge of the
Church's Holy Inquisition and exercising, for a time, a near monopoly over the
bishoprics and universities of the medieval West. This building is, in fact, Toulouse's
original university, home of the theology faculty established by the Dominicans to
strengthen Catholic orthodoxy. Its cavernous thirteenth-century **church** (free)
contains a single file of seven enormous supporting columns, from which a web of
delicate interlacing ribs fan out across the vaulted ceiling (known as "the palm
tree"). In a modest gilt box under the grey marble altar in the centre of the nave rest
the remains of **St Thomas Aquinas** (1225–74), the great Dominican philosopher
who strove to introduce the thought of Aristotle – as interpreted by the Muslim
philosopher Ibn Rushd (Averroes) – into Catholic theology. There's still a pilgrimage
here on his feast day (Jan 28). Next to the reception area (formerly the sacristy) is
the **chapelle de la Vierge,** where you can see the convent's beautifully embroidered
ceremonial robes. Moving on (there's a charge to continue) you enter a low Gothic
cloister, its stubby and unadorned columns as sober in style as the order that built
it. In fact, the cloister isn't original, but the structures along its north side are,
including the large **chapterhouse** and the fourteenth-century **chapel of St-Antonin**.
The old **refectory**, also accessed from the cloister, now houses high-quality
temporary art exhibitions of a decidedly secular character.

Place Wilson and around

Place Victor-Hugo market: Tues–Sun 6am–2pm

East of place du Capitole lies the oblong **place Wilson**, which, edged by modern,
expensive hotels, retains a certain grandeur. Directly north of place Wilson is the
lively triangle of streets centred on the town's main **indoor market** in place Victor-
Hugo. The surrounding area is home to an array of cheap hotels and restaurants, as
well as some great places to pick up regional culinary goodies – look out for
Épicerie Bacquié (see p.71) and Maison Pillon (see p.71). **Rue d'Alsace Lorraine**, the
western boundary of the triangle, is Toulouse's principal shopping street, lined by

TOULOUSE'S VINEYARDS

The nearest **wine-growing area** to Toulouse is around the town of Fronton, 29km to the north of the city. AOP Fronton wines are made with the *Négrette* grape, which is unique to this small part of the world. Legend has it that its ancestor was brought here by the Knights of the Order of St John in the twelfth century but recent research suggests that the grape originated in Fronton. There are now at least forty vineyards in twenty communes producing red wines – with notes of black fruits, violets, liquorice and spices – as well as rosés. A good place to start is at the **Maison des Vins** (Château de Capdeville, route de Villaudric, 31620 Fronton ☎05 61 82 46 33, ⓦvins-de-fronton.com), where you can learn about the wines, taste them and find out which producers you can visit. Alternatively, **Voyages Duclos** (☎05 62 07 08 01, ⓦvoyages-duclos.com), organizes half-day trips from Toulouse on Saturdays in July and August for €45.

tately nineteenth-century apartments whose magnificent facades, with their monumental doorways, elaborately carved cornices and wrought-iron balconies, xude *fin-de-siècle* elegance.

Basilique St-Sernin and around

Leading north out of place du Capitole to **Basilique St-Sernin**, rue du Taur (Occitan for "bull") is a street full of lively studenty cafés and shops, a reminder that Toulouse has ong been a university city. Past **Notre-Dame du Taur**, noted for its wide, turreted steeple, is the Cinémathèque (see p.70) at No. 69, which has an eclectic film programme and holds open-air screenings in July and August.

Basilique St-Sernin

Basilica June –Sept Mon–Sat 8.30am–7pm; Sun 8.30am–7.30pm; Oct–May Mon–Sat 8.30–6pm, Sun 8.30am–7.30pm • Free
Crypts and ambulatory June–Sept Mon–Sat 10am–5.30pm, Sun 11.30am–6pm; Oct–May Mon–Sat 10am–noon & 2–5.30pm,
un 2–5.30pm • €2.50 • ☎05 61 21 70 18 • Metro Jeanne d'Arc

With its wedding-cake bell tower – an emblem of Toulouse – the **Basilique St-Sernin** s arguably southern France's greatest Romanesque church and the largest of its style n Western Europe. It was begun in 1080 to hold the remains of the city's first bishop, who was killed by the Romans in 250 AD – dragged to death by a bull (hence the name of the street rue du Taur). Later, the church was an important stop on the pilgrimage route to Santiago de Compostela, for which it was added to the UNESCO World Heritage Site list in 1998. Despite the fact that the present building was not completed until the fourteenth century, it has almost no Gothic elements: it's this stylistic purity combined with its sheer mass that makes it such a singular monument. The most striking feature of its exterior is the early twelfth-century **Miègeville door**, whose restrained but expressive biblical sculptures mark it as a product of the pivotal era in the evolution of medieval art. Inside, the uniform simplicity of the cavernous nave is impressive; the plain marble altar, still used today, was consecrated by Urban II in 1096. But the real attraction is the church's incredible collection of **reliquaries**, which it amassed over the years under the patronage of kings and with the financial help of donations from Santiago-bound pilgrims. Body parts of all the major saints can be found here, reposing in carved and gilded boxes set into the walls and chapels of the ambulatory and stored in the crypt below the altar.

Musée St-Raymond

Pl Saint-Sernin • Daily 10am–6pm • €4 • ☎05 61 22 31 44 • Metro Capitole or Jeanne d'Arc

On the southwestern side of place St-Sernin, unfortunately used as a car park, is the **Musée St-Raymond**, which holds the city's archeological finds. On the first floor are

1

finds from a Roman town in the region, including an impressive selection of sculpted marble heads. The second floor is dedicated to Roman Toulouse, Tolosa, while in the basement are the remains of a Roman necropolis.

Place St-Pierre and around

Auditorium St-Pierre-des-Cuisines: Aug daily 10am–1pm, 2–6pm; Sept–June Mon 10am–1pm • €3

On the banks of the Garonne sits placid little **place St-Pierre**, home to a couple of small pubs and the **Auditorium St-Pierre-des-Cuisines**, a fourth-century church, reputed to be the oldest ecclesiastical building in southwest France, and now the auditorium for the regional music and dance *conservatoire*. A substantial Gallo-Roman necropolis sits beneath it, accessed via the church's **crypt**.

Just west of the *place*, the languid **Canal de Brienne** angles away from the river through a nineteenth-century industrial area, where newly erected student apartment buildings abut old warehouses and cigarette factories.

Espace EDF Bazacle

11 quai Saint-Pierre • Tues–Sun May–Oct 1.30–7pm, Nov–April 1.30–6pm • Free • ☎ 05 62 30 16 00, ⊕ bazacle.edf.com • Metro Compans-Caffarelli

In 1890 the **EDF Bazacle**, a generating plant that powers up Toulouse to this day, was built on the banks at the former site of the mills, about a ten-minute walk west from St-Pierre. Here you can see both the modern and original turbines churning away, and take in local and international art exhibits, displayed in the main foyer. There are nice views across the river from the terrace; one of the city's pop-up beaches (see box, p.53) is created here in summer.

Place de la Daurade and around

Southeast from place St-Pierre, **place de la Daurade** makes a great spot to take a break and loll by the riverside; better still, take one of the cruises that depart from here (see p.66). Across the Garonne you can see Toulouse's medieval hospital, the Hôtel-Dieu St-Jacques, with the stub of the old bridge still poking out from its walls.

Basilique Notre-Dame-de-la-Daurade

Rue de la Dalbade • Mon–Sat 8.30am–7pm, until 6pm in winter, Sun 8.30am–12.30pm • Free • ☎ 05 61 25 58 05 • Metro Carmes

On the flood banks above place de la Daurade, you'll find the city's oddest church, **Notre-Dame-de-la-Daurade**, a curious compound of disparate architectural styles, disguising a church said to have originated as a pagan temple. Today, the centre of attraction is its *Vierge noire*, or **black Madonna** – a medieval polychrome sculpture of Christ (of the type produced throughout the area in the eleventh and twelfth centuries) seated on Mary's knee, showing Mary's skin tone as black, due to changes in pigment over time. Reputedly empowered to cure ailments and bring good fortune to the unborn child, it is still the object of popular pilgrimage, with many devotional plaques fixed around the entrance.

Hôtel de Bernuy

Off place de la Daurade to the northeast is the sixteenth-century **Hôtel de Bernuy**, one of Toulouse's famed *hôtels particuliers* (see box, p.59), and once the home of Jean de Bernuy. The town's wealthiest woad merchant, de Bernuy was rich enough to literally afford a king's ransom, paying for Francis I's release from captivity at the hands of the Habsburgs in 1526. The palace's 1504 **facade** features an array of sculpted window-frames featuring delicate Gothic details, while its cherub-topped main entrance completes the strange stylistic mix. Stepping back from the building, you'll see its slender tower rising high above the street.

Hôtel d'Assézat

Between place de la Daurade and place du Capitole lies the woad merchants' neighbourhood, the site of the **Hôtel d'Assézat**, home to the *jocs florals* (see p.329) since the nineteenth century. This is Toulouse's most famous and possibly most luxurious *hôtel particulier*, home to a certain (hugely successful) Pierre d'Assézat; his wealth is evident in the predominance of stone over brick, which endows the building with a sense of majesty that many of the town's best mansions lack. It was built in 1555 in cutting-edge style – the weighty, columned facade anticipates the Neoclassicism that would soon dominate European architecture. Inside, the patio is no less splendid, with a magnificent covered porch and columns. Despite his riches, d'Assézat suffered a tragic fate: having taken up Protestantism, he was deprived of his fortune, and Catholic repression forced him into exile.

Fondation Bemberg

Place d'Assézat • Tues–Sun 10am–12.30pm & 1.30–6pm, Thurs until 8.30pm • €8 • ☎ 05 61 12 06 89, ⊕ fondation-bemberg.fr • Metro Esquirol

Today the Hôtel d'Assézat houses an impressive art gallery, the **Fondation Bemberg**. On the first floor up you'll pass through a collection of Renaissance furniture, reaching a gallery displaying fifteenth- and sixteenth-century Flemish art, dominated by portraiture. Highlights include works by Lucas Cranach the Elder, in particular *Venus and Cupid*, and his portrait of a young woman. Further along there's a collection of sixteenth-century decorative statuary, whose kinetic realism bears an odd but striking resemblance to early twentieth-century Art Nouveau. Upstairs you'll find a worthy collection of more recent art, with the Impressionists and their successors well represented, among them Monet, Gauguin and Bonnard, who has a whole roomful of works here. On the museum's covered porch, overlooking the courtyard, you can enjoy a coffee or lunch from mid-April to mid-October.

Along rue St-Rome

Musée du Vieux-Toulouse mid-April to mid-Nov Mon–Sat 2–6pm • €4 • ☎ 05 62 27 11 50 • Metro Capitole or Esquirol • **Musée Paul-Dupuy** 13 rue de la Pleau • Tues–Sun: June–Sept 10am–6pm; Oct–May 10am–5pm • €4 • Metro Carmes

Pedestrianized **rue St-Rome** leads south from place du Capitole to some noteworthy buildings, including – just off the street on rue du May – the sixteenth-century **Hôtel du May**, built by a regent dean of the university's medical faculty, and now home to the hotchpotch **Musée du Vieux-Toulouse**. One of the town's least ornate *hôtels* – with only a simple door decoration to boast – is proof that even then academics were underpaid.

TOULOUSE'S HÔTELS PARTICULIERS

One of the hallmarks of Toulouse is its multitude of luxurious private mansions, or **hôtels particuliers**, scattered throughout the old town, and testament to the tremendous prosperity the town enjoyed in the fifteenth and sixteenth centuries when the *pastel* dye industry turned local merchants and bankers into veritable princes (see box, p.72). The earliest mansions have some sections of timber and daub, but the majority are constructed from local brick, which – ageing badly – detracts somewhat from their majesty. There is often, however, wonderful **masonry**; the mansions' splendour tends to reside in their stone doorways and window frames, embellished with carved figures, statues, coats of arms and floral designs. Stone was relatively expensive here, so more masonry was a sign of greater wealth; the most opulent buildings have facades constructed entirely from stone. In later examples, you'll find Renaissance flourishes, and some of these "mature" *hôtels* have graceful **turrets**, built to reflect the status of the owner; only the chartered elite – those who were wealthy enough to serve as *capitouls* – could add a tower. By the late sixteenth century, however, declining *pastel* production precipitated the end of the woad lords, leaving their magnificent homes to fall into gradual decay. Today they serve a variety of functions, including apartments, offices, schools and museums.

1

More elaborate is the old timber-and-brick mansion down adjacent rue Tripière, studded with stone decorations in the form of rabbits, while a little further south squats the three-storey **Tour de Sarta**, another former palace. **Rue des Changes**, the continuation of rue St-Rome, is evocatively lined by overhanging sixteenth-century homes. South of the modern rue Metz are more *hôtels*, including the Neoclassical **Hôtel de Clary** and the compact but beautiful fifteenth-century **Hôtel du Vieux Raisin.** Nearby, the old Hôtel Pierre-Bresson houses the **Musée Paul-Dupuy**, an applied arts museum containing the knick-knacks collected by its nineteenth-century namesake, including a renowned collection of clocks and watches.

Towards the river, **place du Salin** opens up in front of the massive brick Palais de Justice, built on the site of Toulouse's medieval castle, and its predecessor, the Roman fort. On the adjacent **place du Parlement**, at no. 7, you'll find the house where St Dominic and his early disciples stayed when they arrived in Toulouse in 1215 to preach against Catharism.

Musée des Augustins

21 rue de Metz • Daily expcept Tues 10am–6pm, Wed until 9pm • €3 • ☎ 05 61 22 21 82, ⓦ augustins.org • Metro Esquirol

Southeast of the place du Capitole, the former home of the city's powerful canons of the Augustinian Order now houses Toulouse's second-largest museum, the **Musée des Augustins**, with an important collection of medieval sculpture. The quality of work here is superb and the building itself is well worth a look. An externally featureless fourteenth-century brick precinct, covering an area almost as big as the place du Capitole and dominated by a strikingly huge belltower, the monastery was founded in 1309 on the authority of Pope Clement V. The extensive southern French Gothic style cloister and large chapterhouse are original construction, while its smaller Neoclassical cloister dates from the seventeenth century. The refectory *looks* medieval, though this is, in fact, one of Viollet-le-Duc's (see p.94) dubious nineteenth-century reconstructions.

The collection

The museum's **collection** consists of two disparate sections: superb medieval sculpture and reasonably impressive seventeenth- to-twentieth-century paintings and sculpture. The former is made up of high-quality stone carvings – a legacy of the city's twelfth-century counts. The complex was only restored to its original size in the last thirty years, and in the course of these works, more medieval treasures were discovered and added to the displays. Room 1 houses pieces from around France, and as far afield as northern England. The star attraction, though, is the forest of Romanesque **capitals** (carved column tops) on the bottom floor of the refectory (Room 3), on the west side of the cloister. Rescued from the ruins of the town's various churches, these were crafted by a school of Toulouse sculptors that thrived under the patronage of the counts in the first half of the twelfth century. Moving through the refectory, you can follow the development of the Toulouse school of sculpture, as the elaborate vegetal forms of the 1120s to 1140s give way to busy narrative scenes in increasingly high relief as the century progresses and draws to a close. The latest examples are the most spectacular – wonderfully carved scenes centred around episodes such as the death of John the Baptist. From the refectory, a monumental staircase leads to the upper floor, which contains a collection of French, Italian, Belgian and Dutch **paintings and sculpture**, including works by Rodin, Brueghel, Manet and Delacroix.

Cathédrale St-Étienne

Pl Saint-Étienne • Mon–Sat 8am–7pm, Sun 9am–7pm • Free • Metro François-Verdier

East of the Musée des Augustins, rue de Metz brings you to the curious **Cathédrale St-Étienne**, which, despite holding ecclesiastical priority, has always played second

1

iddle to its rival St-Sernin. The discord between its average-sized brick entrance, which dates from the beginning of the thirteenth century, and the incongruously massive choir plonked on the back some seventy years later is obvious; on entering, you discover that the huge ambulatory isn't even lined up squarely with the older church. The reason for this lack of harmony is that the cathedral was slated to be rebuilt on a much grander scale – the original nave demolished and a new one of the same proportions as the entrance added on – but money ran out, and the church was left as it is today. The **interior** of the cathedral holds few surprises, but is worth a quick look, if only for the Renaissance tapestries which line the walls of the nave, the sixteenth-century carved walnut choir, and the details of some of the chapels behind the main altar: there are several good **stained-glass windows**, going back as early as the fifteenth century, and some carved ceiling medallions date from the 1200s.

Adjacent **place St-Étienne** itself is surprisingly quiet, boasting little more than the city's oldest fountain – the Griffoul – dating from 1546. The streets west of the square offer some of the city's best **shopping** (see p.71). Going south, rue Fermat leads to pretty place Sainte-Scarbes, centre of Toulouse's antique furniture trade.

St-Cyprien

Across the river, the west bank of the Garonne is the site of the old neighbourhood of **St-Cyprien**, which, although enclosed within the medieval city's defensive walls, was always marginalized, owing to its location. Home to tanners and butchers – professionals banned from the main town for sanitary reasons – from the Middle Ages it was also the home of Toulouse's hospitals, where the sick were kept in semi-quarantine. Thus, on this side of the river, you won't find the grand mansions of *capitouls* and merchants.

Les Abattoirs

76 allées Charles-de-Fitte • Mon–Wed & Sun noon–6pm, until 8pm Thurs • €7 • ☏ 05 34 51 10 60, ⑩ www.lesabattoirs.org • Metro St-Cyprien-République

On allées Charles-de-Fitte, the avenue which marks the precinct of the city's former western wall, just behind the great cupola dominating the river's left bank, is **Les Abattoirs**. This splendid venue, opened in 2000, is not only one of France's best contemporary art museums, but also an inspired piece of urban regeneration. The hulking brick complex was constructed in 1831, and functioned as an abattoir until 1988, when environmental concerns forced it to close. The space itself is massive, with huge chambers perfectly suited to display even the largest canvases. Comprising over four thousand works, the collection covers everything from painting to multimedia exhibits. Most European and American schools are well represented, with the major postwar French movements, including Support-Surface, Art Brut and Figuration Libre, plus Italian and Spanish works a particular strength. The most striking piece is undoubtedly **Picasso**'s massive 8.30m-by-13.25m theatre backdrop, *The Stripping of the Minotaur in the Harlequin Suit*, painted in 1936 for Romain Rolland's *Le 14 Juillet* and towering over the lower gallery; it's only on show for six months of the year so check with the museum beforehand. Other avant-garde works that stand out are the untitled canvases of **Tàpies** and **Barceló**, **Bettencourt**'s provocative mosaic *The Conversion of St Paul* and a large collection of **Dubuffet**'s paintings. The collection is so large and varied that, whatever your tastes, you're unlikely to come away disappointed.

In the semi-circular courtyard outside, *L'Hémicycle* is an excellent spot for lunch (see p.69). Next to the museum, the grassy **Jardin Raymond IV**, with its original 1930s merry-go-round, stretches out towards the river along an impressive section of the city's fourteenth-century **walls**; on the quayside you'll find an information panel indicating

1

sites of interest on the opposite bank. From here, the **Passerelle Viguerie**, a 140m-long steel walkway fixed above the water alongside Hôpital de la Grave, is a fun route to get to the Hôtel Dieu St-Jacques.

Hôtel Dieu St-Jacques

Musée d'Histoire de la Médecine de Toulouse Thurs, Fri & Sun 11am–5pm • Free • ☎ 05 61 77 84 25, ⓦ musee-medecine.com • **Musée des Instruments de Médecine des hôpitaux de Toulouse** Thurs & Fri 1–5pm, first Sun of the month 10am–6pm • Free • ☎ 05 61 77 82 72, ⓦ chu-toulouse.fr/le-musee-des-instruments-de-medecine-des-hopitaux

South of Les Abattoirs is the old **Hôtel Dieu St-Jacques**. Modern hospitals grew out of the hospices which cared for pilgrims en route to the Holy Land or Santiago, and which eventually took over the care of sick people in general. Toulouse, being on the pilgrim route and the site of a major university, was a pioneer in medieval medicine. In the plague-ridden centuries preceding the Revolution, the most contagious patients arrived at the hospital directly by boat, so as not to infect the town. Today, these buildings house the administrative offices for Toulouse's centralized medical services, as well as two small **medical museums** with collections of surgical instruments and pharmaceutical equipment.

Château d'Eau

1 place Laganne • Tues–Sun 1–7pm • €3.50 • ☎ 05 61 77 09 40, ⓦ galeriechateaudeau.org

On the western side of the Pont Neuf which crosses over to the old town, you'll see the **Château d'Eau**, a former pumphouse, now a small photographic museum holding exhibitions by internationally renowned photographers. In front of here is the **Prairie de Filtres**; once used to filter the city's drinking water, it's now a green space which also hosts events including one of Toulouse's summer beaches (see box, p.53).

The new town and the Canal du Midi

If you have the time and energy, the areas south and east of the old town are also worth exploring. The southern district is marked off from old Toulouse by the wide allées Jules-Guesde.

Jardin des Plantes

Park Daily 7.45am–dusk • **Muséum de Toulouse** Tues–Sun 10am–6pm • €7/€9 • ☎ 05 67 73 84 84, ⓦ museum.toulouse.fr • **Quai des Savoirs** Tues–Sun 10am–5.30pm • €7 • ☎ 05 67 73 84 84, ⓦ quaidessavoirs.fr • Metro Palais-de-Justice

The town's main park, the formally styled **Jardin des Plantes**, can be entered through a large arch off Jules-Guesde. The park itself is a lively place, complete with kids' rides, ice-cream stands and an ersatz mountain and waterfall. Next to the entrance stands the **Muséum de Toulouse**, which has the largest natural history collection in France and is the city's most visited attraction, though really you need to speak French to get much out of it; it also has a good restaurant. Adjacent is the new science museum, **Quai des Savoirs**. Unfortunately, only French speakers will get much out of a visit, as neither has much information in English.

Musée départemental de la résistance et de la déportation

52 allée des Demoiselles • Mon–Fri 9am–noon & 1.30–5.30pm • Free • ☎ 05 61 14 80 40, ⓦ musee-resistance.haute-garonne.fr • Bus #10 Demouilles

Among the fading glory of the Art Deco mansions on allée des Demoiselles, you'll come across plaques marking the spots where Resistance fighters were shot dead by the Germans in the street-fighting of 1944. About halfway along, you'll arrive at the **Musée départemental de la résistance et de la déportation**, which through photos, artefacts and dioramas commemorates the local resistance; the plight of those living under occupation, including deportation; and the crimes of the occupiers.

1

Musée Georges-Labit

17 rue du Japon • Tues–Sun: June–Sept 10am–6pm; Oct–May 10am–5pm • €4 • ☎ 05 31 22 99 80 • Bus 10 Demouilles

A five-minute walk north from the resistance museum along rue du Japon lies the **Musée Georges-Labit**. This nineteenth-century pavilion is pure Orientalist fantasy, a Gilbert and Sullivanesque vision of the East, while the museum itself holds a small but incredibly varied collection of Asiatica, including Chinese artefacts dating from the tenth century, temple carvings from Northern India and two complete samurai suits of armour.

Canal du Midi

Just a stone's throw from the Musée Georges-Labit, a canal-side path leads up to the remains of the old Canal du Midi port, **Port St-Sauveur**, now a modern pleasure port. The towpath running parallel forms the first leg of the canal-side bike and walking route from Toulouse to the **Seuil de Naurouze** (see box, p.82).

The suburbs

Toulouse has a long history of aviation from its earliest days (*Aéropostale*, which served the French colonies in Africa and South America, was founded here in 1918) and the city has three fascinating aviation-related attractions on its outskirts: the Cité de l'Espace to the southeast and Let's Visit Airbus and Musée Aeroscopia to the northwest near the airport.

Cité de l'Espace

Parc de la Grande Plaine, av Jean-Gonord • Daily 9am–5/6/7/11pm • €21/24/25.50 depending on season • ☎ 05 67 22 23 24, ⓦ cite-espace.com • Take bus #37 from Ramonville metro station; alternatively, there is a private direct Starline Tourist Shuttle from June to August (€19.50 return including entry; ☎ 05 62 07 05 04, ⓦ voyages-duclos.com) from allée Jean-Jaurès (City Tour Toulouse stop).

The **Cité de l'Espace**, east of the city centre by exit 17 of the *périphérique est* ring road, i a massive high-tech science centre packed with scores of exhibits on the theme of space and its exploration, including satellite communications, space probes, a real Ariane rocket and, best of all, a walk-in mock-up of the MIR space station – a fascinating, but absolutely chilling and inhuman, environment. Many of the exhibits are interactive and, though it's on the pricey side, you could easily spend a day here, especially if you've got children in tow.

Let's Visit Airbus

Allée André-Turcat, 31700 Blagnac • Mon–Sat 8am–7pm • €15.50, reservations essential; combined ticket with Musée Aeroscopia €23 • ☎ 05 34 39 42 00, ⓦ manatour.fr/en • Take Tramline 1 to Beauzelle-aeroscopia then it's a 20min walk to the site

Only slightly more down to earth than the Cité de l'Espace is a visit to passenger-jet manufacturer **Airbus**'s headquarters near the airport. You can choose from three

---

TOULOUSE: THE FUTURE OF AIR TRAVEL

Toulouse's **aviation industry** is best known for Airbus, which provides stiff competition to major American airline manufacturers like Boeing, especially since it developed the world's largest passenger jet, the A-380. With a passenger capacity of 853, this two-storey colossus almost doubles the size of Boeing's 747; each plane contains over 500km of wiring. The creation of the super-liner hasn't been an entirely smooth ride, however: the plane's titanic components – manufactured in Germany, Britain and elsewhere in France – can be shipped to Bordeaux, but their size has meant that 250km of highway have had to be altered or built anew to accommodate trucks bearing loads up to 13m in height and 300m long (travelling at the break-neck speed of 20km per hour). The A-380 entered into passenger service in 2007 and so far 190 have been built, with the bulk of them ordered by Emirates.

AN AVIATION LEGEND

Toulouse has long been a centre of innovation in aviation. An early hero was **Antoine de Saint-Exupéry** (born 1900 in Lyon), a pilot who joined a local company and pioneered airmail routes over Africa and the South Atlantic, but is better known today as an author and journalist. Joining up in 1939 to fight the Germans, and despite physical disabilities, he flew reconnaissance missions for the Free French forces from 1940 onwards. A man of courage and conviction, he soon fell out with the authoritarian de Gaulle and, despite his exemplary record, became the subject of accusations of disloyalty. Meanwhile he authored a string of acclaimed books, the most famous of which, the children's fable **The Little Prince** (1943), has become a worldwide classic. A year after the book's publication Saint-Exupéry vanished during a flight over the Mediterranean, and his ultimate fate remained a mystery until 2004, when a Corsican fisherman turned up the pilot's identity bracelet; remains of his plane were found soon after. In 2008, a former German fighter pilot, who had been a fan of the author since his schooldays, regretfully confessed to having shot down Saint-Exupéry's P-38 Lightning on July 31, 1944.

ninety-minute tours: the "Airbus discovery tour" which takes visitors around the Airbus 380 assembly plant (Mon–Sat); "the panoramic tour", a 25km bus tour of the 700-hectare site (Mon–Fri); and "the green tour", a bus tour (first Wed of each month) that looks at Airbus's environmental solutions and commitments. Security is strict and you will need to take ID. It's a good idea to make a day of it and get a combined ticket with the Musée Aeroscopia.

Musée Aeroscopia

Allée André-Turcat, 31700 Blagnac • Daily 9.30am–6pm • €11.50; combined ticket with a Let's Visit Airbus tour €23 • ☎ 05 34 39 42 00, ⓦ musee-aeroscopia.fr • Take Tramline 1 to Beauzelle-aeroscopia then it's a 20min walk to the site; the Starline Tourist Shuttle (€14.50 return including entry; see Cité de l'Espace) also goes here (handy for Let's Visit Airbus too)

Opened in 2015, the **Musée Aeroscopia** next to the Airbus site traces the history of aviation via 25 aircraft. Highlights include a Louis Blériot XI, a huge Super Guppy cargo plane, as used by NASA, and Concorde. There are also five multimedia "discovery islands" where you can learn about different aspects of flying from new technology to the fascinating subject of aerial archaeology.

ARRIVAL AND DEPARTURE

BY PLANE

Toulouse's airport (☎ 0 825 380 000, ⓦ toulouse.aeroport .fr) is 6km northwest of the centre in the suburb of Blagnac. It has better services than many regional airports, with banking and exchange facilities, car rental offices (all the major companies), free wi-fi, family zones, a tourist office and a small selection of shops and travel agencies, but no left-luggage facility.

Getting to the city centre A shuttle bus runs from Toulouse's airport to the bus station (5.40am–12.15am, returning 5am–9.20pm; 20min; €8 one-way, €15 return); buy your ticket directly from the driver. You can use your ticket to continue your journey on the city's bus and tram system. Alternatively, tram T2 runs from the airport to Palais de Justice (6am–midnight Mon–Thurs & Sun, till 12.20am Fri & Sat, returning 5.50am–11.30pm), via the Arènes metro stop. Tickets cost €1.60 in the metro station. A taxi (☎ 05 61 30 02 54) to or from the centre will cost around €25.

BY TRAIN

Trains arrive at the grand old Gare Matabiau on bd Pierre-Sémard along the banks of the Canal du Midi, a 20min walk northeast of the old town. There's a left luggage here (*Espace Bagages*; daily 8.30am–10pm). The nearest metro stops are Marengo on Line A and Jeanne d'Arc on Line B, both of which will take you swiftly into the city centre.

Destinations (TGV stations are indicated with an asterisk) Albi (connections to Carmaux), via Rabastens, Lisle and Gaillac (several hourly; 1hr); Latour-de-Carol/Enveitg (connections to Train Jaune & Perpignan), via Pamiers, Foix, Tarascon-sûr-Ariège, l'Hospitalet-près-l'Andorre and Porte-Puymorens (several daily; 3hr); Mazamet, via Lavaur and Castres (many daily; 1hr 35min); Nîmes* (connections to Le Grau-du-Roi & Tarascon/Beaucaire), via Bram, Castelnaudary, Carcassonne* (connection to Quillan), Narbonne* (connections to Perpignan), Béziers* (connections to Bédarieux), Agde, Sète and Montpellier* (several hourly; 2hr 30min–3hr

1

30min); Paris* (several daily; 5hr 40min); St-Girons/St-Lizier, via Boussens (several daily; 1hr 30min–2hr); Vindrac (Cordes), via Rabastens, Lisle and Gaillac (several daily; 1hr).

BY BUS

Buses pull in right beside the train station at the modern *gare routière*, which has an excellent information desk (Mon–Fri 8am–7pm, Sat 9am–1pm & 2–6pm/Sun 4.30pm).

Destinations Avignonet-Lauragais (several daily; 1hr 20min); Castelnaudary (several daily; 1hr 35min); Castres (several daily; 1hr 40min); Foix (two daily; 1hr 30min); Graulhet (three daily; 1hr 15min); Lavaur (three daily; 50min); Mazamet (several daily; 1hr 50min); Pamiers (two daily; 1hr); Revel (several daily; 1hr 10min); St-Félix-de-Lauragais (several daily; 1hr); St-Girons (one daily; 2hr 20min); Villefranche-de-Lauragais (several daily; 1hr).

BY CAR

If driving in, follow directions for the "Centre" to the A61 ring road – from this take any one of exits 14–17 or 21–30.

There are plenty of car parks, as well as metered street parking and also free parking in cours Dillon and place Viguerie, both in St-Cyprien. There is also free parking at various outlying metro and tram stops so long as you buy a public transport ticket.

Car rental Avis, airport ☎ 0820 611 678, station ☎ 0820 611 677; Budget, airport ☎ 0821 230 499, station ☎ 06 65 31 33 94; Europcar, station ☎ 0825 004 346; Hertz, airport ☎ 0825 801 031, station ☎ 05 62 73 39 47; Sixt, airport ☎ 05 61 49 73 95, station ☎ 05 61 57 88 41.

BY BOAT

Various outfits offer tours on the Garonne and the canals du Midi. Toulouse Croisières offers lunch and dinner cruises from écluse Bayard along the Canal du Midi (€49.50–59.50 lunch, €59.50–69.50 musical dinner; ☎ 05 61 257 257, ⌨ toulouse-croisieres.com). Les Bateaux Toulousains (€10 for 1hr 10min, €29.90 for 5hr or €53.90 for a day cruise including lunch; ☎ 05 61 80 22 26, ⌨ bateaux-toulousains .fr) has a variety of trips on the Garonne from quai de la Daurade (June–Oct) and the Canal du Midi (March–June). For electric boat rental, contact Navicanal (☎ 05 61 55 10 91, ⌨ navicanal.com).

GETTING AROUND

The narrow streets of the old town necessarily make **walking** the best way to see Toulouse.

BY BIKE

Cycling is an excellent option, particularly given the new municipal bike network, which provides free bikes for up to 30min at a time from 253 automated stations, after which you're charged approximately €2 per hour. Subscribe for €1.20 per day or €5 per week at ⌨ velo .toulouse.fr, and pick up a map of cycle paths, sightseeing routes and details on commercial bike rental at the tourist office.

Bike rental La Maison du Vélo (12 bd Bon Repos; ☎ 05 34 40 64 72; ⌨ maisonduvelotoulouse.com), opposite the station, rents bikes from €20 per day and has a nice café in its courtyard. The tourist office will have details of other rental outlets, including those with electric bikes.

BY METRO AND BUS

Both metro and buses – which you're only likely to use when travelling from the bus or train station to the hotel

districts, or to visit outlying sights like the Cité de l'Espace – are operated by the urban transport agency Tisséo (☎ 05 61 41 70 70, ⌨ tisseo.fr), which has several offices including one at Jean-Jaurès metro station (Mon–Sat 6.30am–7.45pm). There is also a free electric nine-seat minibus that serves the city centre (Mon–Sat 9am–7pm); just put your hand out for it to stop. The metro runs until midnight and until 3am on Fridays and Saturdays. You can pick up a transport map from the tourist office or any metro station.

Tickets Available from metro stations, tobacconists and bus drivers, tickets cost €1.60 (one-way), €3.10 (return), and €5.50 (*ticket tribu*, good for two to twelve persons travelling together; it offers twelve journeys in one day). There are also individual passes for a day (€5.50), two days (€8.50) and three days (€10.50), as well as the Ticket Soirée (€3.10) for unlimited travel after 7pm until the last bus/metro.

INFORMATION AND PASSES

Tourist information The large and efficient office at the Donjon du Capitole (June–Sept Mon–Sat 9am–7pm, Sun 10.30am–5.15pm; Oct–May Mon–Fri 9am–6pm, Sat 9am–12.30pm & 2–6pm, Sun 10am–12.30pm & 2–5pm; ☎ 0 892 180 180, ⌨ toulouse-tourisme.com) can help make hotel reservations, sells tickets to many festivals and events and organizes walking tours of the

city (in English, Sat 2pm; €11).

Tourist passes The Pass Tourisme discount card (one/two/three days €15/€22/€29) gives free entry to the city's museums and attractions (discounted entry at Cité de l'Espace, Let's Visit Airbus and Musée Aeroscopia), a free guided tour, free travel on public transport including the airport shuttle and discounts in certain shops

LGBT TOULOUSE

For LGBT information in the city, contact Arc en Ciel (📞 07 83 96 03 00, 🌐 aectoulouse.fr) or the LGBT students' group Jules et Julies (🌐 julesetjulies.fr).

including bike rental. The Pass Premium (one/two/three days €20/€27/€35) also includes a boat trip and a ride on the tourist train. You can book on the tourist office website in advance for pick up at the Tisséo office in the airport or at the tourist office in the city centre. It comes with a handy map.

Tours Free guided tours of the city, according to your interests, are offered by locals through 🌐 toulousegreeters.fr.

Canal information La Capitainerie, 7 port St-Sauveur 📞 05 61 22 22 17.

ACCOMMODATION

There's no shortage of hotels in every bracket of price and comfort. Hotel rooms tend to be cheaper at weekends and during school holidays. The cluster of establishments around the station are good value but the area is rather nondescript. In the old town, the hotels around place Victor-Hugo (just up from the Capitole and place Wilson) are an easy bet, with a wide selection of two-star options.

Albert 1er 8 rue Rivals 📞 05 61 21 17 91, 🌐 hotel -albert1.com; metro Jean-Jaurès. Set in a quiet side-street just off the Capitole and close to the central market in place Victor-Hugo. A small, comfortable and good-value establishment, with foreign cable TV and a/c. Breakfast includes regional products. **€78**

Ambassadeurs 68 rue Bayard 📞 05 61 62 65 84, 🌐 hotel-des-ambassadeurs.com; metro Marengo. Very friendly little hotel just down from the station. Rooms have cable TV and en-suite bathroom. Family rooms and parking are available. **€65**

Athénée 13 bis rue de Matabiau 📞 05 61 63 10 63, 🌐 hotel-toulouse-athenee.com; metro Jeanne d'Arc. This well-renovated hotel offers garage parking, a cocktail bar and carefully chosen contemporary decor. Quiet, despite its location between the station and the old town. **€90**

Beauséjour 4 rue Caffarelli 📞 05 61 62 77 59, 🌐 hotelbeausejourtoulouse.com; metro Marengo or Jeanne d'Arc. Dirt cheap but basic; rooms are sound-proofed, though, and there's a great copper-balconied facade. This is the best of the hotels in this slightly dodgy but engagingly gritty neighbourhood around place de Belfort. **€43**

Camping Le Rupé 21 chemin du Pont du Rupé 📞 05 61 70 07 35, 🌐 camping-toulouse.com; metro La Vache. The nearest campsite to the city is 7km to the north in the Sesquières park. The three-star site, with 181 spaces for tents, caravans and motorhomes, is open year-round and has a jacuzzi, a kids' play area and *boulodrome* but sadly no pool. **€21**

Castellane 17 rue Castellane 📞 05 61 62 18 82, 🌐 castellanehotel.com; metro Jean-Jaurès. A cheerful hotel with a wide selection of room types and sizes (including rooms for up to six people), most of which are bright and quiet. All rooms have a/c and breakfast is free for under-12s. It has outside parking. **€70**

La Chartreuse 4 bis bd Bonrepos 📞 05 61 62 93 39, 🌐 chartreusehotel.com; metro Marengo. Efficient modern choice, right by the station, with a cute little interior patio (it's possible to park bikes here). Each room has free wi-fi, private shower, toilet and TV. **€63**

Le Clocher de Rodez 14 pl Jeanne-d'Arc 📞 05 61 62 42 92, 🌐 hotel-clocher-toulouse.com; metro Jeanne d'Arc. Comfortable and central, with secure parking and a solid range of amenities. All rooms have a/c and the breakfast buffet is excellent. Despite its size, it exudes a very personal hospitality. **€87**

★ **Cour des Consuls** 46 rue des Couteliers 📞 05 67 16 19 99, 🌐 www.cite-hotels.com; metro Esquirol. Opened in 2015, this five-star hotel created from a couple of woad lords' mansions is not only the best in town but one of the classiest in the region. The intimate dining room has a magnificent listed fireplace and the spa uses Graine de Pastel woad-based products (see p.71). **€178**

De France 5 rue d'Austerlitz 📞 05 61 21 88 24, 🌐 hotel -france-toulouse.com; metro Jean-Jaurès. Excellent value-for-money option in the rue d'Austerlitz/place Wilson area. Rooms are clean and functional, if nondescript, with cable TV and a/c. **€60**

Des Beaux-Arts 1 pl du Pont Neuf 📞 05 34 45 42 42, 🌐 hoteldesbeauxarts.com; metro Esquirol. Located in a 150-year-old building, this hotel's contemporary but refined interior contrasts well with its ageing exterior, making for solid, old-world elegance. Each room is individually decorated, some have views of the Garonne, and all have satellite TV. **€155**

Garonne 22 descente de la Halle-aux-Poissons 📞 05 34 31 94 80, 🌐 hotelgaronne.net; metro Esquirol. A chic little hotel tucked away down an alley near the Pont Neuf,

1

with fourteen rooms of understated luxury looking out over the river and the old town. The most romantic of the city's hotels. **€124**

Grand Balcon 8 rue Romiguières ☏ 05 61 21 48 08, ⓦ grandbalconhotel.com; metro Capitole. Just off place du Capitole, this ageing classic was frequented by the *Aéropostale* aviation pioneers, such as *Little Prince* author St-Exupéry (see box, p.65). Now an arty, luxury hotel, it provides chic modern accommodation. **€111**

Lagrange City Toulouse 36 Grande rue St-Michel ☏ 05 34 31 09 09, ⓦ lagrange-city-toulouse .com; metro St-Michel. Excellent-value aparthotel on the southern outskirts of town. The studios and apartments sleep up to six people; some have a balcony or a terrace. Conveniently, there is parking, a gym and a laundry. **€75**

Ours Blanc Victor Hugo 25 pl Victor-Hugo ☏ 05 61 23 14 55, ⓦ hotel-oursblanc.com; metro Jean-Jaurès. Right by the covered market and steps from the Capitole, this welcoming hotel is a good deal, although room quality

varies. The entire building has been renovated and each room has a TV, a/c and a private bath. The owners run two other higher-standard hotels nearby, the *Ours Blanc Centre*, 2 rue Porte Sardane, and the *Ours Blanc Wilson*, 2 ru Victor-Hugo. **€59**

★**Royal Wilson** 6 rue Labéda ☏ 05 61 12 41 41 ⓦ hotelroyalwilson-toulouse.com; metro Jean-Jaurès Well-kept hotel near the theatre with 27 rooms, some o which overlook the very pretty Moorish-style interio courtyard. Decor is a charming mix of traditional an contemporary with a smattering of antiques. Breakfas comes from the nearby market and there is a lock-u for bikes. **€64**

St-Sernin 2 rue St-Bernard ☏ 05 61 21 73 08 ⓦ hotelstsernin.com; metro Jeanne d'Arc. Well renovated old hotel in one of the best districts of the ol town, near the basilica: it's close to all the action, but fa enough away to provide peace in the evening. The decor i modern and coolly understated; amenities include a/c an flatscreen TV. **€79**

EATING

There's no shortage of good eating options in Toulouse, although on Sundays you'll find your choice drastically reduced. A well as French food, the city enjoys a culinary cosmopolitanism thanks to its ethnic mix, and you'll find many bars and café that serve tapas.

Neighbourhoods There are several good areas for restaurants. Rue de la Colombette in the St-Aubin district, just acros boulevard Carnot, has some attractive and fashionable choices. The area surrounding St-Sernin is particularly good; jus north, place Arnaud-Bernard and the tiny adjacent place des Tiercerettes have appealing options; between the basilica an place Bernard there's a compact knot of Arabic and Maghrebi restaurants; and rue du Taur has a number of Vietnames places and sandwich bars. If stuck for a choice, head south of place Wilson to place St-Georges, where you'll find a gaggl of typical terraced eating places, or to the bottom end of rue des Filatiers where there's a cluster of late-night restaurant and tapas bars. Several of the bistrots on place Wilson are distinguished not so much by their food, but by the fact that yo can eat as late as 1am. The best lunchtime bargain is in the covered market on place Victor-Hugo (closed Mon), whose upper floor has a group of very cheap food counters.

CAFÉS

Regular daytime café-lounging can be pursued around the popular student/arty hangout of place Arnaud-Bernard, while place du Capitole is the early evening meeting place. Place St-Georges has been somewhat inundated by restaurant terraces but remains another option, while the more elegant terraces of place Wilson are good if you don't mind the traffic.

Bapz 13 rue de la Bourse ☏ 05 61 23 06 63, ⓦ bapz.fr; metro Esquirol. English-style bakery and tearoom — definitely not your typical "caff". Good-value daily brunch (€17.50) and copious quiches and salads (€11.50). Tues–Sat noon–7pm (open Sun Oct–March).

Bibent 5 pl du Capitole ☏ 05 34 30 18 37, ⓦ maisonconstant.com; metro Capitole. On the south side of the square, this is Toulouse's most distinguished café, with exuberant plasterwork, marble tables and cascading chandeliers. Mon–Wed & Sun 7am–10.30pm, Thurs–Sat until 11.30pm.

Le Café des Artistes Pl de la Daurade ☏ 05 61 12 06 00; metro Esquirol. Lively, young café overlooking the Garonne. A perfect spot to watch the sun set on warm summer evenings, as floodlights pick out the brick buildings along the quays. Mon 7am–10pm, Tues–Fri until 2am, Sat until 3am.

★**Le Florida** 12 pl du Capitole ☏ 05 61 23 94 61, ⓦ leflorida-capitole.fr; metro Capitole. Relaxed café with a nicely retro air. One of the most pleasant places to hang out on the central square. Try the ice creams by artisan *glacier* Philippe Faur. Daily noon–1am.

RESTAURANTS

★**7 Place St-Sernin** 7 pl St-Sernin ☏ 05 62 30 05 30, ⓦ 7placesaintsernin.com; metro Jeanne d'Arc. This intimately romantic restaurant set in a small house behind the basilica serves inventive and original French cuisine based on regional ingredients, with a constantly changing menu including dazzling desserts. *Menus* from €39 and a unchtime *formule* for €24. Tues–Fri noon–1.30pm & .45–9.30pm, Mon & Sat dinner only.

★ **Au Pois Gourmand** 3 rue Émile Heybrard ☎ 05 34 36 2 00, ⊕ pois-gourmand.fr; bus 66 to Ducis stop. Great *cation* in a nineteenth-century riverside house with a eautiful patio. The quality French gastro cuisine does not ome cheap (*menus* from €26–73), but is of a predictably igh standard, and the *carte* presents a pleasant departure rom purely regional dishes thanks to some Asian nfluences. Mon–Fri noon–1.30pm & 7.30–9.30pm, Sat .30–9.30pm.

hez Émile 13 pl St-Georges ☎ 05 61 21 05 56, ⊕ restaurant-emile.com; metro Capitole. One of oulouse's best restaurants, and well situated on this busy blong square. Regional cuisine including cassoulet lownstairs and *gastronomique* with a strong seafood ccent upstairs. Lunch *menu* from €22, dinner from €32. Mon–Sat noon–2pm & 7.30–9.45pm, Sun noon–2pm.

e Colombier 14 rue Bayard ☎ 05 61 62 40 05, ⊕ restaurant-lecolombier.com; metro Jeanne d'Arc. his elegant restaurant, set in the eighteenth-century ormer stables of the *capitole*, is widely regarded as having he best cassoulet in town. Other regional delights include *ésiers* ("gizzards") and foie gras, as well as seafood and jame, all prepared and presented in an imaginative and nodern style. *Formules* from €19. Tues–Fri noon–2pm & '.15–10pm, Mon & Sat dinner only.

a Côte de Boeuf 12 rue des Gestes ☎ 05 61 21 19 61; netro Capitole. This simple and compact street-side estaurant is not the cheapest in the neighbourhood, but he quality of its wood-fire home-cooking (superb duck nd foie gras, not to mention the namesake side of beef) is op notch. Extras (such as coffee and wine) are pricey. Menus €18–55. Mon–Sat 7–10.30pm.

Faim des Haricots 3 rue du Puits Vert ☎ 05 61 22 49 '5, ⊕ lafaimdesharicots.fr; metro Esquirol. An excellent nd unpretentious vegetarian option, with generous all-'ou-can-eat salad and dessert buffets, "bottomless" bowls f soup in winter and a *menu midi* (€14). Daily noon–.30pm & 7–10.30pm.

Le Genty Magre 3 rue Genty Magre ☎ 05 61 21 31 60, ⊕ legentymagre.com; metro Esquirol. A perfect blend of economy and elegance, this restaurant is well-known to locals for its warm service, excellent *gastronomique* cuisine, and superb, well-priced wine list. Evening *menu* from €38, lunch from €16.50. Tues–Sat noon–2pm & 8–10pm.

L'Hémicycle Les Abattoirs (see p.61) ☎ 05 34 51 89 82, ⊕ restaurant-lhemicycle-toulouse.com; metro Saint-Cyprien-République. In the garden of the contemporary

art museum, *l'Hémicycle*, named after the shape of the building, serves *plats du jour* (€11) and *formules* (from €14) from noon to three and tea, coffee and cake before and after. Wed–Sun 10am–6pm.

Les Jardins de l'Opéra 1 pl du Capitole ☎ 05 61 21 05 56, ⊕ lesjardinsdelopera.fr; metro Capitole. The *Grand Hôtel*'s restaurant is one of Toulouse's best and most luxurious eating places. If you want to try some top-class, inventive southern French cuisine at an accessible price this is a good place to go. A basic *menu* starts at €32. Tues–Sat noon–2pm & 8–10pm.

★ **Le Louchebem** In the market at pl Victor-Hugo ☎ 05 67 00 51 75; metro Jean-Jaurès. The best of the market restaurants, this no-nonsense lunchtime establishment is a local institution serving regional specialities such as Toulouse sausage with potato purée. There is also a nice outside terrace. *Menus* from €18. Tues–Sun noon–2.30pm.

Michel Sarran 21 bd Armand-Duportal ☎ 05 61 12 32 32, ⊕ michel-sarran.com; metro Compans-Caffarelli. This famous *gastronomique* is universally acknowledged as the city's best restaurant. Imaginative dishes with a strong Mediterranean streak are served with style and warmth. The desserts are decadent in both constitution and price (€22–€27). *Menus* from €55 at lunch and €100 at dinner. Mon–Fri noon–1.45pm & 8–9.45pm, Wed dinner only.

Sandyan 54b rue Alsace-Lorraine ☎ 05 61 21 45 64, ⊕ sandyan.fr; metro Jeanne d'Arc. Michelin-starred chef Yannick Delpech has dragged Toulouse into the twenty-first century by opening a street-food café. *Menus* are €14.80 at lunch and €26 in the evening; takeaway is also available. Make sure you try one of his spectacular cakes. Mon 11.30am–6pm, Tues–Sat 11.30am–11pm.

★ **Saveurs Bio** 22 rue Maurice-Fonvieille ☎ 05 61 12 15 15, ⊕ saveursbio.com; metro Jean-Jaurès. Toulouse's best vegetarian place, offering everything from spinach quiche to alfalfa salads, made with certified organic produce. You can choose from the casual all-you-can-eat buffet (€12.40) or a range of set meals from €19.70–26.10 served in formal sit-down style. Mon–Sat 11.45–2.15pm & 7–10pm.

Le Ver Luisant 41 rue de la Colombette ☎ 05 61 63 06 73, ⊕ leverluisant.fr; metro Jean-Jaurès. A Fifties-style bar and simple bistro frequented by the arty set. The good food – featuring *gastronomique* spins on regional cuisine – is copious and the atmosphere fun. *Plat du jour* €10 at lunchtime, or €18–30 for an evening meal. Tues–Sat noon–2.15pm & 7.15–10.30pm (until 11pm Thurs & Fri; until 11.30pm Sat), Sun 11am–4pm.

DRINKING AND NIGHTLIFE

The annual influx of university students ensures that the city's nightlife is active, sustaining a whole range of bars and clubs. Things slow down from July to September, when the academic year breaks, but even in the summer you'll have no trouble drinking and dancing as late as you like. Unfortunately some of the city's best venues lie in the suburbs, which

1

means paying for a taxi, though there's no shortage of options closer to the old town. Entrance fees to clubs may be charged depending on the night and event, but generally you're expected to buy a rather expensive drink (€8–10), while at venues which are essentially bars you can enter free of charge.

Au Père Louis 45 rue des Tourneurs ☎ 05 61 21 33 45, ⊛ au-pere-louis.fr; metro Esquirol. A lively, old-fashioned bar with a good selection of *apéritifs* (try the house special: Quinquina) and wine. Mon–Sat 10am–3.30pm & 6–11pm.

Bar de la Lune 24 rue Palaprat ☎ 05 34 41 16 96; metro Jean-Jaurès. This evening drinking spot in St-Aubin draws an arty crowd with its occasional exhibitions and concerts. Mon–Fri 7pm–2am, Sat 8pm–3am, Sun 6pm–2am.

★ **Bar du Matin** 16 pl des Carmes ☎ 05 61 52 72 27; metro Carmes. Great old street-corner bar in the finest beer, peanuts and *pastis* tradition. A friendly and deservedly popular place. Mon–Sat 8am–9.30pm.

Le Bikini Rue Théodore Monod, 31520 Ramonville-Saint-Agne ☎ 05 62 24 09 50, ⊛ lebikini.com; metro Ramonville. On the city's southern outskirts, the eclectic programme includes 70s and 80s nights, electronic music and live gigs from hip international bands. Mon–Thurs 8pm–1am, Fri 8pm–6am, Sat 11pm–6am, Sun 11pm–1am.

Le Cri de la Mouette 78 allée de Barcelone ☎ 05 62 30 05 28, ⊛ lecridelamouette.com; metro Compans-Caffarelli. On a barge on the canal de Brienne, this popular venue features live gigs from a wide range of bands, followed by a DJ. Cover from €5. Thurs 9pm–2am, Fri–Sat 11pm–5am.

The Frog and Rosbif 14 rue de l'Industrie ☎ 05 61 99 28 57, ⊛ frogpubs.com; metro Jean-Jaurès. Stop by this friendly British pub, just off boulevard Lazare-Carnot, for a pint of Darktagnan stout, or one of their other excellent home brews. Quiz nights, football,

and fish and chips draw an international crowd. Daily 5.30pm–2am.

La Luna Loca 9 bis chemin du Prat Long ☎ 06 24 79 14 31, ⊛ lalunaloca.fr; metro Barrière de Paris. Cultural centre and club for lesbians. You'll need to join (€5) if you want to attend. Men admitted on Fri and Sun. Thurs & Fri 8pm–2am, Sat 10pm–3am, Sun 5–10pm.

★ **N5** 5 rue de la Bourse ☎ 05 61 38 44 51, ⊛ n5wineba .com; metro Esquirol. Voted "best wine bar in Europe 2016" by *The World of Fine Wine* magazine, this cosy drinking den has fifty wines by the glass out of a selection of 2,500 wines from twenty countries. Also serves tapas. Daily 6pm–2am.

Puerto Habana 12 port St-Étienne ☎ 05 61 54 45 61, ⊛ puertohabana.fr; metro François-Verdier. Toulouse's hottest salsa venue, in a superb setting beside the Canal du Midi. Also has an excellent restaurant and a house band. Tues–Fri 8pm–2am, Sat until 3am.

Le Purple 2 rue Castellane ☎ 09 67 16 04 67, ⊛ purepurple.fr; metro Jean-Jaurès. Southwest France's temple of cool and Mecca of House, with food, drinks and dancing. Wed–Sat 11pm–7am.

Le Shanghai 12 rue de la Pomme ☎ 05 61 23 37 80; metro François-Verdier. One of the city's most established LGBT clubs, which attracts a mixed crowd including transvestites and transsexuals. Wed–Sun midnight–7am.

★ **Le Télégramme** 1 rue Gabriel Péri ☎ 05 61 20 42 60, ⊛ telegramme-toulouse.com; metro Jean-Jaurès. Stylish cocktail bar and restaurant housed in a print workshop dating from 1912. A great place to spend an evening. Tues–Fri noon–2pm & 7pm–2am, Sat 7pm–3am.

ENTERTAINMENT

As you'd expect for France's fourth-largest city, Toulouse has a wide range of **entertainment** – and festivals (see box, p.53) – to suit all tastes and budgets. To get up-to-date **information** on the latest events check out ⊛ cultures.toulouse.fr and the "Sorties" section at ⊛ toulouse-tourisme.com, ⊛ ramdam.com, ⊛ clutchmag.fr, ⊛ toulousebouge.com and ⊛ toulouse .sortir.eu. **Cinemas** that regularly show films in *v.o.* ("version originale" or undubbed) include ABC at 13 rue St Bernard (☎ 05 61 21 20 46, ⊛ abc-toulouse.fr); Cinémathèque at 68 rue du Taur (☎ 05 62 30 30 10, ⊛ lacinemathequedetoulouse .com) and Utopia at 24 rue Montardy (☎ 05 61 21 22 11, ⊛ www.cinemas-utopia.org).

SPORT IN TOULOUSE

Rugby rules in Toulouse. The local team, Stade Toulousain, is one of Europe's top sides and you can see them in action at Stade Ernest-Wallon, 114 rue de Troènes (☎ 05 61 57 05 05, ⊛ stadetoulousain.fr) with tickets from €19. The city's Ligue 1 **football** team plays at the Stade Municipal, 1 av Gabriel-Biénès (☎ 08 92 70 40 00, ⊛ tfc.info); tickets from €18. There are also several public **swimming pools** in town – try Piscine Nakache at allée Paul-Biénès, which has huge indoor (mid-Sept to mid-June) and outdoor (mid-June to mid-Sept) pools (☎ 05 61 22 31 35).

TOULOUSE MARKETS

Highlights include: place St-Sernin (Sat & Sun) and allées François-Verdier for **antiques** (first Fri–Sun of the month); place Arnaud-Bernard (Thurs morning) and place St-Étienne (Sat 9.30am–6pm) for **books**; place du Capitole (Wed 8am–1pm) for clothes, **food** and general items; and covered markets at place des Carmes, place St-Cyprien and place Victor-Hugo (all Tues–Sun) for fresh produce.

VENUES

Halle aux Grains 1 pl Dupuy ☎ 05 61 63 13 13, ⓦ onct toulouse.fr; metro François-Verdier. Grand home of the Orchestre National du Capitole de Toulouse.

Odyssud 4 av du Parc, 31706 Blagnac ☎ 05 61 71 75 10, ⓦ odyssud.com; tram T1 to "Odyssud". Cultural centre near the airport with an eclectic programme including theatre, music comedy and dance.

Théâtre du Capitole pl du Capitole ☎ 05 61 63 13 13, ⓦ theatreducapitole.fr; metro Capitole. Housed in the Capitole, this theatre is home to the city's opera and ballet companies. Also puts on recitals and chamber music.

Théâtre National de Toulouse 1 rue Pierre-Baudis ☎ 05 34 45 05 05, ⓦ tnt-cite.com; metro Jean-Jaurès. As well as writing and putting on its own works, the theatre company also includes contemporary and classical plays, contemporary dance, circus arts and puppetry in its programme.

Zénith 11 av Raymond-Badiou (box office at 35 rue du Taur) ☎ 05 34 31 10 00; metro Arènes. One of the country's biggest rock music venues; also hosts a wide range of other cultural and sporting events.

SHOPPING

For designer names and classy French high-street brands, head for the streets west and north of place St-Étienne. If you're after antique furniture, place Sainte-Scarbes is a good bet. There are also some good markets (see box above).

The Bookshop 17 rue Lakanal ☎ 05 61 22 99 92, ⓦ bookshop-toulouse.com; metro Capitole. International bookshop with English-speaking staff and works in 35 languages. Tues–Sat 10am–7pm.

Épicerie Bacquié 5 place Victor Hugo ☎ 05 61 23 39 87; metro Jean-Jaurès. As well as eighty kinds of freshly ground coffee, this classy food shop also sells a good selection of local and national products. Mon 2.30–7pm, Tues–Sat 9am–12.30pm & 2.30–7pm.

Graine de Pastel 4 pl St-Étienne ☎ 05 82 75 32 83, ⓦ grainedepastel.com; metro François Verdier. Luxury beauty and body products made from woad oil. With soaps from €6.90 it's a good place to look for gifts. Mon–Sat 10am–1pm & 1.30–7pm.

Maison Pillon 2 rue Ozenne ☎ 05 61 52 68 14, ⓦ maison-pillon.fr; metro Carmes. The place to go for delicious chocolates and cakes. Try the "Fenestra", whose recipe dates back to Roman times. They also have a tearoom here (Tues–Sat 10am–6pm) and there are other boutiques at 2 rue d'Austerlitz and 23 rue du Languedoc. Tues–Sat 8am–7.30pm, Sun 8am–1pm.

DIRECTORY

Hospitals There are two major hospitals, both outside the A61 ring road: CHU Rangueil, av du Pr Jean Poulhès, to the south, and CHU Purpan, pl du Dr Baylac, to the west (for both: ☎ 05 61 77 22 33, emergency ☎ 15, ⓦ chu-toulouse.fr).

Internet café Cyber Copie, 5 pl du Peyrou ☎ 05 61 21 48 80 (Mon–Fri 8.30am–7pm, Sat 10am–7pm).

Laundry Laverie des Lois, 19 rue des Lois (daily 7.30am–9.30pm). Also has a cybercafé (Wed–Sat 1–7pm;

☎ 05 61 23 71 45).

Pharmacy Pharmacie de Nuit, 70–76 allées Jean-Jaurès (entry on rue Arnaud-Vidal) ☎ 05 61 62 38 05 (Mon–Fri & Sun 8pm–8am & Sat 8pm–9am).

Post office 9 rue Lafayette ☎ 36 31 (Mon–Fri 8.30am–6.30pm, Sat 9am–12.30pm).

Police 23 bd de l'Embouchure ☎ 05 61 12 77 77, emergency ☎ 17.

Around Toulouse

Predominantly flat, and ribbed by a multitude of small streams, the hinterland fanning out to the north and east of Toulouse has long been the source of the city's wealth. The woad boom of the fifteenth and sixteenth centuries may have powered its prosperous golden age, but the **cereal farming** carried out in this immensely fertile region has been Toulouse's traditional mainstay. Field after field of wheat dominates the rolling

THE WOAD TO RICHES

From the mid-fifteenth to the mid-sixteenth century Toulouse and Albi experienced an unprecedented wave of prosperity, based on the humble **woad** plant (*Isatis tinctoria* or in French, *pastel*). When craftsmen in Albi discovered that the innocuous weed, which was used for medicinal purposes across the Mediterranean, yielded a rich blue **dye**, they knew they were onto a good thing: blue was one of the colours most in demand for clothing by the growing middle class, and up to that point it could only be produced from rare and expensive raw materials.

With capital from Toulouse, intensive woad cultivation operations were set up across the Lauragais, which had ideal soil and climate conditions for the plant. Once harvested, the process of dye production lasted some four months, involving crushing and rolling the leaves into balls (*coques*) and fermenting them for two weeks. After this the sticky dye was pressed out and rolled into balls (*cocagnes*). Demand from textile manufacturers across Europe brought staggering wealth to the region, which became known in common parlance as the **pays de Cocagne** (a play on words, also meaning "the land of plenty"). Some 30,000–40,000 tonnes were shipped annually, while the woad **merchants**, many of whom became *capitouls* of Toulouse, erected fine mansions, the **hôtels particuliers**, which even today bear witness to their former wealth (see box, p.59). By the late sixteenth century, however, *pastel* began to be superseded by cheaper indigo-based dyes from the Indies. The violent upheavals of the Wars of Religion, ravaging fields and interrupting transport, provided the final blow, and the dye, along with the incredible affluence it generated, became a thing of the past. You can find out more about it at the **Muséum du Pastel** at Terre de Pastel (629 rue Max Planck, 31670 Toulouse-Labège ☎0800 940 167, ⓦterredepastel.com), some 11km southeast of central Toulouse, where there is also a spa, a restaurant and a shop. Take the train (hourly) to Labège-Innopole; the museum is a ten-minute walk north from the station.

landscape, cut across by narrow bands of woodland, and dotted by the church steeples of modest, introverted hamlets. The region is hedged to the north by the River Agout and to the west by the rising peaks of the **Montagne Noire** (see p.157), but is most notable for its southern boundary, the **Canal du Midi** – the engineering marvel constructed in the seventeenth century to link the Mediterranean and the Atlantic, and now a favourite with boating enthusiasts and cyclists.

The northern stretch of the region, known as the "pays de Cocagne" (see box above), is dominated by **Lavaur**, once a stalwart Cathar centre, with its beautifully preserved old town. The easternmost town in the area, sitting on the edge of the Parc du Haut Languedoc, is the old *bastide* of **Revel**, with an impressive medieval covered market place. Just south of here, at **St-Ferréol**, you'll find part of the incredible catchment system of the Canal du Midi. The flat **Lauragais** district stretches southwest of Revel: **St-Félix** is its prettiest town, but **Castelnaudary** – the area's capital – contains a surprising number of monuments and mansions. More significantly, it is also the main town on this stretch of the Canal du Midi.

Lavaur

LAVAUR is the biggest town on the Agout west of Castres, and the traditional capital of the surrounding pays de Cocagne. It's also a key town in the history of Catharism, the twelfth-century heretical movement (see p.315). The town was brutally conquered by Simon de Montfort's crusaders after a two-month siege in 1211 – Guiraude de Laurac, widow of the town's lord and leader of the defence, was thrown down a well and pelted with stones; her brother, along with nearly a hundred knights, was put to the sword; and some four hundred Cathars were burnt at the stake. But the heresy persisted, prompting the papacy and Crown to establish a series of religious foundations here, starting with a Dominican house to run the local Inquisition and finally, in the fourteenth century, a cathedral. In the sixteenth century the town was a Huguenot

1

hotbed, pitting itself once more against the Catholic establishment and the powers of the North. Nevertheless it prospered, profiting first from the lucrative woad industry and, later, **silk manufacture**.

Today Lavaur is an attractive, if quiet, rural centre surrounded by the wheat fields of the Agout valley. The town has a number of timber-and-brick houses, many dating from the fourteenth to sixteenth centuries, and the narrow old streets make for a pleasantly atmospheric whole. Lavaur's **market** is held on a Saturday morning throughout the old town and a **horse fair** is held on the third Saturday of each month near the station.

The Cathedral
Place St-Alain • Mon–Sat 10am–noon & 2–6pm, Sun 2–6pm • Free • ⓦ cathedrale-lavaur.fr

The town's main landmark, the brick-built former **cathedral** of St-Alain, stands on a wide plaza above the river. The present structure was built in 1254, replacing that destroyed by the Crusaders. Some notable features include a wooden door on the south side, which survives from the original pre-Crusade building, an eleventh-century marble altar, a highly stylized fifteenth-century doorway and an incredible mechanical clock, perched high above the ground in one of its two towers. This *jacquemart* – a clock that strikes using a mechanical figure in the form of a soldier wielding a hammer – dates back to 1523 and still marks every half-hour.

Church of St-François
Grand' Rue • Mon–Sat 10am–noon & 2–6pm, Sun 2–6pm • Free

Close by in the old town, you'll find the fourteenth-century **church of St-François**, dedicated to St Francis of Assisi, founder of the Franciscans, the first group established to preach against heretics and the Dominicans' great rivals. Set in the town's old main street, the Grande Rue, this church has weathered the centuries, but the graceful simplicity of its single nave and surviving columns make it worth a look. In the adjoining **garden** keep an eye out for the old dovecote, one of the first along the route des Colombiers (see box opposite).

ARRIVAL AND DEPARTURE   LAVAUR

By train Lavaur's *gare SNCF* is located northeast of the old quarter on place de Stalingrad.
Destinations Castres (several daily; 30min); Mazamet (several daily; 55min); Toulouse (several daily; 40min).
By bus Buses stop at the train station.

Destinations Albi (several daily; 50min–1hr 10min); Castres (several daily; 45min–1hr); Giroussens (several daily; 10min); Gaillac (several daily; 35min); Graulhet (several daily; 30min); Toulouse (several daily; 50min).

INFORMATION

Tourist information In the squat pink brick tower Tour des Rondes (Mon–Sat 10am–noon & 2–6pm, closed Mon April to mid-June & last two weeks of Sept, also closed Thurs Oct–March; ☎ 05 63 58 02 00, ⓦ tourisme-lavaur.fr).

There's also an information kiosk by the cathedral (mid-June to mid-Sept Wed & Sun 2–6pm).
Bike rental Sports Services, 36 av du Pont St Roch (Tues–Sat 9.30am–noon & 2–6pm ☎ 05 63 34 58 70).

ACCOMMODATION AND EATING

Le Jacquemart 3 pl Stalingrad ☎ 05 63 58 04 17, ⓦ le -jacquemart.com. Good quality French cuisine featuring game in season. The *plat du jour* (€8.50) and *menu du jour* (€12–15) are excellent value. Also has five rooms from €45. Tues–Sat 11.30am–3pm & 6–11pm, Sun 11.30am–3pm.

Le Moulin du Carla 747 chemin du Carla ☎ 06 77 57 01 80, ⓦ lemoulinducarla.fr. Set in parkland with a swimming pool 2km from Lavaur, this nineteenth-century country house B&B offers accommodation in two

traditionally furnished rooms. Dinner on request. **€75**
Les Pasteliers 7 rue Alsace-Lorraine ☎ 05 63 58 04 16, ⓦ lespasteliers.com. Two-star hotel with ten cosy recently renovated rooms, including three triples and a family room. The restaurant is noted for its grills. **€62**
La Pitcholina 3 av du Pont St-Roch ☎ 05 64 28 59 42, ⓦ pitcholina-lavaur.fr. Excellent Spanish-Catalan restaurant featuring tapas, burgers, platters, skewers and fish such as *seiche* (squid). Weekday lunch *menus* €14.50 Mon–Sat noon–2pm & 7.30–10pm.

THE ROUTE DES COLOMBIERS

If you're cycling or driving from Lavaur, you should take time to explore the **route des Colombiers**, a loose circuit of approximately 20km which you can start on the southern bank of the Agout heading east out of the town. *Colombiers*, elaborate and varied **dovecotes**, have been constructed here among the farm fields since the Middle Ages to house the pigeons which formed a valuable part of the rural economy, providing food and fertilizer. The tourist office in Lavaur has a map with directions to all of the dovecotes (many are private and hardly visible from the road) as well as some explanatory text. If you don't want to do the whole circuit, which leads about 10km east before looping back, you'll pass a good number of dovecotes by taking the small riverside road from Lavaur towards St-Paul (follow signs for Flamarens). There are also plenty to see right along the main D112 highway which runs between Lavaur and Castres, in addition to half a dozen in Lavaur itself.

Around Lavaur

Accessible by car, bus or bike from Lavaur, the villages of Giroussens and St-Lieux-lès-Lavaur make for an enjoyable day out.

Giroussens

The ancient village of **GIROUSSENS** huddles on the slope of a high ridge. It's been a centre of pottery production for thousands of years – local wares can be purchased at the museum/shop **Centre Céramique de Giroussens** at 7 place Lucie Bouniol (☎05 63 41 68 22; ⓦcentre-ceramique-giroussens.com; €3; July & Aug daily 10am–noon & 2–6pm, Sept–Dec & mid-Feb to June Tues–Sun 10am–noon & 2–6pm) and at the huge **ceramics market** held on the first weekend of June.

ACCOMMODATION AND EATING	GIROUSSENS

Aire Naturelle La Rigaudié lieu dit "La Rigaudiée" ☎05 63 41 67 20, ⓦwww.larigaudie.com. Lovely little bucolic campsite with just 25 spaces. Families will enjoy the pool, the mini farm and the carriage rides. Open May–Sept. **€9.60**

Domaine L'Orguennay Garch-Ségur, St-Anatole ☎05 63 81 84 40, ⓦdomainelorguennay.com. Beautiful three-bedroom B&B in a nineteenth-century *maison de maître* set in parkland with a swimming pool. Wonderful views as far as the Pyrenees. Dinner on request. **€79**

L'Échauguette Grande Rue ☎05 67 67 45 84, ⓦwww.echauguette.fr. Reopened in 2013 with a new chef, this restaurant serving market-fresh regional cusine has a very nice terrace. Lunch *menus* from €16 and dinner from €20. There's usually music on Friday evenings. Mon–Wed noon–3pm, Thurs–Sun noon–3pm & 7.30–9.30pm.

St-Lieux-lès-Lavaur

On the south bank of the Agout, you'll find the hamlet of **St-Lieux-lès-Lavaur**, site of a **steam train** (see website for times; €7; ☎05 61 47 44 52, ⓦcftt.org), which runs a one-hour return trip eastwards along the river valley; it's a fun way to see the gorgeous Tarn countryside, especially on sunny days. The train stops at the **Jardins des Martels** (April & Sept daily 1–6pm, May–Aug daily 10am–6pm, 1–17 Oct Wed, Sat & Sun 1.30–6pm, 17 Oct to 1 Nov daily 1.30–6pm; €8; ☎05 63 41 61 42, ⓦjardinsdesmartels.com), a botanical garden with over 2500 varieties of flowers and plants, as well as a mini farm.

Revel and around

Situated at the westernmost point of the long **Montagne Noire** massif, **REVEL** is a tiny but busy district capital which serves as a regional bus hub and a good base for exploring the surrounding area. It was founded as a *bastide* in 1342 by Philip IV, and the deliberate plan of the town is reflected in its octagonal layout and regular streets; indeed, Revel's original charter prescribed a uniformity which even regulated the size of the houses which could be built. Today, it is still dominated by the immense

1

fourteenth-century **covered market**, which covers the entirety of the town's central square, its rows of stout pillars supporting a single-gabled roof, converging at a stone-constructed tower. The Saturday morning market is classed as one of the most beautiful in France. In the nineteenth century Revel became a centre for finely crafted furniture and **local workshops** such as Monoury (11 av Alexandre Monoury; ☎05 61 83 57 56, ⊚meublesmonoury.fr), whose great grandfather brought the craft here, and still turn out exceptional pieces. If you're interested to learn more about its history and current status check out the **Musée du Bois et de la Marqueterie** at 13 rue Jean Moulin (☎05 61 81 72 10, ⊚museedubois.com; €5; July & Aug daily 10.30am–12.30pm & 2–7pm, Sept–June Tues–Sat until 6pm).

Seven kilometres west of Revel, the tiny picturesque hill-top hamlet of **St-Félix-Lauragais** dominates the flatlands stretching west towards Toulouse. Nothing remains of the time when the town was a meeting place for Cathar clergy, but it does retain a fine wooden **market** with a small stone tower, a curious Gothic-style **church** tucked away among the buildings of the main street and a profusion of timber-frame houses. There are great views across the countryside from the ramparts.

ARRIVAL AND INFORMATION

REVEL AND AROUND

By bus Buses to Revel stop at Salle Claude Nougaro, five minutes' walk northeast of the market.

Destinations Castres (several daily; 45min); Dourgne (several daily; 20min); St-Félix (several daily; 10min); Sorèze (several daily; 10min); Toulouse (several daily; 1hr 10min).

Tourist information Pl Philippe VI de Valois (July & Aug

Mon–Fri 9.30am–1pm & 3–6.30pm, Sat 9am–1pm & 3–6.30pm, Sun 10am–12.30pm; see website for rest of year; ☎05 34 66 67 68, ⊚auxsourcesducanaldumidi .com). Also gives information about neighbouring towns and organizes tours of the tower. There's an exhibition of Revel's history on the second floor.

ACCOMMODATION AND EATING

Auberge du Poids Public Rte de Toulouse, 31540 St-Félix-Lauragais ☎05 62 18 85 00, ⊚auberge-du -poids-public.fr. Located in a big old house beside the town's public weighbridge, this hotel has been restored and decorated in warm luxury, while the restaurant is recommended for its regional gastronomic creations (lunch menus from €27). €78

Camping du Moulin du Roy Chemin de la Pergue, 31250 Revel ☎06 64 16 87 68. Municipal campsite, with hedges to separate pitches, a short walk from the town

centre and opposite the municipal swimming pool. There's a kids' play area as well as a *pétanque* pitch and barbecue area for the grown-ups. €9.10

Du Midi 34 bd Gambetta, 31250 Revel ☎05 61 83 50 50, ⊚hotelrestaurantdumidi.com. Seventeen minimalist, rustic rooms are on offer in this value-for-money *Logis de France* hotel, which arguably has the best restaurant in town. The terrace is the best spot to savour the good-value lunch *menus* (€14–17) in summer. €61

Lac de St-Ferréol

The **Lac de St-Ferréol**, Europe's oldest reservoir and a UNESCO World Heritage Site, was created in 1672 with the completion of a massive 780m-long dam. This was part of the incredible Canal du Midi project (see box, p.79), and took some seven thousand workers five years of hard labour to construct. It was here that run-off from the Montagne Noire was collected to feed the canal, flowing down the Rigole du Canal du Midi (aka la Rigole de la Plaine) to Naurouze, approximately 25km to the southwest. You can find out about its history at the **Musée et Jardins du Canal du Midi** (☎05 61 80 57 57, ⊚museecanaldumidi31.blogspot.co.uk; €5; Feb school hols 2–5pm; March Tues–Sun 10.30am–12.30pm & 2–5pm; April, May & Oct Tues–Sun until 6pm; June & Sept Tues–Sun 10am–12.30pm & 1.30–6pm; July & Aug daily 10.30am–6.30pm; Nov–Dec Sat & Sun and school hols 2–5pm). Nowadays it's a popular weekend spot: the woods make for easy walking, and you can **swim** or **sail** on the lake. The Base de Loisirs (☎06 63 16 54 02, ⊚basedeloisirs -revel.com) will have details of all the activities on offer. A variant of the **hiking** trail

1

GR7 swings by the reservoir, linking up with the G653 west at the Rigole, and passing close to Castelnaudary to the south. A *voie verte* (see p.27), la Rigole de la Plaine, runs from the lake for 42km to the Seuil de Naurouze.

INFORMATION

LAC DE ST-FERRÉOL

Tourist information The office is near the lake (July & Aug 10am–1pm & 2.30–6pm).

ACCOMMODATION AND EATING

Lac de St-Ferréol has a profusion of hotels and campsites, most of them clustered along the northwest corner, where the road from Revel meets the lake.

Camping En Salvan Av du Lac de St-Ferréol ☎ 05 61 83 35 95, ⓦ campingensalvan.com. In an attractive woodland setting near the lake, this three-star campsite has 119 pitches for tents and motorhomes as well as 23 mobile homes and two wooden chalets. There's a swimming pool and plenty of activities for all the family. Open April–Oct. **€10.50**

Hôtellerie du Lac 22 av Pierre Paul Riquet ☎ 05 62 18 80 80, ⓦ hotel-restaurant-saint-ferreol.com. Superior two-star hotel, set back from the lake, with contemporary accommodation in 32 rooms, including four for families. As well as an outdoor swimming pool, there's also a classy restaurant (*menus* €18–50). **€74**

La Renaissance 1 chemin des Dauzats ☎ 05 61 83 51 50, ⓦ hotellarenaissance.fr. On a hill above the lake, this two-star hotel offers budget accommodation in seventeen bright, individually decorated rooms. No views, but there is a pool. The unstuffy restaurant, serving southern French food including cassoulet, has an outdoor terrace. **€50**

Sorèze

In **SORÈZE**, 6km east of Revel, a Dominican **convent-school**, the Abbaye-école (rue St-Martin; ☎ 05 63 50 86 38, ⓦ abbayeecoledesoreze.com; €8; Mon & Wed–Sun April–Sept 10am–12.30pm & 2–6pm, Oct–March 2–5.30pm), once a royal military academy in which the Latin American hero Simón Bolívar trained, is now home to a **museum** dedicated to one of the twentieth century's greatest tapestry makers – Dom Robert (1907–1997), a former monk at the Abbaye de St-Benoît d'En Calcat in nearby Dourgne. His colourful **tapestries** inspired by the flora and fauna of the Montagne Noire are on display alongside those by other top makers such as Aubusson. You can also find out what life was like in the academy in its heyday by exploring its rooms, stopping for a bite or staying the night in its luxury hotel. A weekly open-air **market** takes place on Friday mornings in the town centre.

INFORMATION

SORÈZE

Tourist information In the terracotta-coloured lower Tour Ronde, rue Pierre Fabre (July & Aug daily 9.30am–12.30pm; April–June & Sept Mon–Fri 10am–12.30pm & 2–6pm, Sat & Sun 2–6pm; Oct–March daily 2–5.30pm) ☎ 05 63 74 16 28, ⓦ auxsourcesducanaldumidi.com).

ACCOMMODATION AND EATING

Abbaye-école 18 rue Lacordaire ☎ 05 63 74 44 80, ⓦ abbaye-soreze.fr. In the famous abbey-school, this charming hotel has 72 rooms ranging from two-star minimalist accommodation up to three-star suites decorated with Toile de Jouy fabrics. The restaurant, with a lovely outdoor terrace, specializes in southwestern French dishes (*menus* from €16). **€75**

Camping St-Martin rue du 19 mars 1962 ☎ 05 63 50 20 19, ⓦ campingsaintmartin.com. Friendly three-star campsite in a woodland setting with 54 spaces for tents, caravans and motorhomes. It's also possible to rent chalets and gipsy-style caravans. There's an outdoor swimming pool and plenty of activities in summer. **€19.50**

Dourgne

DOURGNE is home to two Benedictine communities. The larger of the two is the **Abbaye de St-Benoît d'En Calcat** (☎ 05 63 50 32 37, ⓦ encalcat.com), which you can

1

visit to sit in on any of the six daily services and hear a chanted Mass; the abbey is well-known for making zithers. The other community is the **Abbaye Ste-Scholastique** (☎05 63 50 31 32, ⓦbenedictines-dourgne.org), the home of nuns who pass their time in prayer and indulging in arts and crafts. Both communities have shops where you can buy their products.

ACCOMMODATION AND EATING　　　　　　　　　　　　　　　　　　**DOURGNE**

Camp Municipal Travers de St-Stapin ☎05 63 50 31 20. This small municipal campsite has just 16 spaces, a sanitary block and a barbecue area. Its main attraction is its setting beside a river and a lake. Open July to mid-Sept. **€6**

Montagne Noire 15 pl des Promenades ☎05 63 50 31 12, ⓦhotelmontagnenoire.net. Two-star *Logis de France* in an old stone house with eight rooms decorated in warm colours. The hotel is best known for its excellent restaurant which dishes up artistically presented regional specialities and has *menus* from €17. **€59.50**

Castelnaudary and around

The main stop on the Canal du Midi between Carcassonne and Toulouse, **CASTELNAUDARY** holds the joint honours of being the legendary birthplace of that most Occitan of dishes, **cassoulet**, and the capital of the Lauragais region, the flat grain-producing hinterland of Toulouse. With its wide **Grand Bassin**, or reservoir, the town is the major pleasure port on the canal, and a great place to start a waterborne trip towards the Mediterranean.

Brief history

Like the surrounding region, Castelnaudary's past is intimately linked with Cathar history – the town endured no fewer than three sieges during the Albigensian campaigns, and was also the birthplace of Pierre de Castelnau, the papal legate whose murder prompted Pope Innocent III to proclaim the Crusade. When the **Inquisition** arrived here in 1235, the grey-robed Dominicans' efforts to root out heretics were thwarted by the solidarity of the townsfolk, who refused to implicate their fellows. It was also just outside the town that the last dream of **Languedocian independence** died, with the capture in 1632 of the rebellious Henri de Montmorency, who was borne away to Toulouse and executed on orders of Cardinal Richelieu.

Halle aux grains

18 pl de la République

The first sight you're likely to encounter is the **halle aux grains**, the former cereal market built in 1826 and now a **cinema** (films in French only) and cultural centre, with a plain but dignified arcaded front, on the west side of place de la République.

Tour Chappe

Rue des Chantiers de la Jeunesse Française 1940-44

Heading uphill from the *halle* then turning left onto avenue Frédéric Mistral then right up impasse Claude Chappe past the cemetery (about 25 minutes' walk), you'll arrive at the curious **Tour Chappe**. This tower was once part of the immense semaphore network that covered much of France. Napoleon used the system extensively, and on a clear day messages could be passed from Strasbourg to Paris in just over three hours, using over 180 of these signal stations. The network was a huge success, until the introduction of the electric telegraph in 1859 rendered it obsolete.

Moulin de Cugarel

July & Aug only Mon 3–6pm, Tues–Sat 10am–12.30pm & 3–6pm, Sun 10am–12.30pm • Free

Continuing straight uphill from the *halle* along rue des Moulins brings you to the old **Moulin de Cugarel**, the last of the town's wind-powered grain mills. With the building of the Canal du Midi, farmers suddenly had access to markets as far afield as Toulouse nd the Mediterranean, and so 32 mills were built to process the wheat which they rought to be sold. The *moulin* is an attractive stone structure; its superb grinding mechanism was fully restored in 1962. There are lovely views across the surrounding ountryside and an orientation panel to indicate the different places of interest.

lace de Verdun

3elow the mill in the heart of the old town, **place de Verdun** was medieval Castelnaudary's main square. Ringed by handsome townhouse facades (the highly decorated one containing Proxi supermarket was built in 1874 as a branch of the BHV tore in Paris), the *place* is home to the town's main **covered market**, as well as the site f the colourful Monday market.

Collégiale St-Michel

ue du Collège • Mon–Wed & Fri 2–4pm

'o the southeast of place du Verdun sits the southern-Gothic-style **Collégiale St-Michel**, uilt in the thirteenth century. Partially destroyed by the Black Prince in 1355, it has een added to over the years. Its exterior is notable for its beautiful steeple, towering 5m above the neighbouring place Victor Hugo. The bell tower has 35 bells and is one f the largest in France. Inside, there's an eighteenth-century organ by celebrated local rgan maker Jean-Pierre Cavaillé, who also built the organ in the abbey-church in t-Guilhem-le-Désert (see p.236).

résidial: Musée du Lauragais

ampe du Présidial • mid-July to mid-Sept Wed–Mon 2.30–6.30pm • €2 • ☏ 04 68 23 00 42

outheast of Collégiale St-Michel via place Auriol is the **Présidial**, a sombre stone uilding raised on the site of the town's castle in 1585, when Catherine de Médicis, hen Queen of France, made Castelnaudary capital of the Lauragais; it served in turn s a courthouse, a primary school, a prison, and is now the **Musée du Lauragais**, which olds local history and art exhibitions.

THE BUILDING OF THE CANAL DU MIDI

The **Canal du Midi** runs for some 240km from the River Garonne at Toulouse, via Castelnaudary, Carcassonne and Béziers, to the Mediterranean at Agde or Sète, and via its subsidiary, the **Canal de la Robine**, to Narbonne, entering the sea at Port-la-Nouvelle. The waterway was the brainchild of **Pierre-Paul Riquet**, a minor noble and the holder of the lucrative salt-tax concession for Languedoc (the *gabelle* – a tax levied on the sale of salt – was one of the royal treasury's most lucrative sources of income). Riquet succeeded in firing the imagination of Louis XIV (and more importantly, his first minister, Colbert) with the idea of linking the Atlantic and the Mediterranean via the Garonne.

The **main canal**, begun in 1667, took fourteen years to complete using tens of thousands of workers. At the start, an engineering problem automatically presented itself: how to feed the canal with water when the Mediterranean was obviously at sea level, the Garonne at 132m above sea level, and, in the middle, the Col (or Seuil) de Naurouze at 201m. Riquet's solution was to build a system of **dams** and **reservoirs** at St-Ferréol, Lampy and on the Alzeau in the Montagne Noire, channelling run-off water from the heights down to Naurouze. He spent the whole of his fortune on the canal (sacrificing even his daughters' dowries) and died just six months before its inauguration in 1681. Built to accommodate barges of up to 30m in length, the waterway was a success and sparked a wave of prosperity along its course, thanks to the access it provided local farmers, manufacturers and raw material industries to **foreign markets** (via the Mediterranean). Traffic increased steadily until 1856, when it carried 111,000 metric tonnes of material as well as one million passengers, and the official link-up to the Garonne and the Atlantic opened. The next year the Sète–Bordeaux **railway** opened and, rail transport being faster and more cost-effective, traffic on the canal dropped to all but nothing almost immediately.

1

Notre-Dame-de-Pitié

On the corner of rue des Batailleries and rue de l'Hôpital • Ask at the tourist office about guided tours

North of the Musée du Lauragais, the chapel of **Notre-Dame-de-Pitié** should not be missed. Founded in the sixteenth century and a popular stop on the medieval pilgrimage route to Santiago de Compostela, its dazzling interior (which you can peek at through the grilles), contains a feast of eighteenth-century gilt wooden low-relief panels depicting angels and biblical scenes in the most outrageously flamboyant Baroque style.

The Grand Bassin

Castelnaudary's biggest draw is the section of the **Canal du Midi** that runs through town, punctuated by the broad **Grand Bassin**. This roughly oblong pool, some seven hectares in area, is the largest reservoir along the length of the navigable canal. Constructed as a port, where barges could turn around, get repaired and load up with the grain harvested in the Lauragais, it now serves as a **pleasure port**. To the west, the Grand Bassin empties into the Petit Bassin, marked by the two road bridges over the canal, before narrowing to wind its way towards Toulouse. On the east side, a remarkable series of four locks, the **Écluse de St-Roch**, lowers barges and boats bound for the Mediterranean.

ARRIVAL AND INFORMATION

CASTELNAUDARY AND AROUND

By train Trains arrive at Castelnaudary's *gare SNCF*, located on the south side of the Canal du Midi. The town is on the trunk line between Toulouse and Narbonne.

Destinations Bram (many daily; 10min); Carcassonne (many daily; 20min); Lézignan (many daily; 40 min); Narbonne (many daily; 55min); Toulouse (many daily; 40min).

By bus The bus stops at the *gare SNCF*. See ⓦ audelignes .cg11.fr for details.

Destinations Avignonet-Lauragais (several daily; 15min); Bram (three daily; 25min); Carcassonne (three daily; 1hr); Toulouse (several daily; 1hr 40min); Villefranche-Lauragais

(several daily; 30min).

Tourist information Pl de la République (April–June Mon–Fri 9.30am–noon & 2–6pm, Sat 9am–1pm; July–Sept daily 9am–1pm & 2–6.30pm; Nov–Feb Mon–Fri 9.30am–noon & 2–5pm; March & Oct Mon–Fri 9.30am–noon & 2–5pm, Sat 9am–1pm; ☎ 04 68 23 05 73; ⓦ castelnaudary-tourisme.com).

Canal information La Capitainerie, 3 quai du Port ☎ 04 68 23 69 09. Provides information on anything to do with sailing, mooring and environmental issues related to the canal. Also has showers, a library and wi-fi.

GETTING AROUND AND TOURS

By bike You can hire bikes at La Roue qui Tourne, Résidence Habitat Jeune Jean Macé, 70 av du 8 mai 1945 (Mon 9am–noon, Tues & Wed 2–7pm, Fri 10am–noon & 2–7pm; €10 half day; ☎ 07 68 13 87 23).

By boat Le St-Roch at 20 quai du Port (☎ 04 68 23 49 40, ⓦ saintroch11.com) offers trips along the canal in

July & Aug (1hr at 10.30am & 5pm; 2hr at 2.30pm; €8/11).

By car There are car parks (charge) at the train station, Stade Coubertin, rue de l'Horloge and the cemetery on rue de l'Hôpital.

By taxi Taxi Fendeille ☎ 06 20 20 09 20.

CASSOULET

One of the great pillars of southern-French *terroir* ("country" or "local") cuisine is the humble **cassoulet**. A simple but tasty baked dish, made up of white beans and garlic cooked with bits of duck or goose, pork and sausage, cassoulet is a staple you'll find just about everywhere between the peaks of the Pyrenees and the banks of the Rhône. The dish dates back to medieval times and some say it has a Middle Eastern origin. The recipe we know today dates from the sixteenth century, when Catherine de Médicis introduced the *haricot lingots* beans to the Lauragais (she was given some as a wedding present for their apparent aphrodisiac qualities). Its name derives from the dish it was cooked in – a *cassole* – which was made In a nearby village. The "original" recipe is safeguarded by the **Grand Confrérie du Cassoulet** (ⓦ confrérieducassoulet.com), a collective of local chefs who occasionally dress up in distinctive medieval-style robes for culinary events and fairs; a cassoulet festival takes place at the end of August.

1

ACCOMMODATION

Camping Les Fontanilles Chemin des Fontanilles ☎ 04 68 94 11 28. On the western outskirts of town, this two-star campsite has 55 places for tents, caravans and motorhomes. The municipal swimming pool is about ten minutes' walk but there's a kids' playground and a tennis court on site. Open mid-June to Aug. **€11.60**

Du Centre et du Lauragais 31 cours de la République ☎ 04 68 23 25 95, ⓦ hotel-centre-lauragais.com. The best accommmodation in town has just ten rooms, which were redecorated in contemporary style in 2016. The gourmet restaurant is renowned for its cassoulet (€19). **€74**

Le Grand Bassin 301 quai Edmond Combes ☎ 04 68 60 29 27, ⓦ legrandbassin.com. Five-bedroom B&B in an old lock-keeper's cottage next to the canal. Friendly owner Camille speaks fluent English and the place is well equipped for disabled people and cyclists. There's also a small garden. **€70**

EATING AND DRINKING

La Cave du Canal 19 quai du Port ☎ 04 68 23 00 73, ⓦ www.caveducanal.com. Great spot for an *apéro* or a lunchtime snifter thanks to its canal-side terrace and wide selection of regional beers and wines. There's cheese and charcuterie to soak up the alcohol. Mon–Wed, Fri & Sat 10am–11pm, Thurs 4–11pm, Sun 10am–2pm (until 11pm in July & Aug).

★ **Le Petit Gazouillis** 5 rue de l'Arcade ☎ 04 68 23 08 18. Excellent value for money in this little restaurant, always packed with locals, in the town centre. Huge salads, duck with *cèpes* and, of course, cassoulet are on offer. Menus €13.50–23. Daily noon–3pm & 7–11pm.

Le Tirou 90 av Monseigneur de Langle ☎ 04 68 94 15 95, ⓦ letirou.com. On the eastern side of town, this is Castelnaudary's best spot for cassoulet (€26). There's even cassoulet ice cream for dessert, which can be enjoyed on the terrace in summer under the gaze of donkeys and alpacas. Reservations advised. Tues–Fri & Sun noon–1.30pm, Sat noon–1.30pm & 7.30–8.30pm.

Abbaye de St-Papoul

pl Monseigneur de Langle, 8km east of Castelnaudary • July & Aug daily 10am–7pm; April–June, Sept & Oct daily 10am–noon & 2–6pm; Nov–March Sat & Sun and school holidays 10am–noon & 2–5pm • €4 • ☎ 04 68 94 97 75, ⓦ abbaye-saint-papoul.fr

The **Abbaye de St-Papoul** sits on the edge of the Lauragais plain. Founded in the eighth century by Pepin the Short, it became a powerful monastic site after 1317 when its abbot was elevated to the status of bishop. The church itself is impressive, with some sections dating back to the twelfth century and an attractive cloister. The most important feature, however, is the **carved capitals** on the upper rim of the exterior of the apse (which can be viewed without entering and outside of opening hours), executed by the "Master of Cabestany" (see box, p.284) and depicting Daniel in the lions' den. The village itself on the opposite side of the road is worth a stroll.

The Canal du Midi: Toulouse to Carcassonne

Following the dramatic collapse of canal traffic in the mid-1800s (see box, p.79), the Canal du Midi (ⓦ canaldumidi.fr) languished and decayed. In the last twenty years or so, however, it has been revived as a course for pleasure craft, and it's not difficult to see why. It's a gentle, restful chug down a tunnel of greenery with occasional glimpses of a world beyond: a distant smudge of hills or the pinnacles of Carcassonne. There are outfits in all of the major ports which **rent houseboats** and barges – most of which will also rent bikes as an extra. There are many **cruises** too.

The route taken by the canal is roughly straight, passing through the wheat-producing lands of the Lauragais, clearing the compact suburbs of Toulouse and steering its tree-lined course east, parallel to the River Hers, towards its highest point, at the **Seuil** (or "threshold") **de Naurouze**. From here it descends to the basin at Castelnaudary, as the Montagne Noire, the source of the canal's water, comes into view to the north. From the Grand Bassin, the waterway travels eastwards across the plain, bridging the 32km to **Carcassonne**, where it begins to adapt to the contours of the Aude valley, and starts in earnest its descent towards the sea (see box, p.254). The total distance travelled by the canal from Toulouse to Carcassonne is 90km.

1

PRACTICALITIES   THE CANAL DU MIDI: TOULOUSE TO CARCASSONNE

The canal is navigable from mid-March to October, but the high season of July and August is best avoided – boat availability declines, prices rise and the canal gets quite crowded. Generally, locks are open from 9am–12.30pm and 1.30pm–7pm; they open daily from mid-March to October. There's no charge for passage, and you can count on about a quarter of an hour for a basin to fill or empty. With a maximum permitted speed of 8km per hour, you should expect to travel no more than 250km in a week of cruising.

Information Canal information can be found at the port offices of Voies Navigables de France, the government organization in charge of inland waterways. Their head office is at 2 Port St-Étienne in Toulouse (☎ 05 61 36 24 24, ⓦ sudouest.vnf.fr) and there is also an English-speaking port office at Carcassonne (prom Canal, ☎ 04 68 71 27 37).

Boat rental To organize boat rental in Toulouse, contact Navicanal, 139 rue Bonnat (☎ 05 61 55 10 91, ⓦ navicanal .com). In Castelnaudary the biggest boat rental company is Le Boat, Le Grand Bassin (☎ 04 68 94 42 03, ⓦ leboat .com); their fleet consists mostly of modern craft, so if you're hoping for a more authentic-looking barge, you may have to shop around and book well ahead. At Carcassonne you can rent from Les Canalous (☎ 03 85 53 76 74, ⓦ canalous-canaldumidi.com) while Locaboat (☎ 03 86 91 72 72, ⓦ locaboat.com) rents out *pénichettes* (traditional canal boats). Castel Nautique (☎ 04 68 76 73 34,

ⓦ castelnautique.com) in Bram rents out both traditional and electric boats, as well as bicycles. At any of these firms expect to pay between €700 and €3000 per week for a three- to five-person boat depending on the model, amenities and time of year. If you don't want to commit the time and money to rent a houseboat, most ports also rent smaller electric boats, suitable for one to six people by the hour (€20–40) or two hours (around €30–60).

Licences Navigation itself is straightforward (quite literally) and an orientation session by the boat rental company is all you need to get you on your way – no licence is required.

Cruises European Waterways in the UK (☎ 01753 598555, ⓦ gobarging.com) offers weeklong luxury cruises on barges sleeping up to ten people. Prices from £2850 per person including transfers, all meals, drinks, excursions and bike rental.

Along the canal: Toulouse to the Seuil de Naurouze

The quiet and unassuming hamlets lining the canal afford a glimpse of rural France at its most antiquated and peaceful. The first village of any size you'll pass is the old *bastide* of **Montgiscard**, some 10km from the port of Toulouse. If you're tempted to stop, take a look at the medieval church, part of which was remodelled by the same architect who designed Toulouse's Hôtel d'Assézat. Next you'll come to **Ayguesvives** and **Montesquieu-Lauragais**, both of which have impressive nineteenth-century châteaux. Eighteen kilometres from Toulouse you'll reach the **écluse de Négra**, which is where you leave the canal to reach **Villefranche-Lauragais**, and was once the first

---

BIKING AND HIKING THE CANAL DU MIDI

Renting a boat (see p.81) may be the ideal way to enjoy the Canal du Midi, but there are other eminently enjoyable options which involve considerably less time and expense. The easiest part of the canal's route along which to **bike** or **hike** is the initial – paved – stretch **from Toulouse to the Seuil de Naurouze**, following a path from Port St-Saveur (see p.64). The surrounding farmland, which gradually ascends the further you go, doesn't make for the most spectacular of backdrops, but the canal – its tree-lined placidity interrupted only by the "putt-putt" of passing boats – is beautiful in its own right. The total distance along the paved path is 50km, which can be biked in about five hours and walked in under twenty. If you decide on the latter course of action you need not commit yourself to going the whole way – you can stop at Villefranche-Lauragais at the 30km mark to catch a bus back or onwards, or there are several places where you can break the journey and **spend the night** (see opposite). From Port-Lauragais, a further 12km from Villefranche, you have the option of continuing the rest of the journey to the Seuil de Naurouze on a boat cruise (see above). The paved path ends at Écluse Océan, shortly after the port, and a gravel towpath (fine for mountain bikes) continues to Carcassonne, a further 35km along the canal. You can even arrange to have your luggage transported separately with BagaFrance (☎ 06 41 19 20 11, ⓦ midi.bagafrance.com).

1

A MIDI MARVEL

The Canal du Midi is a marvel of engineering and beauty, incorporating no fewer than 99 **locks** (écluses) and 130 **bridges**. The various topographical challenges were met with imagination, including the construction of **canal tunnels** and bridges, the latter allowing water to cross valleys and gullies, suspended in the air. No less beautiful are the stone foot and road bridges, most of which date back to the first era of construction. The graceful oval lock-basins, built in that shape for more strength, are guarded by uniform maisons d'éclusier, where the controls of the mechanism are housed; and, as along any major route, inns and restaurants punctuate the canal's course. Even the double file of plane trees which lines most of the waterway's length, giving it a distinctive "Midi" look, serves a technical as well as an aesthetic purpose: to shade the water and impede its loss through evaporation. The canal was designated a **UNESCO** World Heritage Site in 1996, ensuring its conservation.

post-stop on the way to Agde – several of the old canal-side buildings survive. Just to the southeast, **Avignonet-Lauragais** was once a wealthy woad town, and is notable for being the place where, in 1242, the Cathars, holed up in Montségur, launched an attack on and massacred a contingent of the Dominican Inquisition; the resulting counterattack brought about the destruction of Montségur castle and the mass execution of its garrison and population (see box, p.103). The last stop before you reach the Seuil de Narouze is the modern **Port-Lauragais** (Ⓦlauragais.cepplaisance.fr), built specifically for pleasure boating. Here you'll find an exhibition about the canal, a shop selling regional products, a restaurant and various activities on offer including boat trips. The **Seuil de Narouze**, the highest point on the canal's path, is where the Rigole, or feeder canal, arrives bearing the water gathered on the slopes of the Montagne Noire; it has long been a point of transit, as the vestiges of Roman road here testify. The area around the canal junction has been set up as a **picnic area** and **park** (unfortunately with no toilets), and nearby you'll find a rather sombre monument to the canal's founder, Pierre-Paul Riquet.

ACCOMMODATION	ALONG THE CANAL: TOULOUSE TO THE SEUIL DE NAROUZE
La Maison d'Hôtes de Bigot 31450 Montesquieu-Lauragais ☎ 05 61 27 02 83, Ⓦ hotebigot.chez-alice.fr. Dating from the seventeenth century, and once part of the local castle, this rustic five-bedroom B&B also offers two cottages. Guests can relax in the garden, swim in the pool and even fish. **€55**	**La Pradasse** 39 chemin de Toulouse, 31450 Ayguesvives ☎ 05 61 81 55 96, Ⓦ lapradasse.com. Stunning five-bedroom B&B in a tasteful barn conversion in a bucolic setting with a pool. Couples will love the romantic gipsy caravan and there's a cottage for families or groups. **€99**

Bram

The main place of interest between Castelnaudary and Carcassonne is the ancient village of **BRAM**, a thirteenth-century circulade where the houses are arranged in tight concentric circles around the church. The attraction here is **Eburomagus – Musée Archéologique** at 2 av du Razès (April–June, Sept & Oct Wed–Sun 10am–noon & 2–6pm; July & Aug daily 10am–noon & 4–7pm; Nov–March by appointment; €4; ☎04 68 78 91 19), an archaeology museum displaying finds from the Lauragais area.

ACCOMMODATION AND EATING	BRAM
La Clos St-Loup 69 av Razès ☎04 68 76 11 91, Ⓦ hotel-restaurant-le-clos-saint-loup-bram.fr. Modern two-star Logis de France hotel with twelve bright,	comfortable rooms; ideal for a brief stopover. The restaurant serves specialities from the southwest (menus €17–34). **€67**

Carcassonne, Upper Aude and Ariège

CARCASSONNE

Carcassonne, Upper Aude and Ariège

The citadel of Carcassonne is quintessential Languedoc: a medieval fortress with the foothills of the Pyrenees rising off to the south, the peaks of the Montagne Noire looming to the north, and the languid waters of the Canal du Midi gliding past towards the Mediterranean. Although it fell to Catholic forces early in the Crusade, Carcassonne was held to be the epicentre of the Cathar heresy in Languedoc: the castles which form a far-flung ring in the Corbières and the Pyrenean slopes to the south were referred to as the heretic capital's "daughters"

2

The land fanning southwest of the city rises in a series of ridges and plains, cut through by two **rivers**. The first, the Aude, runs north to Carcassonne, skirting the highlands of the pays de Sault on its way down from the mountains. Journeying up this valley and into the *pays*, a region littered with narrow gorges and high passes, is like flipping through the pages of Cathar history – from the site of their greatest fortified city to the ruins of their last redoubt, **Montségur**. The second river, flowing down from Andorra to Toulouse, gives its name to the *département* – **Ariège** – constituting the remainder of this chapter. **Foix**, once the thriving capital of a proudly independent county, sits at the centre of the *département*, standing sentinel over the course of the rapid river, after it has twisted through the northern slopes of the Pyrenees past the skiing and hiking country around the spa of **Ax-les-Thermes** and **Tarascon-sur-Ariège**, with its incredible array of prehistoric caves – justification alone for a trip to the region. The plain northeast of Foix was once the haunt of troubadours and men of religion: Cathar *parfaits* ("monks"; see p.314) and the Inquisitors sent to hunt them. Reduced to a ruin in the Wars of Religion, today its ancient, near-abandoned villages with their arcaded squares and crumbling walls offer the only faded record of the district's rich past. At the southwestern limits of the *département*, the **Couserans**, whose snowcapped peaks are ranged in breathtaking cirques, form a virtually impenetrable barrier to Spain beyond.

The Aude valley – with the exception of Carcassonne – and the Ariège *département* are two of the least developed and least inhabited areas in France. Isolated by difficult terrain, where vertiginous castles such as the infamous Château de Montségur were the bastions of Cathar heretics in the twelfth to fourteenth centuries, they offer few opportunities apart from farming and herding; the region's youths have long been attracted by the bigger cities. In recent years, **tourism** has rescued the area from its relentless decline, and to a certain extent, the construction of ski resorts, spas and local museums, as well as prehistoric caves being made accessible to the public, has served to improve the region's prospects. But these recent initiatives, if they have stimulated the local economy, have not detracted from the essential flavour of the area – a refuge of mountain tradition.

Highlights

❶ Carcassonne Southern France's most visited monument, this reconstructed medieval citadel is a must-see. **See p.88**

❷ Carnaval Limoux's famous Lenten festival draws crowds from around the Southwest to see its elaborately costumed dancers. **See p.97**

❸ Rennes-le-Château A mecca for occultists and conspiracy theorists following the trail of a nineteenth-century priest. **See p.98**

❹ Rafting The upper Aude and Ariège rivers provide excellent opportunities for a range of skill levels. **See p.102**

❺ Montségur The legendary site of the heretic Cathars' last stand enjoys as dramatic a setting as you're likely to see anywhere. **See p.103**

❻ Mirepoix The region's best-preserved medieval *bastide* features a stunningly carved fourteenth-century town hall, now converted into a hotel. **See p.106**

❼ La Grotte de Niaux The best prehistoric cave art still open to the public. **See p.120**

HIGHLIGHTS ARE MARKED ON THE MAP ON P.88

GETTING AROUND

By train The main rail corridors in this region are Toulouse/Narbonne and Toulouse/Latour-de-Carol/Enveitg (via Foix) which hooks up with the *Train Jaune* (see p.295) to Perpignan. A spur line runs from Carcassonne to Quillan and the Fenouillèdes line (see p.286) from Rivesaltes

terminates at Axat. SNCF buses may run in lieu of trains o[n] these lines; services are reduced on Sundays and holidays

By bus Bus services, even between larger towns, ar[e] infrequent. Weekend services are much reduced, with mos[t] lines having no buses on Sundays and holidays.

Carcassonne

Your first view of **CARCASSONNE**, its fairy-tale citadel perched high above the grassy verges of the River Aude, is likely to be a memorable one. The famous **citadel (cité)**, declared a UNESCO World Heritage Site in 1997, enjoys must-see status on any trip through southwest France, and if it has suffered through the ages – beaten, burnt and dismantled – you'd never guess from looking at it. Descending from here you pass through the medieval suburb of La Barbacane before crossing the river to the **ville basse**, formally La Bastide de St-Louis – a typical grid of thirteenth-century streets,

HIGHLIGHTS

1. Carcassonne
2. Carnaval
3. Rennes-le-Château
4. Rafting
5. Montségur
6. Mirepoix
7. La Grotte de Niaux

CARCASSONNE, THE UPPER AUDE & ARIÈGE

FESTIVALS IN CARCASSONNE AND ARIÈGE

July and August are the best months for festivals in Ariège. The biggest festival is Carcassonne's Bastille Day, but bear in mind that the town gets packed out for the event, with parked cars lining the *route nationale* for several kilometres from the *cité*. Limoux's *Carnaval* is also a unique event, worth planning for if you're in the area.

Mid-Jan to Easter Limoux: *Carnaval* ⓦ carnaval-limoux.com. An extended Lenten celebration featuring vividly costumed dancers in the old town squares. Three sets of performances (11am, 4.30pm & 10pm) on Saturdays and Sundays.

June Couserans: *Transhumances en Couserans* ⓦ transhumances-haut-salat.com. In a revival of the ancient tradition, thousands of sheep are driven up the valleys of the Couserans into the high pasturelands (see box, p.112).

Last Saturday in June Tarascon-sur-Ariège: *L'Ariégoise* ⓦ cyclosport-ariegeoise.com. The *département*'s sporting event of the year: 4500 cyclists racing up and down the *cols*.

Throughout July Carcassonne: *Festival de Carcassonne* ⓦ festivaldecarcassonne.fr. Month-long festival of dance, music and theatre with nightly performances in the castle's amphitheatre and free performances in the squares of the *cité*, with huge fireworks on Bastille Day (July 14).

Third weekend of July Mirepoix: *Les Médiévales de Mirepoix* ⓦ tourisme-mirepoix .com. Medieval horsemanship, pageantry, market and fair in the arcaded squares around the cathedral.

Late July Ax-les-Thermes: *Spectacles de Grands Chemins* ⓦ ax-animation.com. A three-day festival of street theatre celebrating local *montagnard* culture.

Late July Foix: *Festival Trad'Estiu*. A weekend of traditional Occitan music and dance.

Early Aug Limoux: *Vigne et Terroir*. A celebration of local culinary traditions, with concerts, street performances, and good food and drink in abundance.

First week of Aug St-Girons: *Rite* ⓦ bethmalais.com. Five-day festival of traditional culture, including music, song and dance from around the world.

First weekend of Aug St-Girons: *Autrefois le Couserans* ⓦ autrefois-le-couserans.com. Three days celebrating the region's rural traditions, including performances, a market, and horse and donkey races.

Mid-Aug Carcassonne: *Spectacle Médiéval*. Medieval costumes and pageantry and a theatrical re-enactment with a different theme each year.

Early Sept Foix: *Fêtes de Foix*. An annual festival, with produce markets, music and a medieval theme, centred on the illustrious figure of Gaston Fébus (see p.110).

Sept 21 Vicdessos: *Foire de la St-Matthieu*. Transhumant livestock fair, formalized by the Count de Foix in 1313. Nowadays, the tradition continues with a lively market and celebration.

Early Oct Couserans: *Transhumances en Couserans* (see June). The sheep are brought back down from the mountain for the winter.

once contained by a wall. Splayed out around this is the nondescript **new town**, a series of uninteresting suburbs with nothing to tempt you out there. Comparatively good transport links by bus, rail, canal and air also make Carcassonne the best starting point for exploring the surrounding areas: the uplands of the Ariège and the Aude covered later in this chapter, and to the north, the Montagne Noire (see p.157).

Brief history

The city was settled as far back as the sixth century BC, passing through the hands of Romans and Visigoths before its golden age under the great Languedocian family, the **Trencavels**. This family, vassals of the counts of Toulouse (the St-Gilles family) from 1163, used Carcassonne as their principal residence, ensuring the town's prosperity. The town was besieged and taken in 1209 by anti-Cathar Crusaders, eventually passing to the notorious Simon de Montfort, who made it his "**capital**". After the feared warrior died outside the walls of Toulouse in 1218, the Trencavel Raymond-Roger VII briefly recovered the town, only to see it pass to royal control in 1229. Some twenty years later, King Louis IX laid out the *ville basse*, a *bastide* that would serve as a regional market and increase the town's wealth. Carcassonne thus prospered until the Hundred Years' War, when the English **Black Prince** (see box, p.255), frustrated by his inability to

seize the citadel, burnt the *ville basse* to the ground in 1355. Despite this, the citizens rallied and rebuilt, and for the rest of the Middle Ages Carcassonne was an important market town, profiting from its location on the frontier of the Kingdom of France. With the annexation of Roussillon in 1659, however, the border shifted south and Carcassonne stagnated. The citadel was abandoned and eventually quarried for its stones. This is how it remained until it was rediscovered in the nineteenth century by **Viollet-le-Duc**, whose visionary fifty-year restoration project rescued it from obscurity.

Today Carcassonne flourishes largely because of that vision, which brings in two million visitors every year, making it the country's most visited city after Paris – even though there's actually very little to do here. Still, it's a relaxing place, and the *cité* has become something of a symbol of medieval France; its yearly **pageants** and spectacular Bastille Day celebrations (see box, p.89), featuring the second-largest fireworks display in France, keep the streets full of both French and foreign tourists.

The citadel

From whichever direction you approach, Carcassonne's magnificent **citadel**, its stout ramparts and pennant-capped towers piercing the sky, presents one of the South of France's most striking images, straight out of a medieval fantasy. However, much of

THE LEGEND OF DAME CARCAS

The origin of Carcassonne's strange-sounding name has given rise to a number of interesting stories, the most enduring of which is that of **Dame Carcas**. Legend asserts that when the town was under Muslim control in the early Middle Ages, the Emperor Charlemagne arrived to lay siege, knowing that if his army attacked for long enough, eventually the town would run short of food. However, just when defeat looked inevitable, Carcas, the Muslim ruler's wife, ordered a pig to be force-fed with the last of the town's precious grain and tossed over the battlements. When it hit the ground and split open, Charlemagne's troops despaired, believing that the town was well supplied. They lifted the siege and retreated, and as the town's bells pealed in celebration, the townsfolk cried "Carcas, sonne!" ("Ring, Carcas!"). It is pure fantasy of course: a Muslim ruler would never have kept pigs. Nevertheless it is more evocative than the true origin of the name, which derives from the Gaulish *kar* ("rock") and *kassi* ("warrior").

2

Carcassonne is, in fact, fabrication – a piece of imaginative reconstruction by the nineteenth-century restorer Viollet-le-Duc, whose enthusiasm for "the medieval" inspired him to invent inaccurate features like the conical towers and arrow-slits, which the original medieval fortress lacked. Nevertheless, as you cross over the moat, passing the wide grassy verges between the thick double walls, you do feel as though you're entering another world. You can enter through the **Porte d'Aude**, on the citadel's western side, but a more visually impressive option is the main **Porte Narbonnaise** on the far side of the *cité*, where the tourist office, local *navettes* (shuttles from the *ville basse*) and main car park are found.

Château Comtal

rue Viollet-le-Duc • Daily: April–Sept 10am–6.30pm; Oct–March 10am–5pm • €8, guided tours €12.50 • ☎ 04 68 11 70 70, ⌕ remparts-carcassonne.fr

The **Château Comtal** is the twelfth-century castle where Raymond-Roger Trencavel made his last stand against the Catholic Crusaders, and surrendered, in 1209. You enter via the courtyard then head upstairs for a short film about the history and restoration of the site; inside you'll also come across archaeological finds from the area; an impressive scale model of the town; Romanesque frescoes in the keep; and a very worn sixteenth-century bust of Dame Carcas, which was originally outside the Porte Narbonnaise (there's now a replica in its place). The highlight of the visit is a walk along a section of the citadel's three kilometres of **walls** including several of its 52 towers; the views are excellent. Take care along the walls, as stairways can be slippery and the inadequate railings are no match for curious children.

Basilique St-Nazaire

Pl St-Nazaire • Daily 9am–7pm; until 6pm in winter • Free • ☎ 04 68 25 27 65

The **basilica** of St-Nazaire is a late eleventh-century Romanesque church that has undergone major Gothic and Neo-Gothic remodellings. Look out for a stunning series of **gargoyles** along the eaves of the apse, as well as the amusingly carved heads above the door. Inside, you'll find a thirteenth-century choir and rosette window while the central stained-glass window in the choir depicting the life of Jesus, and dating from the thirteenth century, is one of the oldest and best in the region. Propped up against a wall in the south transept is Simon de Montfort's original tombstone.

The lices

The best thing to do in the *cité*, after visiting the castle and church, is to wander the narrow, crooked streets filled with cafés, restaurants and touristy shops. You'll pass a smattering of small "museums" as you walk about, devoted to Middle Ages torture instruments and the like, but you're better off bypassing these and heading for the grassy **lices** between the citadel's two sets of walls. A narrow space some 1100m in length, created with the building of the second set of walls in the 1200s, and divided into two sections, the *lices* make for a beautifully atmospheric stroll. The **lower lices** run from the

2

THE CATHAR "PASSPORT"

If you're planning on visiting a few of the Cathar sites in the region, consider buying a "**Carte Inter-site**" or "Le Passeport des sites du Pays Cathare" pass (€2) from participating sites or local tourist offices. Valid for a year, it gives you reductions of up to €2 on the entrance fee to 21 abbeys, castles and museums of the Ariège, Aude and Tarn *départements* (from your second visit) including Aguilar, Alet, Arques, Carcassonne, Caunes-Minervois, Fanjeaux, Fontfroide, Lagrasse, Lastours, Musée du Catharisme de Mazamet, Musée du Quercorb, Peyrepertuse, Puilaurens, Quéribus, St-Hilaire, St-Papoul, Saissac, Termes, Usson, Villelongue and Villerouge-Termenès. Cardholders benefit from free entry for one child aged 15 and under at each site. For further information see ⓦ www.payscathare.org.

Porte Narbonnaise to the Porte de l'Aude around the northern perimeter of the citadel; starting out from the former, you'll notice a section of brick-and-stone-constructed wall dating back to the end of the period of Roman occupation. Walking along the slightly longer southern circuit of the **upper lices** gives you good views of the elaborate towers added to the citadel's defences under Philip III in the late thirteenth century. Once a space for medieval archery practice and other military exercises, the *lices* now provide a favourite route for horse-drawn *calèches* and a great place to have a picnic.

The ville basse

To reach the **ville basse** upon leaving the *cité*, instead of backtracking through the main gates and past the car park, a better option is to take the gate at the end of rue Notre Dame, off place du Grand Puits, and cut down to rue Trivalle, a world away from the touristy scrum in the fortress above. Spanning the Aude is the picturesque fourteenth-century **Pont Vieux**, adorned on its far side by the small and simple Gothic structure of the twelfth-century Notre Dame de la Santé **chapel**. The riverbanks on the *cité* side have been kept free of building and make a nice grassy spot to relax or have a picnic.

Place Carnot is the heart of the old *bastide* – a wide square with shops, cafés and bars a well as a good **market** (Tues, Thurs & Sat mornings). A couple of blocks south, near the sixteenth-century **cathedral** of St-Michel (bd Barbès; Mon–Sat 8am–noon & 2–7pm, Sun 2–7pm; free), you'll find the most substantial remains of the town's once stout defences; the **Porte des Jacobins**, a medieval gate which was widened and remodelled in Neoclassical style in 1778, is in good shape, while beside it lie the remains of the old ramparts. Otherwise, look for some of the impressive old private **hôtels**; on rue Aimé-Ramond you'll find the plain, medieval-styled facade of the fifteenth-century Maison du Sénéchal, at no. 70, and a more flamboyant Renaissance *hôtel* at no. 50.

Place Gambetta and around

On the southeastern side of the *bastide*, **place Gambetta** is the southern hub of the **ville basse**. It has an airy feel, despite the traffic, as well as some attractive nineteenth-century facades. Keep an eye out for the impressive Art Deco facade of the Groupe Scolaire Jean-Jaurès on the northwest corner.

Musée des Beaux-Arts

1 rue de Verdun • Mid-June to mid-Sept Wed–Sun 10am–6pm; mid-Sept to mid-June Tues–Sat 10am–noon & 2–6pm • Free • ☎ 04 68 77 73 7

Set in an eighteenth-century *hôtel*, the **Musée des Beaux-Arts** has a large collection of paintings and ceramics dating from the seventeenth century. The works are mainly by French and Dutch artists such as landscape painter Van Goyen (1596–1656), Perpignan-born portrait painter Hyacinthe Rigaud (1659–1743) and local boy Jacques Gamelin (1738–1803) – the son of a successful Carcassonne merchant who eschewed a career in business to study art in Toulouse, eventually moving to Rome to become a painter to Pope Clement XIV. There are also temporary exhibitions.

CARCASSONNE: VILLE BASSE

ACCOMMODATION	
45 BB	3
Central	2
De la Bastide	1
Montségur	4

EATING	
Freaks	2
Le Jardin en Ville	1

DRINKING	
Le Black	3
The Celt	1
Le Verre d'Un	2

SHOPPING	
Cabanel	1

Maison des Mémoires

3 rue de Verdun • Tues–Sat 9am–noon & 2–6pm • Free • ☎ 04 68 72 50 83

The **Maison des Mémoires** pays homage to local-born surrealist poet Joë Bousquet (1857–1950). Left paraplegic by battle wounds received at Vailly in 1918, Bousquet lived out the rest of his life bedridden in this house in Carcassonne, comforted by opium and producing dark and mystical poetical reflections which attracted the attention of the interwar intelligentsia including André Gide, Paul Valéry and Max Ernst.

ARRIVAL AND DEPARTURE
CARCASSONNE

By plane Carcassonne's small airport (w aeroport carcassonne.com) is just west of town. A shuttle bus, or navette (30min after each flight arrival; 15min; €5), leaves from outside the terminal and stops in town at the train station, place Gambetta, and the *cité*. A taxi (☎ 04 68 71 50 00) to the centre costs €8–15.

By train The *gare SNCF* is on the north side of the *ville basse*, just over the Canal du Midi from bd Omer Sarraut. SGV stations are indicated with an asterisk.

Destinations Béziers* (connections to Bédarieux); Montpellier* via Agde* and Sète* (many daily; 1hr 30min); Narbonne* (connections to Perpignan); Nîmes* (connections to Grau & Tarascon/Beaucaire) via Lézignan*; Paris* (several daily; 5hr 20min); Quillan, via Limoux and Alet-les-Bains (several daily; 1hr 10min); Toulouse*, via Castelnaudary and Bram (several hourly; 40min–1hr 10min).

By bus Carcassonne has no *gare routière* as such; buses arrive at the Salle du Dôme at the southern end of bd Jean Jaurès in the *ville basse*. For details see w audelignes.cg11.fr.

Destinations Axat (three daily; 1hr 55min); Castelnaudary (several daily; 1hr); Caunes-Minervois (several daily; 30min); Homps (several daily; 50min); Lézignan (several daily; 1hr); Limoux (several daily; 45min); Marseillette (daily; 1hr 35min); Narbonne (daily; 1hr 40min); Quillan (daily; 1hr 30min); Trèbes (several daily; 15min).

By car If you're arriving by car, there's a car park up by the *cité* (free for the first 30min, then €1 per 15min) but there are cheaper options ringing the *ville basse* including free parking at the Parking du Dôme.

2

VIOLLET-LE-DUC

It may come as a surprise that many of the buildings of medieval France are, in fact, nineteenth-century reconstructions. Until then, the Middle Ages was considered a barbaric period best forgotten, but in the early 1800s European intellectuals began to look back at the medieval era as the time when their nations were born, and projects were undertaken to recover its neglected art and architecture. The major figure in this movement in France was **Eugène Emmanuel Viollet-le-Duc**, the prolific restorer-extraordinaire who left his – often fantastical – mark all over the country, but particularly in Languedoc and Roussillon.

Having studied art history at the Sorbonne, Viollet-le-Duc began his career assisting in the renovation of Paris's glorious **Sainte-Chapelle**, and established his reputation as a restorer. In the years that followed he was inundated with contracts to restore buildings such as Narbonne's Hôtel de Ville (see p.243) and the basilica of St-Nazaire in Carcassonne, and in 1853 Louis-Napoléon granted him supervision of the restoration of all of France's medieval buildings. By this time he had already begun the massive reconstruction of the **cité** – a fifty-year project he would not live to see finished.

Viollet-le-Duc's idiosyncratic **theory** of restoration dictated that buildings should not necessarily be returned to their exact previous state, but rather modified according to their essential underlying architectural principles (as he saw them, naturally). As a result, the elaborate restorations – in which he sometimes started from nothing more than a pile of stones – are reflections of Viollet-le-Duc's imagination. In Carcassonne's *cité*, for example, he not only made "improvements", such as adding arrow-slits and crenellation to the walls, but adopted features which, though aesthetically pleasing, are entirely inaccurate: the pointed roofs on the towers are German-style as opposed to the flat Languedocian version. Whatever you think about Viollet-le-Duc's easy attitude to verisimilitude, as you travel around Languedoc and Roussillon, bear in mind that – for better or worse – almost all the great medieval monuments here have "benefited" to some degree from his endeavours.

GETTING AROUND

By bike Generation VTT, port de Carcassonne (April–Oct daily 9.30am–6pm; ☎07 82 32 67 11, ⊛carcassonne.generation-vtt.com) rents out bikes from €10 for two hours; they also have details of cycling routes and organize guided bike tours.

By boat Several companies offer boat trips on the Canal du Midi, from an hour to a day including Le Cocagne (☎06 50 40 78 50, ⊛bateau-cocagne-canal-carcassonne.fr) and Lou Gabaret (☎06 80 47 54 33, ⊛carcassonne-navigationcroisiere.com). You can also hire boats from Les Canalous du Canal du Midi (☎03 85 53 76 74, ⊛canalous-canaldumidi.com) and Le Boat (☎04 68 94 42 80, ⊛leboat.fr). All are located in the pleasure port, where Voies Navigables de France also has an office (☎04 68 25 01 50, ⊛vnf.fr).

By bus La Salle du Dôme at the bottom of bd Jean Jaurès is the main bus stop in the *ville basse*. To get to the *cité* take bus # which leaves around every 30min. Tickets cost €1 or €2.60 f■ a day. There is also a little train shuttle that leaves hourly fro■ André-Chénier gardens near the train station from June to m■ Oct (€2; €3 return). See ⊛carcassonne-agglo.fr for details.

By car Rental companies include the following: AD■ Location, 24 rue Joseph François Duplex ☎04 68 11 71 9■ ⊛ada.fr; Avis, 1 av Maréchal Joffre ☎04 68 25 05 8■ Keolis, 2 bd Paul Sabatier ☎ 04 68 25 13 74, ⊛keolisau■ .com; LOV, 58 av Franklin Roosevelt ☎04 68 11 74 1■ ⊛lovlocation.com; Renault Rent AMDS, rte de Narbonr■ ☎04 68 77 77 68, ⊛renault-rent.com. Most of the■ companies, and others, also have offices at the airport.

By taxi Taxis de Carcassonne ☎04 68 71 50 50.

INFORMATION

Tourist information 28 rue de Verdun (April–June, Sept & Oct Mon–Sat 9am–6pm, Sun 10am–1pm; July & Aug daily 9am–7pm; Nov–March Mon–Sat 9.30am–12.30pm & 1.30–5.30pm; ☎04 68 10 24 30, ⊛tourisme-carcassonne.fr). There's a second tourist office (daily: April–June, Sept & Oct 9am–6pm; July & Aug 9am–7pm; Nov–March 9.30am–1pm & 1.30–5.30pm) in the *cité*, just inside the Porte Narbonnais■ Finally, there's a canal-side tourist information offic■ (daily: April–June 9.30am–1pm; July & Au■ 9.45am–1.30pm & 2–6.30pm; Sept 9.30am–1.30pm ■ 2–6pm) on av Maréchal Joffre.

ACCOMMODATION

Although your first impulse may be to get a room in the *cité*, beware that if you are hoping to pass the evenings in medieval idyll you will most likely be disappointed. What little accommodation there is here is expensive; furthermore, th■

itadel is very busy – verging on lunacy in high season. You may be more satisfied with a room along the slopes down towards the riverbank, or in the *ville basse* (from where you get the view of the *cité*).

★ 45 BB 45 bd Barbès ☎ 04 68 26 41 31, ⊚ 45-bb.com; map p.93. Gorgeous B&B in a nineteenth-century *maison de maître* with two cosy, traditionally furnished bedrooms and a first-floor apartment for two people. The leafy garden has an inviting pool. €90

Camping de la Cité Rte de St-Hilaire ☎ 04 68 10 01 00, ⊚ campingcitecarcassonne.com; map p.90. Exceptional ground with 160 shady sites, 40 chalets and a pool. Tucked away in parkland to the south of town, it's a 20min walk from the *cité*. If you point your tent in the right direction you get a view of the citadel poking up over the trees. Open mid-March to mid-Oct. €28

Central 27 bd Jean Jaurès ☎ 04 68 25 03 84, ⊚ hotel-carcassonne-11.com; map p.93. This nineteenth-century townhouse has 21 bright rooms with wi-fi and a/c, and offers the best budget accommodation in the lower town. They rent out bikes. Closed mid-Dec to Jan. €72

De la Bastide 81 rue de la Liberté ☎ 04 68 71 96 89, ⊚ hoteldelabastide.com; map p.93. This family-run establishment down a quiet side-street not far from the station is a great deal. The clean rooms come equipped with TV, wi-fi and a/c; there's also a lift and car park. €75

De la Cité Pl de l'Église ☎ 04 68 71 98 71, ⊚ hoteldelacite.com; map p.90. If you can afford it, this luxurious hotel with its beautiful enclosed courtyard will separate you from the crowds of the *cité*. Service and amenities are deluxe; there is a beauty spa and an outdoor pool. €329

★ Le Donjon 2 rue du Comte Roger ☎ 04 68 11 23 00, ⊚ hotel-donjon.fr; map p.90. The other *cité* hotel is surprisingly affordable for what you get: a thoroughly renovated establishment with excellent service and an atmosphere of refined luxury. A much better value-for-money choice than *Hôtel de la Cité*. €167

★ Du Pont Vieux 32 rue Trivalle ☎ 04 68 25 24 99, ⊚ hotelpontvieux.com; map p.90. Perhaps the best all-round choice in town, this friendly, traditional-style two-star hotel is on a lively, atmospheric little street which winds up from the medieval bridge towards the *cité*. Expect to pay more for rooms with a view of the turrets. Closed Jan to mid-Feb. €62

HI Hostel Rue Trencavel ☎ 04 68 25 23 16, ⊚ hihostels.com; map p.90. Excellent modern hostel in the heart of the citadel. Its dorms and two- to six-person rooms are clean and bright, and there's a large patio for respite from the crowds outside, plus a bar. Closed last two weeks of Dec. €24.90

Montmorency 2 rue Camille St-Saëns ☎ 04 68 11 96 70, ⊚ hotelmontmorency.com; map p.90. A plain exterior conceals a welcoming and well-kept three-star hotel, with bright, sound-proofed rooms, a/c and a good range of services including a spa and an outdoor pool. Well located for visiting the citadel, as it's just one street north of the *cité*. €130

Montségur 1 av Bunau Varilla ☎ 04 68 25 31 41, ⊚ hotelmontsegur.com; map p.93. Comfortable rooms in an impressive-looking nineteenth-century townhouse. Located a 15min walk west of the cathedral, off bd Barbès, it is not the closest hotel to the *cité*, but it's competitively priced. The decor is decidedly "olde worlde" but all rooms have satellite TV, a/c and wi-fi. €89

Notre Dame de l'Abbaye 103 rue Trivalle ☎ 04 68 25 16 65, ⊚ abbaye-carcassonne.com; map p.90. In a medieval monastery on the way up to the *cité*, this is a good choice for hostel-style accommodation – single, double and family rooms are available. You'll undoubtedly find yourself next to a Santiago-bound pilgrim at breakfast, lunch or dinner (€12). €62

EATING

You'll never have a problem getting something to eat in Carcassonne, whether in the *cité*, where every other facade seems to belong to a bistro, or in the *ville basse*, which has a good selection of simple and smarter establishments.

L'Atelier de la Truffe 51 rue Trivalle ☎ 04 68 25 92 65, ⊚ barriere-truffes.com; map p.90. This truffle shop-cum-wine bar is a firm favourite with locals not just for its rustic dishes such as duck pie with truffles (€23) but also for its excellent selection of local wines. Tues–Sun 11.30am–3pm & 6.30–11pm.

Au Comte Roger 14 rue St-Louis ☎ 04 68 11 93 40, ⊚ comteroger.com; map p.90. Renowned chef Pierre Mesa imaginatively combines local basics with subtle *gastronomique* touches. The excellent cassoulet makes an ideal end to a day in the *cité*. *Menus* €24–41. Tues–Sat noon–1.30pm & 7–9.30pm.

La Barbacane pl de l'Église ☎ 04 68 71 98 71, ⊚ hoteldelacite.com; map p.90. The most elegant (and expensive) of the three restaurants operated by the *Hôtel de la Cité*. Adventurous Mediterranean-inspired *gastronomique* cuisine with first-class service. A three-course lunch with wine and coffee is good value at €38. For €150 chef Jérôme Ryon will treat you to a six-course meal matched up with local wine selections. Daily 12.30–2pm & 7.30–9.30pm.

L'Escargot 7 rue Viollet-le-Duc ☎ 04 68 47 12 55, ⊚ restaurant-lescargot-carcassonne.fr; map p.90. Buzzy, popular wine and tapas bar with street-side tables. Expect to pay around €5 for six snails, €7 for a plate of cheese and €14 for a salad. *Menus* from €12. Mon, Tues & Thurs–Sun 11am–3pm & 7pm–1am.

2

Freaks 30 rue de Verdun ☎ 04 30 18 95 36; map p.93. This tiny hole-in-the-wall with just twenty covers is a restaurant at lunchtime and *salon de thé* in the afternoon. Dishes depend on what's in the market; some have an Asian touch. The *plat du jour* costs €15. Tues–Sat 8am–6pm.

Le Jardin en Ville 5 rue des Framboisiers ☎ 04 68 47 80 91, ⊛ lejardinenville.fr; map p.93. The other side of the train tracks, this hip restaurant and gallery-shop with a leafy garden terrace (hence the name) has a great tapas menu (€18). Otherwise, expect regular meat and fish dishes accompanied by veg from the owner's garden. Tue & Wed noon–2pm, Thurs–Sat noon–2pm & 7–9pm (July & Aug Tues–Sat lunch and dinner).

★**Le St-Jean** 37 pl St-Jean ☎ 09 70 35 92 70 ⊛ le-saint-jean.eu; map p.90. Located in a small squar on the east side of the castle, this restaurant serve traditional regional cuisine in the stone-walled dinin room or on the terrace. The towering salads (€15–19) ar an excellent choice. *Menus* €12–26. Mon & Wed–Su noon–3pm & 7–11pm.

DRINKING AND NIGHTLIFE

Le Black Rte de Limoux ☎ 06 01 31 00 88, ⊛ leblack.fr; map p.93. Carcassonne's leading nightclub offers free entry on Fridays, an open-air dancefloor in summer and a free shuttle to and from town. Fri & Sat midnight–6am.

The Celt 5 rue Armagnac ☎ 04 68 10 96 44, ⊛ thecelt pub.com; map p.93. Just north of place Carnot in the *ville basse*, this Irish pub has forty varieties of bottled beer and thirty brands of whisky. There are two big screens for sport, free wi-fi and live bands most Thursdays. Mon–Fri 4pm–2am, Sat & Sun 2pm–2am.

★**La Métairie** 3 chemin de Montlegun ☎ 04 68 26 8 38; map p.90. A 5min walk uphill from the Port Narbonnaise, this bar has a wonderful view over the *cit* from its garden. Jazzy music and lots of events in summe including a hog roast on Wednesdays and an oyster bar o Fridays. Daily 6pm–2am.

Le Verre d'Un 2 rue de Verdun ☎ 04 68 71 43 99, ⊛ l verredun.com; map p.93. Wine shop-cum-wine bar in th *ville basse* where you can serve yourself from a dispense There's tapas on offer too. Mon–Sat noon–2pm & 6–10pm

SHOPPING

Cabanel 72 allée d'Iéna (ville basse) ☎ 06 01 31 00 88; map p.93. In the same spot since 1905, this wine shop is best known for its artisan *apéritifs* and liqueurs such as Micheline, whose recipe dates back to the fourth century. Mon–Sat 8am–noon & 2–7pm.

Le Panier Gourmand 1 rue du Plô (cité) ☎ 04 68 25 1 63; map p.90. The place to go for good-quality regiona products including cassoulet, beer and *Zézettes de la Cit* (biscuits). July & Aug daily 11am–9.30pm, Sept–Jun Tues–Sun 11am–5pm.

DIRECTORY

Hospital Centre Hospitalier, 1060 chemin de la Madeleine ☎ 04 68 24 24 24.

Laundry Laverie Express, 5 sq Gambetta in the *ville basse* (daily 7am–10pm).

Pharmacy There are several: try Pharmacie SARCOS, 9 pl Carnot in the *ville basse* (Tues–Sat 8.30am–7pm;

☎ 04 68 11 99 99); for night openings see ⊛ pharmacie carcassonne.net/gardes.

Police 4 bd Barbès in the *ville basse* (☎ 04 68 11 26 00).

Post office 40 rue Jean Bringer in the *ville bass* (Mon 9am–6pm, Tues–Fri 8.30am–6pm, Sa 8.30am–noon).

The upper Aude valley

Carcassonne's river, whose course can be followed due south from Carcassonne through the **upper Aude valley**, is like a highway of Catharism – the majority of the most famous sights and ruins associated with the heretical sect lie along its path as it descends from the Pyrenees. The river's lower regions are less visited, making quiet towns like **Limoux** and **Alet-les-Bains** good places to get away from the summer crowds, but as the valley winds its way up to the modern service centre of **Quillan**, more relics of the area's history reveal themselves. On the way you'll pass the mysterious site of **Rennes-le-Château**, a favourite of occultists and treasure-hunters. Just south, the so-called "**Cathar castles**" form a rough chain stretching from **Foix** in the west to the hills of the Fenouillèdes to the east (see p.284). South of Quillan, the valley narrows into a series of gorges as you begin the climb into the mountains, eventually reaching the isolated **Donezan** region – a great area for **hiking**.

Limoux

LIMOUX, the first major town you'll arrive at as you follow the course of the Aude upstream from Carcassonne, has dominated this neck of the woods since the Middle Ages; the same **bridge** which spans the Aude today brought prosperity in the form of merchants and traders as far back as the fourteenth century. Thanks to this, the local consuls were able to construct a formidable set of **defensive walls**, part of which can still be seen along the riverside. The town is known for its sparkling white *blanquette* ("little white") wine, first vinted in 1531, and – pre-dating the sparkling wines of Champagne by a century – claimed the original "Brut". You can try some on a guided visit at local producer Sieur d'Arques (av de Mauzac; ☎04 68 74 63 45, ⓦsieurdarques.com).

Today, Limoux's tranquil old town provides an opportunity to stretch your legs on the way towards the Pyrenees. The heart of the town is the **place de la République**, a wide square with some fine old stone arcading, a number of timber-frame houses and the requisite café and restaurant patios. Just down rue St-Martin, the town's main **church** has some top-notch stained-glass windows and remarkably restrained sixteenth- and seventeenth-century decor in the side chapels. The town is most famous for its Lenten *Carnaval* **festival**, held from January through to March in place de la République, with displays of masked, harlequin-style dancers and live music.

Musée Petiet

Promenade du Tivoli • July & Aug Tues–Sun 9am–noon & 2–6.30pm; June & Sept Mon–Fri 9am–noon & 2–6pm, Sat & Sun 10am–noon & 2–5pm; Oct–May Wed–Fri 9am–noon & 2–6pm, Sat 10am–noon & 2–5pm • €3.50 • ☎04 68 31 85 03, ⓦmusee-petiet-limoux.sitew.fr

On the Carcassonne–Quillan highway you'll find the small **Musée Petiet,** the most interesting of Limoux's several museums. Its collection of paintings, dominated by local nineteenth-century pointillism and allegory, contains some works of surprising quality. The museum is named after Limoux-born Marie Louise Petiet (1854–93) who was best known for her portraits and one of the few women artists celebrated in the nineteenth century.

ARRIVAL AND INFORMATION
LIMOUX

By train Trains arrive at Limoux's *gare SNCF*, on the east bank of the river, a good 20min walk from the old town. TGV stations are indicated with an asterisk. You'll need to change trains in Carcassonne to continue your journey.

Destinations Carcassonne* (several daily; 30min); Quillan (several daily; 40min).

By bus Buses stop outside the cinema on allée des Marronniers, in the old town. See ⓦaudelignes.cg11.fr for details. Tickets cost €1.

Destinations Alet-les-Bains (several daily; 15min); Axat (several daily; 1hr 10min); Carcassonne (several daily; 45min); Couiza (several daily; 20min); Quillan (several daily; 50min).

Tourist information 7 av du Pont-de-France (July & Aug daily 9.30am–12.30pm & 2–6.30pm; Sept–June Mon–Sat 9am–noon & 2–6pm; ☎04 68 31 11 82, ⓦtourisme -limoux-in-aude.fr).

GETTING AROUND

By bike You can rent bikes at Cycles Taillefer, 18 esplanade François Mitterrand ☎04 68 31 02 01.

ACCOMMODATION AND EATING

Camping Le Breil av Salvador Allende ☎04 68 31 13 63. Located on the east bank of the river, this municipal campsite has fifty shaded spaces, a *boulodrome* and a kids' playground. The municipal pool and tennis courts are nearby. Open June to Sept. **€8.80**

Domaine de St-George rte de Malras ☎04 68 20 11 05, ⓦdomainestgeorge.com. The accommodation in the town centre is nothing to shout about so head 2km northwest to this charming four-bedroom B&B. Housed in a seventeenth-century winegrower's house, it's run by

English couple John and Maureen. There's a heated pool too. **€65**

★**Tantine et Tonton** 1 pl du Général Leclerc ☎04 68 31 21 95, ⓦtantinetonton.fr. The *Hotel Moderne et Pigeon* has a brasserie (menus €19–25.50) and a smarter restaurant (menus €32–105) where chef Stéphane Castaing concocts regional-inspired dishes in gourmet style. Elegant fish dishes are a particular strength, and there's a nice outdoor terrace in summer. Brasserie: Mon–Fri noon–2pm; restaurant: Tues–Sat 7.30–9pm and Sat lunch.

SHOPPING

On Fridays a market is held on place de la République, allée des Marronniers and in the covered *halles*.

Maison Bor 15 av Fabre d'Eglantine ☎ 04 68 31 02 15, ⓦ nougatbor.com. Aside from sparkling wine, Limoux is known for its nougat – this is the place to buy it. Mon–Sa 9am–7pm.

Abbaye de St-Hilaire

Twelve kilometres northeast of Limoux on the D104 • Daily: April, May, Sept & Oct 10am–6pm; July & Aug 10am–7pm; Nov–March 10am–5pm • €5 • ☎ 04 68 69 62 76, ⓦ saint-hilaire-aude.fr

Tiny and quiet **ST-HILAIRE** is home to an ancient **abbey-church** whose monks invented Blanquette de Limoux – be sure to take a look around the dank cellar where it was made. This sixth-century church, burial place of at least one of the counts of Carcassonne, contains a splendid sarcophagus, carved in vivid relief by the "Master of Cabestany" (see box, p.284), and depicting the martyrdom of Toulouse's first bishop, St Sernin. The village is worth a wander too, if only to buy some bubbly.

Alet-les-Bains

The ancient village of **ALET-LES-BAINS** still owes its modest prosperity to the **hot springs** that bubble out of the ground on the north side of the town, first harnessed for curative purposes by the Romans, and now harnessed by a spa. From the ninth century the town flourished as the site of a Benedictine abbey, and from the fourteenth as a bishopric, before declining into obscurity with the Wars of Religion. Largely overlooked today, it preserves an atmosphere of antiquity, and its quiet streets conceal some surprising relics. A seventeenth-century **bridge** still connects Alet with the Limoux–Quillan highway, and just across it loom the ruins of the **abbey of Notre-Dame** (daily: March–June, Sept & Oct 10am–noon & 2.30–6pm, July & Aug 10am–12.30pm & 2.30–7pm; €4; ☎ 04 68 69 93 56), destroyed in 1577 and subsequently plundered to strengthen the town walls. Nearby, the town's main **square** is boxed in by timbered houses and the stone **Maison des Consuls**. Along the village's outskirts you'll find **Roman relics**, including a scrap of ancient road, a long section of twelfth-century wall, and a row of tiny **medieval houses**, which housed merchants' families eight hundred years ago.

ARRIVAL AND INFORMATION
ALET-LES-BAINS

By bus Buses arrive at the train station. Alet is one of the stops for several daily buses between Carcassonne and Axat.

By train Trains arrive at the station, on the west side of the river, on the route between Carcassonne and Quillan.

Tourist information Next to the abbey (July & Aug 10am–12.30pm & 2.30–7pm; ☎ 04 68 69 93 56, ⓦ aletlesbains.com).

ACCOMMODATION AND EATING

Camping Val d'Aleth ☎ 04 68 69 90 40, ⓦ www .valdaleth.com. This floral, shady two-star site next to the river has just 37 pitches; facilities run to a sanitary block and a shop. The owners also have a more comfortable B&B in their ancient stone house nearby. €18

Hostellerie de l'Evêché Av Nicolas Pavillon ☎ 04 68 69 90 25, ⓦ hotel-eveche.com. The former bishop's palace has been turned into a charming thirty-room *Logis de France* hotel. Accommodation is a little on the basic side (no TVs) but the excellent restaurant with its gourmet regional cuisine (menus €16–47) makes up for it. €76

Rennes-le-Château

RENNES-LE-CHÂTEAU (not to be confused with the nearby spa town of Rennes-les-Bains) sits at the end of a 4km mountain road winding up from the little village of Couiza.

2

It was here that the enigmatic Bérenger Saunière, Rennes' parish priest, died in 1917 after having lived in luxury for nearly thirty years, building himself a private villa, conservatory and library, and renovating the church in garish style (see box opposite). Together these sites form the mysterious **Domaine de l'Abbé Saunière**, a magnet for treasure-seekers, occultists and crop-circle aficionados, and inspiration for *The Da Vinci Code*.

Ste-Marie-Madeleine church

Daily: March, April, Oct & Nov 10am–1pm & 2–4.30pm; May 10am–6.30pm; June–Aug 10am–7pm; Sept 10am–5.15pm; Oct to mid-Nov 10.30am–1pm & 2–4.30pm • Free • ☎ 04 68 31 38 85, ⓦ rennes-le-chateau.fr

The compact **Ste-Marie-Madeleine church** is entered through the side door, above which a Latin inscription welcomes you to this "terrible place" – perhaps a reference to the decor. Inside, you're greeted by a rather sinister wooden carving of a grimacing demon surmounted by four angels. The interior is painted in medieval style and filled with a healthy contingent of carved Baroque saints. Although these may seem rather ordinary church furnishings, enthusiasts have uncovered a complex code in their details and arrangement, which corresponds – depending on who you ask – to Kabbalistic theory, UFO influence or the secret "Priory of Sion" society.

Musée Domaine de l'Abbé Saunière

Same hours as church • €5

The estate where Saunière lived has now been converted into the **Musée Domaine de l'Abbé Sauniere,** a museum containing important relics, such as the hollow Visigothic pillar that once supported the church's altar. From there you enter the priest's spacious **garden**, where he is buried; it's girded by a fanciful fortified wall capped by two towers, one of which once served as his library and from where there are wonderful views. Next to the house is "Béthania", a more luxurious house where Saunière entertained guests and – banned from conducting the Catholic Mass – installed his own chapel.

ARRIVAL AND INFORMATION

If you have no transport, you can reach Rennes-le-Château by taxi (about €15) from Couiza (☎ 04 68 74 25 36), although, if you are up to it, the demanding 4km uphill walk is enjoyable. Thomas Loisirs (☎ 04 68 74 10 97, ⓦ www.thomasloisirs.fr) in Couiza rents bikes.

RENNES-LE-CHÂTEAU

Tourist information Office de Tourisme du Pays de Couiza, 17 rte des Pyrénées, 11190 Couiza (Mon–Fri 9am–12.30pm & 1.30–6pm, Sat 10am–12.30pm & 1.30–5pm, Sun 10am–1pm; ☎ 04 68 69 69 85, ⓦ paysdecouiza.com).

ACCOMMODATION AND EATING

★**Château des Ducs de Joyeuse** Allée Georges Roux, 11190 Couiza ☎ 04 68 74 23 50, ⓦ chateau -des-ducs.com. Stunning hotel and restaurant in a sixteenth-century château which merits more than its three stars. Some of the rooms are in the towers, while some have four-poster beds and medieval decoration. The cuisine is "gourmet regional" (*menus* €29–83). €108
Domaine de Mournac 11190 Antugnac ☎ 04 68 74 21 10, ⓦ mournac.com. Idyllic B&B in an old coaching inn with wonderful views and a pool, 8km northwest of

Rennes-le-Château. The four rooms are chicly decorated in warm colours; "Magdala" has its own terrace. There's also a studio for two (€598 per week) and a *gîte* sleeping up to ten (€1900 per week). €98
Le Lavaldieu ☎ 04 68 74 23 21, ⓦ lavaldieu.com. Halfway between Rennes-le-Château and Rennes-les-Bains lies Lavaldieu, a restored hamlet set in woodland grazed by horses, where you'll find guesthouse accommodation, a studio and a basic campsite. All food, including dinner, is vegetarian. €34

Arques

The village of **ARQUES** is a little hamlet with a fourteenth-century church, some contemporary buildings and a small exhibition on Catharism housed in the **Maison de Déodat Roché** (daily April–June & Sept 10am–1pm & 2–6pm; July & Aug 10am–1.30pm & 2–7pm; March & Oct to mid-Nov 10am–1pm & 2–5pm; €6; ☎ 04 68 69 84 77, ⓦ chateau-arques.fr).

BÉRENGER SAUNIÈRE AND THE MYSTERIES OF RENNES-LE-CHÂTEAU

Bérenger Saunière arrived to serve as the priest in the tiny and backward hamlet of Rennes in 1885 – at 33, a cranky, royalist reactionary whose political views had already earned him the ire of the Church authorities. But his exile was to take an unexpected turn. Within a few years the humble priest was renovating the tiny and ancient **parish church**, decking it with a collection of eccentric fineries bought on order in Paris. By 1891 he'd begun buying up considerable tracts of land, placing the title under the name of **Marie Denardaud**. Marie, the daughter of his housekeeper, and sixteen years his junior, became his lifelong companion. In 1899, Saunière began work on the house and gardens of **Béthania**, as he called the smartly appointed villa which he raised next to the church. Luxurious by local standards, it was finished in 1904. Meanwhile, the *abbé* and his consort lorded it over the hamlet, dispensing generous donations and throwing magnificent *fêtes*, while keeping an iron grip on its affairs. Such was the awe Saunière inspired that when villagers begged Marie for access to the priest's cistern to put out a fire, she refused them, rather than rouse him from a nap to get his permission.

By 1907 Saunière's activities and outspoken politics provoked an investigation by the bishop of Carcassonne and he was deposed on a string of charges, ranging from abuse of power and finances to traffic of Church offices. His initial appeal failed in 1911 and, **defrocked**, he filed a second appeal to the Holy See in Rome. Meanwhile, work on the villa continued; banned by canon law from celebrating Mass in church, he performed the sacraments in the stained-glass annexe built onto Béthania. On January 22, 1917, after giving his last confession, Saunière died of a heart attack and was buried in the cemetery behind the church (however, to stop the grave from being regularly vandalized, it was moved to the garden of the Domaine in 2004). Marie Denardaud, much to Saunière's family's disappointment, was his only heir, and she remained faithful to her "*chèr disparu*" till her end, refusing to divulge his secrets.

The secret, of course, was where Saunière's money came from. It is generally believed he stumbled upon a cache of medieval coins, perhaps after finding ancient parchments either in the hollow stone **Visigothic** altar-support, in a secret compartment in a wooden column or under a carved flagstone that sat before the altar. After his death, Marie made cryptic references to the "gold" over which the "villagers were walking", which would be enough to "support the village for a hundred years". These tales attracted the attention of a steady string of **treasure-hunters** who became so troublesome and disruptive that even today signs forbid any digging in the vicinity of the town.

The story of the treasure and the bizarre symbolism of the church's decor have spawned scores of occult theories over their origin and significance, including possible links to a secret society called the Priory of Sion, the Templars, **Solomon's treasure**, Cathars, the **Holy Grail** and a Christ who escaped crucifixion. In the last decades this has turned into a small industry and there are dozens of books written on the subject. Inevitably, the town has sparked a series of reports of parapsychological and extra-terrestrial events, including a miraculous image of the Virgin and Child, discernible in a 1967 aerial photograph, UFO visitations and crop circles. The controversy continued in 2009, when Rennes' mayor went public with new documents showing that Saunière died in poverty.

From Arques the road continues (no public transport) through ever more untamed and isolated terrain towards the castles at Termes and Villerouge-Termenès (see p.252), and the abbey-town of Lagrasse (see p.253), a route very much worthwhile exploring either by car or bicycle.

Donjon d'Arques
Same hours and ticket as the Maison Déodat Roché

About ten minutes' walk to the west of the village is the **donjon d'Arques** whose perfectly preserved square **keep** is unmistakable, rising 25m above the surrounding fields. The castle – undoubtedly the most beautiful in the region – was built in perfect northern-French Gothic style by its new lord, Pierre de Voisins, after the Cathar original had been destroyed. Pierre's local reputation was cemented when he burned a

2

SPELUNKING IN THE GROTTE DE L'AGUZOU

While the prehistoric caves around Foix (see p.108) are stunningly impressive, if you're hankering for some real cave exploration, visit the **Grotte de l'Aguzou**, 27km south of Quillan towards the upstream end of the Gorges de l'Aude. The guided tour of this magnificent complex is the real thing – equipped with overalls, helmet and lamp, groups of four to ten people are taken into the unlit **cave system** at 9am, to be conducted through the *grandes salles* of stalactites, stalagmites, columns and draperies, some of which are 20m high. Lunch (you bring your own) is taken 600m underground, and then it's on to the so-called "gardens of crystals" – a fantastic array of forms and shapes, some growing from the rock in long, thin needles; others are like pine cones dusted by hoar frost, or clear and convoluted like a Venetian glass-blower's accident. The full-day **excursions** led by veteran speleologist Philippe Moreno are very popular, so book well in advance, and check the website for details (€60; ☏ 04 68 20 45 38, ⓦ grotte-aguzou.com).

60-year-old local woman as a witch soon after he arrived. The central *donjon*, which dates back to the thirteenth century, is extremely well preserved, with graceful Gothic vaulting sustaining two of its great chambers. The third-floor hall is dominated by an impressively huge **fireplace**.

ARRIVAL AND DEPARTURE ARQUES

By bus Arques to: Couiza (daily; 20min). **By taxi** Taxi from Couiza (☏ 04 68 74 25 36).

Quillan and around

Set on the west bank of the Aude about halfway along its course, **QUILLAN** is the gateway to the spectacular **Aude gorges**, providing ample canoeing and rafting possibilities. It's also a jumping-off point for the isolated region just to the south, known as the **Donezan** and home to a couple of historically important, but decayed, Cathar sites, including **Usson**. The area makes for excellent hiking and driving, but public transport is almost nonexistent.

Quillan itself is a picturesque town, though the only monument of interest is the ruined **castle** on the east bank of the Aude – here a sturdy torrent – just across the Pont Vieux; long reduced to rubble and remnants, it is nevertheless a romantic spot. There's a market on Wednesday and Saturday mornings.

Château d'Usson

About 32km southwest of Quillan in the Donezan • Daily: March–May & Sept to mid-Oct 2–6pm; July & Aug 10am–1pm & 3–7pm • €4 • ☏ 04 68 20 43 92, ⓦ donezan.com

Shrinking and semi-abandoned **USSON** sits in the shadow of its dilapidated **château**, which was the first place of safety for the four Cathars who escaped the massacre at Montségur, and dates back to at least the eleventh century. Inside, the former stables are now the Maison du Patrimoine, which has an exhibition on the history of the area.

ARRIVAL AND DEPARTURE QUILLAN AND AROUND

Quillan's *gare SNCF* and *gare routière* are both central, on bd Charles-de-Gaulle.

Destinations by bus Alet-les-Bains (several daily; 35min); Axat (several daily; 20min); Carcassonne (daily; 1hr 35min); Couiza (several daily; 20min); Limoux (several daily; 50min); St-Paul-le-Fenouillet (two daily; 55min).

Destinations by train Alet-les-Bains (several daily; 30min); Carcassonne (several daily; 1hr 20min); Couiza (several daily; 20min); Limoux (several daily; 40min).

INFORMATION AND ACTIVITIES

Tourist information Quillan: Square André Tricoire (April–June & Sept Mon–Sat 9.30am–noon & 2–6pm; July & Aug Mon–Sat 9am–12.30pm & 2–7pm; Nov–March Mon–Wed & Fri 10am–noon & 2–5pm; ☏ 04 68 20 07 78, pyreneesaudoises.com). Donezan: 09460 Le Pla, around 40km south of Quillan and 4km from the château d'Usson Mon–Fri 8.30am–12.30pm & 1.30–5.30pm, daily in summer; ☎ 04 68 20 41 37, ⊕ donezan.com).

Activities La Forge de Quillan (rte de Perpignan; ☎ 04 68 20 23 79, ⊕ laforgedequillan.fr) organizes a whole range of mountain, river and land-based activities from April to October. Also rents out bikes.

ACCOMMODATION AND EATING

Camping La Sapinette 21 rue Rénée Delpech ☎ 04 68 20 13 52, ⊕ camping-quillan.fr. In an elevated location amid mountain and woodland scenery, this three-star municipal campsite has spaces for campers and rents out chalets too. There's also a swimming pool and a kids' playground. **€11.60**

Casalys 49 grande rue Vaysse Barthélémy ☎ 09 53 71 70 45, ⊕ casalys.com. Three-bedroom B&B in an eighteenth-century townhouse crammed with original

features such as an antique glass ceiling and original floor tiles. The decor is decidedly Mediterranean and there's a view of the Pyrenees from the roof terrace. **€59**

La Chaumière Allée 25 bd Charles de Gaulle ☎ 04 68 20 02 00, ⊕ pyren.fr. Modern three-star *Logis de France* hotel with a distinctive curved exterior and bright, contemporary rooms. There's a Spanish feel to the dining room and the *menus* (from €19) feature Vietnamese specialities as well as well as local *terroir* cuisine. **€85**

Pays de Sault

The magnificent **pays de Sault** is an upland area more or less bounded by the rivers Aude and Ariège and, to the north, the main road (D117) from Quillan to Foix. This is the most accessible route into the area, and offers some of Languedoc's most outstanding scenery, as well as Cathar castles at **Montségur** and **Puivert**. The other main road, the D163, runs southwest from Quillan to Ax-les-Thermes, passing the famous heretic village, **Montaillou**, and the dramatic limestone crevice, the **Gorges de la Frau**.

Montségur

Daily: March & Oct 10am–5pm; April–June & Sept 10am–6pm; July & Aug 9am–7pm; Nov–Feb 11am–4pm • €5.50/6.50 • ☎ 05 61 01 06 94, ⊕ www.montsegur.fr

The ruined castle of **MONTSÉGUR** looms dramatically atop a towering, pillar-like hill, its plain stone walls poised mutely above the straggling village at its foot. It's the best known site in Occitanie after Carcassonne thanks to its turbulent history, myths and legends, and appearance in bestselling novels such as *Labyrinth* by Kate Mosse. The original fortifications were built in the eighth century by Guillaume "Short-Nose", duke of Aquitaine, but between 1204 and 1232 it was reconstructed as a bastion of the Cathars under the direction of Guilhabert de Castres, leader of the sect, who imagined the sheer rocky cliffs of the *pog* ("hill") would render it untakeable. The only access to the ruin is along the western side, where it is possible to walk up to the **summit** (about 30min) through what is now called the *prat dels cremats* ("meadow of the burned"). It was here the surviving Cathars were put to the stake after the castle fell – a modern stone memorial pays tribute to them. What's left of the castle takes no more than a few minutes to explore, but it isn't so much what you see at Montségur that makes the trip unforgettable, as what your imagination can recreate from its remnants.

> ### THE SIEGE OF MONTSÉGUR
>
> In 1242 a band of Cathar warriors struck out from **Montségur** castle and attacked and killed a party of Dominican Inquisitors at **Avignonet-Lauragais**, sparking a series of rebellions across the region. The royal response was swift: a massive force was raised and in May 1243 they laid **siege** to the castle. Inside, 150 knights, led by **Pierre-Roger of Mirepoix**, and several hundred Cathars endured eight months of siege and bombardment before Pierre-Roger negotiated for clemency in exchange for surrender. But the Cathar faithful would not betray their cause and when the castle was opened to the French, some 225 were led out to a field below the fort and **burnt alive**.

The Montségur region is excellent **hiking territory**; you can cross the area in a few days, using a network of walking itineraries – the "Tour du Pays de Sault", the "Tour du Massif de Tabe", the "Piémont" and the GR107. The popular "Sentier Cathare" (Ⓦlesentiercathare.com), meanwhile, is a gentle trail that can be followed from Foix to Montségur, and all the way down to the Mediterranean. Local tourist offices will be able to advise.

2 Archeological museum

Daily: April–June, Sept & Oct 2–6pm; July & Aug 11am–1pm & 2–7pm; Nov–March 2–5pm • €2.50

Down in the village, 1km below, a one-room **archeological museum** displays artefacts excavated since the 1950s from the original village beside the walls, from both pre- and post-Cathar periods – mostly food, bones, personal effects, tools and surviving fragments of houses.

GETTING AROUND AND INFORMATION   MONTSÉGUR

Motoring is by far the best way to explore the region but there is a twice-daily bus service from Pamiers, the main public transport hub, to Montségur (1hr 25min).

Tourist information 104 Le Village (July & Aug 11am–12.30pm & 1.30–5.30pm; rest of the year enquire at the archeology museum; ☎05 61 03 03 03 Ⓦmontsegur.fr).

ACCOMMODATION AND EATING

Camping Point Accueil Jeunes 32 Le Village ☎05 61 01 10 27. Very basic municipal campsite but in a lovely green location with great views. Open May to Sept. €7.60
Costes 52 Le Village ☎05 61 02 66 21. The only hotel in Montségur, with just thirteen simple rooms, is housed in a fifteenth-century building on the east side of the village.

The restaurant serves regional dishes (*plats* from €16) made with ingredients from local producers. Free parking. €68
Le Pèlerin 111 Le Village ☎05 34 14 00 39 Ⓦpelerin111.com. Cosy guesthouse with four rooms named after the elements. The Norwegian owners also have a weaving workshop attached. Breakfast extra. €65

Puivert

The ancient village of **PUIVERT** sits among mountain meadows planted with corn and sunflowers. Its **Musée du Quercorb** (16 rue Barry du Lion; mid-April to mid-July & end Aug to mid-Sept Wed–Sun 10am–1pm & 2–6pm; mid-July to end-Aug daily 10am–7pm; €4.10; ☎04 68 20 80 98, Ⓦmuseequercorb.com) is a folk museum which has reconstructed rooms, displays on local history and reproductions of medieval instruments copied from the castle's sculptures.

> ### HIKING FROM CAMURAC TO MONTSÉGUR
>
> The **GR107 trail** north from the village of **Camurac** – close to Montaillou on the D613 – leads north and west to **Montségur**, a hike of a little over four hours, tracing a stretch of the **Chemin des Bonhommes** ("The Goodmen's Trail"), which recreates the path by which Cathar *perfecti* (see p.314) crossed back and forth over the Pyrenees. Shortly after leaving Camurac, you'll arrive at the hamlet of Comus. Here, the trail drops down as a mule track between fields to a wide gorge that suddenly becomes a defile – the **Gorges de la Frau** – where thousand-metre-high cliffs admit the sun only during the early afternoon. When the gorge widens again, you meet the dead end of the D5 coming south from Bélesta and Fougax-Barrineuf. There are two options for continuing to Montségur: either westwards along the GR107, which runs along a shaded riverbank (turn off at the first farm, "Pelail", 45min along the D5), or via a bridle trail beginning about an hour along the tarmac, offering higher, more open ground. If you want an early start, you can stay at the **gîte**, *de Montaigne*, in Comus (€20; ☎04 68 20 33 69, Ⓦgites-comus.com).

Château de Puivert

Easter to mid-Nov daily 9am–7pm; mid-Dec to Easter Sun–Fri 10am–5pm • €5 • ☎ 04 68 20 81 52, ⓦ chateau-de-puivert.com

Set above the village, 1km to the east, is its romantically sited **château**, which fell to the Albigensian Crusade in 1210, and was rebuilt in the 1300s. More a place of culture than of arms, it was closely associated with the troubadour poets (see p.313), whose preoccupation with love might seem incompatible with the asceticism of the Cathars. What united them was the Occitan language, then spoken all across southern France.

The most interesting part of the castle is its *donjon*. Within it is a chapel with vigil seats at the north and south windows, a wall font and rib-vaulting on the ceiling, culminating in a keystone embossed with images of the Virgin and St George. The highest chamber is dubbed the "**musicians' room**" after its eight *culs-de-lamps* or torch sockets at the termini of more rib-vaulting, each sculpted in the form of a figure playing a different period instrument.

2

ACCOMMODATION   PUIVERT

Camping Puivert ☎ 04 68 20 0058, ⓦ www.camping -puivert.fr. Two-star campsite in an idyllic lakeside location opposite the château. There are 58 shady spaces with a new sanitary block and plenty of activities in summer, including a Wednesday evening market. Open May to Sept. **€15.50**

La Cocagnière 3 pl de Pijol, Hameau de Campsylvestre, 6km southeast of Puivert ☎ 04 68 31 54 58, ⓦ lacocagniere.com. This four-bedroom B&B in a modern stone house is located in an old hamlet, with lovely views across the countryside. *Table d'hôte* is available for €25; the dishes are made with organic produce and home-grown vegetables. **€60**

Montaillou

Sitting on the narrow and sparsely travelled road from Quillan to Ax-les-Thermes, the village of **MONTAILLOU** is only 15km southeast of Montségur as the crow flies, but – unless you're hiking – is reached via a tortuous 40km route through remote territory that vividly evokes a past of heresy and isolation (allow an hour each way by car). Montaillou was home to the last Cathar community until the Inquisition set to work here during the early 1300s. Fewer than twenty people live here permanently now, some of them descendants of the Cathars, as you can see by comparing their surnames (such as Clergues and Belot) with those on the headstones in the ancient graveyard. The village's crumbled **castle** was once the

MONTAILLOU'S SECRET HERETICS

In July 1320, **Béatrice de Planissolles**, a woman of the lower nobility of the Ariège and widow of the lord of Montaillou, was summoned to appear before Jacques Fournier, Bishop of Pamiers, Inquisitor, former abbot of Fontfroide (see p.251) and future Pope Benedict XII on charges of **heresy** and **witchcraft**. Under Fournier's interrogation, Béatrice, who had had a string of lovers, confessed her Cathar tendencies and those of her townsmen. This only served to confirm longstanding suspicions – already in 1308 the entire village of Montaillou had been arrested and hauled off by the **Inquisition** for interrogation. The resulting confessions revealed a village in the grip of heresy, harbouring an adulterous and vengeful parish priest, free-thinking itinerant shepherds, a hypocritical and philandering Perfectus, and the sorts of petty intrigues, violent struggles, and illicit liaisons not untypical of an isolated and insular mountain peasant community. In the end, the villagers suffered various fates: a few were put to death, others condemned to wear yellow crosses on their clothes as a sign of their heresy, while most were absolved after completing some relatively minor penance. Béatrice herself was **immured** ("walled in") for one year, before being freed under the condition that she would wear the yellow crosses.

The copious and detailed records compiled by the inquisitors were so precise that **historian Emmanuel Le Roy Ladurie** was able to recreate every aspect of the villagers' lives from them, from the minutiae of domestic economics to the details of their sexual habits and their conceptions of god and the universe, in his book, *Montaillou* (see p.327).

home of Béatrice de Planissolles (see box, p.105), and the village church is the same one in which she was seduced by the parish priest.

The lower Ariège valley

The **lower Ariège valley** winds a leisurely course through a broad, rolling upland, whose rich dairy and wheat farms set it apart from the dry, vine-dominated scrub of most of Languedoc and Roussillon. East of the Ariège river a broad plain straddles the banks of its tributary, the **Hers**. Centred on **Mirepoix**, these flatlands were home to Cathars and castles; today a series of surprising and unique medieval **monuments** remain. Dominating the river itself is **Foix**, capital of the Ariège *département*. The town's strikingly positioned castle is the only testament to Foix's former role as the centre of a proudly independent principality – now a casualty of history, like the neighbouring County of Toulouse.

Mirepoix

The town of **MIREPOIX** is tucked away among the undulating hills of the Hers valley. History was not kind to this Cathar stronghold: first its townsfolk suffered a massacre at the hands of the Crusaders, then a generation later it was all but destroyed by flood. The present town dates back to 1290, when the noble Jean de Lévis laid out a new *bastide* in a safer location; it's arguably the most beautiful in the region.

There is little in particular to do here, but the beauty of Mirepoix makes it the perfect spot to relax on a terrace, have a drink and soak up the atmosphere. On Monday mornings both of the *places* fill with the **market** stalls of local farmers.

Place Maréchal-Leclerc

At the centre of the village sits the broad **place Maréchal-Leclerc** (or place de Couverts), perhaps the most beautiful town square west of the Rhône. Almost the entire perimeter is rimmed by broad arcades supported by stout old beams, above which rise two storeys of pastel timber-frame houses.

Maison des Consuls

Although the *place* as a whole is beautiful, its star attraction is the fourteenth-century **Maison des Consuls** (now a hotel; see p.106) in the centre of the north side, at no. 6. This former town hall, courthouse and prison dates from the fourteenth century and is decorated by nearly 150 **wooden heads**, carved in high relief at the ends of the beams supporting the second storey. Each carving is individual, the portraits ranging across the gamut of medieval social classes and professions and including exotic and foreign peoples (notably some very early portrayals of black Africans), as well as demons, monsters, animals and assorted grotesques.

Place Philippe-de-Lévis

By passing through an attractive nineteenth-century wrought-iron **market hall** on the south side of place Maréchal-Leclerc, you arrive at another arcaded *place*, **Philippe-de-Lévis** – not as stunning as its larger counterpart, but also impressive.

Cathédral St-Maurice

Mon–Sat 9am–noon & 2–6pm • Free

In the middle stands the fourteenth-century **cathedral of St-Maurice**, whose broad single nave is the widest of any Gothic-style church in France. Local lore attributes the absence of supporting columns to the clergy's desire to monitor parishioners, checking that they were not carrying out forbidden Cathar practices, but this is doubtful given that the cathedral was not consecrated until 1509.

ARRIVAL AND INFORMATION

MIREPOIX

By bus There are several buses daily to Pamiers (30min), or public transport connections, and two daily to Montségur (50min). The bus stops on cours Petitpied to the north of the main square.

Tourist information Pl Maréchal-Leclerc (July & Aug Mon–Sat 9.15am–6.30pm, Sun 10am–6pm; Sept–June Mon–Sat 9.15am–12.15pm & 2–6pm; ☏ 05 61 68 83 76, ⓦ tourisme-mirepoix.com).

ACCOMMODATION AND EATING

★ **BelRepayre** 09500 Manses ☏ 05 61 68 11 99, ⓦ airstreameurope.com. This trailer park filled with retro Airstream caravans sits in a peaceful hilltop location, ten minutes' drive west of Mirepoix. There's an outdoor hot tub with a view, "Lucy's Diner" and the coolest bar you've ever seen – the open-air "Apollo Lounge" – where drinks are served from the windows of a silver trailer lit by neon signs. Open May to September. **€124**

Camping Les Nysades Rte de Limoux ☏ 05 61 60 28 83, ⓦ camping-mirepoix-ariege.com. A short walk to the east of the centre, this two-star campsite has sixty shaded spaces as well as canvas lodges and mobile homes to rent. Open May to September. **€16**

Robet 3 pl Philippe de Lévis ☏ 05 61 69 44 34. Attractive, green-fronted family-run traditional restaurant, usually populated by locals. Lunch, from €16.50, can be enjoyed on the terrace in summer. Mon, Tues & Thurs–Sun noon–1pm, also Fri & Sat 7–9pm.

Maison des Consuls 6 pl Maréchal-Leclerc ☏ 05 61 68 81 81, ⓦ maisondesconsuls.com. Wonderfully atmospheric hotel in an historic building in the main square. Each of the seven rooms is individually decorated from different periods of French history. The wine bar serves up platters of cheese and charcuterie. **€100**

Les Minotiers Av Maréchal-Foch ☏ 05 61 69 37 36, ⓦ hotelmirepoix.com. Good-value two-star contemporary *Logis de France* hotel with free parking. The restaurant is renowned for its traditional cuisine (*menus* €17–38). **€57**

Camon

CAMON, southeast of Mirepoix and one of the Plus Beaux Villages de France, is a tiny settlement of exceptional charm and rich in atmosphere with roses around almost every door; there's a rose festival on the third Sunday in May. Founded by Charlemagne himself, it is still dominated by its thousand-year-old **abbey-castle** and surrounded by parts of its two sets of walls (fourteenth and sixteenth century). The castle is private and operates as a hotel, but its richly appointed sixteenth-century interior, arranged around a vine-draped courtyard, can also be taken in as part of a guided tour (€5), arranged by the small tourist office.

ARRIVAL AND INFORMATION

CAMON

There is no public transport to Camon.

Tourist information 10 rue Georges d'Armagnac (Daily: 10am–12.30pm & 3–6pm; ☏ 05 61 68 88 26, ⓦ camon09.org). As well as organizing tours of the castle, the tourist office runs torch-lit tours of the village on Wednesdays at 9.30pm in July & Aug. There is also a boutique selling regional books and products.

ACCOMMODATION

L'Abbaye-Château de Camon ☏ 05 61 60 31 23, ⓦ www.chateaudecamon.com. English-run luxury B&B and wedding venue in the village's ancient castle. The cloister provides a romantic backdrop for dinner (Mon, Tues & Thurs–Sun; €46) while the pool is a great place to relax at any time of day. Closed Nov–March. **€135**

Vals

Vals, a cluster of farmhouses 12km west of Mirepoix on the north bank of the Hers, has a little-known but very interesting church to its name. About 20m from the main road a small and incredibly ancient **église rupestre** (subterranean church; daily 10am–7pm; free), once a stopping-point on the pilgrims' route to Compostela, is built on a rocky spur. Entering through a hobbit-sized doorway you climb a staircase carved in the rock, passing through a pseudo-crypt of pre-Roman origin before reaching the church itself. When you enter, grope for the light switch to the left of the door to illuminate the curious three-chambered vertical structure; in the arches of some of its windows you'll find well-preserved late eleventh- and early twelfth-century frescoes of saints and angels, which recall the styles of painted churches of the Pyrenees.

Foix and around

FOIX has few specific sights itself but is the most agreeable base in the valley, with connections by train and bus into the mountains. It has a good range of services, and is surprisingly lively for a relatively small town, mainly because of its university. What's more, people tend to hurry past, so that although Foix is located in the midst of the greatest concentration of **prehistoric caves** in France, it is never overwhelmed by visitors and retains an appealing intimacy and freshness.

Foix has a well-preserved **old town** of narrow alleys, wedged in the triangle between the Ariège and the Arget rivers. A few of the overhanging houses here date from the fourteenth to sixteenth centuries, and especially attractive are **place Pyrène** and **place St-Vincent** with their fountains, though many junctions in the old quarter sport some sort of water feature. All lanes seem to lead eventually to the conspicuously large **église St-Volusien** in the east of the old town, originally Romanesque but almost completely reconstructed after being razed during the Wars of Religion. Its eponymous square, along with the Halles aux Grains just off cours

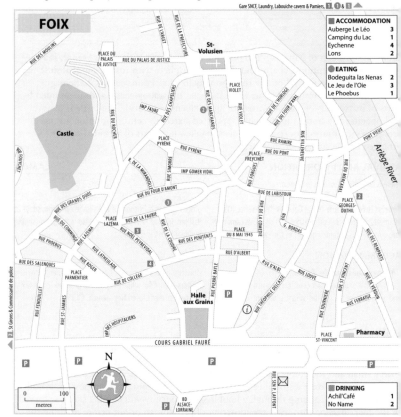

ACCOMMODATION
Auberge Le Léo	3
Camping du Lac	1
Eychenne	4
Lons	2

EATING
Bodeguita las Nenas	2
Le Jeu de l'Oie	3
Le Phoebus	1

DRINKING
Achil'Café	1
No Name	2

Gabriel-Fauré, hosts a lively market on Friday – farm produce and plants at the place, and meat, cheese, savouries and pastries at the metal-roofed *halles*, which on other days is a prime drinking venue.

Château de Foix

Jan Sat & Sun 10.30am–noon & 2–5.30pm; Feb & March Mon & Wed–Sun 10.30am–noon & 2–5.30pm; April, May & Sept daily 10am–noon & 2–6pm; June daily 10am–6pm; July & Aug daily 10am–6.30pm; Oct–Dec (closed Tues Nov & Dec) daily 10.30am–noon & 2–5.30pm • €5.60 • ☎ 05 61 05 10 10, ⓦ sites-touristiques-ariege.fr

Presiding over the old town is Foix's hilltop **castle**, not so much a single fortification as three magnificent, dissimilar towers from different eras: a slender eleventh-century **turret**, a bulky square twelfth-century **keep** and a broad and rounded fourteenth-century tower – dramatic when viewed from any angle. From 1012 the castle on this site was the seat of the counts of Foix, whose association with the Cathar faith led to its being besieged four times by Simon de Montfort, who failed to break the fort's resistance.

The castle is reached by ascending a steep zigzag path lined with river pebbles that can make the climb uncomfortable. Inside, the round tower has **exhibitions** over three floors on the building of the castle, the life of Gaston Fébus and the history of nearby Andorra; if you've got the energy to climb all 134 steps you'll be rewarded with amazing views from the top. The square tower, meanwhile, is home to Henri IV's monumental bed. During the first two weeks of August, the exterior of the castle provides an impressive backdrop for a *son et lumière* show.

ARRIVAL AND INFORMATION

FOIX AND AROUND

By train The *gare SNCF* sits on the right bank of the Ariège, a 10min walk north of the centre. TGV stations are indicated with an asterisk.

Destinations Latour-de-Carol/Enveitg (connections to *Train Jaune* and Perpignan), via Tarascon-sur-Ariège; L'Hospitalet-près-l'Andorre and Porte-Puymorens (several daily; 1hr 40min); Toulouse* (several daily; 1hr 10min).

By bus Most buses stop on bd Ariège by the statue of Lakanal.

Destinations Ax-les-Thermes (several daily; 1hr); Lavelanet (daily; 30min); St-Girons (several daily; 45min); Tarascon-sur-Ariège (several daily; 25min); Toulouse (three daily; 1hr).

Tourist information 29 rue Delcassé (July & Aug Mon–Sat 10am–7pm & Sun 10am–12.30pm & 2–6pm; Sept–June Mon–Sat 10am–noon & 2–6pm; ☎ 05 61 65 12 12, ⓦ foix-tourisme.com). Organizes guided tours of the town by torchlight in July and August (Tues & Thurs 9.30pm) and also has information on all the outdoor activities in the area.

GETTING AROUND

By car You can rent cars at Hertz, RN20 Peysales ☎ 05 61 65 15 99. There's free parking at Champ de Mars, des Moulins and de la Vigne car park.

By taxi Taxi Express ☎ 05 61 02 86 50 (opposite Halle aux Grains).

By bike Although there is no bike rental shop in Foix, there is a 42km *voie verte* (cycling and walking trail) from Foix to St-Girons.

ACCOMMODATION

Auberge Le Léo 16 rue Noël-Peyrevidal ☎ 05 61 65 09 04, ⓦ leodefoix.com. This family-friendly hostel has rooms for one to four persons, each with an en-suite toilet and shower. Other options include studios with a hot plate and fridge. The restaurant serves good-value meals (*menus* €14) and is open to the public at lunchtimes. €54

Camping du Lac Labarre ☎ 05 61 60 09 09, ⓦ vap -camping.fr. Three-star campsite to the north of the town with 135 spaces as well as sixteen chalets to rent. Amenities include a swimming pool and a tennis court; there are plenty of activities in summer. Open March to October. €28

Eychenne 11 rue Noël-Peyrevidal ☎ 05 61 65 00 04, ⓦ hoteleychenne.com. Located in the heart of the old town, this two-star hotel has eighteen recently renovated rooms. Light sleepers should beware: the bar on the ground floor, HQ of the local rugby club, can get noisy in the evening. €55

Lons 6 pl Duthil ☎ 05 34 09 28 00, ⓦ hotel-lons-foix .com The quietest and most comfortable option in Foix is this three-star, set in an old postal *relais* – with unintentionally hip 1970s decor. The restaurant, with a nice riverside conservatory, serves Ariégeoise cuisine (*menus* from €17.80). €85

EATING

Bodeguita Las Nenas 25 rue des Marchands ☎ 09 67 03 83 65. Popular little tapas restaurant with a wide range of good-value dishes (€5.50–7); the homemade *flan* is delicious. Mon–Fri noon–2pm, also Fri & Sat 7–9pm (open Mon–Sat for dinner in July & Aug).

Le Jeu de l'Oie 17 rue Lafaurie ☎ 05 61 02 69 39. In the heart of the town, this unpretentious restaurant serves *cuisine de terroir* (*menus* €11–26) with some

Spanish touches such as salmon crumble with chorizo Mon–Sat noon–2.30pm & 7–10.30pm, closed Mon in winter.

Le Phoebus 3 cours Irénée Cros ☎ 05 61 65 10 42. The best restaurant in town has great views of the castle and fixed-price menus (€19–87) featuring gourmet regional cuisine such as duck *tournedos* with Hypocras *jus*. Tues–Fri & Sun noon–2pm & 8–11pm, also Sat 8–11pm.

DRINKING AND NIGHTLIFE

Achil'Café 2 av République, Labarre ☎ 05 61 03 17 67. Lively music and tapas bar a couple of kilometres north of the town with bands or DJs most nights. Tues–Thurs 9am–midnight, Fri & Sat 9am–2am.

No Name 1 av Lakanal ☎ 05 61 65 59 93. Music bar and restaurant with live entertainment on Fridays. There's also an outside terrace. Mon–Sat 10pm–2am, Sun 10pm–midnight.

DIRECTORY

Hospital Centre Hospitalier du Val d'Ariège, N20, St-Jean-de-Verges ☎ 05 61 03 30 30, ⓦ chiva-chpo.fr.
Laundry Laverie Les Orangers, 35 av Général Leclerc (Tues–Fri 9am–6.30pm, Sat 9am–1pm).
Pharmacy Pharmacie Duferme, 9 cours Gabriel Faure

☎ 05 61 65 12 20, ⓦ pharmacie-foix.fr (Mon–Thurs 9am–12.15pm & 2–7.30pm, Fri 8.30am–12.15pm & 2–7.30pm, Sat 9am–noon).
Police 2 rue Lakanal ☎ 05 61 05 43 00.

Rivière souterraine de Labouiche

April–June & Sept daily 10–11am & 2–4.30pm; July & Aug daily 9.30am–5pm; Oct to mid-Nov Tues–Fri 2–4pm, Sat & Sun 10–11am & 2–4.30pm · €10.80 · ☎ 05 61 65 04 11, ⓦ labouiche.com

If you take the D1 northwest from Foix for about ten minutes, you'll come to the **rivière souterraine de Labouiche**, a subterranean river-cavern said to be the longest navigable example of its kind in western Europe, although the water levels in winter are so high as to block access completely. The same amusement-park atmosphere prevails here as at Lombrives (see p.121): twelve-person boats travel for 1hr 15min in opposite directions along the 1500m of galleries open to the public. Entry is either via the natural entrance, or an artificial one bored at the upstream end, on either side of the ticket office – you're

GASTON FÉBUS

Foix's greatest hero is **Gaston Fébus** (or Phébus, in French), Count of Foix and Viscount of Béarn (just to the west). Fébus is a local legend, revered as a leader who fought hard for regional independence, epitomizing medieval ideals of chivalry. A soldier and poet, he was born in 1331 and died sixty years later. With his dashing, aristocratic image he naturally became a subject for the songs of troubadours and, a relentless self-promoter, he did everything he could to encourage and embroider tales of his own valour and prowess, even inviting Jean Froissart, the great chronicler of the Hundred Years' War, to write his biography. His surname, Fébus, was his own invention, derived from the Occitan word for sun and celebrating his long, golden hair. As a ruler he was very much a medieval nobleman – he had no time for the legislative town councils, which he abolished, and he set himself up as the highest judicial authority in his realms.

Fébus' great ambition was to create an **autonomous kingdom** in the Pyrenees, a goal that was made impossible by the continuing Hundred Years' War, which divided the loyalties of his subjects between the English and French, and emboldened his restless underlings. Despite successes in battle, his ambitions were clearly untenable, and his dreams of dynastic dominance were dealt a final, crushing blow in 1380, when he is said to have killed his only son on discovering the latter's role in a conspiracy to assassinate him. After this, he threw in his lot with the French king. Despite his failures, Gaston Fébus' ideals and endeavours have come to represent all that is romantic about the medieval era, and, in Foix especially, he is celebrated with **festivals** in July and August.

old which to assemble at. Highlights of the cavern are the **waterfall** at the upstream end of the river and a small chamber full of formations below the artificial entry; these and other oddities along the way are described by the English-speaking guides, who do their best to keep up a witty patter while hauling the craft via ceiling-mounted cables.

Le Mas d'Azil

The village of **MAS D'AZIL** is the site of a massive cavern, noteworthy not only for being the most northerly and largest of the great Pyrenean prehistoric *grottes* (see p.121), but also as Europe's only **drive-through cave**. A visit to the cave is best combined with the **Musée de la Préhistoire** on place de l'Église (April–June, Sept & Oct daily noon–2.45pm & 2–6pm; July & Aug daily 11am–12.30pm & 2–7pm; times vary rest of the year; €4.50; same contact details as cave) which features some spectacular finds from the cave including the famous "*faon aux oiseaux*", a fawn sculpted on a deer antler. Nearby on the north bank of the Arize, **Xploria** (rte de Sabarat; April–June, Sept & Oct Tues–Sun 10am–6pm; July & Aug daily 10am–7pm; €8.90; ☏05 61 60 03 69, ⓦxploria.com) offers an educational and fun walk through a forest where you can find out how the natural world has adapted to change through the ages (yes, there are dinosaurs). Note that you'll need a car to explore this area.

The Mas d'Azil cave

Daily: July & Aug 9.30am–8pm (times vary rest of the year; closed mid-Nov to mid-Dec & Jan) · €9 (cave and Musée de la Préhistoire) · ☏05 61 05 10 10, ⓦsites-touristiques-ariege.fr

The **Mas d'Azil cave** (some 50m in height) opens up just to the south of the village, swallowing the D119 road whole, before disgorging it several hundred metres later. Once a lair of the giant cave-bears which populated the south of France in the days of the great mammals and, roughly thirty thousand years ago, a home for our own humble ancestors, historically the cave has provided refuge for a whole series of endangered species, including early Christians, Cathars and Huguenots. Indeed, it was here and in the village that a group of Protestants made a valiant and desperate stand in 1625, fending off a Catholic army which outnumbered them fifteen to one. The caves can be visited on an hour-long **guided tour** (not for the claustrophobic) from the new **interpretation centre**, about ten minutes' walk inside the cave entrance. Also here is a **museum** featuring an exhibition on what life was like for the inhabitants 35,000 years ago and a reconstruction of one of the caves that can't be visited.

INFORMATION

MAS D'AZIL

Tourist information 11 pl du Champ de Mars (July & Aug daily 9.30am–12.30pm & 2–6pm; May, June & Sept Mon–Fri 9am–noon & 2–6pm, Sat & Sun 9.30am–12.30pm & 2–6pm; Oct–April Mon–Fri 9am–noon & 2–6pm; ☏05 61 69 99 90, ⓦtourisme-arize-leze.com).

ACCOMMODATION AND EATING

Camping Le Petit Pyrénéen ☏07 87 06 12 72, ⓦcampinglepetitpyreneen.com. Three-star campsite with 46 spaces and a swimming pool in a lovely elevated rural location. There's a kids' playground, a café-bar and entertainment in July and August. Open April to September. **18.50**

Le Kiwi 5 pl du Bout de la Ville ☏05 61 69 55 82, ⓦrestaurant-lekiwi.com. The menu (*plat du jour* €12) at this village restaurant takes diners on a voyage around the world, with the likes of dhal, wonton soup and Moroccan bread featuring alongside regional staples such as duck. You can eat in the courtyard on warmer days. Mon–Fri noon–2.30pm & Fri from 7pm.

Artigat and Carla-Bayle

Emerging from the south entrance of Mas d'Azil cave, the road meanders through attractively forested uplands before meeting the main highway at Lescure, just 8km east

2

THE RETURN OF MARTIN GUERRE

In 1548 **Martin Guerre**, a surly young farmer who had been accused of theft, suddenly vanished from his home in **Artigat**, abandoning his teenage wife Berthrande and their infant son. Eight years later Martin returned, to the joy of his wife and family. By 1559, however, domestic bliss had given way to family tensions; when Martin sued his uncle for part of his father's inheritance, Pierre Guerre countered with the incredible charge that Martin was, in fact, an **imposter**. After a series of suits and counter-suits the case was brought before the *capitouls* of Toulouse in 1560. Martin was in closing arguments with legal victory in his grasp, when suddenly a man claiming to be the true Martin Guerre appeared in court. And so it was that the defendant was found guilty and sentenced to be **hanged** at the very doors of the house he had fraudulently inhabited. This tale was brought to international attention in the 1980s thanks to historian Natalie Zemon Davis's *The Return of Martin Guerre* (see p.327), acclaimed for its historical accuracy, and the excellent film of the same name, starring Gérard Depardieu and Nathalie Baye – a vivid evocation of rural life in the sixteenth-century Pyrenees and a must-see for travellers to the region. Sadly, little remains of the Artigat of Martin Guerre; the town was captured and all but destroyed by Protestants on March 7, 1621.

of St-Girons (see p.114). Fans of the film and book *The Return of Martin Guerre* (see box above) will want to visit **Artigat**, a bucolic little village, which is best reached via the D919 along 20km of winding lanes. While you're here you should take the D27B west of Artigat then the D26 north to **Carla-Bayle**. This elevated medieval village with great views is known for its art galleries; there's a festival of contemporary art here, along with a Sunday-morning market, in July and August.

EATING ARTIGAT AND CARLA-BAYL

Auberge Pierre Bayle Rue Principale, 09130 Carla-Bayle ☎ 05 61 60 63 95, ⓦ aubergepierrebayle.com. This smart, contemporary restaurant with great views is renowned throughout the region for its gourmet regional cuisine; the steamed local trout is a real treat. Good value for-money *menus* €14–44. June to mid-Sept Tues–Su noon–2pm & 7.30–9.30pm; mid-Sept to May Thurs Sat noon–2pm & 7.30–9.30pm & Sun noon–2pm.

The Couserans

Southwest of Foix, the peaks and the northern slopes of the Pyrenees shelter a series of high river valleys known collectively as the **Couserans**. As the Garbet, Salat, Arac and Ale rivers drain off the high glaciers, they flow down through a country traditionally as poor and isolated as it is majestically beautiful. Cattle farming, herding and forest industries were the original means of subsistence for the meagre population of this area, while later, mineral exploitation and spa development brought tenuous fits of humble prosperity – and they still sustain the area today. The two towns that dominate this region, **St-Giron** and **St-Lizier**, are worth a visit if only to appreciate the subtle cultural shift offered by the mid-Pyrenees – the westernmost zone of Occitan influence coloured by contacts with Navarre, the Basque country and the flatlands of Gascony. The lowlands around the two towns were prosperous in the Middle Ages, as evidenced by the cluster of Romanesque churches in the countryside around them. If you have the time, energy and perseverance, exploring the **highlands to the south** will lead you through some of the most remote and splendid scenery, and distinctive culture, the Pyrenees have to offer.

GETTING AROUND THE COUSERAN

Given the area's isolation, it should come as no surprise that there is little by way of public transport in the region. There a bus links from Toulouse and Foix to St-Girons, and a regular service up into the Couserans (ⓦ www.ariege.fr/Se-deplace /Transports/Lignes-de-bus-regulieres), but unless you have a car, to do any real exploring you'll have to resort to hiking cycling in these hills (*cols*) is strictly for the dedicated.

St-Girons

Apart from its long association with making cigarette papers, the most striking thing about **ST-GIRONS** is its pavements, made of a local dark-grey marble veined with white, and with finely chiselled gullies to carry away the rainwater. And although there are no other memorable sights, it's a far from unpleasant place, with a couple of decent **festivals:** folklore in mid-July and theatre in early August. The simplest centre for orientation is the **Pont Vieux**. Straight ahead on the right bank of the River Salat, the bridge points you into the old commercial centre of the town, with some marvellously old-fashioned shops, their fronts and fittings unchanged for generations. To the right is the typically provincial **place des Poilus**, its cachet largely derived from the faded elegance of the *Grand Hôtel de France* and the equally old-fashioned *Hôtel de l'Union*, opposite. The *Grand Café de l'Union* on the square is a splendidly balconied period café that faces the *mairie*. Beside it, along the riverbank, a wide gravelled *allée* of plane trees, the **Champ de Mars**, provides the site for one of the best **markets** in the area every Saturday morning.

ARRIVAL AND INFORMATION

By train TER-SNCF operates a bus on this route. TGV stations are indicated with an asterisk.
Destinations Toulouse*, via Boussens (several daily; 1hr 35min–2hr).

By bus Buses from Toulouse and the Couserans arrive in St-Girons on the left bank of the river at place des Capots.
Destinations Aulus-les-Bains (several daily; 1hr 10min); Castillon (daily; 20min); Foix (several daily; 1hr); Massat (daily; 1hr); Oust (daily; 25min); Seix (daily; 30min);

Toulouse (daily; 2hr 10min).
Tourist information Esplanade Alphonse-Sentein (July & Aug Mon–Sat 9.30am–1pm & 2–7pm, Sun 10am–1pm; Sept–June Mon & Wed–Fri 10am–noon & 2–6pm, Tues 2–6pm, Sat 10am–1pm & 3–6pm; ☎ 05 61 96 26 60, ⓦ tourisme-stgirons-stlizier.fr). The tourist office can provide information on exploring the Couserans and will have details of walking trails.

GETTING AROUND

By bike Maxi Sport, 16 rue Yvette Garrabé ☎ 05 61 96 49 35. There is a 40km *voie verte*, which runs along the former railway line, between St-Girons and Foix; one of the few spots for relatively undemanding cycling in this hilly region.

ACCOMMODATION AND EATING

★**Château de Beauregard** Av de la Résistance ☎ 05 61 66 66 64, ⓦ chateaubeauregard.net. Charming, turreted *maison bourgeoise* where the bedrooms are named after French writers. Enjoy a dip in the pool before booking a private session in the spa; then relax over dinner in the converted barn – the spit-roast pork is delicious. **€100**
Le Mandala Café 28 rue Joseph Pujol ☎ 05 61 96 58 86. This little café with ethnic decor serves market-fresh food and is well known for its salads; there's always something to suit vegetarians. Menus from €14. Tues–Sun noon–1.30pm & 7.30–9.15pm.

SHOPPING

L'Atelier des Pyrénoust 09200 Moulis ☎ 07 81 04 94 84. About ten minutes' drive southwest of St-Girons is this artisan maker of Pyrenean *santons*: little figures from all walks of life in traditional dress. Daily 9am–noon & 2–7pm.
Brasserie Artisanale d'Ariège-Pyrénées 6 av Réné Plaisant ☎ 05 61 96 60 01, ⓦ biere-ariege.com.
Microbrewery with several beers on offer. Wed–Fri 3–7pm, Sat 10.30am–12.30pm & 3–7pm.
Martine Crespo 38 rue Pierre Mazaud ☎ 05 34 14 30 20, ⓦ croustade.com. The finest maker of *croustade*, a sweet or savoury tart that is a speciality of this area. Tues–Fri 9am–12.30pm & 2.30–7pm, Sat 8am–1pm & 2.30–7pm, Sun 8am–1pm.

St-Lizier and around

A couple of kilometres north of St-Girons along the river Salat is **ST-LIZIER**, its older and prettier sibling, which occupies a little hillock, still partially enclosed by walls and towers built under the Romans in the third and fourth centuries. It's on the **UNESCO World Heritage** list for being an important stop on the pilgrimage route to Santiago de Compostela. Strolling along its narrow streets, keep an eye out for the carved facades of ts numerous fifteenth-century **palaces**, particularly around the places de l'Église and les Entends, and on the rues des Nobles and de l'Horloge.

Le Palais des Évêques

uly & Aug daily 10.30am–7pm; times vary rest of the year; closed Jan to mid-Feb & Nov to mid-Dec • €5.60 • ☎ 05 61 05 50 40, ⓦ sites-touristiques-ariege.fr

Of special note is the eighteenth-century **Palais des Évêques** – bishops' palace – from the terrace of which you get a great view over the Couserans rising to the south, with the snow-capped peaks of the Pyrenees as a backdrop. It functioned as a psychiatric hospital until 1969 but today houses the **Musée départemental de l'Ariège**, which has a fascinating exhibition on two thousand years of local history and contains curious nineteenth-century outfits from the vallée de Bethmale – check out the pointy clogs. The highlight here, though, is the palace's **cathedral**, Notre-Dame-de-la-Sède (not to be confused with the cathedral in the village), which has some stunning sixteenth-century murals. In the **garden**, the former isolation unit for the psychiatric patients now hosts temporary art exhibitions.

Cathédral de St-Lizier

Below the bishops' palace in the village • **Cathedral** Mon–Sat 9am–noon & 2–6/6.30pm, Sun 2–6/6.30pm • Free • **Treasury** Daily guided visits July & Aug • €5.50

The **cathédral de St-Lizier** is an eleventh-century structure built on Roman foundations, with a magnificent array of Romanesque frescoes on the walls and ceiling of its twelfth-century apse; the figure of Christ, as Pantocrator ("Lord of all") presides over angels, apostles and various other figures who descend in hierarchy towards the floor. The adjacent **cloister** is particularly noteworthy for the carvings of its capitals – in addition to the usual floral motifs and monsters are extraordinary narrative scenes illustrating the highlights of the Old and New Testaments. Over the five centuries after its founding the church was completed piecemeal, with sections added on in a strange higgledy-piggledy manner, and though there hardly seems to be a right angle in the floor plan, somehow it all holds together. Apart from the building itself, the church's **treasury** is host to a stunning sixteenth-century reliquary bust of St Lizier, as well as other pieces dating back to the eleventh century.

ARRIVAL AND INFORMATION   ST-LIZIER

TER-SNCF runs a direct bus from Toulouse to St-Lizier (2hr) but you can also get a train to Boussens and continue by bus (1hr 35min–2hr 20min).

Tourist information Pl de l'Église (open daily, times vary; closed Sun Oct–May ☎ 05 61 96 77 77, ⓦ tourisme-stgirons-stlizier.fr). Organizes guided visits of the village and sites in summer.

EATING

Le Carré de l'Ange 6 Palais des Évêques ☎ 05 61 65 65 65, ⓦ lecarredelange.com. The terrace, with its uninterrupted views, is the best place to enjoy a meal at this gourmet restaurant. The *menus* (€19–99) are fish heavy and there are even a few dishes for vegetarians. Tues–Sat noon–1.30pm & 7–9pm and Sun noon–1.30pm.

Montjoie

Four kilometres northeast of St-Lizier, just off the highway to Foix, the tiny, beautifully preserved *bastide* hamlet of **Montjoie** evokes a sense of history which the larger villages and towns of the region have all but lost. Hunkered down within fourteenth-century walls, it boasts a striking fortified **church**.

The southern Couserans highlands

The stunning terrain of the **southern Couserans highlands** buttresses some of the highest peaks in the Pyrenees and, culturally, remains a unique and independent zone, quite different from Languedocian Foix. **Gascon** is still spoken here, and if you have the good

2

DONKEY-TREKKING IN THE PYRENEES

Perhaps the best and most authentic way to explore the amazing mountain trails of the Couserans is to go traditional and avail yourself of one of the low-emission ATVs that have been popular in the region for over a thousand years. Walking with a **pack donkey** allows you to enjoy the countryside unencumbered. Panoram'âne, a family-run outfit (English spoken; ☎ 05 61 04 43 19, ⌨ ariege.com/panoramane) based in Aleu (just west of Massat), can set you up. After an "initiation walk" (€50), you can **hire** a donkey and pack saddle for between one and nine days (€40 and €310, respectively), or opt for a more expensive **guided tour**. **Camping** in tepees and yurts with half-board options is also available, and **children** up to 40kg can ride instead of walk.

---

fortune to visit during local festivities, you'll be treated to the area's singular costume and music: men wearing white embroidered jackets and red *baretos* (hats) sport curious wooden clogs with high (up to 30cm) pointed toes, while women wear long dresses draped with colourful scarves. The Couserans has traditionally been a difficult area to access and even more so to govern, the proud mountain people resentful of any infringement of their liberties or threat to their way of life. As late as the nineteenth century, the villagers waged a guerrilla war against the French government – the so-called **Guerre des Demoiselles** ("war of the girls"), when they dressed up as women in a surprise attack on local property owners, government foresters and police. The magnificent landscape is accessible by **road** and **trail**, with a number of rewarding circuits.

Massat and around

Striking out from the River Salat, south of St-Girons, through the dramatic **Gorges de Riabouto**, brings you to the confluence of the Arac and Riabouto rivers. Here, the more direct of the two routes to Tarascon heads due east to the village of **MASSAT**. The village is renowned for its "baba cool" (hippy) inhabitants, who started moving here in the 1970s; many live "off the grid" in the surrounding forests. As you approach, the fifteenth-century bell tower of Massat's church rises 60m above the village in a marvellous Pyrenean tableau. The **market**, held on the second and fourth Thursday of every month, and also Sundays in July and August, features superb local produce.

Continuing east, the road climbs in a seemingly endless succession of hair-raising bends until you reach the 1250m-high **Col de Port**. On the left rise the wooded slopes of the **Montagnes de l'Arize**, while on the right the barren **Pic des Trois Seigneurs** (2199m) scratches the clouds. A steep 18km descent then brings you to Tarascon, passing the Parc de la Préhistoire (see p.120) at the entrance to the town.

ARRIVAL AND INFORMATION   MASSAT AND AROUND

By bus Massat to: St-Girons (daily; 55min).
Tourist information Rte du Col de Port (Tues–Sat

10am–12.30pm & 3–5.30pm, plus Sun morning in summer; ☎ 05 61 96 92 76, ⌨ tourisme-massat.com).

ACCOMMODATION AND EATING

★ **Auberge de la Sapinière** Col du Port ☎ 05 61 05 67 90. The terrace of this chalet is the perfect place to enjoy spectacular views while you munch on a platter of local ham and cheese from the restaurant kitchen. They also rent out a couple of utterly charming and romantic restored

stone shepherds' huts (B&B) in summer. €98
Maxil Café 4 rue des Faurs ☎ 05 81 29 49 49, ⌨ maxilcafe.com. Cyclist-friendly accommodation in an old village house, which also has a restaurant and bar where they sometimes hold concerts. *Menus* from €13.50. €55

Seix and around

From the mouth of the Riabouto gorge, the road heads further up the Salat to the hamlet of **OUST**. The squat twelfth-century **church** in neighbouring **VIC** (contact the tourist office in Oust for times), one of the most beautiful in the area, is the only real attraction. At Oust, two routes lead to Aulus-les-Bains – a relatively straight road going

TRANSHUMANCE IN THE PYRENEES

Since at least the early Middle Ages, shepherds have capitalized on the change of seasons by moving their herds of sheep and goats up into high mountain pastures to graze for the summer. This practice, **transhumance**, became a focus of social and economic life and a lifeline to the world outside for isolated, rural zones, and continues to be a living tradition in the Couserans, where flocks are taken up in June and descend in October. Both events were causes for **celebration** in peasant villages, and several towns have developed the occasion as an organized event. There is probably no better way for visitors of all ages to experience the rural culture of the Pyrenees.

The best-organized transhumance **festival** takes place at **Seix** on the second weekend of June. On the Friday, herds gather in St-Girons and make their way up the Salat valley. On Saturday morning they arrive at the meadow of Oust, 2km south of Seix. Meanwhile, a series of celebrations are held in Seix including a small livestock fair and demonstrations of **equestrian skill** and mountain **folk-traditions** as well as Landais shepherds **dancing on stilts**. Far from being a packaged tourist event, this is a genuine local celebration and the real protagonists are the townsfolk and shepherds. There is a communal BBQ lunch (€16) in Oust and a dinner and show in the evening (€26) in Seix. On Sunday morning, crowds of walkers accompany the herds south up to the hills, fêted with liqueurs at every hamlet.

Book well ahead to ensure accommodation, and contact the very amenable tourist office in Seix (see opposite) to arrange to buy **tickets** for Saturday lunch and dinner (all of which sell out ahead of the date). See ⓦ transhumances-haut-salat.com for further information.

up the Garbet valley, and a longer route which swings south, via **SEIX** (pronounced "sex"), where the peaks of the **cirque** at the valley's head come into view. This market town, lorded over by a fifteenth-century castle and with a distinctive church tower, makes a good base if you plan to do some hiking in the region; it's also a good spot for white-water sports. In summer, a **market** is held on the second and fourth Wednesday of the month and Sunday mornings. The best time to visit, however, is undoubtedly during the spring **transhumance** (see box above).

ARRIVAL AND DEPARTURE   SEIX AND AROUND

By bus Seix to: Oust (two daily; 2–5min) and St-Girons (two daily; 50min).

INFORMATION AND ACTIVITIES

Tourist information Pl de l'Allée, Seix (July & Aug daily 9am–noon & 3–6.30pm, closed Sun afternoon; Sept–June 9am–noon & 2–5.30pm, closed Thurs and Sun afternoon ☎ 05 61 96 00 01, ⓦ haut-couserans.com). There's also a small office in Oust on rte d'Aulus (July & Aug daily

9am–noon).
Watersports The Haut Couserans Kayak Club (☎ 05 61 66 62 76, ⓦ labasenautiqueducouserans.com) lies 2km south of Seix. White-water rafting (€25), kayaking (from €20) and swimming (€30) are on offer.

ACCOMMODATION AND EATING

Auberge des Deux Rivières Pont de la Taule, Seix ☎ 05 61 66 83 57, ⓦ aubergedesdeuxrivieres.com. In a valley where two rivers meet, this traditional hotel and restaurant has simply furnished rooms and its own private beach. Free parking and free wi-fi. **€45**
Camping Quatre Saisons Rte d'Aulus, Oust ☎ 05 61 96 55 55, ⓦ camping4saisons.com. This three-star campsite has something for everyone: pitches, chalets, apartments and even hotel accommodation. What with mountain

views, a restaurant and a swimming pool, you've got everything on site for a relaxing holiday. **€16.50**
La Gourmandine Pl de l'Allée, Seix ☎ 05 61 66 71 19, ⓦ lagourmandine09.fr. The chef-owner inherited her cooking skills from her grandmother, who also had a restaurant in the village. Expect accomplished traditional dishes (menus €12–23), including vegetarian options. Tues–Sat noon–2.30pm & 7.30–10.30pm and Sun noon–2.30pm.

Aulus-les-Bains and around

From Seix, the road continues up the River Alet to **AULUS-LES-BAINS**, a spa village and adjunct to the mediocre ski station of **Guzet-Neige**, separated from Spain's Vall de

2

Cardós by a 10km-wide mountain wall, and lying among lush and fragrant meadows ringed by dramatic peaks. In summer the station becomes a centre for a variety of sports including mountain biking and orienteering. The most remote point of the traditionally poor Couserans, Aulus was once famous for its bear trainers, who toured the wealthier lowlands. The classic **walk** here involves heading south along the GR10 to the **Cascade d'Ars** waterfall, a round trip of about five hours. There is a Sunday-morning **market** in July and August.

From Aulus, a narrow mountain road and the GR10 wind separate paths along the northern fringe of the **Pic Rouge de Bassiès** (2676m), weaving in and out of the tree line. Looking back, you'll see the high-walled crenellated cirque formed by the peak and its nearest neighbour, the Pic des Trois Comtes. The road rises to the east, then the north, skirting the small Étang de Lers and passing herds of grey Gascon cows grazing the alpine meadow, to arrive at the pass, the **Port de Lers** (1517m). Eventually passing the waterfall, the **cascade d'Arbu**, some 3km beyond, you begin a sharp descent towards **Vicdessos**, the capital of a remote and poor *canton*. There is little to detain you here or at nearby **Auzat**. It is, however, at these villages that the footpath and road route converge again, and where the main road descends the river valley, passing the Grotte de Niaux (see p.120), shortly before entering **Tarascon-sur-Ariège**.

ARRIVAL AND DEPARTURE
AULUS-LES-BAINS AND AROUND

By bus Aulus to: Oust (two daily; 25min); Seix (two daily; 30min) and St Girons (two daily; 1hr 10min).

INFORMATION AND ACTIVITIES

Tourist information Aulus-les-Bains (résidence Ars; July & Aug daily 9am–noon & 3–6.30pm, closed Sun afternoon; Sept–June 9am–noon & 2–5.30pm, closed Thurs and Sun afternoon ☎05 61 96 00 01, ⓦhaut-couserans.com). Guzet-Neige (Mon–Sat and Sun morning 9am–noon & 2–5.30pm; 9am–noon & 1–5pm during ski season; same contact details as Aulus).

Mountain biking The Guzévasion mountain bike park in Guzet (☎05 61 96 00 01, ⓦguzevasion.fr; €14 for a day) is open in July and August.

ACCOMMODATION

Gîte d'étape La Goulue Aulus-les-Bains ☎05 61 66 53 01, ⓦariege.com/la-goulue. Basic, but attractive, accommodation in the village's former casino with rooms sleeping two to four people. The bathroom and kitchen are shared but there is a *table d'hôte* (€12) featuring dishes made with local products. **€16**

Castillon-en-Couserans and around

The longest but most rewarding route over the Couserans to Tarascon begins by heading southwest from St-Girons along the broad Bouigane valley to **CASTILLON-EN-COUSERANS**. This is the most populated and prosperous part of the region, as evidenced by the ancient **churches** clustered around the town. The best are at **Arrout** and **Andressein**, en route to Castillon, and **Ourjout**, where colourful wall murals have recently been uncovered, just beyond.

While hardly a bustling metropolis, Castillon's central position means it has long been an important market town (market second Tuesday in the month). It is set at the crossroads ("Cruz de Camisses" in Gascon) of the four "B" valleys – Biros, Bethmale, Balaguères and Bellongue – and, as such, is the Couserans heartland.

From Castillon, it's a tense 35km drive of hair-raising switchbacks up the **Vallée de Bethmale** to Seix – you'll be rewarded by spectacular views, both in the tree-lined valley and, once the road breaks into open ground, at the **Col de la Core**, just past the halfway mark.

INFORMATION
CASTILLON-EN-COUSERANS AND AROUND

Tourist information Av Noël-Peyrevidal, Castillon-en-Couserans (Mon–Sat 9.30am–12.15pm & 2–6pm, Sun 9.30am–12.15pm, closed mid-July to mid-Aug; ☎05 61 96 72 64, ⓦot-castillon-en-couserans.fr).

EATING

Auberge de la Core Arrien en Bethmale, 4km southeast of Castillon ☎05 61 04 80 53. You can enjoy traditional (meat-heavy) cuisine while admiring the views from the terrace at this mountain restaurant. The fries cooked in duck fat are highly recommended. *Menus* from €13. July & Aug Tues–Sat noon–2pm & 7–9pm, Sun noon–2pm; Sept–June Thurs–Sat noon–2pm & 7–9pm, Sun noon–2pm.

SHOPPING

En Terre d'Abajou Samortein en Bethmale, 6km southeast of Castillon ☎05 61 96 19 53/06 70 25 91 53. Enjoy a sorbet on the terrace before taking away some jams, *sirops* and sauces – all made with hand-picked mountain flowers and herbs. July & Aug daily 3–7pm; rest of year Sat & Sun.

Pascal Justot Aret en Bethmale, 5km southeast of Castillon ☎05 61 96 74 39, ⓦartisan-bois-sabots.fr. Artisan wooden clogs for gardening (from €40), as well as decorative clogs for the home and traditional wooden Bethmale jugs. July & Aug daily 3–7pm; rest of year by appointment.

The upper Ariège valley

South of Foix, the Ariège river narrows rapidly, and forest slopes rise sharply on either side as the riverbed twists and cuts down through gneiss and schist of the Pyrenean foothills towards **Tarascon**. It is along this part of the river that you'll find in thick concentration many of France's best and most famous prehistorically inhabited **caves**, decorated by hand prints, etchings and animal figures left by our ancestors up to a quarter of a million years ago. This, along with the beauty of the countryside, has made the **upper Ariège valley** an extremely popular destination, especially for French tourists. High season, particularly August, is mayhem, and if you're hoping to see the renowned cave art you should plan (and reserve) as far ahead as possible. Further up in the hills towards the Spanish and Andorran frontiers, the high peaks of the Pyrenees loom ever closer. Here, around **Ax-les-Thermes**, there is breathtaking mountain scenery and great possibilities for **walking**.

Tarascon-sur-Ariège and the caves

A small, utilitarian mining and metallurgy centre with traffic roaring past on the bypass highway, **TARASCON-SUR-ARIÈGE** has nothing about it to suggest that this is the heart of one of the most fascinating areas in Europe. Yet any account of the emergence of the human species must include the **caves** around the town, which, taken as a group, constitute an unequalled display of prehistoric painting and artefacts. The *grottes* served as shelters – and, arguably, as places of worship – for early humans, later coming in handy as hideouts for religious dissidents during the Christian era. Their high concentration in the Ariège is due to the limestone which constitutes the hillsides here – permeable rock ideally suited to the work of cavern creation. There are **four main sites**, all accessible in a single day if you have your own transport.

Tarascon itself is a small town, towered over by peaks, with **riverside cafés** providing pleasant vantage points over the Ariège, and a narrow pedestrian lane leading past a string of craft shops into the **old quarter**. Here the church of St-Michel presides over a partly arcaded square, and various surviving bits of the medieval walls, razed in 1632, crop up here and there: the **Tour St-Michel** and **Porte d'Espagne** with a fountain inside. From this former town gate, the short hike past walled orchards up to the **Tour du Castella**, now a clock tower, is worthwhile for the views over the five valleys which converge here. Tarascon is the site of two livestock **fairs**, on May 8 and September 30, timed for the passing of the transhumant herds. A regular **market** is held on Wednesday and Saturday mornings.

2

Parc de la Préhistoire

Lieu-dit Lacombe, rte de Banat, 3km northwest of Tarascon • July & Aug daily 10am–8pm, times vary rest of year, closed Nov–March • €10.80 • 05 61 05 10 10 ⓦ sites-touristiques-ariege.fr

If you can't make it to a cavern, you can still experience the Neolithic era, albeit vicariously, at the **Parc de la Préhistoire**. This rambling park is a great place to spend half a day or so with kids: there are daily workshops of some sort or another including fire-making, archaeology and cave art; you can even spend the night here living like a Stone-Age person. Le Grand Atelier is a museum space with finds from the area including Mas d'Azil, facsimiles of paintings in the Grotte de Niaux and an exhibition with life-size Ice Age animals. There's a picnic area and also a very nice restaurant (*menus* €13–25).

Grotte de Niaux

6km southwest of Tarascon on the D8 • Daily April–June guided visits (90min) in English 1.30pm; July & Aug guided visits in English 9.45am & 12.15pm; times vary rest of the year • €12 • ☎ 05 61 05 10 10, ⓦ sites-touristiques-ariege.fr

Unquestionably the finest of the Pyrenean caves is the **Grotte de Niaux**. The current entrance is a tunnel created in 1968 near the low and narrow natural opening under an enormous rock overhang. Using the flashlights provided, you penetrate 900m (from a total 4km of galleries) to see just some of the famous black outlines of **horse** and **bison**, minimally shaded yet capturing every nuance. Analysis has established that these drawings, and those of the ibex and stag in the recess further back, were produced around 10,800 BC with a "crayon" made of bison fat and manganese oxide. A line of **footprints** left by the artists can be seen in a part of the cave that was opened up in 1970, while their primitive form of **writing** is represented by the dots and bunches of lines on the wall of the main cavity.

Musée Pyrénéen

2 rte du Montcalm • Daily: July & Aug 10am–8pm; Sept–June 2–6pm • €8 • ☎ 05 61 05 88 36, ⓦ musee-pyreneen-de-niaux.com

Niaux village itself, between the cave and Tarascon, has a small, private **Musée Pyrénéen** which displays a splendid collection of tools, furnishings and archival photos illustrating the traditions and daily life of the Ariège until the early twentieth century. Information is only available in French but this doesn't spoil the experience.

Grotte de la Vache

L'Oustal, 09400 Alliat • Closed to the public at the time of writing • ☎ 05 61 05 95 06, ⓦ grotte-de-la-vache.org

The **Grotte de la Vache** is well worth the 2km journey across the valley from Niaux, south on the road to Vicdessos: walkers can slightly shortcut the road, by taking the path beginning 150m or so before the Niaux museum. Excavations here over two decades sifted through the detritus of ten thousand years of habitation, beginning between 15,000 and 12,500 BC and ending in the Bronze Age. In one of the chambers, scientists have uncovered and reconstructed a complete hunting camp dating back some fourteen thousand years. Around thirty thousand fragments of flint tools were unearthed and over six thousand complete tools, mainly for engraving in rock; some pieces are displayed in the cave.

Grotte de Bédeilhac

09400 Bédeilhac-et-Aynat via D618 from Tarascon to Saurat • Visits (90min) July & Aug daily 10.30am, 2.30pm, 3.30pm & 4.30pm; Sept–June by appointment • €10 • ☎ 05 61 05 95 06, ⓦ grotte-de-bedeilhac.org

The **Grotte de Bédeilhac**, above the eponymous village, is a hollow in the ridge of Soudour containing examples of every known technique of Paleolithic art, including polychrome painting (now faded to monochrome). The imposing entrance yawns 35m wide by 20m high, making it easy to understand how the Germans managed to adapt the cavern as an aircraft hangar during World War II. Although the art within is not as immediately powerful as that at Niaux, its diversity compensates, with low reliefs in mud, paintings of bison, deer and ibex, and stalagmites used to model figures.

PYRENEAN CAVE ART

The **painted caves** of the Pyrenees are known to have been created by nomadic and semi-nomadic communities of *Homo sapiens* during the Late Paleolithic period, between 10,000 and 35,000 years ago.

An early hypothesis was that cave art served a **magical function**, to ensure an abundance of game. The frequency with which animals appear on the walls seems to back up this theory, but the animal remains found in the caves show that the species most frequently depicted were not in fact the main food supply. Other theories focused on the **layout** of cave designs. It was observed, for example, that horses were depicted only at the entrance to caves or in the centre, and that mammoths and bison were confined to the centre. To some, this suggested that the arrangement reflected a **sexual polarity**, with bison symbolizing the female element, and horses the male. However, poor lighting would probably not have allowed the artists to see the cave decorations as a unity. Moreover, successive paintings were superimposed to the extent that they became indecipherable, even though suitable areas of blank rock were available nearby. Recently paleo-anthropologists have suggested that the paintings were executed by **shamans** in a **trance state**, and that they reflect the spirit world rather than reality, or alternatively that they are the testosterone-charged **graffiti** of teenage Cro-Magnons.

What is certain is that they did not serve as wallpaper for Neanderthal living rooms, nor were they casual Stone-age doodlings. The zones that are painted are extremely difficult to access, reachable only after hundreds of metres of scrabbling through pitch-black tunnels and galleries. The sense, even today, is that you are in the belly or the womb of the world, and that these works of **art** were executed at great sacrifice to serve a very deliberate purpose – and that they would seldom be seen by human eyes. This, together with the manifest **technical skill** and artistic sensibility displayed by our ancestors tens of millennia ago, makes visiting the caves an intensely moving experience.

Grotte de Lombrives

09400 Ussat-les-Bains via RN20 • July & Aug daily 9am–7pm; June & Sept, weekends, public and school holidays 10am–5pm • From €8 • ☎ 06 70 74 32 80, ⓦ grotte-lombrives.fr

The **Grotte de Lombrives** could only disappoint if you've already seen Niaux, Vache and Bédeilhac. The access by underground train gives it something of an amusement-park feel – as do the nocturnal *spectacles* regularly staged here in July and August – but the stalagmite formations are superb, and the sheer size of the complex is impressive. It is, in fact, the largest cavern in Europe, and would take five days' walking to see it in its entirety. Lombrives was inhabited around 4000 BC, but all the material found here now rests in museums. Its later history is embellished by legends of the last Cathars walled up inside in 1328, and of 250 soldiers subsequently disappearing without trace, the victims of cave-dwelling bandits. There are various **routes for visitors**, ranging from a one-hour visit to a seven-hour underground odyssey.

ARRIVAL AND DEPARTURE

By train Trains call frequently from nearby Ax-les-Thermes (many daily; 25min) and Foix (many daily; 12min), on the line from Toulouse (many daily; 1hr 30min) to Latour-de-Carol (many daily; 1hr 30min); the *gare SNCF* is on the left bank of the Ariège, in the northern half of town.
By bus Buses stop outside the tourist office.

TARASCON-SUR-ARIÈGE AND THE CAVES

Destinations Foix (several daily; 25min) and Toulouse (daily; 2hr 30min).
Tourist information Av Paul Jouclat (Mon–Sat 9am–1pm & 2–6pm, also open Sun July & Aug; ☎ 05 61 05 94 94, ⓦ montagnesdetarasconetduvicdessos.com).

ACCOMMODATION AND EATING

Camping Le Pré Lombard Av de l'Ayroule ☎ 05 61 05 61 94, ⓦ prelombard.com. Well-equipped four-star campsite with a variety of pre-erected tents and chalets as well as spaces. There's a restaurant, plenty of activities and

entertainment in summer and a swimming pool. €38
Les Chataigniers de Florac Hameau du Florac, Surba ☎ 05 61 03 53 49, ⓦ les-chataigniers-de-florac.com. Cyclist-friendly B&B with four chic rooms and a *gîte*, a 5min

drive northwest of Tarascon. Outside, there's a hot tub and a swimming pool. The *table d'hôte* dishes are made with local, organic products. **€70**

★ **Le Manoir d'Agnès** 2 rue St-Roch ☎ 05 6102 32 81, ⓦ manoiragnes.com. Comfortable and charming three-star hotel in a nineteenth-century manor house, originally a family home and then the administration office for the local metallurgy company. The fifteen rooms are decorated in contemporary style and the highly regarded gourmet restaurant serves refined dishes made with regional products (*menus* €16–52); there's even a vegetarian *menu* (€26). **€112**

SHOPPING

Les Biscuits du Moulin Av Paul Berdot, Sinsat, 7km southeast of Tarascon ☎ 05 61 65 37 45, ⓦ lesbiscuitsdumoulin.com. Some of the best biscuits you'll ever taste are made using local, organic flour in this seventeenth-century mill with a tea room. Tues–Sat 10am–noon & 2.30–6pm, Sun 2.30–6pm.

Hypocras Chemin de la Croix de Quié ☎ 05 61 05 60 38, ⓦ hypocras.com. The famous herbal medieval liqueur is now made in Tarascon and you can visit the distillery. Tues–Sat 3–7pm.

Ax-les-Thermes and around

AX-LES-THERMES is a pleasant spa resort with little specifically to see – owing to frequent disastrous fires in centuries past – other than a lively market on Tuesday and Saturday mornings in place Roussel. However, it makes a good base for skiing or walking in the Ariège region, with **hikes** routed in circuits from the town, and several **ski resorts**, both downhill and Nordic, within a convenient distance.

The town itself is small and pleasant enough, but there are few obvious attractions once you've wandered a couple of streets in the quarter to the south of the N20, which forms the main street. Rue de l'École and rue de la Boucarie retain a few medieval buildings, and above place du Breilh, the **church of St-Vincent** is of architectural interest for its Romanesque tower.

The hot springs

Bains du Couloubret: prom Paul Salette; July & Aug Mon–Thurs & Sun 10am–7.30pm, Fri & Sat 10am–8.30pm; Sept–June Mon–Fri 2–7.30pm, Sat 10am–8.30pm, Sun 10am–7.30pm • From €17 for two hours • ☎ 05 61 02 64 41, ⓦ www.bains-couloubret.com

Ax dates back to at least Roman times, while the commercial exploitation of its **hot springs** dates from the thirteenth century; the smell of sulphur that early twentieth-century travellers commented on can still be whiffed from the spring water coursing

---

SKIING AND MOUNTAIN BIKING AROUND AX-LES-THERMES

The nearest **ski resort** to Ax is **Station d'Ax** (ⓦ ax-ski.com), 8km south up the D820, an agglomeration of three resorts, Bonascre, Saquet and Campels. The resort itself is a hideous knot of high-rises, but once you get into the *télécabine* (free with lift pass) and up to the **Plateau du Saquet**, with the beautiful Andorran frontier peaks as a backdrop, it's a different matter. The snow record here is good, there are 75km of pistes (some over 3km long), and the top lift is at 2305m. There's an alternative resort 13km east of Ax at **Ascou-Pailhères** (ⓦ ascou-ski.com), with nineteen downhill runs and a top piste of 2020m. It's a pretty drive up to the resort, and though it only has one black piste, it's quite a challenging one.

Three valleys west of Bonascre, the **Plateau de Beille** (ⓦ beille.fr) has been developed for **cross-country skiing**. The 55km of pistes range in length from one to twenty kilometres, at an altitude of just under 1967m – which should ensure adequate snow. The resort can be reached by *navette* (weekends in the ski season and daily during school hols) from the village of Les Cabannes, 15km north of Ax along the main N20 road. There's also good cross-country skiing to the north of Ax around the **Col de Chioula** (1431m). The resorts usually have a variety of other activities on offer.

When the snow goes, several ski resorts switch over to become summer recreation centres specializing in hiking, paragliding and **mountain biking** (or **VTT**: Vélos Tout Terrain), with runs up to 21km in length, colour-coded for difficulty. See ⓦ vtt-vallees-ax.fr or the Ax tourist office for details.

through the gutters, and the ambience of a spa remains. In total there are more than forty *sources*, producing a volume of water in excess of 600,000 litres per day, some at temperatures of 77°C. Just off the main square, place du Breilh, you can join the locals and dangle your feet for free in the **Bassin des Ladres**, a pool of hot sulphurous water dating to 1250, which was once incorporated into the now-vanished hospital founded in 1260 by Roger IX of Foix for leprous soldiers returning from the Crusades. For a twenty-first-century **spa** experience, the best option is the **Bains du Couloubret**, which offers a range of treatments including massage.

2

ARRIVAL AND INFORMATION

By train The *gare SNCF* is on the northwest side of town, just off the main av Delcassé.

Destinations Foix (several daily; 45min); Latour-de-Carol (several daily; 50min); Tarascon-sur-Ariège (several daily; 30min); Toulouse (several daily; 2hr).

By bus Buses stop in the centre of the town.

Destinations Toulouse (daily; 3hr).

Tourist information 6 av Théophile Delcassé (Mon–Sat

AX-LES-THERMES AND AROUND

9am–7pm, Sun 9am–1pm & 2–6pm; ❶05 61 64 60 60, ⓦvallees-ax.com) provides information on hiking, can contact guides, and sells a range of guidebooks and maps. You can also buy a *Pass Réduc* (€5) giving reductions on a number of activities. The Bureau des Guides et Accompagnateurs de Montagne, Camp de Granou (Mon, Tues, Thurs & Fri 9am–noon & 2–5pm; ❶05 61 01 90 62, ⓦguides-ariege.com) can provide details on mountain activities.

ACCOMMODATION AND EATING

À la Montanha! 3 pl des Platanes, Les Cabannes, 16km northwest of Ax ❶05 34 09 09 09, ⓦlamaisonlacube.com. Head out of town to this superb steak restaurant where the meat comes from the owner's Gascon cows. In summer, he organizes outings into the mountains to meet the grey cattle and have lunch in the open air. Menus €14.50–29. Daily noon–2pm & 7–8.45pm.

Camping Le Malazéou ❶05 61 64 69 14, ⓦcampingmalazeou.com. In a wooded location on the way into town, this four-star campsite has chalets as well

as pitches. There's a bar-restaurant, an outdoor swimming pool and a kids' club in summer. **€30**

★**Le Chalet** 4 av Durandeau ❶05 61 64 24 31, ⓦle-chalet.fr. This chalet-style two-star hotel next to the river is outstanding for its class, but do ask for a renovated room. The restaurant is renowned throughout the region for its excellent traditional cuisine, with *menus* from €15–50 including vegetarian options. There's also a jacuzzi and a special two-night "well being" package is available. **€65**

SHOPPING

La Boutique de la Ferme Pl du Breilh ❶05 61 01 54 63. This town-centre shop has an excellent selection of regional products and hosts regular tastings and

events, including mountain picnics in summer. Mon–Sat 9.30am–12.30pm & 3–7pm, Sun 10am–12.30pm & 4–7pm.

The Oriège valley and Réserve Nationale d'Orlu

Extending east from Ax, the damp, leafy **Oriège valley** is a jumping-off point for hikes into the Carlit peaks and the **Réserve Nationale d'Orlu**, created south of the road in 1975 to benefit a growing herd of isards (Pyrenean chamois, a goat-like animal) as well as roe deer, golden eagles and lammergeiers (Europe's biggest bird of prey, also known as the bearded vulture). The main attractions here are the **Observatoire de la Montagne et son sentier de découverte** (rte des Forges; April–June, Sept & Oct Wed–Fri 10am–1pm & 2–6pm, Sat & Sun 2–6pm; July & Aug Mon–Fri 10am–7pm, Sat & Sun 2–7pm; €7; ❶05 61 03 06 06, ⓦobservatoire-montagne.com), a discovery centre about the mountain environment where they also organize guided walks, and **La Maison des Loups** (rte des Forges; April–June Tues & Thurs–Sun 10am–7pm; July & Aug daily 10am–7pm; Sept & Oct Thurs–Sun 11am–5pm; €8.90; ❶05 61 64 02 66, ⓦmaisondesloups.com) – a wolf reserve.

ACCOMMODATION AND EATING

Le Relais Montagnard Rte des Forges ❶05 34 14 02 94. In the centre of the village, this *gîte d'étape* with dormitory accommodation for thirty people is a good base

from which to explore the reserve. It's worth staying just to enjoy the *table d'hôte* (€18), a showcase for regional products. **€20**

Albi and Haut Languedoc

CATHÉDRALE STE-CÉCILE, ALBI

Albi and Haut Languedoc

Tarn, the *département* to the east of Toulouse, consists of two contrasting zones. The northwest is wine country: the rolling landscape on the banks of the River Tarn is punctuated by towns nurtured on the modest prosperity of the grape and other products of the soil, including woad, sunflowers and garlic. The southeast, on the other hand, is a rugged upland where herding and wool, made into textiles or leather, have been the main way for locals to earn a living since ancient times. Although the *département* remains a sleepy backwater (it's not on a TGV line), there is much to see and do here.

3

In the northwest, you'll find **Albi**, Tarn's principal town, whose name is synonymous with the Cathar sect, or "Albigensians", with which modern *languedociens* still proudly identify. North of here, the former coal-mining town of **Carmaux** is famous for its glass production; to the west, the stunningly preserved medieval village of **Cordes-sur-Ciel** is alive with artists and artisans; and finally, passing Albi, the Tarn flows west towards Gaillac and one of the oldest and best wine regions in the south of France. The *département's* interior, south of Albi, has a scattering of sleepy villages and towns, notably **Lautrec**, one of the Plus Beaux Villages de France. To the southeast, **Haut Languedoc** ("Upper Languedoc"), a wild hinterland of rocky hills, has a history of religious and political nonconformity. On its western side lies **Castres**, Albi's poorer cousin, a lively little provincial town, with a Top 14 rugby team and an important collection of Spanish art. In the uplands, most of which have been incorporated into the **Parc Naturel Régional du Haut Languedoc**, dark woods and high pasture are interspersed with a series of largely forgotten villages including **Lacaune-les-Bains**, famous for its charcuterie. This is easy walking terrain, crisscrossed by *grandes randonnées* and local trails such as the **Gijou Valley Railway Path**. Further south, the densely forested massif of the **Montagne Noire** rises south of Mazamet – the start of the **Passa Païs** walking and cycling trail to Bédarieux.

GETTING AROUND   **ALBI AND HAUT LANGUEDOC**

Despite its isolation, this area is well served by **public transport**. The main Toulouse–Rodez **rail line** follows the course of the Tarn up to Albi and Carmaux, with branch-offs to Cordes-Vindrac and Mazamet via Castres. Castres acts as a **bus hub** (see ⓦ tarnbus.tarn.fr for timetables) for the western part of the Parc Naturel, and there is good transport to St-Pons, which gives access to the heart of the park. Still, getting to smaller villages can be difficult without your own transport. There are also reduced or no services at weekends and in school holidays.

Albi and around

ALBI's sleepy atmosphere belies its role as *préfecture* of the Tarn. In the evening, its streets are deserted, even in summer, lapsing into a village-like slumber. Highlights include the UNESCO-listed **Cité Episcopale**, comprising the hulking brick-built

MUSÉE TOULOUSE-LAUTREC

Highlights

❶ Albi's Cité Episcopale Albi's cathedral, bishops' palace and old town became a UNESCO World Heritage Site in 2010. **See p.126**

❷ Musée Toulouse-Lautrec See the world's largest collection of the diminutive Impressionist's unmistakable work. **See p.131**

❸ Cordes-sur-Ciel Once a refuge for heretics, now a postcard-pretty town of artisans, perched "on the sky" west of Albi. **See p.138**

❹ Gaillac wines Sample one of the country's oldest and most venerable AOPs. **See p.140**

❺ Rabastens Don't miss this village's brilliantly restored, painted church set by the tranquil banks of the Tarn. **See p.144**

❻ Parc Naturel Régional du Haut Languedoc A wild and under-populated area, perfect for hiking and cycling. **See p.150**

HIGHLIGHTS ARE MARKED ON THE MAP ON P.128

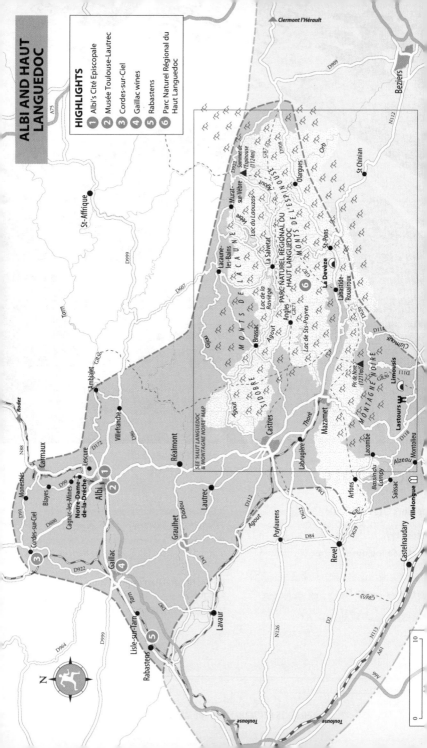

FESTIVALS IN ALBI AND HAUT LANGUEDOC

As elsewhere in Languedoc and Roussillon, most towns have their local **fêtes** between June and August, featuring fireworks and *pétanque* competitions.

Feb to March Albi: *Carnaval*. Albi's traditional French Lenten festival, held from the last Sunday in February to the first Sunday in March.

Mid-July Cordes-sur-Ciel: *Fêtes du Grand Fauconnier* Ⓦgrandfauconnier.com.This two-day medieval festival converts the town into a costumed extravaganza, complete with concerts, banquet, market, exhibitions on medieval crafts and falconry.

Early July Albi: *Pause Guitare* Ⓦpauseguitare.net. One of the biggest pop music festivals in the Occitanie region, featuring French and international acts.

Early July Castres: *Les Extravadanses*. A ten-day free festival featuring music, circus,

dance and cinema in the open air and at the town's theatre.

First two weeks of Aug Castres: *Couleurs du Monde*. Free concerts of folk music, dancing and singing from international groups.

First weekend of Aug Lautrec: *Fête de l'ail rose*. A celebration of the village's famous pink garlic with parades, a market, exhibitions, walks and lots of garlicky food.

First weekend of Aug Gaillac: *Fête des Vins* Ⓦwww.vins-gaillac.com. Gaillac's wine festival offers free tastings, as well as a market, concerts and fireworks.

October Carmaux: Biennale des Verriers. Biannual festival of contemporary glass with exhibitions, demonstrations of glass blowing and sales. Next one in 2017.

cathedral; the **Palais de la Berbie**, the former bishops' palace which houses the Musée de Toulouse-Lautrec; the riverbanks, from where you can take a boat trip; the eleventh-century **Pont Vieux** (old bridge) and the well-preserved **medieval quarter.**

Albi is easily explored on foot, and you can take in the main sights in a single day. Most are within the compact limits of the once-walled **old town**, whose northern boundary is formed by the steep banks of the Tarn, and which is now completely surrounded by the sprawl of the new town. Across the river, the eighteenth-century suburb of **La Madeleine** is also worth a look, primarily for the spectacular views it affords of medieval Albi and the Tarn.

Brief history

After the decline of Roman power, the former Celtic settlement here passed through Visigothic and Frankish hands before coming under the power of the counts of Toulouse in the eleventh century. It was under them that the Pont Vieux was built over the Tarn, stimulating the town's growth as a centre for trade and attracting immigrants from as far away as the Rhine. The **anti-Cathar crusade** provided an opportunity for the town's burghers and bishops to play the counts and kings against each other, increasing their own autonomy. Under the rule of the bishops from the 1300s onwards, Albi rode a wave of prosperity, based on the same woad trade that powered Toulouse (see p.72). But the town's fortunes diminished with the demand for the dye, and by the 1700s the adventurous were turning to the sea, with some, such as Lapérouse (see p.133), becoming renowned navigators. **Industrialization** came with the development of coalfields to the north; glass-working and textiles soon became the mainstay. Today the town is something of a bourgeois backwater, living on under the shadows of its cathedral and the legacy of its most famous son, the artist Henri de Toulouse-Lautrec (see p.132).

Cathédrale Ste-Cécile

Place Ste-Cécile • Daily May–Oct 9am–6.30pm; Nov–April 9am–1.15pm & 2–6.30pm • Free, €5 (inc audioguide) for choir or €6 for choir and treasury • ☏ 05 63 43 23 43, Ⓦcathedrale-albi.com

The rounded arches and towers and red-brick construction of the **Cathédrale Ste-Cécile** dominate Albi, evoking a mix of the Middle Ages and Art Deco that

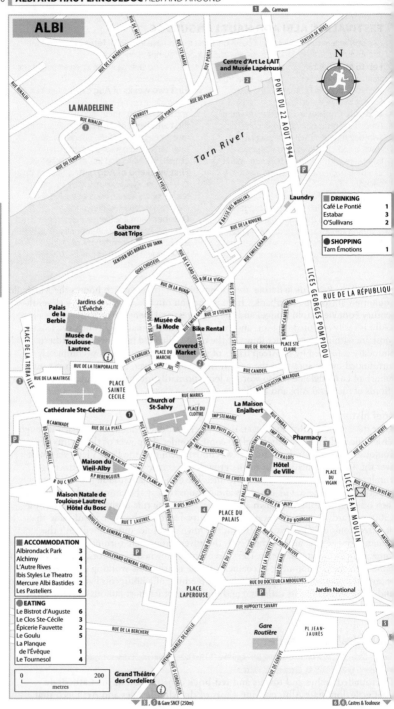

ALBI

Carmaux

N

Centre d'Art Le LAIT and Musée Lapérouse

LA MADELEINE

Tarn River

PONT DU 22 AOUT 1944

Laundry

DRINKING

Café Le Pontié	1
Estabar	3
O'Sullivans	2

SHOPPING

| Tarn Émotions | 1 |

Gabarre Boat Trips

RUE DE LA RÉPUBLIQU

Palais de la Berbie

Jardins de L'Évêché

Musée de la Mode

Bike Rental

Musée de Toulouse-Lautrec

Covered Market

PLACE SAINTE CECILE

Cathédrale Ste-Cécile

Church of St-Salvy

La Maison Enjalbert

Pharmacy

Maison du Vieil-Alby

Hôtel de Ville

Maison Natale de Toulouse Lautrec/ Hôtel du Bosc

PLACE DU PALAIS

ACCOMMODATION

Albirondack Park	3
Alchimy	4
L'Autre Rives	1
Ibis Styles Le Theatro	5
Mercure Albi Bastides	2
Les Pasteliers	6

EATING

Le Bistrot d'Auguste	6
Le Clos Ste-Cécile	3
Épicerie Fauvette	2
Le Goulu	5
La Planque de l'Évêque	1
Le Tournesol	4

Jardin National

PLACE LAPEROUSE

Gare Routière

PL JEAN-JAURÈS

0	200
metres	

Grand Théâtre des Cordeliers

& Gare SNCF (250m)

Castres & Toulouse

makes it without doubt the most curious medieval cathedral you are likely to see. It is the largest brick-built cathedral in the world and the only cathedral in Europe whose walls and ceiling are entirely decorated (the latter with the largest set of Italian paintings created in France). Financed by the proceeds of the Inquisition, the first bricks were laid in 1282, some fifty years after the Cathar defeat, but the 60m-wide nave and 78m-tall tower were not completed until more than a century after. The cathedral's clean lines, narrow windows and hulking mass reflect its role as a bastion of militant Catholicism in a region plagued by heresy, but two alterations spoil its unity: a gaudy and incongruous sixteenth-century stone porch, and a Baroque frenzy of trompe l'oeil festooned about the interior. In better harmony with the structure are the recently restored fifteenth-century **statues** of saints and biblical figures which decorate the rood screen in the **choir**, while the west wall is dominated by a giant contemporary **mural** of the Last Judgement – the largest depiction in existence – complete with nasty devils carrying off teeth-gnashing souls to the Inferno. The **treasury**, reached by a spiral staircase on the north wall, has two rooms of liturgical treasures dating from the thirteenth century including a beautiful brightly painted fourteenth-century reliquary dedicated to Saint Ursula. If you can, catch the free **organ recitals** held in the cathedral in July and August (Wed & Sun at 4pm); built in the eighteenth century, this is the largest classical organ in France.

The Palais de la Berbie: Musée Toulouse-Lautrec

April & May daily 10am–noon & 2–6pm; 1–20 June daily 9am–noon & 2–6pm; 21 June –Sept daily 9am–6pm; Oct–March Mon & Wed–Sun 10am–noon & 2–5/6pm • €8 or €10 inc temporary exhibition • ☎ 05 63 49 58 97, ⏏ museetoulouselautrec.net

Next to the cathedral, the matching brick-built **Palais de la Berbie** ("bishop", in local parlance), the fortified redoubt of Albi's lord-bishops, squats over the slow-passing Tarn. This complex began as a simple keep in the thirteenth century, but was elaborated in succeeding centuries by its wealthy owners, who strengthened its fortifications and linked it to the cathedral.

Today the palace houses the cracking **Musée de Toulouse-Lautrec**, the most important public collection of works by the Albi-born aristocratic nineteenth-century painter, Henri de Toulouse-Lautrec (see box, p.132), and the only part of the palace interior open to the public. Conceived and endowed by the artist's mother and opened in 1922, the museum is comprehensive (boasting both his first and last works) – a must for any fan of the diminutive Albigeois and well worth a couple of hours of any art buff's time. Following HTL's career in **chronological order** from his earliest teenage works (his paintings of cute little dogs are particularly charming), the stars of the show are undoubtedly his famous images of the entertainers and prostitutes of *fin-de-siècle* Paris; same-size preparatory drawings hang next to the finished oil paintings to show his creation process. Among the portraits, look out for *L'Anglaise du Star au Havre*, whose "Cubist" background is said to have inspired Picasso, and *Mr Warner*, which depicts the founder of Warner Bros films who was in France at the time to meet with the Lumière brothers. Also in the collection are 31 **posters,** which naturally include the instantly recognizable cabaret ads. The top floor of the museum's three storeys houses works by other "modern" French artists including Brayer (see also Cordes, p.138), Gauguin and Matisse.

Outside, the palace has a partly covered gallery with views of the old bridge and the far riverbank, as well as a pretty seventeenth-century French-style **garden** (April–Sept 8am–7pm; Oct–March 8am–6pm; free); you enter it from the place de l'Archevêché, on the east side of the complex.

3

3

HENRI DE TOULOUSE-LAUTREC

Undoubtedly the most famous of Languedoc's artists is the painter and illustrator **Henri de Toulouse-Lautrec**. Born into the venerable multititled family of Toulouse-Lautrec in 1864, Henri was deprived of a traditional aristocratic upbringing due to a congenital bone condition; his frailty kept him out of school, and after two falls at his home in Albi resulted in broken legs, any hope of pursuing a "normal" life ended. He thus turned to painting, and his earliest works, scenes from his family's milieu such as *Artilleryman Saddling a Horse*, and portraits – particularly of his mother – showed great promise. With the support of his family and the encouragement of their friend, the painter René Princeteau, Henri moved to Paris to study under Bonnat and Cormon, two successful conservative artists. Settled in bohemian Montmartre and accompanied by his friend and fellow student **Vincent Van Gogh**, he came under the spell both of the Impressionists and of the seedy underside of the city, and it was here that his own vivid style began to flourish. Seduced by the subversive Parisian **nightclubs**, he began to convey their dynamism in charcoal sketches like *Gin-Cocktail* and *Chocolate Dancing*, which were published in popular newspapers and magazines. By the early 1890s he was renowned as an illustrator, doing colourful line-drawn adverts, posters for the famous **Moulin Rouge** cabaret and covers for magazines like *La Revue Blanche*. By 1894, when he began his series of sketches and paintings of Paris **brothels**, including *In the Salon in Moulin Street* and *The Two Girlfriends*, he was already successful.

Henri's disabilities did not prevent him from living life to the full: he travelled widely, drank copiously (one of the creations attributed to him was "the Earthquake" – half cognac, half hallucinogenic absinthe) and, of course, patronized with gusto the brothels he depicted (he was known to Parisian prostitutes as "coffeepot", owing to his short body and big "spout"). In the end his vices aggravated his already fragile state, and by 1899 he was seeking treatment for **alcoholism**. In September 1901, at the age of 36, he died in a family castle near Bordeaux. What compelled Lautrec's dissolute lifestyle is uncertain (it wasn't his family relations, as he remained close to his parents throughout his life) but his contribution to the artistic world is unquestionable; with a unique illustrative style – a peculiar outgrowth of Impressionism – he not only influenced successive movements such as the Fauvists, but set the precedent for innovative poster design: to this day his Moulin Rouge adverts remain some of the most reproduced pictures in the world. His other great legacy is the **chocolate mousse**, a dessert invented by the painter, for whom culinary experimentation was also a passion.

The old town

Albi's **old town** is a chaotic jumble of narrow streets, with some very nice clothes, food and home decoration shops, spreading east and south of the cathedral-palace complex. A couple of minutes' walk east of the bishops' palace, the **Musée de la Mode** (17 rue de la Souque; April–Dec Tues–Sun 9.30am–noon & 2.30–6pm; €6; ☎05 63 43 15 90, ⊕musee-mode.com), housed in a former convent dating from the twelfth century, has annual themed exhibitions of exquisite clothes and accessories from across the ages and is a must for fans of vintage fashion. The old town's most conspicuous landmark is the red-brick spire of the much mistreated **church of St-Salvy**, which marks the old town's centre and is also part of the UNESCO site. Between 474 and 584, it served as Albi's first cathedral, while after the Revolution it was used as a shed for fodder. Its simple Romanesque **cloister** is a great place to read or just take a break (daily 7am–8pm; free).

Townhouses

On the corner of rue des Pénitents and rue Timbal sits the sixteenth-century brick-and-timber **Maison Enjalbert**, once a wealthy merchant's mansion and now a ladies' clothes shop, with playfully carved faces on its wooden beams. South and west of here, narrow cobbled streets overhung with the balconies of medieval houses evoke the age when the bishops and woad merchants held sway. At 1 rue de la Croix Blanche you'll find the restored medieval **Maison du Vieil Alby** (Tues–Sun 2–5.30pm; €2; ☎05 63 54 96 38, albi-patrimoine.fr), a museum displaying items of local interest, including memorabilia of the young Toulouse-Lautrec. Close by to the south, at 14 rue Lautrec, is the artist's childhood home, the **Maison Natale de Toulouse-Lautrec/Hôtel du Bosc** (no entry); for a better view of this grand townhouse head around the corner onto boulevard Sibille.

La Madeleine

Across the river from the main body of the old town lies the eighteenth-century suburb of **La Madeleine**, best reached by the Pont Vieux to the north of the bishop's palace. It's worth a stroll over just for the views back. La Madeleine itself is a compact knot of residential houses, with a number of disused eighteenth-century mill buildings clustered along the riverbank on its eastern side. These now house the *Hotel Mercure Albi Bastides* (see p.134) and the **Centre d'Art le LAIT** (41 rue Porta; Wed–Sun: April–Oct 2–7pm, Nov–March 1–6pm; €2; ☎05 63 38 35 91, ⓦwww.centredartlelait.com), which hosts temporary exhibitions by contemporary artists from around the world.

Musée Laperouse

March–June, Sept & Oct Tues–Sun 9am–noon & 2–6pm; July & Aug Mon–Fri 9am–noon & 2–6pm, Sat & Sun 10am–noon & 2–7pm; Nov–Feb Tues–Sun 10am–noon & 2–5pm • €3.50 • ☎05 63 46 01 87, ⓦlaperouse-france.fr

The **Musée Lapérouse**, in La Madeleine's riverside mill complex, is named in honour of Jean-François de Galaup, comte de Lapérouse, the intrepid navigator (1741–88) who fought the British in New France before embarking on a scientific voyage to Chile, Hawaii, Alaska, California, East Asia, Japan, Russia, the South Pacific and Australia – where he was assumed to have perished in a shipwreck. The museum reviews the admiral's career in a lively display of personal and period artefacts, maps and dioramas.

Notre-Dame-de-la-Drèche

An excellent vantage point from which to take in the panorama of Albi is the octagonal sanctuary of **Notre-Dame-de-la-Drèche**, set on a rise 6km north of town via the D90. Dating from the fourteenth century, it was rebuilt in the nineteenth century after being pillaged during the Revolution. The church is known for its many high-quality bells and you can climb the tower on Sundays (4–6pm; free) when they are being rung. The grassy grounds outside the church are a popular picnic spot, and make an ideal rest stop for those returning by foot or bike from Cagnac (see p.137).

ARRIVAL AND DEPARTURE	**ALBI**
By train Albi's *gare SNCF* is southwest of the old town on place de Stalingrad; you can walk to the town centre in 15min.	**Destinations** Carmaux (many daily; 16min); Toulouse*, via Gaillac (connections for Cordes-Vindrac), Lisle-sur-Tarn and Rabastens (hourly; 1hr).

THE ALBI–CASTRES RAIL LINE TRAIL

The best way to get from Albi to Castres (see p.145) is to follow the *voie verte* (a former rail line), a **trail** perfect for **hiking**, **cycling** and **riding**; it's named *Le Chemin des Droits de L'Homme* (The Human Rights Path). There are no major sights on the way, but the landscape – gently rolling hills with alternating pastures, wheat fields and sunflowers – is beautiful if not breathtaking. The walk is suitable for all ages and fitness levels. The total **distance** is around 44km, which can be walked in approximately sixteen hours, making an overnight stop at Lautrec (see p.144), 26km from Albi. The trail can be picked up 1km south of the Albi ring road, on rue Bourgelat, near the old cemetery, just off the southbound N112. It ends near the *gare SNCF* in Castres. You can pick up a map at the tourist office.

By bus The *gare routière* is on place Jean-Jaurès, southeast of the old town, from where it's a little over 10min by foot to the cathedral and the tourist office.

Destinations Ambialet (several daily; 30min); Cagnac (daily; 30min); Carmaux (daily; 20min); Castres (several daily; 50min); Cordes (daily; 35min); Gaillac (several daily; 30min); Lacaune (daily; 1hr 10min); Lavaur (daily; 1hr 15min); Lisle (daily; 1hr); Rabastens (several daily; 1hr 15min).

INFORMATION

Tourist information Place Ste-Cécile, next to the Palace de la Berbie (March to 19 June & Oct Mon–Sat 9.30am–12.30pm & 1.30–6pm, Sun until 5.30pm; 20 June to Sept Mon–Sat 9am–6.30pm, Sun 9.30am–5.30pm; Nov–Feb Mon–Sat 10am–12.30pm & 1.30–5pm, Sun 10am–12.30pm & 2–4.30pm; ☎ 05 63 36 36 00, ⓦ www .albi-tourisme.fr). There is also an office in the Grand Théâtre des Cordeliers, place Lapérouse (mid-June to mid-Sept Tues–Sat 10am–12.30pm & 1.30–5pm).

Discount cards The "Albi City Pass" gives free entry into the Toulouse-Lautrec museum and the cathedral choir and treasury and provides reductions for more than twenty other sights, as well as discounts on restaurants, boat tours, shopping and other activities. It's available at the tourist office and costs €12. You can also get a "Pass Journée" which includes entry to the Toulouse-Lautrec museum and cathedral, an audioguide (usually €4) to explore the UNESCO site and a three-course lunch plus wine in a partner restaurant – all for €32.

GETTING AROUND

By bike You can rent bikes at Les Vélos de Frédo, 1 place St-Julien (Mon 2–7pm, Tues & Wed 10am–noon & 2–7pm, Thurs–Sat 10am–7pm; ☎ 05 63 54 16 17). From €5 per hour.

Boat trips Albi-croisières (☎ 05 63 43 59 63, ⓦ albi -croisieres.com) offers boat trips along the Tarn in a *gabarre* (traditional riverboat). "Culture" (30 min; 11.45am–5.15pm; €7.50) and "Plaisir" (1hr 30min; 12.30pm; €12; reservation essential), on which you can take your own picnic, depart from the quay by the cathedral from May to Sept.

By car Hire cars are available at Budget, Rond Point de Caussels ☎ 05 63 47 79 30; Europcar, 24 av François-Verdier ☎ 05 63 48 88 33; and Hertz, 15 rue Jacques Monod ☎ 05 63 60 89 89.

By taxi Albi Taxi Radio ☎ 06 12 99 42 46.

ACCOMMODATION

Given its size, Albi offers a wide selection of good hotels, especially at the higher end. Check the tourist office website for details on the "Destination Albi" set-price hotel packages: "Découvrir Albi" offers one night's B&B in a hotel, an audioguide and an Albi City Pass (see box, p.134) from €49 per person.

Albirondack Park 31 allée de la Piscine ☎ 05 63 60 37 06, ⓦ albirondack.fr. Very nice three-star campsite in a woodland location about half an hour's walk northeast of the cathedral. With a North American feel, there are three Airstream caravans as well as wooden lodges, two tree houses and 44 pitches. Facilities include a bar, a restaurant specializing in lobster, a large pool, spa and a shuttle into Albi (charge). Open Feb to mid-Nov and Christmas. **€30**

Alchimy 10–12 place du Palais ☎ 05 63 76 18 18, ⓦ alchimyalbi.fr. You'd be lucky to find a boutique hotel of this quality in a city let alone a provincial town. The seven rooms and suites have been impeccably decorated by two top interior designers and the bar and restaurant (lunch from €15) are the places to be seen in town. **€110**

★L'Autre Rives 60 rue Cantepau, La Madeleine ☎ 06 75 47 01 51, ⓦ lautrerives.com. This large 1920s house across the river has been turned into a very stylish B&B where original features (check out the angular floor tiles) are successfully complemented by twenty-first-century design. As well as five very comfortable rooms, there is a large garden with a saltwater pool. Free parking. **€90**

Ibis Styles Le Theatro 48 Place Jean Jaurès ☎ 05 63 43 20 20, ⓦ ibis.com. Housed in a former office block, the decor at this three-star chain hotel in the new town is quirky and original, with specially commissioned graffiti and a floor mosaic in the reception area. The restaurant hosts a "meet the wine producer" event on Thursday evenings. Breakfast included in room price. **€80**

★Mercure Albi Bastides 41 rue Porta, La Madeleine ☎ 05 63 47 66 66, ⓦ lavermicellerie-hotelmercure.fr. A comfortable four-star hotel in a restored eighteenth-century mill with all mod cons and a grand listed entrance gate. The decor is understated and unremarkable, but the views of the town and cathedral from the restaurant and terrace – or your room, if you can get a riverside window – are spectacular. **€100**

Les Pasteliers 3 rue Honoré de Balzac ☎ 05 63 54 26 51, ⓦ hotelsalbi.com. Attractive, good-value two-star *Logis de France* hotel in a quiet residential street in the new part of town. Some of the individually decorated nineteen rooms have a terrace and jacuzzi. There's also a cute patio for breakfast in summer. Free public parking nearby. **€74**

EATING

Food in Albi is very good and economical, if rather uniform: most restaurants specialize in local *terroir* ("country cooking"), with the usual cassoulet, foie gras and duck, accompanied by fine Gaillac wine.

Le Bistrot d'Auguste 31 rue Général Pont ☎ 09 83 26 57 23. Around the corner from *Hotel Les Pasteliers*, this unassuming *restaurant du quartier* serves good traditional dishes using products from local suppliers, including organic meat. Fantastic duck confit and even better fries. *Plat du jour* €8.80. Mon–Wed noon–1.30pm, Thurs–Sat noon–1.30pm & 7–10pm.

★**Le Clos Ste-Cécile** 3 rue du Castelviel ☎ 05 63 38 19 74. Just to the west of the cathedral, this little restaurant in a former schoolhouse has got the loveliest outdoor eating space in town – the onetime playground is now a tree-shaded, flower-filled garden. Traditional regional food is on the menu, with the €14 lunchtime salads especially recommended ("pastel" includes duck and charcuterie). Mon & Thurs–Sun noon–1.30pm & 7–9pm.

Épicerie Fauvette 7 rue St-Julien ☎ 05 67 87 87 36. Lovely little café-deli in the old town with wines by the glass and a good selection of home-made snacks such as salads, sandwiches and quiches from around €8. Reserve in advance for Sunday brunch (€13). Tues–Fri 10.30am–2pm & 4–7.30pm, Sat 9.30am–2pm & 4–7.30pm, Sun 10am–1pm.

★**Le Goulu** Grand Hôtel d'Orléans, 1 Place Stalingrad ☎ 05 63 54 16 56, ⓦ hotel-orleans-albi.com. Overseen by Guillaume Arguel, who had a Michelin star at his former restaurant *Esprit du Vin*, this smart hotel restaurant is one of Albi's top places to eat. Creative cuisine using local produce matched with international flavours is the name of the game here. Excellent-value €18 lunch *menu*. Tues–Fri noon–2pm & 7–9pm, Sat 7–9pm, Sun noon–2pm.

La Planque de l'Évêque 1 rue de Lamothe, La Madeleine ☎ 05 63 56 89 49, ⓦ laplanquedeleveque .com. Of course the food is good, but the main reason to eat here is to enjoy the views across to the cathedral from the terrace in summer. Main courses such as duck salad from €15 and a copious Sunday brunch featuring home-made desserts for €19. Tues–Sat noon–1.30pm & 7–9.15pm, Sun 10.30am–1.30pm.

Le Tournesol 11 rue de l'Ort en Salvy ☎ 05 63 38 38 14. In an area noted for its top-quality meat, this vegetarian and vegan restaurant is a welcome find. The organic dishes include pâté, salads and lasagnes as well as fruit-based desserts. Menus from €10. Mon–Sat noon–2pm.

DRINKING AND NIGHTLIFE

Café Le Pontié Place du Vigan ☎ 05 63 54 16 34. In business since the eighteenth century, this smart traditional café has the most popular terrace in Albi. It's *the* place to meet during the Pause Guitare festival in July (see box, p.129). Daily 7am–2am.

Estabar 12 av François Verdier ☎ 05 63 38 29 03. Hip student hangout near the university and train station.

There's a DJ at weekends and regular events. Mon–Fri 10am–2am, Sat 7pm–2am.

O'Sullivans 44 Place Jean Jaurès ☎ 05 63 43 46 12, ⓦ osullivansalbi.com. As well as Guinness, this Irish pub has a good selection of beers, including Belgian, and there's tapas on the menu each evening. Regular live music and events. Mon–Fri 11am–2am, Sat & Sun 2pm–2am.

ENTERTAINMENT

Cap Cinéma Lapérouse 60 rue Séré de Rivière ☎ 05 63 54 05 19, ⓦ cap-cine-albi.com. Five minutes' walk east of place du Vigan, this cinema shows independent and arthouse films in their original versions (*vo*).

Cinéma de la Scène Nationale d'Albi Rue des Cordeliers ☎ 05 63 38 55 55, ⓦ sn-albi.fr. This cinema,

on the next road east of the Grand Théâtre, live-screens operas from national and international locations and also shows independent and arthouse films in their original versions (*vo*).

Grand Théâtre des Cordeliers Place Amitié entre les Peuples ☎ 05 63 38 55 55, ⓦ sn-albi.fr. Opened in 2014,

---

SPORTING LIFE IN ALBI

Like the rest of the southwest, Albi is crazy about **rugby** and the town's second-league team, Sporting Club Albigeois (tickets from €25; ☎ 08 92 35 03 42, ⓦ sca-albi.fr), plays at the Stade Municipal, 283 av du Colonel Teyssier. The other big deal here is **motor racing** – both cars and bikes – which use the Circuit d'Albi (☎ 05 63 43 04 04, ⓦ circuit-albi.fr), southwest of the town centre in the Le Sequestre district. For those looking to burn some calories or amuse the kids, the **Espace Atlantis** (☎ 05 63 76 06 09, ⓦ atlantis.grand-albigeois.fr) on route de Cordes has both indoor (year-round) and outdoor (mid-June to mid-Sept) pools and a variety of **water-based activities**.

Albi's state-of-the-art new theatre has two spaces offering an eclectic selection of music, dance and theatre from local and national artists and companies. There's also a roofto bar and restaurant.

SHOPPING

Markets Covered market: rue Émile Grand (Tues–Sun 7am–2pm). Food markets: around the covered market (Sat 7am–1pm); place Fernand Pelloutier (Tues & Sat 7am–1pm); bd de Strasbourg (Sat 7am–1pm). Organic market: place Fernand Pelloutier (Tues 4–8pm). Arts, crafts and books: rue Mariès (Wed & Sat 9am–6pm). Flea market:

Halle du Castelviel (Sat 7am–noon).
Tarn Émotions 15 Place Ste-Cécile ☎ 09 75 94 74 79 ⓦ www.tarn-emotions.fr. Good selection of regiona products including woad-dyed clothes and accessories Daily 11am–7pm.

DIRECTORY

Hospital Centre Hospitalier, bd Général Sibille, southwest of the old town (☎ 05 63 47 47 47, ⓦ www.ch-albi.fr).
Laundry Lavomatique, 10 rue Émile Grand (daily 7am–9.30pm).
Parking There is free parking at La Caserne Teyssier in rue de la Madeleine, la halle du Castelviel, Le Bondidou on bd Sibille and the car park on allée de la Lude. You'll need to

get in early in the morning or be prepared to wait.
Pharmacy Escudie, 2 rue Timbal ☎ 05 63 54 04 55 Mon–Sat 8.45am–12.15pm & 1.45–7.15pm.
Police Police Municipale, 19 Place Ste-Cécil ☎ 05 63 49 15 64.
Post office Place du Vigan (Mon–Fri 9am–6pm, Sa 9am–12.15pm).

Carmaux and around

Lying 16km north of Albi, down-to-earth **CARMAUX** owes its existence to the thirty-square-kilometre coalfield over which it sits, and its few visitors are drawn by the relics of the defunct mining industry around the town: the open pit of **Sainte-Marie** and the museum of **Cagnac**. These sights can be taken in by car, bicycle or even on foot, and, combined with a visit to the church of **Notre-Dame-de-la-Drèche** (see p.133), make a good day's outing from Albi. The countryside hereabouts is flat, scarred by excavation, and not particularly welcoming, but it improves as you head west towards Cordes, passing through **Monestiés**, a small village that's home to a well-preserved ensemble of late medieval statues. Once a hotbed of nationally important industrial action led by Jean Jaurès (see box, p.148), Carmaux itself offers little to visitors aside from a refreshing roughness, counteracted by the striking Belle Époque train station. Come on a Friday morning for the excellent **market** where you should try some *échaudés* or "*petits jeannots*" – triangular aniseed-flavour biscuits whose recipe dates back to the Middle Ages.

Musée/Centre d'Art du Verre

Domaine de la Verrerie, 1km west of the centre • July & Aug daily 10am–noon & 2–7pm; Sept–Nov Mon & Wed–Sun 10am–noon & 2–6pm; glass blowing Mon & Wed–Sun July & Aug 3–7pm; Sept–Nov 2–6pm • €6 • ☎ 05 63 80 52 90, ⓦ museeverre-tarn.com

Apart from the Friday market, the main reason to visit Carmaux is to see the **Musée/Centre d'Art du Verre**, a glass museum housed on the site of the former royal glassworks.

COAL MINING IN CARMAUX

The town's **coal** vein has been used since the twelfth century, but mining on a grand scale didn't begin until the 1700s, when the local squire, Georges Solages, received a royal licence to exploit the deposit. Late in the nineteenth century, the massive coalface at nearby Cagnac was discovered and became the focus of a boom. By the end of that century, though, brutal conditions prompted miners, supported by **Jean Jaurès**, to unionize; in the half-century that followed the mines enjoyed their greatest period of production. In the 1970s things began to wind down, and the last mine, the great open pit, closed in 1987.

which was established in the eighteenth century. In the bowels of one of the industrial buildings, once a hive of activity, you'll find an historical collection of local glass items dating from Gallo-Roman times (who knew that the Montagne Noire was renowned for its glass in the Middle Ages?) and also temporary exhibitions of international contemporary glass art. You can even try your hand at **glass blowing**. The **boutique** has some top-quality items and the Biennale des Verriers, France's leading contemporary **glass fair**, takes place here (next one in October 2017).

Musée-mine départemental

Nine kilometres southwest of Carmaux • May, June, Sept & Oct daily 10am–noon & 2–6pm; July & Aug daily 10am–12.30pm & 1.30–7pm; Nov–April Tues–Sun 10am–noon & 2–5pm; €7; ☏ 05 63 53 91 70, ⊛ musee-mine.tarn.fr

On the D90 between Carmaux and Albi lies the **Cité du Homps**, an industrial suburb of single-storey wooden huts, built for the Polish miners who immigrated in the 1950s. Beyond this, in **Cagnac-les-Mines**, you reach the excellent **Musée-mine départemental**, a vivid recreation of the world of the coal mine, and undoubtedly the region's most original museum. It consists of a stimulating, if claustrophobic, ninety-minute guided tour through 350m of galleries (excavated by out-of-work miners) and over a century of mining history, as you're shown different types of tunnels and machinery, a broad coal face and the miners' day quarters. From Cagnac, the D90 begins a rapid descent, reaching Notre-Dame-de-la-Drèche (see p.133) after 3km, before continuing to Albi.

Monestiés

Some 8km west of Carmaux, the village of **MONESTIÉS**, one of the Plus Beaux Villages de France (see p.46), owes its fame to a magnificent set of fifteenth-century religious **statues** housed in its **Chapelle St-Jacques** (daily: mid-April to mid-June & mid-Sept to Oct 10am–noon & 2–5.30pm; mid-June to mid-Sept 10am–12.30pm & 2–6pm; €3, €4 with museum; ☏05 63 76 19 17). The stone carvings on display are a set of four works representing a group of figures in Christ's tomb, the Crucifixion and a *pietà* (Mary holding a dead Christ in her arms). Commissioned in 1490 by the Bishop of Albi to grace this humble stop on the Chemin de Saint-Jacques, the vivid polychrome statues mark an intermediary step between medieval formalism and humanistic realism – they are not quite portraits, but lifelike, individualized representations. The village is also home to the small **Musée Bajèn-Vega** (same hours and price as Chapelle St-Jacques), displaying unexceptional works by the two locally based twentieth-century artists after whom it is named. There is a **market** on Thursday evenings in July and August.

ARRIVAL AND INFORMATION

CARMAUX AND AROUND

By train Carmaux's *gare SNCF*, on the Albi–Rodez line, sits on the west side of the town centre. Turning left out of the station, boulevard Malroux leads north 100m to avenue Jean-Jaurès, the main street; at the junction turn right and you'll arrive 3min later at the *place* of the same name, the town's centre. There is no public transport to Monestiés.

Destinations Albi (many daily; 15min); Toulouse (many daily; 1hr 20min).

By bus The most convenient bus stop in Carmaux is at the train station.

Destinations Albi (many daily; 30min); Cagnac (many daily; 15min).

Tourist information Carmaux: Place Gambetta (mid-June to mid-Sept Mon–Sat 9.30am–noon & 2–6pm, Sun 9am–1pm; mid-Sept to mid-June Mon–Sat 9.30am–noon & 2–5.30pm; ☏05 63 76 76 67, ⊛ tourisme-tarn-carmaux.fr). Monestiés: Place de la Mairie (daily: mid-June to mid-Sept 10am–12.30pm & 2–6pm; mid-Sept to mid-June 10am–noon & 2–5.30pm; ☏05 63 76 19 17, ⊛ tourisme-monesties.fr).

Discount cards The Pass Musées (€10.50) gives entry to the Musée/Centre d'Art du Verre, Musée-mine départemental, Musée Bajèn-Vega and Chapelle St-Jacques.

Bike rental Patrick Gelac (☏05 63 76 80 10) at 23 bd Augustin-Malroux, near Carmaux station.

ACCOMMODATION AND EATING

Auberge Occitane Lices de l'Est ☎ 05 63 80 73 41, Monestiés. Housed in a pretty coaching inn dating from the fourteenth century, this rustic restaurant offers tasty *terroir* cuisine with lunch *menus* at €13.90 including wine. You can also buy take-away picnics for €8.90. There's a nice outdoor terrace too. April–June & Sept–Nov Mon–Thurs & Sun noon–1.30pm, Fri & Sat noon–1.30pm & 7–9pm; July & Aug daily noon–1.30pm & 7–9pm.

Camping Les Prunettes Monestiés ☎ 05 63 76 19 17. Small basic municipal campsite in a bucolic riverside location with just 22 pitches. Enquiries and bookings at the tourist office. Open mid-June to mid-Sept. €9

Chez Martine 16 Place Jean-Jaurès, Carmaux ☎ 05 63 76 51 08. Traditional, old-fashioned "workers' restaurant" with home-made food using local ingredients. *Plat du jour* €9 or three courses for €13.50. Mon–Fri noon–1.30pm.

Cordes-sur-Ciel

CORDES-SUR-CIEL is the most spectacularly preserved of the Albigeois fortified planned towns, or *bastides*. Dramatically situated on a steep hill, the origin of the town's surname *sur-ciel* ("in the sky") can be appreciated on mornings when fog cloaks the foot of the hill and the medieval *cité* pokes through, apparently suspended in the clouds. Writer Albert Camus, who spent some time in the village in the 1950s, wrote "everything is beautiful here, even regret". More recently, in 2014, it was voted *Le Village Préféré des Français* in the annual TV programme of the same name which aims to find the French people's favourite villages. Camus' words give some idea of the town's allure, and hard though it may be to achieve such a placid state when the streets are packed during summer days, in the evening or out of season the romance of Cordes returns. To watch the sun rise from the ramparts is worth getting up for, and with every other building a medieval mansion, walking the town before the crowds arrive is a delight. No single sight brings people to Cordes; rather, the town as a whole, girded by several concentric medieval walls and endowed with a score of old houses, is something of an open-air museum and artisanal centre. It can be seen in an afternoon, but it makes for an atmospheric place to spend a night or two.

Cordes' layout is simple: the old citadel – the "**upper town**" – runs along and down the sides of the long and narrow ridge which juts up from the plain, while the modern "**lower town**" consists of a clump of streets at the foot of the old town's eastern tip. The best route to the upper town is the knee-cracking Grand-Rue de l'Horloge ascending from the Maison des Producteurs (see p.140), although at busy times, it is more pleasant to take one of the picturesque but less crowded side-streets. Along the way a

---

HIKING THROUGH THE CÉROU VALLEY

From Monestiés to Cordes-sur-Ciel the **Cérou river** meanders down from the scrubby highlands of the Ségala towards the rocky hills of the Tarnais *causses*, before emptying into the Lot. The pleasant and unchallenging 16km trip along the wooded riverbank can be made by **car** or **bicycle**, but can also be **hiked**, following a gentle path, in four to five hours.

Leaving from the sports ground on the north side of Monestiés, follow the disused rail-bed which runs parallel to the D91 highway for 6km to the hamlet of **Salles**. Crossing the river, follow the directions through town for Virac, but turn right when you come to Salles' medieval church. At the end of that street follow the sealed road which ascends towards the Vignasse farm. After 200m or so, take the first trail branching off to the right. After a further 800m or so, following the **yellow trail markings**, you should reach the top of a T-junction. Cross this and proceed 30m, before the trail turns off left through the trees. Regaining a country lane 60m later, turn right, passing a bridge on your right, and a turn on your left, before coming to a T-junction. Here, take the left branch, which descends, becoming a **dirt trail** for 250m before reaching the D7 road. Cordes should now be in view. Descending along the D7 for just over 1km you'll pass a sign saying "virages sur 2000m"; here you can pick up the trail which leads to the town itself (1km further).

series of medieval **gates** leads to the compact upper town. Alternatively, a *petit train* (May–Sept; €3) makes frequent trips from place de la Bouteillerie, where the market takes place on Saturday mornings, to Porte de la Jane on the west side.

Brief history

Founded in 1222 by Count Raymond VII of Toulouse at the height of the war against his Cathar subjects, Cordes provided a durable and defiant stronghold against Simon de Montfort's attacks. Its forename comes from the **leatherworking** industry (a craft associated with Islamic Córdoba, in Spain) that supported and enriched the town, bringing rapid growth; in the 1200s alone the walls had to be enlarged no fewer than seven times. Things took a downturn, however, with the arrival of the plague in the 1300s. Although Cordes later recovered, and had a notable lace industry in the nineteenth century, its real renaissance didn't come until the 1970s, when hippies, including the **craftsmen** and **artisans** whose wood, metalwork and other studios now cram the upper town, arrived to put Cordes back on the map, attracted by the place's beauty and air of antiquity.

3

Musée Charles-Portal – histoire d'une cité

Mid-March to May Fri–Sun 2.30–6pm; June–Aug Mon & Wed–Sun 2.30–6.30pm; Sept to mid-Nov Fri–Sun 3–6pm • €2.50 • musee-charles-portal.asso-web.com

Entering the upper town via the Porte des Ormeaux ("gate of the elm saplings"), just to the south of Port de la Jane, you'll reach the **Musée Charles-Portal**, which has displays of items of local interest from prehistory to the nineteenth century, the village's architecture and a film about the medieval wells that riddle the town, which were used in time of siege for water supply or to store grain. There are fabulous views from the top-floor terrace.

Mansions of the upper town

Continuing up Grand-Rue Raimond VII beyond the Musée Charles-Portal, you'll pass the **Maison du Grand Veneur** ("House of the Great Hunter") whose otherwise plain stone facade is festooned with amusingly sculpted and extremely well preserved medieval caricatures of beasts and hunters. You'll find another impressively carved frontage a few doors along at Raymond of Toulouse's old palace, the **Maison du Grand Ecuyer**, named after the finely sculpted horse.

Musée d'Art Moderne et Contemporain

Mid-March to mid-Nov Mon & Wed–Sun 10.30am–12.30pm & 2–6pm • €4 • ☎ 05 63 56 14 79, ⓦ mamc.cordessurciel.fr

Just after the ancient **covered market** on Grand-Rue Raimond VII, where you can peer down one of the town's famously deep wells, is the elegant and symmetrical arcaded face of the Maison du Grand Fauconnier – now home to the **Musée d'Art Moderne et Contemporain**. The museum's high points include works by Yves Brayer (1907–1990), one of the most important figurative painters of the twentieth century, who lived in Cordes from 1940. There's also a motley collection of modern art, including minor pieces by Picasso, Miró and Klee.

ARRIVAL AND INFORMATION   **CORDES-SUR-CIEL**

By train Trains stop 5km to the west of Cordes at Vindrac, from where it's a pleasant 1hr walk, or you can reserve a taxi the day before: Taxi Cordais ☎ 06 22 42 7211 or Taxi Gilles ☎ 06 16 30 14 90.

By bus Buses from Albi (several daily; 35min) arrive in the lower town in place de la Bouteillerie.

By car There is free parking in the Parking des Tuileries on the northeastern side of town and paid parking around the hill perimeter (meters) and at the Parking du Saint-Crucifix to the north on rue du Cérou. Do not attempt to drive into the upper town.

Tourist information Maison Gaugiran, 38–42 Grand-Rue

(April–June, Sept & Oct Mon 2–6pm, Tues–Sat 10.30am–12.30pm & 2–6pm, Sun until 5pm; July & Aug Mon–Sat 9.30am–1pm & 2–6.30pm, Sun 10am–1pm & 2–6pm; Nov–March Mon–Fri 10.30am–12.30pm & 2–4pm, Sat until 5pm, Sun 2–5pm; ☎ 05 63 56 00 52, ⓦ cordessurciel .fr). Don't miss the impressive interior courtyard.

ACCOMMODATION AND EATING

L'Escuelle des Chevaliers 87 Grand-Rue Raimond VII ☎ 09 66 86 14 40, ⓦ lescuelledeschevaliers.fr. Set foot in this thirteenth-century house and you're transported back to medieval times, either in the five stone-walled bedrooms or in the restaurant, where they hold costumed banquets featuring highly spiced food of the age (menus from €20). Book well in advance. **€68**

Hostellerie du Vieux Cordes 21 rue St-Michel ☎ 05 63 53 79 20, ⓦ hostelleriehvc.com. This three-star, traditionally furnished Logis de France is a good-value option; superior rooms have views over the valley. The terroir restaurant (Tues–Sun), with lunch from €16.90, is the best place to eat in town and has a lovely terrace. **€68**

★ **Le Secret du Chat** 16 Le Planol ☎ 06 95 48 18 10, ⓦ chambres-cordes-tarn-charme-lesecretduchat.com. Fabulous B&B in a seventeenth-century stone house with five stylish, beamed rooms/suites and an apartment with a small terrace and spectacular views. Table d'hôte (€40) is available on request and is served in the "secret" garden in summer. **€120**

SHOPPING

The town has around sixty artists and artisans, whose shops are listed in a free leaflet from the tourist office: Guide des Artistes et Artisans d'Art.

Castan La Souparie, Villeneuve-sur-Vere ☎ 05 63 53 04 61, ⓦ distillerie-castan.com. Off the D600 halfway between Cordes and Albi, this wine producer specializes in AOP organic vino and makes a surprisingly good whisky. Daily: July & Aug 9am–noon & 2–7pm, Sept–June Sat 10am–noon & 2–6pm (call to see if open on weekdays).

Maison des Producteurs du Pays Cordais 8 Place Jeanne Ramels-Cals. Opposite place de la Bouteillerie, this little house showcases products from the region and operates as a seasonal tourist information point. May, June & Sept Tues–Fri & Sun 10am–12.30pm & 2–6pm, July & Aug Tues–Fri 10am–1pm & 2–6.30pm, Sat 10am–1pm, Sun 10am–1pm & 2.30–6pm.

Yves Thuriès 33 Grand-Rue Raymond VII ☎ 05 63 56 02 40, ⓦ thuries.fr. Delicious chocolates and ice cream made by the nationally renowned master chocolatier, who lives in the village. See website for his other shops in the region. Daily: mid-Feb to mid-March, Nov & Dec 10.30am–12.30pm & 1.30–6pm, mid-March to mid-July, Sept & Oct 10am–7pm, mid-July to Aug 10am–8pm.

Gaillac and around

GAILLAC, located at the heart of the wine region bearing its name, is a town built on the grape. It has an ideal climate for viticulture, and its inhabitants started producing wine more than 2500 years ago, making it the oldest French vineyard. The industry really took off in the tenth century with the founding of the Benedictine abbey of St-Michel – as part of their rule, monks were given a healthy daily ration of wine which, along with that needed for Holy Communion, ensured a high demand for the local product. The entrepreneurial order decided to guarantee the quality of their vintage by laying down rules specifying which wines could qualify as Gaillacoises – and thus one of France's most famous AOPs was born. Today, Gaillac continues to live off the deserved reputation of its wine and makes a handy stepping-off point for exploring the old villages of **Lisle**, a *bastide*, and **Rabastens.**

Abbatiale St-Michel

Place St-Michel • Daily 2–5pm but depends on volunteers being available

The focal point of the town is the ponderous **Abbatiale St-Michel**, an abbey-church built in the tenth century, and impressively large for its era. The interior is unadorned, apart from a fourteenth-century painted Virgin and Child on the left-hand side of the nave. **Concerts** (for which there is a charge) are held in the garden on Friday evenings in summer.

Musée de l'Abbaye

Wed–Sun 10am–noon & 2–5pm • €2.50 • ☎ 05 63 57 14 65

The **Musée de l'Abbaye**, next door to the abbey in its former wine cellar, is dedicated to both the history of the town and to wine making, with displays of old presses, barrels, tools and bottles. There's also a very nice fifth-century Gallo-Roman mosaic and some relics from the abbey. But the real centre of attraction in this complex, however, is the **Maison des Vins** (daily 10am–noon & 2–6pm; free; ☎ 05 63 57 15 40, ⓦ vins-gaillac .com), where you can sample (see box below) and buy local vintages. The **tourist office** (see p.46) is also in the building.

Musée des Beaux-Arts

April–Oct Mon & Wed–Sun 10am–noon & 2–6pm; Nov–March Fri–Sun same hours • €2.50 • ☎ 05 63 57 18 25

Behind the abbey, off place Eugénie de Guérin, lies the medieval *faubourg*, whose twisting lanes lack grand monuments but are loaded with atmosphere. On its south side in shady **Parc Foucaud**, a seventeenth-century park with French and Italian-syle gardens and water features, is the surprisingly good **Musée des Beaux-Arts**. This museum, housed in the Château de Foucaud, exhibits the work of nineteenth- and twentieth-century regional artists including Firmin Salabert, who was a pupil of Ingres, and Henri Loubat, who specialized in portraits and bucolic scenes. A free **shuttle bus** #1 links the centre (place de la Libération) with the park.

3

ARRIVAL AND INFORMATION

GAILLAC

By train Gaillac's *gare SNCF* is to the north of the old town, a good 20min walk from the centre.

Destinations Albi (several daily; 20min); Carmaux (several daily; 35min); Lisle (several daily; 8min); Rabastens (several daily; 15min); Toulouse (several daily; 45min); Cordes-Vindrac (several daily; 15min).

By bus Buses stop at the new *gare routière* at Parking La Clavelle about a 15min walk north of the centre. Free shuttle buses #3 and #4 link the bus station with Place de la Libération in the town centre.

Destinations Albi (several daily; 30min); Castres (several daily; 1hr 5min); Lautrec (several daily; 45min);

A QUICK GUIDE TO WINE TASTING

The following quick guide to **wine tasting** is offered to prevent you from reinforcing lingering French stereotypes of Anglo lack of couth and invest you with an air of sophistication which will elicit admiration from even the most haughty Gallic *sommelier*.

Proper wine tasting can be accomplished in **ten easy steps**. When you visit a *domaine* that advertises *dégustation* ("tasting"), you will be offered a selection of different types of wine that are produced there. When your host pours you a glass, be sure to **pick it up by the stem**. Cupping the wine glass will cause your body-heat to warm the wine, which the vintner has taken care to present at the ideal temperature. Next, **study the wine**. Swirl it gently in the glass. Keep an eye out for particulate matter, and for "legs" – the viscous drops that slide slowly down the glass (an indicator of alcohol and glycerin content). **Examine it** against a white background for consistency of colour; hold it up to the light. For the "**first nose**", press your nose deep into the glass and take several short, sharp snorts. Pause, and proceed to the "**second nose**": sniffing the wine slowly while swirling it in the glass. Next, the **taste**. Sip the wine, pursing your lips and slurping loudly, forcing it to mix with air as it enters your mouth. Concentrate on the texture and feel of the wine, but don't swallow yet. **Slosh** it around your mouth, to feel the wine's effect on the different zones of your palate. There are three distinct phases to the taste: the initial "attack," as the wine hits your mouth, the "evolution," as it circulates, and the "finish," or the after-tastes. If you cannot resist, swallow the wine; but a true connoisseur will **spit it out** into the bucket provided. Repeat. **Concentrate** on the sensations you have experienced. Finally, **declaim** your impressions in a stream-of-consciousness deluge (preferably in French, although an evidently enthusiastic English will also serve). While *sommeliers* might employ a specific vocabulary, any adjectives are fair game – the point is to remember your impressions. Then have a cracker and move on to the next vintage.

Lavaur via Giroussens (several daily; 40min); Lisle (several daily; 10min); Rabastens (several daily; 20min).

By car To enjoy 1hr 30min free parking, ask for a *disque de stationnement* (parking disc) from the *mairie* in Place d'Hautpoul; there's also a car park here.

Tourist information Abbaye St-Michel (Easter to June &

Sept daily 10am–12.30pm & 2–6pm; July & Aug daily 10am–1pm & 2–7pm; Oct to Easter Wed–Sun 10am–noon & 2–5pm; ☎08 05 40 08 28 ⓦtourisme-vignoble -bastides.com). There is also an office in Place de la Libération (Easter to June & Sept daily 10am–noon & 2–6pm; July & Aug daily 10am–7pm; Oct to Easter Mon– Sat 10am–noon & 2–5pm).

ACCOMMODATION AND EATING

★**Au Fil des Saisons** 55 rue Denfert Rochereau ☎05 63 42 76 03, ⓦfildessaisons.jimdo.com. In the north of the town near the new bus station, this contemporary restaurant is not only Gaillac's best place to eat but probably the best value, with a two-course lunch *menu* (Mon–Sat) at €13.90 including coffee. Reservations advised. Daily noon–2pm & 7–10pm.

Combettes 8 Place St-Michel ☎05 63 57 61 48, ⓦcombettesgaillac.com. Fans of historical properties will love this B&B in a sixteenth-century townhouse opposite the abbey. The whole place oozes character and the four rooms are decorated in traditional style but with modern bathrooms. €65

Delga 28 rue des Frères Delga ☎06 77 24 65 66, ⓦhoteldelga.free.fr. Boutique B&B in the eighteenth-century birthplace of three Napoleonic war heroes. The four rooms are stylishly decorated with contemporary designer fittings and furnishings. You can work off owner Marie's

yummy breakfast pastries in the pool. Massages are also available, as is free parking. €90

★**Domaine de Perches** 2083 rte de Laborie ☎05 63 56 58 24, ⓦdomainedeperches.com. Six kilometres northwest of Gaillac, this luxury, tastefully decorated B&B in a former wine producer's house, surrounded by vineyards, is the perfect place for a relaxing break. Franco-British owners Alain and Howard are the perfect hosts; Howard's delicious *table d'hôte* (€50) is accompanied by wines from their own vines. There are wonderful views from the pool. €150

Vigne en Foule 80 Place de la Libération ☎05 63 41 79 08, ⓦvigneenfoule.fr. Created by a group of wine producers, this contemporary restaurant and wine bar is the most fashionable address in town. At lunch and dinner, as well as three-course *menus* (€17–29), you can snack on a gourmet sandwich or quiche for around €8. Tues–Sun noon–2pm & 7.30–10pm.

Lisle-sur-Tarn

Only a ten-minute ride (10km) southwest on one of the frequent buses or trains from Gaillac, **LISLE-SUR-TARN** is a tranquil thirteenth-century former port and *bastide* known for its *pountets*, the overhead covered passages which connect many of its brick-built medieval houses. The best way to take it in is with a stroll through the town and a relaxed drink in the arcaded place Saissac, one of the largest medieval squares in the southwest, at its centre. A **market** takes place here on Sunday mornings. The small local museum, **Musée Raymond Lafage** (10 rue Victor Maziès; mid-March to Oct Mon & Wed–Sun 10am–noon & 3–6pm; €4; ☎05 63 40 45 45, ⓦmuseeraymondlafage.wifeo .com) is tucked away to the east of the square and contains works by the native seventeenth-century designer Raymond Lafage; it also hosts some top-quality temporary exhibitions. To the east, a street descends to the riverside to what was long ago the town's pier – an evocative spot.

INFORMATION   LISLE-SUR-TARN

Tourist information 21 Place Paul-Saissac (May Tues–Sat 10am–noon & 2–5pm, Sun 10am–12.30pm; June & Sept Mon–Sat 10am–noon & 2–6pm, Sun

10am–12.30pm; July & Aug daily 10am–12.30pm & 2.30– 6pm; Oct–April Tues–Sat 2–5pm, Sun 10am–12.30pm; ☎05 63 40 31 85, ⓦtourisme-vignoble-bastides.com).

ACCOMMODATION AND EATING

La Jonquière 2 Place de l'Église ☎05 63 40 16 04, ⓦlajonquiere.fr. Charming shabby-chic B&B in an eighteenth-century wine store, which owner François renovated himself. The two rooms – "yellow" and "blue"

– overlook the walled garden. There's a cosy lounge and library with a piano; local produce and home-made jams for breakfast. €78

★**La Pigario** Chemin de la Pigario ☎05 63 40 61 64,

Ⓦlapigario.com. On a hill above the town, this three-bedroom B&B offers spectacular views across the surrounding countryside. What with *table d'hôte* available and a pool, you don't even need to move. But you might want to make an exception to visit the next-door Château de Saurs, one of the best vineyards in the area. **€70**

Le Romuald 6 rue du Port Ⓣ05 63 33 38 85,

Ⓦrestaurant-leromuald-lislesurtarn.fr. Grilled meats, including quail (€12), are the speciality in this traditiona restaurant set in a sixteenth-century house to the southeast of the main square. The rustic dining room has ar open fire and there's a lovely, plant-filled terrace for warmer days. Tues noon–1.30pm, Wed–Sat noon–1.30pm & 8–9pm, Sun noon–1.30pm.

Rabastens

RABASTENS, 8km downriver from Lisle, can be reached easily by bicycle or on foot along the river course. On weekend evenings the village's streets fill with young people, giving it a vivacity surprising for its size and making it a welcome contrast to the sleepier villages of the Albigeois. It's particularly animated on Saturday mornings during the **market**. Still guarded by vestiges of its brick ramparts, Rabastens was founded in the time of the fifth-century barbarian invasions, when it served as a refuge for the inhabitants of a huge Gallo-Roman villa. In the Middle Ages, the tanning industry brought it considerable prosperity, reflected in its surprisingly rich architecture.

Notre-Dame du Bourg

5 rue Toulouse-Lautrec • Mon–Sat 8am–6pm, Sun 2–6pm

The sight that makes Rabastens an obligatory stop is its thirteenth-century church, **Notre-Dame du Bourg**, designated a UNESCO World Heritage Site in 1998 for its importance on the pilgrimage route to Santiago de Compostela. Its incredible painted interior was rediscovered and restored in the 1840s: the magnificent, vibrant **frescoes** cover virtually every surface, and provide a rare chance to see what medieval churches really looked like, before the "puritans" of the Catholic Reformation scrubbed them clean. Check out the "swastikas" on the ceiling of the choir – they represent life and energy. Also of note is a **chapel** dedicated to St Jacques (James), donated by the archbishop of Santiago, grateful for the wealth the pilgrimage route was bringing his diocese.

Musée du Pays Rabastinois

2 rue Amédée Clausade • Jan–Nov Tues–Fri 10am–noon & 2–6pm, Sat & Sun 2–6pm • €2.50 • Ⓣ05 63 40 65 65

Housed in a seventeenth-century mansion (also home to the tourist office), the **Musée du Pays Rabastinois** is just south of Notre-Dame du Bourg and contains a fascinating and diverse collection, which includes local archeological finds, pottery, religious art, nineteenth-century art, Art Nouveau posters and some twentieth-century Parisian haute couture embroidery. Of particular note is a fourth-century **floor mosaic** from a nearby Gallo-Roman villa.

ARRIVAL AND INFORMATION   **RABASTENS**

By bus Buses pass through the centre of Rabastens, while the *gare SNCF* is located just across the river in Coufouleux – about a 10min walk from the centre. The town is on the main rail line between Toulouse and Carmaux so there are frequent trains, and there are several buses a day to Gaillac and Albi.

Tourist information 2 rue Amédée Clausade (mid-Jan to April & Oct to mid-Dec Tues–Fri 10am–noon & 2–5pm, Sat & Sun 3–5pm; May–Sept Tues–Fri 10am–noon & 2–6pm, Sat & Sun 3–6pm (also 10am–noon in July & Aug); Ⓣ05 63 40 65 65, Ⓦtourisme-vignoble-bastides.com).

Lautrec

The most beautiful and inviting of the towns between Albi and Castres, **LAUTREC** enjoys a picturesque setting on a windmill-capped spur, once the site of a twelfth-century castle. Unsurprisingly, it's one of the Plus Beaux Villages de France (see p.46). The little own is a warren of steep, twisting streets, interspersed by compact arcaded squares, making it an agreeable place to spend half a day. It was here that an aristocratic marriage alliance in 1196 established the family of Toulouse-Lautrec (artist Henri's forebears). Nowadays the town prides itself on its pungent **pink garlic** (ⓦailrosedelautrec.com), for which it is a Site Remarquable du Goût. From mid-July to December you'll find it in local produce shops throughout the *département* and also at Lautrec's Friday-morning **market**; it even has its own festival (first Friday in August). The *voie verte* walking and cycling path between Albi and Castres passes near the village.

The windmill

Mid-April to mid-Oct 10am–noon & 2–5.30pm (ask at the tourist office about days) • €2

Lautrec's main attraction is the functioning seventeenth-century **windmill** (*moulin*) perched above the town. As you enter the mill on a windy day, the sight and sound of the large, rapidly spinning wooden mechanisms are exhilarating. The hilltop also offers a superb panoramic **view** towards the south.

3

ARRIVAL AND INFORMATION   LAUTREC

By bus Castres (several daily; 50min); Gaillac (several daily; 45min).

Tourist information Rue du Mercadial (April & Oct Tues–Sat 9.30am–12.30pm & 2–5.30pm; May, June & Sept Wed–Sat 9.30am–12.30pm & 2–6pm, Sun & Tues 2–6pm; July & Aug daily 9.30am–12.30pm & 2–6.30pm; Nov–March Tues–Sat 9am–12.30pm & 2–5pm; ⓣ05 63 97 94 41, ⓦlautrectourisme.com). The tourist office is housed in a seventeenth-century monastery whose gardens were designed by André Le Nôtre, of Versailles fame.

Bike tours Vélotrek (ⓣ06 31 90 78 05, ⓦwww.velotrek .fr). Join Anthony for an active, cultural or gastronomic guided tour (2–7hr) on a mountain bike or electric bike. From €20.

ACCOMMODATION AND EATING

La Caussade 1 rue de la Caussade ⓣ05 63 75 33 21. Good-value B&B with three pretty rooms in a charming old house in the centre of the village. *Table d'hôte* (€20) available. Cash only. **€59**

La Terrasse 9 rue de l'Église ⓣ05 63 75 84 22, ⓦlaterrassedelautrec.com. This seventeenth-century mansion, with listed wallpaper in the lounge and garden said to have been designed by Le Nôtre, has been turned into a smart B&B with four elegant rooms and a *gîte*. There's also a pool. Open mid-April to November. **€105**

★ **Thé Lautrec** 4 rue du Mercadial ⓣ05 63 74 23 29, ⓦlafermeauvillage.fr. Gorgeous little tearoom wedged between two shops selling regional products. Sit in the stylish dining room with its stunning views or in the cute courtyard to enjoy a quiche or a sandwich (€9). The artisan ice creams are delicious. May, June & Sept Sat & Sun noon–6pm, July & Aug daily noon–6pm.

Castres and around

Southeast of Lautrec, the rolling agricultural landscape comes to an abrupt end as the and begins to rise and you approach the Parc Naturel Régional du Haut Languedoc, a highland ridged by peaks rising up to 1120m. **CASTRES**, on the western edge of the uplands, is the Tarn's second "city" (town) whose economy is largely supported by the Laboratoire Pierre Fabre, a **pharmaceutical company** with several international brands including Klorane and Avène. Fabre is also the sponsor of the town's Top 14 rugby team, Castres Olympique (ⓦcastres-olympique.com), who won the league in 2012–13. Boasting an atmospheric medieval core, enhanced by grand mansions dating from the sixteenth century, sleepy Castres is enlivened on match days and by summer **music festivals** (see p.129). In addition, it has a couple of good museums, including the **Musée Goya – Musée d'Art Hispanique**, which has the largest collection of Spanish art in France after the Louvre. Castres is not only a comfortable place to stay for a day or two, but makes an ideal base: **Sidobre**, a granite massif to the east famed for its peculiar

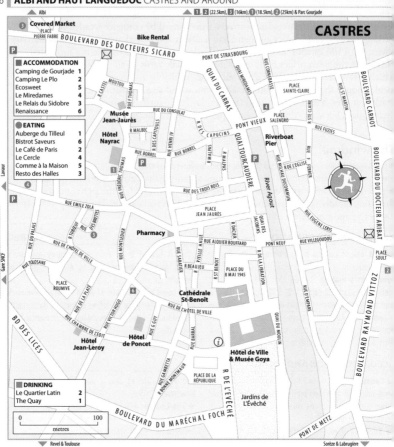

rock formations, is an easy excursion, while the town is also the end-point of the **Gijou Valley Trail**, a hiking, riding and mountain-bike route that leads up into the isolated heights of Haut Languedoc (see p.150).

Brief history

Despite its Latin origins (*castrum* meaning "fortified place"), Castres was not founded by the Romans – even though they were here in 1–2AD. The site was occupied during the Iron Age but the origins of the town go back to the ninth century with the foundation of a **Benedictine monastery**. The monks brought with them the remains of St Vincent of Saragossa and Castres became an important stopover on the Arles route to Santiago de Compostela. In the twelfth century Castres was swept up in the Cathar movement, and it was here that the first Albigensian **martyrs** were burned at the stake in 1209. The ever-rebellious population took up the Protestant banner four centuries later, and the town became an important centre of **Huguenot** administration and also textile production.

The old town

Don't be fooled by the drab suburbs that surround it – Castres' **old town**, spilling over the River Agout to the east, is a delight. The brightly painted riverside **dyers' houses** are

he town's hallmark, while the impressive sixteenth-century mansions hidden among its
arrow streets make the medieval quarter a pleasure to stroll through. Castres' centre is
marked by café-girded **place Jean-Jaurès**, home to a bustling produce market (Tues &
Thurs–Sat), while just south of the square, the unprepossessing **Cathédrale St-Benoît**,
constructed in 1677, stands on the site of the old monastery church. It's a squat and
not especially noteworthy Baroque building, although the marble statues of saints
around the choir are worth a look.

Musée Goya – Musée d'Art Hispanique

April–June & Sept Tues–Sun 9am–noon & 2–6pm; July & Aug daily 10am–6pm; Oct–March Tues–Sun 9am–noon & 2–5pm • €5 •
05 63 71 59 27

Next to the river, the **Hôtel de Ville** reposes within the seventeenth-century former
bishop's palace, a dour, hulking square edifice designed by Jules Hardouin-Mansart
(Louis XIV's chief architect), whose grey sobriety contrasts with the bright formal
gardens, the **Jardins de l'Évêché**, designed by Le Nôtre, which stretch out on its
southern side. The building also houses Castres' foremost museum, the
Musée Goya – Museum of Hispanic Art, which was established a century ago by
private donation, and now holds the biggest collection of Spanish paintings in
France outside the Louvre.

Dominating its largest salon, the core of the exhibition is, as you'd expect, taken up
by the artist after whom it is named, but the paintings here are not the dark, sinister
visions for which **Francisco Goya** is most famous, but rather his portraiture, including
his *Self-portrait with Glasses*, and politically inspired works like *The Junta of the
Philippines Presided over by Ferdinand VII*. Other rooms contain numerous pieces by
other seventeenth-century Iberian masters – including **Velázquez**'s *Portrait of Philip IV*,
Murillo's *Virgin with Rosary* and **Zurburán**'s *Carthusian Martyr*. As well as Flemish-
influenced medieval paintings by fifteenth-century Catalan and Spanish artists, the
collection is rounded off with a modern section featuring Picasso's *Bust of a Man
Writing*. There are also displays of old coins and assorted archeological knick-knacks
including Iberian figurines dating from the sixth century BC, as well as a room
dedicated to local wartime arms. An adjacent gallery houses temporary exhibitions of
impressive quality.

The hôtels particuliers

West of the Goya museum along rue Chambre de l'Édit three palatial **hôtels
particuliers** (mansions dating from the sixteenth and seventeenth centuries) stand
out. On rue Guy, the first street on the right, is the seventeenth-century **Hôtel de
Poncet**, with its classically inspired Renaissance facade and caryatid columns
supporting an elegant Ionic-columned loggia. Further along rue Chambre de l'Édit
you'll find the earlier **Hôtel Jean-Leroy**, notable for its stately carved casement
windows and topped by a defensive tower. Next door to that, **Hôtel de Viviès**, built
along the now-vanished city walls, is the most beautiful of the town's mansions and
was built for an important lawyer. Castres' **shopping** district stretches north from
here, on the far side of which, in rue Thomas, you'll find Castres' grandest *hôtel
particulier*, the **Hôtel de Nayrac**, once the Huguenot judicial court, built in the
brick-and-stone style of the Toulouse mansions, with three sober facades boxing in a
broad, symmetrical courtyard.

Musée Jean-Jaurès

Place Pélisson • Tues–Sat 10am–noon & 2–5/6pm, also Sun May–June & Sept; daily July & Aug • €3 • 05 63 62 41 83

Just beyond the Hôtel de Nayrac is the **Musée Jean-Jaurès**, which pays homage to the
life of Castres' favourite son (see box, p.148), recounting the assassinated activist's
career with newspaper reports, memorabilia and contemporary artefacts. It's a
fascinating and well-planned exhibition but only has information in French.

3

JEAN JAURÈS

Jean Jaurès, the nineteenth-century labour activist, politician and martyr, is a figure whose presence travellers can scarcely escape in Languedoc. Nearly every town has at least one street or square – usually a main one – and a building or two named after this **socialist hero**, whose tireless struggle for workers' rights and international peace eventually cost him his life.

Born in Castres in 1859, Jean Jaurès showed exceptional promise as a student and won a scholarship to complete his studies in Paris. When these were finished, rather than stay in the capital he returned to his home *département* of Tarn and took a post teaching philosophy in **Albi**'s *lycée* (high school), and giving lectures at the University of Toulouse. But the miserable conditions under which his **working-class** neighbours toiled drew him out of the academy; their dangerous working environment, underpayment and near-total lack of rights and representation could have been lifted straight from the pages of **Émile Zola**'s contemporary *Germinal*. Jaurès ran for political office and at the young age of 26 was elected a legislative representative for the Tarn. One of his first projects was to help the glass-workers at Albi found the collectively run V.O.A. bottle factory, which still operates today. Continuing in politics and the cause of social justice, in 1893, as socialist deputy for **Carmaux**, he supported the miners' struggle for better working conditions, and his renown as a social reformer began to spread.

However, Jaurès' desire for reform went beyond simply improving the lives of those around him. Five years later he joined other liberals, including Zola, in defence of the Jewish army captain, **Alfred Dreyfus**, convicted on unfounded charges of espionage. National feelings of resentment against Dreyfus were running high, but despite this, Jaurès persisted in his defence of the underdog, and – eventually – helped him obtain a pardon. The patriotically charged issue temporarily cost Jaurès his popularity, but he was soon back on the stage, founding the Communist daily *L'Humanité* in 1904 (still one of France's major newspapers; ⓦ humanite.fr) and the following year helping found the socialist SFIO party. With the dawn of World War I, however, Jaurès' internationalist brand of socialism revealed itself again in an outspoken and unpopular **pacifist** stand – and led to his **assassination** in Paris by a nationalist extremist in July 1914. On his death he was hailed as a martyr, the perfect hero for the Tarn – a local politician who improved the quality of life in this underdeveloped and marginalized region, and who wasn't afraid to take on the political establishment of Paris in order to defend a higher justice.

The east bank

Over on the far side of the river, the scruffier east bank of the Agout is home to a number of interesting little restaurants and cafés, and although it lacks historical buildings the neighbourhood's proletarian feel is refreshing. The sparsely adorned medieval **fountain** in place Fagerie, just north of the Pont Neuf, is also worth seeking out, if only for the "undiscovered" atmosphere of the square in which it sits. Place Soul has an organic **market** on Thursdays (4–8pm).

The Sidobre

Just to the east of Castres lies the hundred-square-kilometre granite plateau known as **the Sidobre**. This heavily promoted area is known for the boulders that litter it, either eroded into evocative shapes or balancing precariously. Many, including the rock-strewn waterfall, **Saut de la Truite**, are found within a 3km radius of **Lacrouzette**, a nondescript town 15km northeast of Castres. While some of the formations are truly remarkable, others are really rather lame – the **Trois Fromages** ("Three Cheeses"), for example, merely comprises a group of three roundish boulders set on top of each other. South of these groups lies the **Peyro Clabado**, an 800-tonne boulder perched on a smaller stone, and the **Rochers de Sept-Faux**, "logan stones" – two giant rocks balanced in such a way that the upper one, 900 tonnes in mass, can be rocked simply by pushing on it. The wooded paths leading to the sites are well maintained and make for pleasant walking, although on weekends they're crowded with families. Bring sufficient water or be prepared to pay over the odds at the cafés and drinks stands near the trails. To explore the region by foot or bicycle, pick up the free *Les Circuits du Tarn* brochure at the tourist office in Castres or at the Maison du Sidobre, which provides detailed descriptions of routes.

ARRIVAL AND DEPARTURE
CASTRES AND AROUND

By train Castres' *gare SNCF* is at av Albert 1er, a 25min walk west of the old town (bus #2; free).

Destinations Albi (several daily; 2hr); Lavaur (several daily; 55min); Mazamet (several daily; 17–40min); Toulouse (several daily; 1hr 25).

By bus The *gare routière* is on place Soult on the far eastern edge of the centre. Libellus (w libellus.org) runs a free bus #10 from Castres to Mazamet several times a day.

Destinations Béziers (two daily at weekends in July & Aug; 2hr 15min); Dourgne (several daily; 25min);

Gaillac (several daily; 1hr); Lacaune (several daily; 1hr); Lautrec (several daily; 25min); Lavaur (several daily; 50min); Mazamet (several daily; 30min); Revel (daily; 45min); St-Amans-Soult (several daily; 40min); St-Pons (several daily; 1hr); Sorèze (several daily; 35min); Toulouse (several daily; 1hr 40min).

By car For those driving, parking on the street in old Castres is possible, but check the signs carefully: between the market days and street-cleaning schedule, you could easily get your car towed away.

GETTING AROUND

By bike MBK Faury, 6 bd Docteurs Sicard, Castres (t 05 63 59 23 55). Rents bikes from €10 per half-day.

By taxi t 05 63 59 99 25 or 05 81 12 71 27.

By car Rental agencies include the following: Ada,

10 rue de Mélou (t 05 63 51 10 26; Europcar, 67 rue Maillot (t 05 63 72 24 69; Hertz, rte de Mazamet (t 05 63 72 82 21; U-Location, Super-U, av Georges Pompidou (t 05 63 62 52 85.

INFORMATION AND ACTIVITIES

Tourist information 2 place de la République, to the east of the Musée Goya (July & Aug Mon–Sat 9.30am–6.30pm, Sun 10.30am–noon & 2.30–5pm; Sept–June Mon–Sat 9.30am–12.30pm & 2–6pm, Sun 2.30–4.30pm; t 05 63 62 63 62, w tourisme-castres.fr).

Discount card The Passe tourisme en ville (€6.50), valid for one month, gives free admission to the Musée Goya and Musée Jean-Jaurès and also discounts on sporting and cultural activities as well as one hour's free parking. You can buy one at the tourist office.

Maison du Sidobre Vialavert, Le Bez (t 05 63 74 63 38, w sidobre.tourisme-tarn). From Castres, follow the

D622 towards Brassac (20min) to this information centre where you'll find everything you need to know to explore France's largest granite-mining region.

Boat trips The *Miredames* riverboat leaves from the pier by the Pont Vieux on the east side of the river (May–Sept daily from noon; €6 return, €3.50 single; t 05 63 62 41 75) and travels to the Parc de la Gourjade. You can either do a 50min round trip or get off at the park and visit the archeology research centre (Mon–Sat 2–6pm; free), see the miniature rail network (Sat pm) or head to the Archipel swimming pool (daily; €4.30; w larchipel.fr).

ACCOMMODATION

Camping de Gourjade Av de Roquecourbe, Castres (t 05 63 59 33 51, w campingdegourjade.net. Nice three-star riverside campsite in the park of the same name, benefiting from all the activities (golf, archery, horseriding) the latter has to offer. As well as shady pitches, there are mobile homes and tents as well as a pool and a bar-restaurant. Open April to Sept. **€16**

Camping Le Plo Le Bez, Sidobre (t 05 63 74 00 82, w www.camping-leplo.fr. Family-friendly three-star campsite in a quiet, elevated rural location near the village of Le Bez. Just 62 pitches but also a pool and a kids' play area. You can rent bikes here. Open May to Sept. **€25**

Ecosweet 29 rue Jean Soutérène, Castres (t 05 63 35 40 00, w hotel-ecosweet.com. This shiny and new two-

star hotel might be situated 3km east of town on the D612 but it offers spacious, comfortable rooms, free secure parking and a good restaurant serving traditional French food. **€54**

★**Le Miredames** 1 Place Roger Salengro, Castres (t 05 63 71 38 18, w hotel-le-miredames.com. This three-star hotel on the east side of the river has recently been redecorated in contemporary style; some rooms overlook the river. A wine bar-cum-tearoom serving drinks, snacks and artisanal ice cream opened in 2016. **€80**

Le Relais du Sidobre 8 rte de Vabre, Lacrouzette (t 05 63 59 11 68, w relaisdusidobre.jimdo.com. In the "capital" of the Sidobre, this good-value hotel offers contemporary accommodation as well as a restaurant (Fri eve, Sat & Sun) featuring a wide selection of traditional French dishes. Nice views over the hills from the terrace. €47

Renaissance 17 rue Victor Hugo, Castres ☎ 05 63 59 30 42, ⊛ hotel-renaissance.fr. Kitsch-but-charming

four-star hotel in an attractive seventeenth-centur townhouse in the old town. Rooms are individuall decorated in a variety of periods and styles, reflecting th owners' travels. Parking available (charge). €78

EATING

Auberge du Tilleul Guyor Haut, Le Bez ☎ 05 63 74 01 84, ⊛ auberge-tilleul.com. Charming, fifth-generation *auberge* in the heart of the Sidobre, where *poule au pot* (chicken stew) is the speciality, served the first Sun of the month. *Menus* are from €14 and they also have three unremarkable rooms to rent (€42). Daily noon–2pm.

Bistrot Saveurs 55 rue Ste-Foy, Castres ☎ 05 63 50 11 45, ⊛ bistrotsaveurs.com. The best restaurant in town is run by a Brit, Simon Scott, who has worked at the Ritz and the Savoy in London. Contemporary international cuisine using products from small, local, (mainly) organic farmers is the name of the game here. *Menus* €26–85. Mon–Fri noon–1.30pm & 7.30–9.15pm.

Le Café de Paris 8 Place de l'Hôtel de Ville, Brassac ☎ 05 63 74 00 31. On the east side of the Sidobre, this village restaurant, whose chef has worked in some of the world's top hotels, serves traditional French dishes such as beef with shallots. Weekday lunch *menus* €14 and dinner €27. Also has seven rooms (€65). Tues–Sun noon–2pm, Fri & Sat 7–9pm.

★**Le Cercle** 52 rue Émile Zola, Castres ☎ 09 80 78 10

44, ⊛ lecercle81.com. In the chic, contemporary dinin room, Xavier Bories serves semi-*gastronomique* versions o traditional French dishes such as *daube* (beef stew) wit polenta. The *café gourmand*, coffee with three mir desserts, is an excellent choice to finish. Three-cours weekday lunch from €15.50. Mon 7.30–9.30pm, Tues & Sun noon–1.30pm, Thurs & Fri noon–1.30pm & 7.30– 9.30pm, Sat 7.30–9.30pm.

Comme à la Maison 5 rue de Brettes, Castres ☎ 05 6 51 96 25, ⊛ arthome-saveurs.com. As well as offerin organic traditional French dishes, this small restaurar caters for vegetarians. There's a nice terrace in summer an *formules* are around €10. Cookery lessons are available Tues, Wed & Sat 9am–4pm, Thurs 9am–4pm & 7–10pm, Fri 9am–9pm.

Resto des Halles Place Pierre Fabre ☎ 05 63 62 70 70 On the first floor of the covered market, this is the place fo carnivores, as grilled meats reign supreme. A livel atmosphere and good value with lunch *formules* from €13 Mon noon–2.30pm, Tues–Sat noon–2.30pm & 7.30–11pm.

DRINKING AND NIGHTLIFE

Le Quartier Latin 6 Place Soult, Castres ☎ 05 63 51 11 75, ⊛ barquartierlatin.com. Lively industrial-style cocktail and tapas bar on the east side of the river. Wed–Sat 6pm–2am.

The Quay 23 rue Frédéric Thomas, Castres ☎ 05 63 7 91 80. Bright blue Irish pub serving Guinness and Scotc whiskies. There are weekly events, live music and karaoke They also screen rugby matches. Daily 4pm–2am.

DIRECTORY

Hospital Centre Hospitalier Intercommunal Castres-Mazamet, 6 av de la Montagne Noire (☎ 05 63 71 63 71, ⊛ chic-cm.fr). Six kilometres southeast of the centre. Served by bus #10 (free).

Pharmacy Pharmacie Pierre Fabre, 2 rue Victor Hugo

(☎ 05 63 72 65 50). Tues–Fri 8.30am–7.30pm, Sa 8am–7pm.

Police 2 av Charles de Gaulle ☎ 17 or 05 63 71 58 55.

Laundry Lav-Eco, 45 av Lieut Jacques Desplats. Dail 8am–8pm.

Parc Naturel Régional du Haut Languedoc

The southeastern half of the *département* of Tarn is dominated by the mountain-ridged highlands of Upper Languedoc. In this region of isolated hamlets the scant population has traditionally subsisted on herding and agriculture, supplemented nowadays by a growing outdoor recreation industry. The zone is dominated by the sprawling and imprecisely bounded **Parc Naturel Régional du Haut Languedoc**, which over the forty years or so since its establishment has been expanding almost yearly. Its designation as a park is primarily administrative, which can lead to confusion – the boundaries aren't well marked, and there's no change in the landscape or villages which distinguish it from the surrounding area. Essentially, it is defined by the mountains which cross it: the **Monts de Lacaune** in the north, the **Monts de**

'Espinouse to the east, and the north face of the **Montagne Noire** range (see p.157), tacked onto the park's southwest.

INFORMATION   **PARC NATUREL RÉGIONAL DU HAUT LANGUEDOC**

Public transport across the park is poor, but it serves hikers and cyclists well, crisscrossed by a network of paths, notably the Gijou Valley Railway Trail (see box below) and the Passa Païs (see box, p.156). Detailed park **information** can be obtained at the Maison du Parc office (see p.156) in St-Pons, the "capital" of the park.

Lacaune-les-Bains

On the northern edge of the park, slate-roofed **LACAUNE-LES-BAINS** lies east from Castres, at a distance of either 67km along the tortuous Agout and Gijou valley road, or 46km along the mountainous route, which passes through Brassac. At 885m, this lively little village sits just below the source of the Gijou river in the **Monts de Lacaune**, whose sheep are the exclusive source of milk for the famous blue cheese of Roquefort. The town was a curative spa (specializing in urinary tract ailments) in the Middle Ages, a role commemorated by a fourteenth-century iron **fountain** in the town centre known as "Les Pisseurs", featuring four tiny but impressively endowed male figures peeing into a pool below. They still have a spa here, the **Espace des Sources Chaudes** (year round; €7.30; ☎05 63 37 69 90, ⓦpiscine-lacaune.jimdo.com).

3

THE GIJOU VALLEY RAILWAY TRAIL

Half a century ago locomotives still threaded the tortuously meandering Agout and Gijou valleys, steaming up the cliff-hanging **narrow-gauge railway** connecting Castres with Vabre and Lacaune to the east, and branching off to Brassac to the south, 16km up the Agout valley. The trains have long disappeared, but the rail-bed is now an excellent **hiking and mountain-biking** trail – a route best travelled from Lacaune westwards for the simple reason that it's downhill. This defunct railway winds along steep and forested banks, dramatically crossing the riverbed on ancient trestle bridges and only rarely passing tiny hamlets of slate-shingled houses and solitary farmsteads.

THE ROUTE

Leaving Lacaune, the trail arrives at tiny **Gijounet** after a couple of hours' walk, just after a small waterfall. Continuing along for 5km, it skirts the slightly larger **Viane**, with a ruined *château* perched above, and then at **Lacaze**, several hours beyond, a medieval bridge spans the river, beside a once-stately fifteenth-century mansion. Here you'll find the Maison de la Vallée du Gijou (Ponts de Sénégas; ☎05 63 74 54 05), with all the information you need to explore this part of the world. From this point the river gains force and begins to wind erratically through the cliffs girding it; 15km now remain to **Vabre**, a larger town with a twelfth-century bridge. The distance from Lacaze to Vabre is 40km, which will take around **eleven hours on foot**.

At Vabre, the mainline converges with a spur coming from **Brassac**. A few kilometres after Vabre, the Gijou empties into the Agout, and the rail line continues to **Roquecourbe**, threading the gorges which mark the northern limit of the Sidobre; from here the D89 can be followed for 8km to Castres. Alternatively, 3km out of Roquecourbe, take the tarmac road towards Le Carla generating station to regain the river and follow it to Castres via **Burlats** (adding 12km to the route). The Topoguide *Le Tarn…à pied* details the trail with accompanying **maps**.

REST AND REFUELLING

There are few opportunities to pick up **supplies** en route – Lacaze, with a store and café, is the first good spot to refuel. For those planning on making the journey over a night or two, each of the villages along the line has a very basic **campsite**. Vabre has a number of services, including a Thursday-morning **market**, while the best reward for hungry walkers (or drivers) is the **restaurant**, *La Chaumière* (14 allée Généra-de-Gaulle; ☎05 63 75 60 88), in Roquecourbe, featuring superb *terroir* meals (from about €13) and Gaillac wines.

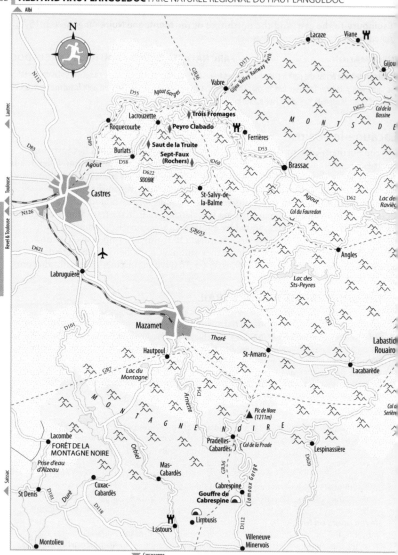

Beside the fountain, in place du Griffoul, is the **Musée du Vieux Lacaune** (May, June & Sept Tues–Sat 3–6pm; July & Aug daily 10.30am–12.30pm & 2–6pm; €2 inc audioguide; ☎05 63 37 25 38, ⊛museeduvieuxlacaune.fr), which offers a look at the town's history from the eighteenth century to 1940 via room reconstitutions. In a similar vein, on rue Rhin et Danube, the **Filature Ramond** is a wool workshop from the nineteenth century, where you can watch various old tools and machines in use (mid-June to mid-Sept 3pm; €2; ☎05 63 37 04 98). The town is also renowned for its pork products and you can find out about the industry – and taste the charcuterie – at **La Maison de la Charcuterie** (3 rue Biarnès; mid-June to mid-Sept Mon 2.30– 6pm, Tues–Sat 11am–1pm & 2.30–6pm; €3; ☎05 63 37 37 46 31). It's also

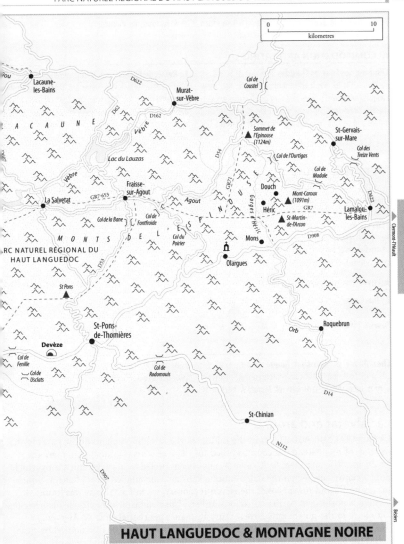

HAUT LANGUEDOC & MONTAGNE NOIRE

worthwhile taking in the Sunday-morning **market** or the larger regional **fair** held on the third Saturday of each month.

ARRIVAL AND INFORMATION   LACAUNE-LES-BAINS

The town has good bus connections, but the best way to explore the area is on foot or by bike along the Gijou Valley Trail, a disused narrow-gauge railway line heading west towards Castres (see p.145).

By bus Buses stop at place de la République.
Destinations Albi (one daily; 1hr); Le Bez (several daily; 30min); Castres (several daily; 1hr 10min).

Tourist information Place du Général-de-Gaulle (mid-June to mid-Sept Mon–Fri 9am–12.30pm & 2–6.30pm, Sat 10am–noon & 2–6.30pm, Sun

10am–noon; mid-Sept to mid-June Tues–Fri 9am–noon & 2–5pm, Sat 10am–noon & 2–5pm; ☏ 05 63 37 04 98, ⓦ www.tourisme-montsdelacaune.com). They rent out bikes.

ACCOMMODATION AND EATING

Camping des Sources Chaudes Domaine de St-Michel ☏ 05 63 37 22 39, ⓦ campinglacaune.fr. Nice new campsite with both pitches and very comfortable wooden chalets. Good facilities including a kids' playground and indoor and outdoor pools filled with water from the hot springs. **€15**

Le Relais de Fusiès 2 rue de la République ☏ 05 63 37 02 03, ⓦ hotelfusies.fr. There are thirty comfortable, renovated rooms in this three-star *Logis de France* hotel dating from 1902. The good *terroir* restaurant is housed in an attractive Art Nouveau dining room. There is also a pool and free public parking. **€75**

Murat-sur-Vèbre

Twenty-six kilometres east of Lacaune lies **MURAT-SUR-VÈBRE**, an ancient hamlet bisected by a tributary of the Vèbre, which undoubtedly saw its heaviest traffic passing through when it was a way-stop on the pilgrim route to Santiago. Hikers who want to relive a bit of the Middle Ages can follow the Chemin de St-Jacques (now the GR653; see box, p.189) east to Castres. The main attractions in the area are the mysterious **standing stones**, dating back to 3500 BC; you can find out about them in the Musée des Mégalithes (part of the tourist office; €3) and pick up a route map.

ARRIVAL AND INFORMATION   MURAT-SUR-VÈBRE

By bus Castres (one daily; 1hr 30min); Lacaune (one daily; 20min).
Tourist information Place de la Mairie (July & Aug

Mon–Fri 9.15am–12.15pm & 3–6pm, Sat 9.15am–12.15pm; Sept–June Mon–Sat 9.15am–12.15pm; ☏ 05 63 37 47 47, ⓦ tourisme-montsdelacaune.com).

ACCOMMODATION

Chez André et Christian Roque Félines ☏ 05 63 37 43 17. Four simple-but-comfortable en-suite rooms on a goat farm, 5min northwest of Murat. A kitchen is

available for guests and you might want to try their home-made goats' cheese. **€45**

La Salvetat and around

LA SALVETAT-SUR-AGOUT, set in the middle of the rambling upland of the park, forms the hub of the **Plateau des Lacs**, so called for the reservoirs that now punctuate the landscape. The attractive little town has not been spoiled by the souvenir shops which dot its centre, and when the daily hubbub subsides, the tangled knot of streets which makes up the old town evokes the eleventh century, when La Salvetat was founded.

There is nothing in particular to look at here, but two historical relics lie just over one kilometre to the north: a twelfth-century Romanesque **chapel** (July & Aug daily 3–7pm), which contains a "black Virgin"– a Romanesque statue discoloured by time – and the stone bridge next to it, used by medieval pilgrims en route to Santiago. There are **markets** on Thursday and Sunday mornings. The town is a short walk from the 12km-long **Lac de la Raviège**, 3.5km west, which has been extensively developed as a holiday spot – here you'll find **beaches**, and plenty of **canoe**, **sail** and **motorboat** rental outlets.

ARRIVAL AND INFORMATION   LA SALVETAT-SUR-AGOUT

By bus Béziers (daily; 55min); St-Pons (daily; 40min).
Tourist information Place des Archers (July & Aug Mon–Fri 9am–1pm & 2–7pm, Sat 10am–12.30pm & 3–6pm, Sun 10am–12.30pm; Sept–June closed Sun; ☏ 04 67 97 64 44, ⓦ www.salvetat-tourisme.fr). Those wishing to explore the surrounding area on foot can

purchase a booklet (€1) with twelve well-laid-out *petites randonnées*.
Bike and boat rental Loca-Surf Loisirs, Les Bouldouïres, Lac de la Raviège (☏ 06 74 57 38 34, ⓦ www.loca-surf -loisirs.com). Canoes, pedalos, motorboats and mountain bikes for rent and boat trips.

ACCOMMODATION AND EATING

Camping Les Bouldouïres Lac de la Ravière ☎ 04 67 97 36 91, ⓦ campingbouldouires.fr. Set back from the lake, this three-star campsite, around 2km to the west of town along the D14E3, has around a hundred pitches and mobile homes as well as a kids' play area and snack bar. There are plenty of activities within walking distance, including tennis and fishing. Open April to Oct. €15

La Plage Lac de la Ravière ☎ 04 67 97 69 87, ⓦ pageloisirs.com/hotel-la-plage. Good-value two-star *Logis de France* hotel with twelve comfortable rooms in an unremarkable modern building about 3km west of town along the D14E3. Excellent regional cuisine, including local charcuterie and fish from the lake, is on the menu (from €14) in the rustic restaurant. €59

Fraïsse-sur-Agout

East of La Salvetat, **FRAÏSSE-SUR-AGOUT** is set at a hilly crossroads only 2km south of **Lac de Lauzas** as the crow flies, though the winding road which crosses the intervening hills clocks in at nearly 10km. This flower-bedecked mountain hamlet has become rather touristy in summer, but still retains its bucolic air, thanks to its diminutive size and the isolated beauty of its surroundings.

3

INFORMATION
FRAÏSSE-SUR-AGOUT

Tourist information Allée des Cerisiers (daily: March–May, Oct & Nov 10am–noon & 2–5pm; June & Sept 9.30am–12.30pm & 2–5pm; July & Aug 9.30am–12.30pm & 2–6.30pm; ☎ 04 67 97 53 81, ⓦ ot-espinouse.fr). Enquire about the many walking trails in the area and also the possibility of donkey-accompanied outings.

ACCOMMODATION AND EATING

Auberge de l'Espinouse Allée des Frênes ☎ 04 67 95 40 46, ⓦ aubergeespinouse.fr. Comfortable, modern two-star *Logis de France* hotel with rooms and *gîtes* on offer. Pork and pizza are the specialities here; you can enjoy

them by the open fire in winter or on the terrace in summer. There's an all-you-can-eat buffet on Sunday lunchtimes for €30. Free parking. €69

St-Pons-de-Thomières

Deep in the folds of the Jaur valley, 35km due east on the N112 from Mazamet, sits **ST-PONS-DE-THOMIÈRES**, separated from the Plateau des Lacs to the north by a high ridge, the western spur of the Monts de l'Espinouse (see p.156). The park's principal information centre, it is also a transport hub, with two main **bus** routes (Béziers–La Salvetat and Castres–Montpellier) intersecting here. This ancient town's curious compound name originates with local count Raymond Pons, who founded a monastery (hence, the "St" part of the name) across the river, north of the hamlet of Thomières in 936.

The old town

St-Pons' **old town** is worth a walk around – at the edge of it, on the north side of the modern road, is poised the twelfth-century **cathedral** (enquire at the tourist office about visits) with its incongruous, slapped-on eighteenth-century façade, around the back of which you can still see the statues on the medieval tympana, faces chipped off by iconoclastic Huguenots in the sixteenth century. The **organ** is reputedly the best in France after Notre-Dame in Paris. The bulk of the old town, however, lies south of the main road on both sides of the Jaur, which is crossed by a medieval **bridge**. The **market** is on Wednesday mornings.

Musée de Préhistoire Régionale

8 Grand'Rue • June & Sept Wed–Fri 10am–noon & 3–6pm, Sat & Sun 3–6pm; July & Aug Tues–Sun 10am–noon & 3–6pm • €3.50 • ☎ 04 67 97 22 61

The new **Musée de Préhistoire Régionale**, housed in a medieval building opposite the cathedral, has an interesting display on the area's *menhirs* (standing stones), which date back to 3500 BC, as well as an exhibition of local Flintstonian relics from the Jaur cave. There's also a video on the daily life of prehistoric man.

Grotte de la Devèze

Around 5km southwest of St-Pons on the D612 • July & Aug daily 11.30am–6pm; enquire for rest of year • €8.50 • ☎ 04 67 97 03 24, ⓦ grottedeladeveze.fr

Cave fans will want to explore **Grotte de la Devèze** and its **Espace Découverte du Milieu Souterrain** ("Underground World Discovery Centre"). Discovered in 1886 by workers building the train line to Mazamet, the cave contains various delicate rock forms, including an impressive stone cascade and several calcite "draperies". The one-hour guided tour takes visitors 35m underground. Back up, take a look around the **exhibition** on speleology.

ARRIVAL AND INFORMATION   **ST-PONS-DE-THOMIÈRES**

By bus Buses stop by the tourist office.

Destinations Béziers (several daily; 1hr 15min); Castres via Mazamet (several daily; 1hr); La Salvetat (daily; 40min); Montpellier via Olargues, Lamalou-les-Bains, Hérépian, Bédarieux and Clermont-l'Hérault (daily; 2hr 35min).

Tourist information 2 Place du Foirail (Tues–Sat 9am–12.30pm & 2–5.30pm, daily in July & Aug; ☎ 04 67 97 06 65, ⓦ www.ot-pays-saint-ponais.fr. Also houses the information office for the park, the Maison du Parc (Mon–Fri 8.30am–12.30pm & 2–5pm; ☎ 04 67 97 38 22, ⓦ www.parc-haut-languedoc.fr).

ACCOMMODATION AND EATING

Les Cerisiers du Jaur Rte de Bédarieux ☎ 04 67 95 30 33, ⓦ cerisierdujaur.com. One of the main attractions at this rural campsite is its nice sandy river beach. As well as pitches, there are gipsy caravans and wooden chalets. Bikes can be rented to work off the wine (twice-weekly tastings in summer). **€29**

Le Somail 2 av de Castres ☎ 04 67 97 00 12, ⓦ hotel -restaurant-lesomail.com. The rooms are pretty basic and OK for a stopover (€25) but the restaurant is a good option with lunch *menus* from €13.50. Specialities include charcuterie, gourmet burgers and baked Camembert. Daily noon–2pm & 7–9pm.

Olargues

From St-Pons, the River Jaur snakes northeast, skirting the **Monts de l'Espinouse** that loom over the north bank, to arrive at **OLARGUES** – one of the Plus Beaux Villages de France (see p.46). Approached from the west, this hamlet presents an impressive vista: a high and gracefully arched medieval **bridge** backed by the steep hill where its castle once stood. From a covered staircase just west of the parking area along the main street, a ten-minute climb through the steep medieval alleys leads up to the lonely **clock tower**, the only remaining vestige of the eleventh-century fortress. Nearby, the Romanesque **priory** of St-Julien makes a good hike or a short drive, its shady wooded surroundings providing a great picnic spot and wonderful **views** of the Jaur valley; take the Bédarieux road east for 2.5km and climb steeply on the left up the narrow signposted road a further 1500m.

The Monts de l'Espinouse

Olargues is a natural place to begin a circuit of the **Monts de l'Espinouse**, an area whose isolated beauty is preserved in part by its inaccessibility; there's no public

---

THE PASSA PAÏS RAILWAY TRAIL

Completed in 2013, the 76km *voie verte* (green route) called the "**Passa Païs**" allows walkers, cyclists and horse riders to cross the *départements* of Tarn and Hérault from Mazamet to Bédarieux. The trail passes through Labastide-Rouairoux (see p.158), St-Pons (see p.155), Olargues (see above), Mons-la-Trivalle (see opposite), Lamalou-les-Bains (see p.268) and Hérépian (see p.268). Starting on the flat in the Thoré valley, the trail rises into the forest and goes through the tunnel in the Col de la Fenille before following the Jaur valley, from where there are wonderful views. You can pick up a **map** in one of the tourist offices.

transport here. From the village, the D14 switchbacks steeply up past slate-covered hamlets clinging to near-perpendicular slopes until you reach the central pass of the **Col de Fontfroide** (971m). Here, **trails** (including the main GR7-71) crisscross the barren hillsides, and a sombre **monument** commemorates the German occupation. To the east on the lonely D53 the forest gets thicker (a picnicker's paradise) as you approach the 1124m **summit** (sommet de l'Espinouse). A few kilometres later, rounding the **Col de l'Ourtigas**, the country opens up dramatically into a series of broad gorges, the vibrant green landscape contrasting with dull grey rock. Continuing for 4km, you come to the turn-off for **Douch**, after which the road descends to **Lamalou-les-Bains**. Douch is a good place to pick up the GR7 trail to reach either **Mont Caroux** (1091m; 2hr round trip) or the **Gorges d'Héric**, which you access via the tiny stone hamlet of Héric, 2km west of Douch. The deep and narrow gully of sparkling red granite shaded by thickly covering oak descends rapidly to the River Orb, 6km below, and the beauty of the gorge accounts for its popularity with day-trippers. Easier access to the trails of the gorge is found at **Mons La Trivalle**, just off the main St-Pons–Bédarieux highway.

3

INFORMATION
OLARGUES

Tourist information Av de la Gare (July & Aug Mon–Sat 9am–1pm & 3.30–7pm, Sun 9am–1pm; Sept Mon–Sat 9am–1pm & 2–6pm; Oct–June Tues–Sat 9am–1pm & 2–6pm; ☎ 04 67 23 02 21, ⓦ www.ot-caroux.fr).

Bike rental Oxygène, chemin de Coulayro (☎ 04 67 97 87 00 or 06 84 39 16 35).

ACCOMMODATION

Camping Les Baous Chemin du Baous ☎ 04 67 97 71 50, ⓦ campingolargues.com. Basic two-star municipal camping ground in a lovely location next to the river. There's a tennis court and electric bikes for rent. Open May to August. **€12**

Laissac-Speiser Av de la Gare ☎ 04 67 97 70 89, ⓦ restaurant-laissac.fr. Old-fashioned French village hotel run by the same family for five generations. Nine basic rooms and a bright restaurant serving good *terroir* cuisine including trout and *cèpes* (mushrooms). Open Easter to Oct. **€44**

Les Quatr'Farceurs Rue de la Comporte ☎ 04 67 97 81 33, ⓦ olargues.net. Two comfortable rooms in an attractive old village house where *table d'hôte* is available (€25, vegetarian options). The owners also have three *gîtes* to rent. **€59.50**

Manoir La Trivalle Rte des Gorges d'Héric, Mons La Trivalle ☎ 04 67 97 85 56, ⓦ monslatrivalle.com. B&B or *gîte* accommodation in a traditional house with a garden and a pool – and lovely views. *Table d'hôte* is available (€22). **€65**

The Montagne Noire

The highlands of Haut Languedoc are bounded on their southwest side by the deep valley of the River Thoré, which empties into the Agout just west of Castres. A separate massif, the **MONTAGNE NOIRE** stretches in a narrow 50km band along the south side of the river course and westwards to Revel (see p.75), its highest peak, the **Pic de Nore** (1211m), located more or less at the centre of the range.

The two sides of the Montagne Noire present a stark contrast: the north face, which has been incorporated into the Parc Naturel Régional du Haut Languedoc, is thickly covered in a mixed forest of oak, beech and spruce, while the south presents a scrubby Mediterranean landscape of brush and vine. This whole district has traditionally been even poorer and more isolated than Haut Languedoc proper: near-subsistence farming and herding continue to be the only activities through most of the zone now that the mining of Salsigne and cloth industry of **Mazamet**, which boomed in the nineteenth century, have been reduced to relics. The Montagne Noire's chief attraction is its **isolated wilderness**, and you'll find that the outdoor facilities that have sprung up in the main park are lacking here. South of Mazamet, the ruin of medieval **Hautpoul** is a popular stop.

Mazamet and around

Lying 17km southeast of Castres, lacklustre **MAZAMET** is an old industrial town whose single sight is the **Musée du Catharisme** (April–June, Sept & Oct Tues–Sat 10am–noon & 2–5pm; July & Aug Mon–Sat 10am–noon & 2–6pm, Sun 2.30–6.30pm; Nov–March Wed & Sat 10am–noon & 2–5pm; €3; ☏05 63 61 56 56) in the old Fuzier family mansion in rue de Casernes, which also houses the tourist office. It's a small but interesting exhibition tracing the tragic history of the Cathars via original documents, short films and a reconstruction of a traditional room. The models of Cathar châteaux are especially good.

Hautpoul

More interesting than Mazamet is **Hautpoul**, a Cathar redoubt with a ruined castle perched on a hillside, which was all but levelled by the unstoppable de Montfort in 1212. The trip up to the village follows the serpentine **Route des Usines**, climbing the course of the Arnette river, where windowless relics of hulking nineteenth-century factories lurk at every hairpin. Like many similar ancient villages, Hautpoul has been colonized by artisans; here they specialize in wooden objects. The **Maison du Bois et du Jouet** (Moulin de l'Oule; June, Sept & Oct daily 2–6pm; July & Aug daily 2–7pm; Nov–May Tues–Sun 2–6pm; €6; ☏05 63 61 42 70), down by the river, is a good place to go with kids. It has an exhibition on wood and its uses as well as wooden toys and a games/play room. Heading east along the D87 for 15km will take you up to the **Pic de Nore**, the Montagne Noire's highest point (1211m).

ARRIVAL AND INFORMATION   MAZAMET AND AROUND

By train Mazamet's *gare SNCF* is in the north of the town on av Charles Sabatié.

Destinations Castres (several daily; 20–40min); Lavaur (several daily; 50min–1hr 30min); Toulouse (several daily; 1hr 30min).

By bus Libellus (☉libellus.org) runs a free bus #10 from Mazamet to Castres several times a day.

Destinations Castres (several daily; 30min); St-Pons (several daily; 35min); Toulouse (several daily; 2hr 10min).

Tourist information Rue des Casernes (April–June, Sept & Oct Mon–Sat 10am–noon & 2–6pm; July & Aug Mon–Sat 9.30am–noon & 2–6pm, Sun 2.30–6.30pm; Nov–March Mon–Wed & Fri–Sat 10am–noon & 2–6pm; ☏05 63 61 27 07, ☉tourisme-mazamet.com).

ACCOMMODATION AND EATING

Camping de la Lauze Chemin de la Lauze ☏05 63 61 24 69, ☉camping-mazamet.com. Three-star municipal campsite in an attractive green space on the edge of town, next to the *voie verte* and near the public pool and tennis courts (free access in July & Aug). Open May to Sept. **€16**

Le Grand Balcon Square Gaston Tournier ☏05 63 61 01 02, ☉restaurant-grand-balcon.com. Previous diners including Généra de Gaulle, Yves Montand and Jacques Brel wouldn't recognize this popular brasserie since its modern makeover, but they could still rely on good traditional French food. Lunch *menus* from €9.90. Mon–Sat noon–3pm & 7pm–midnight, Sun noon–3pm.

Les Jardins de Mazamet 6 rue Henri Gardet ☏05 63 61 26 97, ☉jardinsdemazamet.fr. Luxury B&B in an elegant nineteenth-century *hôtel particulier* with four

stylish rooms as well as a pool and a fitness room. Massages and *table d'hôte* (€30) are available. **€95**

Mets et Plaisirs 7 av Albert Rouvière ☏05 63 61 56 93, ☉metsetplaisirs.wixsite.com. The eleven rooms are perfectly adequate (€56) but the restaurant stands out for its good regional cuisine, such as ravioli with *cèpes*, and variety of local wines. Three-course weekday lunch *menu* €20. Tues–Sat noon–1.30pm & 7.30–9.30pm, Sun noon–1.30pm.

La Taverne d'Hautpoul Hautpoul ☏05 63 97 00 86, ☉restaurant-portugais-tarn.com. This Portuguese restaurant is a welcome sight if you've hiked up to the Cathar village. Traditional French dishes and Portuguese specialities are on the menu (lunch €15), as are stunning views. They also organize *fado* evenings. May–Oct daily 10am–11pm.

Labastide-Rouairoux

Climbing east from Mazamet, the **Thoré valley** still maintains its long-established role as a transport link between Castres and the Mediterranean coastlands, now the N112. About twenty minutes east of Mazamet you reach **LABASTIDE-ROUAIROUX**, a ondescript town famous for its textile production; Chanel and Dior used to buy textiles here. You can find out all about the industry at the **Musée départemental du Textile** (rue de la Rive; mid-Feb to April & Nov to mid-Dec Tues–Sun 2–5pm; May, June, Sept & Oct daily 2–6pm; July & Aug daily 10am–noon & 2–6.30pm; €5; ☎05 63 98 08 60, ⟲musee-textile.tarn.fr), housed in a nineteenth-century factory. The well-planned exhibition takes visitors on a tour of how materials are made and includes examples of finished garments including haute couture. There are also very good temporary exhibitions, on themes such as the development of Japanese kimonos.

ARRIVAL AND INFORMATION

By bus Castres (several daily; 45min); Mazamet (several daily; 25min); St-Pons (several daily; 10min).

Tourist information Bd Carnot (Mon–Sat 10am–noon

LABASTIDE-ROUAIROUX

& 2–6pm; ☎05 63 98 07 58, ⟲www.tourisme-hautevalleeduthore.com).

EATING

★**La Voie Gourmande** 67 av de la Méditerranée, St-Amans-Soult ☎05 63 61 34 87, ⟲www.lavoie gourmande.fr. This unassuming little restaurant with a terrace, off the main road and on the *voie verte* 13km east of Labastide, is recommended for its home-made regional

dishes. The "Menu Tarnais" (€24) features pigs' trotters fried with pink garlic from Lautrec, cassoulet and local cheeses. Tues & Wed noon–1.30pm, Thurs & Fri noon–1.30pm & 7–9pm, Sat 7–9pm.

SHOPPING

Les Toiles de la Montagne Noire 8 rue Gambetta, Labastide-Rouairoux ☎05 63 50 30 13, ⟲lestoilesdela montagnenoire.com. Traditionally made local textiles in

the form of tea towels, tablecloths, bags, dressing gowns and more. They also have shops outside Mazamet and Albi. March–Oct Tues–Sat 10am–6.30pm.

Across the Montagne Noire

If you're heading towards Carcassonne from Mazamet, and you have your own transport, the most direct route is to take the D118. Turning left/east on to the D101 at Les Martys, you travel via the **Orbiel valley**, and further south, the **castles at Lastours**. As you descend the valley, the blanket of iridescent green forest threatens to swallow the steep and narrow stone-buttressed road, and the hairpin curves make the 11km to the attractive village of Mas-Cabardès seem at least twice as long as it should. Driving here is an effort, however, which the scenery makes worthwhile.

The Châteaux de Lastours and around

Daily: April–June & Sept 10am–6pm; July & Aug 9am–8pm; Oct 10am–5pm; see website for winter times • €7 • ☎04 68 77 56 02, ⟲chateauxdelastours.com

Onwards from Mas-Cabardès, the road bends sharply as you approach Lastours. On the right you'll see the old textile mill which serves as the entrance to the grounds of the **Châteaux de Lastours**. A cluster of four separate forts, perched dramatically on the points of the rocky hill dominating the river-bend, these are the northernmost of the Cathar castles, although in fact only two of them, eleventh-century Cabaret and twelfth-century Surdespines, date from the era of the Crusade. Two more castles were built in the fourteenth century. A path climbs the steep and scrubby hill, and leads from one small castle to the next – an exhilarating walk which takes about two hours. The châteaux are quite ruined, and really their location is more evocative than their remains, so if you don't want to climb, you can drive to the look-out point, **Le Belvédère de Montfermier** (same hours and ticket; access just to look-out point €2), set on a ridge to the west, which affords the best perspectives.

Limousis caves

Daily tours March & Oct 2.30–4.30pm; April–June & Sept 10.30–11.30am & 2.30–5.30pm; July & Aug 10.15am–6pm · €10.30 ·
☎ 04 68 26 14 20, ⊛ grotte-de-limousis.com

Before continuing south, take the 5km detour on the D111 to **Limousis**, whose **cave complex** boasts impressive calcite formations, including the largest known cluster of the crystalline mineral, aragonite. The lively English-speaking guides make the visit particularly enjoyable.

ACCOMMODATION AND EATING   THE CHÂTEAUX DE LASTOURS AND AROUND

L'Auberge du Diable au Thym 21 rte des Quatre-Châteaux ☎ 04 68 77 50 24, ⊛ lepuitsdutresor.fr. Housed in a former textile mill next to a river, this smart bistro serving market-inspired dishes is the more affordable version of Marc Boyer's *gastronomique* restaurant, *Le Puits du Trésor*, in the same building. *Menus* €18–27. July & Aug daily noon–2pm & 7.30–9.30pm,

Sept–June Wed–Sat noon–2pm & 7.30–9.30pm, Su noon–2pm.

Camping Le Belvédère 10 rte du Belvédère ☎ 09 6: 01 29 28, ⊛ campingdelastours.com. Small, eco-friendly campsite with pitches and wooden chalets in a stunning location overlooking the castles. Barbecue area an regional products available. €15

Saissac

By traversing the Montagne Noire and heading west along its lower slopes you'll arrive at **SAISSAC**, an ancient hamlet whose steeply sloping lanes lead downhill from the main road to a large ruined fortress looking out towards Carcassonne – the medieval walls and towers can be clearly made out in the distance. Although little remains of the fifteenth-century **castle** (Feb, March, Nov & Dec Sat, Sun & hols 10am–5pm; April–June & Sept daily 10am–6pm; July & Aug daily 9am–8pm; Oct daily 10am–5pm; €5; ☎ 04 68 24 46 01), which can be reached from the road in about ten minutes, the hollow ruin is evocative – and a great place for viewing sunsets. The only sight inside, in two restored rooms, is a display on the "treasure of Saissac", a hoard of thirteenth-century coins found in the area.

ARRIVAL AND INFORMATION   SAISSAC

By bus Carcassonne (several daily; 30min); Montolieu (several daily; 5min).
Tourist information Salle Lagarrigue, Place de la Mairie

(Mon–Fri 10am–1pm & 1.30–5.30pm; ☎ 04 68 76 64 90 ⊛ tourisme-montagnenoire.com).

ACCOMMODATION

Camping La Porte d'Autan Rue Boris Vian ☎ 04 68 76 36 08, ⊛ laportedautan.fr. Three-star campsite in a wooded location 5min to the west of town. There's a pool, a kids' playground and summer activities include a visit to a local farm. Open April to mid-Oct. €21
Domaine de Campras About 2km southeast of Saissac

off the D629 ☎ 04 68 78 48 20, ⊛ chambres-hotes -aude.fr. This modern, architect-designed house has four rooms to rent as well as a gipsy caravan, a wooden cabir and an apartment. Breakfast pastries are home-made and there's a spa, a kids' play area and a picnic area with great views. €49

Montolieu and around

Set between Saissac and Carcassonne, once-sleepy **MONTOLIEU**, an attractive village of eighteenth-century terraced houses, has striven to make a mark since 1990 as a "town of books", a deliberate (if pale) imitation of Wales's famous Hay-on-Wye. As well as around fifteen modern and antiquarian bookshops specializing in all manner of subjects, and twelve or so artists and artisans, the main sight here is the **Musée des Arts et Métiers du Livre** (39 rue de la Marie; April to mid-Nov Mon–Fri 10am–noon & 2–6pm, Sat 2–6pm, Sun 3–6pm; mid-Nov to March Mon–Sat 2–5pm, Sun 3–5pm; €3; ☎ 04 68 24 80 04, ⊛ montolieu-livre.fr), a small museum looking at the history of writing in all its forms and the invention of printing. An antique books fair takes place in the town on Easter weekend.

Abbaye de Villelongue

Hameau de Villelongue, St-Martin-le-Vieil • April–June & Sept Mon–Thurs & Sun 10am–noon & 2–6.30pm; July & Aug daily 10am–noon 2–7pm • €6 • ☎ 04 68 24 90 38, ⓦ abbaye-de-villelongue.com

About ten minutes' drive west of Montolieu, tucked away in a wooded vale down a seemingly endless country lane, lie the ruins of the twelfth-century Cistercian **Abbey of Villelongue** – worth driving to if only for the picturesque location on the banks of the Vernassonne. The remains of the abbey include a thirteenth-century vaulted cellar, a fourteenth-century Gothic cloister and the ruins of the abbey-church, now surrounded by a garden. There are **concerts** here in summer and they also offer **B&B** (€75).

ARRIVAL AND INFORMATION

MONTOLIEU

By bus Carcassonne (several daily; 20min); Saissac (several daily; 10min).

Tourist information Place Jean Guéhenno (April–June, Sept & Oct Tues–Fri 9am–noon & 2–5pm, Sat & Sun 10am–12.30pm & 2–6.30pm; July & Aug daily 10am–12.30pm & 2–6.30pm; Nov–March Tues–Fri 9am–noon & 2–5pm; ☎ 04 68 24 80 80, ⓦ tourisme-cabardes .com).

ACCOMMODATION AND EATING

Les Anges du Plafond Rue de la Mairie ☎ 04 68 24 97 19, ⓦ lesangesduplafond.com. Charming B&B, restaurant and tearoom in an old house in the village centre. All the food is home-made (*menus* from €14.50). The three rooms are cosy and traditionally furnished. €75

Apostrophe Impasse de la Manufacture ☎ 04 68 24 80 18, ⓦ apostrophe-hotel.fr. Arty B&B, restaurant and wine bar in a grand *maison de maître* that once housed the manager of the village's former royal linens factory. There are five spacious rooms with original features, and simple, regional cuisine and tapas (€3–5) are on the menu. Breakfast extra. Open mid-March to mid-Nov. €70

Camping de Montolieu D629 ☎ 04 68 76 95 01, ⓦ campingdemontolieu.com. Five minutes' drive south of the village, this three-star campsite has around forty pitches as well as chalets. Ask for a space away from the road. There's a public pool and a cactus garden nearby. Open mid-March to Oct. €15

Nîmes and around

PONT DU GARD

Nîmes and around

Nîmes is Languedoc's most revitalized city – chock-full of the region's outstanding Roman monuments, it is also a showcase for its most exciting new architecture. On the Mediterranean coast, the Camargue Gardoise – the western section of the Rhône delta dubbed "Little Argentina" by Lawrence Durrell – emerges tentatively out of the sea. Moving inland, the marshes gradually give way to the Costières de Nîmes vineyards and the brushy hills known as the *garrigues*, which in turn are cut through by the deep gorge of the Gardon river. This corner of the south has long been a poorer cousin to neighbouring Provence, and the marginalization is reflected in the faded glory of former medieval port towns Beaucaire and St-Gilles, though a recent revival has drawn developers to Le Grau-du-Roi, the Camargue Gardoise's seaside resort. To the west of Nîmes, meanwhile, the gentle Vidourle valley is dotted by all but forgotten hamlets.

4

The **weather** in the *département* of Gard tends to extremes: hot summers and mild winters, punctuated by violent rainstorms in autumn and the merciless buffeting of the cold mistral wind in spring. The best season to visit is undoubtedly summer, in spite of the heat, but if you want to see Nîmes and Gard at their most traditional, try to visit during the local **festivals**, which invariably entail *tauromachie* – bullfighting, bull games and horsemanship, both Camarguais- and Spanish-style.

GETTING AROUND

Getting around in southern Gard presents some difficulties if you're reliant on public transport and want to get off the main routes. Nîmes is the hub, with good train and bus services to most of the region's towns; services to the coast become more frequent in summer. The flattish terrain makes for relatively easy walking; unfortunately for cyclists, heavy traffic makes the roads unpleasant and dangerous. However, there are several *voies vertes* in the area.

By train Trains run west from Nîmes along the coast to Sète and Béziers, and east to Provence via Beaucaire (hooking up with the north–south Rhône rail corridor), while a secondary line runs north via Alès to the Massif Central. SNCF buses may run in lieu of trains on these lines; services are reduced on Sundays and holidays.

LES ARÈNES DE NÎMES

Highlights

❶ Les Arènes de Nîmes Once the scene of gladiatorial combats, this twenty-thousand-seat amphitheatre still functions after two thousand years. **See p.171**

❷ Pont du Gard France's most famous Roman monument, a testament to brilliant engineering – and to slave labour. **See p.182**

❸ Abbaye de St-Roman An underground monastery cut from the living rock, tucked away in the hills above the Rhône. **See p.186**

❹ Camargue Gardoise Formerly known as the "Petite Camargue", an open expanse of saltpans and marshes, populated by horses, bulls and birdlife. **See p.192**

❺ Aigues-Mortes A picture-perfect medieval walled town, set among the swamps and dunes of the Mediterranean coast. **See p.195**

❻ Tauromachie The "art of the bull" is practised in the Gard with a passion and intensity unparalleled north of the Pyrenees. **See p.196**

HIGHLIGHTS ARE MARKED ON THE MAP ON P.166

By bus The principal bus routes run from Nîmes to Uzès and the Pont du Gard, Le Grau du Roi, Beaucaire and Sommières. Routes are often reduced or cancelled on Sundays and holidays. In summer extra services run from Nîmes to Aigues-Mortes, Grau and La Grande-Motte. For full schedules, see ⓦ edgard-transport.fr.

Nîmes

NÎMES is a city inextricably linked to its Roman past. Its location on the Via Domitia – the main chariot route from Spain to Rome – helped make it a favourite with a series of emperors of the first and second centuries AD, who endowed it with the outstanding collection of monuments which dominate the place today; the **Maison Carrée** and the **amphitheatre** (or "Arènes") are both testament to the city's bright, if short-lived, splendour. Over the eighteen hundred years that followed, however, Nîmes had something of a tough time, having to vie with neighbouring rivals Arles, Avignon and Montpellier, which each in their time stole the city's limelight. In the 1980s and 1990s, two flamboyant mayors drove a local renaissance, engaging in a series of audacious building projects (including a retractable cover for the Roman amphitheatre), and

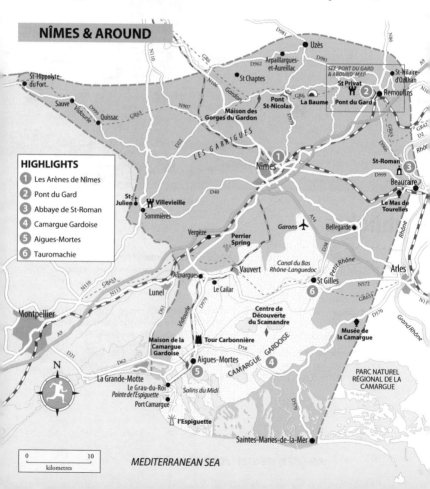

NÎMES & AROUND

HIGHLIGHTS
1. Les Arènes de Nîmes
2. Pont du Gard
3. Abbaye de St-Roman
4. Camargue Gardoise
5. Aigues-Mortes
6. Tauromachie

FESTIVALS IN AND AROUND NÎMES

Festivals in Gard have a decidedly bullish flavour to them. In the bigger places – Nîmes, Beaucaire and St-Gilles – full-blown Spanish-style *corridas* are held for the most important occasions, but otherwise, nearly every small town will somehow involve bulls in their celebrations, whether *courses camarguaises* (see box, p.196) or simply a running of the bulls. Aside from these there are a number of fairs and events which commemorate the area's medieval past or its regional products.

Spring into summer Le Grau du Roi: *Courses camarguaises* are held once a month or more from late March until September to decide the winners of the Trophée des As and the Trophée de l'Avenir.

May Nîmes: *Feria de Pentecôte*. The city's most important festival, a frenzied rite of spring, is held on the fifth weekend after Easter. The *feria* has a heavy emphasis on bullfighting, along with music, dancing and a large street market in the old town.

Mid-May Le Grau-du-Roi: *Fête de la Méditerranée*. Along with traditional *courses camarguaises*, water-jousting competitions are held in the harbour and canals in this three-day celebration of Le Grau's fishermen and their traditions.

Mid-July Uzès: *Autres Rivages* ⓦ autres -rivages.com. A World Music festival held in attractive sites in the town and surrounding area.

Mid-July Nîmes: *Festival de Nîmes* ⓦ festivaldenimes.com. Eleven nights of pop and rock music from international stars in the Roman arena.

Mid-Aug St-Gilles: *Feria de la pêche et de l'abricot*. A four-day harvest festival, celebrating two of the area's major

agricultural products, peaches and apricots, with the emphasis on ranch culture and *tauromachie*.

Late Aug Aigues-Mortes: *Fête de St-Louis*. Held on the closest weekend to August 25, expect a medieval pageant and a reconstruction of St Louis' departure for the Crusades.

First week Sept Fourques (near Beaucaire): *Foires aux Chevaux*. A traditional two-day horse market, which brings together ranch-owners and *gardians* ("cowboys") from across the Camargue.

Second week Sept Le Grau du Roi: *Fête locale*. A major event on the taurine calendar, the twin towns' festivities include bull-running, *courses camarguaises*, water-jousting and the usual markets, street parties and general exuberance.

Third week Sept Nîmes: *Feria des Vendanges*. The second great *feria* in Nîmes, celebrating the wine harvest. Another *tauromachie* extravaganza, with live open-air concerts, parades and a market.

Mid-Oct Aigues-Mortes: *Fête locale*. Twelve-day annual party featuring Gardois *tauromachie*, concerts, dances, meals and much more.

sponsoring grand cultural events. Recently, the city centre has been undergoing a makeover, while a new "trambus" links the town with the suburbs, and a new high-speed rail line has been built between Nîmes and Montpellier on the LGV Méditerranée route. Nowadays, crowds come not only to see the shrines of the Caesars and the dusted-off **mansions** of the cloth-making bourgeoisie, but a collection of provocative contemporary urban architecture in a city that is redefining itself. Not least among these is the new **Musée de la Romanité**, designed by Elizabeth de Portzamparc and due to open in 2018, which will showcase the history of the Roman era in a striking twenty-first-century setting. Nîmes also has two good **art galleries**, and hosts some of the South of France's most colourful **festivals**, when the town is packed late into the night with noisy revellers – undoubtedly including some of its fourteen thousand students.

The heart of Nîmes is a *place* where an august two-thousand-year-old temple, the **Maison Carrée**, faces off against its gleaming twentieth-century doppelganger, the **Carré d'Art**. Fanning out from here to the east, a compact warren of pedestrian streets makes up the city's **old town**, where you'll find most of the sights. Nîmes' **amphitheatre** is southeast towards the station, while the **Temple of Diana** and **Tour Magne** are north of the Jardins de la Fontaine. The town's famous modern architecture is concentrated in the newer suburbs to the south.

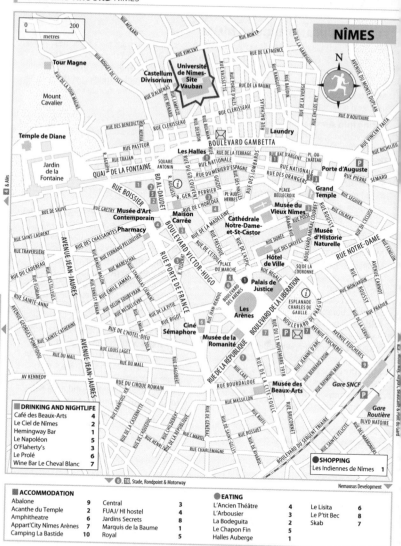

NÎMES

DRINKING AND NIGHTLIFE

Café des Beaux-Arts	4
Le Ciel de Nîmes	2
Hemingway Bar	1
Le Napoléon	5
O'Flaherty's	3
Le Prolé	6
Wine Bar Le Cheval Blanc	7

SHOPPING

Les Indiennes de Nîmes	1

ACCOMMODATION

Abalone	9	Central	3
Acanthe du Temple	2	FUAJ/ HI hostel	4
Amphitheatre	6	Jardins Secrets	8
Appart'City Nîmes Arènes	7	Marquis de la Baume	1
Camping La Bastide	10	Royal	5

EATING

L'Ancien Théâtre	4	Le Lisita	6
L'Arbousier	3	Le P'tit Bec	8
La Bodeguita	2	Skab	7
Le Chapon Fin	5		
Halles Auberge	1		

Brief history

Nemausus had been a Roman colony since 40 BC, but didn't really take off until Augustus Caesar (then, Octavian, and not yet emperor) defeated Mark Antony and Cleopatra at Actium in 31 BC, bringing Egypt under his power. As a reward, he settled his veterans here, laying out a Roman grid-plan city and endowing it with powerful fortifications. In honour of their victory in Egypt, his soldiers adopted the ensign of a crocodile (the Nile) chained to a palm tree, which subsequently became the city's **symbol**.

Changing fortunes

As the town grew, water-demand outstripped the resources of its sacred spring and, under Claudius, a 50km-long canal, of which the Pont du Gard (see p.182) is part, was constructed to supply water. A century later the city was at its zenith, enjoying the special patronage of the emperor Antoninus Pius, whose mother's family hailed from these parts. It was a sprawling city enclosed by some 7km of thick walls (which survived as late as 1786), reinforced by thirty stout towers and pierced by seven monumental gates. From that glorious era, however, things went rapidly downhill. Within a decade of Antoninus's death, the Roman Empire spun into a temporary political crisis, and by the time the situation had restabilized, Christianity had replaced paganism in the empire, and Christian Arles had supplanted pagan Nîmes as the local capital.

Counts of Toulouse

With Roman decline, Nîmes passed to the Visigoths, who were in turn displaced by Muslims coming up from Spain in about 724. Only seven years later the Muslims were forced out, and for the next four hundred years the town was incorporated into a series of rapidly dissolving Germanic principalities. In 1185 it came under the control of the **counts of Toulouse**, and briefly flirted with Catharism; the mere sight of de Montfort's powerful army, however, was enough to make it "repent" and return to the Catholic fold. Nîmes was absorbed by the French Crown in 1226, but by this time little was left of the glorious Roman city – only two clusters of houses huddled around the cathedral and amphitheatre.

Wars of Religion

After three sleepy centuries, Nîmes discovered a new vocation as a textile centre – until the **Wars of Religion** wracked the region. Calvinist preachers found eager ears among Nîmes' prosperous cloth-makers, to the extent that local Huguenots destroyed the eleventh-century cathedral and, on St Michael's Day of 1567, massacred some two hundred clergy. Following their repression in the wake of the Wars, Protestants from Nîmes as well as exiles from Haut Languedoc rose up together in the Camisard rebellion, brutally suppressed by royal forces in 1704, following its leader's defection to the Catholic forces at Nîmes. Many Protestants fled, while others persevered, having to disguise their faith.

Denim de Nîmes

After the Revolution, religious issues were laid aside, and Nîmes, still predominantly Protestant, got back down to making money, which it did by spinning silk and cotton. The town's product became so successful that the cotton cloth "de Nîmes" (thus, "denim") went west, where in 1848 an American, Levi Strauss, hit upon the idea of attaching small red labels to trousers made out of the material.

Maison Carrée

Daily: March & Oct 10am–6pm; April, May & Sept 10am–6.30pm; June 10am–7pm; July & Aug 9.30am–8pm; Nov–Feb 10am–1pm & 2–4.30pm • €6 (€12 combined with amphitheatre and Tour Magne) • ☎ 04 66 21 82 56, ⓦ arenes-nimes.com

The **Maison Carré** ("square house"), a tiny but perfectly proportioned temple, once the centrepiece of the city's forum, was likely founded around 3 AD. Size, of course, is not everything, and as Henry James remarked, it is precisely because of its compactness that "it does not overwhelm you, you can conceive it." This is perhaps the world's best-preserved Roman temple (rivalled only by the Temple of Apollo at Baalbek), and can still boast all of its columns, an intact roof and *cella* (inner sanctum). If, over the ages, its functions – including use as a stable – haven't always done it justice, its aesthetic perfection has long drawn admirers: Colbert, Louis XIV's powerful finance minister, wanted to carry it off lock and stock to Versailles; Thomas Jefferson modelled the Virginia Capitol building on it; and Napoleon took it as inspiration for the Madeleine church in Paris. Inside you can watch a film, *Nemausus*, about the history of Nîmes. You can also download a free app from the website to give you more in-depth information.

AVANT-GARDE ARCHITECTURE IN NÎMES

Through the mid-1980s and 1990s Nîmes embarked on an audacious project of **urban renewal**, contracting high-flying architects from around the world to construct public housing developments, sports centres and civic spaces. These new buildings – Nîmes' modern pride – vary in originality and effect; you may judge them to be either wonders or monstrosities, while the scheme itself saddled the city with huge debts. Some of them you'll pass as you make the rounds in the centre, while the rest (which are really only of interest to hardcore modern architecture fans) are scattered around the southern edge of the city and are best visited either by bike or taxi – the tourist office can point them out on a map.

The best work by far is Norman Foster's great **Carré d'Art** (see p.170). Also in the old town are two remodelled urban *places*: Martiel Raysse's **la place d'Assas** (1989) and Philippe Starck's **Abribus** (1987), both offering simple landscape architecture and decidedly underwhelming modern sculpture. The peripheral sites include the whale-like and rapidly ageing social housing development **Nemausus 1** (Jean Nouvel, 1987), its monstrous rejoinder, **Nemausus 2** (Alain Amedeo and Jacek Padlewski, 1989), and three sports complexes – **Stade des Costières** (Vittorio Gregotti and Marc Chausse, 1989), **Salle Omnisports** (Gregotti, 1993) and already-dated **Le Colisée** (Kisho Kurokawa, 1991) – which, with their lunging surfaces of concrete and glass, complete the discordant collection. The latest addition to the collection is the new **Musée de la Romanité** on boulevard des Arènes.

Carré d'Art

Pl de la Maison Carrée • Tues–Sun 10am–6pm • Free • ☏ 04 66 76 35 70, ⓦ carreartmusee.com

On the far side of boulevard Victor-Hugo towers Norman Foster's 1993 **Carré d'Art**, a twentieth-century *riposte* to the Roman temple. Four fine columns support its high portico with seeming effortlessness, contrasting the chunkier Corinthian columns of the smaller Maison Carrée, reflected in the inscrutable glass face of Foster's building. Home to a library and resource centre, the top two floors house the city's **Musée d'Art Contemporain** (€5), which contains an impressive survey of French and Western European art of the last four decades. Emphasis is on Gallic movements such as Nouveau Réalisme and Support-Surface but Mediterranean and northern European art is also strongly represented. The l'Accrochage exhibition, which highlights the collection's new acquisitions and lesser-seen works, is a good option if you are short on time.

The cathedral and around

Place aux Herbes • Mon 3–7pm, Tues 9am–noon & 3–6pm, Wed 11am–1pm, Thurs 9–10am & 3–6pm, Fri 9am–noon & 3–6pm, Sat 9am–noon & 2–6pm, Sun 9am–12.30pm & 2–6pm • Free

With the core of the Roman city long built over, and most of the medieval buildings destroyed in the course of the Wars of Religion, Nîmes' **old town** is testament to the success of the local cloth merchants of the seventeenth to nineteenth centuries – the builders of the grandiose *hôtels particuliers* which pepper the streets south and west of the **Cathédrale de Notre-Dame et St-Castor**, a five-minute stroll east of the Maison Carrée. This church was constructed on the foundations of the former temple of Apollo; of the original cathedral, founded in 1069, only the bell tower and the badly chipped friezes of the facade survived the Huguenots' wrath – the rest was rebuilt in the 1700s. The new building is rather nondescript and the interior of little interest.

South of the cathedral on rue du Chapitre is **Hôtel Régis**, a former merchant's house with a stately sixteenth-century courtyard. Close by, on Grande Rue, you'll be confronted by the clean Neoclassical lines of the former **Jesuits' Chapel** (Tues–Sun 10am–6pm; free). Inside, there's a spacious and luxuriously appointed Baroque interior, now used for exhibitions and concerts. In rue des Greffes, to the south, sits the late Renaissance **Hôtel de Ville**, built in 1700 – look for the stuffed crocodiles suspended above the staircase inside the entry hall, gifts to the city from contented (and rich) eighteenth-century burghers.

West from here, the saurian theme continues in place du Marché, where a twentieth-century homage to the city's emblem has been paid in a **fountain** designed by Martiel Raysse and Silvio and Vito Tongiani. A couple of blocks north sits **Hôtel Bernis**, one of the town's earliest surviving mansions, its fifteenth-century facade studded by casement windows and concealing an atmospheric old courtyard with a well in the centre. Nearby, at 8 rue de l'Aspic, you can see three early Christian sarcophagi incorporated into the walls of the **Meynier de Salinelles** mansion, as well as a splendid staircase leading up from its courtyard. Further along rue de l'Aspic is the place de l'Horloge, whose solitary eighteenth-century **clock tower** is now crowded by the tables of café terraces.

Musée du Vieux Nîmes

Pl aux Herbes • Tues–Sun 10am–6pm • Free (€5 for exhibitions) • ☎ 04 66 76 73 70

On the south side of place aux Herbes sits the **bishop's palace**, now home to the **Musée du Vieux Nîmes**, whose lively collection focuses on the city's artisanal and industrial past (including, of course, denim), and will appeal to both adults and children. It is a well-organized exhibition, rounded out by a noteworthy furniture collection, including a nineteenth-century billiard table and sedan chairs.

Porte d'Auguste

Northeast of the cathedral is the excavated **Porte d'Auguste.** This surprisingly well-preserved triumphal entryway into the city, sunk by the rising ground level, was only discovered in the eighteenth century with the destruction of a later palace that had been built around it. The **Via Domitia** entered Nîmes through this gate: the larger central passages were for chariots and the smaller side entrances for pedestrians.

Musée d'Histoire Naturelle

13 bd Amiral Courbet • Tues–Sun 10am–6pm • Free (€5 for exhibitions) • ☎ 04 66 76 73 45

Abutting the back of the Jesuits' Chapel is the **Museum d'Histoire Naturelle**. The quirky natural-history exhibition comprises a jumbled collection of Polynesian masks and spears, and a hotchpotch of stuffed animals, including a Royal Bengal Tiger. In fact, the museum rather resembles a large curio cabinet – a journey into the nineteenth-century European mind, which saw the world beyond its borders as a hunting ground for collectables. The same building also used to house the now-closed **archeology museum**, whose collection will transfer to the new **Musée de la Romanité.**

Les Arènes and around

Bd des Arènes • Daily: March & Oct 9am–6pm; April, May & Sept 9am–6.30pm; June 9am–7pm; July & Aug 9am–8pm; Nov–Feb 9.30am–5pm • €10 inc free audioguide (€12 combined with Maison Carrée and Tour Magne) • ☎ 04 66 21 82 56, ⊛ arenes-nimes.com

The city's most famous Roman monument, **Les Arènes**, may not be the largest surviving Roman amphitheatre but it's certainly one of the best preserved – even if UNESCO has still not seen fit to include it or the city's other Roman remains on the World Heritage list. Dating from the first century AD, the 133m-long and 101m-wide oval surges 21m above the street, thanks to its uniquely intact upper galleries, and still

> ## NIMEÑO II
>
> Outside the main entrance of Les Arènes you'll see a sombre reminder of the seriousness of the *corrida* – the statue of Christian Moncouquiol, a successful young *torero* who had fought in France, Spain and Latin America. "**Nimeño II**" as he was known (his brother, Alain, was "Nimeño I"), was paralyzed after landing on his head when tossed by a bull in the ring in Arles in September 1989. He eventually regained the used of his legs and right arm but committed suicide in 1991 at the age of 37. Nimeño II is best remembered for taking on six bulls in one bullfight after his co-fighter was injured.

4

holds the crowds of twenty thousand spectators for which it was designed. An ingenious access system allows the public to enter and exit through the *vomitoria* – the great arched entryways that ring the building – quickly and with minimal jostling.

Before the Christians banned them in the fourth century, **gladiatorial matches**, along with spectacles involving killing exotic animals, were the big draw. Since the decline of these games the building has managed to escape destruction thanks to its more or less continued use. The Visigoths used it as a fortress (in the east section, two contemporary windows remain); from the twelfth century it filled up with houses, shops and churches, coming to constitute a veritable slum, which was only cleared out when restoration work began in 1809. Since the nineteenth century, the amphitheatre has been used again for public spectacles, including bullfights.

The best time to visit is during the **grands jeux Romains** in April, a weekend re-enactment of Roman games, or to see one of the rock concerts during the **Festival de Nîmes** in July (see box, p.167). But whatever time of year you come here you can't fail to be impressed by the vast, near-identical passages, stairways and bench-rows – a tribute to Roman engineering. To enhance your experience you can hire a "visioguide" (€5) for a tour using a tablet or download a free app onto your own device from the website. In July and August there are daily **guided tours** (no booking required) when the amphitheatre is open.

Musée des Cultures Taurines

6 rue Alexandre Ducros • May–Oct Tues–Sun 10am–6pm • Free (€5 for exhibitions) • ☎ 04 30 06 77 07

Even if you don't want to see a matador in action, you might like to check out the **Musée des Cultures Taurines**, which explores the significance of the bull to local life. Dedicated to *tauromachie*, including bullfighting and *courses camarguaises*, it houses a permanent collection of posters and relics, and engagingly themed annual exhibitions. The posters, designed by local artists, and other memorabilia available in the boutique, can make attractive souvenirs.

Musée des Beaux-Arts

Rue de la Cité Foulc • Tues–Sun 10am–6pm • Free (€5 for exhibitions) • ☎ 04 66 28 18 32

From the amphitheatre, it's a five-minute jaunt south to the **Musée des Beaux-Arts**, whose highlight is a huge Roman mosaic depicting the mythical "marriage of Admetus". The rest of the collection – mostly Flemish, Italian and French paintings

---

BULLFIGHTING IN FRANCE

The traditions of the **bullfight**, which seem now to be so essential to the spirit of Gard, are in fact almost exclusively recent innovations. The first real **corrida** (Spanish bullfight) in France was held in 1853 at Bayonne under the patronage of a Spanish nobleman. It was a great success and soon spread throughout the Midi and into Provence. Nîmes' first official *corrida* was held at Les Arènes in 1865, and by 1880 the spectacle could be seen across the south. The main places for bullfighting are Arles, Béziers and Nîmes.

The "art" reached its zenith in the first half of the twentieth century when well-known fans such as Pablo Picasso and **Ernest Hemingway**, along with their rich and famous friends, brought an air of glamour to the proceedings. When in Nîmes, the latter used to stay at the *Hotel Imperator*, where the bar is now named after him (see p.176). His name has also been given to a writing prize, the Prix International Hemingway, which was launched at the Nîmes *feria* in 2004 and celebrates excellence in writing about bullfighting.

Bullfighting is only legal in France in towns where it is part of a long tradition – but for how much longer? In 2011, it was added to **UNESCO**'s list of Intangible Cultural Heritage; but in June 2016 it was removed following a successful court challenge by the Comité Radicalement Anti-Corrida (CRAC). And increasingly, many smaller towns and villages are refusing to have *corridas* in their arenas.

from the sixteenth to eighteenth centuries – is endowed with works of surprising quality, including Rubens' uncharacteristically static *Portrait of a Monk*, and a fine example of the transition from medieval to humanist style in Giambono's *Mystical Marriage of St Catherine*.

Along the way, in rue Porte de France, you'll pass through the **Roman gate** of the same name. It's worth pausing here to consider the immense size of the Roman city – the whole area between here and the Tour Magne was contained by its walls.

The castellum divisorium and Jardin de la Fontaine

North of boulevard Gambetta, beside the cold, sinister facade of the town's eighteenth-century **fortress** – now the Université de Nîmes' Site Vauban – sits the **castellum divisorium**. The rare remains of a first-century waterworks (the only similar ones are at Pompeii in Italy and Tiermes in Spain), this is one of Nîmes' most important but least known Roman artefacts. It was from this unremarkable-looking open basin that the water carried to the town via the Pont du Gard was distributed to the various parts of the Roman city by lead pipes, which are still partly visible – multimedia installations at the Pont du Gard museum (see p.183) show how the complex worked. Following the quiet residential streets west from here takes you to the **Jardin de la Fontaine**: this formal eighteenth-century garden with a complex series of fountains and pools, at the foot of forested **Mont Cavalier**, was the first public garden in France.

La Tour Magne

4

Daily: March & Oct 9.30am–1pm & 2–6pm; April, May & Sept 9.30am–6.30pm; June 9am–7pm; July & Aug 9am–8pm; Nov–Feb 9.30am–1pm & 2–4.30pm • €3.50 (or €12 combined with amphitheatre and Maison Carrée) • ☏ 04 66 21 82 56, ⓦ arenes-nimes.com

From the *place* at the foot of Mont Cavalier, a serpentine path leads up to the ruins of **La Tour Magne**. This **watchtower**, based on an earlier Celtic structure, dates from about 15 BC; as the Roman settlement grew, it was eventually incorporated into the city walls. The tower has suffered its share of indignities, including the loss of the top fifteen of its original 45m height and the frantic diggings around the foundations by a treasure-hunting seventeenth-century gardener deluded by a prediction of Nostradamus, but it is impressive even in its ruined state. Broken off and eroded, the tower evokes the romantic etchings of the nineteenth-century travellers who marvelled at it, and it is still the best place from which to survey Nîmes and its surroundings. Download the free app on the website to get the most out of your visit.

The Temple of Diana

At the foot of Mont Cavalier, on its west side, sit the shambolic ruins of the "**Temple of Diana**". Originally a *nymphaeum*, a sacred fountain dedicated to Nemausus (the god of the spring), the structure was taken over by Benedictine monks in the Middle Ages, in whose care it remained until destroyed by Huguenot mobs. Today the hulking half-arches and ruined walls are the only remnants of the temple, but are enough to give you an impression of the scale of the building in Roman times.

ARRIVAL AND DEPARTURE

NÎMES

By plane Located 8km south of the city, Nîmes airport (☏ 04 66 70 49 49, ⓦ aeroport-nimes.fr) has few facilities other than an ATM, a café and car rental desks. From here the trip to the city can be made by *navette* (€6.50), or by taxi (at least €40, or €45 at night).

By train Nîmes' *gare SNCF* is about ten minutes' walk south of the old town. TGV stations are indicated with an asterisk.

Destinations Agde* (many daily; 1hr 5min); Beaucaire (several daily; 15min); Béziers*, with connections to Bédarieux (many daily; 1hr 20min); Carcassonne* with connections to Quillan (many daily; 2hr–2hr 30min); Castelnaudary* (many daily; 2hr 40min–3hr 40min); Le Grau du Roi, via Aigues Mortes (several daily; 45min–1hr); Montpellier* (many daily; 30min); Narbonne*

AQUATIC FUN IN NÎMES

You can go swimming at **Némausa** (☏ 04 66 70 98 80, ⊚ vert-marine.com; adults/kids €4.40/2), 120 av de la Bouvine, an Olympic-size pool which is open daily year round. A good place to take the kids is **Parc Aquatropic** (☏ 04 66 38 31 00, ⊚ aquatropic-equalia.fr; adults/kids €5.25/1.40), a water park with indoor and outdoor pools and a spa near the Nîmes-Ouest *autoroute* exit, also open daily year round.

(many daily; 1hr 45min); Paris* (hourly; 3hr); Perpignan* (several hourly; 2hr–2hr 30min); Sète* (many daily; 40–55min); Toulouse*(many daily; 2hr 40min–3hr 20min).

By bus Nîmes' *gare routière* is at the back of the station. To find out where your bus goes from call into the shop of Edgard Transport (☏ 08 10 33 42 73, ⊚ edgard-transport .fr) at 5 av de la Méditerranée.

Destinations Aigues-Mortes (several daily; 1hr); Beaucaire (several daily; 30min); Collias (daily; 1hr 5min); Ganges (several daily; 1hr 20min); La Grande Motte (several daily; 1hr 30min); Le Grau du Roi (several daily; 1hr); Pont du Gard (many daily; 45min); St-Gilles (several daily; 40min); Sauve (several daily; 50min); Sommières (several daily; 45min); Uzès (many daily; 40min); Vauvert (daily; 45min); Villevieille (several daily; 45min).

GETTING AROUND

By bike Vélo TANGO (Mon–Sat 7.30am–8pm) at the *gare SNCF* has regular bikes for €3 per day and electric bikes for €7.50 a day. There is a 20km *voie verte* trail to Sommières from Caveirac, 11km west of Nîmes, which you can access by bike along busy roads from the city.

By car There are five car parks in the centre including Arènes, Maison Carrée, Porte Auguste, Halles and Coupole. The first 30 mins are free. Rental agencies include the following: ADA, 2614 rte de Montpellier ☏ 04 66 04 79 99; Avis, *gare SNCF* ☏ 08 20 61 16 40; Budget, *gare SNCF* ☏ 04 30 92 02 35; Europcar, *gare SNCF* ☏ 04 66 26 29 07 94; Hertz, *gare SNCF* ☏ 04 66 76 25 91. Avis and Hertz also have airport offices.

By taxi TRAN (☏ 04 66 29 40 11, ⊚ taxinimes.fr), besides operating as a regular taxi, can take you to the area's tourist sites.

INFORMATION

Tourist information 6 rue Auguste (April, May & Sept Mon–Sat 9am–7pm, Sun 10am–6pm; July & Aug Mon–Fri 9am–7.30pm, Sat 9am–7pm, Sun 10am–6pm; Oct–March Mon–Fri 9am–6.30pm, Sat 10am–6pm, Sun 10am–5pm; ☏ 04 66 58 38 00, ⊚ ot-nimes.fr). There is also an office on the Esplanade Charles de Gaulle (Mon–Fri 10am–5pm). Up-to-date information on Nîmes and other places covered in this chapter can be found at ⊚ tourismegard.com.

ACCOMMODATION

Accommodation options in Nîmes are plentiful, although rock-bottom budget places aren't so easy to come by, and you should book ahead as far as possible for any of the city's celebrations, when you may have to resort to the cluster of chain motels around the Nîmes-Ouest exit of the A9. In addition to the HI hostel (see opposite) there are several private hostels (*résidences*), some for under-25s, others with self-catering suites (contact the tourist office for details).

Hotel packages The "Pass Romain" (from €60 per person, depending on hotel rating) includes admission to the city's attractions, the Pont du Gard, an audioguide to explore the city, and one night's B&B accommodation. The "Pass Vin & Patrimoine" (from €47 per person depending on hotel rating) includes a visit to a wine cellar with tasting, entry to the city's attractions, an audioguide to explore the city and one night's B&B accommodation. Both can be booked on the tourist office website.

Abalone 23 av Feuchères ☏ 04 66 69 20 14, ⊚ nimes -hotel.com. Right by the train station, this is a recently renovated two-star hotel with contemporary decor and attentive staff. Amenities include cable TV and wi-fi. **€63**

Acanthe du Temple 1 rue Charles Babut ☏ 04 66 67 54 61, ⊚ hotel-temple.com. One of the old town's best bargains: friendly, well-kept and quiet, set in a seventeenth-century house. Rooms have fans, TV and en-suite showers. Closed Jan. **€65**

★**Amphitheatre** 4 rue des Arènes ☏ 04 66 67 28 51, ⊚ hoteldelamphitheatre.com. This three-star hotel with just eleven rooms is probably the best value for money in town, thanks to its tasteful, southern French decor in muted tones. Rooms have king-size beds, cable TV and a/c. **€90**

Appart'City Nîmes Arènes 1 bd de Bruxelles ☏ 04 56 60 26 70, ⊚ appartcity.com. The flagship accommodation of this French aparthotel chain is housed in a Haussmannian-style building just south of the amphitheatre. Rooms, featuring small kitchens, are chic and boutique; some have original features and there are several specially adapted studios for disabled people. Breakfast is available. **€80**

Camping La Bastide Route de Générac, 5km south of the centre, beyond the A9 autoroute ☎ 04 66 62 05 82, ☺ camping-nimes.com. Facilities include a laundry, a pool, grocery store, bar and restaurant, as well as a playground for kids. Open year-round. Take bus #D ("La Bastide" stop). **€31**

Central 2 pl du Château ☎ 04 66 67 27 75, ☺ hotel -central.org. Just behind the temple and the Porte d'Auguste, with English-speaking management, this small but cosy three-star hotel features simple but comfortable rooms which were renovated in 2013. **€70**

FUAJ/HI hostel Chemin de la Cigale, 2km northwest of the centre ☎ 04 66 68 03 20, ☺ hihostels.com. A comfortable hostel set in an olive grove, with private rooms as well as single-sex dorms. Non-members are required to purchase membership on arrival. Take bus #I, direction Alès or Villeverte, to "Stade". **€18.75**

Jardins Secrets 3 rue Maruéjols ☎ 04 66 84 82 64, ☺ jardinssecrets.net. Nîmes' best and most luxurious hotel is hidden behind a huge gate in an unremarkable street. As well as the fourteen dimly lit, lavishly decorated rooms in this former coaching inn, there is a small pool in the "secret garden" and a spa. **€250**

Marquis de la Baume 21 rue Nationale ☎ 04 66 76 28 42, ☺ bookinnfrance.com. This four-star hotel in a seventeenth-century mansion was about to undergo refurbishment at the time of writing. Whatever the result (think "contemporary luxe"), the rooms on the first floor will still keep their original high ceilings with painted beams. **€100**

★ **Royal** 3 bd Alphonse-Daudet ☎ 04 66 58 28 27, ☺ royalhotel-nimes.com. The *Royal* is the hippest place to stay in town, with original contemporary art adorning the walls and chic, modern rooms. It's also home to the *Bodeguita* tapas bar, which is one of *the* places to be seen during the *ferias*. **€50**

EATING

Three culinary traditions – Spanish, *gastronomique* and, of course, Gardois *terroir* – dominate Nîmes' restaurants, with Indian and North African establishments adding a cosmopolitan flavour. Many of the cheapest places, including self-service cafés and budget sandwich stands, can be found along the boulevard Amiral-Courbet, and the whole of the old town is stuffed with small restaurants and brasseries, with a veritable colony of street-side bistros in the narrow alleys around place du Marché (many in the €14–20 range).

L'Ancien Théâtre 4 rue Racine ☎ 04 66 21 30 75. Just a five-minute stroll west from the Maison Carrée, with solid Gard cuisine, and featuring home-made breads and pastries. *Menus* from €20. Tues–Fri 11.45am–1pm & 7.45–9pm plus Sat dinner.

L'Arbousier 18 rue de l'Horloge ☎ 09 50 14 43 78. Middle Eastern restaurant and tea room serving snacks and sweet treats, with vegetarian and vegan options available. Falafel *galette* €7. Tues–Sat 10–7pm.

La Bodeguita 1 pl d'Assas, in the Royal Hotel ☎ 04 66 58 28 27, ☺ royalhotel-nimes.com. A reliable choice for Spanish food and tapas – Manchego cheese, octopus, *patatas bravas* – with a good view of the Maison Carrée. Tapas from €4. Tues–Fri noon–2pm & 7–10pm plus Sat eve.

Le Chapon Fin 3 rue Château Fadaise ☎ 04 66 67 34 73, ☺ chaponfin-restaurant-nimes.com. Basic but hearty *terroir* cuisine in simple surroundings; a good

value-for-money choice. *Menus* €17.50–31.50. Mon & Tues noon–2pm, Wed–Sat noon–2pm & 7–9pm.

★ **Halles Auberge** Les Halles, allée du Paprika ☎ 04 66 21 96 70. Buzzy, popular restaurant in the covered market where you sit elbow-to-elbow around the counter with other diners. Local, traditional dishes are on the menu including fried vegetables. *Menus* from €13. Tues–Sun 10am–2.30pm.

Le Lisita 2B bd des Arènes ☎ 04 66 67 29 15, ☺ lelisita .com. No longer the best address in town but still a good place to go for refined traditional food. High points include *brandade*, local veal and strawberries from the *garrigues*, which can be enjoyed on a terrace with views of the Arènes. *Menus* start from €29. Tues–Sat noon–2pm & 7–10pm

Le P'tit Bec 87 bis rue de la République ☎ 04 66 38 05 83, ☺ restaurant-lepetitbec.fr. The best mid-range place for typical French cuisine. *Menu* options from €18, plus children's meals. The dining room is pleasant and airy and

4

LOCAL CUISINE

The cuisine of Gard has a distinctly **Mediterranean taste**, with a strong current of olive and garlic, plus rosemary, basil, bay and mint, all of which sprout up in the *garrigues*. Look out for *gardiane de taureau* (slow-cooked bull meat in red wine) served with Camargue rice; bull steak; *soupe au pistou* (vegetable soup with pesto); *brandade de morue* (cod and olive-oil purée); and Pélardon cheese from the Cévennes. Wash these down with the wines of the Costières, or with the famous Côtes-du-Rhône vintages.

THE FERIAS

The most important dates in the Nîmes calendar are those of the **ferias**, lively street festivals featuring parties, music and *tauromachie*. The city is the French capital of the *corrida*, and during the two great annual *ferias*, **Pentecôte** (seven weeks after Easter) and **des Vendanges** (mid-Sept), the best local and Spanish *toreros* come to Les Arènes to practise the brutal pageantry of their art. During the *ferias*, particularly Pentecost, the centre of Nîmes becomes a massive round-the-clock party, and the best hotels get booked a year in advance.

there's a courtyard terrace. Tues & Thurs–Sat noon–2pm & 7–9pm plus Sun lunch.

★**Skab** 7 rue de la République ☏ 04 66 21 94 30, ⓦ restaurant-skab.fr. In spite of its unfortunate name, this contemporary gourmet restaurant is one of the best places to eat in town. The lunch menu (from €31) and seasonal tasting menu (€80) feature delicate, creative dishes made with local ingredients. Tues–Sat noon–2pm & 7–9pm.

DRINKING AND NIGHTLIFE

Since 2008's smoking ban went into effect, the blue haze of Gauloise and Gitane smoke that used to hang in the air of Nîmes has disappeared, and with it, a piece of local heritage – the person who introduced tobacco to France in the sixteenth century was Nîmes native Jean Nicot (also the drug's namesake). Nevertheless, the city's traditional drinking establishments remain lively, if somewhat less atmospheric. A generous selection of quiet, neighbourhood café-bars, and louder and larger music-bars is scattered throughout the city.

Café des Beaux-Arts 17 pl aux Herbes ☏ 04 66 67 97 97. A cheerful and airy place in the medieval heart of Nîmes with a good patio that's well located for people-watching. Mon–Sat 7am–11pm.

★**Le Ciel de Nîmes** 16 pl de la Maison Carré ☏ 04 66 36 71 70, ⓦ lecieldenimes.net. Great views of the city from inside the glassed-in interior or outside on the patio atop the Carré d'Art. Tues–Sun 10am–6pm (open evenings in summer).

Hemingway Bar Hotel Imperator, 15 rue Gaston Boissier ☏ 04 66 21 90 30, ⓦ hotel-imperator.eu. Follow in "Papa's" footsteps and soak up the atmosphere (and check out the memorabilia) in the bar of this legendary hotel where he spent many a "happy hour" with his bullfighting chums. Daily 24hr.

★**Le Napoléon** 46 bd Victor Hugo ☏ 04 66 67 20 23. Famous old neighbourhood café – complete with Second Empire decor, old men in cardigans and unbeatable Gallic ambience. Great place for a refreshing mid-afternoon *pastis* break. Daily 7am–midnight.

O'Flaherty's 21 bd Amiral-Courbet ☏ 04 66 67 22 63, ⓦ pub-oflahertys.com. British beer – seven kinds on tap – plus food and regular Thursday concerts of Irish, country and bluegrass (except July & Aug). Mon–Wed 11am–1am, Thurs & Fri 11am–2am, Sat 5pm–2am, Sun 5pm–1am.

Le Prolé 20 rue Jean Reboul ☏ 04 66 21 67 23. Young, lively neighbourhood bar to the west of the amphitheatre where they have live music every Friday in the courtyard in summer. Mon–Sat 8am–11pm.

Wine Bar Le Cheval Blanc 1 pl des Arènes ☏ 04 66 76 19 59, ⓦ winebar-lechevalblanc.com. Historic wine bar in a vaulted cellar where they not only serve around fifteen wines by the glass but also have a good range of traditional French dishes such as steak tartare on offer. Mon–Sat noon–2pm & 7–11pm.

ENTERTAINMENT

Les Arènes Bd des Arènes ☏ 04 66 28 40 20, ⓦ arenes-nimes.com. Hosts music concerts, bullfights and other events throughout the year.

Ciné Sémaphore 25 rue Porte de France ☏ 04 66 67 83 11, ⓦ cinema-semaphore.fr. Cinema showing some films in their original version (*vo*).

SHOPPING

There is a covered market at 5 rue des Halles (Mon–Sat 7am–1pm, Sun 7am–1.30pm; ☏ 04 66 21 52 49, ⓦ leshallesdenimes .com) and several weekly outdoor markets including a flea market on Monday mornings and a farmers' market on Friday mornings on boulevard Jean Jaurès. On Thursday evenings (6pm–midnight) in July and August, "Les Jeudis de Nîmes" sees farmers' markets around town as well as musical entertainment.

Les Indiennes de Nîmes 2 bd des Arènes ☏ 04 66 21 69 57, ⓦ indiennesdenimes.fr. The place to go for traditional Camargue *gardian* gear as well as clothes and home furnishings in the colourful, patterned fabrics that are made in this area. Mon–Sat 10am–12.30pm & 2.30–7pm.

Hospital Hôpital Universitaire Carémeau, 4 rue du Professeur Robert Debré (⊙ 04 66 68 33 44, ⊚ chu-nimes.fr).

Laundry There are self-service launderettes (daily 8am–9pm) at 4 rue Bachalas and 85 rue de la République.

Pharmacy Grande Pharmacie de l'Horloge, 1 pl de l'Horloge (Mon–Sat 8am–7.30pm; ⊙ 04 66 36 11 71, ⊚ grandepharmaciedelhorloge.pharminfo.fr).

Police 245 av Pierre Gamel (⊙ 04 66 27 30 00).

Post office There are several post offices including one at 1 bd de Bruxelles (Mon–Fri 9am–6pm, Sat 9am–12.30pm).

Around Nîmes

For such a small area, the southern portion of Gard contains a surprising number of attractions. Just across the River Gardon to the north of Nîmes lies **Uzès**, the "First Duchy" of France, its castle still in the hands of a family which traces its roots back to Charlemagne. A few kilometres east of the city lies the **Pont du Gard**, perhaps the most famous of all Roman aqueducts, now developed into a major attraction, while along the Rhône, medieval **Beaucaire**'s castle and the uniquely sculpted facade of the church of **St-Gilles** deserve a visit. The southern edge of the *département*, sweeping west of here, is dominated by the westernmost branch of the swampy Rhône delta, the **Camargue Gardoise** – an important way-station for migratory birds. On the edge of the Camargue, the medieval walls of **Aigues-Mortes**, once attacked by allies of the English, are now besieged only by invading sun-seekers who crowd the beaches south of the town, around **Le Grau-du-Roi**. Upstream from Le Grau, on the River Vidourle, **Sommières** and **Sauve** lie quietly languishing in forgotten obscurity, far from the bustle of the coast.

4

Uzès

Long disdained by the French literati as the proverbial "middle of nowhere", **UZÈS**, nestled among the rocky *garrigues* 20km north of Nîmes, has now been discovered by well-heeled expats and turned into the *gardois* equivalent of St-Rémy-de-Provence – as attested by the house prices in the area. At the time of writing, a local mansion, the Château de Castille, with original Picasso frescoes on the terrace wall, was on the market for around €9 million.

Today the town fairly packs out with tourists in summer months; each medieval stone arcade now conceals a bistro or chic boutique, and when the weather is good the restaurant patios that dominate the squares are frequented by buskers. The compact **old town**, which can be walked in about an hour, is still dominated by the twelfth-century castle, **the Duché**, just south of the tourist office, while its other focal point, the **place aux Herbes**, lies southwest of the fortress. The **cathedral** overlooks the Alzon river on the eastern edge of the old town, as if pushed aside by the power of the town's dukes.

Saturday's traditional **market** is particularly lively, while gourmands will want to sample the **truffles** for which the town is renowned. If you're reliant on public transport and short on time the town is best visited on a day-trip from Nîmes that also takes in the **Pont du Gard**, 20km southwest.

Brief history

Like so many of Gard's towns, Uzès traces its history back to the time of the toga, when it served as an agricultural and local market centre. It became the seat of a bishop in the fifth century, eventually coming under the control of the counts of Toulouse. Under the kings of France, who took over in 1229, the lords of Uzès distinguished themselves as loyalists and were rewarded in 1632 with the title "**First Duchy of France**", which the Dukes of Montmorency had held until Henri de Montmorency's failed revolt (see p.319). Like Nîmes, Uzès violently embraced Calvinism – becoming the fifth most

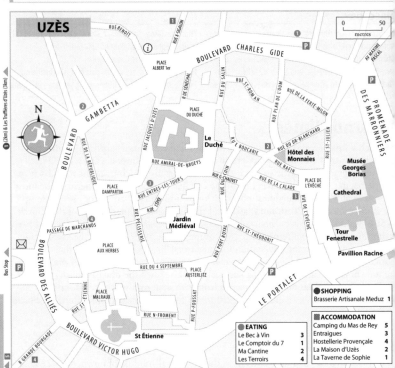

important Huguenot centre in France – but once the movement was suppressed and the majority of Protestants fled, those "Catholics" that remained turned it into a wealthy **silk town**, which it remained for the next three hundred years. The early twentieth century brought depression, and when the railway bypassed the town, the writing of Uzès' decline was on the wall.

The history of the town's celebrities is also one of near misses: Guillaume de Grimoard, later to become Pope Urban V, was not from Uzès, but did live here for a while; the great seventeenth-century poet Jean Racine had an uncle from the town, and spent a year and a half here; and Charles Gide, father of Nobel-laureate author André, was a native – Gide Junior passed his childhood summers here.

The Duché

Daily: July & Aug 10am–12.30pm & 2–6.30pm; Sept–June 10am–noon & 2–6pm • €18 (€10 on Sat) • ☏ 04 66 22 18 96,
Ⓦ duche-uzes.fr

The old ducal castle of the de Crussol family, **the Duché**, remains the centrepiece of Uzès, and the sight of its towering *donjon* topped by the family's red-and-yellow-banded pennant makes a Hollywoodesque but authentic tableau. The compact walled *enceinte* rises dramatically from amid the old town's buildings, concealing a courtyard presided over by a majestically columned Renaissance facade and a small garden, as well as the bulky and crude keep.

Claiming roots that go back to Charlemagne and St Louis, the de Crussols are proud of their long lineage, and their motto *ferro non auro* – "by iron [i.e. the sword], not gold" – sets them apart from the later families who bought rather than fought their way into the aristocracy. Their stay in Uzès has not been continuous, however, as the

Revolution precipitated a hiatus which lasted until 1954. Among the most colourful of the family's members was the Duchess Anne, grandmother of the present duke: monarchist, suffragette and enthusiastic hunter (she killed over two thousand animals), she rode until the age of 87, and was France's first female driver – and the first to receive a speeding ticket.

Still a part-time residence for the seventeenth duke, the castle can be visited on an interesting hour-long **guided tour** (an English-language hand-out is provided) through the family's apartments, which offers an intimate look at a disappearing aristocratic world, with personal effects set among the rare furnishings and ancient books. The visit ends in the castle's ancient cellars. The budget-conscious may opt only to climb the tenth-century **Tour Bermonde** (€13 without castle visit), whose summit gives fine views from between the battlements

Place aux Herbes and around

The arcaded **place aux Herbes** (where Wednesday and Saturday markets take place) was the setting for some scenes in the 1990 film *Cyrano de Bergerac* starring Gérard Depardieu. Southeast of here on café-lined boulevard Victor Hugo lies the recently restored **St-Étienne church**, with its curved Baroque facade and thirteenth-century belfry, and just behind, in quiet place St-Étienne, is the old Gide house (look out for wall plaque).

Jardin Médiéval

Impasse Port Royal • Daily: April–June & Sept Mon–Fri 2–6pm, Sat & Sun 10.30am–12.30pm & 2–6pm; July & Aug 10.30am–12.30pm & 2–6pm; Oct 2–5pm • €4.50 • ☎ 04 66 22 38 21, ⓦ jardinmedievaluzes.com

Set in the courtyard of the former bishop's palace, the **Jardin Médiéval** contains 450 varieties of herbs and plants that were collected or cultivated in the area during the Middle Ages and makes a great stop for children. In summer, the garden provides an attractive venue for events including exhibitions and concerts.

The cathedral

de la Cathédrale • Daily: 9am–6pm • Free

East of the Jardin Médiéval, past the dour entrance to the plain **Hôtel des Monnaies** (the former bishop's mint), you'll find the **cathedral**. Like so many in the region, the medieval cathedral of Uzès fell victim to the violence of the Wars of Religion but, thankfully, the twelfth-century bell tower, the **Tour Fenestrelle** (not open to the public), survived. Rising 42m, the six levels of arched windows on this round structure – unique in France – strongly recall the Leaning Tower of Pisa. The cathedral, which dates from the seventeenth century and is now a parish church, has little of interest, apart from its flamboyantly styled seventeenth-century organ.

ANDRÉ GIDE

André Gide was born in Paris in 1869, the son of a wealthy Huguenot family from Uzès. A sensitive, nervous soul, the young Gide's introspection and uncertainty was nourished by tensions he felt regarding his sexual identity. His disquietudes came to be expressed through literature, and his exceptional promise was reflected in the fact that he published his first work at the age of 20. His *Si le grain ne meurt* ("If It Die"; 1924–26), recalls in part the summers of his youth, spent in Uzès. Like so many nonconformist contemporaries he was drawn to exotic and liberating French North Africa, where he confronted and eventually came to celebrate his bisexuality, as in the landmark *The Fruits of All Earth* (1897) – a work that decisively influenced both Camus and Sartre. In the English-speaking world his best-known **novels** are *The Immoralist* (1902) and *The Counterfeiters* (1926). He died in 1951, recognized as a seminal moral and social iconoclast of the modern age, four years after having received the Nobel Prize for Literature. In 1952 his books were placed on the Catholic Church's "Index of Forbidden Books".

Musée Georges Borias

Ancien Évêché • Tues–Sun: March–June, Sept & Oct 3–6pm; July & Aug 10am–noon & 3–6pm; Nov, Dec & Feb 2–5pm • €3 • ☏ 04 66 22 40 23, ⊚ uzesmusee.blogspot.co.uk

On the north side of the cathedral, the sombre and hulking episcopal palace houses the **Musée Georges Borias**, which holds a good selection of local pottery, Polynesian relics carried home by local missionaries, some decent eighteenth-century portraiture and a room full of Gide family memorabilia.

ARRIVAL AND INFORMATION   UZÈS

By bus Uzès' bus stop is located just west of the old town on avenue de la Libération, a short walk east from the tourist office.

Destinations Nîmes (several daily; 50min); Pont du Gard (several daily; 20min).

Tourist information Chapelle des Capucins, pl Alber ler (June–Sept Mon–Fri 10am–6/7pm, Sat & Su 10am–1pm & 2–5pm; Oct–May Mon–Fri 10am–12.30pr & 2–6pm, Sat 10am–1pm; ☏ 04 66 22 68 88, ⊚ pays-uze -tourisme.com).

GETTING AROUND

By bike Bikes can be rented from British-run Village Vélo, 32 av Général Vincent (daily 9am–6pm; ☏ 06 86 45 13 10, ⊚ villagevelo.com). Rental from €18 per day.

ACCOMMODATION

Most of the town's hotels reflect its noble past – which is to say, luxurious but pricey.

Camping du Mas de Rey Rte d'Uzes, chemin du Pré des Mières ☏ 04 66 22 18 27, ⊚ campingmasderey .com. Four-star campsite in a rural location 3km from town with 60 pitches, six chalets and some ready-erected tents. There's a bar and an outdoor pool. Open Easter to mid-Oct. €27.50

★ **Entraigues** 4 pl de l'Evêché, rue de la Calade ☏ 04 66 72 05 25, ⊚ hotel-entraigues.com. This boutique hotel, set in a fifteenth-century mansion opposite the cathedral, has been completely renovated and reopened in 2016. Rooms are contemporary and fairly minimalist, there is a small rooftop pool and pretty, simple dishes are on the menu (€38). €129

Hostellerie Provençale 1 rue de la Grande Bourgade ☏ 04 66 22 11 06, ⊚ www.hostellerie provencale.com. A simple-looking facade disguises one of the area's most highly praised hotels, with attractive rooms decorated in traditional Provençal style. Breakfa is served on the roof terrace and the restaurant, L Parenthèse, specializes in market-fresh cuisine (menu €23–47). See website for special packages including truffle break in winter. €140

La Maison d'Uzès 18 rue du Docteur Blanchar ☏ 04 66 20 07 00, ⊚ lamaisonduzes.fr. The town's be hotel is set in a seventeenth-century mansion, complet with monumental staircase, a gourmet restaurant, La Tab d'Uzès, serving refined southern French cuisine (menu €28–117) and a spa in the original Roman cellar. €203

★ **La Taverne de Sophie** 4 rue Xavier Sigalon ☏ 04 6 22 13 10, ⊚ lataverne-uzes.com. This easy-going two star hotel with nine rooms is the best value for money i Uzès. An excellent location within the old town, with small shaded garden, perfect for escaping the high-seaso hordes. €95

EATING AND DRINKING

The best restaurants are in the top hotels (see above). Among the terraces that clutter the old town and line the ring road a number of establishments stand out (see below). For a drink, take your pick from any of the cafés in place aux Herbes o along boulevard Gambetta.

Le Bec à Vin 6 rue entre les Tours ☏ 04 66 22 41 20, ⊚ lebecavin.com. Well regarded by locals for its innovative Mediterranean food (*menus* from €22); you can dine indoors here or in one of several outdoor courtyards. Mon 7–9pm, Tues–Sun noon–2pm & 7–9pm.

Le Comptoir du 7 7 bd Charles Gide ☏ 04 66 22 11 54, ⊚ le-comptoir-du-7.fr. The main attraction here is a menu which changes daily (lunch €21) and features original, creative dishes made with seasonal products There's a nice courtyard outside too. Tues–Sun noon– 2pm & 7–9pm.

★ **Ma Cantine** 22 bd Gambetta ☏ 04 66 01 00 07 ⊚ restaurant-ma-cantine.com. You'll need to get her early to secure a table at this local favourite. It's all abou regional products and dishes in this modern restauran whether in tapas or more substantial meals. The long win

FROM TOP BLACK TRUFFLES (P.182); ABBATIALE ST-GILLES (P.189) >

THE BLACK DIAMONDS OF UZÈS

The eighteenth-century Brillat-Savarin, one of the founders of modern gastronomy, called them "the diamonds of cuisine" and *épicures* the world over worship their pungent, earthy taste – southern France's **Black Truffle**, or *tuber melanosporum*, is among the most desirable natural products in the world. This dark lumpy fungus grows only wild in certain oak forests and is all but undetectable to the human eye; gatherers use trained pigs and dogs to sniff out these truffles, some of which grow to 7cm in diameter, and which can easily sell for **€1000 per kilo**. Fortunately, not much is needed, and modest quantities of Black Truffle can raise a pasta, rice, egg or meat dish from *quotidien* to *extraordinaire*.

Nevertheless, Uzès and the truffle trade that is so much a part of the town's soul is under threat from much cheaper imported **Chinese** truffles (a distinct species), which are a mere shadow of their Gallic cousins. Not only are they sold fraudulently as "real" truffles, local restaurateurs have even been caught substituting them. The problem is, so few people have tried real Black Truffles, not many can spot the difference.

If you want to meet a truffle producer, visit **Les Truffières d'Uzès** (830 rte d'Alès; July & Aug Wed–Fri 10am–noon & 6–8pm; €7; ☎04 66 22 08 41, ⓦlestruffieresduzes.fr) where you can learn about truffles on a guided tour and buy truffle products in the boutique. Or best of all, come to town on the third weekend of January for the **truffle festival**, which includes live demonstrations of truffle hunting and, of course, the best and freshest "black diamonds" for sale.

menu has many choices from local vineyards. Mon–Wed, Fri & Sat 8.30am–9pm, Sun 8.30am–4pm.

Les Terroirs 5 pl aux Herbes ☎04 66 03 41 90, ⓦenviedeterroirs.com. Very popular deli and café underneath the arcades in the town's most atmospheric spot, serving tapas and salads made with local ingredients. Dishes from €9. Daily: July & Aug 9am–11pm, Sept–June 9.30am–6.30pm.

SHOPPING

Brasserie Artisanale Meduz 42 chemin du Mas des Tailles ☎06 76 03 12 23, ⓦmeduz.fr. This brewery, a 20min walk northwest of town, offers Belgian-style beers featuring flavours of the south. The free 30min tour ends with a tasting. Mon–Sat 10am–7pm.

The Pont du Gard and around

No one with even a passing interest in history or architecture should travel through Gard without seeing what is arguably the world's most famous Roman aqueduct, the **PONT DU GARD**, 20km northeast of Nîmes. The area around the Pont was devastated by serious flooding in 2000, but since then the site has been developed as a major tourist attraction, with an activities centre and an impressive modern **museum** which, together with the stony but pleasant river-beach (a great spot to cool down in summer), excellent **picnic** and **hiking** possibilities and a wide range of nearby accommodation and activities including **via ferrata** and **kayaking**, make it a good base, particularly if you are travelling with children. Several of the **surrounding hamlets** are worth checking out too, as is the **medieval bridge of St-Nicholas**, further up the Gardon river. The most intriguing of the hamlets along the Uzès–Remoulins road (and also the one where the most buses stop) is **Vers**, 4km north of the Pont, where you'll find bits of ruined arches and chunks of Roman road lying around town, and an eleventh-century church. Other nearby villages include **St-Hilaire** and **Castillon-du-Gard**, ancient and picturesque farming settlements which don't have any particular sights, but are worth wandering around.

Brief history

When the Romans needed to supply growing Nîmes with water, they found that the nearest suitable source was some 50km away on the Eure river, near Uzès. Despite the deep Gardon gorge which cut through the route, with Roman single-mindedness (and slave labour), they set about constructing a waterway. This remains nothing short of a technical marvel, descending only 17m in altitude along its course and bridging the Gardon with a monumental aqueduct, the **Pont du Gard** – now a UNESCO World Heritage Site and one of the Grands Sites de France. Most likely constructed in the mid-first century, the Pont's three tiers of arches span an incredible 275m in length, carrying water 49m above the riverbed below. Pillaged for stone through the ages, and first used as a bridge in 1295, the aqueduct has suffered various misfortunes, including an earthquake of 1448, but there was enough of the structure remaining to begin a comprehensive restoration by the eighteenth century. Such was its impact that when Rousseau passed by shortly after this work had been undertaken, the sight of the monument was enough to make him say he wished he'd "been born a Roman". A visit here used to be a must for French journeyman masons on their traditional tour of the country, and many of them have left their names and home towns carved on the stonework. Among these, the markings made by the original builders to facilitate construction can also still be found.

The aqueduct

Site open daily: March, April & Oct 8am–8pm; May–Sept 7.30am–midnight; Nov–Feb 8.30am–7pm; cultural activities and shops daily: March–May & Oct 9am–6pm; June & Sept 9am–7pm; July & Aug 9am–8pm; Nov–Feb 9am–5pm • €18 for up to five people and a car; €7 on foot or by bike • ☎ 04 66 37 50 99, ⓦ pontdugard.fr

The whole point of visiting the Pont du Gard site is to behold the incredible **aqueduct** which spans the Gardon. You can swim or kayak under it, hike alongside and walk over it, although you can only cross the broad lower level. The best way to enjoy this ancient engineering wonder, however, is to take it in from different perspectives, climbing up to the lookout areas at the top of either end, or viewing it upriver from the pebbly bed of the Gardon. Seen from here on a sunny day, the utilitarian but gracefully symmetrical beauty of the aqueduct's yellow-stone structure presents a striking contrast to the blue sky.

The modern **Site du Pont du Gard** visitors' complex offers a whole range of activities and attractions. The **museum** is an incredible multimedia installation, fully

4

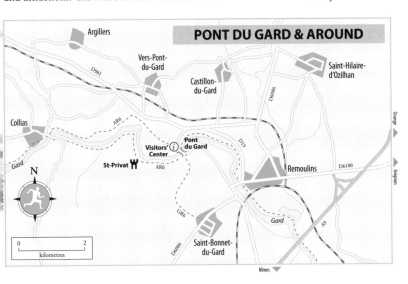

PONT DU GARD & AROUND

HIKING THE GORGES DU GARDON

Moving on from the aqueduct, the best way to leave is to hike west along the **Gardon gorge** to the commune of Ste-Anastasie (about 20km on foot). The GR6 on the north bank and the AR6 on the south (passing St-Privat) lead to **Collias** 4km away, formerly a hippie mecca, from where the GR6 can be followed upriver. Aside from the rugged beauty of the riverbed's red cliffs, look out for the **Grotte de la Baume St-Vérédème**, a medieval chapel next to a cave on the north bank just west of Collias; its frescoes, dating from the twelfth century, have recently been restored. Some 10km after Collias, you reach the ponderous thirteenth-century **Pont St-Nicolas**, now incorporated into the main Uzès–Nîmes highway. It's worth continuing a few kilometres west to Ste-Anastasie as you'll find, in an old stone village house, the **Maison des gorges du Gardon** (2 rue de la Pente, hameau du Russan; Tues–Sun 10am–6pm; ☎04 48 27 01 00, ⓦwww.gorgesdugardon.fr) where you can find out all about this Grand Site de France and buy local products in the shop.

multilingual and incorporating archeological finds, working models, film, sound effects and interactive terminals. Themes include the role of water in Roman society and culture, the building of the aqueduct, and its later decay and then revival as a tourist destination. In the same building you'll find the Ludo (an interactive activity centre for **children**), a resource centre, and a cinema. Out back, the **Mémoires de Garrigue** is a fifteen-hectare garden with **nature trails** highlighting the local fauna. There are also a number of activities and displays particularly suited to children including **workshops** for making Roman-style crafts and weapons. The whole site is suitable for visitors with disabilities.

Château de St-Privat

Av du Pont du Gard, Rive Droite • Mid-Aug to Oct (by appointment only) • €6–10 (guided visits) • ☎04 66 37 36 36

Two kilometres west of the aqueduct lies the **château de St-Privat**, the site where Cardinal Richelieu – Louis XIII's most powerful minister – signed the Peace of Alès with the Huguenots in 1629 (the lords of the castle, the Faret family, were Protestants). The château is famous for its elaborate formal garden, which dates back to 1644. One of its three sections, the "Avant-park", is home to the **War Sacrifice Chapel**, commissioned after World War I by then-owner Jacques Rouché; its walls are decorated with painted works of metaphysical allegory, mixing biblical figures with depictions of *poilus* (French common soldiers). Unfortunately the property can only be visited on a ninety-minute **guided tour**.

ARRIVAL AND DEPARTURE

The Pont itself can be reached by **bus** direct from Nîmes or Uzès – get off at "Rond Point Pont du Gard" then it's a 20-minute walk down a quiet lane. If you are coming by **car** there is secure parking at the entrance to the site, which is included in the entry price.

INFORMATION AND ACTIVITIES

Tourist information In the first unit on the left as you enter the main concourse of the "discovery area". There is a larger tourist office in place des Grands Jours in Remoulins (June, Sept & Oct Mon–Fri 9am–12.30pm & 2.30–6pm, Sat 10am–1pm; July & Aug Mon–Fri 9am–1pm & 2–6pm, Sat & Sun 10am–1pm & 2–5/6pm; Nov–May Mon–Fri 9am–12.30pm & 2–5.30pm, Sat 10am–1pm; ☎04 66 37 22 34, ⓦot-pontdugard.com).

Activities For canoe rental, Kayak Vert in Collias (☎04 66 22 80 76, ⓦkayakvert.com) can arrange trips (including pick-up or drop-off) in either direction, the best being the downstream paddle from Pont St-Nicolas. Canoes can also be rented from Natu-Rando in Remoulins (☎06 67 11 49 19, ⓦnatu-rando.com) who also rent out mountain bikes. Daredevils might like to try climbing the via ferrata – a series of iron ladders secured into the rocks high above the gorge. Contact the Bureau des Moniteurs du Gard (☎06 29 77 25 15, ⓦmoniteurs -gard.com) for details.

ACCOMMODATION

The websites of the Uzès (ⓦpays-uzes-tourisme.com) and Remoulins (ⓦot-pontdugard.com) tourist offices are great for accommodation – which tends to be on the pricey side. Lovers of luxury will find many stylish boutique hotels and B&Bs in this area. There are also many campsites around, most with cabins or trailers for rent, though in high season they get booked up very quickly.

HOTELS

★La Bégude St-Pierre 295 chemin des Bégudes, Vers ⓣ04 66 02 63 60, ⓦhotel-begude-saint-pierre.com. Stylish four-star boutique hotel in a seventeenth-century coaching inn on the edge of Vers village. Art exhibitions, a swimming pool and a well-regarded gourmet restaurant (lunch *menu* €23) make for a great stay. **€147**

Le Castellas 30 Grand'Rue, Collias ⓣ04 66 22 88 88, ⓦlecastellas.com. Three luxuriously if idiosyncratically restored seventeenth-century houses contain thirteen rooms, individually decorated in the style of a different era. As well as a gourmet meal (lunch from €25), you can have a body treatment in the wellness area and even take a cookery lesson. **€115**

Le Colombier 24 av du Pont-du-Gard, Remoulins ⓣ04 66 37 05 28, ⓦhotelrestaurant-pontdugard.fr. The best of Remoulins' hotels: a three-star *Logis de France* with seventeen rooms, a good restaurant (lunch from €12) and a pool. **€95**

Coteaux des Ânesses 150 chemin de Vazilliers, St-Hilaire ⓣ06 86 51 89 94, ⓦcoteaux-des-anesses.fr. This contemporary B&B with two simple rooms lies in the middle of a Côtes du Rhône vineyard and is named after the owner's donkeys who graze in the nearby *garrigue* (their milk makes beauty products). It's one of the best-value and most charming places to stay in the area. **€60**

Le Gardon 9 rue de Campchesteve, Collias ⓣ04 66 22 80 54, ⓦhotel-le-gardon.com. Another excellent mid-range choice at an old farmhouse in a village just up river from Remoulins. Lovely views over the countryside from the pool and a restaurant serving traditional French cuisine (*menu* €24). **€87**

Le Mas de Mon Père La Bégude de Vers ⓣ04 66 74 18 70, ⓦmasdemonpere.fr. This nineteenth-century farm has two *gîtes* for rent: the smaller one sleeps eight while the larger one sleeps fourteen. Both are rustically charming with all mod cons and the garden is a nice spot for dinner in summer. **€700**

★Le Vieux Castillon 10 rue Turion Sabatier, Castillon-du-Gard ⓣ04 66 37 61 61, ⓦvieuxcastillon.com. Owned by the same company as *La Maison d'Uzès*, this ultra-stylish four-star hotel is the perfect spot for a luxury break. There are wonderful views from the pool and creative dishes using local ingredients in the restaurant (lunch from €28). Previous guests include U2 and The Rolling Stones. **€224**

CAMPING

Le Barralet Chemin des Grès, Collias ⓣ04 66 22 84 52, ⓦcamping-barralet.com. This site wins out on both location and value – set on the riverside, it is far from the crowds and has excellent facilities including a pool and restaurant. Open April to Sept. **€25**

Gorges du Gardon 762 chemin Barque Vieille, Vers ⓣ04 66 22 81 81, ⓦcamping-gorges-gardon.fr. This is the cheapest campsite around yet has good amenities, including a pool and kids' activities. Open April to Sept. **€22**

La Soubeyranne 1110 rte de Beaucaire, Remoulins ⓣ04 66 37 03 21, ⓦsoubeyranne.com. A good choice if *La Sousta* is full. Decent facilities including indoor and covered heated pools as well as a bar and restaurant. Open April to Sept. **€29**

La Sousta 28 av du Pont-du-Gard, Remoulins ⓣ04 66 37 12 80, ⓦlasousta.com. This campsite is the closest to the Pont and has the widest range of facilities, including a shop, pool, recreational activities and wi-fi. Open April to Oct. **€26**

EATING AND DRINKING

The most pleasant option for eating is to have a picnic on the banks of the river. However, there are many good options for eating out in the area, including the local hotels (see above).

Les Clos des Vignes 9 pl du 8 mai, Castillon-du-Gard ⓣ04 66 37 02 26, ⓦleclosdesvignes30.fr. This reliably good *terroir* restaurant sits right at the heart of attractive little Castillon. There are some excellent salads and options for vegetarians. A two-course *menu* is €26. Noon–2pm & 7–9pm: May–Oct Tues, Wed & Fri–Sun; Nov–April Mon, Tues & Fri–Sun.

★La Grange de Vers 1 pl de la Fontaine, Vers ⓣ04 66 72 65 45, ⓦlagrangedevers.com. Popular wine bar in the main square, with artisan coffee and an excellent selection of local wines. Snacks such as platters of ham and cheese are available and there's sometimes live music. Mon, Wed & Thurs 9am–8pm, Fri & Sat 9am–9pm, Sun 10am–5pm.

La Petite Gare 435 rte d'Uzès, Vers ⓣ04 66 03 40 67, ⓦlapetitegare.net. The village's nineteenth-century former train station has been turned into a quirky, railway-themed restaurant. The Mediterranean ingredients are combined with Asian flavours and *menus* start at €20. Mon–Sat noon–2pm & 7–9pm.

4

Beaucaire and around

BEAUCAIRE doesn't necessarily merit making a special effort to visit, but can be a rewarding stop for those passing through. This is particularly worth considering if you have your own transport, as the interesting **Roman** and **medieval** vestiges around the town are better reached by car, although **hiking** and **biking** are possible as well. The best time to visit Beaucaire is during the Fête de la Madeleine at the end of July, a medieval pageant celebrating the town's once-famous fair.

Today, the tree-lined **canal** running through town is lined with a few waterfront restaurants and the busy leisure of the boaters who are going to or returning from Sète, while the **old town** continues to languish in semi-neglect. In July and August, the quaysides come alive on Friday evenings with musicians, street entertainers and a market. There are also weekly **markets** on Thursday and Sunday mornings.

While there's not much to see and do in the town itself, there are some interesting sights within a few kilometres' drive. The nearest place of interest is the well-preserved **Château de Tarascon**, just across the Rhône, while 4km to the northwest is the underground **Abbaye Troglodytique de St-Roman**. Wine lovers will want to make a beeline for the **Mas des Tourelles**, a reconstructed Roman winery, which also produces AOP Costières de Nîmes.

Brief history

From the second century BC Beaucaire was a Roman wine entrepôt known as Ugernum, but this disappeared along with the empire. Centuries later, the town thrived under the patronage of the counts of Toulouse. During the Albigensian Crusade, it was the site of a rare defeat for the fierce Simon de Montfort at the hands of Raymond VII – the jubilant count granted the town the right to hold a yearly **trade fair** as a reward. Bringing merchants from all over Europe, the Middle East and North Africa, the market survived the town's transition to the French Crown in 1229 and continued to be held through the nineteenth century. Trade routes shifted, however, and by the time Richelieu ordered the castle torn down in 1632, Beaucaire was already a backwater.

The castle

Museum April–June Wed–Fri 9.30am–12.30pm & 2–6pm, Sat 2–6pm; July–Sept Wed–Sun 9.30am–12.30pm & 2–6pm; Oct–March Wed–Sat 2–5pm • €5.40 • ☎ 04 66 59 90 07

Poised on a rocky promontory rising 35m above the Rhône, Beaucaire's partially ruined **castle** – the main attraction here – provides dramatic views of the surrounding countryside and Tarascon's own castle. Parts of the fourteenth-century **curtain wall** survive, as do several towers, including the striking **Tour Polygonale**, shooting dramatically skyward out of the living rock of the hill. The castle and its eighteenth-century listed **gardens** which fill the outer courtyard can be visited free of charge. Also here is the **Musée Auguste-Jacquet**, a museum which features archeology and local history.

L'Abbaye Troglodytique de St-Roman

4km northwest of Beaucaire • See website for dates and times • €5.50 • ☎ 07 81 56 44 51, ⊕ abbaye-saint-roman.com

The underground **Abbaye Troglodytique de St-Roman**, founded in the fifth century, is one of the oldest monasteries in France. Later covered over by a castle that was subsequently destroyed, the huge abbey was not rediscovered until 1966. The subterranean main chapel – built to house the sacred remains of St Roman – still contains the impressive carved seat from which the abbots presided over their community until the sixteenth century. Inside you'll also find small tombs carved in the floor, and set with recesses in which oil lamps were placed in honour of the dead. This church, the monks' cells and other chambers were cut into the living rock of the hill in what must have been gruelling labour. The terrace of the monastery offers a sweeping panorama of **the Rhône**, with the hills of Provence easily visible in the distance.

Le Mas des Tourelles

Around 8km west of Beaucaire on the D38 • April–June & Sept Mon–Fri 10am–noon & 2–6pm, Sat & Sun 2–6pm; July & Aug Mon–Sat 10am–noon & 2–7pm, Sun 2–7pm; Oct daily 2–6pm; Nov–March Sat 2–5.30pm • €5.80 • ☎ 04 66 59 19 72, Ⓦ tourelles.com

The recreated Roman winery of **Le Mas des Tourelles**, on the site of an original Roman villa, is an entertaining stop. You can take a walk around the garden and vineyard, check out the ancient methods in the winery, visit the Gallo-Roman perfume workshop and taste some wines made to original Roman recipes. On the second Sunday of September (2–5pm) you can watch toga-clad types treading grapes and eat Roman food.

From the vineyard it's a thirty-minute signposted walk north to a well-preserved 8km stretch of the **Via Domitia** that leads west from Beaucaire, and still boasts three Roman **milestones**; when you reach the road, turn right and you will find them.

Château de Tarascon

Bd du Roi Réné, Tarascon • Daily: Feb–May 9.30am–5.30pm; June–Sept 9.30am–6.30pm; Oct 9.30am–5.30pm; Nov–Jan 9.30am–5pm • €7.50 • ☎ 04 90 91 01 93, Ⓦ chateau.tarascon.fr

4

While visiting Beaucaire it would be a shame not to walk or drive across the bridge that spans the Rhône to visit the **Château de Tarascon** (look to your left – you can't miss it). This immaculately preserved thirteenth-century fortress, rising majestically from the banks of the Rhône, provides a stunning contrast to the ruins of Beaucaire's fortress. It was here that the anonymous medieval poem (possibly a musical play), *Nicolette and Aucassin*, was written, recounting the tale of the star-crossed love affair between Aucassin, a fictional heir of Beaucaire, and Nicolette, a beautiful Muslim slave girl who had been bought by the viscount of Tarascon and raised as a Christian. As well as a display on the castle's history and heritage, there is also an (annually changing) exhibition of contemporary artworks that have been inspired by the building.

ARRIVAL AND INFORMATION

BEAUCAIRE AND AROUND

By train The *gare SNCF* is on av Lech Walesa, south of the canal next the river. TGV stations are indicated with an asterisk.

Destinations Montpellier* (several daily; 1hr); Narbonne* (several daily; 2hr 10min); Nîmes* (several daily; 16min).

By bus Arriving by bus get off at "Fontêtes" (the old town is on your left and the canal is to the east) or "Passarelle" stop (the footbridge).

Destinations Nîmes (several daily; 40min); St-Gilles (several daily; 40min).

Tourist information On the north side of the canal that runs along the southern edge of the old town at 24 cours Gambetta (Mon–Fri 9am–12.15pm & 1.30–5.30pm, Sat 9.30am–12.30pm; also open Sat 2–6pm April–Oct; ☎ 04 66 59 26 57, Ⓦ provence-camargue -tourisme.com).

ACCOMMODATION AND EATING

Auberge L'Amandin 1076 chemin de la Croix de Marbre, 2km southwest of Beaucaire ☎ 04 66 59 55 07, Ⓦ auberge-amandin.com. Highly regarded restaurant in an attractive, bucolic setting; the terrace is next to a swimming pool. Mediterranean seafood is the speciality here, but there's something to suit most tastes. Lunch menu €19. Tues, Wed, Fri & Sat noon–2pm & 7–9pm, Thurs & Sun noon–2pm.

Domaine des Clos 911 chemin du Mas de la Tour ☎ 04 66 01 14 61, Ⓦ domaine-des-clos.com. Lovely boutique hotel in a seventeenth-century winery surrounded by parkland. The nine rooms are individually decorated in tasteful southern French style; there are also nine apartments. The pool is long enough to swim decent lengths. **€136**

4

THE RHÔNE–SÈTE CANAL

Although not as famous as its sister to the west, the **Rhône–Sète canal** is an inland waterway which also offers great sightseeing and leisure possibilities, either on its own or combined with a trip along the Canal du Midi. Not only is the Rhône–Sète waterway less crowded than its more popular counterpart, but the general evenness of the landscape means that there are no locks (on the main line) and fewer queues to contend with, even in high season. The various **subsidiary canals** also offer the opportunity to explore the backwaters of the Camargue in relative isolation.

The canal begins in **Beaucaire**, heading southwest through the flat Camarguais wine-country to **St-Gilles**, where you can turn off on a secondary canal to **Vauvert**, a handy stop for supplies, particularly when its market is in full swing on Wednesday and Friday mornings. Otherwise, the main canal crosses 30km of salty marshland, rich in birdlife, to pass the medieval **Tour Carbonnière**, just before **Aigues-Mortes**. From here, St Louis' thirteenth-century canal (or *grau*) can be followed to **Le-Grau-du-Roi** and **Port Camargue**.

Alternatively, from Aigues-Mortes follow the main canal west as it weaves its way past the Étang de Maugaio, before arriving at **Palavas-les-Flots**, which provides a handy base for exploring **Montpellier**, and whose branch canals lead inland to **Villeneuve-lès-Maguelone** and Lattes. Heading west, the canal threads a series of *étangs*, gliding past the ancient cathedral of **Maguelone**, and **Frontignan**, an ancient *circulade* with a **medieval church**. Finally, the canal arrives at its terminus, **Sète**; from here you can continue into the broad expanse of the Bassin de Thau, skirting the oyster beds, to visit its colourful fishing towns: Balaruc, **Mèze** and Marseillan. At the far end of this saltwater lagoon, an access canal leads 5km to **Agde** (Chapter 6), from where the **Canal du Midi** can be accessed.

Boats can be rented at most of the ports of call along the canal, which also have sanitary facilities and fresh-water supplies. At Beaucaire there is En Bateau (☎ 04 67 13 19 62, ⓦ en-bateau.com) and River and Boat (☎ 01 70 80 97 38, ⓦ river-and-boat.fr). Arolles Marine is at Bellegarde (☎ 04 66 01 75 15, ⓦ camargue-fluvial.com) and Le Boat (☎ 04 68 94 42 80, ⓦ leboat.fr) is in St-Gilles. The local *capitaineries* can also direct you to the nearest **bicycle** rental, handy for exploring the canal-side towns.

Épicerie de Cécile Place de la République/place Vieille ☎ 06 80 04 09 04. On sunny days, sit on the terrace of this popular deli-restaurant and admire the medieval architecture around the attractive square. Salads, soups and light meals are on the menu, with main courses around €13. Tues–Sun noon–2pm.

St-Gilles and around

Like Beaucaire, **ST-GILLES** is another town whose candle blew out in the late Middle Ages, and whose present attraction is the magnificent and fortunately preserved facade of its former **abbey-church** – once the most important place of pilgrimage after Rome, Jerusalem and Santiago de Compostela and now a UNESCO World Heritage Site. Other than the church and the **Maison Romane** museum, it's well worth wandering around the narrow lanes and arch-covered streets of the **old town** – many of the tiny houses here retain their medieval details and it won't take long for you to discover small doors set in slowly sagging walls, and half-open windows revealing pastel-toned plaster walls and ceiling beams within. St-Gilles is also one of the gateways to the swampy **Camargue Gardoise**, formerly known as the "Petite Camargue", which stretches from Nîmes airport 12km to the north of the town as far as Aigues-Mortes in the southwest, and covers a surface area of around four hundred square kilometres. Today the town's two principal roles have been revived: it has both a busy canalside **pleasure port** and the still-functioning **pilgrim route** to Compostela, which lives on as the GR653, coming into town from Arles and heading on west through the flat vineyards to Montpellier.

The biggest festivities in St-Gilles take place in mid-August, with the Feria de la Pêche et de l'Abricot ("The Peach and Apricot Festival") featuring *abrivados*, *encierros* and full-blown *corridas*. Throughout the year there are lively **markets** on Thursday and Sunday mornings.

Brief history

Perched on the edge of the Camargue, quiet St-Gilles takes its name from a legendary sixth-century hermit who converted the Visigothic king Wamba to Christianity. The ever-astute Cluniac monks promoted the **cult of the saint** in order to make the town (already on the Arles-to-Santiago de Compostela pilgrim route) a lucrative stopping point early in the twelfth century. By this time it was a favourite of the counts of Toulouse – the Crusader Raymond IV used "de St-Gilles" as his surname. A good port and liberal market privileges further boosted prosperity and drew traders from around the Mediterranean, but within a few hundred years the unstoppable silt of the Rhône and the tide of the Reformation conspired to kill both the port and the pilgrim route. The **Wars of Religion** were especially bitter in St-Gilles – at one point a Protestant mob is said to have thrown the church's choristers down a well – and by the time the great abbey-church was virtually destroyed by Huguenot mobs in 1622, the town had already passed into history.

Abbatiale St-Gilles

Place de la République • April–Sept Mon–Sat 9.30am–12.30pm & 2–6pm, Sun 2–5.30pm; Oct–March Mon–Sat 9.30am–12.30pm & 2–5.30pm • Free for the church but €5 for the crypt, €6 combined ticket with Maison Romane

The main attraction in St-Gilles is its spectacular **Abbatiale St-Gilles,** the abbey-church, in the heart of the old town. Although the Religious Wars destroyed almost the entire building, fate spared the most interesting work of medieval art in the region: the great twelfth-century Romanesque **frieze** that graces the church's west entrance. Spreading between and over the three great doorways (reminiscent of a Roman triumphal arch), a series of bas-reliefs conveys the story of Jesus' return to Jerusalem and subsequent Crucifixion, representations of the Apostles, the three Marys and St Paul, and scenes

---

THE CHEMIN DE ST-JACQUES

The pilgrimage route to Santiago de Compostela (known in Spain as the Camino de Santiago and in France as the **Chemin de St-Jacques**) was Languedoc's and Europe's first grand tourism venture (and inspired the first European guidebooks). It all started in the ninth century when a priest in northwestern Spain miraculously "discovered" the burial site of **St James the Greater**, the Apostle, in a local cemetery. The remains were shifted to a nearby hamlet, which was subsequently renamed as **Santiago** (St James) **de Compostela** (from the Latin for "little burial ground"). The tomb became a rallying point for the Christians of northern Spain, but it was in the late eleventh century that things really got going. By this time the Church was prescribing pilgrimage as a way of doing penance for sins, and both common folk and nobles saw it also as a way to see the world and escape the banalities of daily existence. The volume of travellers brought wealth and prosperity not only to Santiago, but also to the churches and monasteries along the route which, like **St-Sernin** in Toulouse (see p.57), **St-Guilhem** in Hérault (see p.236) and **St-Gilles** in Gard, made showcases of their own relics to attract the faithful along the way. Other notable stops on the pilgrim route include **Vals** in the Aude (see p.107), **St-Lizier** in Ariège (see p.114), **Rabastens** in the Tarn (see p.144), **Joncels** (see p.269), **Murat** (see p.154), **La Salvetat** (see p.154) and **Clermont l'Hérault** (see p.231) in Haut Languedoc, and **Santa María Vilar** in Roussillon. Today, hikers continue to follow the route, designated a UNESCO World Heritage Site in 1998, and a fascinating window into a world long past. Most towns and hamlets along the route have a **pilgrim hostel** where you can sleep for about €12. In the old days these might be signalled by a carved scallop shell, the symbol of the pilgrimage, but nowadays look for signs which say "accueil pèlerins".

4

based on the Old Testament and medieval iconography. These carvings are of superlative workmanship, a unique blend of Byzantine, Classical and medieval styling setting them apart from the mass of contemporary work. They're best viewed (and photographed) in the afternoon, when the sunlight plays across the carvings. Aside from this, two other noteworthy remains of the medieval church can be seen: the **choir** and the **crypt**, one of the largest in France, which contains the **tombs** of St Gilles and Pierre de Castelnau (see p.314). Located behind the modern building, the ruins of the former choir hint at the grandeur of the medieval church. On the north side stands the *vis* ("screw"), a massive self-supporting **spiral staircase** built in the 1100s to access the church's upper gallery. An architectural marvel, the abbey-church was, like the Pont du Gard, a mandatory stop on the masons' tour of the country.

Musée de la Maison Romane

Place de la Maison Romane • April–Oct Wed–Fri 10.30am–12.30pm & 2–4pm; Nov–March Wed–Fri 2–4pm • €2; or €6 combined ticket with abbey • ☎ 04 66 87 40 42

Opposite the church sits the **Musée de la Maison Romane**, a restored medieval house in which it is claimed Gui Foucois, a.k.a. Guy Foulques, who became Pope Clement IV in 1265, was born. Restored in the nineteenth century and one of France's "historic monuments", it now houses a municipal **museum** featuring a musty mix of local archeology, carvings from the abbey and Camargue birdlife. The twelfth-century top floor, with its original features and a fourteenth-century statue of St-Gilles, is a highlight.

ARRIVAL AND DEPARTURE

ST-GILLES AND AROUND

By bus Take a Tango bus #42 (several daily; 40min; ⓦ tangobus.fr) from Nîmes or Edgard #C31 (several daily; 45min; ⓦ edgard-transport.fr) from Beaucaire. Get off at the "Mistral" stop, by the tourist office.

By car There is free, secure parking at Parking Charles de Gaulle, accessed via rue Gambetta or rue Sadi Carnot.
By boat St-Gilles is one of the main stops on the Rhône-Sète canal (see box, p.188).

INFORMATION AND ACTIVITIES

Tourist information 1 pl Frédéric Mistral (April–Oct Mon–Sat 9.30am–12.30pm & 2–6pm, also Sun 9.30am–1pm in July & Aug; Nov–March Mon–Fri 9.30am–12.30pm & 2–5.30pm; ☎ 04 66 87 33 75,

ⓦ ot-saint-gilles.fr).
Bike rental Le Barjonaute, 282 rue Carnot, Vauvert (daily 8.30am–noon & 1.30–7pm; ☎ 06 03 53 65 64, ⓦ lebarjonaute.com). Mountain bikes, electric bikes and

PERRIER

Set amid the shadeless countryside of vineyards and indistinguishable hamlets west of St-Gilles is one of France's proudest commercial institutions, the **Perrier spring and bottling plant**, located a few minutes' drive north of **Vauvert**. The source of France's second most famous bubbly stuff, the much-advertised **spring** (mid-April to Sept Mon–Fri 9.30am–12.30pm & 1.30–5pm, guided visits to reserve in advance10am, 11am, 2pm, 3pm & 4pm; €3–4; ☎ 04 66 87 61 01, ⓦ visitez-perrier.com) is a site venerated by Gallic hordes who arrive daily, blissfully shelling out for the thirty-minute **tour** (although you can do a self-guided visit), sharing vicariously in the glory of the water which has come to signify France abroad. The spring was known in Roman times, but subsequently languished in obscurity until 1894, when a certain Dr Perrier of Nîmes bought the property and set up the Perrier Spring Company in partnership with a young, disabled English aristocrat, who came up with the distinctive shape for the bottle inspired by the dumbbells he used for his physiotherapy. The **tour or self-guided visit** includes a walk through the vast and modern bottling complex, a visit to the spring itself and ends at the former owner's mansion, this last now the Perrier "museum" – a thinly disguised shop where you can pay inflated prices for various bits of merchandising.

trikes from €12 per half-day. You can cycle from St-Gilles to Le Grau-du-Roi via a new section of the Via Rhôna cycle path.

Walking From April to October you can follow a path (4km), "Le sentier du Cougourlier", along the canal and through the marshes where horses and bulls graze. The path starts 4km west of St-Gilles by the N572.

Wine tasting and tours Château l'Ermitage, 1301 chemin dit le Saou (☏ 04 66 87 04 49, ⊕ chateau-ermitage .com). Explore a Costières de Nîmes vineyard guided by the producer in his 1970s open-top Land Rover.

Visit an olive producer Oliverae Jeanjean, 2373 chemin des Loubes (☏ 04 66 87 42 43, ⊕ oliveraie-jeanjean.com). Visit the olive groves on your own or in a golf buggy with the owner (€20 for up to five people). The olives are pressed, and the oil and its other products are sold, in the on-site shop.

ACCOMMODATION AND EATING

Camping La Chicanette 7 rue de la Chicanette ☏ 04 66 87 28 32, ⊕ campinglachicanette.fr. Good-value three-star campsite with a mix of pitches, chalets and apartments. There are two pools, a kids' play area and entertainment in summer. Open April to Oct. €20

★ **Le Cours** 10 av François Griffeuille ☏ 04 66 87 31 93, ⊕ hotel-le-cours.com. This reliable *Logis de France* hotel makes a good-value base but the real reason to come here is for the food – their *gardiane de taureau* (slow-cooked bull meat in red wine) is hard to beat. €61

Domaine de la Fosse 111 rte de Sylvéréal, 7km south of St-Gilles ☏ 04 66 87 05 05, ⊕ domainedelafosse .com. Luxury B&B in a former Templar commandery in the middle of the countryside, with six tastefully furnished rooms and two *gîtes*. There's a pool and individual yoga classes; also *table d'hôte* (€35). €135

The Camargue Gardoise

4

The **CAMARGUE GARDOISE**, which Lawrence Durrell called "Little Argentina", is a forbidding expanse of marshes, crisscrossed by canals, and dominated by great saltwater *étangs* ("lagoons"), spreading from the banks of the Petit Rhône, an off-shoot of the larger river. The Camargue as a whole, most of which is in the Bouches du Rhône *département* in Provence, is a lightly populated and isolated area, whose capital is the village of **Saintes-Maries-de-la-Mer** (the other side of the river in Provence), with a scattering of ranches (*manades*), rice paddies, fruit farms and salt works. It is temporary

---

EXPLORING THE CAMARGUE GARDOISE

The easiest way to get around the Camargue Gardoise is with your own vehicle; however, don't be tempted onto the **unpaved roads** and lanes leading out through the fields – quite often they are deceptively soft and you may find yourself walking back to civilization. The best way to visit the more remote areas is on an organized one-day **safari** or **boat tour**. Several of the horse farms near **St-Gilles** offer half- and full-day horseback and carriage tours around their land – ask at the tourist office there (see p.190).

BULL FARMS

A visit to a **bull farm** (*manade*) is an interesting experience – a chance to see the traditional lifestyle of the ranches of the delta, and witness the impressive equestrian skills of the *gardians* ("cowboys") who manage the herds, which are raised for meat or to take part in *courses camarguaises*. The tourist office in St-Gilles has a list of the twenty or so ranches in the area, and can indicate which have English-speaking guides and which charge admission to visitors. Some also organize **dinners** accompanied by flamenco music.

OPERATORS

Cabane du Boucanet Le Grau ☏ 04 66 53 25 64, ⊕ cabaneduboucanet.com. Organizes horseback rides of the area (€20/hr).

Camargue Découverte 6 rue des Alliés, Le Grau ☏ 04 66 53 04 99, ⊕ camargue-decouverte.com. Runs expeditions by 4x4, quad bike or carriage, and also offers tours of a working bull farm.

Isle de Stel Aigues-Mortes ☏ 04 66 53 60 70, ⊕ croisiere-de-camargue.com. From April–Sept, ninety-minute tours of the nearby *étangs* and canals (€9) are offered on the good ship *Isle de Stel*.

GARDIAN TRADITIONS

The Rhône delta is where the Gard's strong traditions of **horsemanship** and *tauromachie* originate, on the great ranches where wild bulls are left to graze the salty scrub freely. The *gardians* (Camargue cowboys) whose simple huts dot the plain have been the proud masters of the delta since at least 1512, when they established a formal confraternity. Riding their distinctively small "Camargue" ponies they pursue and corral the black bulls, rounding them up for branding in the springtime *ferrade*. The local tourist offices will have details of *manades* where you can watch these traditions in action.

home, however, to an incredible variety of **waterfowl** – some four hundred different species – including a steady stream of migrating birds crossing the Mediterranean between Europe and Africa in spring and fall; look out especially for pink flamingos, herons, grand cormorants and egrets. In 2014, the Camargue Gardoise became a **Grand Site de France**.

Maison de la Camargue Gardoise

Rte du Môle, beyond Aigues Mortes • Tues–Sun 10am–12.30pm & 1.30–6pm • Free • ⓣ 04 66 77 24 72, ⓦ camarguegardoise.com

Marking the region's citation as a Grand Site de France in 2014, the **Maison de la Camargue Gardoise** now gives visitors the chance to learn all about this fascinating area. There is an exhibition, a shop and a "discovery path", as well as guided tours (mid-July to mid-Aug 7–9am; €6) which include breakfast. However, if you have kids or problems walking, the path at the **Centre de Découverte du Scamandre** (rte des Iscles Gallician, Vauvert; Tues–Sat 9am–6pm; free; ⓣ 04 66 73 52 05, ⓦ camarguegardoise .com), with picnic spots and one-kilometre raised walkway through the marsh, is much easier to negotiate and is also a more attractive spot.

4

Parc Naturel Régional de la Camargue

A large slice of the Camargue proper, which lies officially in Provence, has been incorporated since 1970 into the **Parc Naturel Régional de la Camargue** (ⓦ parc -camargue.fr), but there is no visible characteristic that distinguishes the official parkland from the rest of the Rhône delta.

Musée de la Camargue

Mas du Pont du Rousty, Arles • Mon & Wed–Sun: April–Sept 9am–12.30pm & 1–6pm; Oct–March 10am–12.30pm & 1–5pm • €5 • ⓣ 04 90 97 10 82, ⓦ parc-camargue.fr

The **Musée de la Camargue** provides an excellent orientation to the area. Located in an old sheep-farm, Mas du Pont du Rousty, and surrounded by nature trails, the museum reopened after renovation in 2013 and now contains a permanent exhibition on the ecology and economy of the Rhône delta. Outside is a ninety-minute "discovery path" where you can learn about local farming and see a *cabane de gardian* (traditional thatched cottage), as well as birds and animals.

Saintes-Maries-de-la-Mer

The furthest the road will take you in the Camargue is **Saintes-Maries-de-la-Mer**, an ancient seaside village the population of which swells to over fifty thousand in July and August, from the less than three thousand inhabitants it has the rest of the year. The windswept fishing village, dominated by its fortress-like medieval **church**, attracted the likes of Van Gogh in the late nineteenth century and bullfighting fans Hemingway and Picasso in the early twentieth century, and now brings in crowds of summer sun-worshippers. The crypt of the ancient church

---

SARA AND THE THREE MARYS

A legend going back five hundred years recounts how after the Crucifixion, Joseph of Arimathea and Jesus' female followers – Mary Magdalene, Mary Salomé and Mary Jacobé – had set sail from Egypt and landed near the mouth of the Petit Rhône at the town of Ra. In 1838 the town's name was changed to **Saintes-Maries-de-la-Mer**, and soon after **Roma** ("Gipsy") peoples began to gather here to mark the feast of St Sara, or "**Black Sara**," who they hold to have been an Egyptian servant-girl belonging to Mary Magdalene, and considered to be their patron saint. Black Sara is still commemorated every year on May 24 and 25, when thousands of Roma from around Europe converge on the town for a **celebration** marked by baptisms, music and dancing, culminating in the statue of Sara (and subsequently with those of Mary Salomé and Jacobé) being taken from the town's church and carried in **procession** by crowds down to the sea. The following day, May 26, is celebrated with an *abrivado* (bulls, contained by horses, running through the streets), folk dancing and displays of **horsemanship** by *gardians*.

(daily 8am–7pm; free) is worth visiting to see the statue of **Black Sara** (see box above), bedecked in colourful robes and surrounded by offerings of the faithful. There's enough here to keep you occupied for at least a day, including **sandy beaches** and **markets** on Monday and Friday mornings. The biggest event of the summer is the **Feria du Cheval**, a three-day celebration of horses, which takes place around 14 July.

4

ARRIVAL AND INFORMATION
SAINTES-MARIES-DE-LA-MER

By bus There are no direct buses from the Gard *département* to Saintes-Maries. You will need to get a bus or a train to Arles and then take bus #20 onwards (on the way it stops at the Musée de la Camargue). Get off at the "Razeteurs" stop for the village.

Tourist information 5 av Van Gogh (daily: April, May & Oct 9am–6pm; June & Sept 9am–7pm; July & Aug 9am–8pm; Nov–March 9am–5pm; ☎04 90 97 82 55; ⓦsaintesmaries.com).

ACCOMMODATION AND EATING

Camping Le Clos du Rhône D85 rte d'Aigues Mortes ☎04 90 97 85 99, ⓦcamping-leclos.fr. Well-equipped four-star campsite next to the beach with lodges and pitches on offer. As well as a pool, there's a small spa and a free shuttle into the village (1.5km) in summer. Open April to Oct. **€27**

Casa Romana 6 rue Joseph Roumanille ☎04 90 97 83 33. The place to go in the village for good-quality Camargue specialities such as bull steak, *gardiane de taureau* or *tellines* (local shellfish). Lunch *menu* €19. Tues–Sun noon–2.30pm & 7–9pm.

Hôtellerie du Pont Blanc Chemin du Pont Blanc ☎04 97 89 11, ⓦpont-blanc.camargue.fr. A good budget hotel with fifteen simple, ground-floor rooms around the pool and three rooms in a *cabane de gardian*. **€67**

Mas de Calabrun Rte de Cacharel ☎04 90 97 82 21, ⓦmas-de-calabrun.fr. Good mid-range hotel with 3 individually decorated rooms and three romantic gipsy caravans for rent. The restaurant, with a nice outside terrace, serves gourmet versions of Camargue dishes. There's a pool too. **€129**

The Camarguais coast

Set by the **Camarguais coast** amid the flat swampy land of the westernmost reaches of the Rhône delta, is **Aigues-Mortes**, its perfectly intact rectangular walls rising out of the plain like a storybook image of a medieval town. From here, an ancient canal leads southwest to **Le Grau-du-Roi**, once a humble fishing town, now a teeming **summer resort**, exploiting the great unbroken band of dunes which stretches along the coast from the town's eastern limits all the way to the mouth of the Petit Rhône. **Port Camargue**, a modern adjunct to Le Grau, is a purpose-built yachting complex – the biggest pleasure-port in Europe.

Aigues-Mortes and around

Originally intended to be France's principal Mediterranean port, walled-town **AIGUES-MORTES** was swallowed up in short order by the silt of the Rhône, which pushed the sea south and consigned the town to stagnation among the "dead waters" surrounding it. Today it is a mandatory photo-stop, and a tour of the **fortifications** and the rectangular grid of thirteenth-century streets is a pleasant way to pass an hour or so, combining well with a trip to the **beaches** to the south. It is well maintained, but its success as a day-trip and weekend destination has cluttered the streets with postcard and souvenir boutiques and restaurants. If you have the good fortune to visit during the **Fête locale** in October, try to catch a *course camarguaise*; watching the crowds and the bulls beneath the medieval ramparts is a truly evocative sight. There are **markets** on Wednesday and Sunday mornings as well as Saturday in the summer.

Brief history

Founded by **Louis IX** in 1246, it was from here that the saint-king embarked on two of his expeditions: to Cyprus on the Seventh Crusade of 1248 and to Tunis in 1270, where he met his death (by diarrhoea). His son, Philip, gave the medieval town its present form, commissioning Genoan engineers to build walls in emulation of those of Damietta in Egypt, the site of Louis' early (but Pyrrhic) triumph. Local salt beds and trade privileges brought initial success, but by the end of the fourteenth century it had become a backwater, stranded by the waves of silt brought downriver by the Rhône. Aigues-Mortes' misfortune, however, has preserved the town's striking profile, which may have otherwise been built over and around.

Tour de Constance

Daily: May–Aug 10am–7pm; Sept–April 10am–1pm & 2–5.30pm · €7.50 · ☎ 04 66 53 61 55, ⓦ monuments-nationaux.fr

On the far side of the open *place* where the tourist office sits, looms the massive **Tour de Constance**, the main fortress of the town – once a lighthouse and for many years a prison for uncooperative nobles and stalwart Huguenots. Protestant women were confined in the cells on the top floor, including one stoic Marie Durand who spent almost forty years here in the eighteenth century, and whose graffiti remain etched in the stone to this day. It is also through the tower that you access the walk along the **town walls**, which provides sweeping views over the flat terrain of the delta and allows a close-up look at the city's defences: arrow-slitted battlements, and stone ducts for pouring boiling oil on would-be attackers. Those on a budget, however, should skip this steeply priced visit; a pleasant (and free) option is to walk across town from the Porte de la Gardette and take in the walls from the fields to the south.

La Tour Carbonnière

1km northeast of Aigues Mortes on the D979 then D46

Heading northeast from Aigues-Mortes towards the Camargue Gardoise will take you to the curious **Tour Carbonnière**. Once the guard-post on the only land access to

---

THE SALTED BURGUNDIANS

In the southeastern corner of the town is "**the tower of the salted Burgundians**", the curious nickname dating back to a grisly episode of the Hundred Years' War. When the town was seized in a raid by English-allied Burgundian forces in 1418, royalist Armagnacs came to try to retake the town. They were foiled by the strong fortifications, but one night a local citizen opened one of the smaller gates to let their forces in. Sneaking up on the sleeping Burgundian garrison, the Armagnacs slaughtered them before they knew what was happening, but rather than bury the bodies (no easy task in the fetid marshes surrounding the town), the victorious forces stuffed them into this tower, and layered them with salt so they would not putrefy – leaving them, literally, in a pickle.

4

the medieval port-town, this 20m-high tower, perched on a rare mound of terra firma and pierced by a gate through which the road once led, is now a popular place for a walk.

Les Salins du Midi

Rte du Grau-du-Roi, 3km southwest of Aigues Mortes • Daily: March & Oct 10.30am, 11.30am, 2.30pm & 4pm; April–June & Sept 10am, 10.30am, 11am, 11.30am, 2pm, 2.30pm, 3pm, 3.30pm, 4pm, 4.30pm & 5pm; July & Aug 10am, 10.30am, 11am, 11.15am, 11.30pm, noon, 1.30pm, 2pm, 2.30pm, 3pm, 3.30pm, 4pm, 4.30pm, 5pm, 5.30pm & 6pm • €10 • ☎ 04 66 73 40 24, ⓦ visitesalinsdecamargue.com

Heading southwest from Aigues-Mortes towards Le Grau-du-Roi you'll see the salt pans of the **Salins du Midi**, which can be visited on a 75-minute tour by *petit train* with a guide explaining their history and the techniques of salt harvesting. In July and August, you can take the train tour at sunset (Tues–Fri 7.30pm). It's also possible to have a three-hour guided tour by bike (April & Oct 9am & 2.30pm; May & June 8.30am & 3pm; July–Sept 8.30am & 4pm; €25).

ARRIVAL AND DEPARTURE — AIGUES-MORTES AND AROUND

By train The *gare SNCF*, on the spur line that runs down from Nîmes to Le Grau-du-Roi, is on the route de Nîmes, just north of the old town.

Destinations Le Grau-du-Roi (several daily; 7min); Nîmes (several daily; 40min–1hr).

By bus This route is served by Edgard and stops at the To de Constance.

Destinations La Grande Motte (several daily; 40min Le Grau-du-Roi (several daily; 10min); Montpellier (seve daily; 1hr 10min); Nîmes (several daily; 55min).

INFORMATION AND GETTING AROUND

Tourist information Pl St-Louis (April–June & Sept Mon–Fri 9am–6pm, Sat & Sun 10am–6pm; July & Aug daily 9am–7pm; Oct–March Mon–Fri 9am–5pm, Sat & Sun 10am–5pm; ☎04 66 53 73 00, ⓦ ot -aiguesmortes.com).

Bike rental Veloc, 296 rte de Nîmes (☎ 06 76 67 40 23/☎ 66 23 77 58). From €3 for an hour. You can cycle fro St-Gilles to Le Grau-du-Roi via Aigues Mortes on the V Rhôna cycle path.

TAUROMACHIE AND LES COURSES CAMARGUAISES

Bulls have been raised in the Camargue Gardoise and the plains to its north for centuries, and for the people of the ranchlands around St-Gilles, **tauromachie** or *la bouvine* – the art of bull-handling – has come to represent a measure of virility, testament to their proud rural roots. Its significance however, is also region-wide: the growing cultural awareness of the mid-nineteenth century prompted intellectual Occitan patriots to find in it a further mark of the uniqueness of their local culture, thus investing *tauromachie* with iconic status throughout Languedoc and Roussillon. Although the imported Spanish tradition of the *corrida* (see box, p.172) has come to dominate, the bloodless **course camarguaise** – an expression of what locals call La fé di bioù ("love of the bull") – is quite distinct.

Less expensive and elaborate than the *corrida*, the *course* is common in village *fêtes*, such as at **Sommières** or **Aigues-Mortes**. Here, the bulls (or cows) are first led to the ring (an *abrivado*), herded by a tumult of mounted *gardians* – if this takes place within a confined area, it is called an *encierro* (a "running" of the bulls). Once in the ring the animals are outfitted with a rosette and tassels suspended between their horns, and for fifteen minutes *raseteurs* (named after the hooked handgear they wear) provoke the animal into charging, and attempt to snatch the rosette or tassels without getting trampled or gored. When all is complete, the bulls are herded out with great fanfare and frenzy (the *bandido*) and back to the pen.

Aside from these entertainments, a rather more workaday manifestation of *la bouvine* has also become a staple of local springtime festivals. This is the **ferrado**, in which year-old bulls are driven from their pens by mounted *gardians*, wrestled to the ground by their colleagues on foot and then branded with a hot iron, marking them with the arms or initials of the *manade* to which they belong.

CCOMMODATION AND EATING

amping La Petite Camargue Rte de Cacharel
04 66 53 98 98, ⓦyellohvillage-petite-camargue
om. Five-star campsite in a wooded location a couple of
lometres from the beach. The main attraction is a massive
wimming pool with slides and jacuzzis; there's even an
n-site horseriding centre. **€31**

e Duende 16 rue Amiral Courbet ☎04 66 51 79 28.
osy, rustic restaurant with good-quality Camargue cuisine
n the menu. *Crème brûlée à l'orange* is an excellent choice

for dessert. Daily noon–2.30pm & 7.30–9pm.

Les Templiers 23 rue de la République ☎06 61 51 63
94, ⓦhotellestempliers.ellohaweb.com. The pick of the
mid-range hotels is this boutique number in an eighteenth-
century merchant's house. "Boho chic" is the theme here;
the comfortable rooms are dotted with antiques and
there's contemporary artwork on the walls. Market-fresh
dishes are on the bistro menu. **€125**

.e Grau-du-Roi and Port Camargue

E GRAU-DU-ROI, and its marina **PORT CAMARGUE**, merge seamlessly into one another,
omprising, between them, a bustling contrast to Aigues-Mortes. Like its fortress
eighbour, Port Camargue is also a purpose-built port complex, but one dedicated to
acific hedonism rather than violent idealism. The marina is the largest in Europe and
he second largest in the world after San Diego. Le Grau (Occitan for "channel") has
een a fishing village since the time of Henri IV in the sixteenth century, but it was
nly with the building of Port Camargue in 1969 that prosperity finally arrived. Today
t's the second largest **fishing port** in the Mediterranean with around 25 boats; there
s a fish market every morning on the left bank of the canal. The summer months fill
he town with boaters and sun-worshippers from around the world who seek out the
luned expanses stretching off towards the mouth of the Rhône in the east. If on the
ne hand the town resembles a package-tour nightmare, on the other, there's no
hortage of bars, cheap food and beachside fun. Off-season, it's another story entirely;
hings wind down quickly and, as happens in so many seaside towns, a certain air of
old desolation sets in.

4

The beaches

Basically, the only reason to stay in Le Grau or Port Camargue – which to all intents
and purposes form a single town – is to enjoy the Blue Flag **beaches** and their
watersports. West of the mouth of the canal which passes through Le Grau's centre,
a narrow band of sand, hemmed in closely by road, leads 5km west to **La Grande-
Motte** (see p.217), whose curious triangle-shaped buildings can easily be made out
on a clear day. This is the most accessible swimming area, but the best **beaches** are
east of town, once you pass the busy little bay between Le Grau and Port Camargue.
Just beyond Pointe de l'Espiguette, the spur of land jutting westwards on the south
edge of Port Camargue, is where the real sand starts – an uninterrupted swathe of
dunes stretching 10km east to the lighthouse and from there towards the horizon.
The busiest area is around the **lighthouse** itself, which can be accessed by road from
Le Grau, and where you will be charged a €5 fee to park. The further east you go,
the more the crowds thin out, and the more laidback the beach etiquette becomes.
Nudists have staked their claim on one stretch of beach to the east of the lighthouse,
and if you are prepared to go far enough away you can find seclusion even at the
busiest time of year.

Seaquarium

Av du Palais de la Mer • Daily: April– June & Sept–Oct 9.30am–7.30pm; July & Aug 9.30am–11.30pm; Nov–March 9.30am–6.30pm •
€13.90 • ☎04 66 51 57 57, ⓦ seaquarium.fr

Other than the seaside, the main attraction in town is the **Seaquarium**, one of the
biggest indoor aquariums in Europe, located in the Palais de la Mer between the old
town and the port. The fairly steep admission price also gives access to the **Requinarium**
in the same building, where you can learn all about sharks and see about thirty

---

WATER AND BULLS

Le Grau and Port Camargue have facilities for a wide range of **watersports**, including outfits which rent sail-boards, kite-surf boards, SUPs, sailing boats, kayaks and jet-skis, many offering instruction, as well as waterborne jousting competitions during the *fêtes* of mid-June and September. For children, there are no fewer than three nearby **water parks**. Le Grau/Port Camargue is also a big centre for **bull**-related activities, including a series of *courses* (held every weekend from the end of March to September), the climax of which is the Trophée des As competition in mid-August, and *corridas* held throughout July and August.

---

different species swimming in the huge tanks; there's also a petting pool with the less vicious varieties. Watching the seals and sea lions in the outdoor pool is great fun too.

ARRIVAL AND DEPARTURE   **LE GRAU-DU-ROI AND PORT CAMARGU**

Both buses and trains approach Le Grau/Port Camargue along the narrow sand spit leading from Aigues-Mortes an deposit passengers more or less smack in the middle of Le Grau, at the small *gare SNCF*, just off the canal on the east side

Destinations by bus Le Grau-du-Roi to: La Grande Motte (several daily; 20min); Nîmes, via Aigues-Mortes (several daily; 50min).

Destinations by train TGV stations are indicated with a asterisk. Le Grau-du-Roi to: Nîmes*, via Aigues-Morte (several daily; 50min).

INFORMATION AND GETTING AROUND

Tourist information Villa Parry, rue Sémaphore (daily: April, May & Oct 9.30am–12.30pm & 2–6pm; June & Sept 9am–7pm; July & Aug 9am–8pm; Nov–March 9am–12.30pm & 2–5.30pm; ☎ 04 66 51 67 70, ⊛ letsgrau .com), on the west side of the canal on the seafront. There is also an office at the Maison du Nautisme on quai de l'Escale in Port Camargue (daily: April–June & Sept 9am–12.30pm

& 2–6pm; July & Aug 9.30am–noon & 3.30–8pm; O 9.30am–noon & 2–5.30pm; ☎ 04 66 51 10 06).

By bike Vélo Évasion, 1291 av de Camargue (☎ 04 66 5 48 65), is one of several local outfits which rent bicycle You can cycle from Le Grau to St-Gilles, via Aigues Morte and there is also a *voie verte* (5km) which crosses marshe and runs along part of L'Espiguette beach.

ACCOMMODATION

Les Acacias 21 rue de l'Égalité ☎ 04 66 51 40 86, ⊛ hotel-les-acacias.fr. In a quiet street five minutes from the beach, this two-star hotel has 28 bright rooms with contemporary decor. There's no restaurant or pool but the attractive courtyard is a pleasant place to sit. **€81**

Camping Le Boucanet Rte de Carnon ☎ 04 66 51 41 48, ⊛ campingboucanet.fr. There are several campsites in Le Grau and the main attraction of this one is that it's on l'Espiguette beach. The most desirable accommodations

are the thatched cabins that face the sea. Plenty o activities and entertainment on site. Open April to Sep **€30**

L'Oustau Camarguen 3 rte des Marines ☎ 04 66 51 5 65, ⊛ oustaucamarguen.com. The town's best hotel is se in a collection of low-rise tile-roof white buildings an decorated in classy Camargue style. There is a pool and hot tub and the restaurant menu is a showcase for regiona products (main courses from €19). **€125**

EATING AND DRINKING

L'Assiette Amoureuse 11 rue Victor Granier ☎ 04 66 53 88 46. In the market place, this friendly restaurant is good value for money (lunch *menu* €15) and specializes in Mediterranean cuisine. Try the Provençal-style grilled fish. Mon, Tues & Thurs–Sun noon–1.30pm (also evenings in July & Aug).

Bamboo Beach Bd du Docteur Jean Bastide ☎ 04 66 53 04 12. This Bali-themed beach bar-restaurant is the place to go for cocktails and partying in summer. There's live music or DJs on Friday and Saturday evenings. Mid-June to Aug 9am–2am.

L'Oyat Plage Parking Les Baronnets, l'Espiguette

☎ 06 02 60 55 72, ⊛ oyat-plage.com. Eco-friendly hippie-chic private beach (sunbeds €10) with good-value snacks (sandwiches from €4.50). Possible to rent SUF boards, kayaks and pedaloes. May–Sept Mon–Thurs 9am–8.30pm, Fri–Sun 9am–10.30pm.

Le Petit Nice 36 quai Généra-de-Gaulle ☎ 04 66 80 0C 04. The owner of this quayside restaurant is a fisherman so you can guess what's on the menu (from €19) – seafood fresh off the boat (which is opposite the restaurant). Mon, Tues & Thurs–Sun noon–2.30pm & 7–10.30pm (closed Mon–Fri eve Oct–May).

SHOPPING

Markets are held year round Tues, Thurs and Sat mornings in place de la République; on Mon, Wed and Fri in the Centre Commercial du Boucanet; and on the promenade in Port Camargue on Wednesdays from June to Sept.

Maison Méditerranéenne des Vins 3430 rte de Espiguette ✆ 04 66 53 51 16, ⊛ maisondesvins espiguette.com. Don't leave town without visiting this supermarket-size treasure trove of local wines (cost price) and regional products, both food and home. You'll need a car to get here. Daily: April–June & Sept 9.30am–12.30pm & 2.30–7pm; July & Aug 9.30am–1pm & 2.30–7.30pm; Oct–May 9.30am–12.30pm & 2.30–6.30pm.

The Vidourle valley

West of Nîmes, the border of Gard is marked by the **Vidourle valley**, whose river begins as a trickle on the southern edge of the Cévennes mountains at the northwest of the *département*. This is a quiet corner of Gard, relatively unexplored, and on the whole the villages here, some of which are impressively ancient, lack both the sights and amenities to draw travellers. Notable exceptions, though, are **Sommières**, where the breadth of the river is still spanned by a Roman bridge and watched over by the richly preserved castle of Villevieille, and **Sauve**, an ancient hamlet that makes a convenient stopping-point en route from Nîmes to Ganges, in the upper Hérault valley.

Sommières and around

SOMMIÈRES, the largest town along the Vidourle, lying halfway between Nîmes and Montpellier, is one point on the way west from Nîmes which definitely merits a stop. Its easy, unspoilt charm seduced the English author Lawrence Durrell into spending the last 33 years of his life here, and prompted him to remark, in *Spirit of Place*, that he had seen "nothing prettier". Walking through the old town or along the riverbank it's hard not to sympathize with Durrell's judgement – Sommières remains a peaceful, idyllic village. Part of Claude Berri's 1985 film *Jean de Florette*, starring Yves Montand, was shot here. Strongly Protestant, it was all but destroyed during the Wars of Religion as it repeatedly changed hands before being conquered personally by Louis XIII in 1622. Today Sommières makes a pleasant stop for a bite to eat and a wander around, and those looking for a few days of quiet relaxation could fare a lot worse than to spend some time here, away from the crowded beaches of Le Grau and the busy streets of Nîmes. April through to September is the season for *courses camarguaises*, held on Sunday afternoons.

Roman bridge

The **Roman bridge** spanning the river remains an integral feature of Sommières, uniting the newer town on the west bank with the old town on the east. Something of a curiosity, it was built in the first century and originally consisted of at least 21 arches, but half a dozen or so have been gradually covered over by the encroaching town. A testament to Roman engineering, it continued to carry all of the car and truck traffic passing through the town up until the recent opening of a new bypass.

The old town

At the bridge's eastern end, the walled **old town** is entered by passing through the **tour de l'horloge**, home to a ponderous seventeenth-century clock. From here you can descend to the left to place des Docteurs M. et G. Dax, or proceed along the course of the old Roman road to place Jean-Jaurès – both arcaded squares still serve as **market places** on Saturday mornings for local farmers. There is also a market on Wednesday evenings in July and August.

The castle

June & Sept Mon–Fri 10am–1pm & 2–5pm; July & Aug Wed–Fri & Sun–Mon 10am–1pm & 4–7pm, Sat 2–7pm • €3 • ☎ 04 66 53 78 32, ⓦ chateau-sommieres.fr

From place Jean-Jaurès, an alley leads to the steep stairs at the foot of the town's **castle**. Not much remains of this fortress, built in the tenth century and all but destroyed by Catholic forces in 1573, but you can climb to the top of the square **tower** for a dramatic panorama of the Vidourle plain. The chapel has recently been restored and inside you can watch a film about the castle's turbulent history. There are sometimes evening **music concerts** in the courtyard.

Château de Villevieille

1 rue du Château, Villevieille • Daily: July–Sept 2–7pm • €8 • ☎ 04 66 71 65 23, ⓦ chateau-de-villevieille.fr

Perched on the rise that dominates the old town of Sommières, the **Château de Villevieille** is in **Villevieille**, a beautiful little hamlet of stone-built houses. Owned by the same family for some 750 years, it is one of the few noble castles to escape appropriation or destruction during the Revolution (due to the lord's friendship with Voltaire and Condorcet, who interceded on his behalf). Today it boasts a sumptuous interior: the furnishings, including sixteenth-century Flemish leather "wallpaper" and the first mirror in France, are classed as national monuments, and the beds in which three kings of France and Cardinal Richelieu slept are still in their respective rooms. One of the best things about the visit is that you're shown around by members of the family – an unassuming, friendly bunch who are disarmingly frank and genuinely welcoming.

ARRIVAL AND DEPARTURE

SOMMIÈRES AND AROUND

By bus Buses drop passengers off on the opposite side of the river to the tourist office and old town.

Destinations Le Grau-du-Roi (one daily in summer;

40min); Montpellier (several daily; 45min); Nîmes (several daily; 1hr); Villevieille (several daily; 5min).

INFORMATION AND ACTIVITIES

Tourist information 5 quai F. Gaussorgues (June to mid-July & mid-Aug to Sept Mon–Sat 10am–12.30pm & 2–6pm; mid-July to mid-Aug Mon–Sat 10am–12.30pm & 2–7pm, Sun 10am–1pm; Oct–May Mon–Fri 10am–12.30pm & 2–5.30pm, Sat 10am–12.30pm; ☎ 04 66 80 99 30, ⓦ ot-sommieres.com).

Bike rental Vaunage Passion Vélos, 1 rue des Marchands,

Calvisson (☎ 04 66 81 43 78, ⓦ vaunagepassionvelos.fr). Not in Sommières but in a town along the *voie verte* (see box below). From €10 per half-day.

Watersports Kayak-Tribu, rte de Montpellier (☎ 06 28 35 05 75, ⓦ kayak-tribu.com). Kayak or SUP tours on the Vidourle from €10.

ACCOMMODATION AND EATING

Camping Municipal Le Garanel Chemin de la Princesse ☎ 04 66 80 33 49. There are several campsites in the area but this one owned by the *mairie* is the closest to town. Sixty spacious, shady pitches and a

heated pool for less than €20 – bargain. Open from April to Sept. €18.50

★**L'Orange** 7 rue des Baumes ☎ 04 66 77 79 94, ⓦ hoteldelorange.com. Gorgeous, boho-chic B&B in a

---

WALKING AND CYCLING AROUND SOMMIÈRES

The best of the **local walks** (detailed in the tourist office's brochure) is an excursion to the twelfth-century **church of St-Julien**, 5km north of Sommières along the right bank of the Vidourle (the turn-off is marked on the left after 3km). It makes a good stop for a picnic, though the church itself is usually closed. The villages of the *garrigues* stretching north from Sommières do not contain any sights of particular interest, but the relative tranquillity of the highways makes for very pleasant **cycling**. There is also a *voie verte* between Sommières and Caveirac, through forests and past vineyards; you can continue to Nîmes, if you can face the busy roads from there on.

MAKING SILK

During the eighteenth and nineteenth centuries, **silk farming** was big business in the northern part of the Gard *département*. The first evidence of sericulture in France dates back to the thirteenth century in Anduze but it was in 1709 that the industry really took off, when local farmers looked for a new way to earn a living after the local chestnut and olive trees were destroyed during a harsh winter. Originally produced by family businesses, it was carried out on an industrial scale in the nineteenth century to supply the burgeoning weaving and hat-making companies in this area; two thirds of the local population was employed in silk production. However, the industry eventually died out in the 1960s for several reasons including the appearance of synthetic materials. You can find out about its fascinating history at **Le Musée de la Soie** (pl du 8 mai 1945; Tues–Sun 10.30am–12.30pm & 2–6pm, open daily in summer; €5.50; ☎04 30 67 26 94, ⓦmuseedelasoie-cevennes.com) in St-Hippolyte-du-Fort; the shop sells some lovely scarves.

seventeenth-century mansion run by arty English couple Liz & Tom. There are five en-suite rooms and two *gîtes* and lovely views over the town from the roof terrace pool. **€125**

Sansavino 9 place des Docteurs Dax ☎04 66 80 09 85.

Excellent Italian restaurant in this very pretty square, where everything is made on the premises with local products. The antipasti is recommended. Mon & Thurs–Sun 8.30am–11pm.

Sauve

SAUVE is a quiet little town, once fortified and still presided over by the castle which was centuries ago the summer retreat of the bishops of Maguelone. The **old town** is a maze of twisting alleys, some of which are covered, and the **view** from the other side of the bridge over the Vidourle is inspiring. In recent years an influx of cosmopolitan urban refugees has revived the town, which is known for making big wooden forks for stacking hay – you can find out about this ancient craft at **Le Conservatoire de la Fourche** (rue des Boisseliers; April–June & Oct Tues–Sat 10am–noon & 2–5pm; July & Aug Tues–Sat 10am–noon & 2–6pm; Nov, Dec & March Mon–Fri 10am–noon & 1.30–5pm; €4; ☎04 66 80 54 46). There is a **market** on Saturday mornings.

ARRIVAL AND INFORMATION

SAUVE

By bus Ganges (several daily; 1hr 20min); Nîmes (several daily; 45min); St-Hippolyte-du-Fort (several daily; 15min).

Tourist information 26 rue des Boisseliers (April–June, Sept & Oct Mon–Fri 9am–12.30pm & 2–6pm, also Sat 9.30am–12.30pm in last two weeks of June & first two weeks of Sept; July & Aug Mon–Sat 9am–12.30pm & 2.30–6.30pm, Sun 10am–12.30pm; Nov–March Mon–Fri 9am–noon & 2–5pm; ☎04 66 77 57 51, ⓦpiemont -cevenol-tourisme.com).

ACCOMMODATION AND EATING

Le Comptoir de l'Evèsque Domaine de l'Evèsque ☎06 45 50 83 75, ⓦcomptoirdelevesque.fr. Top-notch traditional French food with Italian touches is on the menu at this attractive former farm. Lunch menu €14.50. Tues 7–9.15pm, Wed–Sun noon–1.30pm & 7–9.15pm.

La Magnanerie ☎06 47 22 42 54, ⓦla-magnanerie -dhotes.com. B&B with both rooms and *gîtes* in a former silk farm dating back to the seventeenth century. There's also a pool, kids' play area and beauty treatments are available. **€90**

Montpellier and around

CIRQUE DE NAVACELLES

5

Montpellier and around

Together, Montpellier and the surrounding country comprise the most varied and exciting region in Languedoc. The capital of Languedoc-Roussillon before it became part of the new Occitanie *région*, Montpellier is a zesty centre of commerce and, best of all, it is minutes from the beach. Languedoc's coast is forty kilometres or so of nearly uninterrupted sandbar, punctuated by fishing ports that produce some of the best shellfish in France, and provides ample opportunities for sun-soaking and watersports. Just inland, well-preserved Pézenas is one of the most beautiful towns in the Southwest.

The River Hérault gives its name to the *département* of which Montpellier is the administrative centre, and dominates its interior, whose beautiful highlands are home to a wealth of natural wonders and historic sites – notably the **Cirque de Navacelles**. East of the cirque, you can visit one of France's most celebrated caverns, the **Grotte des Demoiselles**, before following the dramatic Hérault gorge southwest past the ancient pilgrimage site of **St-Guilhem-le-Désert**.

GETTING AROUND   MONTPELLIER AND AROUND

Getting around by public transport in the region around Montpellier is easy. The city sits on the main coastal rail artery, uniting it with Sète to the west and Nîmes to the east, while the area of greater Montpellier, the *agglomération*, is served by the city's transport network (TAM), whose far-ranging buses reach Palavas and Maguelone on the coast. Inland, the lack of train lines is compensated for by regular bus services connecting the bigger towns. Only the smaller villages, such as the hamlets around Lac du Salagou and Navacelles, do not have useful bus services; to explore these you'll need a car or bike.

By train The main coastal rail line (with TGV) connects Montpellier to Perpignan and Nîmes. SNCF buses may run in lieu of trains on secondary lines; services are reduced on Sundays and holidays.
By bus Hérault's bus hubs are in Montpellier and Béziers.

Many lines have no Sunday service; service on Saturdays and holidays may be reduced. For a route map, full schedules and information on discount tickets, see ⓦ herault-transport.fr or call ☎ 04 34 88 89 99.

Montpellier

Home to a youthful and dynamic university culture and a host of artistic festivals and events, **MONTPELLIER** is one of France's most exciting cities. It boasts a beautiful architectural fusion of the classical and the avant-garde, and is even close enough to the Mediterranean to have the beach within reach of public transport. With fine museums, a charming old centre and a bouncy rhythm of life, Montpellier works just as well

BEACH NEAR MONTPELLIER

Highlights

❶ L'écusson Montpellier's shield-shaped old town is one of the oldest and best preserved in France. **See p.210**

❷ Seafood Whether cultivated in the Bassin de Thau or fished from the sea, the coastal cuisine of this area is a gourmet's delight. **See p.225**

❸ Beaches A long swathe of sand girds the Mediterranean coast: you can find both solitude and crowds here. **See p.217**

❹ Water-jousting This curious Sétois sport has grown in the last centuries into a regional tradition. **See p.219**

❺ Pézenas Walk the streets of Languedoc's old capital for a taste of life in the age of Molière. **See p.228**

❻ Cirque de Navacelles A spectacular ox-bow canyon, etched deep into the *causse* of upper Hérault. **See p.234**

HIGHLIGHTS ARE MARKED ON THE MAP ON P.206

5

either for a longer, relaxing stay, or a whirlwind two-day tour of its highlights, notably the **Musée Fabre** and many Renaissance **mansions** of the old town.

By tradition solidly socialist, Montpellier has garnered kudos for its ecological initiatives, such as the development of its public transport system as far as the coast and the effective banning of cars from the historic centre – now the largest pedestrianized area in France. You can stroll around the medieval city soaking up the atmosphere, free from exhaust fumes, tooting horns and traffic.

More or less everything you will want to see in Montpellier can be found in or on the edge of its compact and largely pedestrian **old town**, which spreads out north and west from the **place de la Comédie**, at the heart of the city. Bounded to the north by the boulevards Pasteur and Louis Blanc, to the east by the **Esplanade Charles de Gaulle** and to the west by the **Jardin des Plantes** and **place du Peyrou**, the terminus of the town's old aqueduct, the old centre is marked off into two unequal halves by the avenue made up of rues de la Loge and Foch. The north side was the most prosperous part, to which the **mansions** which pepper it testify, and it is also home to the city's old university buildings and **cathedral**. The crowded lanes of the south side were inhabited by the city's workers and artisans; its buildings are correspondingly less showy. East of the place de la Comédie

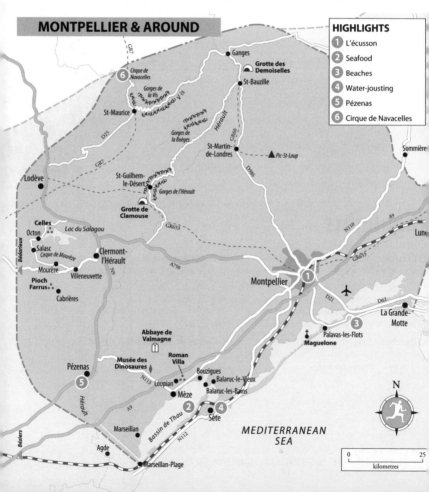

MONTPELLIER & AROUND

HIGHLIGHTS
1. L'écusson
2. Seafood
3. Beaches
4. Water-jousting
5. Pézenas
6. Cirque de Navacelles

5

FESTIVALS IN AND AROUND MONTPELLIER

Most of the action in Hérault *département* is centred on Montpellier, which is renowned for its cultural vitality, hosting a range of annual **festivals**. Also worth looking out for are the *fêtes* on the coast, which invariably feature the local tradition of **water-jousting** – throughout July and August in Palavas and Sète (see box, p.219) – as well as *tauromachie* (both Spanish and Camargue styles; see box, p.196). The uplands of the Hérault valley also have a few small local festivals.

Feb or March Pézenas: *Carnaval*. Lent kicks off with a four-day Mardi Gras (Shrove Tuesday) festival here, featuring folkloric displays and a parade led by the local totem-animal, Le Poulain.

May, July, Sept, Oct & Dec St-Guilhem-le-Désert: *Saison musicale* ⊛ amisdestguilhem. fr. Classical and World Music in and around St-Guilhem.

Late June to mid-July Montpellier: *Montpellier Danse* ⊛ montpellierdanse.com. A three-week festival of traditional music and dance from around the world, held in various venues around town.

First weekend in July Sète: *Fête de la St-Pierre*. Traditional fishermen's festival with a religious procession, street party and water-jousting.

Second Sun in July Palavas: *Fête de la Mer*.

Religious procession and blessing of fishing boats, followed by water-jousting, fireworks and *tauromachie*.

Mid- to end July Montpellier: *Le Festival de Radio-France et Montpellier* ⊛ festivalradiofrancemontpellier.com. Music festival representing styles from classical to jazz. Half the concerts are free.

Late July Bassin de Thau: *Festival de Thau* ⊛ festivaldethau.com. Annual week-long World Music festival, held in Mèze, Marseillan, Loupian and Frontignan.

Mid-Aug Sète: *Fête de St-Louis*. Six-day extravaganza of fireworks, street parties, water-jousting and medieval pageantry.

End Sept Palavas: *Feria d'Automne*. Local Camarguais-style festival of horsemanship and *tauromachie*.

you'll find the Polygone shopping mall and sprawling **Antigone** development, Montpellier's boldly designed but sterile modern quarter. Beyond the old town are mixed commercial and residential quarters, which provide interesting backdrops to stroll past, if lacking in significant sights, while further out still, various **châteaux** ring the town.

Brief history

Montpellier is a medieval city, and can't claim the same venerable Roman past of rival Nîmes. Starting off as a market town for nearby **Maguelone** in the tenth century, in 1204 it was acquired by marriage by the count-kings of Barcelona, who favoured it as a residence – both Jaume I "the Conqueror" and his son Jaume II of Mallorca were born here. By the late thirteenth century it had become second only to Paris in size, thanks partly to its famous **university**, and a major centre for medicine, law and the arts. With Jaume I's posthumous division of his realms, the city was incorporated into the Kingdom of Mallorca until 1349, when Jaume II sold it – afflicted with plague, banditry and famine – to the French Crown. In the era that followed, the city was sustained by its university, through whose doors passed the pioneering Renaissance poet **Petrarch** and, later, the satirist **Rabelais**, who received his doctorate here in 1537. Despite the transfer of the bishopric of Maguelone here in 1537, Montpellier became strongly **Protestant** in the sixteenth and seventeenth centuries, losing many of its old church buildings in factionalist struggles, and was only saved from destruction at the hands of Louis XIII, who had personally waged war on the Huguenot stronghold in 1622, by an eleventh-hour truce.

The city's **leftist tradition** began with a bang in 1789, and the revolutionary anthem known as "La Marseillaise" was in fact first sung by a local medical student. Another wave of serious unrest came during the wine crisis of 1907, during which it was the strongest centre of popular agitation in reaction to plummeting grape prices (see p.323). The last shake-up was in 1962: with the dismantling of the **Algerian colony**, thirteen thousand French (*pieds-noirs*) and Maghrebi (*harki*) refugees arrived in the city, two

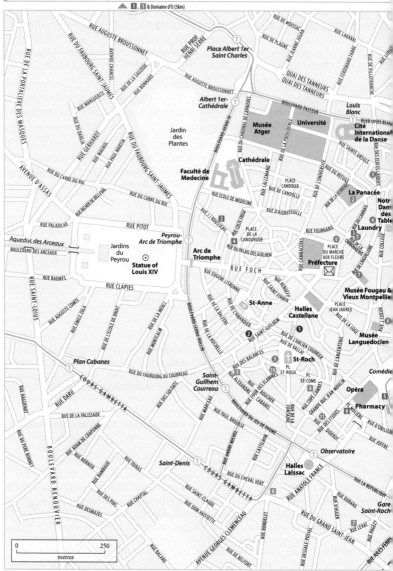

groups whose integration into Montpellier society generated considerable friction, but whose presence brought a revitalizing dynamism to the city. Until 2016, Montpellier was the capital of the administrative *région* of Languedoc-Roussillon; however, since the region combined with Midi-Pyrénées to create Occitanie, Toulouse is now top dog.

Place de la Comédie

The **place de la Comédie** is a broad plaza that was opened up in the mid-nineteenth century with the inauguration of the then new **opera hall** at its southern end. Although

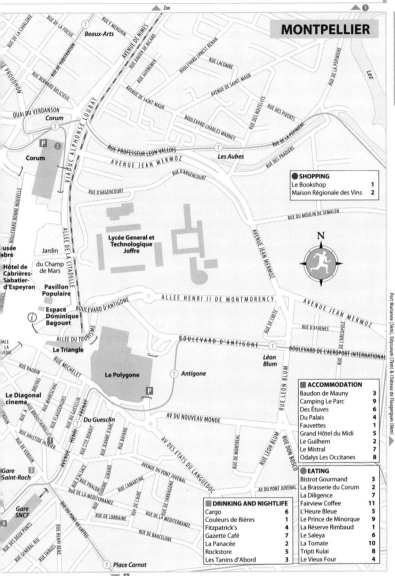

MONTPELLIER

SHOPPING

Le Bookshop	1
Maison Régionale des Vins	2

ACCOMMODATION

Baudon de Mauny	3
Camping Le Parc	9
Des Étuves	6
Du Palais	4
Fauvettes	1
Grand Hôtel du Midi	5
Le Guilhem	2
Le Mistral	7
Odalys Les Occitanes	8

EATING

Bistrot Gourmand	3
La Brasserie du Corum	2
La Diligence	7
Fairview Coffee	11
L'Heure Bleue	5
Le Prince de Minorque	9
La Réserve Rimbaud	1
Le Saleya	6
La Tomate	10
Tripti Kulai	8
Le Vieux Four	4

DRINKING AND NIGHTLIFE

Cargo	6
Couleurs de Bières	1
Fitzpatrick's	4
Gazette Café	7
La Panacée	2
Rockstore	5
Les Tanins d'Abord	3

superseded by the new Corum hall, the gaily domed building still hosts music and theatre performances. Today the *place* to its northeast is a busy crossroads for both pedestrians and trams, and is lined on each side by a series of old cafés and fast-food joints, although it retains its traditional role as a marketplace (Mon–Sat 9am–4pm).

Esplanade Charles de Gaulle

The tourist office's pavilion marks the beginning of the **Esplanade Charles de Gaulle**, also known as the **Champ de Mars**, a park with both a formal promenade and a network of

5

paths and ponds which attract sunbathers and strollers in good weather. On its south side are the **Pavillon Populaire** (Tues–Sun 10/11am–1pm & 2–6/7pm; free; ☎04 67 66 13 46), which hosts photography exhibitions by internationally renowned photographers, and **Espace Dominique Bagouet** (Tues–Sun 10/11am–1pm & 2–6/7pm; free; ☎04 67 63 42 78) featuring exhibitions by local nineteenth- and twentieth-century artists.

Musée Fabre

Esplanade Charles de Gaulle • Tues–Sun 10am–6pm • €7 • ☎ 04 67 14 83 00, ⓦ museefabre.fr

The main attraction in the vicinity of the park is the huge **Musée Fabre**, situated halfway up its west side. The museum's important collection of nearly a thousand paintings ranges from the Renaissance to the present day, and is particularly strong on post eighteenth-century French art. Works by better-known names include David's *Portrait of Doctor Alphonse Leroy* and Delacroix's *Fantasia*, as well as pieces by Dufy, Maillol and the local Frédéric Bazille – a talented Impressionist painter who died in battle at the age of 28 during the Franco-Prussian war. In addition to these, there are works by well-known foreign artists such as Reynolds, Zurbarán and Rubens. The museum also owns a palace next door, the **Hôtel de Cabrières-Sabatier-d'Espeyran** (mid-June to mid-Oct Tues–Sun 2–6pm; mid-Oct to mid-June Tues, Sat & Sun 2–5pm; same ticket as Musée Fabre), which houses its decorative arts collection.

Le Corum

Esplanade Charles de Gaulle • Open during events and concerts • ☎ 04 67 61 67 61, ⓦ montpellier-events.com

At the northern end of the park looms the concrete-and-pink-granite **Le Corum**, designed by Claude Vasconi to house the city's two-thousand-seat opera hall – the Opéra Berlioz – plus a convention centre and exhibition hall. When it's open you can poke around the building and take in the sweeping **views** of the old city from its terrace. There's also a very nice restaurant, *Brasserie du Corum* (see p.215).

The old town

Montpellier's greatest attraction is its **old town**, richly adorned by elaborate mansion facades and home to a maze of medieval streets and a series of small museums. This area is also known as "*l'écusson*" as it is shaped like a shield.

La Panacée

14 rue de l'École de Pharmacie • Wed–Sat noon–8pm, Sun 10am–6pm • Free • ☎ 04 34 88 79 79, ⓦ lapanacee.org

Opened in 2013 in the former royal medical college, **La Panacée** is dedicated to the research and creation of visual arts, writing and digital technology. As well as the artists' studios and five exhibition spaces, there is a **café** with a courtyard terrace, which is the hippest place to drink in town (see p.216). The building, which dates back to the twelfth century, was rehabilitated with the help of architect Jean-Luc Lauriol, who has designed many public buildings and spaces in the city and region.

Hôtel de Varennes

Musée du Vieux Montpellier Tues–Sun 10am–1pm & 2–6pm • €3 • ☎ 04 67 66 02 94 • **Musée Fougau** Wed & Thurs 3–6pm • Free

Five minutes' walk south of La Panacée, the compact, triangular place Pétrarque is closed in by a clutch of palaces, the largest of which is the **Hôtel de Varennes**, at no. 2, whose ground floor is almost entirely Gothic in style, and includes the beautiful fourteenth-century **salle de Pétrarque**, a long hall vaulted with delicate stone ribs. On the first floor is the **Musée du Vieux Montpellier**, whose grand rooms are probably more interesting than the collection of city-related objects from the Middle Ages to the twentieth century. On the second floor is the **Musée Fougau**, a small, privately run folk museum. The tragedy is that this gem of a building, like many others in the old town, is in such a poor state of repair.

Musée Languedocien

rue Jacques Coeur • Closed for renovation • ☎ 04 67 52 93 03

The impressive fifteenth-century facade of the Hôtel des Trésoriers de France is now home to the best of the city's historical museums, the **Musée Languedocien**, whose fine seventeenth-century courtyard can also be visited. This museum is worth a look not only for its collection of medieval artefacts, which include thirteenth-century ceramics and a curious lead baptismal font, but for the impressively vaulted Gothic interior of the main exhibition room. You'll also find luxurious Flemish tapestries, pre-Revolution furniture – including a seventeenth-century Italian celestial globe – and a collection of *faïence* (tin-glazed pottery) whose manufacture was an important industry here throughout the 1700s.

The mansions

You'll find a concentration of mansions in the old town, particularly on **rue du Cannau** (north of the colourful place du Marché aux Fleurs), whose string of facades, decked out with ornately carved doorways and casement windows, attest to the one-time wealth of this street – it was a prestigious neighbourhood three centuries ago. Further west, the **Hôtel de la Vieille Intendance**, the former governor's mansion at no. 9 on the street of the same name, is a stately palace which was later home of the philosopher Auguste Comte and writer Paul Valéry. Close by, the larger **place de la Canourgue** served as the eighteenth-century administrative hub of the city. This is one of the city's prettiest squares and a lovely spot for a drink. Its eastern side is dominated by the huge **Hôtel de Richer de Belleval**, the former town hall, whose broad, square courtyard is decorated in the finest Neoclassical pomp of the late 1700s; at the time of writing, it was being turned into a luxury hotel.

Cathédrale St-Pierre and around

Cathedral Mon–Sat 9.30am–noon & 2.30–6.30pm, Sun 9am–noon • Free • ☎ 04 67 66 04 12, ⏾ cathedrale-montpellier.fr • **Musée Atger** Mon, Wed & Fri 1.45–5.45pm • Free • ☎ 04 34 43 35 80

On the northwest side of the old city in place St-Pierre sits Montpellier's **cathedral**, with its strikingly bizarre entrance, a porch flanked by two straight towers capped with a high conical roof, dating back to its fourteenth-century foundation. Next door in rue de l'École de Médecine is the **Faculty of Medicine**, a stately Neoclassical faculty building which is home to the **Musée Atger**, named after the local collector Xavier Atger, whose acquisitions include paintings by important Flemish artists such as Rubens and Van Dyck.

Jardin des Plantes

Tues–Sun: June–Sept noon–8pm; Oct–May noon–6pm • Free

Lying at the end of rue de l'École de Médecine, which is lined with nineteenth-century university buildings, the **Jardin des Plantes** marks the transition to the new town. The garden dates back to 1593, when it was founded by order of the former Huguenot king, Henry IV, in order to cultivate and study herbal remedies. Today, you can stroll orderly lines of botanical specimens, cool down beside the pond of its English garden, and wander among tropical and Mediterranean trees.

Place du Peyrou and around

Rising above the Jardin des Plantes on the edge of the old *enceinte*, the flat paved expanse of the **place du Peyrou** stretches west, dominated by a Roman-style equestrian statue of the "Emperor" Louis XIV – an 1838 replacement of the original statue of 1692, which was destroyed during the Revolution. The great bronze king is frozen in

5

motionless stride towards the **Arc de Triomphe**, opposite the eastern end of the park, at the head of rue Foch. The arch, designed on the ancient Roman model, consists of a single, free-standing entryway, whose sides are covered with low-relief sculptures celebrating the military victories of the "Sun King" over the Dutch and the Huguenots, the revocation of the Edict of Nantes and the construction of the Canal du Midi. Behind Louis' statue, at the western end of the place du Peyrou, an octagonal, colonnaded pavilion marks the terminus of the 880m-long **aqueduct** of St-Clément, built in the late eighteenth century to carry water to the city from a nearby spring. Passing through the triumphal arch you'll come face to face with the striking Neoclassical **Palais de Justice**, which features a Doric-columned facade capped by an impressive tympanum in relief.

Quartier Ste-Anne

The nearby plain stone nineteenth-century **church of St-Anne** is only really of interest for the occasional art exhibitions it houses; also here is the **Conservatoire Régional de Montpellier** and workshops making fine stringed instruments. South of the church on rue de l'Huile, you'll enter the city's old **artisanal quarter**, containing houses that survive from as early as the thirteenth century – look out for the outline of the (filled in) medieval arched windows, which were uncovered during restoration, as you wander around.

Quartier St-Roch

South of rue St-Guilhem, a street of functional, quotidian shops, you'll find a succession of attractive squares – good territory for restaurant-hunting. At the northernmost of these, place St-Ravy, are the scant remains of the **palace** of the kings of Mallorca. The area is named after the unremarkable nineteenth-century church in the middle of **place St-Roch** – check out the huge mural on the wall opposite.

Tour de la Babote

To the southeast of place St-Roch you'll come upon a final small *place*, set in the shadow of the **Tour de la Babote**, the only surviving portion of the town's twelfth-century defences. Crowned by an observatory in the 1700s it was also incorporated into the same semaphore system used at the Tour Chappe in Castelnaudary (see p.78).

Antigone

Cut off from the main part of the old city by the sprawl of the Polygone shopping complex and defended on the north and south by a whizzing expressway, the **Antigone**, twenty-first-century Montpellier, is a world away from its medieval origins. Laid out on an esplanade stretching east from the city for almost 2km, this self-contained and car-free development of residences, shops, services and restaurants is endowed with an uncompromising unity of form and design. The Catalan architect **Ricardo Bofill** has created a massive low-rise building complex, drawing largely on Classical motifs, including smooth columns and roof cornices reminiscent of ancient temples, but with a net effect that looks somehow futuristic-Georgian. The first section, the westernmost part of the complex, was inaugurated in 1984, and the latest, a library designed by Paris-born architect Paul Chemetov, opened in 2000. The whole thing, a striking if not entirely convincing Utopian landscape of broad cypress-lined courtyards, culminates in the monumental **Esplanade de l'Europe** on the bank of the River Lez.

The suburbs

Beyond Montpellier proper, the majority of worthwhile sights are in the east, notably the new **Port Marianne** district and the **Odysseum** leisure complex. North of the centre lies the city's **zoo**, set in a typical Mediterranean forest.

Port Marianne

The area east of the river, **Port Marianne**, has now become a desirable place to live, with dozens of swish apartment blocks springing up around an artificial lake. Although a bit soulless, there are several interesting futuristic buildings housing designer shops and fashionable restaurants, including **Philippe Starck**'s "Nuage" fitness club (daily: 9am–11pm) and **Jean Nouvel**'s RBC Design Center and *mairie*.

Odysseum

The eastern end of Tram 1 takes you to **Odysseum**, which is a good destination in bad weather. Here you'll find a shopping mall, cinema complex, bowling alley, ice rink, planetarium, restaurants and **Aquarium Mare Nostrum** (daily: July & Aug 10am–8pm; Sept–June 10am–7pm; €15.50; ☎04 67 13 05 51, ⓦaquariummarenostrum.fr), where in two and a half hours you can explore the world's seas – the recreation of being caught in a storm is actually quite scary.

Château de Flaugergues

744 av Albert Einstein, 4km east of the centre • **Château** June, July & Sept Tues–Sun 2.30–7pm; Aug & Oct–May by appointment • €9.50 • **Vineyards** Mon–Fri 9.30am–6pm, Sat 2.30–6/7pm • €7 • ☎04 99 52 66 37, ⓦflaugergues.com

The main attraction of Montpellier's hinterland is the series of **follies** raised by the town's wealthiest citizens as summerhouses in the 1700s. In a game of social one-upmanship, merchants and aristocrats vied to construct ever more luxurious estates, a few of which have been opened to the public, and are accessible by city transport. The oldest and most elegant is the **Château de Flaugergues**; it is still owned by the original family who built the palace in 1696. You can have a ninety-minute guided tour of the luxurious apartments, decked out with contemporary tapestries and *objets d'art*, or just visit the formal French gardens, set amid the vineyards of its *domaine*. There is also a very nice restaurant, *Folia* (Mon–Fri noon–2pm), and a wine cellar, where you can taste and buy their products. Details of other follies in the area can be obtained from the tourist office.

Parc Zoologique de Lunaret

50 av Agropolis, 5km north of the centre • Tues–Sun (daily during school hols) Feb, Mar & Oct 10am–6pm; April–Sept 9.30am–6.30pm; Nov–Jan 10am–5pm • €6.50 • ☎04 67 54 45 23, ⓦzoo.montpellier.fr

More than 140 species are kept in this huge park, dotted with pine trees and *garrigue*, in zones split into their continents of origin. Latest developments include a new enclosure for the cheetahs and three new male giraffes from Chester Zoo, as the park is actively involved in preservation programmes. Also here is France's largest Amazonian greenhouse, where visitors can experience this unique environment, with its vegetation and animals, for themselves.

ARRIVAL AND DEPARTURE
MONTPELLIER

By plane The city's airport (ⓦmontpellier.aeroport.fr) is 8km southeast of the centre, beside the Étang de Mauguio: from here a *navette* (timed for flights; 15min; €1.60 or €2.60 plus tram) runs to the stop at place de l'Europe by Antigone from where you can get tram Line 1 or 4. A taxi (☎04 30 96 60 60) costs €18–38.

By train The *gare SNCF* (left luggage; daily: 9am–8pm; €5.50–9.50), Gare St-Roch, is at the southern end of rue

Maguelone – it's a five-minute walk along this street to the central place de la Comédie. TGV stations are indicated with an asterisk.

Destinations Nîmes* (connection to Beaucaire; several hourly; 30min); Paris* (many daily; 3hr 30min); Perpignan*, via Sète, Agde*, Béziers* (connections to Bédarieux) and Narbonne* (several hourly; 2hr); Toulouse*, via Sète*, Agde*, Béziers* (connections to Bédarieux),

5

Carcassonne* (connection to Quillan) and Castelnaudary* (several hourly; 2hr 15min).

By bus Buses depart from outlying tram stops, depending on which direction you are travelling. For details contact Hérault Transport (☎ 04 34 88 89 99, ⓦ herault-transport.fr).

Destinations Aigues-Mortes (many daily; 1hr 5min); Bédarieux (several daily; 1hr 25min); Béziers (several daily; 1hr 55min); Clermont-l'Hérault (many daily; 45min); Ganges (several daily; 1hr 10min); La Grande-Motte (many daily, in summer hourly; 30min); Lamalou-les-Bains

(several daily; 2hr 5min); Le Grau-du-Roi (many daily 45min); Lodève (several daily; 1hr); Pézenas (several daily 1hr); St-Bauzille (several daily; 55min); St-Guilher (several daily; 55min); St-Martin-de-Londres (several daily; 30min); St-Pons (daily; 2hr 25min); Sète (several daily; 1hr) and Sommières (several daily; 45min).

By car If you're driving, the simplest option for parking to head for the "Corum" or "Polygone" car parks – i however, you want to avoid paying the hefty daily rate outlying P+ Tram car parks charge only €4.60 for parkin (including a return tram fare for each passenger).

GETTING AROUND

By tram and bus Montpellier's four tramlines (Mon–Thurs & Sun 4.30am–1.30am, Fri & Sat until 2.30am) are the signature of its efficient and modern public transport system, run by TAM (ⓦ tam-voyages.com). Tickets valid on trams and buses (single €1.60, ten tickets €10) can be purchased from machines at the stops, while passes (one-day pass €4.30; weekly pass €16.50) are available at the TAM office, 27 rue Maguelone (Mon–Sat 9am–noon & 2–5pm). Unless you're planning on visiting specific outlying sites, however, you won't need to use the system,

as the centre of town is compact and eminently walkable.

By bike Montpellier's municipal Vélomagg (ⓦ tam -voyages.com) stations around town rent bikes free for th first hour then €0.50 per hour thereafter.

By taxi Les Taxis du Sud ☎ 04 67 42 80 00; Taxi du Coi ☎ 06 58 10 50 10; Taxi Bleu Midi ☎ 04 67 03 20 00.

By car ADA, 58 bis bd Clemenceau ☎ 04 67 58 34 35; Avis 22 av de Maurin ☎ 0820 611 643; Europcar, Gare St-Roc ☎ 04 67 06 89 05; Hertz, 18 place August Gibert ☎ 04 67 0 87 90; Rent-a-Car, 111 av de Palavas ☎ 04 67 22 42 52.

INFORMATION

Tourist information 30 place de la Comédie (Mon–Sat July–Sept 9.30am–7.30pm; Oct–June 9.30am–6pm; Sun year round 10am–5pm; ☎ 04 67 60 60 60, ⓦ montpellier -france.com). There are two-hour guided tours in English on Sat at 3pm (€7), with extra tours in summer. They also sell

one-, two- and three-day "City Cards" (covering buses an trams, admission to many city sights and other discounts €13.50–25.20), as well as handing out the fortnightl Sortir, with entertainment listings. You can also ren portable wifi access (€8 per day or €4 with the "City Card").

ACCOMMODATION

★ **Baudon de Mauny** 1 rue de la Carbonnerie ☎ 04 67 02 21 77, ⓦ baudondemauny.com. Stylish B&B with five-star service in an eighteenth-century mansion in the heart of the old town. There are four rooms and four apartments, all with original features set off by contemporary design classics. **€265**

Camping Le Parc Rte de Mauguio, Lattes ☎ 04 67 65 85 67, ⓦ leparccamping.com. Three-star campsite in a woodland location with 68 pitches and 34 chalets. There's a heated pool, a kids' play area, a small gym and entertainment in summer. Open year round. **€30**

Des Étuves 24 rue des Étuves ☎ 04 67 60 78 19, ⓦ montpellier-hotel.com. Simple, spotless rooms in the

south of the old city, all with en-suite bathrooms, free wi-f and TV. **€49**

★ **Du Palais** 3 rue du Palais ☎ 04 67 60 47 38 ⓦ hoteldupalais-montpellier.fr. Tastefully renovated eighteenth-century mansion on the west side of the old town, blending modern and antique touches. Cosy rooms most with en-suite facilities. An excellent mid-range option. Free wi-fi. **€90**

Fauvettes 8 rue Bonnard ☎ 04 67 63 17 60, ⓦ hote -lesfauvettes.fr. Charming budget hotel in a quiet stree near the Jardin des Plantes. Rooms are small, simple and TV-free but there's an attractive courtyard where breakfast is taken in summer. **€44**

Grand Hôtel du Midi 22 bd Victor-Hugo ☎ 04 67 92 69

SPORT AND SWIMMING IN MONTPELLIER

Montpellier has a top-flight **football** team (ⓦ mhscfoot.com), who play at Stade de la Mosson, and a Top 14 **rugby** team (ⓦ montpellier-rugby.com), who play at the Altrad Stadium. For **swimming**, try the Piscine Olympique d'Antigone, av Jacques-Quartier (Mon–Fri 9am–9.30pm, Sat 9am–7.15pm, Sun 9am–1.15pm & 3–7.15pm; adults €5, kids €2.70; ☎ 04 67 15 63 00; tram to "Léon Blum"), which is part of a massive indoor swimming and sports complex.

51, ⓦgrandhoteldumidimontpellier.com. Renovated in 2015 with a theatrical theme, this four-star hotel is the most glamorous address in town. The most prized room overlooks the place de la Comédie. **€139**

Le Guilhem 18 rue J-J-Rousseau ⓞ 04 67 52 90 90, ⓦleguilhem.com. Beautifully restored sixteenth-century townhouse whose cheerful rooms mostly overlook quiet gardens, and with a sunny breakfast terrace. Free wi-fi. A good alternative to the *Du Palais*, if full. **€124**

★**Le Mistral** 25 rue Boussairolles ⓞ 04 67 58 45 25,

ⓦhotel-le-mistral.com. A comfortable and attractively decorated two-star hotel offering satellite TV, free wi-fi and garage parking. They also sell regional products in reception. An excellent economy choice. **€69**

Odalys Les Occitanes 20 rue de la République ⓞ 04 67 02 92 50, ⓦodalys-vacances.com. Opposite the station, this new four-star aparthotel is great for families or for longer stays. Rooms, with a kitchen area, are set in two buildings around a courtyard. There's no bar but there is a breakfast room and a launderette. **€90**

EATING

No other city in Languedoc and Roussillon, with the possible exception of much larger Toulouse, can compete with Montpellier in terms of either dining possibilities or cultural life. Eating in Montpellier is a pleasure, with local cuisine combining the bounty of the sea, the rich garden produce of the plain and the meats of the hills and Camargue – and practically all the squares in Montpellier's old town have a restaurant or two.

★**Bistrot Gourmand** 7 place de la Chapelle Neuve ⓞ 04 67 66 08 09. Excellent-value Languedocian cuisine (both inland and coastal varieties) with a wonderful shaded terrace. The *pâtés de canard* are particularly notable, and the wine list is excellent. *Menus* €17 at lunch and €27 at dinner. Daily noon–2pm & 7–10.30pm.

La Brasserie du Corum Le Corum, place Charles de Gaulle ⓞ 04 67 02 03 04. On the ground floor of the new opera building, this contemporary restaurant serves up modern Mediterranean cuisine and has *menus* (from €22) that change with the seasons. Highlights include monkfish seasoned with rosemary, and sardines and preserved lemons on t°ast. Mon–Sat noon–2.30pm.

La Diligence 2 place Pétrarque ⓞ 04 67 66 12 21, ⓦla-diligence.com. Atmospheric, vaulted medieval setting for innovative French dishes. Look out for the roast partridge with apricot sauce. *Menus* are €39–69 (€23 at lunch), and offer a good-value dip into the finest French cuisine. Mon & Sat 7.30–11pm, Tues–Fri noon–2pm & 7.30–11pm.

Fairview Coffee 6 rue Loys ⓞ 09 80 56 39 39. A stone's throw southwest of place de la Comédie, this independent café is a good place to go for American-style coffee. On the menu are pancakes and bagels. Tues–Sat 9.30am–7pm, Sun 11am–5pm.

★**L'Heure Bleue** 1 rue de la Carbonnerie ⓞ 04 67 66 41 05. Quirky café and tearoom in a vintage clothes and furniture shop named after Guerlain's famous perfume. Excellent salads (around €16), not to mention the home-made cakes – try the lemon meringue. Tues–Sat 10.30am–7pm.

Le Prince de Minorque 1 rue des Tessiers ⓞ 04 67 66

05 77. Great-value Mediterranean food, in a cheerful setting with a streetside patio. Solid *plats du jour* at only €8, and *menus* from €12 featuring grilled meat and fish. Tues–Sun noon–2.30pm & 7–11pm.

La Réserve Rimbaud 820 av de St-Maur ⓞ 04 67 72 52 53, ⓦreserve-rimbaud.com. In a bucolic location on the outskirts of town, this is the place to go for fine dining. The *menus* (€32–100) showcase the best regional products. In summer, there's an outdoor cocktail and tapas bar. Tues–Fri noon–2pm & 7–10pm, Sat 7–10pm, Sun noon–2pm

Le Saleya Place du Marché aux Fleurs ⓞ 04 67 60 53 92. In fine weather, join the locals at the outdoor tables to feast on a daily selection of market-fresh fish and regional fare for €12. A long-standing Montpellier institution. Mon–Sat noon–2pm & 7–10pm.

La Tomate 6 rue Four des Flammes ⓞ 04 67 60 49 38. Unmissable with its tomato-coloured facade, this restaurant serves solid, *terroir* standards from only €10.50 at lunch and from €15.50 at dinner. Daily noon–10.30pm.

Tripti Kulai 20 rue Jacques-Coeur ⓞ 04 67 66 30 51, ⓦtriptikulai.com. Quirky, friendly, women-run vegetarian/vegan restaurant. Dishes with oriental flair, including a good choice of salads, from €10.50. The lassis and home-made chai are superb. Mon–Sat noon–3pm & 6–10pm.

Le Vieux Four 59 rue de l'Aiguillerie ⓞ 04 67 60 55 95, ⓦlevieuxfour.fr. Carnivores will love this cosy, candlelit place specializing in *grillades au feu de bois* – meats roasted on an open spit. The *carte* is dominated by beef, but the duck breast with thyme *jus* is excellent. *Menus* €24–30. Tues–Sun 7.30–9.30pm.

DRINKING AND NIGHTLIFE

The nightlife in Montpellier is also excellent, with an incredible number of bars, clubs and live music options. You'll be able to find everything you need in the old town and its environs, but die-hard clubbers will want to head for the string of nightclubs on the route de Palavas in Lattes. Fortunately, many of these are served by l'Amigo, TAM's night

5

LGBT MONTPELLIER

After Paris, Montpellier might be France's most gay-friendly city. Contact **ANGEL**, 21 bd Pasteur (drop in Sat 4–7pm ☎06 29 66 16 56, ⓦangel34.com) and see ⓦmontpelliergay.com for information.

bus (until 6am in July & Aug), so you may not have to take a taxi home (TAM can provide a list of nightclubs served by the route).

Cargo 5 rue du Grand St-Jean ☎04 67 29 96 85. Montpellier's best nightclub and cocktail bar, which is mainly geared towards the city's student population. Regular theme nights and often free entry. Wed–Sat 11pm–5am.

Couleurs de Bières 48 rue du Faubourg St-Jaumes ☎04 67 03 31 54. North of the Jardin des Plantes, this is a must for lovers of craft beer, with more than eight hundred on offer. Mon 5–11pm, Tues–Sat 5pm–1am.

Fitzpatrick's 5 place St-Côme ☎04 67 60 58 30, ⓦfitzpatricksirishpub.com. The place to go if you're craving Guinness. There's a nice outside terrace in a small square and live music on Friday evenings. Daily noon–1am.

★**Gazette Café** 6 rue Levat ☎04 67 59 07 59, ⓦgazettecafe.com. Hip wine bar, restaurant, literary café and general cultural hotspot with film screenings, live music and exhibitions. Tues–Sat 10am–1am.

★**La Panacée** 14 rue de l'École de Pharmacie ☎04 99 63 45 68, ⓦlapanacee.org. The hippest place to drink in town is this café in the new contemporary art centre of the same name. Enjoy a glass of wine or tapas indoors underneath an original sculpture "24 Lignes", or in the courtyard. Wed–Sat 10am–1am, Sun 10am–6pm.

Rockstore 20 rue Verdun ☎04 67 06 80 00, ⓦrockstore .fr. Legendary Montpellier club and concert venue. You can't miss the half-Cadillac protruding from the front of this former Calvinist temple. Free except for concerts. Tues–Sat midnight–6am.

Les Tanins d'Abord 10 rue Roucher ☎09 70 38 60 88, ⓦlestaninsdabord.com. New wine bar in an attractive stone cellar with a good selection of French wines as well as international spirits. The more mature clientèle soaks it up with a platter of ham and cheese. Tues–Sat 6pm–1am.

ENTERTAINMENT

Centre Chorégraphique National de Montpellier Agora, Cité Internationale de la Danse, 18 rue Ste-Ursule ☎08 00 60 07 40, ⓦccnmlr.com. In the grand surrounds of a former convent, this experimental centre for the creation and performance of contemporary dance is unique in Europe.

Le Diagonal 5 rue de Verdun ☎04 67 58 58 10, ⓦcinediagonal.com. Screens international independent films in their original versions (vo).

Domaine d'O 178 rue de la Carriérasse, 5km north west of the centre ☎08 00 20 01 65, ⓦdomaine-do-34 .eu. Open-air theatre hosting dance and plays by international companies as well as several festivals.

JAM (Jazz Action Montpellier) 100 rue Ferdinand-Lesseps ☎04 67 58 30 30, ⓦlejam.com. Concert venue for jazz and World Music, with several gigs a week, free on Thursdays. Oct–June Wed–Sun.

Opéras de Montpellier 11 bd Victor Hugo ☎04 67 60 19 99, ⓦopera-orchestre-montpellier.fr. The excellent local opera company performs at the Opéra Comédie or Le Corum.

Orchestre National de Montpellier Le Corum, Esplanade Charles de Gaulle ☎04 67 60 19 99, ⓦopera -orchestre-montpellier.fr. The regional orchestra performs at Le Corum.

Park & Suites Arena Rte de la Foire, Pérols ☎04 67 17 69 69, ⓦps-arena.com. France's second largest indoor arena hosts concerts by international bands as well as handball and tennis matches.

SHOPPING

Covered markets: Castellane, rue de la Loge, and Laissac, place A. Laissac (both Mon–Sat 7.30am–1pm). Outdoor markets: place Albert ler (Wed, Fri & Sat 7am–1.30pm); bd des Arceaux (Tues–Sat 7am–1.30pm); place du Nombre d'Or, Antigone (Wed 7am–1.30pm); place de la Comédie (Mon–Sat 9am–4pm); av d'Heidelberg, Mosson (Tues, Fri & Sat 7am–1.30pm). Books: Esplanade Charles de Gaulle (Sat 9am–6pm). Fleamarkets: Esplanade du Peyrou (Sun 7.30am–2pm); Espace Mosson (Sun 6am–1pm); Les Arceaux (Tues 8am–5pm).

Le Bookshop 8 rue du Bras de Fer ☎04 67 66 22 90. English bookshop which holds free French-English conversation evenings (Mon & Fri 5–7pm). Mon 2–7pm, Tues–Sat 11am–7pm.

Maison Régionale des Vins 34 rue St-Guilhem ☎04 67 60 40 41. Regional wine and products. Mon–Sat 9.30am–8pm.

DIRECTORY

Hospital Centre Hospitalier Universitaire de Montpellier, 191 av du Doyen Gaston Giraud (☎ 04 67 33 95 00, ☯ chu -montpellier.fr). Call ☎ 15 in an emergency.
Laundry Wash In, 68 rue de l'Aiguillerie (☯ washin.fr;

daily 7am–10pm). Also at several other locations.
Pharmacy Pharmacie de la Comédie, 1 rue de Verdun (☎ 04 67 58 54 94; Mon–Sat 8.30am–7.30pm).
Police 206 rue du Comte-de-Melgueil ☎ 04 99 13 50 00.

The coast: La Grande-Motte to Marseillan-Plage

From its narrowing point at Le Grau-du-Roi, south of Nîmes, the Camargue Gardoise trails off westwards in fits and starts – a string of salty *étangs* and scrubby flats populated by birds and bulls respectively, passing close by Montpellier and continuing as far as Agde (see p.265). The easternmost town along this stretch is **La Grande-Motte**, a bizarre 1960s planned resort. The other towns along this coast – **Palavas**, **Sète** and **Mèze** – have been fishing centres for generations, and their maritime heritage lives on in popular local traditions, such as the water-joust. Only **Maguelone**, once a bustling port, was unable to stand the test of the ages, and has been reduced to an ancient and romantically sited **cathedral**. Extremely popular and flooded with people in the summer months, all of these towns offer the makings of a good beach holiday, yet are far from being soulless seaside resorts.

La Grande-Motte

LA GRANDE-MOTTE is undoubtedly the oddest resort town on the French Mediterranean. A Sixties-era beachside version of Montpellier's Antigone development, this "futuristic" planned community, executed by Jean Balladur, was awarded the "Twentieth Century Heritage Site" label by the Ministry of Culture in 2010. The town consists of an immense array of weirdly shaped sand-coloured condos and apartment complexes with evocative names like "Le Calypso" and "Temple du Soleil", set on a long boardwalk; the whole place feel like an enormous shopping mall that just happens to have a beach. Putting its architecture to one side, La Grande-Motte is a run-of-the-mill family-holiday seaside resort. It's as good a place as any to stop for a swim, and if you want to spend a couple of days on the beach, you'll find all the facilities and services you would expect.

ARRIVAL AND INFORMATION | LA GRANDE-MOTTE

By bus Buses stop at "La Poste" or "Le Port".
Destinations Aigues Mortes (several daily; 20min); Le Grau-du-Roi (several daily; 10min); Montpellier (several daily; 40min). There's a beach shuttle in summer.

Tourist information 55 rue du Port (July & Aug daily 9.30am–1pm & 3–7.30pm; Sept–June Mon–Sat 10am– noon & 3–6pm, Sun 10am–1pm; ☎ 04 67 56 42 00, ☯ lagrandemotte.com).

ACCOMMODATION AND EATING

Camping Le Garden Av de la Petite Motte ☎ 04 67 56 50 09, ☯ legarden.fr. About ten minutes' walk north of the beach, this four-star campsite has chalets to rent as well as pitches in the middle of a pine forest. Facilities include an on-site shopping centre with a bar and restaurant, and a pool. Open April to Sept. **€49.50**
L'Entre Potes 35 av Pierre Racine ☎ 04 67 84 36 60, ☯ restaurant-grandemotte.com. The *menus* (€23.60– 30.90) at this wine bar and restaurant near the port are inspired by the Mediterranean. They do tapas too. Daily noon–2pm & 8–10pm.

Saint Clair Av de l'Europe ☎ 04 67 56 57 77, ☯ hotelsaintclair.com. Lovely two-star hotel with a "boutique" feel and 27 light, bright rooms; some face the sea, as does the breakfast room. There's also a pretty interior courtyard. **€100**
Saveurs Marines 438 quai Georges Pompidou ☎ 04 34 11 27 36, ☯ restaurant-saveursmarines.fr. Owned by an oyster farmer, this is the place to go for fresh-off-the-boat shellfish. Expect to pay around €20 for a "discovery platter". Daily 10.30am–6pm (call for winter times).

5

Palavas-les-Flots

PALAVAS-LES-FLOTS is the closest seaside resort to Montpellier. The town is built on a sandbar that encloses a series of *étangs* replete with birdlife, including flamingos. Palavas has been a popular summer destination for almost a century, a fact attested to by the satirical caricatures of its inhabitants and visitors drawn by Montpellier artist Albert Dubout (1905–76). Almost entirely surrounded by water (it's attached to the mainland by a road), Palavas is not as peculiar as first impressions suggest, either, for once you penetrate the surrounding developments you'll find that the oldest part, where the banks of the canalized River Lez reach the sea, still retains the air of a pretty old fishing town. There are **markets** on Sunday (April–Nov) and Monday in the parking des Arènes.

Musée Albert Dubout

Rue de l'Abbé Brocardi • April–June & Sept–Oct Tues–Sun 2–6pm; July & Aug daily 10am–1pm & 4–8pm; Dec–Feb Sat & Sun 2–6pm • €5 • ☎ 04 67 07 73 82, ⓦ dubout.fr

The smallest of the *étangs*, the Lac du Levant, on the north side of the old quarter, has a small eighteenth-century fort, La Redoute de Ballestras, in the middle. Reached by a long causeway, the fort now houses the **Musée Albert Dubout**, where you can see the artist's work. The themed exhibitions, which look at daily life in the resort in times gone by, change every spring. You can buy a variety of good-quality items featuring Dubout's images in the on-site shop; his drawings of cats are particularly cute.

The beach

The most interesting section of **beach** and the best for swimming and sunbathing lies west of the main town, past the campsite. You can walk or cycle there or, if you drive, you will be obliged (mid-June to mid-Sept; €3) to use the car park. From the parking area, a narrow sand-spit stretches west, separated from the *étang* behind by a shrubby embankment; the beach here is a popular gay and naturist spot.

Maguelone

A road runs along the inland side of the embankment on which a free *petit train* runs every twenty minutes in summer, ferrying people from their cars to the beach and on to the peninsula of **Maguelone**, dominated by its twelfth-century **cathedral** – a lone survivor of the days when the former port was an important religious centre (see box opposite). The rest of the peninsula is a verdant idyll, and on the north shore some restored fishermen's huts evoke the Maguelone of the early twentieth century, when it was a poor fishing hamlet.

The cathedral

Daily 9am–6pm • Free (audioguide €3) • ☎ 04 67 50 49 88, ⓦ www.compagnons-de-maguelone.org

Pass beneath Maguelone **cathedral**'s marble portal, with its excellent mid-twelfth-century low-relief carvings of apostles Peter and Paul, to enter an **interior** that has suffered total looting through the ages. Its most striking feature is its huge overhanging gallery, and you'll also find some ancient tombstones down by the altar. From the gallery you can look down through the sluices over the entrance, which were intended to have hot oil poured through them onto the heads of attackers. In June, a festival of **choral singing** takes place here. There is also a **restaurant** (June to mid-Sept daily noon–3pm) where you can taste the monks' wine and shellfish.

ARRIVAL AND DEPARTURE

PALAVAS

By bus Take bus #131 from Montpellier's Line 3 tram stop "Garcia Lorca".

INFORMATION

Tourist information Place de la Méditerranée (April– June & Sept daily 10am–1pm & 2–6pm; July & Aug daily 10am–8pm; Oct–March Mon–Sat 10am–1pm & 2–6pm; ☎ 04 67 07 73 34, ⓦ ot-palavaslesflots.com). The office is

5

MAGUELONE'S PAST GLORY

You wouldn't guess it, but the Romanesque **cathedral** that looms over the green peninsula of Maguelone was for centuries one of the most important churches in medieval Christendom. Before accumulated silt linked it to the mainland, Maguelone was an **island**, most likely first settled by the Phoenicians. In the early eighth century, the town here was taken by Saracen forces, but Charles Martel, court chamberlain and de facto ruler of France, pushed back their advance and destroyed the settlement in 737 to prevent its recapture and use as a forward base for further attacks. Refounded in 1030, the strongly fortified church became an important **religious centre** and a place of refuge for bishops and popes in their quarrels with the nobility and kings of Europe. In 1096, Pope Urban II proclaimed Maguelone as the second church after Rome – an indulgence which guaranteed the complete forgiveness of sins of whoever was buried there. With the papal blessing and in its recovered role as **port**, the town thrived from the Middle Ages until the Wars of Religion, when Louis XIII destroyed it for its unrepentant Protestantism. Nowadays, all that remains is the ancient cathedral.

in the unmistakable lighthouse building that towers above the port.

Bike rental There are several places to hire bikes including Cycloloc, 49 rue Sire de Joinville (☎ 04 67 68 55 84; €15 per day).

ACCOMMODATION AND EATING

Camping Les Roquilles 267 bis av St-Maurice ☎ 04 67 68 03 47, ⓦ camping-les-roquilles.fr. Well-equipped four-star campsite in a pine forest next to the sea. There are two large pools with water slides and numerous activities including guided tours on Harley-Davidsons. Open mid-April to mid-Sept. €38.10

★ **Glacier Catalan** 5 quai Paul Cunq ☎ 04 67 68 44 45, ⓦ glaciercatalan.fr. The artisan ice-cream maker at this waterfront café is regarded as one of the finest in France – try the Mojito sorbet. Daily 9am–2am in summer (call for winter times).

Le Piccolino 3 bd Maréchal Foch ☎ 04 11 75 80 52. French, Spanish and Italian cuisine is on the menu at this popular restaurant and tapas bar next to the casino. Lunch from €13.90. Reservations recommended. Wed–Fri noon–1.45pm & 7–10pm, Sat noon–2.15pm & 7–10pm, Sun noon–2.15pm.

Tanagra 2 rue St-Louis ☎ 04 67 68 00 16, ⓦ hotel -tanagra-palavas.com. In the centre of town but next to the sea, this two-star hotel has been welcoming guests for over a hundred years. The sixteen bright rooms are decorated with warm Mediterranan tones. €72

Sète

SÈTE is the largest fishing port on France's Mediterranean coast and the second largest commercial port. Entering town from the north, where the station is situated, you find

WATER-JOUSTING

The origins of the curious Sétois sport of **water-jousting** date back to the time of the Crusades when it was developed as a means of training for soldiers. The practice seems to have caught on here in the late seventeenth century, when Sète was thriving as a port thanks to its link to the Canal du Midi and the Canal du Rhône. The sport consists of two sleek boats, each manned by eight oarsmen, charging at each other on a near head-on course. At the stern of each boat, a long, raised tail supports the platform on which a jouster stands, dressed in white. Six other jousters provide a counterweight to the platform, while the rest of the crew, a coxswain and two musicians, keep the boat on course and in time. As the boats approach each other, the jousters steady their small shields, aim their long lances and attempt to strike their adversary from his mount. The spectacle is repeated seven times in each **tournament**, or *joute*, and the winning team is the one that unseats its opponents the most times. There are seven *sociétés des joutes* in Sète (other Languedocian ports also have their own teams). The **season** runs from mid-June to mid-September with more frequent tournaments taking place in the summer. The most important championships are held here on August 25, the Fête de St-Louis.

Musée International des Artes Modestes & Midisport

Gare SNCF

SÈTE

Espace Brassens

Ferry Terminal

QUAI LATTRE-DE-TASSIGNY

RUE HONORÉ EUZET

QUAI LÉOPOLD SUQUET

RUE GEN DE GAULE

AV MAX DORMOY

RUE DÉPUTÉ SALIS

R COL FABIEN

RUE JEAN JAURÈS

R ALSACE LORRAINE

RUE GAMBETTA

RUE DOUMET

RUE LEFEBVRE

R F MISTRAL

RUE MAURICE CLAVEL

R DE LAPEYRADE

R P SEMARD

RUE LAZARE CARNOT

QUAI DE LA RÉPUBLIQUE

Bike Rental

QUAI DE LA RÉSISTANCE

Market

R DE METZ

RUE P VALERY

PL L-BLUM

RUE LOUIS BLANC

CH DU MAS ROUSSON

RUE VILLEFRANCHE

RUE PASCAL

RUE DU PALAIS

R RIBOT

GRAND RUE

Sète Croisières

RUE SAVONNERIE

QUAI CH LEMARESQUIER

RUE R ROLLAND

QUAI D'ALGER

Nouveau Bassin

RUE J-F BAZILLE

RUE GARENNE

RUE DU PARC

GRANDE RUE HAUTE

R E BONNET

RUE FRANKLIN

RUE 3 JOURNÉES

R RAPIDE

RAMPE P VALERY

QUAI GÉNÉRAL DURAND

Canal Royal

QUAI M LICCIARDI

QUAI ASPIRANT HERBER

RUE MARTIN

RUE RICHELIEU

Centre Régional d'Art Contemporain

RUE VILLARET JOYEUSE

RUE LACAN

GRAND RUE

R DES MARINS

R DES PÊCHEURS

RUE ÉLIE D'ÉLIA

QUAI DE LA MARINE

QUAI RICHELIEU

Citadel

RUE TRAVERSIÈRE

Bike Med

PROM DE J B MARTY

RUE R PINEL

Vieux Port

Musée Paul Valéry

GRANDE RUE HAUTE

Cimetière Marin

ACCOMMODATION
Auberge de Jeunesse	3
Le Grand Hôtel	2
Mira Ceti Yurt	4
Le National	1
Venezia	5

EATING
Brasserie Victor Hugo	2
La Cantine de l'Etonnoir	3
Chez François	4
La Coquerie	6
Le Social	5
Tielle Cianni Marcos	1

0 _____ 250
metres

N

Musée de la Mer, Théâtre de la Mer, Plage de la Corniche, Bassin de Thau & Agde

yourself surrounded by grey warehouses, fenced-in storage yards and stacks of freight containers; cranes dominate the skyline and moveable bridges cross canals. Once across the wide Canal Maritime, however, you'll arrive at the colourful **old quarter**, which straddles the westernmost of the two north–south canals, the Canal Royal.

On the west bank, the land rises dramatically, hedging in the historical centre. This slope is the eastern side of the 175m-high rocky promontory, **Mont St-Clair**, whose presence has determined the growth of the town. Sète grew as a long corniche completely circling the *mont*, but recently suburbs have begun to climb its steep slopes. The attractive town has several interesting museums and a park, but primarily makes a good base for enjoying the 12km-long unbroken stretch of beach west towards Agde – it also has excellent pleasure-port facilities and lively nightlife in summer. It's worth trying to time your visit to coincide with one of the many **water-jousting** tournaments (see box, p.219) held on the town's canals; the quaysides jam with people watching the boat-borne combatants, and afterwards the bars fill with boisterous revellers.

Canal Royal and around

You're likely to spend most of your time in Sète along the **Canal Royal**, which is lined on the west side by restaurants and bars, or in the tight scrum of streets between the water and the hill. On the east-side waterfront, the **Centre Régional d'Art Contemporain** (26 quai Aspirant-Herber; Mon & Wed–Fri 12.30–7pm, Sat & Sun 3–8pm or 2–7pm in winter; free; ☎04 67 74 89 69) is dedicated to the creation of contemporary art and hosts temporary exhibitions, while the quirky **Musée International des Arts Modestes** (23 quai Maréchal-Lattre; April–Sept daily 9.30am–7pm; Oct–March Tues–Sun 10am–noon & 2–6pm; €5.50; ☎04 99 04 76 44, ⓦmiam.org), on the west side, contains a quirky collection of art made from cast-off goods.

Musée Paul Valéry

Rue François Desnoyer • April to mid-Nov daily 9.30am–7pm; mid-Nov to March Tues–Sun 10am–6pm • €5.50 (€9 during exhibitions) • ☎04 99 04 76 16, ⓦmuseepaulvalery-sete.fr

On the southern side of Mont St-Clair, about ten minutes' walk from the old port, lies the **Musée Paul Valéry**. As well as editions and manuscripts written by the renowned local writer (see box below), you'll find a small but impressive collection of contemporary paintings, including works by Courbet and Dufy. Outside is a pricey restaurant, *Brasserie des Arts*, which is best visited to sip a drink on the terrace and admire the view. Valéry's remains lie in the **cimetière marin** across the street from the museum, along with those from the town's grandest families – check out the marble tombs.

Musée de la Mer

Rue Jean Vilar • Tues–Sun May–Oct 10am–7pm; Nov–April 9.30am–6pm • €3.50 • ☎04 99 04 71 55.

At the **Musée de la Mer**, below the **cimetière marin**, you can find out about water-jousting and the history of the port from the eighteenth century. There are some lovely little replicas of boats here too. Nearby is the open-air **Théâtre de la Mer** which hosts music concerts and festivals in the summer; you can get a free boat bus to shows from quai Paul Riquet.

PAUL VALÉRY

Though of Corsican and Italian parentage, **Paul Valéry** was born in Sète in 1871, and spent his childhood and adolescence in the town. An introspective youth, he whiled away his hours contemplating the sea. On reaching adulthood, he moved to Paris, where he took up work as a legal clerk; by this time he had already begun writing **Symbolist poetry** influenced by Poe and Mallarmé. His great and largely unrequited love, however, was for science, and despite his literary successes, he turned towards more pragmatic intellectual pursuits in the sciences. He was a great admirer of da Vinci, in whom he saw the "universal man" – a cerebral Renaissance figure whom he brought to life in his stylized novel *Monsieur Teste* (1895). Valéry did his best to live up to the da Vincian ideal which he professed. In his forties, at the urging of André Gide, he returned to poetry, while his scientific pursuits brought him into personal contact with contemporaries such as Albert Einstein. His acute observational powers and political insights made him a popular *salon* guest in interwar Paris, and official accolades followed with his election in 1925 to the Académie Française and his appointment to the Collège de France as the first Professor of Poetry. Valéry remained in Paris through the Nazi occupation and, having lived to see the Liberation, died the following year and was buried as a national hero.

5

Mont St-Clair and around

Bus #5 from the Hôtel de Ville or the museum

Looking over the Valéry museum, on a broad plateau on the west of Mont St-Clair, you'll see the park of **Pierres Blanches**, a scrubby habitat for thyme, which provides impressive views over the shellfish beds of the Bassin de Thau to the north, particularly towards sunset. This is also a great spot for a picnic, but if you come without supplies, you can get a snack at the small on-site café. Further east, at the summit of the *mont*, you'll find the nineteenth-century church of **Notre-Dame-de-la-Salette** (bus #5), built on the remains of a medieval fort; the church is nothing special but the views from here over the ports, old and new, are spectacular. West of here, the best **beach** reachable by public transport (buses #9, #915 and #323) – with showers and other amenities – is the **Plage de la Corniche**, where you'll also find restaurants and accommodation.

Espace Georges-Brassens

67 bd C amille Blanc • June–Sept daily 10am–6pm; Oct–May Tues–Sun 10am–noon & 2–6pm • €5.60 • ☎ 04 99 04 76 26, ⓦ espace-brassens.fr

From the canal front, it's a long ride (bus #3 or #7) to the northwest side of Mont St-Clair, where you'll find another local shrine, the **Espace Georges-Brassens**. Local-born Brassens (1921–81) was perhaps France's most popular folk singer of the postwar era, a sort of Gallic Bob Dylan, whose simple guitar melodies served as platforms for irony-edged sentimental lyrics. He's buried in the "poor people's" cemetery opposite.

ARRIVAL AND DEPARTURE
SÈTE

By train Sète's *gare SNCF* is on quai Maréchal-Joffre, on the north bank of the Canal Latéral; from here it's a 40min walk into town so your best bet is to take bus #2, #3, #6, #9, #915 or #323 to the "Passage Le Dauphin" stop, near the tourist office. Sète is on the main TGV line between Nîmes and Perpignan.
Destinations Agde (several daily; 12min); Marseillan-Plage (several daily; 10min); Montpellier (several daily; 25min); Nîmes (several daily; 55min); Perpignan, via Béziers and Narbonne (several daily; 1hr 35min).
By bus There is no *gare routière* as such – the main bus hubs are the train station and the following stops: "Noël Guignon" (for buses to Montpellier), "Passage Le Dauphin" and "Épi d'Or".
Destinations Balaruc-les-Bains (many daily; 15–30min); Bouzigues (several daily; 35min); Loupian (several daily; 40min); Marseillan (several daily May–Sept; 30min); Marseillan-Plage (several daily May–Sept; 15min); Mèze (several daily; 45min).
By ferry Across the Canal Maritime, to the east of the *gare routière*, you'll find the ferry terminal, Gare Maritime Orsetti (☎ 04 67 46 15 22, ⓦ gnv.it), which has regular departures for Morocco.

GETTING AROUND

By bike You can rent bikes at several places including BikeMed, 19 quai de la Consigne (☎ 04 67 74 49 23, ⓦ bikemed.fr), and scooters at Midisport, 3 av Victor Hugo (☎ 04 67 74 93 52).

INFORMATION AND ACTIVITIES

Tourist information 60 Grand'rue Mario Roustan (April–June & Sept Mon–Sat 9.30am–6pm, Sun 10am–5pm; July & Aug 9.30am–7pm; Oct–March Mon–Sat 9.30am–5.30pm, Sun 10am–1pm; ☎ 04 99 04 71 71, ⓦ tourisme-sete.com). As well as organizing their own guided tours of the town, fish market and street art, you can also book a free tour with an English-speaking "Greeter" here.
Glass-bottom boat tours Sète Croisières on quai Général-Durand (☎ 04 67 46 00, ⓦ sete-croisieres.com) runs a number of regular trips in the summer for €9–14.

ACCOMMODATION

Surprisingly, given its seaside setting and the activity of its port, Sète is not overflowing with accommodation. As a consequence, booking ahead is crucial in summer, and far in advance should you be planning to stay during one of the town's festivals.

Auberge de Jeunesse 7 rue Général Revest ☎ 04 67 53 46 68, ⓦ fuaj.org. The main reason to stay in this youth hostel, in a traditional villa on Mont St-Clair, is for the wonderful view from its terrace. You can camp here in July

5

> ## MARKETS IN SÈTE
>
> There is a daily **covered market** at Les Halles, rue Gambetta (7am–1pm). **Outdoor markets** take place on Wednesdays throughout the town centre, and on Fridays in place Stalingrad and on avenue Victor Hugo. On Sundays there are **flea markets** in place de la République and on quai des Moulins. On Thursday evenings in July and August, an **arts and crafts** market is held on place du Galion aux Quilles.

and August. Closed Nov to March. **€23**

★**Le Grand Hôtel** 17 quai de Lattre ☎04 67 74 71 77, ⓦlegrandhotelsete.com. Alongside the northwestern part of the Canal Royal, this elegant three-star hotel with original Art Nouveau features and a lovely interior courtyard is the town's smartest accommodation. There's also a gourmet restaurant (*menus* €30–47). **€128**

Mira Ceti Yurt 805 chemin des Pierres Blanches ☎06 03 13 60 87, ⓦmiracetiyurt.com. Three romantic, eco-friendly yurts in an idyllic location on Mont St-Clair. Welcome *apéritif* and breakfast included. Closed Nov to

March. **€130**

★**Le National** 2 rue Pons de l'Hérault ☎04 67 74 67 85, ⓦhotellenational.fr. This friendly family-run two-star hotel five minutes' walk south of the train station, across the canal, is the best value for money in town. Rooms are simply decorated and there's a good spread at breakfast. **€72**

Venezia 20 La Corniche de Neuburg ☎04 67 51 39 38, ⓦhotel-sete.com. Steps from the sand, this family-run two-star boutique hotel makes a good alternative to staying in the centre of town. Each room has its own patio and car parking space. **€92**

EATING AND DRINKING

Brasserie Victor Hugo 30 av Victor Hugo ☎04 67 51 18 97. Busy on market day (Fri), this quintessential *café du quartier* is an elegant spot for breakfast or lunch, or coffee in the afternoon. The *plat du jour* is €11. Mon–Sat 7.30am–8pm.

★**La Cantine de l'Entonnoir** Halles de Sète, rue Gambetta ☎06 73 14 91 43, ⓦhalles-sete.com. In the covered market, this tiny restaurant uses ingredients from the stallholders to create tasty traditional dishes, accompanied by local wines. Main courses are around €18. Wed–Sun noon–1.30pm.

Chez François 8 quai Général Durand ☎04 67 74 59 69. This is where the locals go to eat their shellfish – fresh out of the Bassin de Thau. Sit elbow-to-elbow on the buzzy terrace in summer and share a seafood platter (from €38). Mon & Wed–Sun noon–10pm.

La Coquerie Chemin du cimetière marin ☎06 47 06 71

38, ⓦannemajourel.fr. With a market-inspired *menu* (€65) that changes daily, Anne Majourel's restaurant is the place to come for fine dining. Lovely views over the sea. Reservations recommended. June–Sept daily (closed Sun eve) noon–2pm & 8–10pm; Oct–May Thurs–Sun noon–2pm. Closed Dec and Feb.

★**Le Social** 35 rue Villaret Joyeuse ☎04 67 74 54 79. Hip café-bar with a youngish clientele who come here for drinking as much as for eating; it's the HQ of one of the water-jousting societies. Tapas, charcuterie and traditional French dishes are on the menu (around €20 per person). Mon–Sat noon–2pm & 6pm–1am, Sun noon–3pm.

Tielle Cianni Marcos 24 rue Honoré Euzet ☎04 67 74 16 23. The speciality of Sète is *tielle*, a spicy octopus pie, and this little shop and restaurant is the place to try it. Reservations recommended, unless you want to take one away. Daily 8am–8pm.

Around the Bassin de Thau

The **BASSIN DE THAU**, at 19km long and some 5km wide, is one of the biggest **salt lakes** in Languedoc. From its northeastern end above Sète it extends along the town's 12km stretch of beach southwest to Agde. One of the best times to visit is in July, when the **Festival de Thau** (ⓦfestivaldethau.com) livens up the local towns and villages with a week-long series of World Music concerts. Around the lagoon you'll find **Balaruc-les-Bains**, France's leading spa town; **Bouzigues**, one of the country's main centres for oyster farming; and **Marseillan**, the most attractive town in the area and a good spot for shopping. The main attraction is the **Musée-Parc des Dinosaures**, the largest dinosaur museum in Europe.

GETTING AROUND
AROUND THE BASSIN DE THAU

By bus You can get around the Bassin by bus #302 from Sète (several daily), which goes to Balaruc-les-Bains (15min), Bouzigues (35min), Loupian (40min) and Mèze

(45min). Bus #103/4 leaves from Montpellier and Béziers to the same towns (several daily).

By bike There is a cycle path around the Bassin (except

5

SHELLFISH FARMING

The Bassin is one of France's "Sites Remarquables du Goût" thanks to its **shellfish cultivation**, with approximately eight thousand tonnes of oysters raised here annually, eighty percent of which are the larger Pacific variety. At the eastern end of the lagoon, between Bouzigues and Sète, the wooden **oyster racks** protruding from the water make a curious aquascape. The oysters are harvested using a nineteenth-century technique of cementing them to ropes which hang from the racks: the strong winds which blow along the surface of the water compensate for the lack of tidal movement, which the shellfish depend on to move water through their gills.

for a section between Marseillan and Mourre-Blanc), which is 60km heading east clockwise from Mèze to Marseillan. You can rent mountain bikes and tandems from €5 per day from Galexia Bien-Être (104 av Vauban, Frontignan ☎ 06 19 98 75 88, ⓦ galexiabienetre-deferlantes.fr), which can be delivered to your accommodation. They also organize guided bike tours.

Balaruc

BALARUC consists of two villages: **Balaruc-le-Vieux**, a tiny *circulade* set dramatically on a low spur just inland and **Balaruc-les-Bains**, an ancient fishing port which has become France's leading spa town. The main attraction here (apart from the spa) is the **Jardin Antique Mediterranéen** (rue des Pioch; Tues–Sun: March–June 9.30am–noon & 2–6.30pm; July–Sept 9.30am–12.30pm & 3–7pm; Oct & Nov 9.30am–noon & 2–5.30pm; €4.70 or €6.80 with audioguide; ☎ 04 67 46 47 92), a beautiful and fascinating reconstructed Mediterranean garden from antiquity.

INFORMATION AND ACTIVITIES   BALARUC

Tourist information Rue Romaine, Pavillon Sévigné (Jan, Feb & Dec Mon–Fri 9am–noon & 2–6pm; March–June & Sept–Nov Mon–Sat 9am–noon & 2–6pm, Sun 9am–1pm; July & Aug Mon–Sat 9am–1pm & 2–7pm, Sun 10am–1pm & 3–7pm; ☎ 04 67 46 81 46, ⓦ balaruc-les-bains.com).
Spa O'balia, allée des Sources (☎ 04 67 18 52 05,

ⓦ www.obalia.fr). Opened in 2015, these hi-tech thermal baths are a good place to spend a few hours whether or not you are ill. Beauty treatments are also available.
Watersports Centre Nautique Manuréva, av de la Gare (☎ 04 67 48 55 63). Sailing, windsurfing, kayaking and stand-up paddle for all ages.

ACCOMMODATION AND EATING

Neptune 5 rue Montgolfier ☎ 04 67 48 53 17, ⓦ hotelneptune-balaruc.com. Modern three-star hotel next to the new spa in the town centre. Rooms are simply decorated in contemporary style. There's a pool and a rooftop sun terrace; they also offer spa packages. Closed mid-Nov to mid-March. **€65**

Le Point de Thau 55 av du Port ☎ 04 67 18 08 42. Good-value fish restaurant on the waterfront with the *plat du jour* at €10. Gorgeous views from the first-floor dining room and second-floor terrace. Mon, Tues & Fri–Sun noon–1.30pm & 7.30–10.30pm.

Mèze and around

The largest village on the Bassin de Thau's northern shore, **MÈZE** is an ancient fishing village whose old quarter is a dense maze of narrow streets flanked by low houses. As it isn't directly on the sea it gets relatively few visitors, and provides some respite from the crowded coastal towns. The village is an excellent stop for families, with a pleasant, laidback feel, two beaches, a beautiful old fishing port and a fine **covered market** (rue Garibaldi; Tues–Sun 6.30am–1.30pm). There's also a market at the port on Thursday evenings in July and August.

Musée-Parc des Dinosaures

Rte départementale 613 • Daily: Feb–June & Sept–Oct 2–6pm; July & Aug 10am–7pm; Nov–Dec 2–5pm • €9.80 (for either the park or museum) or €16.50 combined • ☎ 04 67 43 02 80, ⓦ dinosaure.eu

The **Musée-Parc des Dinosaures** is the largest dinosaur museum in Europe and was established on the site of a major paleontological find: one of the biggest caches of

5

dinosaur eggs yet discovered. As well as a forest route past reconstructions of the creatures and a 25m-long skeleton of a brachiosaurus, there is also the **Musée de l'Évolution,** which traces the origins of man. Well worth a visit.

Musée de Site Gallo-Romain Villa-Loupian

RD 158 E4, Loupian • July & Aug daily 1.30–7pm; Sept–June Mon, Mon & Wed–Sun 1.30–6pm • €5 • ☎ 04 67 18 68 18

The **Musée de Site Gallo-Romain Villa-Loupian** is on the site of a Gallo-Roman villa, built between the first and sixth centuries BC, where wheat and wine were cultivated. You can see finds from the site as well as reconstructions of what the place once looked like, but the stars of the show are the polychrome **mosaics**.

INFORMATION

MÈZE AND AROUND

Tourist information Nord du Bassin de Thau, quai Baptiste Guitard (May, June & Sept Mon–Fri 10am–noon & 1.30–5.30pm, Sat 10am–noon; July & Aug daily 9.30am–12.30pm & 2.30–6.30pm; Oct–April Mon–Fri 10am–noon & 2–5pm; ☎ 04 67 43 93 08, ⓦ tourism -nordbassindethau.fr).

EATING AND DRINKING

★**Atelier & Co** Zone Conchylicole Ouest, Loupian ☎ 04 67 43 81 67, ⓦ ateliernco.com. There's no better place to eat shellfish than at the farm of this third-generation producer with views across the lagoon. The €15 platter includes twelve oysters (gold medal winners in a national competition, no less), six mussels and a glass of Picpoul de Pinet. Mon–Thurs & Sun noon–2pm, Fri & Sat noon–2pm & 7–9pm.

La Barque Bleue 39 av de Montpellier, Mèze ☎ 04 67 43 87 10, ⓦ labarquebleuemeze.sitew.com. In the north of the town, you don't come here for nice views or decor but simply for good seafood – try the oysters or mussels *gratinés*. Reservations are recommended. They also do takeaway. Daily 8.30am–8.30pm.

De la Pyramide 8 promenade Sgt Jean-Louis Navarro, Mèze ☎ 04 67 46 61 50, ⓦ hoteldelapyramide.fr. Comfortable three-star hotel with a pool. The bright rooms have either a terrace or balcony and overlook the garden or lagoon. Free parking. €88

★**Mèze Maison** 2 rue François Besse, Mèze ☎ 06 21 16 43 42, ⓦ mezemaison.com. Chic B&B in a nineteenth century wine merchant's house in the centre of the old town. The four rooms have been individually decorated and the whole place oozes good taste. Bikes are available and there is free parking nearby. €140

Les Palmiers 31 bis av Montpellier, Mèze ☎ 04 34 53 55 65, ⓦ villa-lespalmiers.fr. Mediterranean food is on the menu at this restored Italianate villa with a lovely courtyard terrace (desserts such as roast fig with honey parfait and rosemary cream are a speciality). There's three-course lunch *menu* for €21 and they have five rooms to rent too. Mon–Tues, Thurs & Fri noon–1.30pm & 7.30–9.15pm, Wed noon–1.30pm, Sat 7.30–9.15pm.

Bouzigues

BOUZIGUES has the appearance of a fishing town that's slept through the last century, with its narrow, laundry-strung streets and strong salt air. It is also *the* place to eat **shellfish**, and the long waterfront boulevard, avenue Louis-Tudesq, is girded by a phalanx of colourful **restaurants** offering generous, fresh *coquillages*. The best time to come is in August for the Foire aux Huîtres, a weekend of eating, drinking (mainly Picpoul de Pinet) and street entertainment.

Musée de l'Étang de Thau

Quai du port de pêche • Daily: March–June & Sept–Oct 10am–noon & 2–6pm; July & Aug 10am–12.30pm & 2.30–7pm; Nov–Feb 10am–noon & 2–5pm • €5 • ☎ 04 67 78 33 57

The **Musée de l'Étang de Thau** has an array of imaginative multimedia displays which explain the art of shellfish-raising (including tanks with live specimens) as well as traditional fishing techniques. They also organize a day-long guided tour which includes a visit to an oyster farm, a boat trip on the lagoon and a wine tasting.

ACCOMMODATION AND EATING

BOUZIGUES

Camping Lou Labech Rte de Stade ☎ 04 67 78 30 38, ⓦ lou-labech.fr. Family-run campsite with 48 pitches as well as some chalets and ready-erected tents. There's no pool but it is a stone's throw from the lagoon. Open April to Oct. €29.90

La Côte Bleue Av Louis Tudesq ☎ 04 67 78 30 87, ⓦ la cote-bleue.fr. Modern three-star hotel where most of the rooms overlook the pool and have a private terrace. The restaurant is the best place in town for seafood, with platters from €16 per person. **€110**

★**Les Glaces de la Bouline** 8 av de la République,

Bouziques ☎ 04 99 02 63 16. Artisan ice-cream maker with over fifty flavours, which change with the seasons. Try one of the regional specialities such as olive oil, pumpkin or saffron. May, June & Sept Tues–Sun 10.30am–12.30pm & 3–7pm; July & Aug daily 3.30–7.30pm & 9–11.30pm; March & April Sat & Sun 10.30am–12.30pm & 3.30–7.30pm.

Marseillan and Marseillan-Plage

MARSEILLAN and **MARSEILLAN-PLAGE**, which anchor the southern end of the Bassin, reflect how the economy of the region has shifted in the last generation. Once a flourishing fishing town, Marseillan now lies all but forgotten, ignored by the masses of weekenders who inundate the seashore at its namesake, Marseillan-Plage. This is good news for the few who do come to Marseillan, now the most picturesque and atmospheric town in the area, with a very evocative **old port**. There's little to do here aside from soak up the atmosphere, although a trip to the famed **Noilly Prat distillery** at 1 rue Noilly (see box p.228; daily: March–April & Oct–Nov 10–11am & 2.30–4.30pm, May–Sept 10–11am & 2.30–6pm; €4.50; ☎ 04 67 77 20 15, ⓦ noillyprat.com) is a good excuse to soak up the local vermouth as well. Separated from Marseillan by 6km of marshy reeds, **Marseillan-Plage**, by contrast, is the epitome of noisy Mediterranean hedonism. Its one sight, other than the hordes of near-naked bodies that crowd its beaches, is the **débouché**, the terminus of the great Canal du Midi, whose earthworks protrude strikingly into the Mediterranean here. It's a quick drive or a nice, level bike-ride between the two towns and there are several buses a day from May to September.

INFORMATION AND ACTIVITIES

Tourist information Av de la Méditerranée, Marseillan-Plage (April–June & Sept daily 9am–noon & 2–6pm; July & Aug daily 9am–7pm; Oct–March Mon–Fri 9am–noon & 1.30–5pm; ☎ 04 67 21 82 43, ⓦ marseillan.com). There is also a seasonal information point in Marseillan (Théâtre municipal Henri Maurin; July & Aug 10am–1pm & 3–7pm).

MARSEILLAN AND MARSEILLAN-PLAGE

Bike rental Denis à votre service, rue Arc-en-Ciel, Marseillan-Plage (☎ 06 46 30 23 93). From €8.50 per half-day.

Watersports There are plenty of watersports on offer including kite-surfing, jet-skiing, kayaking, sailing and diving. Ask at the tourist office for details. There are also boat trips on the lagoon.

ACCOMMODATION AND EATING

Camping Beauregard Plage 250 rue de l'Airette, Marseillan-Plage ☎ 04 67 77 15 45, ⓦ camping-beauregard-plage.com. Three-star campsite next to the beach, which has been run by the same family for fifty years. There are no permanent structures, just two hundred pitches for tents, caravans or motorhomes. **€23**

La Chaumière 1150 av de Sète, Marseillan-Plage ☎ 04 67 98 35 63, ⓦ hotel-la-chaumiere.com. Family-run two-star hotel about five minutes' walk from the beach. Rooms have a contemporary feel and the bright, airy restaurant has *menus* from €23. There's a kids' play area and free parking. **€90**

★**Coqui Thau** 30 chemin de l'Étang Port, Marseillan ☎ 04 67 77 68 58. Make like the locals with a visit to this lagoon-side producer for eat-in or takeaway shellfish. Six oysters for €5 and "discovery platters" from €10. Mon–Sat: May–Sept 9am–12.30pm & 5–8pm, Oct–May 9am–12.30pm.

★**Cosy** 16 rue du Capitaine-Bages, Marseillan ☎ 04 67 31 76 75, ⓦ cosy-chambresdhotes.fr. Four individually decorated, stylish bedrooms and an apartment are on offer in this design-conscious B&B run by a couple of graphic artists. They can arrange on-site massage and boat trips. **€100**

LOCAL MARKETS

Marseillan: covered market (place du 14 Juillet; Tues–Sun 7am–1pm); weekly market (town centre; Tues 8am–1pm); arts and crafts market (port; July & Aug Thurs 7pm–midnight); food market (town centre; July & Aug Wed 7–11pm). **Marseillan-Plage**: food market (market place; June–Sept daily 8am–1pm); weekly market (allées Fillol; June–Sept Tues 8am–1pm) and arts and crafts (market place; July & Aug Fri 9pm–midnight).

5

STIRRED, NOT SHAKEN...

The dry martini is not an association most of us would make with Languedoc, but, in fact, Marseillan-Plage is home to what British author and lifelong cocktail researcher **Somerset Maugham** described as a "necessary component" of the drink – and connoisseurs around the world agree. The secret is **Noilly Prat** (pronounced "nwah-lee prah") vermouth, created in 1813 by taking white Languedoc wine, ageing it in vats for eight months, and then for a further year outdoors in oaken barrels. The *apéritif* gets its distinctive taste from the twenty **herbs and spices** with which it is infused. For those in the know, it is the best vermouth for cocktails, although locals typically enjoy it on a hot day **on the rocks** with seafood. You can tour the Noilly Prat facility (see p.227) and buy some to take home; be warned, however, it is best consumed within a month of opening. Bond fans, incidentally, will be interested to know that according to Somerset Maugham, shaking a dry Martini destroys its "molecular characteristics" – Martinis should *always* be stirred.

La Table d'Emilie 8 place Carnot, Marseillan ☎ 04 67 77 63 59. The best restaurant in town is situated in an attractively decorated medieval house with a patio. *Menus* (lunch €22) are imaginative and feature the likes of shrimp and grapefruit sorbet. Carnivores won't be disappointed either. Tues–Sun noon–1.30pm & 7–10pm.

Pézenas and around

PÉZENAS is the last large inland settlement on the Hérault river, as it meanders south to Agde through the vineyards of the Languedoc plain. One of the most singularly beautiful towns in the French Southwest, endowed with an almost overwhelming concentration of grand architecture, it is also a centre for **arts and crafts**, and thus very popular. Although it had been an important market centre for centuries, Pézenas catapulted to glory when it became the seat of the Languedoc parliament and the residence of its governors in 1456, and reached its zenith in the mid-seventeenth century, when Armand de Bourbon, prince of Conti and governor of Languedoc, made it a "second Versailles," drawing artists and writers of the stature of **Molière** to his court with his wealthy patronage. On and off, the playwright spent a good four years here performing for the prince and garnering inspiration for the plays that would later make him famous. But with the prince's death in 1666, stagnation soon set in, and Pézenas reverted to the sleepy provincial town which – in winter – it remains today.

On Saturday mornings, there is a huge **general market** in the town centre as well as an organic market in place Gambetta. The rolling countryside around Pézenas is dotted with atmospheric old villages as well as medieval castles and one of the oldest vineyards in Languedoc, the **abbey of Valmagne**. The immediate surroundings of Pézenas offer good possibilities for walking, cycling or exploring by car.

Hôtel des Barons de Lacoste

8 rue François Oustrin • Free

Of the several fine *hôtels particuliers* dotted around town, the first you'll likely encounter is the **Hôtel des Barons de Lacoste**, a sixteenth-century palace with a beautiful but compact vaulted courtyard framed by a monumental staircase. Opposite is the former barber's shop where Molière idled away his afternoons.

La Maison des Métiers d' Art

6 place Gambetta • Tues–Sat 10am–6pm, July & Aug until 8pm • ☎ 04 67 98 16 12, ⓦ www.ateliersdart.com

Across the narrow, cobblestoned *place* stands the handsome seventeenth-century council HQ, whose broad and square-vaulted interior once held sessions of the Estates of Languedoc, but now houses the **Maison des Métiers d'Art**, a showcase for national

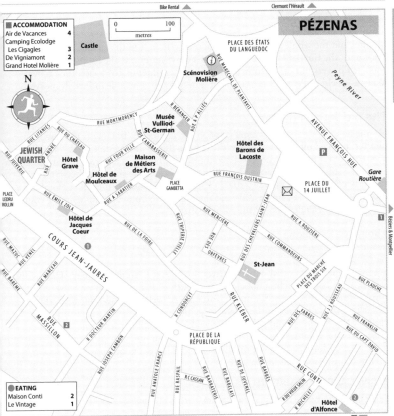

arts and crafts, including painting, decorative sculpture, stained-glass items, jewellery and fashion accessories. It's a good place to shop for classy, unique souvenirs or gifts.

Musée Vulliod-St-Germain

3 rue Albert-Paul Alliés • Tues–Sun mid-Feb to May & Oct to mid-Nov 10am–noon & 2–5.30pm, June–Sept 10am–noon & 3–7pm, until 9pm Wed & Fri in July & Aug • €1 • ☎ 04 67 98 90 59

North of the square is the mansion housing the **Musée Vulliod-St-Germain** containing all manner of sixteenth- and seventeenth-century artefacts, from classically themed Aubusson tapestries to displays dwelling on the daily life of the humbler classes. Taking pride of place upstairs is the chair from the barber's shop in which Molière once sat. But the main reason to visit is to get an idea of what a magnificent mansion like this once looked like. On the hill at the end of rue Béranger lie the ruins of the **castle** (closed) destroyed by Richelieu and dating back to as early as 1500 BC.

Scénovision Molière

Place des États de Languedoc • Daily: July & Aug 9am–7pm, until 8pm Wed & Fri; Sept–June Mon–Sat 9am–noon & 2–6pm, Sun from 10am • €7 • ☎ 04 67 98 35 39, ⓦ scenovisionmoliere.com

Turning left at the end of rue des Alliés, you'll come to the tourist office. On the top couple of floors is the **Scénovision Molière**, which recreates the world of one of France's

5

most famous playwrights. Fittingly, Molière's story is told like a play, in five acts via 3D films, with the audience moving from room to room. The tours start every fifteen minutes and the whole experience lasts about an hour. On the far side of town at 32 rue Conti, the **Hôtel d'Alfonce** (guided visits only; enquire at the tourist offce) is where Molière's players put on performances during the winter of 1655–56. The **Festival Molière** is held in Pézenas each June but is only really accessible to French speakers.

The old Jewish quarter

On the far side of the castle's base, through rue Litanies, is the town's **old Jewish quarter**, marked off by gates, as was the custom during the Middle Ages – snaking east, between the gate of rue Juiverie and place Gambetta, is a warren of narrow streets jammed with little boutiques and magnificent *hôtels*; make sure you check out the doorway of the **Hôtel Grave** at 9 rue du Château, the fourteenth-century **Hôtel de Jacques Coeur** at 7 rue Émile-Zola and the impressive ironwork railing in the courtyard at the **Hôtel de Moulceaux**, 12 rue Alfred-Sabatier.

Abbaye de Valmagne

On the D5 between Montignac and Villeveyrac, 13km east of the centre • Mid-June to Sept 10am–7pm; Oct to mid-June Mon–Fri 2–6pm, Sun 10am–6pm • €7.90 • ☎ 04 67 78 47 32, ⓦ valmagne.com

Set in a romantic wooded park, the twelfth-century Cistercian **abbey of Valmagne** was once one of the richest abbeys in the South of France and is now owned and run by descendants of the Count of Turenne. As well as a one-hour tour, the entry ticket includes a tasting of the estate's organic wines, a visit to the Gothic church, cloister, chapterhouse and medieval vegetable and herb gardens, and access to the temporary art exhibitions. The terrace of the restaurant (mid-June to Sept Tues–Sun noon–2pm, Thurs & Fri 7–9pm; *menus* from €20) is a good spot for a Mediterranean-inspired lunch.

ARRIVAL AND INFORMATION **PÉZENAS**

By bus Buses stop in Pézenas at the open-air *halte routière* on promenade du Pré St-Jean.
Destinations Béziers (several daily; 35min); Clermont-l'Hérault (several daily; 35min); Montpellier, via Bouzigues, Loupian and Mèze (several daily; 1hr). See ⓦ herault-transport.fr for details.
Tourist information Place des États du Languedoc (July & Aug Mon–Sat 9am–7pm, Sun from 10am; Sept–June Mon–Sat 9am–noon & 2–6pm, Sun from 10am; ☎ 04 67

98 36 40, ⓦ pezenas-tourisme.fr). Also in the building is the Centre d'Interprétation de l'Architecture et du Patrimoine (CIAP; same hours as tourist office; free), which has an interesting exhibition on how the town's mansions were built. There are guided tours of Pézenas in English on Thursdays in July & Aug at 10am (€6).
Bike rental Planète Vélo, av Émile-Combes (Tues–Sat 9am–noon & 2–7pm ☎ 04 67 98 34 04). From €8.50 per half day.

ACCOMMODATION

Air de Vacances 1 rue Calquières Basses ☎ 09 50 58 99 11, ⓦ air-de-vacances.com. Friendly B&B in a nineteenth-century stone house southeast of the old town, with two bedrooms and two suites. "Le Poisson" has high ceilings, exposed beams and huge windows. Breakfast is served on

the terrace in summer. **€65**
Camping Ecolodge Les Cigales 2 impasse des Cigalous, Hameau de Conas ☎ 04 67 98 97 99, ⓦ campinglescigales.com. Set amid the vines, this attractive eco-friendly campsite has modern, very

---

> ### LE POULAIN
>
> If you happen to be around for one of the local festivals (see box, p.207), keep an eye out for **Le Poulain** – the town's traditional totemic animal, which was added to UNESCO's list of Intangible Cultural Heritage in 2005. A mock horse constructed of a cloth-draped wooden frame, borne through the streets by a bunch of burly men, Le Poulain was adopted in honour of a foal that King Louis VIII's favourite mare gave birth to here in 1226.

5

LE PETIT PÂTÉ DE PÉZENAS

One of the local specialities is the **petit pâté**, a bite-sized mince tart based on the recipe of an Indian cook in Lord Clive's household – the British Governor of India holidayed here in 1768 and the recipe stuck around. The best place to pick these up, piping hot, is at Maison Alary, 9 rue St-Jean.

comfortable wooden chalets as well as pitches. There's also a heated pool and a bar. Open April to Oct. **€28**

★**De Vigniamont** 5 rue Massillon ☎04 67 35 14 88, ⓦhoteldevigniamont.com. Tastefully decorated B&B in a seventeenth-century mansion with five bedrooms. The breakfast buffet, featuring home-made cakes, is served on the terrace in summer. The owners hold wine tastings each

evening and can organize on-site massages. **€95**

Grand Hôtel Molière 40 place du 14 juillet ☎04 67 98 14 00, ⓦhotelmoliere.fr. Renovated in 2016, this three-star hotel in a nineteenth-century Haussmann-style building opposite the bus stop has 22 comfortable, contemporary rooms. There's no restaurant but there is a bar and a small spa. Parking is available (€8). **€92**

EATING AND DRINKING

Maison Conti 27 rue Conti ☎04 99 41 11 12, ⓦmaisonconti.eu. Near the theatre where Molière's plays were once performed, this family-run restaurant specializes in imaginatively presented French cuisine made with seasonal, organic products (where possible). Good-value lunch *menu* at €16. Mon–Sat 11.45am–1.30pm & 6.45–9pm.

★**Le Vintage** 20 cours Jean-Jaurès ☎04 67 31 71 98, ⓦlevintagepezenas.com. Buzzy bar serving local wines and craft beers as well as tapas (from €3.50), platters of cheese and charcuterie (from €8.50) and salads (from €10.50). The home-made panna cotta with salted caramel is delicious. Tues–Sat 10.30am–10.30pm.

Clermont-l'Hérault and around

The area inland from Montpellier is dominated by two rivers: the mighty **Hérault**, which cuts down southwest from the Cévennes mountains through the plains above the city, and the **Vis**, which runs along the northern rim of the *département* and into the Hérault at Ganges. Between them, their underpopulated and lesser-travelled valleys – a world apart from the fishing towns and beaches of the coast – offer some remarkable scenery and attractions; taken in conjunction with a couple of absorbing towns, they also form a naturally circuitous tour of the region by car, with plenty of hiking opportunities along the way. Quiet **CLERMONT-L'HÉRAULT** itself, a short distance from the banks of the River Hérault, is a dull little cantonal capital whose only recommendation is as a jumping-off point for visiting the area.

Villeneuvette

VILLENEUVETTE is a model factory town founded by Colbert (Louis XIV's finance minister) in the seventeenth century to produce high-quality wool for sale in the Mediterranean; it stayed in business until 1954 and still has seventy inhabitants. The walled-in compound is entered through a monumental gate bearing the legend *Honneur au Travail* ("honour to work"). Inside, a square, flanked by the church and *mairie*, opens onto neat rows of low, flower-bedecked workers' houses. In its wooded surroundings, the little settlement presents a curious but enchanting idyll.

Mourèze

The village of **MOURÈZE** is in the midst of an eerie zone of eroded dolomite known as the **Cirque de Mourèze**, featuring a landscape of ancient seabed eroded by rainfall into a forest of rocky pinnacles. Along with the **Lac du Salagou**, it's working towards becoming a Grand Site de France (see p.47). You can stroll along the myriad paths that crisscross the area, or enjoy an impressive panoramic view from the **Courtinals**, a series of huge, pointy rock formations. Mourèze was also the first town that the Resistance

5

THE WAR IN LANGUEDOC ROUGE

In 1942, with the dissolution of the puppet **Vichy regime**, the formal **German occupation** of Languedoc began, and once again the natives of the region found themselves fighting an outside power against enormous odds. Embittered by labour conscriptions that had sent local men to German factories and concentration camps, many locals joined or supported the Communists, deserters and refugees who made up the local **Resistance** – called "*maquisards*" or "**maquis**", in reference to the scrubby Mediterranean landscape which was their home and refuge.

The main resistance group here, the "**Maquis Bir Hakeim**", was extremely active until surprised by German forces and wiped out in May 1944. In the Sidobre (see p.148) and Tarn, the feared "Maquis de Vabre" carried out a campaign of raiding and sabotage despite the brutal retaliations such acts provoked. Two months after D-Day, fifteen OSS (the forerunner of the CIA) commandos parachuted into Vabre (see p.151), one day before a British agent, Major Davies, arrived. Davies' notebook, which he called a report on "the war in Languedoc Rouge", recalls the fighters as "mainly youths…upstanding fellows with fresh keen faces, from all social classes". Despite their lack of arms and equipment, in August 1944, *maquis* action turned the German withdrawal from Albi into a military debacle – many vehicles were lost and the 4500-strong garrison of Castres surrendered.

---

group, the Maquis Bir Hakeim (see box above), liberated from the Germans – a monument to 140 of their dead (including one English officer) sits a kilometre or two south of the entrance to town.

Lac du Salagou

Renowned for its red rocks, the **Lac du Salagou** is actually a reservoir, whose shallow waters teem with birdlife, as well as fish and tiny crabs. The area has become a centre for watersports and mountain biking. The north shore, east of the larger village of **Octon**, is more developed and the landscape less striking. As the road follows the cliffs above the shore, it passes the ghost town of **Celles**, which was expropriated in the 1970s when the reservoir was built. The waters, however, never reached the hamlet, which now sits abandoned.

ARRIVAL AND DEPARTURE

CLERMONT-L'HÉRAULT AND AROUND

By bus Buses arrive at the *gare routière* on place Jean-Jaurès. Destinations Clermont-l'Hérault to: Bédarieux (several daily; 35min); Herepian (45min); Lamalou (several daily; 50min); Lodève (several daily; 25min); Montpellier (several daily; 50min); Pézenas (several daily; 35min); St-Guilhem (two daily; 30min).

INFORMATION

Tourist office Clermont: place Jean-Jaurès (July & Aug Mon–Fri 9am–12.30pm & 2–6pm, Sat 9.30am–12.30 & 3–6pm, Sun 9am–1pm; Sept–June Mon–Fri 9am–noon & 2–6pm, Sat 9am–noon & 2–5pm; ☎ 04 67 96 23 86, ⓦclermontais-tourisme.fr). Mourèze: on way into village (daily: July & Aug 9.30am–5.30pm, April–June & Sept–Nov 10am–5pm; ☎ 04 67 96 61 48). Lac du Salagou: rives de Clermont (daily: mid-June to mid-Sept 10am–6pm). The offices can advise on walks and sights in the area.

Bike rental Ozone, 1 rte du Lac, Clermont (☎ 04 67 96 27 17, ⓦvtt-salagou.com). From €16 per day.

Watersports Base de Plein Air du Salagou (☎ 04 67 96 05 71, ⓦbasedusalagou.com).

ACCOMMODATION AND EATING

★ **L'Ami Paradis** 6 rte de la Dolomie, Mourèze ☎ 04 67 88 77 26. Organic, local, seasonal ingredients go into the dishes (often spicy) at this quirky café-deli by the Courtinals. At weekends in season there's usually brunch or dinner with entertainment. Lunch is from €15.50 and there are vegetarian offerings too. Daily 9am–midnight in summer (ring ahead in winter).

Camping Les Vailhés Baie de Vailhés, Lac du Salagou ☎ 04 11 95 01 82, ⓦcampinglesvailhes.com. Next to the watersports centre and supervised beach, this family-friendly two-star campsite is in a great location on a hill extending down to the lake. There are no structures to rent, just pitches. €20

La Source Villeneuvette ☎ 04 67 96 05 07,

w hoteldelasource.com. Comfortable three-star *Logis de France* hotel in a seventeenth-century manor surrounded by parkland; there's a pool too. Beautifully presented Mediterranean food is on the menu (lunch from €17.90). **€90**

Lodève

Located on the eastern spur of the massif that forms the bulk of the Parc Naturel Régional du Haut Languedoc (see p.150), and just 10km north of Lac du Salagou, **LODÈVE** is a pleasantly situated and friendly little town with several surprisingly good sights including a museum with an internationally important collection of fossils and one of the French government's carpet-making workshops. From the cathedral, the **old town** spreads out east, bounded on three sides by a dramatic bend in the Lergue river. To the southeast, you'll find the beautiful medieval bridge, **Pont de Montifort**. There is a general **market** every Saturday morning and a farmers' market on Tuesday from June to September in place de la Républiique from 4pm.

Cathédrale St-Fulcran

Heading southwest from the *gare routière*, you'll arrive in a few minutes at the **Cathédrale St-Fulcran**, built in the town's second great period of prosperity in the twelfth and thirteenth centuries (the first was under Nero in the first century BC, when it had been important enough to have an imperial Roman mint). The current cathedral was raised on the riches of the woollen cloth industry. Although it's mostly late medieval, traces of an earlier cathedral's sixth-century foundations can be seen, while the **cloisters** preserve part of the cathedral building raised by the saint himself in the tenth century. The nave's dimensions are impressive – 58m in length and 25m high – and its biggest bell weighs in at 2000kg; in a small interior chapel opposite the door, you'll find where the remains of the town's 84 bishops lie interred.

Musée de Lodève

Square Georges Auric • Closed for renovation until 2017 • ☎ 04 67 88 86 10, ⓦ museedelodeve.fr

The **Musée de Lodève** has three collections: archeology, paleontology (this area is particularly rich in rare

5

fossils) and art, centred around local-born artist Paul Dardé (1888–1963). You can can also see his work in the **Halle Dardé** (daily 9am–7pm; free), the former covered market in place du Marché. His controversial war memorial, consisting of five women with two children and the body of a dead soldier, stands solemnly in the park next to the cathedral.

Manufacture Nationale de la Savonnerie, Atelier de Lodève

Impasse des Liciers • Guided visits Thurs 10.30am, 2pm & 3.30pm, Fri 10.30am & 2pm; book at the tourist office • €5 • ☎ 04 67 88 86 44

Installed here in 1966, the **Manufacture Nationale de la Savonnerie**, an annexe of the original workshop in Paris, makes and restores carpets for France's embassies and residences of the president and prime minister. The carpets are hand woven on looms by a small, mainly North African, female workforce and can take up to ten years to make; the most interesting designs are those created by renowned contemporary artists.

ARRIVAL AND INFORMATION   LODÈVE

By bus Lodève's *halte routière* is on place de la République, opposite the tourist office. See ⓦherault-transport.fr for details.
Destinations Clermont-l'Hérault (several daily; 25min); Montpellier (several daily; 1hr).

Tourist information 7 place de la République (April, May & Oct Mon–Sat 10am–1pm & 2–6pm; June–Sept daily 10am–1pm & 2–6pm; Nov–March Mon–Fri 10am–1pm & 2–6pm, Sat 10am–1pm; ☎ 04 67 88 86 44, ⓦtourisme-lodevois-larzac.fr).

ACCOMMODATION AND EATING

De la Paix 11 bd Montalangue ☎ 04 67 44 07 46, ⓦhotel-de-la-paix.com. The best hotel in town is this three-star *Logis de France* in a former coaching inn, now decorated in contemporary style. The food is a delight with a lunch *menu* from €17; try the organic trout. There's a small pool and parking is available (€8). **€80**

★ **Le Soleil Bleu** 39 Grand'rue ☎ 04 67 88 09 86. On the main shopping street, this little café serves simple market-fresh meals at lunchtimes, as well as tea (35 varieties) and cake in the afternoon. They also sell ceramics by local artists. *Menu* around €13. Mon–Sat 10am–6pm.

The Cirque de Navacelles

Taking the D25 eastwards from just north of Lodève, you'll climb 15km up the wooded Brèze valley before reaching an open plain stretching a similar distance to the hamlet of **St-Maurice-Navacelles**. If you turn off to the north at St-Maurice, you'll come to the **CIRQUE DE NAVACELLES** (ⓦcirquedenavacelles.com), a breathtaking section of the valley where the river, carving down sharply through the surrounding plain, has doubled back on itself, leaving a small hillock stranded in the middle of the cirque; at its base huddles the ancient hamlet of **Navacelles**. The cirque, which is working towards becoming a Grand Site de France and is also part of UNESCO's "Causses and Cévennes Mediterranean agro-pastoral Cultural Landscape", can be reached in a day's **hiking**; the GR653 east from Lodève links up with the GR7, which winds its way north, entering the Vis valley near St-Maurice before heading on into the Cévennes. Arriving by **car**, you'll first reach the belvedere on the south side of the cirque, **La Baume Auriol**, from which you can contemplate the incredible sweep of the gorge and look down on the village 600m below. From the lookout point, the road follows a dramatic series of switchbacks descending to Navacelles itself – a tiny stone hamlet with a medieval bridge – before climbing to another lookout point, **Blandas**, on the north side.

INFORMATION   THE CIRQUE DE NAVACELLES

The cirque has two **Maisons du Grand Site**: Belvédère de la Baume Auriol (March Wed–Sun 10am–6pm; April–June & Sept–Nov daily 10am–6pm; July & Aug daily 10am–7pm; ☎ 04 67 88 86 44, ⓦbaumeauriol.com) and Les Belvédères de

Blandas (same hours as La Baume Auriol; ☏ 04 99 51 60 36, ⓦ lerelaisducirque.fr). They both have lots of information on the area as well as shops selling **local products**; the one at Blandas also has a restaurant.

ACCOMMODATION AND EATING

Auberge du Causse de Blandas Blandas ☏ 04 67 81 51 55. It's all about the local *terroir* in this village restaurant with a roadside terrace. A two-course lunch with coffee is good value at €12.50. Try one of the local *apéritifs* made with chestnut *sirop*. Mon–Thurs & Sun 9am–4pm, Fri & Sat 9am–8.30pm.

L'Oustal del Passejaire Hameau de Navacelles ☏ 04 67 13 25 92, ⓦ chambres-hotes-navacelles.com. Charming B&B in an old stone house in a time-forgotten hamlet at the bottom of the cirque. There are four cosy rooms, two sharing a bathroom, and *table d'hôte* is available (€22) – a good opportunity to sample local products. **€60**

Ganges and around

The road snakes down from the cirque into the **Vis gorges** for the remaining 26km to **GANGES**, the largest town in the Hérault valley. Contrasting with the open scrub around Navacelles, this section of the valley is a steep and lush canyon, whose tree-clad banks at times close off the sky above with thick boughs. As you continue, it gradually widens, passing occasional signs of life – riverside *relais* (inns), ancient bridges and abandoned factories. Ganges itself is primarily of interest as a transport hub and service centre for the more interesting places just to the south, and for the busy recreation industry which has grown up on the banks of the river. The best time to visit is on Friday morning when the farmers of the Cévennes come to sell their produce.

The Grotte des Demoiselles

St-Bauzille-de-Putois • March & Oct daily 11am–5.30pm; April–June & Sept daily 10.30am–7pm; July & Aug daily 10am–7.30pm; Nov–Feb Mon–Sat 2–5pm, Sun 11am–5.30pm • €10.80 • ☏ 04 67 73 70 02, ⓦ grotte-des-demoiselles.fr

A few kilometres south of Ganges, you'll come upon the area's biggest draw, the **Grotte des Demoiselles**. This incredibly vast cavern, discovered in 1770, stretches out below the plateau de Thaurac, the highland southeast of Ganges, and is famous for its huge stalactite and stalagmite formations. Due to its excellent acoustics, concerts are held here during the summer. The obligatory eighty-minute **guided tour** (expect a long wait in high season; last departure 1hr before closing) is made aboard an underground funicular, which lends the whole thing an amusement-park air, and though the cave is spectacular, the whole experience can be a bit of a let-down, having to put up with all of the crowds and fuss. Whatever, make sure you take warm clothes.

ARRIVAL AND INFORMATION

GANGES AND AROUND

By bus Buses stop at the *mairie* on av Généra-de-Gaulle, to the north of the town.

Destinations Ganges to: Montpellier (several daily; 1hr); Nîmes (several daily; 1hr 15min); St-Bauzille-de-Putois (several daily; 10min); St-Hippolyte (several daily; 15min); St-Martin-de-Londres (several daily; 25min);

Sauve (several daily; 25min).

Tourist information 25 av Pasteur (Mon 9.30am–1pm & 3–6.30pm; Tues–Fri 9.30am–1pm & 2.30–6.30pm, Sat 10am–1pm; ☏ 04 67 73 00 56, ⓦ ot-cevennes.com). There are many activities in this area including kayaking, climbing and caving.

ACCOMMODATION

Auberge de la Filature 57 rue Agantic, St-Bauzille-de-Putois ☏ 04 67 73 74 18, ⓦ aubergedelafilature .com. In summer, the four stone village houses are only available to rent as *gîtes*, but in winter the owners offer B&B (€52). Meals are available to guests for €19 and can be eaten in the garden in summer. **€500**

De la Poste 8 plan de l'Ormeau, Ganges ☏ 04 67 73 85 88, ⓦ hotel-ganges.fr. "No frills" hotel in the main square, where the 22 minimalist rooms are nonetheless bright and comfortable. Parking is available and there's a lock up for bikes. **€55**

5

St-Guilhem-le-Désert and around

The route from Ganges to St-Guilhem follows the course of the Hérault via the D4. Hugging the western bank of the river, the road follows the tortuous **Gorges de l'Hérault** to reach the stunningly situated **ST-GUILHEM-LE-DÉSERT** – le of the Plus Beaux Villages de France (see p.46) and a Grand Site de France (see p.47). There is no mistaking the great antiquity of St-Guilhem; as you descend a steep wooded ravine, the reddish roofs of its medieval houses contrast with the electric green of the trees. The village grew up around the abbey founded by Charlemagne's counsellor Guilhem, who returned from Rome in 800 with three pieces of wood said to be remnants of the Cross. Thanks to these relics, the monastery and the community around it thrived, both as a pilgrimage destination in its own right, and a stopping point en route to Santiago de Compostela – for which the abbey was added to the UNESCO World Heritage Site list.

Abbaye de Gellone

Abbey Daily 8am–6pm, cloister closed Mon–Sat noon–2pm & Sun 11am–2.30pm • Free audioguide when you show your receipt for the car park **Museum** April–Oct daily 10.30am–12.30pm & 1.30–6.30pm, closed Sun am • €3

The eleventh-century **Abbaye de Gellone**, crowned by a chunky, fifteenth-century bell tower, is the only surviving part of the once powerful monastic house. Its magnificent entryway, flanked by columns pillaged from Roman ruins, passes through a small vaulted narthex and opens into the cavernous but plain nave, ending in a curiously oversized transept and apse. Inside the church is the casket holding the remains of Guilhem (who was canonized after his death) and a reliquary holding one of the famous bits of wood. From the church you can climb down to the **crypt**, which dates from the eighth century, as well as the ruined **cloister**, whose north and west galleries are still in place (the rest are in The Met Cloisters in New York).

Pont du Diable – Maison du Grand Site

Maison du Grand Site, Pont du Diable, Aniane, 4km south of St-Guilhem • Daily: April–June & Sept 10.30am–1pm & 2–6pm; July & Aug 9.30am–7pm; Oct & Nov 10am–1pm & 2–5pm • ☎ 04 67 56 41 97, ⓦ saintguilhem-valleeherault.fr/maison-du-grand-site

The stone **Pont du Diable** ("devil's bridge"), another UNESCO World Heritage Site and Grand Site de France, was built in the eleventh century to make the Santiago pilgrimage route easier and is one of the oldest medieval bridges in France. You can access it from the **Maison du Grand Site**, via the *passerelle des Anges*, a rare high-tension bridge designed by architect Rudy Ricciotti. Then you can continue to the pebbly river beach below for some sunbathing.

Grotte de Clamouse

Around 3.5km south of St-Guilhem • Daily: Feb–May & Oct 10.30am–4.20pm, June & Sept 10.30am–5.20pm, July & Aug 10.30am–6.20pm • €10.20, audioguides €1.50, combined ticket with Argileum €10.70 • ☎ 04 67 57 71 05, ⓦ clamouse.com

Famous for its immense and delicate crystalline formations, the **Grotte de Clamouse** cavern is worth ninety minutes of anyone's time – just remember to take warm clothing. In 2016, the owners opened "Spéléopark", where you can explore the caves via climbing, abseiling and zipwires on a two-hour guided tour (€30).

Argileum

6 av du Monument, St-Jean-de-Fos • April–June & Sept–Oct Tues–Sun 10.30am–12.30pm & 2–6pm; July & Aug daily 10am–7pm; Nov, Feb & March Tues–Fri 2–5.30pm • €5.50 • ☎ 04 67 56 41 96, ⓦ www.argileum.fr

Some 4.5km south of St-Guilhem, **St-Jean-de-Fos** has long been a centre for pottery. **Argileum** is a new attraction in the village that brings to life the original studio of a

5

nineteenth-century potter via multimedia exhibits. They run workshops and can provide a list of potters still working in the village

ARRIVAL AND DEPARTURE

ST-GUILHEM AND AROUND

By bus Clermont-l'Hérault (several daily; 40min); Montpellier (several daily; 50min). See ⓦherault -transport.fr.

By car There is a car park at the top of the village which

charges a fee. You can also park at the Maison du Grand Site (free except weekends June & Sept and daily July & Aug; €5 when applied) from where you can get a free shuttle to St-Guilhem, the Grotte de Clamouse and Argileum in summer.

INFORMATION AND ACTIVITIES

Tourist information 2 place de la Liberté (daily: April–June & Sept 9.30am–1pm & 2–6pm; July & Aug 9.30am–7pm; Oct–March 9.30am–1pm & 2–5.30pm; ⓣ04 67 56 41 97, ⓦsaintguilhem-valleeherault.fr). You can get a voucher for €1.50 off the entry to the Grotte de Clamouse.

Watersports Several companies rent out kayaks for descents of the Hérault gorges, including Base Nautique, av

d'Aniane (ⓣ06 50 76 75 66, ⓦbase-nautique.com). Most also offer canyoning and rafting.

Vineyard tour Take a trip through the vines, followed by a wine tasting, aboard "Le Petit Train des Vignes" from the shop, Domaine Alexandrin, opposite Argileum (July & Aug 10.30am–6pm; €5; ⓣ04 67 57 72 09, ⓦdomaine-alexandrin.com).

ACCOMMODATION AND EATING

Guilhaume d'Orange 2 av Guillaume d'Orange ⓣ04 67 57 24 53, ⓦguilhaumedorange.com. At the bottom of the village, this quaint hotel has ten comfortable, individually decorated rooms as well as a restaurant renowned for its market-fresh cuisine (*menu* €23). **€73**

★**Le Village d'Antan** 15 rue Chapelle des Pénitents ⓣ04 67 57 77 07, ⓦmuseestguilhem.fr. As well as its charming collection of *santons* (traditional figures from the south), this "museum" in a twelfth-century house has a small tearoom with a lovely terrace. Light meals, salads and yummy fruit tarts are on the menu. Daily 10am–7pm.

Pic-St-Loup and St-Martin-de-Londres

The **Pic-St-Loup** (658m) is a hulking limestone ridge which, dominating the plain of Hérault, can be seen from Béziers almost to Nîmes. **ST-MARTIN-DE-LONDRES** makes the best base for hiking (tricky in parts) the remaining 10km to the *pic*'s wooded summit – a site from which you can enjoy impressive panoramas, but which can only be reached by foot (drivers can get as close as 4km away by taking the D113 to the hamlet of Cazevieille). St-Martin is another town of great antiquity and, contrary to appearances, its name has nothing to do with England's capital, London ("Londres" in French); it is named after the Plaine de Londres (from the Celtic word for "swamp") in which the town is located. The main sight here is the eleventh-century Romanesque **church** surrounded by a beautiful knot of buildings.

INFORMATION

PIC ST-LOUP AND ST-MARTIN-DE-LONDRES

Tourist information Place de la Mairie (mid-Feb to March, Nov & Dec Mon–Fri 9.30am–1pm & 2–5.30pm; April–June, Sept & Oct Mon 2–5.30pm, Tues–Fri

9.30am–1pm & 2–5.30pm, Sat 9.30am–12.30pm; July & Aug daily 10am–12.30pm & 1.30–6.30pm; ⓣ04 67 55 09 59, ⓦtourisme-picsaintloup.fr).

ACCOMMODATION AND EATING

Camping le Pic St Loup Rte du Pic St Loup ⓣ04 67 55 00 53. Friendly, family-run two-star campsite in a rural location with eighty pitches and a dozen chalets to rent. There's a heated swimming pool, a bar-restaurant and a shop. Open May to Sept. **€18.50**

Le Coin Perdu 19 rte des Cévennes ⓣ04 67 55 23 10,

ⓦle-coin-perdu.fr. Fine-dining restaurant where the young chef turns top-quality ingredients into beautifully presented dishes, sometimes with Asian flavours. Three-course *menus* from €31 and vegetarian meals on request. Wed–Sun noon–2pm & 7.30–9pm.

Narbonne, Béziers and around

BÉZIERS

Narbonne, Béziers and around

The provincial towns of Narbonne and Béziers dominate the flat expanse of marshy alluvial plain formed by the outpourings of the Hérault, Orb and Aude rivers, whose mouths all reach the Mediterranean within a 15km strip. The former town, once an important Roman capital, is the smaller, with a compact medieval core; the latter is the oldest town in the region, boasting a turbulent history, and springs to life each summer with its *feria*. Narbonne is best situated for excursions into the Corbières, an isolated range of hills, famous for its vineyards, stretching west towards the River Aude and south to Roussillon; once forming the Cathar heartland, the area harbours the idyllic abbey of Fontfroide, the magnificent castle of Villerouge-Termenès (where the "last" Cathar was burnt) and the strikingly beautiful village of Lagrasse.

Swinging southeast at Carcassonne, the **Canal du Midi** takes you past the various monuments of the Minervois – the region squeezed in between the Corbières and Haut Languedoc – and vine-dotted countryside, before splitting north of Narbonne: here, the Canal de la Robine heads south to Port-la-Nouvelle, where it enters the sea, while the main waterway meanders on, via Béziers, to the Bassin de Thau. Port-la-Nouvelle is also the start/end of the 250km **Sentier Cathare** (see p.28) trail to Foix.

Skirting Béziers, the road up the **Orb valley** threads north to the southeastern border of the Parc Naturel Régional du Haut Languedoc; along the way it passes a succession of villages including Roquebrun, which has a canoeing centre. The coastal stretch curving between Narbonne and Béziers is dominated by the Massif de la Clape, another area known for its wine production; at either end, the ancient ports of **Agde**, to the east, and **Gruissan**, to the west, have modern beach-resort alter egos as well as more sedate old towns. The latter is surrounded by the Parc Naturel Régional de la Narbonnaise en Méditerranée, which stretches south to Fitou, and offers plenty of outdoor activities.

GETTING AROUND

NARBONNE, BÉZIERS AND AROUND

Public transport facilities in this region vary considerably. At Narbonne, the busy coastal rail line to Perpignan branches off from the main Toulouse–Marseille route on which Béziers can be found. In the hinterland, you'll have to depend on bus services, which are fairly good for the major towns along the coast and the Orb valley. Out-of-the-way sites are more difficult: Minerve, for example, isn't served at all by public transport. But in any case – if you have time – the best way to travel through the region is by canal, either by piloting a houseboat, or biking or hiking along the towpath.

By train Main lines link Narbonne to Béziers/Montpellier and Perpignan, as well as to Carcassonne/Toulouse, while a secondary line climbs the Orb from Béziers towards the Massif Central. SNCF buses may run in lieu of trains on these lines; services are reduced on Sundays and holidays.

By bus Main bus lines in the Aude *département* run up the valley to Quillan and down to Narbonne. Services may be reduced on Saturdays and school holidays. No buses run on

LAGRASSE

Highlights

❶ **Lagrasse** This "Plus Beaux Village de France", tucked among the hills of the Corbières, sits beside an ancient and once-powerful monastery. **See p.253**

❷ **Canal du Midi** France's seventeenth-century engineering wonder is now a sublimely beautiful thoroughfare for cyclists, walkers and boaters. **See pp.254–260**

❸ **Oppidum d'Ensérune** These ruins of a pre-Roman settlement of "civilized" barbarians sit

perched on a ridge above the vineyards of Béziers. **See p.260**

❹ **Béziers** A city of atmospheric streets whose splendid cathedral provides views as far west as the peak of Le Canigó. **See p.260**

❺ **The Orb valley** Rarely visited, this river course boasts unique microclimate zones and near-forgotten hamlets. **See p.267**

HIGHLIGHTS ARE MARKED ON THE MAP ON P.242

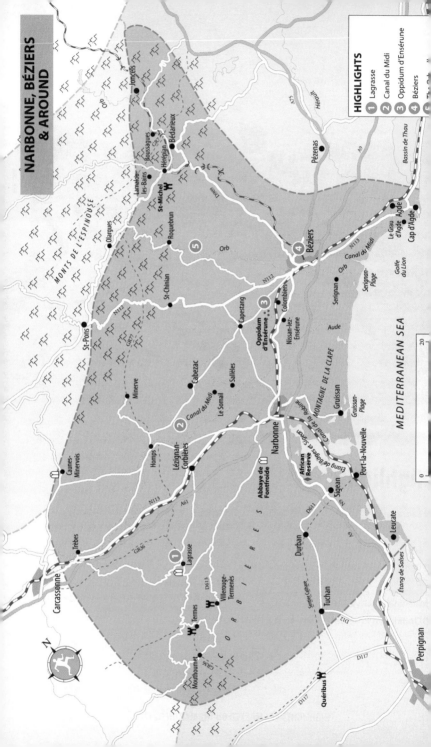

undays in the Aude, and on many lines in the Minervois. In ummer, extra services run from Béziers and Narbonne to the beach towns. For travelling in Aude, see Ⓦ audelignes.cg11 .fr and for travelling in Hérault, see Ⓦ herault-transport.fr.

Narbonne and around

There's no mistaking **NARBONNE** as you approach it, its towering cathedral rising up over the rooftops and dominating the coastal plain for miles around. Once the capital of the Roman province of Gallia Narbonensis, it flourished as a port and communications centre from ancient times into the Middle Ages, and was home to an important Jewish university in the twelfth and thirteenth centuries. But in the mid-1300s things suddenly went awry: the Jews were expelled, the plague struck, the Black Prince burnt down the town, the dykes of the Aude burst and the port silted up, a series of disasters which brought ruin to Narbonne's economy. A tentative prosperity returned only in the late 1800s with the birth of the modern wine industry, which continues to support the town. Today, it's a pleasant, rugby-mad provincial town with a small but well-preserved old core, centred on the great truncated choir of the **cathedral** and bisected by the **Canal de la Robine** (see p.257), whose banks provide a grassy esplanade running through the city centre.

If Narbonne's name lends itself to a certain sense of grandeur, thanks to its past as an important Roman capital, you'll be surprised by its diminutive size. The whole of the **old town** – which is where all the sights are – fits snugly into a 1km-by-750m rectangle, bisected north–south by the **Canal de la Robine**, with the **Archbishop's Palace**, its **museums** and the **cathedral** dominating affairs.

Palais des Archevêques

The broad square of the place de l'Hôtel de Ville, in the centre of which you'll find an uncovered section of the Roman Via Domitia, is overwhelmed by the great facade of the **Palais des Archevêques** (Archbishop's Palace), peppered by pointed ogival windows and decorated with Gothic-looking vegetal flourishes. But its "authentic" charms are the result of one of Viollet-le-Duc's imaginative repair jobs (see box, p.94) – an ersatz bit of medieval fantasy. Today the palace's rambling complex currently incorporates the city's two major museums, plus the entrance to the cathedral (see p.245).

The donjon
June–Sept daily 10am–6pm; Oct–May Mon & Wed–Sun 10am–noon & 2–5pm • €4

Passing through the main doors of the palace, which are directly on the square, on the left you'll find the entrance to the towering **donjon**, commissioned in the late thirteenth

---

THE SINGING MADMAN

Charles Trenet, one of France's most popular singers of the mid- to late-twentieth century, was born in Narbonne in 1913. Best known for his songs *Boum!* and *La Mer*, Trenet developed his talent for music and art while recovering from typhoid as a child. After studying art in Berlin, he moved to Paris where he enjoyed success as part of a duo before going solo after his National Service – during which time he earned the nickname **Le Fou Chantant** ("The Singing Madman") due to his exuberant style. After World War II, Trenet moved to the United States where he also enjoyed some success and forged lifelong friendships with Hollywood stars including Charlie Chaplin. Returning to France, his career flourished, in spite of being imprisoned for 28 days in 1963 for "corrupting the morals of young men under the age of 21", and he continued to perform until suffering a stroke in 2000. Trenet, whose breezy songs were inspired by jazz, the surrealist poetry of Max Jacob and his beloved Roussillon, died in 2001. You can find out more about him at his birthplace, **Maison Natale Charles Trenet** (13 av Charles Trenet; June–Sept daily 10am–6pm; Oct–May Mon & Wed–Sun 10am–noon & 2–5pm; €4).

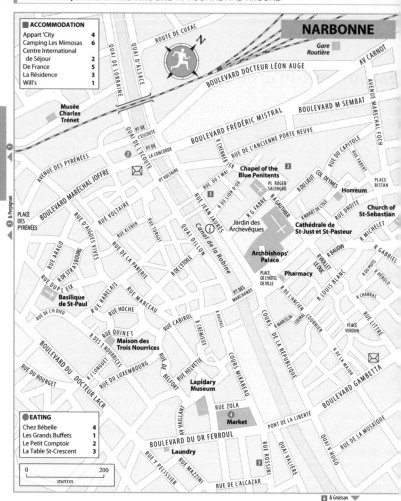

century by the town's lord and archbishop, Gilles Aycelin. This ponderous 41m defensive tower is a fine example of late thirteenth-century military architecture – its splayed-out base was designed to prevent battering and undermining. After climbing the 162-step keystone staircase you can enjoy excellent **views** of the cathedral and the surrounding countryside.

Musée d'Art et d'Histoire

Same hours and price as the donjon

To the left of the *donjon*, you'll see the entrance to the **Musée d'Art et d'Histoire**. The main attraction here is the luxurious interior of the palace itself, with its *artesonado* (see p.341) and other details; rooms to look out for in particular are the audience hall, the king's chamber – with seventeenth-century painted walls – and the eighteenth-century dining room. That said, the **Orientalist collection** in the last two rooms alone almost justifies the admission price: paintings depicting sultry Berber girls staring enigmatically at the viewer, or eyes flashing from under turbans, as bearded men pose with cruel-looking swords on horse- or camel-back.

Musée Archéologique
Same hours and price as the donjon

A much better collection can be found just across the courtyard in the **Musée Archéologique**. The highlight is its **Roman collection**, whose strong maritime streak reflects the role Narbonne played as a major port of Roman Gaul. Various stone carvings illustrate ships of the period, and there's a towering 3.5m wood-and-lead ship's anchor on display. Combined with the seafaring items is a collection of first-century BC **Roman mosaics** – the best of its kind outside of Italy. In 2019, the exhibits will relocate to the new €49 million **Musée de la Romanité**, aka MuRéNa, designed by Foster + Partners, in the east of the town.

6

Cathédrale de St-Just et St-Pasteur
Daily 9am–noon & 2–6pm • Free

From the archeological museum a narrow alley, the passage de l'Ancre, leads further into the complex, towards the entrance to the **Cathédrale de St-Just et St-Pasteur**. Christianity in the city dates back at least to the time of Constantine; as a provincial capital Narbonne became seat of an archbishop, and a cathedral was raised.

The exterior
The **exterior** is pure Gothic – the tall and narrow core of the building, dominated by expanses of stained-glass window, is braced by sturdy buttresses, from which delicate-looking flying buttresses launch up to support the highest points on the walls. The building you see today was begun in 1272. With the completion of the hulking 41m choir some fifty years later, construction of the nave, which was meant to extend westwards, was held up after the first couple of stages, because extending it would have involved knocking down the old Roman defensive wall – still very useful in those uncertain times. Thus, as with Toulouse's cathedral, the project was never completed, leaving the church with its strikingly odd form. As you climb the short flight of stairs from the street you'll arrive first at the compact **cloister**, from where there's a good view of the flying buttresses. A door on the west side of the cloister leads to the formal-style **Jardin des Archevêques**, with even better views, and around to the so-called **Cour St-Eutrope**, which is in fact the sealed-off stub of the aborted nave.

The interior
Treasury July–Sept Mon–Sat 10–11.45am & 2–5.45pm, Sun 2–5.45pm; Oct–June closed Tues • €4

The first thing that will strike you about the **interior** is the tremendous space inside the unfinished building – its soaring ceiling the third-highest for a French cathedral. Along with the upward dynamic of the design, the predominance of stained glass over stone on the walls is a hallmark of high Gothic style – some of the windows date from the original construction. Directly behind the altar, a badly damaged but nevertheless beautiful fourteenth-century stone **retable** illustrates themes of the Redemption with exceptionally carved and incredibly kinetic high-relief figures. Around this is a series of chapels hung with fine Gobelin and Aubusson **tapestries**. From the southernmost of these, a spiral stair leads up to the cathedral's **treasury**, the centrepiece of which is a sumptuous late fifteenth-century tapestry depicting the Holy Trinity, personified as three kings. Other fine pieces include a ninth-century ivory panel and an eleventh-century pyx of Muslim origin.

Around the palace and cathedral
It's worth taking time to explore the lesser sights in the vicinity of the palace and cathedral. First among these is the small **chapelle des Pénitents Bleus** (hours vary), on

the west side of place Salengro; an eighteenth-century chapel which is now used for exhibitions and concerts. South of the square two small streets lead directly away from the massive east wall of the cathedral into a compact **medieval neighbourhood**, once the *quartier* of the choristers and other functionaries of the great church: rue du Lieutenant-Colonel-Deymes and the next street along, rue Rouget de l'Isle, both contain houses with distinctly medieval windows and doors.

Horreum

7 rue Rouget de l'Isle • Same hours and price as donjon

Despite Narbonne's importance in Roman times, the **Horreum** is the only structure in the city to have survived from that era. Its name means "granary" in Latin, and that's what it is thought to be: an underground grain store which was most likely attached to a market building or depot above the ground. As you stroll down the long corridors sounds and plaques will bring to life this undoubtedly once-busy cavern. In the north wing is an impressive collection of amphorae.

West of the Canal de la Robine

Narbonne's old town extends over the **Canal de la Robine** to the west, a humbler section of town, even in the Middle Ages. To get there you can cross the **Pont des Marchands**, a one-arch bridge with houses built on it. Today, the narrow lanes and crooked streets west of the bridge are home to the city's gypsy community, and wear a certain air of neglect; there are fewer shops and restaurants here, and the tiny windows of the ageing buildings hang with laundry. Even so, the area is eminently explorable, with two parish churches that are well worth visiting.

Basilique de St-Paul

Rue Dupleix and rue de l'Hôtel-Dieu • Mon–Sat 9am–noon & 2–6pm • Free

The **Basilique de St-Paul** is a tall thirteenth-century construction, chipped and battered on the outside over the years, but inside possessing a pleasant mixture of Romanesque and Gothic. The main attraction is the **crypt** (ask the caretaker for the key; €4.50 donation requested): built over a paleo-Christian necropolis and dating back to the fourth century, it is where the town's first bishop was buried.

Notre-Dame-de-Lamourguier

Close by on rue des Trois Nourrices you'll find the magnificent sixteenth-century facade of the **Maison des Trois Nourrices**, and continuing southeast to place Lamourguier, the former abbey-church of **Notre-Dame-de-Lamourguier**. This is currently home to the town's **Musée Lapidaire** (same hours as *donjon*; €4), housing a large, but rather monotonous, collection of over a thousand statues, inscriptions, tombstones and sarcophagi, most dating back to Roman days. The collection will transfer to the **Musée de la Romanité** (see p.167) when it opens in 2019.

ARRIVAL AND DEPARTURE

NARBONNE

By train Narbonne's *gare SNCF* is situated northeast of the city centre, from where it's about a 15min walk to the place de l'Hôtel de Ville in the centre. TGV stations are indicated with an asterisk.

Destinations Nîmes*, via Béziers* (connections to Bédarieux, Agde*, Sète* and Montpellier* (several hourly; 1hr 40min); Paris* (many daily; 4hr 30min); Perpignan*, via Salses (hourly; 30–45min); Toulouse*, via Carcassonne* (connection to Quillan) and Castelnaudary* (many daily;

1hr 15min–1hr 45min).

By bus To the southwest of the train station you'll find the *gare routière*. In summer, extra services run to the beach resorts.

Destinations Carcassonne (several daily; 1hr 25min); Gruissan (several daily; 30min); Homps (daily; 50min); Narbonne-Plage (several daily; 15min); Sallèles (several daily; 30min); Sigean (daily; 35min); Le Somail (daily; 35min); Villerouge-Termenès (daily; 1hr 25min).

6

MARKETS IN NARBONNE

The city's **covered market** is the Halles de Narbonne (daily 7am–1.30pm; ⦿ halles-de -narbonne.com). On Tuesdays a **general market** takes place in the car park on the boulevard du Roussillon; there's another (no food) on Sundays on promenade des Barques and cours Mirabeau. On Thursdays there's a **flower market** on cours de la République. Thursdays also see a **food market** on Plan St Paul, promenade des Barques and cours Mirabeau. For **organic products** head to place du Forum on Saturdays.

GETTING AROUND

By bike Languedoc VTT Évasion, 12bis rue Guiraut Riquier (daily 8am–8pm ⦿ 06 74 89 75 98). From €14 per half-day. There is a *voie verte* along the Canal de la Robine between Narbonne and Port-la-Nouvelle (22km) and from Narbonne to St-Pierre-la-Mer (29km) via Narbonne-Plage and Gruissan.

By bus Local buses are operated by Citibus (8 av Maréchal Foch; Mon–Fri 8.30am–noon & 1.30–5pm; ⦿ 04 68 90 18 18, ⦿ citibus.fr). There is a free shuttle, La Citadine, that serves the town centre (Mon–Sat 7.40am–7.20pm).

By car There is free parking at the Théâtre and Victor Hugo car parks Mon–Sat and free parking in all car parks in the city centre on Saturdays. Rental agencies: ADA, 10 av Carnot ⦿ 04 68 65 80 48; Avis, 21 bd Marcel-Sembat ⦿ 04 68 32 43 36; Europcar, 14 av Carnot ⦿ 04 68 32 34 54; Hertz, 92 bd Frédéric Mistral ⦿ 04 68 42 43 92.

By boat For canal trips, rent an electric boat from Les Petits Bateaux du Canal, promenade des Barques (⦿ 06 15 65 12 51). From €29 per hour.

By taxi Renaud Grenier ⦿ 06 73 22 33 78.

INFORMATION

Tourist information 31 rue Jean Jaurès (April to mid-Sept daily 9am–7pm; mid-Sept to March Mon–Sat 10am–12.30pm & 1.30–6pm; ⦿ 04 68 65 15 60, ⦿ narbonne-tourisme.com).

Discount cards The "Pass Monuments & Musées" costs €9

and gives entry to the Musée Archéologique, Horreum, Musée Lapidaire, Le Trésor de la Cathédrale, the Donjon, the Musée d'Art et d'Histoire and Maison Natale de Charles Trenet. It is valid for fifteen days and you can get one at the tourist office or at the participating sights.

ACCOMMODATION

Appart'City 18 bd du Généra-de-Gaulle ⦿ 04 57 38 37 11 ⦿ appartcity.com. This good-value and modern three-star aparthotel lies a 10min walk north from the archbishop's palace. There's a breakfast room, laundry and car park. **€69.90**

Camping Les Mimosas Chaussée de Mandirac ⦿ 04 68 49 03 72, ⦿ camping-les-mimosas.fr. Big four-star site with all mod cons, including an aquatic park and a "wellness centre", located 6km south of town on the Étang de Bages (no public transport). Open mid-March to Oct. **€44**

Centre International de Séjour Place Roger-Salengro ⦿ 04 68 32 01 00, ⦿ cis-narbonne.com. Modern hostel with a nice lounge. There's also a simple self-service restaurant where you can get a three-course lunch *menu* for €12. **€24.40**

De France 6 rue Rossini ⦿ 04 30 37 01 47,

⦿ hotelnarbonne.com. A quiet nineteenth-century establishment south of the old town, close to the covered market and the canal. It's basic but has a spread of amenities including a/c, wi-fi and parking nearby (charge). **€80**

La Résidence 6 rue du 1er Mai ⦿ 04 68 32 19 41, ⦿ hotel-laresidence-narbonne.fr. An early nineteenth-century converted house, in a great location on a quiet street near the Pont Voltaire. Comfortable rooms with a/c, and there's a garage and lift. **€105**

★**Will's** 23 av Pierre-Sémard ⦿ 04 68 90 44 50, ⦿ willshotel-narbonne.com. Friendly, good-value two-star hotel set in a nineteenth-century townhouse right by the station. The seventeen bright, contemporary rooms have aircon, a desk and double glazing; family rooms sleeping up to six are available. It's popular so book in advance during high season. **€69**

EATING

★**Chez Bébelle** Halles de Narbonne ⦿ 06 85 40 09 01, ⦿ chez-bebelle.fr. Owned and run by former "rugbyman" Gilles Belzons aka Bébelle, this lunch spot in the covered market is an essential stop for meat eaters and egg chasers. Steak, fries and salad for €12.50. Tues–Sat noon–1.30pm.

Les Grands Buffets Espace de Liberté ⦿ 04 68 42 20

01, ⦿ lesgrandsbuffets.com. Good-value self-service, all-you-can-eat restaurant where you can help yourself to a huge range of France's traditional dishes; there's just one *menu* at €32.90. The region's best wines are available by the glass at cost price. Mon–Fri noon–2pm & 7–10pm, Sat & Sun 11.30am–2.30pm & 7–10pm.

★**Le Petit Comptoir** 4 bd Maréchal Joffre ⦿ 04 68 42

FESTIVALS IN AND AROUND NARBONNE AND BÉZIERS

In this little corner of Languedoc, Béziers is the hotspot for popular **festivals**, with its five-day **feria** the prime attraction. There are summer music cycles and parties throughout the area and, as can be expected from a wine region, local festivals to celebrate the **grape harvest**.

Mid-April Leucate: *Mondial du Vent* ⓦ www .mondialduvent.fr. Annual world championships of windsurfing, kitesurfing and SUP in this seaside resort 37km south of Narbonne.

Late April Béziers: *Fête de la St-Aphrodise*. The feast day of the town's patron saint, usually held on the third Sunday, and featuring a curious procession with a camel float.

Mid-May Gruissan: *Les Festejades*. A three-day festival of traditional and contemporary Occitan music.

Mid-July Abbaye de Fontfroide: *Fêstival Musique et Histoire* ⓦ fontfroide.com. Five-day festival of ancient music played by international musicians in the beautiful surrounds of the abbey.

Late July Lagrasse: *Abracadagrasses* ⓦ www.abracadagrasses.fr. A lively weekend of World Music in the main square.

Late July Narbonne: *Jazz Festival à L'Hospitalet* ⓦ chateau-hospitalet.com. Four days of jazz concerts by internationally renowned artists in the attractive setting of this well-known vineyard.

Late July Cap d'Agde: *Fête de la Mer*. An open-air Mass for victims of the sea, boats are blessed and there is water-jousting.

Mid-Aug Béziers: *La Feria*. Five-day festival with street entertainment, fireworks, music and a daily Spanish-style *corrida*.

Mid-Oct Gruissan: *Fête des Vendanges*. A weekend of wine-themed activities to celebrate the grape harvest.

30 35, ⓦ petitcomptoir.com. Excellent modern bistro and wine bar (300 labels, no less) where the market-inspired menu changes with the seasons and dishes are made with local products. Two-course lunch at €16. Tues–Sat noon–2pm & 7.30–10pm.

La Table St-Crescent 68 av Général-Leclerc ☏ 04 68 41 37 37, ⓦ la-table-saint-crescent.com. This *gastronomique* is located in an ancient eighth-century oratory about 1km south of the canal, in the local wine producers' Palais des Vins, where you can shop for fine local vintages. Lunch *menu* €31, otherwise €59–89. Tues–Sun noon–3pm & 8pm–midnight, closed Sun eve.

DIRECTORY

Hospital Centre Hospitalier de Narbonne, bd Docteur-Lacroix (☏ 04 68 42 60 00, ⓦ www.ch-narbonne.fr).

Kids Espace de Liberté, rte de Perpignan (☏ 04 68 42 17 89, ⓦ espacedeliberte.fr). This complex includes pools and a water park (€7.60), a bowling alley (€6.50) and an ice rink.

Laundry 24 bd du Généra-de-Gaulle; 25 bd Docteur Ferroul; 47 av Anatole France.

Pharmacy Pharmacie de l'Hôtel de Ville, 3 pl de l'Hôtel de Ville. For night-time and weekend opening hours, check the notice on the door.

Police Hôtel de Police, 1 rue Pierre Benet ☏ 04 68 90 38 50.

Gruissan

The fishing village of **GRUISSAN** cuts a striking figure from the distance, with its circular streets huddled around a thirteenth-century hilltop tower, overlooking the inland *étang* which bears its name. In summer it becomes a busy seaside resort and nightlife hub with the youth of Narbonne and the surrounding area flocking to open-air La Villa (see p.250). As you arrive, you'll first pass the 1970s marina on your left before reaching Gruissan-Village, which, although small, is a pleasant place to stroll around and browse the individual shops. There is a **market** in place Gibert on Monday, Wednesday and Saturday mornings and some interesting cultural events and festivals throughout the year.

Gruissan-Plage

The salty Étang du Grazel separates Gruissan from a narrow spit of sand, **Gruissan-Plage**, marking the Mediterranean's shore. This area is known for its 1300 chalets on stilts, which featured in the 1986 cult French film *Betty Blue*. Apart from the appeal of its beach and watersports, there is a **market** here on Sunday mornings from mid-June to mid-September.

ARRIVAL AND DEPARTURE   GRUISSAN

By bus Buses from Narbonne stop on bd du Pech Maynaud, opposite the tourist office.

INFORMATION AND ACTIVITIES

Tourist information 80 bd Pech Maynaud (April–June & Sept daily 9am–noon & 2–6pm; July & Aug daily 9am–8pm; Oct–March Mon–Fri 9am–noon & 2–6pm, Sat & Sun 10am–noon & 2–4pm; ☎04 68 49 09 00, ⊛gruissan-mediterranee.com). The tourist office organizes guided tours of the town and area on Segways and electric bikes, and also visits to vineyards.

Bike rental Cycle Aventure, rue du Loch (☎04 68 49 17 26). From €8 for two hours. There are plenty of cycling paths in this area including a *voie verte* to Narbonne.
Kids Espace Balnéoludique, av des Bains (☎04 68 75 60 50, ⊛gruissan-mediterranee.com/espace-balneoludique). Waterpark with several pools, spa facilities and massages on offer.

ACCOMMODATION

Camping LVL Les Ayguades Av de la Jonque ☎04 68 49 81 59, ⊛camping-soleil-mer.com. Four-star campsite right next to the beach, with a mix of pitches and chalets to rent. There's a heated pool, restaurant and kids' play area, as well as entertainment in summer. Open April to mid-Nov. **€22**
De la Plage 13 rue du Bernard L'Hermite ☎04 68 49 00 75, ⊛hotelplagegruissan.fr. Friendly, comfortable two-star hotel at Gruissan-Plage with 25 rooms sleeping up to five people. Free storage for bikes, motorbikes and boards. Open mid-March to Sept. **€90**
★La Grussan-Hôtes 5 av du Général Azibert ☎04 68 90 76 68, ⊛la-grussan-hotes-gruissan.com. Stylish B&B in a nineteenth-century townhouse in the heart of the village. Minimalist, contemporary furniture complements the original features in the four rooms. **€80**

EATING AND DRINKING

Aux Deux Oliviers 1 bd de la Corderie ☎04 68 75 85 53, ⊛auxdeuxoliviers.com. Beautifully presented market-fresh southern French cuisine is on the menu at this popular restaurant at the entrance to the village. Excellent "deconstructed" lemon meringue tart. Expect to pay €20–40 for three courses. Wed–Sun noon–2.30pm & 7.30–9.30pm (July & Aug Tues–Sun).
★La Cambuse du Saunier Rte de l'Ayrolle ☎04 84 25 13 24, ⊛lesalindegruissan.fr. In the famous salt fields, this rustic restaurant with communal tables is the place to go for seafood. There's also an ice-cream parlour (try the sheep's milk flavour), a shop and guided tours. Daily 10.30am–5pm & 7–9.30pm.
Le Paparazzo Pôle Nautique, Gruissan-Plage ☎04 68 65 25 10, ⊛lepaparazzo.fr. Fashionable beachside bar and restaurant with something to suit most tastes and pockets including tapas (€4–15), pizzas (€11) and salads (€13). There's usually music and events at weekends. April–October daily 10am–1.30am.
La Villa 1 av des Noctambules, Gruissan. Open-air summer-only nightclub whose dance music attracts the youth from right across the area. Entry is €15 including a drink. May & June Fri & Sat; nightly July & Aug.

Sigean

Heading south from Narbonne, the road hugs the base of the rising hills, separated from the sea by a wide buffer – a series of salty *étangs* – and accompanied by a landscape characterized by scrubby trees, red soil and an impossibly blue sky in summer. This area is the main part of the **Parc Naturel Régional de la Narbonnaise en Méditerranéee** (⊛parc-naturel-narbonnaise.fr), which offers plenty of opportunities for outdoor activities including birdwatching. The main town is **SIGEAN**, a quiet wine town on the Roman Via Domitia with attractive old streets, whose only sight is the **Musée des Corbières** (pl de la Libération; Mon, Tues, Thurs & Fri 2–3.45pm; Wed 9am–noon; €3; ☎04 68 41 59 89), a seven-room museum of local history from prehistoric times to the Middle Ages.

Réserve Africaine

13 chemin Hameau du Lac • Daily 9am–4/6.30pm • €32 • ☎04 68 48 20 20, ⊛reserveafricainesigean.fr

Eight kilometres north of Sigean lies the **Réserve Africaine**, an immense drive-through park (no motorcycles) with almost four thousand animals that recreates several equatorial habitats, including brushland, savanna and plain. You'll see lions, giraffes, rhinos and hippos lazing around, as well as graceful oryx and springboks. For those without cars, a series of footpaths have been laid out among the habitats providing up to three hours of walks.

INFORMATION SIGEAN

Tourist information Place de la Libération (Mon–Fri 9am–1pm & 3.30–6.30pm, Sat 9am–12.30pm & 3–5.30pm, Sun 9am–1pm; ☎ 04 68 48 14 81, ☉ tourisme -sigean.fr).

ACCOMMODATION

Andemar 41 av de Narbonne, Sigean ☎ 04 68 27 08 73 ☉ sigeanhotel.com. Opened in 2015, this disabled-friendly four-star aparthotel in a renovated townhouse has twelve bright rooms. There's also a bar and an attractive courtyard garden. Parking is available (€10). **€92**

Terra Vinéa Chemin des Plâtrières, Portel-des-Corbières ☎ 04 68 26 22 24, ☉ terra-vinea.com. A few kilometres southwest of the Réserve Africaine, this wine "theme park" in a converted mine offers good-value lunches (€14.90–19.90) and platters of cheese and charcuterie (€10–12). April–Oct daily noon–2pm.

The Corbières

To journey into the heart of the hilly **Corbières** region, which fans out southwest of Narbonne, bordered to the west by the upper Aude valley and to the south by the Fenouillèdes hills of northern Roussillon, is to enter a world very distinct from the coastal plain. As the land rises, the roads narrow, twisting and writhing up into the forests of the low mountains, tenaciously following the stream beds which cut into the slopes. Once the heart of **Cathar territory**, this area has suffered centuries of abandonment and neglect, and many hamlets lack even a café or a proper payphone, let alone a restaurant or hotel. For all of this, it is a splendid place to drive through, offering the ancient monasteries of **Fontfroide** and **Lagrasse**, and the Cathar sites of **Villerouge-Termenès** and **Termes**. Without your own **transport**, however, the Corbières is difficult to access, the only bus route following the D613 from Narbonne.

Abbaye de Fontfroide

Daily: April–June, Sept & Oct 10am–6pm; July & Aug 9.30am–7pm; Nov–March 10am–12.30pm & 1.30–5pm • €11 • ☎ 04 68 45 11 08, ☉ fontfroide.com

Passing through the rocky *garrigues* west of Narbonne, the D613 leads you past the narrow turn-off to the **Abbaye de Fontfroide**. Following this road south for 4km, you'll come across the stout walls of the ancient Cistercian foundation, tucked inside a shallow valley hidden among cypress groves. Founded in the late eleventh century by a count of Narbonne, it saw its greatest prosperity in the two subsequent centuries, after which, like so many monastic centres, it began to decline. The monastery's best-known abbot was Jacques Fournier, who as Bishop of Foix commanded the Inquisition which investigated the Cathars of Montaillou (see box, p.105), and went on in 1337 to be elected pope as Benedict XII.

In private hands for the last hundred years or so, Fontfroide can be explored with a leaflet, a tablet or on a 75-minute **guided tour** (€13). Even if you're not interested in religious architecture, this beautiful abbey is well worth half a day's visit for its **rose garden**, wine (tastings in the shop), excellent **restaurant** (lunch from €21) and surrounding walks; you can even rent a *gîte* in the grounds. It's best to come early in the morning or late in the day in order to avoid crowds. In summer, there is a wide variety of **events** including music concerts, night-time guided tours (10pm) and demonstrations of medieval trades.

Villerouge-Termenès

Heading inland along the D613, the road forks right for Lagrasse (see p.253), and left towards the hills. Following this second route will lead you into some of the wildest back-country of the region, where forested uplands are capped by the tumbled remains of nameless castles. As you round the top of the 404m-high Col de Villerouge you'll get a startling view of the village of **VILLEROUGE-TERMENÈS** below, dominated by the tall keep of its impressively restored **castle**

The castle

April–June, Sept & Oct Mon–Fri 10am–1pm & 2–6pm, Sat & Sun 10am–6pm; July & Aug daily 10am–7.30pm; Oct–March Sat & Sun 10am–5pm • €6 • ☎ 04 68 70 09 11, ⓦ chateauvillerouge.wix.com/termenes

The earlier Cathar fort here was destroyed in the wake of its conquest by Crusaders in 1210, and the present **castle**, dating from the 1300s, was designed not to protect but to dominate the inhabitants of the surrounding hills. A visit involves an engaging and educational audiovisual show (with an audioguide), which recaps the history of the area and recounts the tale of Guilhem Bélibaste, the Cathar *parfait* who was burned at the stake here in 1321. Afterwards it's worth taking a walk through the village huddled around the castle; the town was almost certainly fortified in the twelfth century, but the walls that are visible today were built to fend off the English and their allies during the Hundred Years' War in the 1300s. South of the *enceinte* you'll find the **church** of St-Étienne, which houses an immense sixteenth-century retable.

EATING   **VILLEROUGE-TERMENÈS**

La Rôtisserie Médiéval At the castle ☎ 09 81 64 09 11, ⓦ restaurant-medieval.com. Theme restaurant serving dishes from the thirteenth and fourteenth century served on crockery based on architectural finds.

Grills, usually spit-roast chicken or beef skewers, go for €16–20 and *menus* €35–42. They sometimes have medieval music concerts. Daily July & Aug noon–2pm & 7–9pm.

Termes

Leaving Villerouge, another steep ascent takes you to the **Col de Bedos** (485m), where a narrow paved road veers off to the right. Carefully following this relentless succession of hairpin curves will take you over hill and into valley until you make a sharp descent to **TERMES**. Little more than a cluster of ancient houses set on cramped but orderly streets, this extraordinarily beautiful hamlet would be worth a visit even if it weren't for its famous **castle**. Trees crowd over the narrow stream, spanned by a centuries-old stone bridge, and the sharply rising slopes above are covered by a blanket of beech, ash and stunted oak. The only thing that ruins the effect is the modern reception centre across the river, where you begin the arduous ascent to the ruins of the castle.

The castle

March & Nov Sat & Sun 10am–5pm; April–June & Sept–Oct daily 10am–6pm; July & Aug daily 10am–7.30pm • €4 • ☎ 04 68 70 09 20, ⓦ chateau-termes.com

You wouldn't know it from either the ruins or the village, but Termes **castle** was one of the greatest feudal domains of Languedoc. Ruled by an unrepentant heretic lord, Raymond, it was a prime target for de Montfort, who besieged it for four months, until the disease-ravaged garrison could resist no more. The castle remained in use until destroyed by Richelieu in the seventeenth century. The visit starts with a short introductory film followed by an exhibition on the siege. Then, clambering among the remains of the two concentric sets of walls, you'll find the chapel and can enjoy breathtaking **views** over the gorges.

Lagrasse

Just over halfway between Narbonne and Carcassonne, **LAGRASSE** is the largest and most beautiful village of the Corbières highlands; it's one of the Plus Beaux Villages de France (see p.46). A compact walled settlement set idyllically where the Orbieu opens up in a broad hollow, it hugs the right bank of the shallow river, where you can swim in summer, while its magnificent **abbey** squats on the far side. The grid of streets in the old town is almost completely residential, with at least thirty nationalities living here, and around fifteen artisans. Much of the old *enceinte* is intact, and is best appreciated as you cross the early fourteenth-century bridge; the town's riverside fortifications are now pierced by scores of windows of the houses built against them. There is a **market** on Saturday mornings and a good **cultural events** calendar, thanks to the village's active arty community.

6

Abbaye Ste-Marie d'Orbieu

Daily: mid-Jan to March & Nov to mid-Dec 10am–5pm; April to mid-June & mid-Sept to Oct 10am–6pm; mid-June to mid-Sept 10am–7pm • €4 • ☎ 04 68 32 63 89, ⊛ abbayedelagrasse.com

It's only about a five-minute walk from the far side of the river to the **Abbaye Ste-Marie d'Orbieu**. This is one of the region's oldest monastic houses, founded in an era when it was a dangerous, under-populated frontier of the eighth-century Carolingian empire. Cultivating the extensive lands with which they had been endowed, the monks slowly increased the monastery's wealth until its golden age in the fourteenth century. The complex is now a pastiche of styles, with components dating from the tenth to eighteenth centuries. Inside the publicly owned section (entrance on the left), you will discover a huge dormitory and the **chapelle de St-Barthélemy**, which has well-preserved wall murals; the *dépôt lapidaire* has examples of work by the "Master of Cabestany" (see box, p.284). Three times a year the abbey hosts the "Banquet du Livre" **literary festival** and in the garden is the *Café Littéraire* (see below). The private part of the abbey (entrance on the right) is inhabited by an order of monks who admit visitors to the church, cloister and garden (April–Oct Fri–Wed 3.15–6pm; €4; ⊛ lagrasse.org). You can hear them sing Gregorian chant daily at 6.30pm.

INFORMATION AND TOURS

Tourist information Maison du Patrimoine, 16 rue Paul Vergnes (April–June & Sept daily 10.30am–1pm & 2–6pm; July & Aug daily 10.30am–1pm & 2.30–7pm; Oct–March Mon–Fri 10.30am–12.30pm & 2–5pm; ☎ 04 68 43 11 56, ⊛ lagrasse.com). Check out the fifteenth-century painted ceiling in the room on the left as you enter.

Tours Entre Les Vignes (☎ 06 33 06 60 22, ⊛ entrelesvignes .fr). Guided 90min walking tours of the village in English with Carlos or Sam (€20).

ACCOMMODATION AND EATING

★Café Littéraire At the Abbaye Ste-Marie d'Orbieu ☎ 04 68 32 63 89. The café in the publicly owned part of the abbey is a "café du pays", a café-bookshop which serves simple dishes such as platters of cheese and charcuterie for around €12; all produce is local. The café regularly hosts literary and live music events. Mid-June to mid-Sept daily 11am–7pm; mid-Sept to mid-June Sat & Sun.

Camping Boucocers Rte de Ribaute ☎ 04 68 43 10 05. Basic municipal campsite with just forty pitches but good views over the village. It's on the way to Ribaute, which has excellent river swimming. Open mid-March to mid-Oct. **€13**

La Cocotte Fêlée 2 bd de la Promenade ☎ 04 68 75 90 54. Local products and regional cuisine with Asian influences; the chicken with coconut is a good choice and

there are vegetarian options too. Lunch *menu* €14 and dinner €27. Tues 7.30–9pm, Wed–Sat noon–2pm & 7.30–9pm, Sun noon–2pm.

Les Glycines Bd Charles Cros ☎ 04 68 43 14 54 ⊛ gites -les-glycines.fr. Owned by a pianist who organizes the annual piano festival, this charming old townhouse is a veritable warren of rooms with both B&B and *gîte* options. **€60**

Hostellerie des Corbières 9 bd de la Promenade ☎ 04 68 43 15 22, ⊛ hostellerie-des-corbieres.com. Comfortable *Logis de France* hotel in a townhouse with six TV-free rooms. The restaurant is renowned for its creative regional cuisine and overlooks a vineyard; *menus* are €17– 39 and include vegetarian options. Closed Oct–Apr Wed & Thurs. **€75**

SHOPPING

Cyril Codina 13 bd de la Promenade ☎ 04 68 32 18 87, ⓦ 1900-lagrasse.com. Artisan flavoured vinegars and olive oils used by some of the region's top chefs. Daily 10am–noon & 2–6pm.

Les Vins sur le Fruit pl de la Halle ☎ 04 68 49 80 76, ⓦ les -vins-sur-le-fruit.fr. Good selection of top-quality national and local wines from small producers at cost price. Daily 10.30am–12.30pm & 3–7.30pm, closed Wed in winter.

6 | Along the Canal du Midi east from Carcassonne

Heading east from Carcassonne, the **Canal du Midi** follows the course of the lower Aude valley, past the tree-shaded port at **Trèbes**, and on into the wine country of the **Minervois**, bounded by Haut Languedoc to the north and the hills of the Corbières to the south. Here the small port of **Homps** provides a jumping-off point for the old Cathar stronghold of **Minerve** and the monastery at **Caunes**. Just after the old way-station of Le Somail the canal splits; the offshoot **Canal de la Robine** glides past the ancient wine centre of **Sallèles**, and on through Narbonne to reach the sea near Gruissan, while the main channel edges on to pass the magnificent **Oppidum d'Ensérune**, before reaching Béziers and, eventually, Agde (see p.265). As with the western leg of the canal system, you needn't commit yourself to boating to enjoy this archetypal southern French landscape, since the two towpaths which run along the canal's length make for wonderful **cycling** and **walking**.

Trèbes

The first and prettiest port of call along the eastern stretch of the Canal du Midi is **TRÈBES**, just a few kilometres east of Carcassonne. The canal makes a broad curve here, following the wide meander of the Aude; arriving at Trèbes, two canal bridges, the

---

NAVIGATING THE CANAL DU MIDI EAST OF CARCASSONNE

The section of the Canal du Midi east of Carcassonne is the most interesting, and the best for **cycling**, **hiking** and **boating** (see box, p.82). Almost all of the towns along the way have boat rental facilities. **Voies Navigables de France**, the government organization in charge of inland waterways (☎ 04 67 11 81 30, ⓦ www.vnf.fr), has an office in avenue du Prado, Béziers, and is the best place for further **information**.

TRÈBES

At Trèbes, head to the canalside boat basin, where the port office (☎ 04 68 78 83 08) and Le Boat (☎ 04 68 94 42 80, ⓦ leboat.fr) have a selection of houseboats. For boat trips, contact Bateau Le Cathare, avenue Pierre Curie (July–Oct; €10; ☎ 04 68 78 89 50).

HOMPS

In Homps, you can rent boats from Les Canalous (☎ 03 85 53 76 74, ⓦ canalous-canaldumidi.com).

LE SOMAIL

In Le Somail, Minervois Cruisers, at 38 chemin des Patiasses (☎ 04 68 46 28 52, ⓦ minervoiscruisers.com), rents out cruising boats for longer trips, while Comptoir Nature (☎ 04 68 46 01 61, ⓦ comptoirnature.free.fr), at 1 chemin de Halage, hires electric boats by the hour for €22.

COLOMBIERS

In Colombiers, cruisers can be rented from En Bateau (☎ 04 67 13 19 62, ⓦ en-bateau.com), who also rent out boats in the other ports along the way. Also here, Sunboat (☎ 04 67 37 14 60, ⓦ sunboat.fr) rents out electric boats, bikes and offers cruises.

THE BLACK PRINCE: LANGUEDOC'S FIRST ENGLISH TOURIST

Not long after the dust of the Cathar Wars settled, events far off at the courts of Westminster and Paris brought warfare once again to the already severely devastated region. This time the occasion was the **Hundred Years' War**, which flared up in 1330 when Edward III of England claimed that he, rather than Philip VI, was the rightful king of France. At that time, Edward III's eldest son and heir, also named Edward, was only two years of age, but by the time he was 16, he was a veteran warrior.

Young Edward, Duke of Aquitaine, and the second heir to the throne to carry the title "Prince of Wales" (the first was Edward II), was sent off to Bordeaux to take command of the province. Here the local Gascons were only too happy to join the English in looting and pillaging their neighbours. Edward, by then known as the **Black Prince** after the colour of his armour, would give them every opportunity, mounting a massive scorched-earth campaign into Languedoc in 1355. Striking out towards Toulouse, he and his men covered nearly 675 miles in 68 days of raiding. Castelnaudary, as well as the *bastide* of Carcassonne, Trèbes, Limoux and Narbonne, were just a few of the towns he and his troops sacked and torched, and his five thousand men laid waste to nearly eighteen thousand square miles of territory. The following year Edward went on to further glory by capturing the French king, John II, in battle at Poitiers. With Gallic aplomb, the contemporary chronicler, Froissart, summed up the expedition as proof of "the great haughtiness of the English, who are affable to no other nation than their own".

6

second designed by the military architect Vauban in 1686, carry the watercourse over the Frequel and Orbiel rivers. For boaters the town is a well-equipped stage post, just as it was in the seventeenth century, with mooring facilities and a range of services. There is a market on Sunday mornings.

Église St-Étienne

Mid-June to mid-Sept Mon–Fri 2.30–6.30pm • Free guided visits (ask at the tourist office)

Aside from being an attractive place with a canal port overlooked by the town walls at its western end, Trèbes is home to a remarkable church, the **Église St-Étienne**, the wooden-beamed ceiling of which, dating back to the early fourteenth century, has 320 individual faces painted on the ends of its roof supports, including caricatures of various professions and social classes, exotic foreigners and grotesques.

INFORMATION

TRÈBES

Tourist information 12 av Pierre Curie (March, April & Oct Mon–Sat 10am–noon & 2–6pm; May–June & Sept daily 10am–noon & 2–6pm; July & Aug daily 10am–7pm; Nov–Feb Mon–Fri 10am–noon & 2–5pm; ☎04 68 78 89 50, 🔗ot-trebes.fr).

Bike rental 3 rue du Plô d'Orbiel (☎04 68 78 68 81, 🔗locavelo.fr). From €12 per half-day.

ACCOMMODATION AND EATING

Camping à l'Ombre des Micouliers ☎04 68 78 61 75, 🔗audecamping.com. Four-star campsite in the southeast of the town with pitches and chalets to rent. There's a bar, a kids' playground, a small shop and free access to the covered municipal swimming pool. **€23**

Le Moulin de Trèbes 2 rue du Moulin ☎04 68 78 97 57, 🔗lemoulindetrebes.com. Gourmet regional cuisine is on the menu at this former water mill with a lovely covered terrace. Main courses, such as roast kid with thyme, are €19–24. *Menus* start at €17 for lunch. Tues–Sun noon–2.30pm & 7–9pm.

Riverside Home Cottage 6 rue Lamartine ☎04 68 78 99 39, 🔗riverside-home-cottage.fr. Two romantic rooms ("Le Loft" has a terrace) and a *gîte* are on offer in this utterly charming B&B in a riverside townhouse. Free parking. **€60**

The Minervois

Named after the beautiful village of Minerve, the **Minervois** is a sun-bleached wine-producing territory stretching from the north bank of the Aude up to the hills of Haut Languedoc. The Canal du Midi runs through it northwest to southeast.

6

Homps

As the Canal du Midi arcs northward it passes **HOMPS**, a town which suffered destruction in the Crusade and the Wars of Religion, but revived with the construction of the waterway. It's the main port of the Minervois region. The main sight here is Le Chai – La Maison des Vins du Minervois (35 quai des Tonneliers; May–Oct Mon–Fri 9am–12.30pm & 2–7pm, Sat 2–7pm; Nov–April Mon–Fri 9am–12.30pm & 2–6pm; ☎04 68 91 29 48, ⊛lechai-portminervois.com), where you can learn about, taste and buy wines from this area. Northwest of town is the **Lac de Jouarres**, with a pebble beach and watersports in summer.

ACCOMMODATION AND EATING   HOMPS

★**En Bonne Compagnie** 6 quai des Négociants ☎04 68 91 23 16, ⊛in-good-company.com. British-run restaurant in a stone village house with a canalside terrace. On the menu is traditional French cuisine with international influences from chef Craig's travels. Two-course weekday lunch from €14. Tues–Fri noon–2pm & 7–10pm, Sun noon–2pm, Sat 7–10pm.

Le Jardin d'Homps 21 Grand Rue ☎04 68 75 30 76, ⊛jardinhomps.fr. Luxury B&B with five minimalist, stylish rooms overlooking a lush garden. In summer, take a dip in the pool before enjoying breakfast on the patio. **€110**

Minerve

The former Cathar stronghold of **MINERVE** is a tiny medieval hamlet located at the cirque where the deep gorge of the River Cesse doubles back on itself. Unsurprisingly, given its stunningly dramatic location, Minerve is on the Plus Beaux Villages de France and Grand Site de France lists. Only a single pile of stones remains of its **fortress**, which resisted Simon de Montfort for five months in 1210. When it was taken, 140 Cathars who refused to recant their beliefs voluntarily jumped into the fire the Crusaders had prepared for them. Once you've had a stroll, head for the **canyon** that surrounds the town, where you can walk in natural tunnels bored through the cliffs – the **trail** can be picked up just over the bridge which enters town. It's best to avoid Minerve in August, when the volume of visitors threatens to obliterate its charms.

INFORMATION   MINERVE

Tourist information 9 rue des Martyrs (daily 10.30am–1pm & 3–6.45pm ☎04 68 91 81 43, ⊛minervois-tourisme.fr).

ACCOMMODATION AND EATING

Relais Chantovent 17 Grande Rue ☎04 68 91 14 18, ⊛relaischantovent-minerve.fr. Top-class restaurant in the heart of the village with a terrace overlooking the gorge. On the menu (€22–62) is the likes of slow-cooked pork with rosemary *jus*, and there is a special truffle *menu* (€51) in winter. They also have ten comfortable rooms (from €53) nearby. Tues 12.15–2pm, Mon & Thurs–Sat 12.15–2pm & 7.15–9pm.

Caunes-Minervois

CAUNES-MINERVOIS, the region's capital, lies on the far western edge of the Minervois. It has some very nice hotels and restaurants and makes a good base to explore the surrounding area. The centre of Caunes, which has some beautiful mansions, is dominated by a hulking **abbey** (daily: April–June & Sept–Oct 10am–noon & 2–6pm; July & Aug 10am–7pm; Nov–March 10am–noon & 2–5pm; €5; ☎04 68 78 09 44). The crypt holds the foundation of the original eighth-century church, and some eleventh-century pavement has been uncovered in the cloister. There is also a space for temporary exhibitions on famous comic strips and in summer there are classical music concerts in the grounds on Fridays (⊛lesvendredisdecaunes.fr).

Caunes is most famous for its **marble quarries**, which supplied red stone to the Capitole in Toulouse, the Opéra in Paris, the mosque in Cordoba and St Peter's in Rome. You can take a one-hour guided tour at the **Villerambert quarry** (June–Sept 4pm; €10; ☎06 30 13 95 78, ⊛visitecarriere.fr). The Fête de la Sculpture et du Marbre takes place in June.

INFORMATION

CAUNES-MINERVOIS

Tourist information 3 ruelle du Monestier (Daily: April–June & Sept–Nov 10am–1pm & 2–6pm; July & Aug 10am–1pm & 2–7pm; Dec–March 10am–1pm & 2–5pm; ☏ 04 68 76 34 74, ⓦ tourisme-haut-minervois.fr). Here you can pick up a free guide to the town and ask about visits to local vineyards.

ACCOMMODATION AND EATING

L'Ancienne Boulangerie 20 rue St-Gênes ☏ 04 68 76 27 17, ⓦ ancienneboulangerie.com. Lovely English-run B&B in a former bakery. The four rooms are attractively furnished with antiques and quality bed linen. There's a guest lounge, a pretty walled terrace, and dinner is available (€22). **€80**

D'Alibert Rue St-Gênes ☏ 04 68 78 00 54, ⓦ hotel-dalibert.com. The rooms at this hotel-restaurant are fine but really you come here to experience the stunning surrounds of this sixteenth-century mansion, where they often hold concerts in the courtyard. The regional cuisine is excellent (*menu* €29) and there's a good wine list. **€90**

La Marbrerie Av de l'Argent Double, 2 rue du Chasselas ☏ 04 68 79 28 74, ⓦ la-marbrerie.fr. Elegant three-star *Logis de France* in a former marble-polishing workshop. There's a very good *terroir* restaurant (*menus* from €16.90) and also a tearoom, an exhibition on marble and a shop selling marble products. **€85**

La Table d'Emilie 10 av de l'Argent Double ☏ 04 68 78 70 10. Well-regarded small restaurant with an English lady at the helm ("Emilie" is her daughter). There are French dishes with international influences on the daily-changing menu, all made with local products where possible. Lunch from €15. Mon & Thurs–Sun 11am–2pm & 6–9pm.

Le Somail

East from Caunes Minervois, this leg of the canal crosses the aqueduct of Répudre – France's first, and an invention of Riquet himself – on to **LE SOMAIL**, the last port before the Canal de la Robine splits off to head south towards Narbonne. Here a single-arched stone **bridge** dating from the eighteenth century spans the canal, still attached to the old post-house *auberge* on the east bank and a small **chapel** on the west. There's little to do here aside from browsing antiquarian bookshop Le Trouve Tout du Livre (28 allée de la Glacière; Wed–Sun April–mid-Nov 10am–noon & 2.30–6.30pm; July & Aug daily; Dec–March 2.30–6.30pm) then enjoying a drink or meal and soaking up the canalside ambience before moving on.

INFORMATION

LE SOMAIL

Tourist information 168 allée de la Glacière (April to mid-Nov Mon–Fri 9am–1pm & 2–6/7pm, Sat & Sun 2–6pm; mid-Nov to March Mon–Fri 2–5pm ☏ 04 68 41 55 70, ⓦ tourisme-corbieres-minervois.com).

EATING

Le Comptoir Nature 1 chemin du Halage ☏ 04 68 46 01 61, ⓦ comptoirnature.free.fr. Next to the canal, this popular "*café de pays*" serves simple dishes using ingredients from local and regional producers (*menus* €14.50–32.50); try the goats' milk ice cream. There's live music on Wed and Fri evenings in summer. Daily April–Oct from 10am.

Along the Canal de la Robine

From Le Somail, the **CANAL DE LA ROBINE**'s short trajectory heads almost directly south, crossing the course of the wide and, here, tame Aude, then continuing through Narbonne before penetrating the marshy extent of the Étang de Bages et de Sigean. After Narbonne there are two legs; the longer tracks the same spit of land as the railway, skirting the bird-lovers' paradise of **Île de Ste-Lucie**, before arriving at Port-la-Nouvelle and the sea, while the shorter cuts east past the vineyards of La Clape, passing **Gruissan** (see p.249) and the saltpans of St-Martin before reaching the Mediterranean.

Sallèles-d'Aude

The only major port of call on the Canal de la Robine, a few kilometres before it merges with the Aude, is **SALLÈLES-D'AUDE**. Sallèles is a **wine town** of great antiquity, whose vintages graced the tables of Rome more than two thousand years ago. A festival – Eau, Terre et Vin – celebrates the town's assets every July.

Musée des Potiers Gallo-Romains Amphoralis

Allée des Potiers • June–Sept Tues–Sun 10am–noon & 3–7pm; Oct–May Tues–Fri 1.30–5pm, Sat & Sun 10am–noon & 2–6pm • €5 • ☎ 04 68 46 89 48, ⓦ amphoralis.com

The **Musée des Potiers Gallo-Romains Amphoralis** bears testimony to the town's wine-making heritage. Named after the distinctively tapered vessels (amphorae) once made here, it's a well laid out and entertaining museum, which includes the excavation site of the pottery itself. The walk out to the museum, which is northwest of the centre is interesting too, thanks to the six sets of **locks** which grace that part of the canal. There is a **pottery festival** in Sallèles every August.

INFORMATION   SALLÈLES-D'AUDE

Tourist information Av du Gailhousty (irregular hours; ☎ 04 68 58 73 13, ⓦ sallelesdaude.fr).

Bike rental L'Oc Évasion, 2 av du Gailhousty (☎ 06 83 2 51 81). From €15 per half-day.

EATING

Cook'n Roll Near the Canal de Jonction, off av Gailhousty ☎ 06 21 49 09 18. Local seasonal food is on the menu at this "slow food" truck, which has been set up in a tree-shaded garden with seating. Mains such as mackere or duck are around €12. Call to check location, and opening dates and times. Daily June–Sept noon–10pm.

The Canal du Midi from Le Somail to the sea

East of Le Somail, the Canal du Midi enters its most picturesque stretch, snaking through a rugged landscape of low and rocky vine-clad hills whose only reminder of civilization is an occasional bell tower. Beyond Béziers, the canal finally empties into the Bassin de Thau, from where you can reach the sea or connect with the other great inland waterway of Languedoc, the Rhône–Sète Canal (see box, p.188), which carries on past the Camargue Gardoise into Provence.

Capestang

Sixteen kilometres before reaching Béziers, the Canal du Midi passes under the old hilltop town of **CAPESTANG**, whose small castle is capped by a distinctive tower. With a tree-lined square snuggled up against its medieval church, Capestang is an exceedingly pleasant little town – you can climb the church's **bell tower** (43m) to enjoy sweeping views over the Aude valley, or simply enjoy a snack or drink and observe the unhurried life of the *place*. There is a **market** on Wednesday and Sunday mornings in place Jean-Jaurès.

The castle

Mon–Fri 9am–6pm • Free • ☎ 04 67 93 40 90

The nondescript-looking **castle** was once a residence of the archbishops of Narbonne. Despite centuries of neglect, the incredible artwork of the old great hall has survived the ages – the 161 fourteenth-century **ceiling paintings** are a must-see for those following the canal route. These vivid caricatures depict monsters, musicians, court ladies and even a mischievous jester pulling a rather exaggerated "moon" at the viewer.

INFORMATION   CAPESTANG

Tourist information Quai Élie-Amouroux (April–June Mon–Sat 9.30am–noon & 2–5pm; July & Aug daily 10am–12.30pm & 3–6.30pm; Sept & Oct Mon–Sat 9.30am–noon & 2–5.30pm; Nov–March Mon–Fri 9am–noon & 2–5pm; ☎ 04 67 37 85 29, ⓦ tourismecanaldumidi.fr).

Bike rental Vélogénie, 2 av de Béziers (☎ 06 99 67 53 50, ⓦ velogenie.com). From €15 per half-day.

ABBAYE DE FONTFROIDE (P.251) >

EATING

La Table du Vigneron 3 rue Paul Bert ☎ 04 67 93 48 90. Traditional French cuisine is on the menu at this rustic restaurant run by a family of wine producers. Sit in the lovely courtyard and savour a main course for around €1▮ accompanied by one of their own Domaine Clos-Rebou wines. Daily: May–Sept 6–9pm.

Colombiers

After cutting through the ancient hamlet of Poilhes, some 5km beyond Capestang, the Canal du Midi passes through a long tunnel, eventually arriving at the tiny village of **COLOMBIERS**, where you can visit the **Maison du Tourisme** and the **Cave du Château** (March–Oct daily 9.30am–12.45pm & 3–6.45pm; €3; ☎ 04 67 37 00 90) in place du Millénaire, a sumptuous nineteenth-century *bodega* designed by woodcarvers who studied under Eiffel, which hosts art and archeological exhibitions.

ACCOMMODATION AND EATING

COLOMBIERS

Au Lavoir Rue du Lavoir ☎ 04 67 26 16 15, ⓦ au-lavoir .com. A good choice for top-class southern cooking with a *plat du jour* and a glass of wine for €15 on weekdays. They also have four comfortable rooms decorated i▮ contemporary style, with king-size beds and jacuzzi▮ (€110). Daily noon–2pm & 7–9pm.

Oppidum D'Ensérune

Excavations: April & Sept daily 10am–12.30pm & 2–6pm; May–Aug daily 10am–7pm; Oct–March Tues–Sun 9.30am–12.30pm & 2–5.30pm • €5.50 • ☎ 04 67 37 01 23, ⓦ enserune.fr

Set on a long ridge towering over the surrounding plains, the site of the **OPPIDUM D'ENSÉRUNE** (*oppidum* being Latin for "town", referring generally to pre-Roman hilltop settlements) has attracted settlers for over 2500 years. Even before Hannibal and the Romans took it over in turn, it was an important centre for trade, maintaining commercial ties with Greece, while under the Romans it served as one of the postal way-stations on the busy Via Domitia. The site itself, a rocky spur crowned with cypress and brambles, is characteristically Mediterranean, and climbing to the top, looking north, you'll get a view of a strange array of fields resembling a spoked wheel. This was once the *étang* of Montady, one of the many salt lagoons of the lowlands here that were drained and cultivated in the thirteenth century. The **excavations** of the ancient ruins, covering most of the hilltop, are impressive, with remains of defensive walls, villas and a large number of cisterns and sunken grain stores. The small **site museum** inside the grounds holds a collection of statuary found here, including small devotional pieces and larger civic portraits. On the way to the oppidum, the **Maison du Malpas** (July & Aug daily 10am–7pm; Sept–June Mon–Fri 10am–6pm, Sat 10am–5pm ☎ 04 67 32 88 77, ⓦ ladomitienne.com) has an exhibition of the site and can organize guided tours (April–Sept); there is also tourist information and a shop selling regional products.

The neuf écluses

As it arrives at the foot of Béziers' ridge, the canal descends six locks known as the **neuf écluses** (originally nine, hence its name) – arguably Riquet's greatest achievement and the third most visited sight in the former Languedoc-Roussillon region. The canal paths along it are currently undergoing a €13 million restoration and are inaccessible (until summer 2017) but that doesn't stop the families and tour groups who dutifully stand around watching the boats make their slow descent. A new car park opened in 2016 and is where the "Béziers City Tour" (☎ 06 33 75 72 50, ⓦ lepetittraindebeziers.fr) stops.

Béziers and around

Just inland from the mouth of the Orb river and dominating the strip of plain between the coast and Haut Languedoc, **BÉZIERS** could be held up as a metaphor for Languedoc – it has a long and proud past and a history of independent spirit, which it has more than once paid for in blood. Until the early Noughties, the city had fallen into decay, its dusty streets and deteriorating shop-fronts betraying the slump into which the town had settled in the last century or so. Determined civic efforts have turned the situation around, however, and Béziers is once more a delight, its atmospheric **old quarter** now bustling with busy shops. Modern Béziers is the home of two great Languedocian adopted traditions: English **rugby**, and the Spanish **corrida**, both of which it follows with a passion. The best time to visit is during the mid-August **feria**, a raucous five-day party.

As you approach Béziers, its impressive **cathedral** towers over the Orb river, high up on a dramatic ridge. The vaguely semi-circular **old town** snuggles into a gentle meander of the Orb, which, along with the canal – the Ruisseau de Bagnols – bounds it on three sides. The eastern limit is marked by allées Paul-Riquet, which has a broad pedestrian concourse running down its centre.

There are open-air **markets** in the city every day and a covered market, Halles de Béziers, place Pierre Sémard (Tues–Sun 7am–1pm).

6

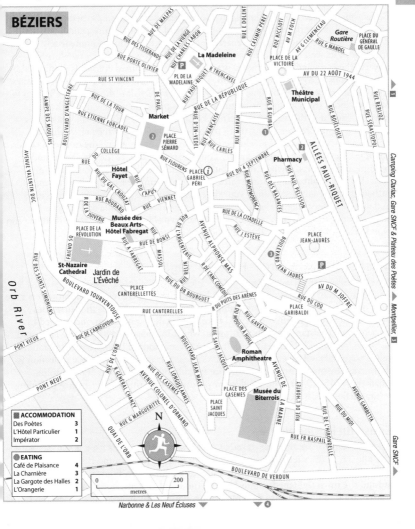

BÉZIERS

▪ ACCOMMODATION	
Des Poètes	3
L'Hôtel Particulier	1
Impérator	2

● EATING	
Café de Plaisance	4
La Charnière	3
La Gargote des Halles	2
L'Orangerie	1

0 — 200 metres

6

Brief history

Béziers has been inhabited since neolithic times and is one of the oldest cities in France, dating back to 575BC. Like neighbouring Narbonne, it was already a sizeable settlement when the Romans took it over in the second century BC (the remains of the amphitheatre were uncovered in the 1990s); it thrived under *pax Romana*, and was the seat of a bishop and a prosperous market town through the Middle Ages. After the horror of the attack it suffered in the Albigensian Crusade, Béziers went on to become the richest city in Languedeoc in the latter half of the nineteenth century thanks to its **wine production** (until phylloxera took its toll), whose wealth created the grand buildings, *allées* and park. The town also produced two men who shaped France: **Pierre-Paul Riquet**, the genius behind the Canal du Midi, and **Jean Moulin**, one of the leading figures in the Resistance.

Cathédrale St-Nazaire

Place des Albigeois • Daily: July & Aug 9.30am–6pm; Sept–June 9.30am–noon & 2–5pm • Free

Béziers' main attraction is undoubtedly the majestic Romanesque **Cathédrale St-Nazaire**. Constructed in the thirteenth century on the site of a tenth-century church that was destroyed in 1209, the cathedral's marriage of style and function is immediately apparent in its west face, which has a great rosette window flanked by two fortified towers. The cathedral's voluminous, predominantly unadorned **interior** is dominated by an outrageous Baroque retable – a gaudy starburst of saints and cherubs, which clashes with the sobriety of the building. The high point of the visit is the dizzying climb to the **upper galleries** (free) – a rare opportunity to get a pigeon's-eye view of a cathedral's interior. Climbing the well-worn, narrow keystone staircase (169 steps), you traverse a small landing before continuing up to the top – the balconies which circle the pinnacles afford spectacular **views**. Almost directly below the cliffs on which the cathedral stands, you'll see the evocative twelfth-century Pont Vieux as it crosses the Orb below and, beyond to the west, the whole of the Biterrois plain stretching off into a haze – on a clear day you might make out the form of Le Canigó on the horizon. Leaving the cathedral by the south-side door, you will enter the unfinished cloister. Within its low and austere gallery, there's a collection of old funerary stones while on its east side a stairway descends into the airy gardens, the **Jardin de l'Évêché**, from where there are also wonderful views for those without a head for heights.

Musée des Beaux-Arts – Hôtel Fabrégat

Place de la Révolution • June–Aug Tues–Sun 10am–6pm; Sept–May Tues–Fri 9am–5pm, Sat & Sun 10am–6pm • €3 • ☎ 04 67 28 38 78

At the far end of the pleasant place de la Révolution – where republican protesters were fired upon in 1851 – is the Hôtel Fabrégat, a mansion that houses the **Musée des Beaux-Arts**. The highlight, on the top floor, is a small art collection once owned by Béziers-born Resistance hero Jean Moulin, which includes works by Raoul Dufy and Suzanne Valadon. The museum's sculpture annexe is lodged in another aristocratic residence, the **Hôtel Fayet** (rue du Capus; same hours and ticket), whose collection is dominated by nineteenth-century works, notably by local sculptor Jean-Antoine Injalbert (1845–1933), whose public works can be seen throughout France including several major pieces in Paris.

Église de la Madeleine

Place de la Madeleine • June–Sept daily 10.30am–12.30pm & 4–6pm; Oct–May Wed & Fri 10am–noon & 2–4pm, Sat & Sun 10am–noon • Free

On July 22, 1209, the papacy sent an army of knights to surround Béziers, led by the Abbot of Cîteaux, the most powerful monastery in northern France. As the noose around the town tightened, around several thousand citizens, both Catholic and Cathar, took refuge in **Église de la Madeleine**, within which, according to law, no blood was to be shed. The abbot, however, gave the order to set fire to the church, exclaiming "Burn them all, God will know his own!". The church was also the site of the murder of Raymond Trencavel, Viscount of Béziers, in 1167 by the local bourgeoisie (his long-gone castle was in place Jean-Jaurès).

Along allées Paul-Riquet

Heading east from La Madeleine, rue Trencavel takes you towards the pretty Art Nouveau-style **Théâtre Municipal** at the top end of **allées Paul-Riquet**, a broad, leafy esplanade lined with cafés and restaurants; on Friday mornings the weekly **flower market** is held here. The boulevard ends at the gorgeous little park of the **Plateau des Poètes**, whose ponds, palms and lime trees were laid out in the so-called English manner by the brothers Denis et Eugène Bühler, who created Paris's Bois de Boulogne. Check out the sculptures of the Occitan poets after whom the park is named and also Injalbert's grand, ornate fountain.

Musée du Biterrois

Rampe du 96ème • June–Sept Tues–Sun 10am–6pm; Oct–May Tues–Fri 10am–5pm, Sat & Sun 10am–6pm • €3 • ☎ 04 67 36 81 60

To the west of the park you'll find the impressive **Musée du Biterrois**, housed on the ground floor of an old barracks. It traces the town's history – including sections on natural history, ethnography and archeology – from prehistory until the Second World War. The most interesting sections cover Riquet and the Canal du Midi, the nineteenth-century wine industry and the Gallo-Roman period, whose highlight is the "treasure of Béziers" – a rich cache of **silver platters** found in a nearby field (removed for restoration at the time of writing). Although this is a fantastic town history museum, unfortunately there is no information in English.

ARRIVAL AND DEPARTURE   BÉZIERS

By plane Béziers Cap d'Agde Airport (☎ 04 67 80 99 09, ⓦ beziers.aeroport.fr) is 14.5km southeast of the town. Shuttle buses, which serve Béziers, Agde and Marseillan, leave 30min after the flights arrive and cost €1.60. Many taxis serve the airport (see website for details) and a one-way journey costs around €25.

By train If you arrive at the *gare SNCF* on bd de Verdun, the best way to enter the old town is via av Gambetta – about 10min walk northwest uphill. TGV stations are indicated with an asterisk.

Destinations Bédarieux (several daily; 35min); Nîmes*, via Agde*, Marseillan-Plage, Sète* and Montpellier* (several hourly; 1hr 15min); Paris* (many daily; 4hr 30min); Perpignan*, via Narbonne* and Salses (many daily; 1hr);

Toulouse*, via Narbonne, Carcassonne* and Castelnaudary (hourly; 1hr 30min–2hr 20min).

By bus The *gare routière* is on pl du Généra-de-Gaulle, on the eastern side of av Clemenceau.

Destinations Agde (several daily; 40min); Bédarieux (daily; 1hr); Bouzigues (several daily; 1hr 50min); Capestang (several daily; 30min); Castres (weekends; 2hr 15min); Colombiers (several daily; 20min); Hérépian (daily; 1hr); Lamalou (daily; 1hr 10min); Loupian (several daily; 1hr 45min); Marseillan (several daily; 50min); Mèze (several daily; 1hr 40min); Montpellier (several daily; 2hr 15min); Pézenas (several daily; 35min); Roquebrun (several daily; 50min); St-Pons-de-Thomières (several daily; 1hr 15min).

GETTING AROUND

By bike Relax Bike Tours & Rentals, 70 allées Paul Riquet (☎ 06 38 12 32 82, ⓦ relaxbiketours.com). From €15 per half-day. They also organize itineraries and tours.

By car There are car parks (charge) at pl Jean Jaurès, the train station and La Madeleine church. Rental agencies: ADA, 23 bd Verdun ☎ 04 67 62 65 39; Avis, 18 bd Verdun

☎ 04 67 28 65 44; Budget, *gare SNCF* ☎ 04 67 28 14 41; Hertz, 83bis av Président-Wilson ☎ 04 67 62 82 00. There are also car rental agencies at the airport.

By taxi Taxis Radio de Béziers (☎ 04 67 35 00 85, ⓦ taxisbeziers.fr).

INFORMATION

Tourist information 2 place Gabriel Péri (daily: July & Aug 9am–7pm; Sept–June 9am–6pm; ☎ 04 99 41 36 36,

ⓦ beziers-in-mediterranee.com). There is also an office at the "neuf écluses" (see p.260; April & May daily 10am–1pm

6

& 2–5pm; June–Sept daily 10am–7pm; Oct–March Wed–Sun 10am–1pm & 2–5pm). As well as a good selection of themed guided tours, you can also book a free guided tour in English, based on your interests, with a "Greeter"

(w beziers-mediterranee-greeters.com).

Museum pass The Pass Musées (€5) allows entry to both the Musées des Beaux-Arts and the Musée du Biterrois.

ACCOMMODATION

Des Poètes 80 allées Paul Riquet ☎04 67 76 38 66, w hoteldespoetes.net. An all-round excellent choice with recently renovated rooms and amenities including wi-fi and a good breakfast for €8. Book ahead. €60

★**L'Hôtel Particulier** 65bis av du 22 août 1944 ☎04 67 49 04 47 w hotelparticulierbeziers.com. Elegant four-star boutique hotel in a nineteenth-century mansion in the north of the town. The nine spacious rooms are

tastefully decorated in plain minimalist style with splashes of colour. There is a small garden with a pool and also beauty treatments and parking (€10). €130

Impérator 28 allées Paul Riquet ☎04 67 49 02 25, w hotel-imperator.fr. This three-star hotel is well located and has a fascinating history, which includes being the local Nazi HQ during World War II. Rooms exude classy comfort, just shy of luxury. Parking from €15. €125

EATING AND DRINKING

★**Café de Plaisance** 1 quai du Port Neuf ☎04 67 76 15 90, w cafedeplaisance.fr. Canalside café with an original zinc counter – the kind of place you'd see in an old film. Traditional dishes on the menu (lunch for €13.50) and there's even a *pétanque* pitch outside. July & Aug Mon–Sat noon–2.30pm (café 8am–10pm), Sept–June Mon–Fri noon–2pm (café 8am–8.30pm).

La Charnière 22 bd Jean Jaurès ☎07 85 06 37 65, w lacharniere.fr. Owned by former Northampton and Béziers "rugbyman" Johnny Howard, this café-bar not only has a good selection of beer but does pretty decent food too including steak or fish and chips, tapas and huge salads. Naturally, rugby matches are shown in season. Wed–Sun 9am–3pm & 7–11pm.

La Gargote des Halles Halles de Béziers, place Pierre Sémard ☎04 67 36 64 90, w la-gargote-des-halles .com. Buzzy café-restaurant in the covered market where the dishes are mainly made with products from the stallholders. Excellent-value tapas (€8–15), delicious fries and regional wines from €2 per glass. Mon–Fri 7am–3pm, Sat & Sun 6am–5pm.

L'Orangerie 5 rue Guibal ☎04 67 49 07 20. Charming little bistro in a narrow street in the old town. The food is traditionally French (but with vegetarian options) and the wine is good and inexpensive. Expect to pay around €30 for three courses. Tues–Thurs 8am–3pm, Fri 8am–3pm & 6.30pm–midnight, Sat 10.30am–3pm & 6.30pm–midnight.

DIRECTORY

Hospital Centre Hospitalier, 2 rue Valentin Haüy, ZAC de Montmiran (☎04 67 35 70 35, w ch-beziers.fr).

(Mon–Sat 8.30am–7.30pm; ☎04 67 28 32 28).
Police Rue Georges-Mandel (☎04 67 49 54 00).

Sérignan

Lying some 11km southeast of Béziers, **Sérignan** is worth a stop to visit the **Musée Régional d'Art Contemporain** (146 av de la Plage; July & Aug Tues–Sun 11am–7pm; Sept–June Tues–Sun 10am–6pm; €5; ☎04 67 32 33 05, w mrac.languedocroussillon.fr) whose eclectic permanent collection includes Abstract Landscape, Narrative Figuration and Conceptual Art by a wide range of French and international artists.

There are **markets** in Sérignan on Monday, Wednesday and Friday mornings, and the beaches at nearby **Sérignan-Plage**, especially those in the west that are part of the Réserve Naturelle des Orpeillières, are a great place to get away from it all.

INFORMATION

Tourist information La Cigalière, 1 av de Béziers (April–Sept daily 9am–1pm & 2–6pm; Oct–March Wed–Sat

10am–noon & 2–5pm; ☎04 99 41 36 36, w beziers-in -mediterranee.com).

EATING AND DRINKING

Latino Beach Plage de la Maïre, Sérignan-Plage ☎04 67 32 15 99. This beach restaurant has a great atmosphere and is the perfect spot to chill out over

seafood (mains around €15) or tapas. There's usually a DJ or live music in the evening. May–Aug daily 9am–2am.

Agde and around

Thanks to the few kilometres that separate it from the sea, **AGDE** is one of the most unspoilt towns on the Languedocian coast. It boomed as a port 2500 years ago under the Phoenicians and on through the Middle Ages, until competition from neighbouring towns and the silting up of the Hérault pushed the seashore from its walls. Today, its compact **old town** has resisted intensive development and remains a quiet respite from the crowds. There is a **market** on Thursdays year round (daily in summer).

A series of *places* follows the Hérault from east to west: the lively Jean-Jaurès, with its sidewalk cafés; Picheire, where you'll find the small porticoed medieval **market**; and de la Marine, a grittily authentic fishermen's quarter. Heading south from place de la Marine, the residential rue de la Poissonnerie is a step back in time – a neighbourhood of fishermen's families living in modest and ancient houses. Continuing, you'll pass the new market building and the **church of St-André**, occupying a site on which there's been a church since as far back as 506 AD, when an episcopal council was held here. Just south is the wide tree-lined La Promenade, with its multitude of terraced bars, while close by, rue de l'Amour and rue Jean-Roger are lined with tacky souvenir shops. If you're looking to escape the crowds, head to the shady nineteenth-century gardens of **Château Laurens**, set on Belle-Isle, a twelve-hectare park bordered by the Hérault and the Canal du Midi, just across the bridge from the old town.

Cathédrale St-Étienne

Quai du Chapitre • March–Oct guided tour Fri 3pm • Free

Set along the now canalized river, the town is dominated by the twelfth-century fortified **Cathédrale St-Étienne** on its south bank, whose appearance is more castle than church, its 3m-thick walls and hot-oil sluices having formed the strongpoint of the town's defences; you can climb the **bell tower** to get striking views of the town and coastal plain.

Musée Agathois

5 rue de la Fraternité • Tues–Sat 9am–noon & 1.30–5.30pm • €5 • ☏ 04 67 94 82 51

A Renaissance mansion houses the **Musée Agathois**. It's one of the better of the region's "local" museums, renovated in 2012, with 27 rooms of exhibitions on life in the area from its origins to the twentieth century. Highlights include traditional costumes, the Asian room with Japanese armour, and Art Nouveau furniture from Château Laurens.

Cap d'Agde

Some 5km south from Agde, **CAP D'AGDE** is a sprawling modern resort, its one concession to visual charm coming from the abundance of colourful plants and flowers which line its broad streets. But the Cap has everything you would want for a holiday, with an abundance of nightclubs, watersports and restaurants. The best **beaches**, sheltered from the often-overwhelming Mediterranean winds, are on the west side of the cape stretching over towards La Guirandette.

Musée de l'Éphèbe

Mas de la Clape • July & Aug daily 10am–6pm; Sept–June Mon–Fri 10am–noon & 2–6pm, Sat & Sun 9am–noon & 2–5pm • €5 • ☏ 04 67 94 69 60, ⊠ museecapdagde.com

The **Musée de l'Éphèbe**, in the central Parc de la Clape, holds an impressive collection of Greek and Roman relics retrieved from the local seabed. Highlights include the Hellenistic bronze statuette known as the *Éphèbe d'Agde*, formerly housed in the Louvre.

6

CAP D'AGDE'S NAKED CITY

Founded in 1958 by a caravan-load of German naturists looking for a quiet place to strip off, Cap d'Agde's **quartier naturiste** has a population which swells to forty thousand in summer. The *quartier* took shape over the Sixties and Seventies and has now become a small town in its own right, with supermarkets, restaurants, cafés, bars, discos, a hotel and a campsite with more than 2500 places, all catering to a naturist clientele. Nudity is permitted – although not absolutely required – at all times anywhere within the confines of the resort.

Until about the early 1990s most of the people who came to Cap d'Agde's *quartier naturiste* did so simply because they enjoyed spending their time naked. Gradually, however, another type of naturist, described by French commentators as "*à poilistes*", began to arrive. For these people **nudity and sex** were inextricably linked, and soon the beach became unofficially segregated into various sections: for families, for sexually liberated heterosexuals and for gays. Now there are more boutiques selling X-rated clothing in the *quartier naturiste* than in most large cities, and some of the raunchiest and most famous **swingers' clubs** in Europe are located here.

The nudist **season** in Cap d'Agde runs all year long. One-day access is €18 with a car or €8 for pedestrians and cyclists. No tickets are sold after 8pm. For more **information**, contact the Bureau d'Accueil (☎04 67 26 00 26).

Grau d'Agde

Nearby **GRAU D'AGDE** is the beach-town antithesis of the Cap: a dispersed settlement of weathered houses and ageing bungalows, this dissipating suburb distils into an old fishing town as you reach the lighthouse-capped wavebreak. The main sight here is the **Belvédère de la Criée** (quai du Commandant Méric; April–Oct Mon–Fri 9am–noon & 2.30–6pm; €4–5; ☎06 16 07 09 62, ⓦlebelvedere-agde.com) where you can learn all about the fish market; there are also guided tours most days. To the west, across the river (there's a shuttle boat: April to mid-Nov 9am–midnight; €1.50), is the lovely, pine-fringed **Tamarissière beach**, which is a popular spot for kitesurfing.

ARRIVAL AND DEPARTURE
AGDE AND AROUND

By plane Béziers Cap d'Agde Airport (☎04 67 80 99 09, ⓦbeziers.aeroport.fr) is 13km northwest of the town. Shuttle buses leave 30min after the flights arrive and cost €1.60. Many taxis serve the airport (see website for details) and a one-way journey costs around €25.

By train The *gare SNCF* is on rue de la Digue and you'll need to head south across the Hérault river to reach the town. Most of the buses from the station go into Agde Town but you'll need #3 or #4 (the latter also serves the naturist

village) for Cap d'Agde and #2 for Grau d'Agde. TGV stations are indicated with an asterisk.

Destinations Béziers* (hourly; 16min); Nîmes*, via Marseillan-Plage, Sète* and Montpellier* (several hourly; 1hr 10min); Paris* (many daily; 4hr); Perpignan*, via Narbonne* and Salses (many daily; 1hr 20min); Toulouse*, via Narbonne*, Carcassonne* and Castelnaudary* (hourly; 2hr).

By bus The *gare routière* is in front of the train station.
Destinations Marseillan (several daily; 10min).

GETTING AROUND

By bus A shuttle links the towns and the beaches in summer.

By bike You can rent bikes at Cap Aventure, 19 av des Sergents ☎04 67 26 36 00. There are 34km of cycle paths.

By boat Le Millésime, 11 quai du Commandant Méric (☎04 67 01 71 93, ⓦagde-croisiere-peche.com) offers educational boat tours, fishing trips and *sardinades* or barbecues on the nearby island of Fort Brescou.

INFORMATION

Agde There's a tourist office at place de la Belle Agathois (April & May daily 9am–12.30pm & 2–6pm; June Mon–Fri 9am–12.30pm & 2.30–6.30pm, Sat 9am–7pm, Sun 10am–1pm & 2.30–6.30pm; July–Sept Mon–Sat 9am–7pm, Sun 10am–1pm & 2.30–6.30pm; Oct–March Mon–Fri 9am–noon & 2–6pm, Sat 10am–noon & 2–5pm,

Sun 10am–noon & 2–6pm; ☎04 67 31 87 50).

Cap d'Agde The main tourist office for the area is at Rond Point du Bon Accueil, a 5min walk from the port (April, May & Sept daily 9am–12.30pm & 2–7pm; June daily 9am–7pm; July & Aug daily 9am–8pm; Oct, Nov, Feb & March Mon–Fri 9am–noon & 2–6pm, Sat & Sun

10am–noon & 2–5pm; Dec & Jan closed Sun; ☎04 67 01 04 04, ⓦcapdagde.com). There is also an information point at the port (April–June & Sept daily 10am–12.30pm & 2–6.30pm; July & Aug 10am–9pm).

Grau d'Agde There is an information point on quai Antoine Fonquerle in Grau d'Agde (June–Sept daily 8.30am–noon & 1.30–5pm; ☎04 67 94 33 41).

ACCOMMODATION

Bellevue 12 impasse des Gabelous, Cap d'Adge ☎04 67 26 39 10, ⓦhotel-lebellevue.fr. The seventeen rooms are nice enough in this two-star hotel, but the main reason to stay here is for the wonderful sea views. Good value for money in these parts. Open March–Nov. **€90**

★Capaô 1 rue des Corsaires, Cap d'Agde ☎04 67 26 99 44, ⓦcapao.com. Very comfortable three-star hotel with direct access to the beach, where they have a private area

with sun loungers, a restaurant and bar. Most of the rooms have a sea view and they also have a spa and offer yoga classes. An excellent choice. **€115**

Rosa 62 chemin de Janin, Agde ☎04 67 35 22 10, ⓦchambresrosa.com. Charming B&B in the old town with three rooms decorated in bright, contemporary style. There are sunbeds and a hot tub in the garden and a tapas and wine bar within staggering distance. **€80**

EATING AND DRINKING

Le Bistrologue 5 rue Louis Dejean, Cap d'Agde ☎06 22 98 21 48. Excellent open-air tapas bar away from the port with a good selection of local wines and Belgian beers. Dishes from €4. April–Sept daily 11am–2.30pm & 6–10.30pm.

L'Écailler Place du Barbecue, Cap d'Agde ☎04 67 26 55 42. At the port, this outdoor restaurant is the place to go for seafood; expect to pay around €16. Popular with locals and a buzzy atmosphere.

April–Oct daily 10am–2.30pm & 5.30–9pm.

La Table de Stéphane 2 rue des Moulins à l'Huile, Agde ☎04 67 26 45 22, ⓦlatabledestephane.com. Good-value *gastronomique* restaurant serving inventive French cuisine such as veal kidneys in raspberry vinegar and a special lobster *menu* with summer truffles (€70). Two-course lunch from €18. Tues–Fri noon–2.30pm & 7–9.30pm, Sat 7–9.30pm, Sun noon–2.30pm.

The Orb valley

The **River Orb** winds a twisting path down from its source in the hills of Haut Languedoc north of Béziers, descending some 120km through the highlands and across the broad coastal plain to skirt the city before emptying into the Golfe du Lion. Heading up its valley from Béziers provides rapid access from the coast to the lesser-travelled uplands of Haut Languedoc. Just after **Roquebrun**, a centre both for viticulture and rafting, the valley delves into the rugged uplands, wheeling off to the east to pass **Hérépian** and the old spa town of **Lamalou-les-Bains** – both good bases for walks into the **Parc Naturel Régional du Haut Languedoc**. From here the valley follows the park's edge round until the land opens up into a compact but fertile plane around **Bédarieux** – another possible departure point for exploring the highlands. Heading further north into the **upper valley** you eventually reach a series of tiny hamlets high up at the river's origins. The **Passa Païs** walking and cycling trail (see p.156) from Mazamet passes through Lamalou and Hérépian and ends in Bédarieux.

Roquebrun and around

Clumped on a hillside beneath the ruins of its medieval tower, **ROQUEBRUN** is located in an exceptionally mild microclimate, making the valley floor an ideal place for vine cultivation – you can sample the local award-winning vintages (AOP Saint-Chinian) at the various *domaines* scattered around the valley. The good weather also provides a suitable climate for the town's **Jardin Méditerranéen** (rue de la Tour; mid-Feb to June & Sept to mid-Nov 9am–noon & 1.30–5.30pm; July & Aug 9am–7pm; €5.50; ☎04 67 89 55 29), a collection of exotic, primarily arid-climate plants from around the world; in winter the valley around the town bursts into colour with the blooming of mimosas. There's a general **market** on Friday mornings.

6

INFORMATION AND ACTIVITIES

Tourist information Av des Orangers (daily 9am–1pm & 3.30–7pm; closed Mon in winter; ☎ 04 67 23 02 21, ⓦ ot-caroux.fr).

Kayaking Canoe-Roquebrun, chemin de la Roque (☎ 04 67 89 52 90, ⓦ canoeroquebrun.com) offers kayak rental from €23 for ninety minutes.

ACCOMMODATION

Camping Le Nice Rte du Temps Libre ☎ 04 67 89 61 99, ⓦ camping-lenice.com. Small campsite next to the river. As well as 25 pitches there are chalets and *gîtes*. Activities include tennis, *boules* and kids' games. Nice views. **€13**

Les Mimosas 12 av des Orangers ☎ 04 67 89 61 36,

ⓦ lesmimosas.net. Lovely B&B in a nineteenth-century *maison de maître* ("gentleman's residence"). The five spacious rooms are tastefully decorated (it's also possible to rent a studio for two and an apartment for four) and breakfast is served on the terrace in summer. **€75**

Lamalou-les-Bains

LAMALOU-LES-BAINS came into fashion in the late nineteenth and early twentieth century, with notables such as Alphonse Daudet and André Gide coming to enjoy its curative waters. It's still a popular therapeutic spot today, and the constant parade of ailing people moving among its faded *fin-de-siècle* mansions gives it the air of a large outdoor hospital. The beautiful parish church, **St-Pierre-de-Rhèdes**, displays a pastiche of stylistic touches overlaying its basic Romanesque form, resulting from immigrants to the region, including Mozarabs from Spain, who left Christian inscriptions written in Arabic.

INFORMATION

Tourist information 1 av Capus (mid-June to mid-Sept Mon–Fri 9am–noon & 1.30–6.30pm, Sat 9am–noon & 2–5pm, Sun 9am–1pm; mid-Sept to mid-June Mon–Fri

9am–noon & 2–5/6pm, Sat 9am–noon; ☎ 04 67 95 70 91, ⓦ www.ot-lamaloulesbains.fr). The tourist office can advise on walking routes in the area.

ACCOMMODATION AND EATING

L'Arbousier 18 av Alphonse Daudet ☎ 04 67 95 63 11, ⓦ arbousierhotel.com. Housed in a Belle Époque building, this three-star *Logis de France* has comfortable, contemporary rooms. The restaurant serves traditional French dishes (two-course lunch €15). Spa packages available. **€75**

La Chemin'hôte av de la Gare ☎ 04 67 97 39 08, ⓦ lacheminhote.com. Quirky B&B in the town's old train station, complete with original features. There are just two rooms and a *gîte*. Guests can benefit from a fifteen percent discount on treatments at the spa. **€70**

Hérépian

HÉRÉPIAN is a pleasant workaday town with a less clinical air than its neighbour Lamalou. It's home to one of the country's last functioning bell foundries, the **Bruneau-Garnier foundry** (May–Oct Tues–Sun 2–7pm; ☎ 04 67 95 39 95), which has been owned by the same family since 1600 and has a small museum. From here you can hike up to the twelfth-century **chapel of St Michel** above the village of Les Aires, which is best known for its spring water. There are great views from the orientation panel.

ACCOMMODATION

Des Lits sur Place 12 pl de la Croix ☎ 06 41 61 43 44, ⓦ deslitssurplace.fr. Very nice B&B in a nineteenth-century

coaching inn with five traditionally furnished – but dimly lit – rooms. Local products for breakfast. **€67**

Bédarieux

BÉDARIEUX, the biggest place north of Béziers on the course of the Orb, is a busy administrative and transport hub. The town's one tourist attraction is the mediocre **Maison des Arts** (19 av Abbé Tarroux; Tues 2–6pm, Wed & Fri 9.30am–noon & 2–6pm, Thurs 9.30am–noon, Sat 10am–12.30pm & 2–6pm; €3; ☎ 04 67 95 48 27), which looks at local life in the nineteenth century including the famous writers who visited the area. The town's **market** is on Monday mornings. Otherwise, the tourist office can set you up with detailed information on **walks** in the local countryside. One of the better short ones is the trail, through vines and bulrushes, to the twelfth-century pre-Romanesque **chapel** of St-Raphaël, on the far bank of the river, while a more challenging option is the ascent of the Pic de Tanajo (518m) to the southwest.

ARRIVAL AND INFORMATION
BÉDARIEUX

By train Bédarieux's *gare SNCF* is on rte de St-Pons in the north of the town.

Destinations Béziers (several daily; 35 min).

By bus Buses stop at the *gare routière* on rte de Clermont.

Destinations Béziers (daily; 1hr 20min); Clermont-l'Hérault (several daily; 50min); Hérépian (several daily; 10min); Joncels (several daily; 45min); Lamalou-les-Bains

(daily; 15min); Montpellier (several daily; 1hr 30min); St-Pons (daily; 1hr 20min); Salasc (several daily; 25min); Villeneuvette (several daily; 35min).

Tourist information 1 rue de la République (Mon–Fri 9am–noon & 2–6pm, Sat 9am–noon; ☎ 04 67 95 08 79, ⓦ bedarieux.fr).

GETTING AROUND

By car You can hire cars at Carrefour, rte de St-Pons (☎ 04 67 95 00 18).

By bike Hire bikes at Cycles Horizon, 13 av Abbé-Tarroux (☎ 04 67 95 24 25).

ACCOMMODATION AND EATING

De l'Orb Parc de Pharos, rte de St-Pons ☎ 04 67 23 35 90, ⓦ hotel-orb.com. Modern two-star hotel with an old-fashioned atmosphere and bright rooms sleeping up to four. It's near the train station and ideal for a short stay. €53

La Forge 22 av Abbé Tarroux ☎ 04 67 95 13 13,

ⓦ restaurantlaforgebedarieux.fr. Good *terroir* restaurant in an old forge with a lovely vaulted ceiling and outdoor terrace. *Menus* €18–37. They also have an apartment for rent. Tues–Sun noon–2pm & 7–9pm, closed Wed and Sun eves in winter.

The upper Orb valley

Moving north, the **valley** continues to rise, with the river petering out to little more than a brook near its sources in the Monts d'Orb. This is one of Europe's biggest **cherry-growing** areas, dotted with tranquil villages. A fun way to explore is in the company of a donkey with **Balladanes** (Mas de Riols, La Tour-sur-Orb; ☎ 04 67 23 10 53, ⓦ balladanes.fr).

Boussagues

BOUSSAGUES is an extremely well preserved, walled town, replete with church, fountain and *donjon*, which is surprisingly off the tourist radar; the only service you'll find here is a (frequently closed) café. The ruins of its castle, on the hill above, are little more than foundations overgrown by vine and bramble, but the views they provide are great. **Hikers** on the GR7 will pass by Boussagues as they make their way between Lamalou and Lodève.

Joncels

The evocative mountain hamlet of **JONCELS** grew up around the seventh-century Benedictine **monastery of St-Pierre**, and became an important stop on the Chemin de St-Jacques pilgrim route (see p.189). In the thirteenth century the town was fortified, with further amendments made in the eighteenth century. The monks still live here today (forbidden by papal order from leaving the confines of the abbey) and still provide rest for passing pilgrims.

INFORMATION AND ACCOMMODATION
JONCELS

Tourist information July & Aug ☎ 04 67 23 80 60, ⓦ avene-orb-gravezon.com.

Villa Issiates ☎ 04 67 23 87 32, ⓦ villa.issiates.free.fr.

Rambling, arty B&B with plenty of character and a pretty garden with a pool. Rooms have jacuzzis and there are occasional weekend music concerts. €80

Roussillon

TRAIN JAUNE

Roussillon

Roussillon, bordered by the Mediterranean to the east, the hills of the Corbières along the north, and the upper Aude and Ariège valleys to the west, is France's southernmost region, sometimes known as French Catalonia; the peaks of the eastern section of the Pyrenees, which it shares with Spain, mark its southern limit. Although absorbed by France some three and a half centuries ago, and now known officially as the *département* of Pyrénées-Orientales, it hasn't entirely lost its Catalan flavour: in the mountains there are many people whose language of choice is Catalan, and even in the larger towns you'll find the survival of customs such as the *sardana* dance and unique Paschal rituals. You'll also notice the influence of traditional Catalan ingredients and recipes in the region's *terroir* cuisine. But despite these particularities, and recent efforts by Catalan speakers to broaden the currency of the language, Roussillon is fundamentally French in cultural orientation.

Roussillon is marked by the variety and contrasts of its landscape. North of its attractive main city, **Perpignan**, a marshy coastline hems in the **Fenouillèdes** hills – home to the easternmost Cathar castles and the world-famous Tautavel prehistoric site. Southwest of the capital you can follow the course of the River Têt (or Conflent), up the valley to **Canigó**, the peak which symbolizes all of Catalonia. In the south and west of the *département* lie the mountains, which offer excellent hiking and skiing. The **Tech valley** runs vaguely parallel to the Têt, leading up from the plains and along the Spanish border; its villages are some of the most traditionally Catalan in the region. Finally, the rugged **Côte Vermeille** is ideal for swimming and relaxing.

GETTING AROUND   ROUSSILLON

The main transport routes run along the coast and up the major valleys. Travelling between the valleys is more problematic, and unless you have your own transport you'll have to resort to hiking or hitching. The main road and rail links to Spain head south from Perpignan, the latter passing through the towns of the Côte Vermeille.

By train The main railway line runs along the coast via Perpignan. SNCF buses may run in lieu of trains on these lines; services are reduced on Sundays and holidays. The *Train Jaune* (see p.295) also runs a service up the Têt valley to Latour-de-Carol/Enveitg (linking with the Ariège valley rail line to Toulouse), and the *Train du Pays Cathare et du*

Fenouillèdes (see p.286) serves the Fenouillèdes to Axat. **By bus** Bus fares across the *département* have been set at €1. Many lines have no or reduced service on Saturdays, Sundays and holidays, and in summer months. Main bus lines follow the coast or run up the Fenouillèdes, Tech and Conflent valleys. See ⑫ bus1euro.cd66.fr for a route map and full schedules.

COLLIOURE

Highlights

❶ Le Canigó The Catalans' sacred mountain, now a Grand Site de France, towers above Roussillon; join the midsummer firelight pilgrimage. **See p.292**

❷ Train Jaune A revived narrow-gauge line takes you up through stunning mountain terrain to a string of villages that make perfect hiking bases. **See p.295**

❸ Vauban fortifications France's finest military architect left his mark on several sights

in the area, notably Villefranche-de-Conflent. **See p.297**

❹ La Fête de l'Ours This ancient winter festival in the Tech valley is hoping to make it onto UNESCO's list of Intangible Cultural Heritage. **See box, p.299**

❺ Collioure At the region's most beautiful coastal town you can soak up the atmosphere that inspired the town's Fauvist artists. **See p.304**

HIGHLIGHTS ARE MARKED ON THE MAP ON P.274

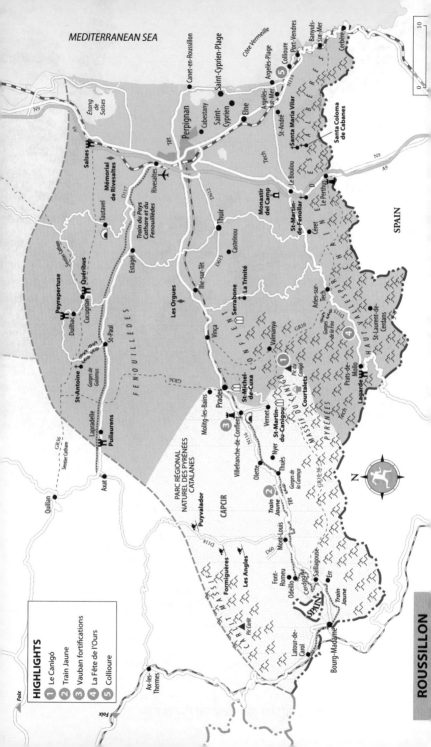

ROUSSILLON

MEDITERRANEAN SEA

HIGHLIGHTS
1 Le Canigó
2 Train Jaune
3 Vauban fortifications
4 La Fête de l'Ours
5 Collioure

ROUSSILLON'S FESTIVALS AND TRADITIONS

The Roussillonais seem to have inherited a penchant for **festivals** from their Spanish cousins south of the Pyrenees, as just about every village has at least one cheerfully energetic celebration – usually the local saint's day, or *festa major* (*fête majeure*, in French). It is in these that the region's Catalan and Spanish character comes to the fore, with *sardanas* (traditional Catalan dancing), *corridas* and processions.

First weekend in Feb Arles-sur-Tech, Prats-de-Mollo and St-Laurent-de-Cerdans: *Fête de l'Ours*. This ancient festival, rooted in prehistoric shamanistic ceremonies and hunting traditions, marks the time when bears come out of hibernation (see p.299).

April Perpignan: *Sant Jordi*. Festival of Catalonia's patron saint, St George. Men present their sweethearts with a red rose, and women reciprocate with a book.

June 23 Têt valley: *Nit de Sant-Joan*. On the eve of St John's Day people come from all over Catalonia for the torchlight pilgrimage from the Castillet in Perpignan to the peak of Le Canigó – one of the symbols of the Catalan nation.

End June Arles-sur-Tech: *Fête de St-Éloi*. This three-day festival culminates in the blessing of the mules – traditionally indispensable as transport here.

End July Céret: *Festival International de la Sardane*. Hundreds of dancers descend upon the town to dance this traditional Catalan dance in the arena.

July 30 Arles-sur-Tech: *Festa Major*. Typically boisterous Catalan festival, featuring processions and loaded with medieval traditions.

End July to mid-Aug Prades: *Festival Pablo Casals* ☎ 04 68 96 33 07, ⓦ prades-festival -casals.com. A world-famous classical music festival.

Sept Perpignan: *Trobades Médiévales*. The old town centre is transformed into a medieval open-air market replete with costumed vendors, jugglers and street entertainers.

First two weeks Sept Perpignan: *Visa pour l'Image* ⓦ visapourlimage.com. International festival of photojournalism.

Perpignan and around

PERPIGNAN (or Perpinyà, in Catalan), situated in the centre of the Roussillon plain, is the most multicultural city in the Southwest. A substantial portion of its population is descended from Spanish Catalans who poured across the border in the final days of the Spanish Civil War, desperate to avoid reprisals at the hands of Franco's Castilian and Moroccan troops. There's also a sizeable Romany contingent, while some of the suburbs were settled by French colonists who fled the upheavals associated with the Maghrebi independence movements of the 1950s and 1960s. A less touristy zone in the centre is home to some of the more impoverished Romany and Arab communities but has also been the recent subject of **redevelopment** efforts, including the reconstruction of the Law Faculty of the University of Perpignan.

The melting-pot atmosphere of the city is accentuated by the many **festivals** that Perpignan shares with Catalonia, just across the border, including the festival of St-Jean and St-Jordi and the many other folk and musical traditions that can be seen on feast days. Perpignan's **multiculturalism** has, on occasion, been a source of tension but this is the exception rather than the norm despite the recent shifting political climate in Europe. The city is currently in a great phase of renewal and projects such as Jean Nouvel's **Théâtre de l'Archipel**, the new TGV station and its Centre del Mon shopping mall, and the renovation of **Musée Rigaud**, have improved the city's attractiveness. In addition, Perpignan is the principal **transport hub** of the region and serves as a handy base for exploring both inland and the many Blue Flag **beaches** of the Côte Vermeille.

Brief history

Perpignan has had a quiet history. Too far from the sea to serve as a port itself, it was a sizeable if unremarkable town until the thirteenth century, when it began to boom as a **cloth-making** centre. Jaume II of Mallorca and Roussillon enhanced this prosperity in 1276, when he made the town his alternative mainland capital (Montpellier being the other, and Palma de Mallorca the king's principal residence). When that kingdom evaporated in 1349, however, the city was absorbed by the Catalan-Aragonese crown, whose own main capital was nearby **Barcelona**, bringing an end to Perpignan's elevated status. In the centuries that followed it was the object of repeated campaigns of conquest by France, finally becoming French territory in 1659 with the Treaty of the Pyrenees.

Place Arago and around

The heart of the city is café-lined **place Arago**, on the flower-decked bank of the canalized Basse river; it's where you'll find the tourist office. South of this is a tiny thirteenth-century *faubourg*, whose quiet grid of streets contains well-restored houses and **Notre-Dame-des-Anges** (32 rue Maréchal Foch; Tues–Sat 9am–12.30pm & 1.15–5pm; free), the chapterhouse of a Franciscan monastery built by the Kings of Majorca and featuring a tympanum attributed to the Master of Cabestany; it is now the **Maison du Patrimoine Catalan** (Catalan heritage centre).

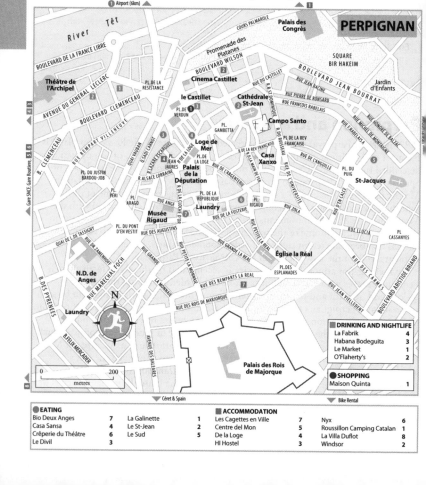

DRINKING AND NIGHTLIFE
La Fabrik	4
Habana Bodeguita	3
Le Market	1
O'Flaherty's	2

SHOPPING
Maison Quinta	1

EATING
Bio Deux Anges	7	La Galinette	1	
Casa Sansa	4	Le St-Jean	2	
Crêperie du Théâtre	6	Le Sud	5	
Le Divil	3			

ACCOMMODATION
Les Cagettes en Ville	7	Nyx	6
Centre del Mon	5	Roussillon Camping Catalan	1
De la Loge	4	La Villa Duflot	8
HI Hostel	3	Windsor	2

PERPIGNAN ORIENTATION

Perpignan's medieval walls, though spared by Richelieu, were demolished early last century to allow for expansion, and replaced by wide boulevards. This, in fact, maintained the separation of the city's older districts from the new, and it's still easy and enjoyable to get around the compact **old town** on foot. Most of the city's sights are concentrated in the dense clutch of pedestrian streets northeast of riverside **place Arago**, and stretching towards the geographical centre of the old town, while between **place de la Loge** and **place Rigaud**, just to the southeast, you could be on the Left Bank in Paris, the old streets now a maze of chic boutiques. On the north side of the pedestrian area you'll find the **cathedral**, from where you can follow the course of the old walls through the **Romany and Maghrebi quarter** to the church of St-Jacques, marking the eastern limit of old Perpignan. To the south of this the land rises towards the massive **Palais des Rois de Majorque**, crowning the hill that dominated the southern quarter of the medieval town. In the **new town**, to the west of the Basse river, you won't find many sights, but the avenues leading west towards the train station make for excellent hotel- and restaurant-hunting.

Musée Rigaud

16 rue de l'Ange • Closed for renovation until 2017

The **Musée Rigaud** is housed in a seventeenth-century palace, originally the workshop of local artist Hyacinthe Rigaud, a favourite of Louis XIV, and it later served as studio and living space for Picasso, Dufy and Cocteau. Since 2014, the museum has been undergoing a €10 million **renovation** to triple its size by integrating the Hôtel de Mailly next door. When it reopens, there will be three collections: Catalan Gothic; Baroque, with paintings from the court of Versailles; and Modern Art, including works by Picasso, Dufy and Maillol. Visitors will also be able to access a "hanging garden" and the studio where Picasso lived and worked. Outside, rue de l'Ange has some lovely boutiques and **artisan food** and coffee shops.

Place de la Loge and around

The **place de la Loge** was the centre of activity in fourteenth-century Perpignan: on its southeastern side, you'll find three of the city's most important administrative buildings. The first of these is the fifteenth-century Gothic-style **Palais de la Députation**, where the Catalan count-kings once convened the Roussillon parliament, while next door, the sixteenth-century **Hôtel de Ville** (Mon–Thurs 8am–6pm, Fri 8am–5pm) is worth a peek for the Aristide Maillol bronze, *La Méditerranée*, which sits in the courtyard (there is also a copy on the artist's tomb in Banyuls-sur-Mer). The last of the three great buildings is Roussillon's famous **Loge de Mer**.

The square long served as the scene of grisly executions, notably of the rebels housed in Le Castillet (see p.278), while during World War II, the *place*'s busy pavement cafés were the place to find *passeurs*, the men and women who guided refugees across the Pyrenees into Spain.

Loge de Mer

Place de la Loge • Mon–Fri 8am–6pm, Sat & Sun 9am–5.30pm • Free

The **Loge de Mer** was built in 1397 and served as the region's stock exchange – the meeting place and court for its merchants. High on the south wall is a blazon bearing three arms, which stand for the three classes of city folk who ran the town council: merchants and drapers; doctors and notaries; and artisans and gardeners. The building remains a marvel, with a gracefully vaulted interior and **gargoyles** adorning the upper parts of its facade – a fine and rare example of Gothic civic architecture whose ground floor is now home to a restaurant.

Le Castillet and around

Place de Verdun • June–Sept daily 10.30am–6.30pm; Oct–May Tues–Sun 11am–5.30pm • €2, free first Sun of the month

A series of ancient lanes run off towards the river from place de la Loge, including tiny **rue Fabriques d'en Nabot**, where you'll come across a number of notable thirteenth- and fourteenth-century houses, with magnificent doorways and ogival windows. Following any of these streets, or taking the wider rue Louis-Blanc at the north end of place de la Loge, will lead you to Perpignan's distinctive red-brick **Le Castillet**, the lone surviving tower of the old town walls. Also known as the Casa Païral ("The House of the Ancestors"), it now houses a **museum** celebrating Roussillonais rural culture and in particular commemorating the anti-French rebellions of 1661–74, when the tower held captured Catalan insurgents. If you can face walking the 142 steps to the top, you will be rewarded with great views. The **place de Verdun**, on the south side of Le Castillet, is the setting for summer evening performances of the *sardana*: the simple, repetitive Catalan folk dance. Nearby, at 1 boulevard Wilson, is the battered but splendidly Art Nouveau **Cinéma Castillet**, now converted into a seven-screen arthouse complex (see p.282).

Cathédrale St-Jean and around

Place Gambetta • Daily June–Sept 8am–7pm, Oct–May 8am–6pm • Free

Two hundred metres east of Le Castillet, but most easily accessed from the north end of place de la Loge, lies another ancient square, **place Gambetta**, scene of the town's open-air **market** since the Middle Ages. At its eastern end towers the **Cathédrale St-Jean**, commissioned in 1324 and elevated to cathedral status in 1602 when the diocese of Elne was transferred to Perpignan. Next door, its predecessor, the impressive Romanesque **St-Jean le Vieux** (currently closed for renovation), is linked to the cathedral by mammoth buttresses. The cathedral's striking exterior sports bands of rounded river stones sandwiched by brick, while inside there's a majestically columned nave, whose side chapels, though badly damaged, retain some elaborate sixteenth- and seventeenth-century retables. Leaving through the south transept, poke your head in the **chapel** on the left, which is presided over by an excellent fourteenth-century polychrome Crucifixion, known as the *Dévot Christ*, and most likely the work of a Rhineland sculptor.

Campo Santo

Rue Amiral Ribeil • June–Sept daily 10.30am–6.30pm; Oct–May Tues–Sun 11am–5.30pm • Free

Past the chapel, on the left, is the entrance to the **Campo Santo**, one of France's oldest cemeteries, going back some six hundred years. This cloister-cemetery is unique in

---

THE KINGS OF MAJORCA

The history of Perpignan is more or less synonymous with that of the palace, originally built in the late thirteenth century as a residence for **Jaume II of Mallorca**, son of Jaume I ("The Conqueror"), Count of Barcelona and King of Aragón and Valencia, who captured Mallorca from the Muslims. At his death "The Conqueror" divided his kingdom between his two sons: to the elder, Pere II, went the titles of King of Aragón and Valencia and Count of Barcelona, but only a portion of the actual kingdom; the remainder, including Roussillon and Mallorca, went to the younger Jaume. The two branches of the family were immediately at each other's throats, and stayed that way until Roussillon was **reunited** with Aragón and Catalonia in the early fourteenth century by the powerful Pere III. Having passed to the French, then back to the Catalans, Perpignan changed hands for the last time in 1642, a couple of years after France had occupied Roussillon in the wake of the Catalans' revolt against the Habsburg rulers of Madrid; in September, after a **siege** that was at times commanded personally by Louis XIII and Richelieu, Perpignan fell. Vauban, military engineer to Louis XIV, constructed the imposing outer walls in the fit of over-enthusiastic fortification that followed consolidation of French sovereignty accorded by the 1659 Treaty of the Pyrenees.

THE CATALAN CHRISTMAS CAGATIÓ

Among the many Catalan folkloric customs that have survived centuries of French domination are two rather strange practices associated with **Christmas**. Like the Provençals, the Roussillonais are known for their elaborate **Nativity** scenes (*pessebres*), populated by hordes of figurines. However, if you look carefully at the Catalan version, among the various shepherds, angel choirs and wise men you'll note a small figure, usually dressed in peasant garb and sporting a traditional Catalan red cap. This is the **caganer**, a crouching man, poised with pants around his ankles, in some stage of the act of defecation. Similarly, although Catalan children customarily receive presents on the Epiphany (Jan 6), the **cagatió** (literally, the "shitting log") ensures that they don't go completely empty-handed at Christmas. It consists of a log with a painted-on face, draped with a red cloth at its posterior end. As children gather round the *cagatió*, beating it with sticks and singing a song invoking bowel movement, the blanket is withdrawn to the delight of all, revealing the sweets it has apparently excreted. You can purchase your own *caganers* (which now come in various forms, including policemen, referees and political figures) and *cagatiós* at Perpignan's Christmas market, held in front of the cathedral during the four weeks of Advent.

7

France and was used up until the Revolution. The grand families were buried in the alcoves – you can still see their coats of arms – and there was a general burial "pit" in the middle for your regular parishioner. It is now used for concerts and the "Visa pour l'Image" photojournalism festival (see box, p.275).

Casa Xanxo
8 rue de la Main de Fer • June–Sept daily 10.30am–6.30pm; Oct–May Tues–Sun 11am–5.30pm • Free • ☎ 04 68 62 37 98

On the other side of Campo Santo, **Casa Xanxo** is a luxurious residence constructed by the local merchant Bernat Xanxo in the sixteenth century and renovated in the seventeenth century; it now houses a replica of Perpignan in 1686 (the original is at Les Invalides in Paris) and hosts temporary exhibitions. Close by, the lively **rue de la Révolution Française**, populated by arty cafés and hip bars, runs east to the *place* of the same name.

Place du Puig and around

East of place de la Révolution Française you can ascend into a substantially more rundown area which runs south as far as the great palace, and east to place Cassanyes, at the former limits of the city walls. Several urban renewal projects are at work and the area is slowly improving. Centred around **place du Puig** (pronounced "pooch"), this district is almost exclusively inhabited by a Romany community. **Place Fontaine-Neuve** dates back some seven hundred years to the time when the "new well" after which it is named was dug here.

Église St-Jacques
Rue de l'Église St-Jacques • Tues–Sun 9–11am • Free

Northeast of place Fontaine-Neuve and just east of place du Puig is the fourteenth-century **Église St-Jacques**, the nucleus of Perpignan's oldest parish, originally founded by Jaume I in honour of his patron saint (Jacques being French for Jaume) a hundred years earlier. The king was also a donor to the confraternity of Sanch – a parish-based social organization typical of the Middle Ages, dedicated to the Holy Blood of Christ ("sanch" means "blood" in old Catalan). On Maundy Thursday each year they hold a Spanish-style procession of penitents, who walk from the church through the town hooded (so as not to take pride in their piety) and barefooted, carrying heavy candles or crosses.

Palais des Rois de Majorque

Rue des Archers • Daily: June–Sept 10am–6pm; Oct–May 9am–5pm • €4 • ☎ 04 68 34 48 29

Perpignan's most famous sight (but arguably not the most interesting), and the kernel around which the city grew, is the massive **Palais des Rois de Majorque** on the southern fringe of the old city. After ascending an impressive zigzagging ramp, large enough for several cavalry to ride abreast, you enter a grassy park, with the square thirteenth-century **castle** ahead of you, standing incongruously with its curious stone-and-mortar construction. Passing into the splendid two-storey **courtyard**, whose upper level opens into graceful Gothic galleries on the east and west sides, you ascend the stairs to the former kings' apartments, which now host temporary exhibitions. Across from these you'll find the unsullied but sparsely furnished queens' apartments, which have delicately vaulted period ceilings and windows. Between the two sets of royal apartments are the so-called king's and queen's **chapels**, one on the upper floor and one on the lower, and both with interesting details in Gothic style, from carved corbels to fading frescoes. It's useful to pick up a free plan of the castle in the ticket office before you start exploring.

7

Église la Réal

Rue Grande la Réal • Daily 11am–6pm • Free

Just below the fortress is the **Église la Réal**. Restored in 2012, this fourteenth-century foundation was the parish church of the castle, and contains contemporary frescoes, fifteenth-century wooden polychrome sculpture and a fine, carved baptismal font.

ARRIVAL AND DEPARTURE

PERPIGNAN

By plane Perpignan's small airport, Perpignan-Rivesaltes (☎ 04 68 52 60 70, ⓦ aeroport-perpignan.com) lies 7km north of town. An airport *navette* #7 (shuttle service) makes the 20min trip (€1.20) into the centre about every 30min from 7.10am–22.10pm, stopping at place de Catalogne, a 10min walk west of the train and bus stations at the end of avenue Général-de-Gaulle. A taxi into the centre will cost around €22–28.

By train Perpignan's new *gare SNCF*, at the west end of av Général-de-Gaulle, was once dubbed "the centre of the world" by Salvador Dalí, and is now attached to a shopping mall called "Centre del Mon". Thanks to the youths hanging around and sometimes begging for money, this isn't one of the most comfortable of places to pass through. To get into the heart of the city from here is a 20min walk – or you can take the free "P'tit Bus 1" to "Castillet".

Destinations Barcelona, via Girona (hourly; 1hr 20min); Cerbère, via Elne, Argelès, Collioure and Banyuls-sur-Mer (hourly; 35min); Latour-de-Carol, via Ille-sur-Têt, Prades and Villefranche-de-Conflent/Vernet (several daily; 4–6hr); Nîmes*, via Rivesaltes, Salses, Narbonne*, Béziers* (connections to Bédarieux), Agde*, Sète* and Montpellier* (several hourly; 2hr 10min–2hr 45min);

Paris* (many daily; 5hr); Toulouse*, via Rivesaltes, Salses, Narbonne*, Carcassonne* (connection to Quillan) and Castelnaudary* (several hourly; 2hr 20min–3hr 30min); Villefranche-de-Conflent/Vernet, via Ille-sur-Têt and Prades (several daily; 50min).

By bus The *gare routière* is next to the train station. Bus tickets cost €1.

Destinations Argelès (several daily; 40min); Arles-sur-Tech (several daily; 1hr 10min); Banyuls-sur-Mer (several daily; 1hr 20min); Cabestany (many daily; 20min); Céret (daily; 45min); Collioure (several daily; 45min); Elne (many daily; 20–45min); Font-Romeu (daily; 2hr 20min); Ille-sur-Têt (hourly; 35min); Latour-de-Carol/Enveitg (many daily; 3hr); Le Boulou (several daily; 30min); Le Perthus (one daily; 45min); Passa (daily; 45min); Maureillas (several daily; 40min); Mont Louis (several daily; 1hr 45min); Prades (several daily; 1hr 10min); Prats-de-Mollo (daily; 1hr 55min); Puilaurens-Lapradelle (two daily; 1hr 20min); Quillan (two daily; 1hr 50min); Rivesaltes (several daily; 35min); St-Cyprien (several daily; 50min); St-Paul-de-Fenouillet (several daily; 50min); Salses (several daily; 30min–1hr); Thuir (several daily; 25min); Vernet-les-Bains (several daily; 1hr 25min); Villefranche-de-Conflent (several daily; 1hr 20min).

GETTING AROUND

By bus A free *navette*, "P'tit Bus", circulates through the old town and to the station.

By bike Perpignan has a municipal bike system, Bip! (ⓦ bip-perpignan.fr), with fifteen hubs including the train station and Palais des Rois de Majorque. The first 30min are free. There are several *voies vertes* in the area.

By car The major car rental agencies are at the train station: Avis (☎ 04 68 35 61 48), Budget (☎ 04 11 30 02 70); Europcar (☎ 04 68 34 89 80) and Sixt (☎ 04 68 61 34 34). They also have branches at the airport.

By taxi Perpignan Taxi ☎ 04 68 35 15 15 or Taxi Direct Perpignan ☎ 04 68 83 83 83.

INFORMATION

Tourist information Palmarium, place Arago (June–Sept Mon–Sat 9am–7pm, Sun 10am–5pm; Oct–May Mon–Sat 9am–6pm, Sun 10am–1pm; ☎ 04 68 66 30 30, ⓦ perpignantourisme.com). They offer guided tours of the historic centre and you can enquire about renting four-person electric boats (€12) on the Basse river.

ACCOMMODATION

Les Cagettes en Ville 8 rue des Rois-de-Majorque ☎ 06 09 35 67 44. Hip B&B above a vintage clothes shop, decorated in 1950s style, with three simply furnished rooms including one for families. Breakfast is served in the lovely garden in summer. €80

Centre del Mon 35 bd St-Assiscle ☎ 04 11 64 71 00, ⓦ www.hotels-centredelmon.com. Part of the new train station and shopping mall complex, this hotel has three-star ("Comfort") and four-star ("Quality") rooms – both categories with ultra-modern decor. There is a bar, an atrium terrace and parking is available (charge). €75

★ **De la Loge** 1 rue Fabriques d'En Nabot ☎ 04 68 34 41 02, ⓦ hoteldelaloge.com. This well-priced option in the heart of the old town occupies a gorgeous sixteenth-century townhouse with a magnificent listed wrought-iron staircase. Factor in the pretty flower-filled courtyard and this is easily Perpignan's most charming accommodation. €79

HI Hostel Av de la Grande-Bretagne ☎ 04 68 34 63 32, ⓦ fuaj.org. Modern, well-run hostel beside a park, fifteen minutes' walk from the centre but with a noisy road running behind it. Open mid-April to mid-Oct. Free parking. €23

Nyx 62 bis av Général-de-Gaulle ☎ 04 68 34 87 48, ⓦ nyxhotel.fr. Stylish boutique hotel near the station with seventeen rooms decorated on the themes of night and day; one has wheelchair access and a couple have private terraces. The service is friendly and the (mainly home-made) breakfast is delicious. Parking available (charge). €89

Roussillon Camping Catalan 3252 av de la Salanque ☎ 04 68 62 16 92, ⓦ camping-catalan.com. Large two-star site, 8km northeast of the city, with shop, swimming pool and laundry service. Also rents chalets and is wheelchair accessible. Open mid-March to Oct. €24.76

La Villa Duflot Rondpoint Albert Donnezan ☎ 04 68 56 67 67, ⓦ villa-duflot.com. Halfway between the city centre and the airport, Perpignan's most luxurious hotel is set in one hectare of parkland and has an excellent *gastronomique* restaurant (*menu* from €30). There is also an outdoor pool and a fitness room. €200

Windsor 8 bd Wilson ☎ 04 68 59 25 94, ⓦ hotel-windsor-perpignan.com. Near Le Castillet, this four-star Best Western is a very comfortable city-centre option. The rooms were renovated in 2012 and boast top-quality bedding, bathrobes and eco-friendly products. Good selection of local wines in the bar. €125

EATING

Perpignan has eating places to suit all tastes and budgets but for an authentic experience head to tiny rue Paratilla and graze on oysters, charcuterie or tapas at the counters of the cheek-by-jowl shops and bars.

Bio Deux Anges 39 rue des Augustins ☎ 04 68 08 78 32, ⓦ biodeuxanges.com. Organic vegetarian and vegan restaurant where the wonderful local ingredients are put to good use. There is a choice of salads or pasta (around €13.50) as well as a good selection of desserts (from €7). You can also drop in for tea or coffee. Tues–Sat noon–3pm.

Casa Sansa 2 rue Fabriques-Nadal ☎ 04 68 50 48 01. The city's best Catalan cuisine is served up in this comfortable establishment, founded in 1846, in one of the old town's most beautiful streets. Two-course lunch €14.95. Tues–Sat noon–2pm & 7–11pm.

Crêperie du Théâtre 12 rue du Théâtre ☎ 04 68 34 29 06, ⓦ creperie-du-theatre.fr. What's great about this crêperie is that, as well as the traditional Breton fillings, it also offers seasonal crêpes made with local products; there are several vegetarian options too. The *galettes* are gluten-free and start at €7.50. Tues–Sat noon–9.30pm.

Le Divil 9 rue Fabriques d'En Nabot ☎ 04 68 34 57 73, ⓦ restaurant-le-divil-66.com. An excellent old-town choice, this popular bull-themed restaurant specializes in fantastic grilled meats, but it also has seafood options such as grilled sardines. The *plat du jour* is €12 and there are lunch *menus* from €14. Mon–Sat noon–2pm & 7–11pm.

La Galinette 23 rue Jean Payra ☎ 04 68 35 00 90, ⓦ restaurant-galinette.com. The best restaurant in town creates artistically presented dishes using the finest local products with some international influences. The "Saveurs de Saison" *menu* (€48) contains the likes of tomato sorbet with eighteen spices. Good-value weekday lunch at €25. Tues–Sat noon–2pm & 7–9.30pm; closed July.

★ **Le St-Jean** 1 rue cité Bartissol ☎ 04 68 51 22 25, ⓦ lesaint-jean.com. Refined cuisine with a southern accent, which you can enjoy on the romantic terrace underneath the cathedral's flying buttresses in summer. Wines from the owner's vineyard are on the menu. Two-course lunch from €15. Mon–Sat noon–2pm & 7–9pm, closed Mon–Wed eve off season.

Le Sud 12 rue Louis Bausil ☎ 04 68 34 55 71, ⓦ restaurantlesud.fr. Eclectic and delicious

7

Mediterranean cuisine served up in the heart of Perpignan's Romany quarter. Check ahead as the restaurant hosts many

exhibitions and events. Main courses €18–28. Mon–Sat 7–9pm.

DRINKING AND NIGHTLIFE

La Fabrik 53 av Maréchal Leclerc ☎ 04 68 64 24 04. Excellent tapas and wine bar with more than three hundred labels and also a cocktail menu. They have weekly events and music in summer. Mon–Fri 11.30am–3pm & 5pm–2am.

Habana Bodeguita 5 rue Grande des Fabriqués ☎ 04 68 34 11 00. Lively tapas, wine and cocktail bar with DJs playing salsa music; there are regular party nights. Tues–Sat 6pm–2am.

Le Market 15 av Maréchal Leclerc ☎ 06 01 64 86 55. This chic club, which plays a wide selection of dance music, is up in the north of the city – an area which, thanks to its new bars and restaurants, is fast becoming Perpignan's centre for nightlife. Thurs–Sun 11pm–6am.

O'Flaherty's 27 av Maréchal Leclerc ⓦ oflahertys -perpignan.com. An Irish pub with live music or DJs at weekends and major sports matches streamed. Tues–Sun 6pm–1am.

ENTERTAINMENT

Cinema Castillet 1 bd Thomas Wilson ☎ 08 92 68 75 35, ⓦ castillet.cine-movida.com. This famous Art Nouveau cinema now hosts arthouse and independent films in their original version (*vo*).

Théâtre de l'Archipel Av Maréchal Leclerc ☎ 04 68 62

62 00, ⓦ theatredelarchipel.org. Jean Nouvel's new theatre runs an eclectic programme including theatre, dance, circus and classical music while its El Mediator concert hall (ⓦ elmediator.org) hosts current touring French bands.

SHOPPING

There's a general market in place de la République (Tues–Sun 7.30am–1.30pm), plus a flea market on av du Palais des Expositions (Sun 7.30am–1.30pm). The most colourful market takes place daily (7.30am–1.30pm) in place Cassanyes, with a mixture of French, Arab and African traders selling cheap clothes, crafts and all sorts of local produce. Plans are afoot to build a new covered market.

Maison Quinta 3 rue Grande des Fabriqués ☎ 04 68 34 41 62, ⓦ maison-quinta.com. Over three floors in a gorgeous old mansion, this lifestyle shop sells a mix of

traditional and modern Catalan home deco items including the colourful stripy fabrics. Tues–Sat 9.45am–noon & 2.15–7pm.

DIRECTORY

Hospital Centre Hospitalier, av du Languedoc (☎ 04 68 61 66 33, ⓦ www.ch-perpignan.fr).

Laundry Au Tambour, 19 rue de la Fusterie (daily 7am–10pm; ☎ 06 52 02 89 15) and Foch Pressing, 60 rue

Maréchal Foch (Mon–Sat 8am–7pm; ☎ 04 68 51 19 68).

Pharmacy Grande Pharmacie de la Loge, 4 place de la Loge (Mon–Sat 8am–7.30pm; ☎ 04 68 34 42 17).

Police Av de la Grande Bretagne ☎ 04 68 35 70 00.

Around Perpignan

Heading north from Perpignan towards Narbonne along the N9, the main attraction is the enormous stronghold of **Salses-le-Château**, built to dominate the strategic strip of land between the Étang de Leucate and the uplands of the Corbières. East of Perpignan is its beach resort, **Canet-en-Roussillon**, with a good if rather windswept beach, while the village of **Cabestany**, to the southeast, has a museum dedicated to the eponymous medieval master-sculptor.

Salses-le-Château

Daily: April–Sept 10am–6.30pm; Oct–March 10am–12.15pm & 2–5pm • €7.50 • ☎ 04 68 38 60 13, ⓦ forteresse-salses.fr

The fortress of **SALSES-LE-CHÂTEAU** was constructed by the Spanish in the fifteenth century to guard the northern border of Roussillon from French attack. It's a curious structure – set low within a deep moat, like a cannon-age fortress, but with the basic design and overall squareness of a medieval castle, it represents an intermediary stage in the evolution from early to modern fort. Salses withstood four sieges before it was taken by the French in 1642; with the shift of the frontier south to the mountains, the fortress was first abandoned and then later used as a prison until it was declared a monument in 1886.

ARRIVAL AND INFORMATION

SALSES-LE-CHÂTEAU

By train The *gare SNCF* is just west of the fortress. The town is on the main coastal line via Perpignan (many daily; 12min).

By bus The main stop is at place de la République. There are frequent departures to Perpignan (1hr).

Tourist information place de la République (July & Aug daily 9am–7pm; ☎04 68 38 66 12, ⓦsalses-le-chateau.fr).

ACCOMMODATION AND EATING

Casa Montes 1 clos des Abricotiers ☎04 68 35 24 58, ⓦcasa-montes.com. At the foot of the fortress, this attractive old farmhouse has been turned into a tasteful B&B by a couple of antique dealers. There's a small pool in the lush garden and *table d'hôte* is available. Secure parking. €80

★**La Loge** 38 av Xavier-Llobères ☎04 68 38 62 86, ⓦlalogesalses.com. Aside from the decent *terroir* food, the main reason to eat here is to admire the listed Art Nouveau interior. Lunch is from €14.50. They also have a boutique selling regional products and host art exhibitions. July to mid-Oct daily noon–3pm & 7–9pm; days vary off season.

Canet-en-Roussillon

CANET-EN-ROUSSILLON is made up of two parts: **Canet-Ville**, with its ruined castle and thirteenth-century church, and **Canet-Plage**, which has everything you'd expect from a beach town: sun, fun, bars and music. The main sight here is the **aquarium** (bd de la Jetée; daily: July & Aug 9.30am–8.30pm; Sept–June 10am–noon & 2–6pm; €6.50; ☎04 68 80 49 64, ⓦaquarium-canet.com), home to over three thousand species, including shark, piranha and coral. There are morning **markets** on Wednesdays and Saturdays in Canet-Ville and Tuesdays, Thursdays and weekends in Canet-Plage, as well as at the port on Friday in summer.

ARRIVAL AND INFORMATION

CANET-EN-ROUSSILLON

By bus Served by bus #6, which leaves Perpignan every 30min.

By bike Sun Bike 66, 122 prom de la Côte Vermeille (☎04 68 73 88 65, ⓦsunbike66.fr). From €10 per half-day.

Tourist information 1 bis av de la Méditerranée (July & Aug daily 9am–7pm; Sept–May Mon–Sat 9am–noon & 2–6pm, Sun 9.30am–12.30pm & 2.30–6pm; ☎04 68 86 72 00, ⓦot-canet.fr).

ACCOMMODATION AND EATING

Le Bouchon Catalan 18 av de la Méditerranée, Canet-Plage ☎04 68 73 37 16. This attractive restaurant with a street-side terrace is noted for its fish and Catalan cuisine, especially the *parillade* and delicious desserts; try the *crema catalana*. Lunch from €14. Noon–1.30pm & 7.30–11pm; July & Aug Tues–Sun; Sept–June Mon & Thurs–Sun.

La Brasilia 2 av Anneaux de Roussillon, Canet-Plage ☎04 68 80 23 82, ⓦbrasilia.fr. Huge five-star campsite in a pine forest next to the sea. As well as "standard" and "comfort" pitches, there are several kinds of chalets for rent. Excellent facilities including a waterpark, a spa, a football pitch and entertainment. €57

La Frégate 12 rue de Cerdagne, Canet-Plage ☎04 68 80 22 87, ⓦhotel-la-fregate.fr. Good-value three-star hotel in a pedestrian street about five minutes from the beach. The 27 rooms were renovated in 2010 in contemporary style. As well as the bar, there's a billiard table and a piano. Secure parking. €102

Cabestany

Fans of medieval art and sculpture will want to make a pilgrimage to **CABESTANY**, where the eleventh- to fourteenth-century church of **Notre-Dame-des-Anges** is home to a remarkably vividly carved **tympanum**, the discovery of which in 1930 led to the identification of the Master of Cabestany (see box, p.284). You can see further examples of his sculpture at the museum and resource centre, the **Centre de Sculpture**

7

> **THE MASTER OF CABESTANY**
>
> The actual name of the **Master of Cabestany** has long been forgotten, but the work of this genius of masonry comprises one of Languedoc's most important medieval legacies. The twelfth-century itinerant **sculptor**, whose speciality was human figures in high relief, worked as far afield as Tuscany and Catalonia, but the greatest concentration of his works can be found in a wide band of territory stretching from Castelnaudary to the sea. Doorways, cloisters, tombs and tympanums – over 120 works found so far – all bear the distinctive mark of his vivid style. His large-handed, bulbous-eyed portraits are remarkable not so much for their realism as for the obvious brilliance with which they were executed, which seems to endow the mute stone figures with a life and soul of their own. The most dramatic example of his work can be found at **St-Hilaire** (see p.98), while others survive at Cabestany (see p.283), Lagrasse (see p.253), Passa (see p.301), St-Papoul (see p.81) and Le Boulou (see p.301). Several works have been identified just over the border in Catalonia, including at the magnificent monastery of San Pere de Rodes (only 25min by car from Le Boulou), and one piece now resides in the Cloisters collection of the Metropolitan Museum of Art in New York.

Romane – Maître de Cabestany (Parc Guilhem; 10am–12.30pm & 1.30–6.30pm: May, June & Sept Tues–Sun; July & Aug daily; Oct–April Tues–Sun closes at 6pm; €3; ☎04 68 08 15 31, ⓦwww.maitre-de-cabestany.com).

The Fenouillèdes

Stretching out to the northwest of Perpignan, the **Fenouillèdes** is the range of scrubby limestone hills that marked the inland border between France and Spain until the Treaty of the Pyrenees gave Roussillon to France in 1659. It is a rich area to discover, with highlights including the caves at **Tautavel**, where some of Europe's earliest hominids have been discovered, and several Cathar castles, the most famous being **Quéribus** and **Peyrepertuse**. Further west, you can explore the dramatic **Gorges de Galamus** and continue to another Cathar stronghold at **Puilaurens**. The main artery through the Fenouillèdes is the D117, running westward from Perpignan to Quillan (see p.102); all the sights can be accessed from various points along this road, whether you're driving or reliant on the bus. If you have time to take the hills in by foot, however, head out on the **Sentier Cathare**, which leads west into the pays de Sault (see p.103), or the **Tour du Fenouillèdes**, a seven-day circuit that links the main sights of the region (for information on this see the tourist office in Perpignan, or visit their website; see p.281).

Tautavel

In 1971, archeologists working at the Caune de l'Arago, a cave near the village of **TAUTAVEL**, on the edge of the Fenouillèdes, discovered the front part of a skull of *Homo erectus* – an evolutionary midpoint between the African *Homo habilis* and modern *Homo sapiens* – which dated back half a million years, making him France's earliest known inhabitant. The reconstructed skull, with its enormous cranial ridge and low eye sockets, is displayed in Tautavel's **Musée de Préhistoire** (av Léon-Jean Grégory; daily: July & Aug 10am–7pm; Sept–June 10am–12.30pm & 2–6pm; €8; ☎04 68 29 07 76, ⓦ450000ans.com), the centrepiece of a moving exhibition across 22 rooms which includes stone tools, animal bones and a reconstructed cave as well as films and information on the digs. The **cave** where the discovery was made, La Caune de l'Arago (July & Aug; ask at the museum about visiting), is situated in a low hill on the opposite side of the Verdouble valley. **Excavations** take place every year from May to August and in 2015 a teenage volunteer found two human teeth dating back 550,000 years – some of the oldest remains ever unearthed in Europe.

Cucugnan and the castles

CUCUGNAN makes a good base for visiting two of the region's most famous **castles** – the **Château de Quéribus** and the **Château de Peyrepertuse**. Cucugnan itself is a typical southern French hill village with ancient streets, terracotta roofs and a windmill at its summit. Near the church, the **Horto del Bitou** (daily dawn to dusk; free) is a hanging garden with a lovely collection of roses.

Château de Quéribus

Quéribus is a short detour off the D117, from the turn-off at Maury • Daily: Jan–March, Nov & Dec 10am–5pm; April 10am–6pm; May, June & Sept 9.30am–7pm; July & Aug 9am–8pm; Oct 10am–6.30pm; • €6.50 • ☎ 04 68 45 03 69 • If you don't have your own transport take the Perpignan–Quillan bus to Maury, from where it's a steep two-hour walk

Visible on its turret of bare rock long before you reach it, the **château** in the Cathar stronghold of **QUÉRIBUS** is much bigger than it looks, since much of the **interior** is below ground level. A single stairway links all the various structures, including the so-called **salle du palmier** in the polygonal keep, where the vaulted ceiling is supported by a graceful pillar sprouting a canopy of intersecting ribs.

Quéribus was constructed at the end of the tenth century, and belonged successively to the count-kings of Barcelona and Aragón and the counts of Fenouillèdes. After the fall of Montségur in 1244 it became the refuge of some of the last surviving Cathars, an affront that **King Louis IX** decided to erase. His opportunity came in 1255, when the local lord who sponsored the Cathars, Chabert de Barbaira, was captured by royal forces and forced to cede this and other castles as his ransom. But, unlike at Montségur, the Cathar garrison here had time to escape, probably south across the mountains.

Château de Peyrepertuse

Signposted from Duilhac; 15min uphill walk from ticket office • Daily: Jan, Nov & Dec 10am–4.30pm; Feb 10am–5pm; March & Oct 10am–6pm; April 9.30am–7pm; May, June & Sept 9am–7pm; July & Aug 9am–8pm • €6.50–12 • ☎ 04 30 37 00 77, Ⓦ chateau-peyrepertuse.com

The **Château de Peyrepertuse** is the largest and one of the best preserved of the **Cathar castles**. Its age and history are nearly identical to those of Quéribus, with Paris assuming definitive control here by treaty with Catalonia-Aragón in 1258. The setting of the castle, draped the length of a jagged ridge with sheer drops at most points, is its most impressive feature. No single architectural feature among various cisterns, chapels and towers claims attention, but from the highest chamber, the **Chapelle San Jordi**, there are sweeping views east to the Mediterranean and Perpignan, with Quéribus perched on its rock stalk in between. Try and coincide a visit with the **Festival Médiéval** in August.

INFORMATION

CUCUGNAN AND THE CASTLES

Tourist information 2 rte de Duilhac, Cucugnan (April, Oct & Nov Mon–Sat 10am–5pm; June & Sept Mon–Sat 10am–6pm; July & Aug daily 10am–7pm; Dec–Feb Fri & Sat 10am–5pm; ☎ 04 68 45 69 40, Ⓦ www.corbieres -sauvages.com).

ACCOMMODATION AND EATING

L'Auberge du Vigneron 2 rue Achille Mir, Cucugnan ☎ 04 68 45 03 00, Ⓦ auberge-vigneron.com. Very nice *Logis de France* hotel in an old stone wine warehouse with five attractive, comfortable rooms. There are lovely views from the restaurant terrace and elegant *terroir* cuisine on the menu (Tues–Sun; lunch from €15). Closed mid-Nov to mid-March. €90

L'Hostellerie du Vieux Moulin 24 rue de la Fontaine, Duilhac, 4km west of Cucugnan ☎ 04 68 45 03 00, Ⓦ auberge-vigneron.com. Owned by the same family as the *Auberge du Vigneron*, this two-star hotel

has thirteen simple-but-comfortable rooms, some of which have views of Peyrepertuse. Closed mid-Nov to mid-March. €59

Le Patio des Créateurs – Les 3 Cathares Av St-Félix, Rouffiac-des-Corbières, 10km northwest of Cucugnan ☎ 04 68 70 71 04, Ⓦ les3cathares.fr. Cool and arty youth hostel (12 beds; €15–20) and café serving good-quality burgers, snacks, tapas and yummy desserts. There's live music on Friday evenings on the courtyard terrace and plenty of other events throughout the summer. July–Sept daily 10am–10.30pm.

> ## THE FENOUILLÈDES RAILWAY
>
> The best and most relaxed way to appreciate the rugged landscape of the Fenouillèdes is the **Train du Pays Cathare et du Fenouillèdes**, a narrow-gauge rail line refurbished as a tourist route. Starting from the station at **Rivesaltes**, 7km north of Perpignan, it climbs along the vine-clad route of the Agly river before turning up the valley of La Boulzane. Climbing through forests of fir, it arrives at **St-Paul-de-Fenouillet** (see below) and threads the **Gorges de Galamus**, before stopping at Caudiès-de-Fenouillèdes. From here it continues to **Lapradelle** (from where a stiff 3km walk leads up to the castle of **Puilaurens**) before the final 7km leg takes it to the end of the line, at Axat, near Quillan (see map, p.102).
>
> The train, which was inaugurated in 1904, runs irregularly from mid-April to October, but most days in July and August. The full return fare is €20.80 per adult and €14.50 for under-14s, and the journey takes around 2hr 30min each way. They also run shorter trips. See ⓦtpcf.fr for **information** on departures and reservations.

7

SHOPPING

Les Maîtres de mon Moulin 3 rue du Moulin, Cucugnan ☎04 68 33 55 03, ⓦfarinesdemeule.com. The town's old mill has been brought back to life and now produces artisan bread, cakes, biscuits and pasta made with organic, traditional grains. They also run bread-making courses. Daily 9am–7pm.

Gorges de Galamus

The **Gorges de Galamus** (ⓦgorgesdegalamus.fr) is a short but impressive limestone *défilé* worn through the ridge by the river La Boulzane. The narrow road, which clings to the rock face, is not for the faint of heart. Most visitors enter the gorge at its downstream end, 3km out of St-Paul-de-Fenouillet. Here there's a free car park and the start of a path to the exquisitely sited **Ermitage de St-Antoine**, about halfway down the gorge's east flank (daily: mid-March to April & Oct to mid-Nov 10am–5pm; May–Sept 10am–7pm) – a huge, sanctified grotto thrusting deep into the cliff, from where a steep path, culminating in a rock ladder, drops down to pools below. The river is deep enough for swimming, and the gorge is also a popular **canyoning** venue: contact Pyrénées Outdoor Sports (☎06 19 36 16 47, ⓦpyrenees-outdoor-sports.com). There is a market in St-Paul-de-Fenouillet on Wednesday and Saturday mornings.

ARRIVAL AND INFORMATION   THE GORGES DE GALAMUS

By bus There are regular services to St-Paul-de-Fenouillet. Destinations Axat (daily; 25min); Maury (several daily; 15min); Perpignan (several daily; 55min); Quillan (daily; 50min).

Tourist information 26 bd de l'Agly, St-Paul-de-Fenouillet (July & Aug Mon–Sat 10am–noon & 3–7pm; Sept–June Tues–Sat 10am–noon & 2–6pm ☎04 68 59 07 57, ⓦst-paul66.com).

ACCOMMODATION AND EATING

Camping Agly Av du 16 août 1944 ☎04 68 59 09 09, ⓦcamping-agly.com. This small riverside campsite has pitches, caravans and *gîtes*. They can advise on activities including via ferrata, canyoning and rafting. €16.55
Le Châtelet Rte de Caudiès ☎04 68 59 01 20,

ⓦhotel-lechatelet.com. One of two hotels in town, this contemporary *Logis de France* is well equipped for walkers, cyclists and fishing enthusiasts. There's an inviting outdoor pool and a restaurant showcasing local produce including trout. €66

Château de Puilaurens

Feb & March Sat, Sun & hols 10am–5pm; April & Oct to mid-Nov daily 10am–5pm; May daily 10am–6pm; June & Sept daily 10am–7pm; July & Aug daily 10am–8pm • €5 • ☎04 68 20 65 26

At tiny **Lapradelle** you'll find the turn-off for the **castle** of **Puilaurens**, perched majestically on a 700m-high ridge. Built originally by the Visigoths, Puilaurens was enlarged not long before its captured lord, the Cathar Chabert de Barbaira, turned it over to Crusader forces as a condition of his release. You enter from the west, via a stepped maze of *chicanes* (staggered low walls); much of the interior is dilapidated, but make sure you catch the **view** east over pined hills from outside the southeastern gate, and the point on the **western donjon** complex where you're allowed briefly on the curtain wall to take in the vista in the opposite direction.

The lower Têt valley

From Perpignan, the Têt valley (also known as the Conflent), provides a fast if initially not very scenic route southwest into the Pyrenees. The **lower Têt valley** is that stretch running up to the peak of Canigó, and its most interesting parts are found some 30km west of Perpignan, where **Ille-sur-Têt** provides a jumping-off point for the spectacular rock formations of **Les Orgues** to the north and, just west, the narrow Boulès gorge climbs south to the region of Les Aspres, within whose wooded isolation you'll find the magnificent Romanesque **Prieuré de Serrabona**. Further west along the valley, you'll come to **Prades**, a good access point for the Canigó mountain and, skirting the north side of the famous massif, you reach **Villefranche-de-Conflent**, which marks the transition to the upper valley (see p.289).

Ille-sur-Têt and around

ILLE-SUR-TÊT has an attractive medieval quarter of narrow alleys, within which the seventeenth-century **Hospici d'Illa** (see website for opening times; €4; ☎04 68 84 83 96, ⓦtourisme.ille-sur-tet.com) – the local headquarters of the medieval Hospitaller Knights – houses a **museum** of exquisite medieval and baroque religious art. A farmers' market takes place on Saturday mornings. More remarkable are the clay cliffs just across the River Têt, a kilometre or so on the road north towards Sournia, and which the elements have eroded into extraordinary figures known as **Les Orgues**, so called because of their resemblance to organ pipes. Rising dramatically up from a deep tributary of the Têt, they can be explored by a series of **footpaths** laid out within the gorge (daily: Jan & Nov 2–5.30pm; Feb–March & Oct 10am–6pm; April to mid-June & mid-Sept to mid-Oct 9.30am–7pm; mid-June to mid-Sept 9.15am–8pm; €5; ☎04 68 84 13 13).

Thuir

THUIR is known chiefly as the main producer of the red aperitif wine called Byrrh (pronounced "beer"), and you can visit the **winery** at 6 boulevard Violet (April–June, Sept & Oct daily 9.30–11.30am & 2.30–5.30pm; July & Aug daily 10–11.30am & 2–6.30pm; Nov–March Tues–Sun 10.45am–3.30pm; €4.50; ☎04 68 57 51 73, ⓦcaves-byrrh.fr) and taste the sweet ferment that is aged in a cathedral-like gallery designed by Gustave Eiffel.

Castelnou

Capping a hilltop, **CASTELNOU** is one of the Plus Beaux Villages de France (see p.46). It has a strong medieval ambience, with a well-preserved gate and walls, as well as a tenth-century **castle** (daily: April–Sept 10am–6.30pm; Oct 11am–5pm; Nov–March 2–5pm; €5.50; ☎04 68 53 22 91, ⓦchateaudecastelnou.fr), with good views and a shop selling their own wines. The best day to come is Tuesday, when a local **market** breathes extra life into the village (mid-June to mid-Sept).

Prieuré de Serrabona

Daily 10am–6pm • €4 • ☎04 68 84 09 30

The most compelling stop en route to Prades involves a detour south from Bouleternère up a perilous 8km track to Roussillon's celebrated **Prieuré de Serrabona**. The location of the simple church, set as it is on a high hilltop, against a precipitous and wooded drop, is impressive; in the grounds around the priory, a **botanical garden** has been set up to showcase the region's diverse flora. The building's modest facade conceals a strange cloistered gallery, which looks out on the hills, and leads inside to the church's equally curious interior. Here, the almost windowless nave is dominated by an exquisitely decorated tribune of rose marble – an unusual "indoor" **cloister**, reminiscent of some Spanish Mozarabic churches and perhaps a faint echo of Córdoba's great mosque. Excavated columns found here suggest that much of the original priory – founded in the twelfth century – was as elaborate as the tribune.

ARRIVAL AND INFORMATION

ILLE-SUR-TÊT AND AROUND

By train Ille's *gare SNCF* is a 5min walk southeast of the town centre. The town is on the regional line between Perpignan (20min) and Villefranche–Vernet-les Bains (25min).

By bus Ille is on the main bus route between Perpignan (35 min) and Vernet-les-Bains (50min), via Prades (30min) and Villefranche (40min). There is also a regular bus service from Perpignan to Thuir (20min).

Tourist information Ille-sur-Têt: place Henri Demay (July & Aug Mon–Sat 9.30am–12.30pm & 2–6pm, Sun 9.30am–12.30pm; Sept–June Mon–Thurs 9am–noon & 2–6pm, Fri until 5pm; ☎ 04 68 84 02 62, ⓦ tourisme.ille -sur-tet.com). Thuir: bd Violet (April–June, Sept & Oct Mon–Sat 9.30am–12.30pm & 2.30–6.30pm; July & Aug daily 10am–12.30pm & 2–6.30pm; Nov–March Tues–Sun 9.30am–12.30pm & 2–6pm ☎ 04 68 53 45 86, ⓦ aspres -thuir.com).

ACCOMMODATION AND EATING

Camping Le Colomer Rte du Colonel Fabien, Ille-sur-Têt ☎ 04 68 84 72 40. No-frills municipal campsite with pitches and chalets to rent. There's a kids' playground and some games including *pétanque*. Closed Oct. **€11.35**

★ **Cortie** 3 rue Jean-Jacques Rousseau, Thuir ☎ 04 68 34 58 66, ⓦ hotel-cortie.fr. Totally charming, brightly coloured two-star hotel with twelve rooms decorated in contemporary style. The airy, high-ceilinged restaurant specializes in Catalan cuisine and has *menus* from €14.50. **€65**

El Pinyol d'Oliva 10 rue Petite Place de l'Huile, Ille-sur-Têt ☎ 04 68 84 04 17. Chic, contemporary B&B in a medieval townhouse, which has graced the pages of lifestyle magazines, with four stylishly but simply furnished rooms. There is a roof terrace and dinner is available. **€100**

La Figuera 3 carrer de la font d'Avall, Castelnou ☎ 04 68 53 18 42, ⓦ la-figuera.com. Lovely B&B in an old stone village house. There are five rooms decorated in warm, southern colours and a terrace with great views. *Table d'hôte* is available. **€75**

Le Patio Catalan 4 place du Général-de-Gaulle, Thuir ☎ 04 68 53 57 28. Opposite the Byrrh winery, this well-regarded restaurant serves refined Catalan dishes in an attractive patio setting. Naturally, there's a good selection of Roussillon wines on the menu. Lunch from €14.50. Mon, Tues & Fri–Sun noon–2pm & 7–9pm.

Saveurs des Orgues 1 rue Gutemberg, Ille-sur-Têt ☎ 04 68 84 10 48. The refined and inventive Catalan cuisine served here in an unassuming, contemporary dining room is excellent value. The *menus* (lunch from €14.90) include the likes of calamari carbonara. Tues–Sat noon–1.30pm & 7.30–9.45pm, Sun noon–1.30pm.

Prades and around

Midway along the Têt valley, **PRADES** is by far its biggest town. Distinctively pink with its marble masonry and pavements, it is the birthplace of Thomas Merton, the twentieth-century Catholic mystic who eventually settled in a Trappist monastery in Kentucky. It is best known, however, for hosting the annual summer **music festival** (see p.275) founded in 1950 by the Catalan cellist **Pablo Casals** (or Pau Casals in Catalan). In exile from Franco's Spain, Casals spent the second half of his life here, composing such works as the oratorio *The Crib* and the popular *Song of the Birds*. The **Espace Pablo Casals** (33 rue de l'Hospice; July & Aug Tues–Fri 10am–noon & 2–5pm, Sat 10am–noon; times vary off-season; free; ☎ 04 68 96 28 55) in the *médiatheque* (library) commemorates the virtuoso, who died in 1973. In the main place de la République you'll find the **church of St-Pierre**, which contains a huge and sumptuous seventeenth-century retable, a masterpiece by the Catalan sculptor Joseph Sunyer. Prades is in fact conspicuously Catalan in feel, hosting a summertime Catalan university course (last two weeks of August; ⓦ uce.cat) and having established the first

Catalan-language primary school in France. On Tuesday and Saturday mornings there's an excellent produce **market** in the square and surrounding streets.

St-Michel-de-Cuxà

Rte de Taurinya, Caudalet • Daily: 9.30–11.50am & 2–5/6pm • €6 • ☎ 04 68 96 15 35, ⓦ abbaye-cuxa.com

Much of the music festival takes place at the restored ninth-century Benedictine monastery of **St-Michel-de-Cuxà**. St-Michel reached its peak in the eleventh century and then went into slow decline: closed and abandoned in 1790, much of its stone was pillaged during the Revolution, some of it eventually finding its way – like many other Romanesque fragments from the region – to The Met Cloisters in New York. Today the highlights of a visit include a subterranean **crypt** consisting of a circular chapel dating back to the monastery's foundation, and the remains of the broad **cloister**, whose columns are capped by fine twelfth-century details. If you're around in early May, don't miss the iris **garden**.

ARRIVAL AND INFORMATIONS

By train The *gare SNCF* is at the southern edge of Prades, about ten minutes' walk from the centre. Prades is on the main line from Perpignan (several daily; 40min) to Villefranche – Vernet-les-Bains (several daily; 8min).

By bus Buses set you down on av Général-de-Gaulle (RN116), the main road through the centre of town.

Destinations Casteil (daily; 30min); Font-Romeu (several daily; 1hr 20min); Ille-sur-Têt (several daily; 35min); Latour-de-Carol (several daily; 2hr); Mont-Louis (several daily; 55min); Perpignan (many daily; 1hr 5min); Thuès

PRADES AND AROUND

(daily; 35min); Vernet-les-Bains (several daily; 25min); Villefranche (several daily; 10min).

Tourist information 10 place de la République (mid-June to mid-Sept Mon–Sat 9am–1pm & 2–7pm, Sun 10am–1pm; mid-Sept to mid-June Mon–Fri 9am–noon & 2–6pm, Sat 9.30am–12.30pm; ☎04 68 05 41 02, ⓦ prades-tourisme.fr). For information on the Massif du Canigó (see p.292), head to the Syndicat Mixte Canigó Grand Site on bd de la gare (Mon–Fri 9am–noon & 2–5pm; ☎04 68 96 45 86, ⓦ canigo-grandsite.fr).

ACCOMMODATION AND EATING

Camping La Plaine St-Martin Chemin du Gaz ☎ 04 68 96 29 83, ⓦ camping-prades.sitew.com. Municipal campiste in a bucolic setting with sixty pitches and nineteen chalets. There's fishing nearby, as is the local swimming pool (reduced rates for campers). Entertainment in summer. Open April to Dec. **€14**

La Galie 3 av Général-de-Gaulle ☎04 68 05 53 76, ⓦrestaurantlegalie.com. Named after the chef's wife, this renowned restaurant serves refined dishes made with regional products, such as smoked trout cannelloni; the local peach tart is not to be missed. Lunch from €18. Mon & Tues noon–1.45pm, Thurs–Sun noon–1.45pm & 7.30–9.30pm.

Villa Lafabrègue 15 av Louis Prat ☎04 68 96 29 90, ⓦ villafrench.com. Attractive, British-run B&B in an Italianate villa set in lush grounds with a pool. The five rooms are traditionally furnished; three have their own terrace and "Canigou" has a view of the mountain of the same name. There are also two *gîtes* for rent. **€65**

SHOPPING

Calvet 140 av Général-de-Gaulle ☎04 68 96 07 18, ⓦ bijouterie-calvet.com. This part of the world is known for its garnets and Calvet is the oldest garnet workshop in the region. As well as buying some jewellery, you can visit the small museum (free) and see the artisans at work. Tues–Sat 9am–noon & 2–7pm.

Villefranche-de-Conflent and around

Beyond Prades, the Têt valley narrows dramatically, becoming a gorge 6km further on, where the high walls of **VILLEFRANCHE-DE-CONFLENT** almost block the way. As there's almost no construction outside the walls, externally at least the town, one of the Plus Beaux Villages de France (see p.46), looks much as it did three hundred years ago: an elongated, two-street place squeezed between the palisade just to the south and the river. Within the ramparts, the most evocative area is along the bank of the Têt, by the thirteenth-century **church of St-Pierre**; the best view is from the far side, from where the weathered red-tiled roofs and the tower of the twelfth-century **church of St-Jacques** peer over the ramparts.

Villefranche dates from 1092, when Guillaume Raymond, Count of Cerdagne, granted the charter for the town, meant as a strategic bulwark against the counts of

Roussillon. Some remnants from that period still stand, notably the **Tour d'en Solenell** on the little square known as the **Placette**. In 1654 Villefranche – then controlled by Spain – was besieged by Louis XIV's troops, and fell after eight days' fighting. After the Treaty of the Pyrenees confirmed their annexation of Roussillon, the French rebuilt the Spanish fortifications according to plans drawn up by Vauban; they are now a UNESCO World Heritage Site.

The ramparts

2 rue St-Jean • Daily: Feb & Nov 10.30am–12.30pm & 2–5pm; March–May & Oct until 6pm; June & Sept 10am–7pm; July & Aug until 8pm; Dec 2–5pm • €4.50 • ☎ 04 68 05 87 05

Dating from the eleventh century, reinforced in the thirteenth century then "modernized" by Vauban in the seventeenth century with six bastions, the **ramparts** are the only remaining ones in France over two levels; part of the walkway is covered and built into the wall.

Château-fort Libéria

Daily: May & June 10am–7pm; July & Aug 9am–8pm; Sept–April 10am–6pm • €7 or €9.50 inc shuttle • ☎ 04 68 96 34 01, ⓦ fort -liberia.com • Take the shuttle from Café Le Canigou (89 place du Génie) or Restaurant Le Relais (39 rue St-Jean) and then descend by the underground staircase "Mille Marches" (734 steps, actually), although there is also an outdoor path

Rising high above the main town on the steep northern bank of the Têt, **Château-fort Libéria,** which was built by Vauban and remodelled by Napoleon III, has seen more service as a prison than as a fortress; its interns have included a group of seventeenth-century noblewomen of the court of Versailles, locked up in isolation and silence for over thirty years, on allegations of witchcraft and poisoning. From June to Sept you can enjoy lunch on the terrace. Back in town, the **Musée du Château** (17 rue St-Jacques; daily 10am–6pm; €2.30; ☎ 04 68 05 74 29) exhibits finds from the château and is worth visiting to see a replica of the eighteenth-century model of Villefranche; the original is in Les Invalides in Paris.

Cova Bastéra

Daily: April, June, Sept & Oct 11am–4pm; July & Aug 10am–5pm • €7

The most celebrated incident in Villefranche's history was the 1674 revolt against French rule, which culminated in the betrayal of the rebellion's leader, Charles de Llar, and his co-conspirators by Llar's own daughter, Inès. His hiding place was the **Cova Bastéra**, a cave which he could enter and exit from within the walls of the town – today the entrance is opposite the public park on the N116. Incorporated into Villefranche's defences during the time of Vauban, the cave has a film on the famous engineer as well as evidence of its prehistoric past including life-size dinosaurs.

Grottes des Grandes Canalettes

Rte de Vernet-les-Bains • Daily: April–June 10am–5pm; July & Aug 10am–5.30pm; Sept & Oct 10am–4pm; Nov–March Sat, Sun & hols 11am–4pm • €10 • ☎ 04 68 05 20 20, ⓦ grottescanalettes.com

The spectacular **Grottes des Grandes Canalettes** are located across the highway from Villefranche. Entry is via a 160m passageway, hollowed out by water over the past four hundred million years; the water dripping down the sides is now directed over moulds to create limestone images for sale at the shop. Beyond a door you then enter a succession of huge chambers crammed with stalactites, stalagmites, pillars and tiny, feathery formations. There is a *son et lumière* show at 6pm every evening in July and Aug.

| **ARRIVAL AND DEPARTURE** | **VILLEFRANCHE-DE-CONFLENT AND AROUND** |

By train Mainline trains from Perpignan (several daily; 55min), via Ille-sur-Têt and Prades, terminate at the *gare SNCF*, 400m north of the town; for onward *Train Jaune*

services (see box, p.295), simply change platforms.
By bus Buses run to Perpignan (several daily; 1hr 20min) via Ille-sur-Têt and Prades and also to Vernet-les-Bains (5min).

FROM TOP LES ORGUES (P.287); ESPADRILLES FOR SALE (P.299) >

INFORMATION AND ACTIVITIES

Tourist information 33 rue St-Jacques (March–May Mon–Sat 10am–12.30pm & 2–6pm; June–Sept daily until 6.30pm; Oct–Feb Tues–Sat until 5pm; ☎ 04 68 96 22 96, ⓦ villefranchedeconflent-tourisme.fr).

Activities Exploration Pyrénéenne, 73 rue St-Jean (☎ 06 22 45 82 02, ⓦ ex-pyr.com) offers canyoning, caving and hikes from €33 per person.

ACCOMMODATION AND EATING

Camping Mas de Lastourg RN116, Serdinya ☎ 04 68 05 35 25, ⓦ camping-lastourg.com. Well-equipped three-star campsite in parkland next to a river, five-minutes' drive west of Villefranche. There are 75 pitches and various structures to rent, as well as a pool, mini-golf, a kids' play area and a restaurant. Open April to mid-Oct. **€20**
Casa Penalolen 3 Domaine Ste-Eulalie ☎ 06 89 16 38 57, ⓦ casapenalolen.fr. Idyllic B&B in a

nineteenth-century mansion surrounded by a large garden with a pool. The four bedrooms are decorated in contemporary style, enhanced with the odd antique. **€80**
Le Patio 32 rue St-Jean ☎ 04 68 05 01 92, ⓦ lepatio-66 .com. In a listed building dating back to the twelfth century, with a patio, this Catalan restaurant offers the best value in town (*menus* €16.50–34.50). Try the *cargolade* (grilled snails), followed by chestnut cake. Daily noon–2pm & 7–9pm.

Massif du Canigó and around

Rising to a height of 2784m between the Tech and Conflent valleys, the **Massif du Canigó** (Catalan for "dog's tooth"; "Canigou" in French) is the great landmark of Catalonia, dominating the whole of the Roussillon lowlands. It was inscribed on the Grand Site de France list in 2012. Situated well inside French territory, the mountain became a symbol for Catalonia's lost independence in the course of the nineteenth-century literary renaissance, and came to signify Catalan cultural unity, endorsed today by the small flags and other patriotic paraphernalia festooned from its summit cross. The massif has been protected as a nature reserve and the peak (when not clouded) affords breathtaking views; if you're intent on reaching the summit, you must **hike**, and the most direct route is from the 2150m **Refuge des Cortalets** (see box below) on the peak's northeastern slopes – you can get to this by vehicle or on foot. **Vernet-les-Bains** on its northwestern slopes is the place from which to get to the key sight around Canigó – the **monastery of St-Martin-du-Canigou**, easily accessible by car.

TO THE SUMMIT VIA THE REFUGE DES CORTALETS

Most hikers tackle Canigó from the *Refuge des Cortalets*, a busy **refuge** a couple of hours from the summit. You can get to the chalet from either the east or the north. The easternmost route is the quiet and impressively steep (but not difficult) approach from **Valmanya**, which you can drive or **hike** to (along the GR36) from Vinça, some 20km to the north. From the village, a narrow road climbs a further 5km west, before petering out – you must then use the GR36 to complete the remaining 8km to the *refuge*. Approaching from the north, there is a jeep track to the *refuge* from near **Prades**. If you're **driving**, take the D35 out of the south side of Prades to Villerach (8km; signposted as "Clara-Villerach"), from where an unpaved *route forestière* dirt track rises to the chalet – an hour's drive. An ordinary car can easily get as far as the ruined hut at Prat Cabrera (1650m), an hour's walk from the *Refuge des Cortalets*, and – with extra care and ideal conditions – all the way to Cortalets itself. The well-marked hike to the summit goes past a lake, with its fine view up to the summit of the cirque, then climbs south along the ridge connecting with Pic Joffre. It takes about ninety minutes and provides only a slight sense of exposure as you reach the wrought-iron summit cross and orientation table.

Before setting out towards the summit, be sure to check the **weather conditions**. In general, the best time of year to hike up is the autumn, when there is no snow on the summit (as in late spring); summer is not the best of times to make the ascent, as the heat can be uncomfortable and humidity reduces visibility from the top.

THE FLAMA DEL CANIGÓ

At midsummer, for the Fête de St Jean (23 June) and the weekend before, the *refuge* and the peak are a frenzy of activity as seemingly half the population of Catalonia congregates for merrymaking and the kindling of the traditional **bonfire** that is then relayed to light numerous others in Catalan villages on both sides of the frontier. The flame used to light the bonfire is the Flama del Canigó, which was lit in 1960 and is kept in the village of Castillet. The **sharing of fire** is a symbol of Catalan unity. For further information see ⓦ feuxdelasaintjean.com.

Vernet-les-Bains and around

The biggest village on Canigó's slopes and the major stop en route to the famous abbey of St-Martin is the pleasant if slightly stuffy spa-town of **VERNET-LES-BAINS**, whose easiest approach is via the D116 for 10km south from Villefranche. English visitors such as Rudyard Kipling made the place fashionable during the last century and a waterfall, 3km out of town on a well-marked track, is even called the **Cascade des Anglaises**. Along with the thermal paraphernalia of plunge-pools and institutional adjoining therapy wings – first installed in 1377 – a range of more contemporary pastimes is now offered (mountain biking, canyoning, hydrospeed and caving), though the baths are still the focus of activity. Often overlooked, the old quarter's warren of alleys is capped by the ninth-century but much-restored double church of **Notre-Dame del Puig/St-Saturnin**, which incorporates the remaining bits of a castle.

Monastery of St-Martin-du-Canigou

Three kilometres southeast of Vernet-les-Bains • Visitors are allowed only on guided tours (hourly departures: June–Sept Mon–Sat 10–noon & 2–5pm, Sun 10am & 12.30pm; Oct–May Mon–Sat 10am, 11am & 2–4pm, Sun 10am & 12.30pm • €6 • ☎ 04 68 05 50 03, ⓦ stmartinducanigou.org

From the village of **Casteil**, an appealing, quiet hamlet, it's a thirty- to fifty-minute walk uphill along a paved path (you can also book a jeep transfer; see below) to the **monastery of St-Martin-du-Canigou**, a ubiquitous sight on local book covers, postcards and posters. Inaccessibility, and its continuing use by an active religious community, helps protect the place from becoming over-commercialized. Built from tan stone and roofed with grey slates, the monastery ranks as one of the most gorgeous monuments in the eastern Pyrenees, and the surrounding woods of sweet chestnut, beech and aspen form an unbeatable backdrop to the pinnacle of rock on which it stands. Founded in 1001 by Count Guifred de Cerdagne, it was severely damaged by an earthquake in the fifteenth century and thoroughly pillaged after abandonment in 1782. Restored through the twentieth century, the glory of the place resides in its **cloister capitals**, reassembled in unity by a bishop of Perpignan. The monastery is now occupied by an unusual mixed order of monks and nuns, called the "Beatitudes", with a sprinkling of lay workers.

ARRIVAL AND DEPARTURE
VERNET-LES-BAINS AND AROUND

By train The nearest train station is Villefranche–Vernet-les-Bains, the end of the regional train line from Perpignan (several daily; 55min).

By bus Vernet-les-Bains to: Perpignan (several daily; 1hr 40min), via Villefranche, Prades and Ille-sur-Têt. Casteil: to Perpignan (two daily; 1hr 25min), via Vernet-les-Bains, Villefranche and Prades.

INFORMATION AND ACTIVITIES

Tourist information Your first stop should be the Syndicat Mixte Canigó Grand Site in Prades (see p.289). Vernet-les-Bains: Maison du Patrimoine, 2 rue de la Chapelle (May, June & Sept Mon–Fri 9am–noon & 2–5pm, Sat 9am–noon & 3–5pm; July & Aug 9am–12.30pm & 2–6.30pm, Sat 9am–12.30pm & 3–6pm, Sun 9am–1pm; Oct–April Mon–Fri 9am–noon & 2–5pm; ☎ 04 68 05 55 35, ⓦ vernet-les-bains.fr). Also see ⓦ tourisme-canigou.com.

Jeep-taxis To the Chalet des Cortalets: M. Bouzan (☎ 04 68 05 99 89/06 50 33 95 79); La Caravelle du Conflent (☎ 06 11 22 48 79); M. Dard (☎ 06 09 71 91 62); Montagne et Transport (☎ 04 68 30 02 82/06 10 19 60 85) and

Villacèque (☎ 04 68 05 51 14). To the monastery: Montagne et Transport (☎ 04 68 30 02 82/06 10 19 60 85); €90 return from Casteil for up to six people.

Donkey-trekking Caravanigou (☎ 06 02 29 34 54, ⓦ caravanigou.fr) runs guided and self-guided donkey treks from two to five days, with tent accommodation.

ACCOMMODATION AND EATING

Bistrot Le Cortal Rue du Château, Vernet-les-Bains ☎ 04 68 05 55 79, ⓦ bistrot-lecortal.fr. Very popular British-run restaurant specializing in *pierrade* (meat cooked on a hot stone), with *menus* from €21.50. Lovely views from the terrace of this former stable. Reservations recommended. April–Oct Mon & Wed–Sun noon–1.30pm & 7–9pm, Nov–March Wed–Sun noon–1.30pm & 7.30–9pm.

Domaine St Martin 6 bd de la Cascade, Casteil ☎ 04 68 05 52 09, ⓦ domainestmartin.com. Friendly, family-run three-star campsite in a wood of chestnut trees. As well as pitches, there are several types of accommodation including bivouacs. There's also a pool, restaurant and plenty of activities on offer. Open mid-March to Oct. **€24.50**

Princess Rue des Lavandières, Vernet-les-Bains ☎ 04 68 05 56 22, ⓦ hotel-vernet-les-bains.com. Modern three-star hotel with bright, comfortable rooms, some of which have balconies and mountain views. The restaurant serves decent French cuisine from €14.50 for lunch. Open mid-March to Nov. **€84**

Le Refuge des Cortalets ☎ 04 68 96 36 19, ⓦ www .refugedescortalets.ffcam.fr. A *maquisard* hideout in the last war, and consequently heavily shelled by occupation forces, this restored *refuge* is run by the Club Alpin Français. Breakfast, lunch picnics and dinner available. Reserve in advance. You can park at the car park "Ras des Cortalets" then it's a 10min easy walk up. Open mid-May to mid-Oct. **€17.30**

The upper Têt and the Capcir

The lower Têt valley finishes at Villefranche-de-Conflent, above which the shaggy flanks of the **upper Têt** (Conflent) close dramatically around the narrow-gauge *Train Jaune* rail line and N116, which forge their separate ways along the river up to **Mont-Louis**, at the top of the Têt. En route, interspersed with abandoned villages colonized by hippies and New Age travellers, are a number of small hamlets, on the valley floor or perched just above, which make serviceable bases for excursions into the hills. Of these, the hot springs and the splendour of the nearby **Carança gorge** make **Thuès-entre-Valls** one of the most accessible and rewarding. North of Mont-Louis, a sedimentary plateau called the **Capcir** spreads towards the gorges of the upper Aude. Bare and extremely flat, dominated in the centre by the large artificial lakes of Matemale and Puyvalador, it is cradled by densely wooded slopes that sweep up to Pic Madrès and the Carlit massif, with only the pistes of the **ski resorts** Les Angles, Formiguères and Puyvalador interrupting the trees. One of the harshest winter climates in southern France also makes this excellent **cross-country skiing** terrain. The Capcir woodlands, with their sprinkling of *gîtes* and hotels, provide ample opportunities for **hiking** during warmer months, well within the capabilities of a novice walker.

Gorges de la Carança and around

Less than an hour from Villefranche the *Train Jaune* stops at **Thuès-Carança**, from where a clearly signposted path leads just west of the village of **Thuès-entre-Valls** to the

---

A NATURAL PARK

In 2004, the three upland regions of the Haut Conflent, Capcir and Carlit were incorporated into the **Parc Naturel Régional des Pyrénées Catalanes**, covering almost 1400 square kilometres including 64 communes and villages and their 23,000 inhabitants. The aim of the park is to protect and preserve the fragile habitat and indigenous traditions of the region, and to provide services for visitors. The park's **administrative office** is at 1 rue Dagobert, Mont-Louis (☎ 04 68 04 97 60, ⓦ parc-pyrenees-catalanes.fr).

THE TRAIN JAUNE

The best way to move into the uplands of the Parc Naturel Régional des Pyrénées Catalanes (see box opposite) is on the **Train Jaune**, once an essential local service, but now more of a fun ride – in summer some carriages are open-air. Built in the early twentieth century, the railway climbs for 62km from **Villefranche** (427m) up to **Latour-de-Carol** (1231m), where it connects with the Transpyrenean railway (Toulouse–Barcelona).

From July to September there are two **departures** a day in each direction (several other daily departures go as far as Font-Romeu); at 9.58am and 5.49pm from Villefranche and 8.28am and 3.13pm from Latour-de-Carol. There is a reduced service in winter. The descent takes just over two hours and the ascent an extra thirty minutes (note that there are no toilets on the train); there are connections with the Villefranche–Perpignan line within ten to twenty-five minutes of each arrival and departure. Return **fares** cost around €45 from Villefranche to **Latour de Carol** and around €27 to **Mont-Louis** (the most attractive stretch). For **information** on timetables and prices check ⓦwww.ter-sncf.com.

7

entrance to the spectacular **Gorges de Carança**. The gorge, as the signs at the entrance advise, is to be visited at your own risk. After a short walk from the car park (charge) the path divides: the left-hand path (signposted for Roc Madrieu) climbs steeply up the wooded side of the valley, while the right-hand path (over a small bridge) follows the more spectacular corniche route; the two paths converge at the Pont des Singes, a suspension bridge. The first ninety minutes of corniche walkway are the most amazing, poised over sheer 400m drops – not for the vertigo-prone. Next is a series of nerve-racking catwalks, ladders and wobbly, metal suspension bridges (these last not advisable for heavily laden walkers). The nearby **Réserve Naturel de Nyer** (ⓣ04 68 97 05 56, ⓦcatalanes.espaces-naturels.fr) consists of over 22 square kilometres of mountain wilderness between 700m and 2663m and is home to rare and varied Pyrenean flora and fauna, including the Pyrenees lily, bearded vulture and royal eagle as well as wildcats.

ACCOMMODATION

GORGES DE LA CARANÇA AND AROUND

Mas de Bordes Rue de la Soulane, Thuès-entre-Valls ⓣ04 68 97 05 00. This restored farm is part of a substantial property that includes its own hot springs, B&B

accommodation, *gîtes*, a log cabin and a meadow for pitching tents. *Table d'hôte* is available (€20). **€50**

Mont-Louis

At 1580m, the garrison town of **MONT-LOUIS** is the highest fortified town in France. Known as the gateway to the Cerdagne, Mont-Louis is the quintessential work of Louis XIV's military engineer Vauban (see box, p.297), for which it is a UNESCO World Heritage Site, and its massive moat-ringed **ramparts** (always open; free), built between 1679 and 1682, represent a glorious but failed effort to close off the Spanish frontier. Though promoted as a resort, Mont-Louis is still essentially a military town (now a commando training centre), and apart from the walls, its only other attraction is the world's first **solar oven** (*four solaire*), built in 1949 and now open for one-hour **guided tours** (daily from 10am; see website for last tour times; €6.50; ⓣ04 68 04 14 89, ⓦfour-solaire.fr); the huge mirror for the *four* stands in the moat, just to the left of the main gate, the Porte de France.

ARRIVAL AND INFORMATION

MONT-LOUIS

By train The *Train Jaune* to: Villefranche–Vernet-les-Bains (five daily; 1hr 30min) or Latour-de-Carol (two daily; 2hr).

By bus Several daily to: Font-Romeu (20min);

Formiguères (30min); Ille-sur-Têt (1hr 30min); Latour-de-Carol (1hr 5min); Les Angles (10min); Perpignan (2hr 10min); Thuès (25min); Prades (1hr) and Villefranche (50min).

THE CAPCIR SKI RESORTS

Les Angles (W lesangles.com) is the area's largest resort and a favourite with snowboarders: it has 55km of pistes, with the top run at 2325m. Chalets predominate rather than high-rises, but the old village has still been almost completely swamped. Six kilometres further north, **Formiguères** (W formigueres.fr) is far more attractive, with its shops, cafés and crêperies giving it the feel of a provincial town. The pistes here total just 22km, with no really tough runs. Moreover, standing at the heart of 110km of marked trails, Formiguères is the perfect place for **cross-country skiing**. Meanwhile, **Puyvalador** (W puyvalador.com), at the end of the north Capcir plateau, is 5km west of its namesake village. There are only 32km of pistes, but with a top station at 2380m, it has breathtaking views and is known for its excellent off-piste skiing. For further information about winter and summer activities in the Capcir area see W www .capcir-pyrenees.com).

7

Tourist information 6 bd Vauban (April–June & Sept Mon–Sat 9.30am–12.30pm & 2–6pm; July & Aug daily 9.30am–12.30pm & 1.45–6pm; Oct–March

Mon–Fri 9am–12.30pm & 2–5pm; ☎ 04 68 04 21 97, W mont-louis.net). Guided visits throughout the year (€5.50).

ACCOMMODATION

Camping Pla de Barrès Rte des Bouilloses ☎ 04 68 04 26 04, W pladebarres.com. Two-star municipal campsite in a relaxing woodland setting next to the Têt river. This a great spot for walking, mountain biking and fishing and there are shuttles to the nearby lake. Open mid-June to mid-Sept. €13.50

La Volute 1 place d'Armes ☎ 04 68 04 27 21, W lavolute.wixsite.com/lavolute. Two utterly charming *gîtes*: *La Volute* is in the former governor's house and sleeps up to fifteen people while *Le Pont Levis* is in the old toll gate and sleeps up to four. Off season they do B&B from €50. €1350

The Cerdagne

The French **Cerdagne** is half of the ancient Catalan county of La Cerdanya, chopped in two by the seventeenth-century Treaty of the Pyrenees. It is the highest point of the Sègre watershed, which descends south to Catalan Lleida, and is the sunniest area in the French Pyrenees, the ripe colours of summer grain and hay on its treeless, rolling hills reinforcing this impression. Curiously, the Cerdagne consists of the hamlets and countryside surrounding the sizeable Spanish enclave of Llívia – the result of a technicality in 1659's Treaty of the Pyrenees. To its northeast, the ski-centre of **Font-Romeu** is the biggest town in the region.

Font-Romeu

Sprawling at the foot of Roc de la Calme, in the southeast corner of the Carlit massif, **FONT-ROMEU** is one of the best-known ski areas in the Pyrenees and the second oldest ski resort in France after Chamonix. With 43km of pistes, but few of them challenging, these days the resort is best known for its cross-country skiing – there are 111km of marked trails. The resort is also the home of the **Centre National d'Entraînement en Altitude** (W cnea-fontromeu.com), which provides top-class training facilities for elite athletes including Mo Farah. Naturally, Font-Romeu has a range of other winter and summer activities. **Market** day is Wednesday.

ARRIVAL AND DEPARTURE
FONT-ROMEU

By train The *Train Jaune* station is at Via, from where it's a fairly steep 2km walk north to Font-Romeu. Or you can get a taxi from M. Salvat (☎ 06 22 86 85 40) or M. Leber (☎ 04 68 30 22 15).

Destinations Latour-de-Carol (two daily; 1hr 10min) and Villefranche (several daily; 1hr 45min).
By bus The bus stops at the Tourist Office and is on line #260 from Perpiganan to Porte-Puymorens.

IMPERIAL DESIGNS

Sébastien le Prestre de Vauban was born in 1633 to a family of the lower nobility, who, after initially supporting a rebellion against Louis XIV, went over to the service of the king. A professional soldier, Vauban joined the fledgling **engineering** corps and soon distinguished himself by constructing innovative siege works, fortifications and war tactics, such as richochet cannon fire. He was rewarded by being granted the rank of field marshal, and in 1680 undertook a comprehensive campaign to **fortify** France's frontiers, peppering the country's borders with his low-profile zigzag walled redoubts. While his most famous creations are in the northeast, such as Strasbourg and Landau, there are several impressive sites in Roussillon, including the walls of Perpignan's palace (see p.280) and the forts at Villefranche (see p.289), Mont-Louis (see p.295) and Prats-de-Molló (see p.300). **Mont-Louis** is unique because he designed not only the fortress, but the entire town. Vauban served until a year before his death in 1707 and was remembered as a modest, generous and conscientious officer in an age of vain, glory-seeking aristocrats. In 2008, twelve of Vauban's works were inscribed as **UNESCO World Heritage Sites**, including Villefranche and Mont-Louis. For more, see Ⓦsites-vauban.org.

7

Destinations Several daily to: Ille-sur-Têt (1hr 50min); Latour-de-Carol (45min); Mont Louis (20min); Perpignan (2hr 30min); Prades (1hr 20min); Thuès (45min); Villefranche (1hr 10min).

Tourist information 82 av Emmanuel Brousse (daily 9am–noon & 2–6/7pm, closed Sun May, Oct & Nov; ☎04 68 30 68 30, Ⓦfont-romeu.fr).

ACCOMMODATION AND EATING

Camping Huttopia Rte de Mont Louis ☎04 68 30 09 32, Ⓦfrance.huttopia.com. Pitches, cabins, bivouacs and trapper lodges are all on offer at this lovely natural site with great views. There's a small grocery store, a bar-restaurant and a communal lodge with sofas, games and a TV. Open mid-June to mid-Sept and mid-Dec to mid-March. €20.50

★**La Ferme des Lloses** 3 av du Maréchal Joffre ☎04 68 04 79 51. "Mountain" foods are on the menu at this fabulous restaurant/wine bar/deli/cheese shop, where

everything is organic and artisan or farm-produced. Vegetarian options. *Menus* from €19. Winter: daily 10am–11.30pm; summer: Tues–Sat 10am–2.30pm & 5–10.30pm.

Le Grand Tétras 14 av Emmanuel Brousse ☎04 68 30 01 20, Ⓦhotelgrandtetras.fr. This modern three-star hotel has 36 comfortable rooms, including a family suite, which either overlook the mountains or forest. The glass-covered top-floor pool is the perfect place to relax with a view. €113

The Tech valley

The **Tech valley** (or Vallespir) is the southernmost in France, endowed with exceptional sunshine (three hundred days a year) and relatively low rainfall, which nurtures a flora that includes oranges, cacti and bougainvillea, as well as dense forest on the higher, wetter slopes. Heading up the valley will take you through artistic **Céret**, and on to **Arles-sur-Tech**, the gateway to the exciting **Gorges de la Fou**. Further upstream, the upper Tech is dominated by **Prats-de-Mollo**, where the main road departs from the river to reach the Spanish frontier.

Céret

The cherry capital of southern France, **CÉRET** is a friendly, bustling place with a shady old town of narrow and winding streets and cute squares, still dominated by its much-built-into medieval fortifications. It's best known for its early twentieth century artistic expat residents, notably Picasso and, as a result, has several art galleries and public sculptures dotted around. You can easily spend half a day here. The best time to visit is during any of the town's famous **festivals** (see box, p.275), which have a markedly Catalan and Spanish flavour, including *sardanas* and *corridas* held in the arena to the north of town – but you'll have to plan ahead, as accommodation sells out well in advance. A market takes place on Saturday mornings.

Pont du Diable

On the northern outskirts of town over the Tech river, the single-arched **Pont du Diable** (45m) was said to have been built by the Devil in 1321 in return for the soul of the first Cérétan to cross. The engineer who made the bargain duly sent a cat over first, but the trick backfired as none of the locals would then risk the Devil's vengeance by using the bridge themselves.

Musée d'Art Moderne

8 bd Maréchal Joffre • July–Sept daily 10am–7pm; Oct–June Tues–Sun 10am–5.30pm • €8 • ☎ 04 68 87 27 76, ⓦ musee-ceret.com

Like Prades on the Têt, Céret was a place of refuge for escapees from Franco's fascist regime, with many artists passing through or staying here. At that point, the town was already a creative colony, having been a temporary home to luminaries such as Pablo Picasso, Marc Chagall and a clutch of Catalan and French artists, including Pierre Brune, who in 1950 opened the **Musée d'Art Moderne**. This museum's small but varied collection includes works by the Fauvists, Cubists and Surrealists, as well as pieces by recent artists such as Tàpies, but the highlight is a series of painted bowls with bull motifs by Picasso. The museum boutique is a good place to shop for unique gifts.

ARRIVAL AND INFORMATION   CÉRET

By bus The bus stops at place de la Résistance, 10min northeast of the town centre along bd Général-de-Gaulle.
Destinations Several daily to: Argelès-sur-Mer (1hr 30min); Arles-sur-Tech (40min); Le Boulou (10min); Maureillas (10min); Perpignan (55min) and Prats-de-Mollo (55min).
Tourist information 1 av Georges Clémenceau (May,

June & mid-Sept to Oct Mon–Sat 9am–12.30pm & 2–6pm; July to mid-Sept Mon–Sat 9am–7pm, Sun 9.30am–1pm; Nov–April Mon–Fri 9am–12.30pm & 2–5pm, Sat 9am–12.30pm; ☎ 04 68 87 00 53, ⓦ ot-ceret.fr). There are guided tours (€5) throughout the year. Pick up a free leaflet on the town's "art trail".

ACCOMMODATION AND EATING

Le Cérétan 7 rue de la République ☎ 04 68 87 11 02, ⓦ leceretanhotel.com. Two-star hotel with seventeen tastefully renovated rooms behind a listed nineteenth-century facade; check out the wrought-iron staircase. The best-value accommodation in town. **€50**
Le France 35 bd Maréchal Joffre ☎ 04 68 87 11 27.

Aside from the delicious Spanish and French food on offer (the huge salads are a treat), the main reason to come here is to sit under the trees on the terrace in this pretty square and watch the world go by. Around €16 for a main course. Daily 7am–2am.

Arles-sur-Tech and around

ARLES-SUR-TECH is renowned for having preserved the curious folk traditions of the eastern Pyrenees – along with Prats-de-Mollo and St-Laurent-de-Cerdans, it celebrates the Fête de l'Ours (see box, p.275) in February. There is a market on **Wednesday** mornings.

Abbaye Ste-Marie

July & Aug Mon–Sat 9am–7pm, Sun 2–5pm; Sept–June Mon–Sat 9am–noon & 2–6pm, Sun 2–5pm; Nov–March closed Sun • €4 • ☎ 04 68 83 90 66

The heart of the town is formed by its compact medieval quarter, centred on the eleventh-century **Abbaye Ste-Marie**. Before passing through the main door built into its impressive facade, check out the grilled-off marble block just to the left. This is the *sainte tombe*, a fourth-century sarcophagus, revered for the pure water which miraculously issues from it, and which plays a key part in the town's ancient religious rituals. Look out also for the curious *simiots*, half-human, half-monkey creatures carved on the church. The interior has a number of good **chapels**, as well as an elegant thirteenth-century **cloister**.

Gorges de la Fou

April–Nov daily 10am–5.30pm (July & Aug 9.30am–6.30pm), weather permitting · €10 · ☎ 04 68 39 16 21 · Follow the signposted turning off the main highway west of Arles or ascend the trail leading off the D115, 3km west of town

From Arles, you can access the nearby **Gorges de la Fou**, one of the great – if touristy – spectacles of the eastern Pyrenees. You need at least an hour to cover the 1500m of metal walkway to the end and back, squeezing between 200m-high walls, so close together that they have trapped falling rocks. In places, water erosion has made the walls as smooth as plaster, and the force of the torrent during storms in 1988 swept part of the walk away – when storms threaten, the route is closed.

St-Laurent-de-Cerdans

A tortuous road ascends through forests of sweet chestnut to the village of **ST-LAURENT-DE-CERDANS**, an important junction on the World War II refugee route to Spain. Here the local history museum, **La Maison du Patrimoine et de la Mémoire André Abet** (at tourist office; July & Aug Mon–Sat 10am–noon & 2–6pm; Sept–June Mon–Fri 10am–noon & 2–5pm; €1; ☎04 68 39 55 75), preserves rural arts such as the manufacture of espadrilles, the traditional esparto-woven shoes favoured by refugee guides (*passeurs*). The **market** is held on Saturday.

ARRIVAL AND INFORMATION

ARLES-SUR-TECH AND AROUND

By bus Arles-sur-Tech (several daily) to: Le Boulou (35min); Céret (30min); Maureillas (35min); Perpignan (1hr 10min); St-Laurent-de-Cerdans (30min).

Tourist information Arles-sur-Tech: Le Palau, opposite the *mairie* (July & Aug Mon–Sat 9am–7pm, Sun 2–5pm; Sept–June Mon–Sat 9am–noon & 2–6pm, Sun 2–5pm;

Nov–March closed Sun; ☎04 68 39 11 99, ⓦtourisme-haut-vallespir.com). St-Laurent-de-Cerdans: 7 rue Joseph Nivet (July & Aug Mon–Sat 10am–noon & 2–6pm; Sept–June Mon–Fri 10am–noon & 2–5pm; ☎04 68 39 55 75, ⓦsaintlaurentdecerdans.fr).

ACCOMMODATION AND EATING

Camping Le Vallespir Av Alzine Rodone, Arles ☎04 68 39 90 00, ⓦcampingvallespir.com. The pick of several campsites in the area, this two-star site is in a lovely woodland location with two pools, tennis courts and a kids' playground. You can also enjoy swimming and trout fishing in the river. Open April to Oct. **€20.90**

Les Glycines 7 rue du Jeu de Paume, Arles ☎04 68 39 10 09, ⓦlesglycines-arles-sur-tech.e-monsite.com. Comfortable *Logis de France* hotel, which has a six-bed dormitory (€24) as well as double rooms. Light sleepers should ask for a room at the back. Good traditional French food in the restaurant and *menus* from €19.50. **€56**

SHOPPING

Création Catalane Chemin du Baynat d'En Pouly, St-Laurent ☎04 68 54 08 68, ⓦespadrille-catalane .com. Traditionally made espadrilles and fashion accessories. Free guided tours of the workshop (mid-April

CELEBRATING THE BEAR

Until the early 2000s, when they were hunted to extinction, **indigenous bears** roamed the wooded slopes of the Pyrenees, preying on game and herds, and inspiring awe among village-dwellers. Today, ursine totems and costumes are standard features of folk festivals in the mountains, the most famous being the February **Fête de l'Ours**, or "bear festivals", celebrated in Arles-sur-Tech, Prats-de-Mollo and St-Laurent-de-Cerdans. The ancient festivals mark the date when hungry bears emerged from hibernation. Traditionally, village youths would go out to capture a live animal to prove their masculinity, but gradually this was transformed into a symbolic hunt, in which three men dressed as bears are chased by a gang of hunters and eventually tamed by the town's butchers. In 2016, the local mayors applied to have the festival added to UNESCO's list of Intangible Cultural Heritage.

to mid-Oct Mon 3pm). May–Sept Mon–Sat 10am–noon & 2–7pm, Sun 3–7pm; Oct Mon–Fri 10am–noon & 2–5.30pm; Nov–April Mon–Fri 3–5pm.
Les Toiles du Soleil Av Jean Jaurès, St-Laurent ☎ 04 68

39 33 93, ⍈ toiles-du-soleil.com. In the courtyard of the factory that makes them, this is the place to buy colourful, stripy Catalan textiles for the home. Mon–Sat 10am– noon & 2.30–7pm, also Sun 2.30–7pm July & Aug.

Prats-de-Mollo

Located on the left bank of the River Tech, the medieval fortified town of **PRATS-DE-MOLLO**, together with its sister town of **La Preste**, has been famous as a spa since 1302. The present road up follows the path of a former railway (the station houses can be seen along the way), since the old road, along with houses and bridges, was washed away in the disastrous floods of October 1940. In the seventeenth century, when the Treaty of the Pyrenees subjected this area to the outrageous tax policies of Louis XIV, Prats-de-Mollo and a number of other towns and villages revolted against the French crown.

With Canigó at its back and the River Tech in front, the picturesque town, though a tourist attraction, is still surprisingly unspoilt – particularly the old *ville haute* within the city wall, with its steep, cobbled streets and ancient **fortified church**. In summer, the pedestrianized streets buzz with activity; the rest of the year the hotels are locked up, and the locals pass the time playing *boules* under the plane trees of **El Foiral**, the huge square outside the walls, where markets and fairs have been held since 1308.

Fort Lagarde

A 15min walk uphill • Mid-June to mid-Sept daily 11am–1pm & 2–6pm; mid-Sept to Oct Wed–Sun 2–5pm • €3.50 or €5–7 guided visits • ☎ 04 68 39 70 83

Fort Lagarde, which dominates the town from above, was built in 1680 under the direction of Vauban, as much to subdue the local population as to keep the Spanish at bay; the town walls, raised on fourteenth-century foundations, are another Vauban relic from this period. The fort has been beautifully restored, and the superb views all around from the ramparts compensate for the walk up. An additional attraction here is the ninety-minute **Visite-Animée** (July & Aug Mon–Thurs & Sun 3.30pm), led by an eighteenth-century cavalier who demonstrates the weapons of the era and horse-riding.

ARRIVAL AND INFORMATION   **PRATS-DE-MOLLO**

By bus Arles-sur-Tech (30min); Le Boulou (1hr 10min); Céret (50min); Perpignan (1hr 35min).
Tourist information Place du Foiral (Jan–March Mon–Fri 9.30am–12.30pm & 2–5pm; April to mid-June Mon–Fri 9.30am–12.30pm & 2–6pm, Sat & Sun 10.30am–12.30pm

& 2–6pm; mid-June to mid-Sept daily 9.30am–1pm & 2–6.30pm; mid-Sept to Dec Mon–Sat 9.30am–12.30pm & 2–5pm, Sun 10.30am–12.30pm & 2–5pm; ☎ 04 68 39 70 83, ⍈ pratsdemollolapreste.com).

ACCOMMODATION AND EATING

Le Bellevue Place du Foiral ☎ 04 68 39 72 48, ⍈ hotel -le-bellevue.fr. Good-value three-star *Logis de France* hotel in a traditional Catalan house with sixteen renovated rooms; some have their own balcony with great views. The highly regarded restaurant serves Catalan cuisine and has *menus* from €20. Breakfast included. **€56**

★ **Maison Mauro** 1 rue du Jardin d'Enfants ☎ 06 14 62 63 21, ⍈ maisonmauro.fr. This dreamy B&B has three stylish, bright, spacious rooms and a suite. With arts and crafts exhibitions, a bar, panoramic terrace and dinner on offer, what's not to like? **€70**

The Albères

The northern face of the Pyrenees, rising out of the sea at the rugged Côte Vermeille and bordered by the Tech river to the north, is known as the **Albères**. Here, a myriad of paths – a traditional route of shepherds, refugees and smugglers – cross the frontier into Spain, marked officially by the village of **Le Perthus**.

Le Boulou and around

The cork capital of France, **LE BOULOU**, is a fairly nondescript little spa town, although it is worth stopping at the **Église Ste-Marie**, the doorway of which features a fine frieze attributed to the "Master of Cabestany" (see box, p.294). There is also a small **history museum**, the Espace des Arts (rue des Écoles; Mon–Fri 9am–noon & 2–6pm, Tues–Sat in school hols; free; ☏04 68 83 36 32), with more works by the master. Die-hard fans should head 14km north to the outskirts of **Passa**, where the cloister, **Monastir del Camp** (Mon–Wed & Fri tours 3–6pm; €4; ☏04 68 38 80 71), features more of the anonymous sculptor's work.

From Le Boulou, head a few minutes south, where the Tech cuts by on its way to the sea, to visit the remarkable **chapel of St-Martin-de-Fenollar** (July & Aug daily 10am–noon & 2.30–6.30pm; Sept–June Wed–Sun 2–5pm; €3.50 ☏04 68 87 73 82) in **Maureillas-las-Illas**, an ancient village of stone-clad houses. Its twelfth-century frescoes are the best Romanesque wall paintings in Roussillon, and their clarity and simplicity of line may well have influenced Picasso, who sometimes stayed in nearby Céret.

7

ARRIVAL AND INFORMATION

LE BOULOU AND AROUND

By bus Le Boulou (several daily) to: Argelès-sur-Mer (1hr 10min); Arles-sur-Tech (40min); Céret (20min); Le Perthus (10min); Maureillas (10min); Perpignan (35min); Prats-de-Mollo (1hr 15min).

Tourist information 1 rue du Château (March–June;

Sept & Oct Mon–Fri 9am–noon & 2–6pm, Sat 9am–12.30pm; July & Aug Mon–Sat 9am–12.30pm & 2.30–6pm, Sun 9am–12.30pm; Nov–Feb Mon–Fri 9am–noon & 2–6pm, until 3pm on Mon; ☏04 68 87 50 95, ⓦ tourisme-leboulou.fr).

ACCOMMODATION

Le Relais des Chartreuses 106 av d'en Carbouner ☏04 68 83 15 88, ⓦ relais-des-chartreuses.fr. Stylish three-star boutique hotel in a seventeenth-century Catalan

farmhouse with fifteen chic, romantic rooms. Both massages and dinner are available to guests by request. There's also an attractive garden with a pool. Open April to Oct. **€65**

Le Perthus

LE PERTHUS (ⓦ le-perthus.com) was marked in history on the night of February 5, 1939, when a column of twenty thousand Spanish Republicans arrived at the border post to seek sanctuary in France. Nowadays consumer armies descend here every day, disgorging from coaches to spend their money on foodstuffs, booze and perfume, or to cross the border to fill up their tanks in Spain. The main landmark hereabouts is **Fort de Bellegarde** (daily mid-June to mid-Sept 10.30am–6.30pm; €4), which looms on a peak above the town. Built in the sixteenth century and later reinforced by Vauban, it comprises two rows of dilapidated buildings and the deepest well in Europe (63m) within an enclosure of mighty walls, and gives superb views south into Spain and north across Roussillon.

ARRIVAL AND DEPARTURE

LE PERTHUS

By bus Le Boulou (10min) and Perpignan (1hr 5min).

By car If you decide to head into Spain, take the *autoroute*

(less than €3) to avoid queues at Le Perthus.

The Côte Vermeille

When the nineteenth-century Fauvists discovered the **Côte Vermeille**, which extends southeast from Argelès-sur-Mer to the Spanish border, they found natural inspiration for their revolutionary use of colour: the sunsets (from which the coast earned its name) are a gentle red, the sea is turquoise and, as Matisse wrote, "no sky is more blue than that at Collioure". **Elne**, inland, once Roussillon's main town, is the gateway to the coast, and proceeding south you'll pass the broad sandy Blue Flag beaches of **Argelès**, before reaching the characteristically rocky coves of **Collioure** and **Banyuls**. The beauty of this stretch of coastline has inevitably been exploited, but cut up along the trails into the hills at the back of the resorts and you'll often be on your own. **Public transport** along the coast is good, with a regular train and bus service connecting all the major points of call.

Elne

Standing on a hill just 6km from the sea, the first stop on the coastal transport line is **ELNE**, an ancient fortified town that was once the capital of Roussillon. The main attraction here is the **cathedral cloister** (see below) but you might also want to check out the **Musée Terrus** (3 rue Porte Balaguer; same times as the cathedral; €3 or €6.50 combined with the cathedral; ☎04 68 22 88 88), dedicated to the landscape painter Étienne Terrus (1857–1922), a contemporary of the Fauvists and friend of sculptor Aristide Maillol (whose bust of Terrus stands on the Plateau des Garaffes, nearby). There are **markets** on Monday, Wednesday and Friday.

Cloister of the cathedral of Ste-Eulalie

May–Sept daily 10am–12.30pm & 2–6.30pm; Oct–April Tues–Sun 10am–12.30pm & 2–5pm • €4.50, or €6.50 combined with the Musée Terrus (see above) • ☎ 04 68 22 70 90

The **cloister** of the **cathedral of Ste-Eulalie** is one of the most beautiful in the region and all original, never having been restored. Built from Céret marble, one intact side of twelfth-century Romanesque pillars and capitals, immaculately carved with motifs such as foliage, lions, goats and biblical figures, is complemented on the other sides by fourteenth-century Gothic work. The eleventh-century cathedral was the seat of Roussillon's bishops until their transfer to Perpignan in 1602.

ARRIVAL AND INFORMATION   ELNE

By train The *gare SNCF* is a 10min walk west of the tourist office.

Destinations Many daily to: Argelès-sur-Mer (5min); Banyuls-sur-Mer (20min); Collioure (10min); Port-Vendres (15min); Perpignan (8min).

By bus Buses stop at the *mairie*.

Destinations Many daily to: Argelès-sur-Mer (5min); Banyuls-sur-Mer (1hr); Collioure (35min); Perpignan (30min); Port-Vendres (50min); St-Cyprien (20min); Thuir (30min).

Tourist information Place Sant Jordi (May, June & Sept daily 9.30am–12.30pm & 2–5.30pm; July & Aug daily 9.30am–6pm; Oct–April Mon–Fri 9.30am–noon & 2–5pm; ☎04 68 22 05 07, ⓦelne-tourisme.com). You can buy a pass for the two sights for €6.50.

ACCOMMODATION AND EATING

Au Remp'Arts 3 place Colonel Roger ☎04 68 22 31 95, ⓦremparts.fr. Popular French-Catalan restaurant with a nice terrace and a good-value three-course weekday lunch *menu* (€15). They also have studios and apartments to rent. Tues–Sun noon–2pm & 7–9.30pm.

Camping Le Florida Rte de Latour-Bas-Elne ☎04 68 37 80 88, ⓦcampingleflorida.com. Well-equipped four-star campsite with a waterpark where you can have diving lessons. Many activities in summer including pony rides and evening entertainment; also a free shuttle to the beach and excursions in summer. Open April to Oct (year round for motorhomes). **€39**

Can Oliba 24 rue de la Paix ☎04 68 89 44 76, ⓦcan -oliba.fr. B&B in a stone village house with four bright, spacious and stylishly decorated rooms. Home-produced pastries, jam and honey are on the breakfast menu. There's also a pool and a hot tub. **€70**

Saint-Cyprien

In the sleepy old village of **SAINT-CYPRIEN**, clumped around a tiny square, the place de la République, you'll find **Les Collections de Saint-Cyprien** (rue Zola; Tues–Sun: July & Aug 3–7pm; Sept–June 2–6pm; €4; ☎04 68 21 06 96, ⓦwww.collectionsdesaintcyprien.com).

THE DEATH OF A POET

As Francisco **Franco**'s fascist forces tightened the noose on Catalonia in early 1939, Republican refugees, both soldiers and civilians, poured over the French border. Far from being welcomed, they were herded into **concentration camps** that sprang up through Languedoc-Roussillon and along the Pyrenees, including those at Argelès, Agde, Vernet and Rivesaltes. Republican soldiers, suspected of being Communists (illegal in France), were immediately disarmed and detained, and many were sent to the special "punishment" camp set up in Collioure castle, where up to five hundred men were subject to **forced labour**. In the other camps, some of which had capacities of ten thousand, malnutrition and disease were rampant. Among the civilians who crossed in February 1939 was **Antonio Machado**, one of the leading figures of Spain's "Generation of '98" cultural movement. The 64-year-old poet and playwright, widely famous for his literary output and his characterization of "the two Spains" locked in conflict, would not survive. Exhausted, only four days after his arrival and internment he died and was buried in the Collioure cemetery, and thus became, alongside Lorca, a cultural martyr of the Spanish Civil War and a symbol of the blind destructiveness of such struggles.

In 2015, the camp at Rivesaltes opened to the public as a memorial (av Christian Bourquin, Salses-le-Château; April–Oct daily 10am–6pm; closed Mon Nov–March; €8; ☎ 04 68 08 34 90, ⓦmemorialcamprivesaltes.eu). As well as taking in the partly restored camp, visitors can explore a new windowless, concrete bunker-like building, designed by Rudy Ricciotti, which houses exhibitions and a café. Information is available in English.

Its tiny permanent collection contains a few pieces of interest, notably Dalí's sculpture *Venus de Milo with Drawers*, but it also hosts excellent and often provocative temporary exhibitions of contemporary and modern art. Three kilometres east of the village is the beach town of **Saint-Cyprien-Plage** with a long, Blue Flag sandy beach. It's the second largest pleasure port in the French Mediterranean, has abundant activities and is well equipped for families and disabled visitors. There are plenty of different **markets** in summer; throughout the year, there are also markets on Thursdays in the village and on Fridays at the beach.

ARRIVAL AND INFORMATION   SAINT-CYPRIEN

By bus Saint-Cyprien (several daily) to: Cabestany (40min); Elne (30min); Perpignan (1hr); Thuir (1hr). In July & Aug bus #410 runs to Argelès Plage, Collioure, Port-Vendres and Banyuls-sur-Mer.
Tourist information Quai Arthur Rimbaud (July & Aug daily 9am–1pm & 2–7pm; last two weeks of June and first two weeks of Sept daily 9am–noon & 2–6pm; mid-Sept to mid-June Mon–Sat 9am–noon & 2–6pm; ☎ 04 68 21 01 33, ⓦtourisme-saint-cyprien.com).

ACCOMMODATION

Le Belvedere Rue Pierre Benoît, St-Cyprien-Village ☎ 04 68 21 05 93, ⓦhotellebelvedere.com. Friendly, family-run two-star hotel in an elevated position with nice views over the coast and mountains. The thirty rooms are decorated in minimalist Catalan style and the restaurant serves decent Catalan food and grills (April–Oct). There's a pool, a kids' play area and free parking. **€49**
Camping Cala Gogo Av Armand Lanoux, St-Cyprien-Plage ☎ 04 68 21 07 12, ⓦcamping-le-calagogo.fr. Large five-star campsite with direct access to the beach; there's also a heated pool. Activities include diving lessons and evening entertainment. Open May to Sept. **€47.10**

Argelès-sur-Mer and around

Poised on the northern edge of the Côte Vermeille, **ARGELÈS-SUR-MER** has the last wide, sandy beach on the coast. At the end of the Spanish Civil War thousands of refugees lived in camps here, their numbers including the Republican poet Antonio Machado, who failed to survive the first harsh winter of his arrival (see box above). Nowadays, more than any other resort on this section of coast, this is a mass-tourist town, wooing its visitors with holiday essentials like mini-golf, gambling tables and beauty contests. It's also equipped for disabled visitors.

The town itself is divided in two: the old **Argelès-Ville**, a little inland, and the new **Argelès-Plage**, which receives an annual inundation of up to 300,000 French, Belgian, Dutch and English visitors. Plage Nord and Plage des Pins are **beaches** of the smooth, sandy and potentially windblown variety, whereas **Le Racou** – the first bay of the Côte Vermeille – is more intimate and offers a taste of mountain coastline. Either way, Argelès-Plage is a centre for noisy, ebullient, youthful hedonism, a landscape of neon lights and fast food with a background of loud music and the rattle of scooters.

ARRIVAL AND INFORMATION
ARGELÈS-SUR-MER AND AROUND

By train The *gare SNCF* is a few minutes' walk west of the centre of Argelès-Ville. The town is on the main line that runs along the coast from the Spanish frontier.
Destinations Many daily to: Banyuls-sur-Mer (15min); Collioure (5min); Elne (5min); Perpignan (15min); Port-Vendres (8min); Rivesaltes (25min); Salses-le-Château (35min).
By bus Several daily to: Banyuls-sur-Mer (35min); Céret (1hr 30min); Collioure (15min); Elne (25min); Le Boulou

(1hr 10min); Maureillas (1hr 15min); Perpignan (45min); Port-Vendres (30min); St-Cyprien (30min).
Tourist information Argelès-Plage: place de l'Europe (April–June & Sept daily 9am–12.30pm & 2–6.30pm; July & Aug daily 8.30am–8pm; Oct–March Mon–Fri 9am–noon & 2–6pm, Sat 9am–noon; ☎04 68 81 15 85, ⊕argeles-sur-mer.com). Argelès-Ville: Salle Cardonne, place St Côme (mid-June to mid-Sept Mon–Sat 9.30am–1pm).

ACCOMMODATION AND EATING

There are around sixty campsites in the area, with something to suit most tastes and budgets. Book in advance, as they get full in summer.

★**La Bartavelle** 24 rue de la République, Argelès-Ville ☎06 19 25 70 13, ⊕restaurant-labartavelle.fr. This stylish little restaurant is the best place to eat in town. Creative Catalan cuisine is on the menu (lunch from €15), accompanied by carefully chosen local wines. Reservations essential. Tues, Thurs & Fri 7.30–9.15pm, Wed 12.15–1.15pm, Sat 12.15–1.15pm & 7.30–9.15pm.
Menja Aqui 12 av Torre d'En Sorra, Le Racou, the

southernmost beach in Argelès ☎04 68 81 65 07. Lively waterfront tapas bar (from €5) with a party atmosphere in the evenings. Decent selection of regional wines. Daily May–Sept 10am–midnight.
Les Mimosas 51 av des Mimosas, Argelès-Plage ☎04 68 81 14 77, ⊕hotel-mimosas.com. Simple but welcoming two-star hotel with "beach house" decor and 27 white, minimalist rooms ("Standard" and "Confort" have a/c). It's a couple of minutes' walk to the sea. **€79**

Collioure

Sitting nestled in a picturesque cove, **COLLIOURE** is a true Côte Vermeille town, which to a certain extent still banks on its maritime and artistic past. Established as a trading port by the Phoenicians and ancient Greeks, Collioure was later occupied by Romans, Visigoths and Arabs. Altogether, the place has been the focus of nearly a dozen territorial squabbles, including four invasions by the French and two by the Spanish. The sixteenth-century **Fort St-Elme** overlooking the town from the south, and the seventeenth-century **Fort Miradou** to the north (still used by the military), are reminders of this turbulent past.

The artistic tradition of Collioure survives today, albeit with less distinction; however, there are a few serious commercial galleries. Many of these are in the old quarter of the town, the **Mouré**, whose steep, narrow streets are lined by pastel-tinted houses, restaurants and assorted clothing and regional produce shops. Lateen-rigged fishing boats might be moored in the **harbour** itself, or drawn up on the palm-lined beach; those no longer used by fishermen are now beautifully restored and sailed as pleasure vessels by their new owners. **Markets** take place on Wednesday and Sunday.

Musée d'Art Moderne – Fonds Peské
Rte de Port-Vendres • Daily 10am–noon & 2–6pm, Oct–May closed Tues • €3 • ☎04 68 82 10 19

Housed in the beautiful Villa Pams on the eastern edge of the town about five minutes'

THE FAUVISTS

In the early 1900s, invaders of a different sort came to Collioure; the group of painters – including Matisse and Derain – known as the **Fauvists** (*les Fauvistes*) made the town (also an inspiration to Picasso) their summer base. Some of their original work adorns the bar at *Les Templiers* (12 quai de l'Amirauté; ⓦ hotel-templiers.com); you can also follow the "Chemin du Fauvisme" around the town, a trail of nineteen reproductions of paintings by Matisse and Derain placed on the sites where they were painted (a **map** is available from the tourist office). For further information and guided tours (€10), drop by the Maison du Fauvisme (10 rue de la Prud'homie; daily: June–Sept 9.30am–1pm & 2.30–6pm; Oct–May until 5.30pm; ☏ 04 68 98 07 16).

walk uphill from the port, Collioure's **Musée d'Art Moderne**, has several temporary exhibitions a year which alternate with displays of works from the permanent collection. You might want to check what's on before you head up; otherwise it's one strictly for avid fans of modern and contemporary art.

Château-royal

Daily: June–Sept 10am–6/7pm; Oct–May 9am–5pm • €4 • ☏ 04 68 82 06 43

The **château-royal**, the imposing fortress which dominates the harbour, was founded by the Templars in the thirteenth century, rebuilt and used as a sometime residence by the kings of Mallorca and Aragón two hundred years later, and modernized by Vauban after the Treaty of the Pyrenees. Inside, there are usually temporary exhibitions – for example on local archeology – and it's also used for events and concerts. The two **beaches** which bookend the castle are attractive and worth whiling away an hour or two, although they become hopelessly crowded in summer months. One is sandy and the other stony.

Fort St-Elme

Daily: April–Sept 10.30am–7pm; Oct–March 10.30am–5pm • €6 • ☏ 06 64 61 82 42, ⓦ fortsaintelme.fr • It's a 30min walk or you can take the *petit train*

High above Collioure, **Fort St-Elme** was built in the sixteenth century by Charles V to defend his Spanish Empire from the French. These days, although it's privately owned and inhabited, the fort is open to the public who come to enjoy the marvellous views, the impressive collection of weapons and the **gardens** filled with South American plants and flowers. There are regular **events** throughout the year including medieval tournaments in August.

Église Notre-Dame-des-Anges

On the north side of the harbour, the **Église Notre-Dame-des-Anges** was erected in the seventeenth century, replacing the ancient Sainte-Marie, razed on the orders of Vauban. The distinctive round bell tower – once doubling as the lighthouse – onto which it was grafted has been damaged many times by storm and war: the base dates from the thirteenth century, the middle from the fourteenth to seventeenth centuries, and the bell chamber from the nineteenth. It's worth taking a look inside to see the magnificent gilt retable, carved and painted in three tiers by Joseph Sunyer.

ARRIVAL AND INFORMATION
COLLIOURE

By train The *gare SNCF* is less than ten minutes' walk west of the centre, along av Aristide Maillol.

Destinations Many daily to: Argelès (5min); Banyuls-sur-Mer (8min); Elne (12min); Perpignan (22min); Port-Vendres (2min); Rivesaltes (32min); Salses-le-Château (40min).

By bus Buses stop at the central car park, Les Glacis, off av Général-de-Gaulle.

Destinations Several daily to: Argelès (15min); Banyuls-sur-Mer (25min); Elne (35min); Perpignan (1hr 5min); Port-Vendres (15min).

By car The car parks fill up quickly and are expensive. There is free parking at Cap Dourats (2km to the east) and a free shuttle bus from May to Sept to get into town.

7

THE SCOTTISH CONNECTION

Glasgow-born **Charles Rennie Mackintosh** (1868–1928) – architect, designer and artist – first arrived in Roussillon in 1923. Disillusioned with his work, and looking for somewhere warmer and cheaper to live, the spa town of Amélie-les-Bains in the Tech valley seemed a good option. "This lovely coloured land … with its warmth and its sun", Roussillon went on to provide the inspiration for his watercolours over the next few years. Going on to Collioure for the summer, he spent the next winter in Ille-sur-Têt (see p.287). While exploring the Têt valley, Mackintosh discovered Mont-Louis, which became his home for the next three summers; Port-Vendres was his base for the winters. You can find out more about the artist's time in the region at the **interpretation centres** in Amélie-les-Bains and Port-Vendres (see p.306). See ⓦ crmackintoshfrance.com for details.

Tourist information Located just behind the harbour on place du 18 Juin (April–Sept daily 9am–8pm; Oct–March Mon–Sat 9am–noon & 2–6pm; ☎ 04 68 82 15 47, ⓦ collioure.com).

ACCOMMODATION AND EATING

La 5ème Péché 16 rue de la Fraternité ☎ 04 68 98 09 76, ⓦ le-cinquieme-peche.com. Japan meets Catalonia at this *gastronomique* hole-in-the-wall in Collioure's old town. Creative dishes, well-chosen wines and lunch from €25. Tues–Sat 12.15–1.30pm & 7.30–9pm.

★ **Casa Païral** Rue des Palmiers ☎ 04 68 82 05 81, ⓦ hotel-casa-pairal.com. The town's nicest hotel is in a nineteenth-century gentleman's residence, with a peaceful garden and pool, in a quiet location off the west side of rue de la République, the main shopping street. Local products feature in the excellent breakfast buffet. €125

La Cuisine Comptoir 2 rue Colbert ☎ 04 68 81 14 40. In the maze of streets behind the port, this tiny tapas and wine bar with a courtyard is a fun spot to while away a couple of hours. Expect to pay €15–20. Daily noon–midnight.

SHOPPING

Anchois Roque 17 rte d'Argelès ☎ 04 68 82 04 99, ⓦ anchois-roque.fr. Collioure is famous for its anchovies (*anchois*) and this is the place to buy them, along with many other regional products. You can also visit their workshop (Mon–Fri 8.15–11.45am & 2–4.45pm; free). Mon–Sat 8am–7.30pm, Sun 9am–noon & 2–7pm.

Port-Vendres and around

A five-minute ride southeast from Collioure, **PORT-VENDRES** (the Roman Portus Veneris: "Port of Venus") is marred by the busy main road, but for a genuine, unsophisticated fishing port, this is your best (indeed only) choice on the Côte Vermeille – though you probably won't want to stay longer than it takes to have a look around the port and tuck into a fish lunch. A huge fish-processing **factory** dominates one side of the harbour, while sardine- and tuna-fishing boats are moored under the Maillol-designed war memorial opposite, with nets and other paraphernalia piled along the harbour wall. The general **market** is on Saturday mornings.

Four kilometres south of town is one of the region's most original attractions: the listed **Site de Paulilles** (daily: April & Oct 9am–7pm; May, June & Sept 9am–8pm; July & Aug 9am–9pm; Nov–March 9am–5pm; free), which is working towards becoming a Grand Site de France. It is centred on a nineteenth-century **dynamite factory** (founded by Nobel) that is being allowed to revert to nature. Here you'll find nature trails, a Blue Flag beach, and a workshop that restores traditional fishing boats. Call into the Maison du Site for information.

ARRIVAL AND INFORMATION   PORT-VENDRES

By train The *gare SNCF* is less than ten minutes' southwest of the port.
Destinations Many daily to: Argelès (8min); Banyuls-sur-Mer (4min); Collioure (2min); Elne (15min); Perpignan (25min); Rivesaltes (35min); Salses-le-Château (43min).
By bus Several daily to: Argelès (30min); Banyuls-sur-Mer (10min); Collioure (15min); Elne (40min); Perpignan (1hr 15min).

Tourist information 1 quai François Joly (April–Sept daily 9am–8pm; Oct–March Mon–Sat 9am–noon & 2–6pm; ☎ 04 68 82 07 54, ⓦ port-vendres.com). Maison du Site de Paulilles: on the RD914 (daily: April & Oct 9am–1pm & 2–6pm; May & Sept 9am–1pm & 2–7pm; June 9am–1pm & 2–8pm; July & Aug 9am–8pm; Nov–March 9am–noon & 2–5pm; ☎ 04 68 95 23 40).

EATING

Chez Pujol 16–17 quai Forgas ☎ 04 68 82 01 39, ⓦ chezpujol.com. At the port, this fishmonger-brasserie is the place to go to sample *fruits de mer* – even better in fine weather, when you can enjoy your meal on the terrace. If it's on, try the *fricassée* of cuttlefish (*seiche*) with chorizo. *Menus* from €18.50. Daily 11.45am–3pm & 6.30–10.45pm.

Banyuls-sur-Mer

As the road crosses the Col du Père Carnère and drops down towards the Plage des Elmes, the once-elegant wine town of **BANYULS-SUR-MER** comes into view, with dry-stone walls and orderly rows of vines stretching into the hills behind it. Banyuls is famous for its dessert wine, which the French tend to drink as an aperitif; if you fancy a tipple, take a forty-minute **guided tour** of one of the larger cellars, such as Terres des Templiers (rte du Mas Reig; mid-March to early Nov daily 10am–7.30pm; early Nov to mid-March Mon–Fri 10am–1pm & 2.30–6.30pm; in English in the afternoon; €5; ☎ 04 68 98 36 92, ⓦ terredestempliers.fr). The coastal waters of this area, rich in marine life due to the Pyrenees' steep underwater descent, were the first *réserve marine* to be created in France. You can experience and explore them for yourself via an **underwater trail** (you'll need a snorkel) from Peyrefitte beach. Sunday is **market** day.

Maillol's tomb

To get here, walk the length of av Général-de-Gaulle, until you pass under a bridge. Shortly afterwards, where the road curves around to the right, take the left-hand road, following the line of a river: signs from here point to the "Musée et Tombeau de Maillol". The round trip takes about 2.5hr.

Striking out of town, the 4km **hike** from Banyuls to **Maillol's tomb** and house makes a pleasant excursion up into the vine-clad Albères. Sculptor **Aristide Maillol** (1861–1944) was a Banyuls native famous for his fleshy nude sculptures. He is buried at his farm, La Métairie, now restored as the **Musée Maillol** (Tues–Sun: May–Sept 10am–noon & 3–6pm; Oct–April 10am–noon & 2–5pm; €5; ☎ 04 68 88 57 11), which contains his personal art collection, featuring works by Duchamp, Bonnard and Picasso. The artist's tomb is topped by his *La Méditerranée*.

ARRIVAL AND INFORMATION

BANYULS-SUR-MER

By train The *gare SNCF* is at the very western edge of town.
Destinations Several daily to: Argelès (13min); Collioure (8min); Elne (20min); Perpignan (30min); Port-Vendres (4min); Rivesaltes (40min); Salses-le-Château (47min).
By bus Several daily to: Argelès (45min); Collioure (35min); Elne (1hr); Perpignan (1hr 20min); Port-Vendres (15min).
Tourist information Av de la République (July & Aug daily 9am–7pm; Sept–June Mon–Sat 9am–noon & 2–6pm; ☎ 04 68 88 31 58, ⓦ banyuls-sur-mer.com). The office can provide information on walking, cycling, diving, kayaking and sailing.

ACCOMMODATION AND EATING

Le Jardin de Saint Sébastien 10 av du Fontaulé ☎ 04 68 55 22 64, ⓦ lejardindesaintsebastien.com. This portside restaurant owned by a wine estate has a good range of dishes, from freshly caught fish to tapas (*menu* €18.50). They have a sister restaurant in Collioure (see website). Daily noon–2pm & 7–9pm.
Les Pêcheurs 5 av du Fontaulé ☎ 04 68 88 02 10. Overlooking the sea, this traditional resort hotel has been renovated to give it a bit of contemporary style, though there are few facilities. **€88**

7

ONENSIS GALLIÆ VETUSTISSIMA

LaTour Romaine, ou Tourre Magne.

ANTIQVES.

PANS DE MVRAILLE.

1582 MAP OF NÎMES

Contexts

History

The two areas of Occitan Languedoc and Catalan Roussillon, in addition to their own cultural particularities, have strong historical differences. Languedoc was traditionally ruled by a native aristocracy, while Roussillon fell into the ambit of Catalonia, fated to become part of modern Spain. Even before they were integrated into the nation-state of France, though, their geographical proximity meant there were parallels and connections; each enjoyed its "golden age" in the Middle Ages, which may account for the nostalgia with which the inhabitants regard the period, and their shared borders saw considerable movement and contact.

Prehistory

The earliest traces of the human occupation of Languedoc and Roussillon date from the early **Paleolithic era** (Stone Age): the cranial remains of the slight but upright *Homo erectus*, discovered in the 1970s at Tautavel, near Perpignan, date back nearly half a million years. These early ancestors, who do not appear to have harnessed fire, hunted with the aid of simple stone weapons and tools and lived off the abundant (and dangerous) fauna of the region, which included wolves, hippos, rhinos, wild sheep and goats and the ferocious cave bear, whose claw marks are still visible on cave walls in the region (for example at Limousis, in the Montagne Noire). As the evolutionary tree branched off, taller and smarter **Neanderthal** humans appeared, dominating the local scene during the mid-Paleolithic era (approximately 150,000–35,000 BCE). With a better tool-making capability than *Homo erectus*, the Neanderthals were able to pursue the mammoths and elephants of the Languedocian plain, and the remains of burial places scattered about the Pyrenean foothills dating from this time point to the beginnings of culture and religion.

It was not until the late Palaeolithic era that **modern humans** (*Homo sapiens*) came to monopolize the area, thriving especially in the Magdalenian period, some 14,000 years ago, which followed the last retreat of the glaciers. The earliest **cave paintings** of the Ariège valley (at Niaux and Mas d'Azil) date from this period and show the preoccupation of this early people with the hunt. In addition to cave art, they fashioned the small corpulent "Venus" statuettes, which are generally considered to relate to fertility rites.

With the invention of the harpoon, the development of fishing began to draw people towards the coasts of modern Roussillon. Nevertheless, the mid-altitude caves remained the favoured habitat into the Mesolothic and Neolithic (middle and new Stone Age) periods, which lasted here until about 1500 BCE. Several important innovations occurred in the Neolithic era: **agriculture** and **animal husbandry** came into being in the fifth millennium BCE, as did the use of grain-storage facilities. **Mining** and smelting were developed for the crude utilization of metals, such as copper, and better management of fire also permitted the manufacture of ceramics. Technical

450,000 BCE	150,000 BCE	13,000 BCE
"Tautavel man", *Homo erectus*, is one of Europe's first known inhabitants	Neanderthals appear, whose tool-making ability allows them to hunt large animals	Magdalenians are painting caves in the Ariège valley

improvements encouraged specialization and this, in turn, trade, which seems to have first arisen among the lowland settlements of the Narbonnais plain. It was also in the last millennium of the Stone Age that the **dolmens** (megalithic henges) and **tumuli** (burial mounds) which dot the mid-level Pyrenees and Haut Languedoc appeared.

The Bronze Age

The Bronze Age in Languedoc and Roussillon was an era of great movement and change. Around 800 BCE, the **Celts** arrived and began displacing the indigenous peoples, and an area stretching from Nîmes in the east past Toulouse in the west came under the hegemony of the Volcae, one of several large Celtic tribal groups who dominated the south of France. Meanwhile, **Phoenicians** and **Greeks** began to arrive on the region's shores. They set up outposts (such as Maguelone and Port-Vendres) and began to trade with natives, who lived for the most part in fortified hill-top towns now known as **oppida** (plural of the Latin *oppidum*, or "town"), such as the settlement of Ensérune. As archeological finds have confirmed, the native tribes were not uncivilized "barbarians" as Romans were later wont to claim, but participants in complex, technologically capable societies linked to extensive trade networks. Their rich culture is evinced by the objects that have survived them: skilfully worked bronze weapons and jewellery. Although perhaps not comparable with contemporary civilizations of the eastern Mediterranean, they had their own diversified agricultural and craft-based economies and stratified social structures. Their one weakness was that they were not oriented towards the sea and so needed intermediaries such as the Phoenicians to reach foreign markets.

The Romans

In the fourth century BCE, the **Romans** embarked on a series of campaigns of conquest which brought the whole Iberian peninsula and the bulk of Greek possessions under its power and set it against the **Carthaginians**, heirs of Phoenicia in the western Mediterranean. The Romans were the ultimate victors, and the rumble of **Hannibal**'s elephants across the length of Languedoc in 218 BCE presaged the beginning of a long colonial period in southern France. A few decades later the **Via Domitia**, the Rome–Cadiz superhighway, was built along the Languedoc coast, facilitating Roman military and economic expansion, and the Roman city of Narbo was founded. By about 70 BCE all of what is now France south of Lyon and Toulouse constituted Narbonensian Gaul. With the completion of the conquest by **Julius Caesar** and his successor, the Emperor **Augustus**, the zone was elevated to the rank of an imperial province, and subdivided (in 27 BCE), so that Narbonne became the capital of the lands from the Rhône to the Pyrenees.

With the benefits of Pax Romana, the region enjoyed an easy prosperity under the first emperors. Trade flourished (wine was a big export item) and there were major settlements at Baeterra (Béziers) and Nemausus (Nîmes). Nîmes became the region's most important city in the mid-second century under Antoninus Pius – an emperor who lavished favours on his home town. During this period, Roman organizational infrastructure and slave labour permitted the elaboration of architectural projects of a scale and complexity that would not be duplicated for fifteen hundred years. This is particularly true in the case of public civic architecture, such as Nîmes' huge amphitheatre, **Les Arènes**, the nearby

800 BCE	575 BCE	120 BCE	118 BCE
The Celts arrive and take over the area from Nîmes to Toulouse	Foundation of Béziers	The Romans annexe the south of France	The Via Domitia, the Roman road linking Spain with Italy, is built and Narbonne is founded

aqueduct, the **Pont du Gard**, and the **bridge** at Sommières. Religious buildings, the finest surviving example of which is Nîmes' **Maison Carrée**, were based on Greek styles – temples usually consisting of a *cella* or inner sanctum (the abode of the god), ringed by a colonnade of columns which were topped by decorative capitals.

But rocky times lay ahead for the empire, as the expansion on which its prosperity had depended slowed. Domestic economic crises were compounded by the growing threat of neighbouring powers: Persia in the east, and "barbarians" in North Africa and northwest Europe. While the frontiers under attack by **Franks** and **Goths** were far from Languedoc, the disruption of the empire's stability had economic repercussions which reached Gallia-Narbonensis. The growing dissatisfaction and malaise in the empire encouraged a certain trend towards new religions such as the Mithras cult and **Christianity**, which spread rapidly through urban Languedoc. The latter was seen as a threat to the imperial order and a series of emperors set about trying to quash it. The fiercest persecutions, which saw Christians submitted to all manner of brutal public tortures and executions, were carried out under Valerian and Diocletian between 257 and 311 – many of the area's martyred saints date from this era.

When **Constantine the Great** became sole emperor in 324, he proclaimed Christianity a tolerated religion and it quickly took hold in the towns and cities of Languedoc. With the capital of the empire now in far-off Constantinople, the bishops, who were appointed in each Roman town after 391, helped hold together the decaying fabric of administration. In the new, contracting Christianized empire, Nîmes and Narbonne waned, as Roman cities in Provence, such as Arles, came to the forefront. But great changes were afoot, and as central power declined, people left the cities, taking refuge in smaller fortified towns and villas, and frequently trading off their liberty for the protection of a powerful patron. Imperial policy in the east was to deflect the waves of semi-nomadic steppe peoples westward, a tactic which saved the core of the empire, but brought about its disappearance in the west.

After the Romans

In the fifth century wave after wave of these small but aggressive invading bands passed through Languedoc and Roussillon: first the Suevi, then the Vandals and finally the **Visigoths**. It was the last of these who set up a durable kingdom, which in its greatest extent covered the southwest of France and most of Iberia. Their first capital was **Tolosa** – modern Toulouse – and they initially ruled, in name, as Roman imperial governors. At this time, however, a rival group, the **Franks**, had coalesced in the Low Countries and, led by King Clovis (482–511), drove southwards, incorporating Toulouse into their Kingdom of Aquitaine. Most of Languedoc and Roussillon, however, known then as **Septimania** (either after its seven great cities: Narbonne, Agde, Béziers, Maguelone, Lodève, Nîmes and Uzès, or after the Roman Seventh Legion which was garrisoned in the area), remained under the Visigoths.

The weak and conflictive Visigothic kingdom was dealt a deathblow by **Muslim armies**, which arrived in Iberia around 711. Wiping out the Spanish Visigothic nobility in a single battle, they quickly conquered most of modern Spain and Portugal, and small raiding parties crossed the Pyrenees, taking Toulouse and Septimania in the 720s. The most northern of these groups was turned back near Poitiers by Charles Martel in 732.

1 AD	**257–311 AD**	**324 AD**
The Pont du Gard aqueduct is built to supply water to Nîmes	Christians are persecuted and executed by the Romans who want to eradicate this "threat"	Constantine the Great becomes Emperor and declares that Christianity should be tolerated

Numerically too few to hang onto such an extensive area, the Muslims occupied the towns, exacting tribute and using them as raiding bases. In the years that followed the battle of Poitiers, the Muslims were turned out of Toulouse, Carcassonne and eventually their coastal enclaves as one by one these fell to the Franks; it was to prevent their return that Martel destroyed the town of Maguelone (see p.218). This long campaign was carried out under the leadership of **Pepin the Short**, the first Carolingian king (751–68), and it was his successor, **Charlemagne** (Charles the Great), who pushed the Muslims back over the Pyrenees. Languedoc was absorbed into the **Frankish Empire** and Roussillon became part of the semi-autonomous frontier region known as the **Spanish Marches**. After the decline of Roman power in the west, the empire continued in the east, but despite the fact that Constantinople was now its capital, its rulers continued to bear the title "Emperor of Rome". During Charlemagne's era, it so happened that it was a woman, Irene, who was in power in Constantinople; seeing an opportunity to enhance his prestige – given that no one actually held the title of "Emperor" – Charlemagne journeyed to Rome and had the pope crown him as "Holy Roman Emperor" in 800. Thus, his dominions, which covered almost all of western Europe, came to be known as the **Holy Roman Empire**, and the papacy, which up till then had been little more than an ordinary bishopric, gained justification for its later claims to be the power which could (or not) crown emperors.

The counts and feudalism

Despite his centralizing policies, Charlemagne followed Germanic custom, separating his kingdom among his heirs, and Languedoc fell into the **Kingdom of the Western Franks**, more or less contiguous with modern France. When its second king, Louis the Stammerer, died heirless in 879, the kingdom rapidly disintegrated, leaving power in the hands of local **counts**, although nominally Charlemagne's other descendants held the highest authority. Among the local nobility, one family, the "**Raymonds**" or "dynasty of St-Gilles", eventually came to dominate. They had ruled Toulouse since 840, thanks to a grant by Pepin II, and by the late 900s they were to all intents and purposes independent rulers. As such, they began to expand, absorbing neighbouring territories, such as Albi, or co-opting other, lesser noble lines, such as the **Trencavels** of Carcassonne, as vassals. **Raymond IV** ruled a realm which stretched from Toulouse to the banks of the Rhône; it was he who adopted the surname of "St-Gilles", in honour of his favourite possession (the abbey). Meanwhile, the most powerful lord of the Spanish March, **Guifré el Pelós** ("Wilfred the Hairy"), Count of the Cerdagne, Girona and Barcelona, was granted independence from the empire. Roussillon, then dominated by Elne, came under his power; it is at this point that Languedoc's and Roussillon's histories as separate regions begin, and over the course of the centuries that followed their paths would be linked, but not united again until Louis XIV's formal annexation of Roussillon in the 1600s.

In these early medieval centuries, what little industry and urban life existed under the Romans all but disappeared. Western Europe became overwhelmingly agrarian, developing an economy of near subsistence in which the noble class siphoned off the meagre surplus and provided military protection to the masses. Local magnates obtained warriors by granting lands in exchange for loyalty, and **feudal** structures developed. Learned culture all but vanished with the disappearance of towns, and was maintained only by the monks who lived in isolated communities.

391 AD	5th century AD	7th century AD	8th century AD
Bishops are appointed in each Roman town	The Visigoths take over the rule of the region	Muslim raiding parties from Iberia take Toulouse and Septimania	Charlemagne pushes the Muslims back over the Pyrenees and is crowned Holy Roman Emperor

Twelfth-century revival

In the twelfth century the picture began to change rapidly. A shift away from subsistence, possibly as the result of climatic change and aided by improvements in agricultural technology, allowed the population to grow, while under the counts the region began to enjoy a stability which stimulated **trade** and **industry**. People started to move around Europe looking for better opportunities; towns expanded, shaking Toulouse and the cities of Septimania back to life. The agrarian social structures which had developed in the previous period were not suitable for town life, and the counts, anxious to promote economic growth, recognized that by extending liberties and privileges to the townsfolk, their own position could be improved. Oligarchic **town councils**, such as the **Capitolo** in Toulouse, were formed, sharing in or taking over urban administration and further stimulating growth.

The papacy, meanwhile, was in the process of becoming a geopolitical power, with control over the resources and policies of local churches – traditionally the turf of the nobles. On the popular level, **pilgrimage** played an important role, carrying ordinary believers across Europe, to Rome or Santiago de Compostela, and visiting local churches such as that at St-Gilles. A wave of reformation also swept over the **monasteries**, where the degenerate and locally independent Benedictines were replaced by pious, well-controlled orders, most importantly the Cistercians.

Secular and religious culture began to revive. Great churches were raised in the towns, and old cathedrals were replaced by more elaborate structures. The courts of the counts' palaces became the focus of a new culture as well, one which sought refinement in the **courtly traditions** of elaborate manners, rich clothes and imported luxuries. The most visible manifestation of this new culture was the tradition of courtly love and the **troubadours**. These singing poets – the first of whom is said to have been Guilhem de Peitieu, count of Poitiers and father of Eleanor of Aquitaine, Queen of France and, later, England – composed odes of yearning, unrequited love to anonymous "dark ladies", and satirical barbs aimed at local nobles. Their language of choice was not Latin, which had previously been the only voice of culture, but the local vernaculars, Occitan and Catalan.

Better educated than before, the newly wealthy and increasingly literate craftsmen, the **burghers**, began to look for more satisfying theological answers than the still feudal-oriented Church could provide. The peasants, too, were dissatisfied; although increasingly interested in Christianity, a shortage of priests meant they were frustrated by a lack of pastoral care. In short, the Church was seen as **corrupt** by everyone but the nobility.

Neighbouring Roussillon, though it went through most of the same social and economic processes as Languedoc, followed a distinctive political and religious course. In the centuries following Guifré el Pelós, his descendants, the **counts of Barcelona**, had been struggling to gain supremacy over their various rival counts in Catalonia, who did not want to recognize them as overlords. They were aided in this campaign in 1142 when Ramon Berenguer IV married the princess of Aragón, obtaining the title of King of Aragón for his heirs. Thus Barcelona became the capital of a multinational monarchy and its rulers, the count-kings, were to govern one of the great powers of the medieval Mediterranean. Linked by ties of marriage to noble houses in Languedoc and further east in Provence, they angled for political expansion, and for a time their holdings included Montpellier and various parts east of the Rhône. Indeed, the counts

879	9th century AD	11th century AD	12th century AD
Louis the Stammerer dies heirless and the Kingdom of the Western Franks is up for grabs	The counts of Toulouse expand their area as far as the Rhône	The Pilgrimage to Santiago de Compostela becomes popular with Catholics	Towns expand and town councils, such as the Capitolo in Toulouse, are formed

of Toulouse became their vassals – although this was merely a formality, amounting more to a pact of mutual assistance than a recognition of the count-kings' authority.

Catharism and the Albigensian Crusades

In the climate of dissatisfaction with the Church, popular **heresies** began to spring up, led by men who preached to the people in their own language and led lives of austerity and poverty, in emulation of the Apostles and in contrast to the wealthy and aloof Catholic clergy. The Church tried at first to quash the problem with force, but then, co-opting the impulses which drove the heretics, licensed two new groups, the Dominican and Franciscan preaching friars who – in contrast to the isolated monks – were to minister and preach among the common people. But the damage had already been done, and the most successful of the new heresies, **Catharism**, had become firmly entrenched. This doctrine was a variant on ancient Middle Eastern beliefs combined with Christianity, a dualistic creed which portrayed the material world as evil and the spiritual world as good. It resonated among the common folk as well as nobles (who wanted to set themselves apart from the influence of Rome and its northern French political allies), and a shadow counter-Church began to organize itself, holding its first Council at St-Félix-de-Lauragais in 1167. In most of the major towns of Languedoc, and the countryside around Toulouse and south of the Aude, this new Church gained a strong presence. Here, the nobility, including the counts of Toulouse, the Trencavels of Carcassonne and a whole array of minor barons, remained Catholic themselves, but gave free reign to Cathar preachers to spread their religious message. As Roussillon did not develop an urban society as quickly as Languedoc and the count-kings had a more favourable political attitude to the papacy, Catharism was discouraged from gaining a strong hold here. Preachers and refugees did arrive in Catalan lands, but they could not live openly in their faith, for fear of persecution.

The Albigensians

By the end of the 1100s the Catholic Church had become a powerful corporation, and it was not about to brook the loss of Languedoc to the heretic Cathars – or **Albigensians**, as they are commonly known. When persuasion failed to convert the heretics or influence the Cathar-protecting lords of Languedoc, and excommunication had little effect, the papacy turned to military force. Although it hardly had a formal army, the papacy could count on the support of powerful multinational monastic organizations such as the Cistercian Order, whose headquarters, Cîteaux, was in northern France, and which was dominated by noble families from the north. These same families, which had been united under the Capetian kings of France, began to look hungrily at the extensive but fragmented lands of the counts to the south. Papal efforts to bring the Cathars back into the fold began as early as 1150, and in 1204 **Raymond VI** of Toulouse was excommunicated for refusing to persecute his Cathar subjects. However, the Albigensians and their lords would not cave in – the papal legate Pierre de Castelnau was murdered at a parley in 1208 – and **Pope Innocent III** called a Crusade, providing the northern nobles with the ideological justification to wage war on Languedoc. They were joined by knights from across Christendom, drawn by the allure of religious redemption and loot.

1167	1204	1208
The first Cathar council is held at St-Félix-de-Lauragais	Raymond IV of Toulouse is excommunicated for refusing to persecute his Cathar subjects	The papal legate, Pierre de Castelnau, is murdered by an agent of Raymond

TOP 10 CATHAR SITES

Montségur The defiant Cathar redoubt. See p.103.
Carcassonne De Montfort's headquarters. See p.88.
Lavaur The capital of the Cathar heartland. See p.72.
Les Jacobins The Dominican headquarters in Languedoc. See p.53.
Lastours Cathar fortresses that defied de Montfort. See p.159.
The Madeleine church, Béziers The site of the massacre. See p.262.
Minerve Breathtaking, canyon-girded Cathar village. See p.256.
Quéribus castle The rebels' last refuge. See p.285.
Villerouge-Termenès Site of the last burning in 1321. See p.252.
Montaillou A Cathar hamlet in the Pyrenees. See p.105.

The campaign was led initially by **Arnaud Amaury**, abbot of Cîteaux, whose campaigns carried him rapidly across the littoral from Nîmes, which gave up without a fight, to Béziers. Here, faced by the refusal of the town's Catholics to give up their Cathar neighbours, he ordered the wholesale slaughter of the town's occupants; some twenty thousand are said to have perished.

Simon versus Raymond

At about this time, the ageing Crusader **Simon de Montfort** set his sights on the Cathar lands and, taking up leadership of military operations, embarked on a campaign marked by its terror and efficiency. Carcassonne was taken, and with it **Count Raymond VI**; thereafter Cathar towns and fortresses were besieged one by one, including Lastours, Minerve, Hautpoul, Lavaur, Termes and Puivert. Almost without exception they fell or surrendered, and the unfortunate defenders were executed or mutilated and sent on as blunt warning to the next victims; the only survivors were those on the inaccessible southern border: Quérigut, Peyrepertuse and Montségur.

After a brief exile in England, **Raymond VII** returned to lead a counter attack, calling on the aid of various allies, including his liege-lord **Pere the Catholic**, Count-King of Catalonia-Aragón. Fresh from a decisive victory against Spanish Muslims at Las Navas de Tolosa, Pere went into the field at Muret (14km south of Toulouse) in 1213, but was singled out and killed by de Montfort's men, dealing a grievous blow to Raymond's forces.

It took five more years of fighting to turn the tide against the northern forces, who were deprived of their leader de Montfort (who had assumed the title of Count of Toulouse), when his head was smashed in by a missile outside the walls of Toulouse. His son Arnaud attempted to carry on the campaign, but could not sustain his position and returned to his lands in the north, carrying with him his father's dead body and broken dreams. After this long-drawn-out battle, Raymond had no choice but to make **peace** with the papacy in order to recover his lands, reaffirming his Catholicism and recovering his scarred and battered territories. These he began immediately to fortify, founding strategic strongholds such as Cordes-sur-Ciel.

Back in royal hands

However, **Occitan independence** was not to last. By the mid-1220s the French king, **Louis VIII**, swelled by victories over the English Crown, turned his own sights south,

1209	1220s	1229
Béziers' inhabitants are massacred for refusing to hand over the Cathars	Louis XIII launches a new, successful crusade against the Cathars	A university is founded in Toulouse, the second in France after Paris

proclaiming a fresh Crusade against the Occitan Cathars, who continued to live discreetly in Raymond's lands, or openly under the defiant and unconquered barons of the south. This time the exhausted forces of the counts and local nobility could not respond, and after a brief campaign much of Languedoc came under the direct power of the king of France. Louis VIII's aggressive policy was followed up by his heir, Louis IX (later St Louis), who came to the throne in 1226 and finished off the job. With the counts out of the way, the papacy sent in the **Inquisition**, led by the Dominican Order.

Their job was to investigate and root out heretics, employing torture if necessary, and urging them to recant before turning them over to the king's forces to execute. When a band of renegade Cathars sallied out of their stronghold at Montségur in 1242 to **massacre** a band of Inquisitors at Avignonet-Lauragais, the royal reaction was immediate: an army of six thousand was assembled and laid siege to the fortress in 1243. Nine months later, when it fell, the garrison of two hundred was burnt alive. Subsequent mopping-up operations finished with the surrenders of Puilaurens and Quéribus in 1256. Catharism had disappeared as a political force and was hunted into extinction over the next century.

But royal policy was not wholly destructive in Languedoc. From the time of de Montfort's death, the kings had worked to rehabilitate the area, particularly through the founding of royal **bastides**, such as Revel and Réalmont. These planned and usually fortified towns were set up by royal charter. Ruled by a council, they answered directly to the king rather than to an intermediary noble, and were given privileges such as the right to hold a market.

On the fringes of Languedoc, mountainous **Foix**, like Toulouse, had been an independent county since about the time of the Carolingian disintegration. Over the following centuries, it remained isolated, even more than Roussillon, from the modernizing trends which were shaping Languedoc. That said, the counts of Foix were sworn enemies of the French Crown and allied themselves with the Raymonds during the Albigensian Crusade; in the campaigns that followed, the county managed to escape more or less unscathed, and when the French Crown threatened in the 1270s, the ruling house eluded their control by forging a marriage alliance with the neighbouring kingdom of Béarn.

Roussillon under Mallorcan rule

Except for the loss in battle of Count-King Pere, **Roussillon**, too, all but escaped the effects of the Albigensian Crusades. The death of Pere, and the period of uncertainty that followed, when his five-year-old son, Jaume, was made king, entailed the end of any Catalan-Aragonese pretensions in Provence, so the French Crown had a long breathing period in which to consolidate its power there. Roussillon, however, remained for the moment firmly in the Catalan-Aragonese ambit, and its nobility was drawn towards the campaigns of conquest which the count-kings carried out against their Muslim neighbours (Valencia, Mallorca and Menorca), and Sardinia and Sicily. When **Jaume the Conqueror** died after a 63-year reign, he divided his kingdom between his elder son Pere (who received the mainland holdings south of the Pyrenees) and Jaume, who became **king of Mallorca** and count of Roussillon and Montpellier. Perpignan served as his mainland capital. The kings of Mallorca allied with the French against their

1244	1200s	1276	1328
The nine-month siege at Montségur ends in the death by burning of around 200 Cathars	Royal *bastides*, fortified towns, are founded in the region	Perpignan becomes capital of the Kingdom of Majorca	Charles IV dies childless, which leads to the Hundred Years' War

Barcelona-based rivals, and in the 1280s Roussillon served as the springboard for the French invasion of Catalonia, launched in retribution for Catalan seizure of French-ruled Sicily.

The Hundred Years' War

Under **Philip le Bel** (1285–1314), France became a superpower. The astute king managed his treasury well, disbanded and appropriated the funds of the wealthy Knights Templar and brought the papacy under his ominous protection in Avignon.

But royal domination of Languedoc brought only short-lived peace and prosperity to the region. Philip's male line had failed when his son Charles IV failed to produce an heir, and Edward III of England, Philip's grandson through his daughter, claimed the throne. Edward's family, the Plantagenets, were French in origin, and the language and culture of their court were northern French, but the prospect of Edward taking the throne was highly undesirable to a large section of the French nobility, who stood to see themselves marginalized by such a turn of events. So they invoked (or, rather, invented) the "ancient" French Salic Law, which forbade succession to the throne through the female line, and resisted the English claim. These were the circumstances that provoked the series of conflicts which came to be known as the **Hundred Years' War** – essentially a struggle between two French royal houses.

England took the early advantage, defeating the French at Crécy in 1346 and capturing the French king shortly afterwards. Meanwhile, the king's son, Edward, Prince of Wales (known as the **Black Prince**), was unleashed on Aquitaine and ravaged the Aude valley. These military campaigns coincided with a series of disasters, including **crop failures**, the arrival of the **Black Death** and the Jacquerie peasant uprising. In 1360, a **truce** was called and part of western Languedoc remained under English control until nine years later, when **Charles V** began a campaign, which all but expelled the English from France.

Unfortunately, Charles' successor, **Charles VI**, was considered mentally unfit to rule, and a struggle ensued between the dukes of Burgundy and Orléans, who had been entrusted with the care of the realm. The English intervened on the side of the Burgundians, against the Duke of Orléans and his Armagnac allies, and began to reconquer the country. After a series of defeats, including Agincourt in 1415, all seemed lost for the French Crown. It was then that the peasant girl **Joan of Arc** appeared on the scene, and helped to turn the tide against the invaders, claiming divine guidance and rallying the French forces in a campaign to push the English off the mainland. Five years later, **Charles VII** entered Toulouse in triumph; a French king was once again master of Languedoc, and although the reconquest of the former royal territories dragged out over the length of the fifteenth century, France emerged from the struggle as a unified, powerful national kingdom.

In this protracted period of **crisis**, the people of Languedoc coped as best they could. Population decreased, agriculture suffered and traditional industries, such as leather-working, which accounted for the prosperity of the Tarn region, were almost extinguished. However, in the mid-fifteenth century it was discovered that a local plant, **woad**, could be made to yield a fine blue dye, *pastel*, a high-priced luxury commodity much in demand by the fabric industry of the day, thus provoking an

1355	1422	1400s
England's Black Prince carries out military campaigns in the Aude valley	Charles VII is crowned King of France, eventually regaining control of the country	The woad industry brings great prosperity to Tarn and later Toulouse

economic renaissance which lasted for over a century. Toulouse, still ruled over by a council of burghers, took the lead in this industry. Fortunes were made, fine palaces were raised, and the city's famous university was founded, turning Toulouse into a centre of culture. On the Occitan coast, Montpellier (which had been bought by the French Crown in 1349) was also driven by the growing textile industry and set up its own prestigious university.

As had happened with the Albigensian Crusade, Catalonia was not involved directly in the Hundred Years' War, but it did have to contend with France's relentless efforts to chip away at its holdings north of the Pyrenees, Cerdanya and Rosilló (the **Cerdagne** and **Roussillon**), and through the fourteenth and fifteenth centuries, they were shifted back and forth between the two powers. In 1462, when **Louis XI** mounted a military campaign against Roussillon – seizing it in response to the Catalan-Aragonese capture of French-dominated Naples – Catalonia was on the verge of a major realignment. The marriage of Ferran (Ferdinand) of Aragón and Isabel of Castile in 1469 laid the foundations for the creation of the Kingdom of Spain, and the ultimate submission of Catalonia and its dependencies to Madrid; it thus became a secondary concern, and Roussillon was set further on the periphery.

The rise of Protestantism and the Wars of Religion

Despite the peace which came with re-establishment of a strong monarchy in France under **François I** (1515–47), there was much dissatisfaction in Languedoc and Roussillon. This resentment took two forms: that towards the Church on the part of the people, and that towards the Crown and the northern nobility on the part of local lords and magnates. As had happened in the Cathar period, the interests of these two groups coincided, and even more so after 1483, when the Crown gained direct control over the Church in France. So social and political discontent was once again voiced on religious terms – this time the revolutionary movement was **Protestantism**.

The new faith first arrived in Haut Languedoc close on the heels of **Martin Luther**'s defiance of Church authority in 1519. However, French Protestantism, or the **Huguenot** movement (named after an obscure Swiss political event), tended to follow the teachings of **John Calvin** (Jean Cauvin), which had a clearer political message. Calvin had studied theology at the conservative University of Paris and had been swept up in the wave of reforming theology which very quickly provoked a clampdown by the religious and royal authorities. He fled into exile in Geneva, which became a hotbed for the Protestant creed that he formulated. His beliefs focused on the omnipotence of God and predestination, denying hierarchies and earthly elites and concentrating on hard work and pastoralism – a recipe for success among the artisanal classes – and it spread like wildfire in Paris and through Occitania.

By 1559, **Calvinism** was established as a religion and organization in France, and had the support of some of the kingdom's greatest noble houses, despite the persecution which had been carried out by François I's son Henri II. When Henri died (in an accident allegedly presaged by Nostradamus), the succession of two weak child-kings gave the rival **noble factions** led by the Protestant Bourbons and the Catholic Guises the opportunity to battle for control of the realm. Forty years of bloody and relentless civil war followed.

1464	**1483**	**1562**
Creation of Beaucaire fair	Crown gains control over the church in France resulting in the rise of Protestantism	The start of the French Wars of Religion

The wars were finally concluded by the victory of Henri, King of Béarn (or Navarre, and a successor of Gaston Fébus of Foix), the leader of the Protestant faction. It was, however, politically impossible for him to become king as a Huguenot, so having decided that "Paris is worth a Mass", he converted and was crowned as **Henri IV** of France in 1593. Thanks to his accession, Foix was incorporated into the French realm. Six years later, he proclaimed the **Edict of Nantes**, which granted political and religious freedom to the Huguenots and the right to maintain certain fortified strongholds.

Although most of Languedoc had been ruled by the Catholic Guises, its population was strongly Protestant. Castres became a "protected zone" for Huguenots, and home to one of the four **courts** empowered to mediate legal disputes between Catholics and Protestants. In Nîmes, some three-quarters of the population converted to Calvinism, while Montpellier was home to the Protestant Theological Institute. In the east, most of the towns – mainly herding and textile centres – were firmly Huguenot but, despite regional imbalances, the new pluralistic French society seemed to function well.

The Age of Absolutism

The liberal vision of Henri IV was not to last, however. When he was assassinated by a Catholic reactionary, his year-old son **Louis XIII** came to the throne under the strict control of his staunchly Catholic mother, Marie de Medici. In 1624, that supreme Machiavellian **Cardinal Richelieu** managed to wrest control from the queen. Richelieu made it his mission to establish France as an absolutist Catholic state, and for almost two decades he was the sole power behind the Crown. He immediately set about stripping the towns and cities of their defensive walls (to prevent revolt) and then began reducing Protestant strongholds. He also adopted an aggressive foreign policy, attacking France's neighbours and taking Roussillon. But his heavy-handedness provoked reaction at home. In 1622, the Protestant Duke of Rohan raised a **revolt** in the Cévennes (just north of Hérault) and although after seven years of fighting he was forced to make a settlement with Richelieu that stripped the Huguenots of political power, he maintained their freedom to worship.

Heavily Protestant Languedoc was not pacified, however, and shortly thereafter its royal governor, **Henri de Montmorency**, raised a revolt against Richelieu which spanned the region from Nîmes to Toulouse. He was no match for the cardinal, who defeated him in battle at Castelnaudary in 1632 and led him off to be beheaded on the place du Capitole in Toulouse. The vindictive Richelieu then exacted revenge on Henri's heirs by transferring the title of First Duchy of France from the house of Montmorency to the loyally Catholic dukes of Uzès.

In 1643, the "Sun King" and supreme absolutist **Louis XIV** came to the throne. Continuing the centralizing policies initiated by Richelieu, he hamstrung the French nobility by obliging them to take up residence at his palace in Versailles and to participate in its expensive and regimented court life. His megalomaniac tendencies ("I am the state") led him to embark on a series of costly and ultimately disastrous military adventures, the successful episodes of which are recorded on the Roman-style monuments, such as the equestrian statue and triumphal arch of Montpellier, which he erected to commemorate his grandeur. He waged **war** in Flanders, Germany and Spain,

1598	1593	1624
The Edict of Nantes grants rights to the Protestants and ends the war	Protestant Henri IV converts to Catholicism in order to become King of France	Cardinal Richelieu seeks to establish France as an absolutist Catholic state

managing to secure the permanent annexation of the Cerdagne and Roussillon with the **Treaty of the Pyrenees** in 1659.

The able management of his successive prime ministers, Mazarin and Colbert, managed to preserve the kingdom from financial ruin, and it was Colbert who gave the green light to Riquet's visionary project of linking the Atlantic and Mediterranean by canal. The main channel of the **Canal du Midi**, which stretched from Toulouse to Agde, was opened in 1666, sparking an economic recovery in the region, which had languished in depression since the wane in demand for the local *pastel* dye (thanks to the discovery of cheaper alternatives in the Indies); the canal allowed locally grown grain to be shipped to distant markets. But on the whole, Louis' reign was not a happy one for Languedoc and Roussillon. In 1674, the **Catalans** rose up against French rule, which they found even more oppressive than that of the Spanish Habsburgs, against whom they had risen a generation earlier. The **uprising** was brutally crushed, and its leaders imprisoned and executed in Perpignan.

The Camisards

A decade after the Catalan uprising, Louis moved against the Protestants by issuing a **Revocation of the Edict of Nantes** (1685), which deprived the Huguenots of their rights and outlawed their religion. Half a million Protestants chose to flee the country, including many merchants and textile workers, dealing a grievous blow to the industry on which the prosperity of eastern Languedoc depended. Those who remained were subjected to **oppression**; they were spied on and hounded, forced to carry on their services in secret and brook the humiliation of having soldiers billeted in their homes. Intransigent Protestants were imprisoned, among them Marie Durand, locked up for over thirty years in a tower in Aigues-Mortes. Some feigned conversion, some were deported to the colonies, and others fled to the "desert" – the wild and isolated hills of the Cévennes. It was here that they rose again in protest, in what is known as the **Camisard revolt**. The spark came in July 1702 when the parish priest of Chayla arrested and detained a small group of fugitive Protestants. A group of villagers stormed the castle to free them and in the course of the struggle the priest was killed. Knowing that retribution would be swift and cruel, Protestants across the Cévennes (mostly refugees from Languedoc proper) began a guerrilla war which pitted their forces, numbering between three and five thousand, against some thirty thousand royal troops. The shirts they wore as a sign of recognition earned them the popular name of Camisards (from *chemise*, French for "shirt"). Battles raged across the region, with one of the greatest confrontations taking place at **St-Hippolyte**. The guerrillas and civilian population took refuge where they could, hiding in the remote hills or in caverns, like the Grotte des Demoiselles, south of Ganges.

In the course of the struggle two leaders emerged: the aristocratic **Jean Cavalier**, and the commoner **Roland**. Unable to conclude the struggle militarily, the French commander Villars began to negotiate with Cavalier at Nîmes, offering him the rank of colonel, command of a Protestant legion which would fight for the French abroad, and a hefty annual salary in exchange for submission. Cavalier accepted, greatly undermining the uprising. The former leader left France and served the English,

1632	1659	1666
Protestant Henri II de Montmorency, governor of Languedoc, is beheaded in Toulouse	Following the Treaty of the Pyrenees, Roussillon is handed back to the French	Work begins on the Canal du Midi and the port of Sète is founded

eventually being named governor of Jersey. Roland continued the struggle, but later the same year was killed in battle, bringing an end to the revolt.

In the century or so before the Camisards episode, Languedoc had been tamed into discontented submission by France, ruled by the princes of Conti, members of the ruling Bourbon family, since the defeat of Montmorency. Pézenas, which had been the region's capital since the 1450s, became a paler southern Versailles, especially in the 1650s when **Armand de Bourbon** lavished his patronage on the town, playing host for a time to the playwright Molière and his company.

The absorption of Roussillon, while it aggrandized France, struck a blow against the towns of the Aude valley, which up until then had enjoyed a trade-based prosperity thanks to their position on the Spanish frontier. As part of Madrid's empire, in which Church institutions like the Inquisition kept a very tight lid on any potential sources of dissent or heterodoxy, Protestantism was basically unknown in Roussillon during its efflorescence, and by the time of the region's annexation, it was virtually a spent force.

The Revolution

Languedoc and Roussillon were not the only areas which chafed against the Sun King's absolutism. As the **economic crisis** deepened, taxes were driven up, forcing the masses of the kingdom, the *sans-culottes* ("trouserless"), into an ever more desperate state of poverty. A series of bad harvests compounded the problem, and indebted smallholders had their lands repossessed and were reduced to penury and near-servitude. In order to gather the revenue necessary to maintain the court, fund expensive military adventures and service the spiralling national debt, the ruling class resorted to **tax-farming**.

Speculators paid the Crown a set sum upfront and were then free to extract as much as they could from the area under their control. This excluded most of the nobility, many of whom enjoyed hereditary exemptions, and the largest single land-holder, the Church, which paid no royal taxes and continued to collect its own. At the same time, the Crown's growing obsession with control bred a fear of rebellion, which became self-fulfilling. Law was completely subverted to royal authority, and suspected troublemakers were imprisoned indefinitely without charges, by writ of the feared *lettres de cachet*, or orders of detention.

These **dictatorial** tendencies worsened over the course of the eighteenth century, as Louis XIV's successors continued his absolutist style of ruling and his disastrous policy of foreign intervention. **Louis XV** (1715–74) carried France into the Polish and Austrian Wars of Succession and the Seven Years' War, as a result of which the kingdom lost all of its colonies.

Poor grain harvests continued after Louis XV's death in 1774, provoking riots and unrest. Royal finance ministers attempted to institute reforms, but to little avail. In Languedoc, the new king Louis XVI's conciliatory policies were chiefly noted in the form of the **Edict of Toleration** (1787), which was aimed at diffusing the rebelliousness of the Protestants by restoring their rights and liberties. The situation was such that the king was forced in 1789 to summon the Estates General (the equivalent of parliament) for the first time in nearly two centuries. The newly constituted Third Estate, made up of commoners, who for the first time joined the nobility and clergy in government, called for the formation of a National Assembly.

1685	1702	1787
The Revocation of the Edict of Nantes outlaws Protestantism and many flee the country	The Camisard revolt begins eight years of battles between Protestants and Catholics in the Cévennes	The Edict of Toleration restores the rights and liberties of Protestants

When in the months that followed the country rose in **revolution**, Languedoc and Roussillon were solidly Jacobin (revolutionary). The Revolution was a focus for the discontentment of diverse groups in the south: the Protestants, the poor, the Occitans and the local magnates, all of whom had a bone to pick with Paris or the monarchy. But although the monarchy fell, Paris persevered, emerging as the capital of a sharply centralized and thoroughly French state.

The short and bloody revolutionary experiment was centred in Paris, and Languedoc felt its influence chiefly in the administrative novelties which were introduced, the most durable of which was the division of the region (as with the rest of the country) into administrative **départements**. The rationalist (and centralist) policies of the new government ensured a break with historical traditions in defining these areas. They were based on geography, for the most part on the major river valleys. Roussillon became the culturally neutral Pyrénées-Orientales.

The Napoleonic era and the nineteenth-century republics

The rise of revolutionary France did not, however, bring about a change in foreign policy, which remained aggressive. The **armies** of the Republic, among whose leaders figured a young **Napoleon Bonaparte**, lashed out against their neighbours on all sides. Back at home, power had devolved to a five-member **Directory**, whose heavy-handed governance was met with growing resentment by the populace. When Bonaparte returned from his defeat by the British in Egypt, he set a coup d'état in motion, which saw him elevated initially, in 1799, to First Consul, and subsequently, to **Emperor**. His campaign of European domination brought him up against practically every other power in Europe and, after initial successes in Germany and Spain, his campaign in Russia brought about the destruction of his Grand Army and his ultimate ruin.

Although most of the Napoleonic Wars took place on foreign soil, Languedoc was to feel the sting of the emperor's defeat. **Wellington**'s British expeditionary force, which had been sent to aid Spain and Portugal, pushed its way across the peninsula and dealt the French a severe defeat at Toulouse in 1814.

For the next forty years France and Languedoc returned to monarchy, with the reigns first of the Bourbon **Louis XVIII** (1814–24) and **Charles X** (1824–30), and then **Louis-Philippe** (1830–48) of the house of Orléans. The Bourbons, who had obviously learnt nothing from previous experience, immediately embarked on a heavy-handed Catholic-oriented policy, and were brought down by popular revolution in 1830. The throne was then taken by Louis-Philippe, the candidate of the middle-class elite, a commercial nobility no less despised than their aristocratic forebears. He was unseated in the **revolution of 1848**, European socialism's *annus mirabilis*, which saw uprisings in capitals across the continent. But the Second Republic quickly gave way to the **Second Empire**, when Bonaparte's crafty nephew gained the throne as **Napoléon III** in 1852. Protests followed his seizure of power, such as the one in Béziers, where troops opened fire on a crowd of republican demonstrators led by the town mayor. As a tactician, Napoléon III proved as unsuccessful as his namesake, first embroiling the country in the bitter Crimean War, and then in 1870 provoking the ignominious **Franco-Prussian War**, which saw his own capture and the subsequent German siege of Paris.

1789	1791	1814
Come the revolution, Languedoc and Roussillon are firmly Jacobin (revolutionary).	The French Republic is declared and administrative *départements* are created	Wellington's armies, on their way to assist Spain, defeat Napoleon's troops in Toulouse

Although Roussillon continued to drift in agrarian poverty, Languedoc weathered all these events with some measure of good fortune. While the bulk of the population suffered in poverty, the **textile industry**, based on wool and cotton and later on silk, boomed. The herds of the uplands of the Cévennes and Haut Languedoc were the chief source of raw material, and the fast-flowing rivers provided the energy to run the newly mechanized factories. All along the fringe of the mountains, towns which had up to then been insignificant villages – Castres, Mazamet, Ganges, St-Hippolyte – enjoyed unprecedented good fortune. As coal was discovered, new industries, such as **mining** and **glassmaking** (at Albi and Carmaux), sprang up, and when the railways arrived in the middle of the century, the towns along their route benefited additionally from better access to distribution networks. Of course, this good fortune tended to remain in the hands of a relative few – the factory owners and merchants – and this fact contributed to the popularity of egalitarian and **socialist ideologies** among the masses of the region.

The era of the **Third Republic**, which followed France's defeat at the hands of the Prussians, was one of introspection, not least because of the massive war indemnities which the state was forced to pay. Socialists were scapegoated, and there were mass executions at the hands of the new reactionary regime: in excess of twenty thousand were killed in Paris alone. Nor was all well in Languedoc and Roussillon, as outside the industrial areas the people of the countryside still eked out only the most meagre of livings. Many left, frequently for Paris, compounding the capital's social and economic problems. The new, modern **wine industry** which had developed along the littoral provided a seasonal source of income for many, and stimulated related industries, such as bottle-, cork- and barrel-making, but in 1875 the vineyards were destroyed by phylloxera. This was followed by a second epidemic which attacked mulberry trees, the silkworm's staple food, precipitating a crisis in the silk industry.

A marked tendency towards the Left continued to colour local politics, partially fuelled by resentment towards remote and indifferent Paris. These political trends were personified in **Jean Jaurès** (see box, p.148).

The wine revolts

Popular politics in Languedoc and Roussillon were not divided strictly across ideological lines, however, as the cross-class solidarity of the **wine revolts** would show. As the wine industry recovered in the last years of the nineteenth century from the blow dealt by disease, it received further setbacks. A series of abundant harvests drove down the price of grapes, and the combination of competition from cheap Algerian vintages and a law permitting sugar to be added during fermentation (reducing the amount of grape pulp required) decreased demand. Wages plummeted and underar rose. Led by the innkeeper, Marcellin Albert, half a million protesters turned out in Montpellier in 1907, and similar numbers rose up in other wine towns, like Béziers and Narbonne. People across the class spectrum depended on the wine industry, so the uprising had the character of a regional revolt. The interior minister, Georges Clémenceau, responded by sending in the troops, but the locally levied 17th Infantry Regiment sympathized with their countrymen and mutinied. They were packed off to Tunisia in short order, and troops from the north were sent in to quell the "Midi madness". In the confrontations between army and civilians, shots were fired and there

1851	**1864**	**1899**
Louis Napoléon's troops kill republican supporters in Béziers	Birth of Henri de Toulouse-Lautrec in Albi	Birth of Jean Moulin, one of France's great Resistance figures, in Béziers

were some casualties, but the episode served to instigate the creation of a regional wine board to manage prices and quality and to bring stability to the industry.

The two world wars

Although no fighting took place in Languedoc and Roussillon during **World War I**, the **cenotaphs** which mark the centre of every hamlet and village bear dramatic testimony to the price they paid in the struggle.

Languedoc and Roussillon limped through the 1920s and 1930s, suffering along with the rest of Europe in the postwar **flu epidemic** (which claimed more lives than the war) and the **Great Depression**. Weak postwar democracies arose in Italy and Germany and were quickly replaced by dictatorial fascist regimes, and a prelude of the struggle to come took place in Spain, where General Franco's attempted coup set in motion a civil war in 1936. The bitter struggle, from which France – along with the rest of the Allies – remained aloof and uncommitted, lasted until 1939. As fascist troops took over Catalonia and the Basque country, tens of thousands of **refugees** poured over the border, the Catalans arriving initially in Roussillon.

A few months later, German soldiers stormed over the Polish border, initiating **World War II**. The following year they circumvented France's defensive white elephant, the Maginot line, and arrived in Paris in June. For the first time in seven hundred years Languedoc and Roussillon found themselves independent of Paris as they were incorporated into the puppet **Vichy Republic**, which enjoyed a fictitious independence under the World War I hero turned traitor, **Henri Pétain**. He collaborated with the **Nazis**, facilitating the repression of their opponents, the deportation of "undesirable elements" and the wholesale transportation of southern French citizens to labour camps and factories in Germany.

In 1942, the Germans decided to dispense with even the illusion of autonomy in the South and brought the whole region under their direct control. Repression was intensified, but the local guerrilla **resistance**, the **Maquis**, benefited from a stiffened resolve on the part of the populace. Across France as a whole there were about as many active collaborators with Nazi rule as resisters, but Resistance activity in Languedoc and Roussillon was considerable, the efforts of local companies like the famed Maquis Bir Hakeim of Haut Languedoc, or of individuals like Jean Moulin of Béziers, who founded the National Committee for Resistance, proving a significant element in the war. In their mountain redoubts in the Pyrenees and Cévennes and in the hills of Haut Languedoc, they withstood German air attacks and pacification missions, while the civilian population suffered direct reprisals for their collusion with the rebels. In the Cerdagne and Roussillon, clandestine *passeurs*, motivated by either ideals or profit (or a combination of the two), helped to slip people and contraband back and forth over the frontier with neutral Spain.

From 1943 on, the disasters of the Russian campaign focused German manpower in the east, and with the **allied invasions** of Italy in 1943 and Normandy in 1944, the underarmed Maquis finally had a chance, and began to mount an open military campaign. The first towns that they managed to recover were mere mountain hamlets, like Mourèze, near Clermont-l'Hérault, but when the Germans sent a column of three thousand troops to retake the upper Hérault, they were fended off after a fierce day-long battle with the local Resistance. Memorial plaques which pepper the streets of

1907	**1914–18**	**1939–45**
Half a million people take to the streets of Montpellier to protest about the state of the wine industry	Like the rest of France, the region loses many young men in the Great War	Refugees fleeing Hitler make the hazardous journey on foot across the Pyrenees

Toulouse and other major towns recall the Maquis who fell in the widespread **street-fighting** of 1944. By the end of that year, France had been liberated.

Recent history

In the postwar **Fourth Republic** France endeavoured to recover from the damage wrought by four years of occupation and two invasions. Europe's colonial age was coming to an end and for France this signalled nationalist revolts in Indochina and Algeria. In Languedoc and Roussillon, the wine industry recovered and mining continued, but with the advent of cheaper synthetic fibres, the textile industry all but disappeared. **Poverty** and **depopulation** continued and served to channel political consciousness ever more to the Left.

Former general and self-proclaimed liberator of France **Charles de Gaulle**'s conservative **Fifth Republic**, which came in 1958 on the heels of France's entry into the new European Common Market, gradually became something of a dictatorship. In the South, certain progressive economic policies were embarked upon, including the construction of **reservoirs** and **hydroelectric facilities** and the articulation of a region-wide irrigation plan.

Meanwhile in **Algeria**, native unrest led to open rebellion, and when de Gaulle reacted by announcing the abandonment of the **colony**, the *pieds-noirs* (so-called by the natives for their custom of wearing black shoes) – the French population who had ruled it since 1830 – felt betrayed and carried out a brief armed resistance. With the **Accord of Évian** (1962), they agreed to be settled, along with the **harkis**, their native Algerian allies, in Languedoc. The influx of this population – a largely educated and skilled workforce – gave new life to the cities of the coast (notably Montpellier, Narbonne and Perpignan), although the welcome which the *harkis* received was hardly warm.

The **Student Revolution** of 1968 presaged the departure of de Gaulle, who resigned in 1969 after a failed attempt to widen his already broad powers by popular referendum. The unrest of that summer also heralded an era of openly **left-wing politics** in Languedoc and Roussillon. In the elections of the years that followed, Languedoc voted massively in favour of the socialists and communists, encouraged by the area's traditional economic marginalism and an antipathy to the conservative north.

The nation, however, remained under **conservative rule** through the presidencies of Georges Pompidou (1969–74) and Valéry Giscard d'Estaing (1974–81). In this era of baby boom and general prosperity, the infrastructure of Languedoc and Roussillon was improved by the construction of *autoroutes* and the improvement of roads. The **tourist industry** also received stimulus through the revitalization of the abandoned Canal du Midi and the creation of regional parks, such as that of Haut Languedoc. The area still retains a shadow of its former textile industry, but manufacturing has been dominated in the west by the high-profile **aviation industry**, based in Toulouse. The city had been a pioneer of flight since before the days of St-Exupéry, and served as a hub for Africa and South America between the wars. It was here that the Concorde was first tested, and the European joint-venture Airbus Industries was founded.

Despite these recent successes, the region remains **underpopulated** and relatively poor, and *départements* such as Aude, Ariège and significant parts of Hérault are now actively stimulating tourism as a way of bringing investment and employment. Whether as a result of these efforts, or as a consequence of overcrowding and rising

1940	**1962**	**1970**
Languedoc and Roussillon become part of Vichy France	Following the Accord of Evian, Algeria's French population and their allies, the *harkis*, are resettled in Languedoc	European aircraft builder Airbus founded at Blagnac, near Toulouse

prices in traditional Anglo destinations like the Dordogne, British travellers and property investors have moved into Languedoc and Roussillon, both as a holiday destination and as somewhere to set up home.

As the French population ages, waves of northern retirees are heading south to the affordable property and agreeable climes of Languedoc and Roussillon – a trend which is seen with a jaundiced eye by many natives, who perceive in it a modern reprise of the invasions of the past. Some also see the massive influx of North African immigrants from France's former colonies and protectorates as an invasion, and this has served to divert part of the traditional extreme Left vote, paradoxically, to the **extreme Right**. The 1995 municipal elections gave a surprisingly high return to the parties of the far Right, dominated then by Jean-Marie Le Pen's **Front National**. At the *région* level, the Right scored well in the 1998 elections; the UDF–FDR coalition's (President Chirac's power base) 22 seats added to the FN's thirteen made for a narrow majority over the 31 seats won by the socialists and resurgent communists.

As parties geared up for the 2002 elections, it appeared that the region would return to its traditional socialist orientation, with the FN splintered and the **Chirac government** discredited by an influence-peddling **scandal** involving government contracts which seemed to point at the president's office. Few were prepared for what was to come. The first electoral round was met with record voter apathy and abstention, particularly among socialist voters. This knocked out Jospin's party from the race and catapulted Le Pen into second position. In a typical irony of politics, leftist voters came out for the second round and voted in Chirac, seen as the lesser of two evils.

In the April 2007 election, right-of-centre **Nicolas Sarkozy** succeeded in trouncing the internally fractured socialists, and neutralizing the far-Right parties by leaning in their direction on certain issues. In Languedoc and Roussillon, the affluent coastal areas tended to support the conservative candidate, while the struggling interior was largely socialist. This trend was reflected by the election in 2008 of a socialist to the *mairie* of Toulouse (the first in a half-century).

In the 2012 legislative elections there was a big swing to the left, with virtually all of Languedoc and Roussillon voting socialist. Nationally, the Parti Socialiste took the majority of votes and François Hollande became president. However, all that looks set to change during the next elections in 2017. Thanks to Hollande's unpopularity, the social unrest caused by the government's controversial planned labour reforms, the migrant crisis, and the terror attacks in Paris and Nice, the **right and far right** have been gaining significant support. In the 2014 municipal elections, the right won the most seats; regionally, Toulouse moved to the right, and far-right Front National mayors were elected in Béziers and Beaucaire. Even Sarkozy, who retired from politics after his 2012 defeat, made a comeback with views and plans that made him sound more Front National than centre right.

In 2016, France saw a big change on an administrative level with new "super" regions being created. Midi-Pyrénées, in this book comprising Haut-Garonne, Tarn and Ariège, joined with Languedoc-Roussillon, made up of Aude, Gard, Hérault and Pyrénées-Orientales, to create a new region named "**Occitanie**", with Toulouse as its capital. While they've never shown any inclination towards gaining independence in the way that Brittany and the Basques have, it seems that the regional inhabitants, who voted for this name, very much identify with their roots.

1973	**1996**	**2014**	**2016**
Creation of Parc Naturel Régional du Haut-Languedoc	The Canal du Midi becomes a UNESCO World Heritage Site	Far-right Front National mayors are elected in Béziers and Beaucaire	The administrative regions of Midi-Pyrénées and Languedoc-Roussillon are combined to create "Occitanie"

Books and film

HISTORY

Jean-Vincent Blanchard *Eminence: Cardinal Richelieu and the Rise of France*. An interesting look at Richelieu's rise to power, presenting the cardinal as a complex Machiavellian figure, who was not without his convictions.

Anthony Crubaugh *Balancing the Scales of Justice: Local Courts and Rural Society in Southwest France, 1750–1800*. Engaging new academic study of local court documents, revealing the subtleties of peasant life in Languedoc in the era of the Revolution.

Emmanuel Le Roy Ladurie *Montaillou*. Village gossip of who's sleeping with whom, tales of trips to Spain and details of work, all extracted by the Inquisition from Cathar peasants in the fourteenth century.

George Millar *Maquis: An Englishman in the French Resistance*. Gripping first-person account of what life was like as a Resistance fighter.

Felix Platter *Beloved Son Felix*. Fascinating diary of a young Swiss man who sets out to study medicine in sixteenth-century Montpellier.

Graham Robb *The Discovery of France*. Based on the academic author's exploration of France by bike, this book looks at France's development as a nation from the perspective of ordinary people and features anecdotes from the South West.

Janet Shirley *Song of the Cathar Wars*. Translation of two contemporary accounts of the Cathar wars of 1204–1218, written by a Crusade supporter and an Occitan sympathizer.

Edward Stourton *Cruel Crossing*. The BBC Radio Four presenter recounts the (often moving and harrowing) tales of those who tried to escape Hitler by fleeing across the Pyrenees.

Jonathan Sumption *The Albigensian Crusade*. Concise but eloquent portrayal of the Albigensian Crusades from the beginnings of the Cathar movement through to the fall of Montségur.

SOCIETY AND POLITICS

Jose Bové *The World is Not for Sale: Farmers Against Junkfood*. A manifesto by the US-raised self-proclaimed saviour of French ecology and cuisine.

Andrew Hussey *The French Intifada: The Long War Between France and its Arabs*. A fascinating and readable account about the complex relationship between secular France and its Muslim North African population.

Geoffrey Kurtz *Jean Jaurès: The Inner Life of Social Democracy*. An insightful overview of the life and work of one of France's most important politicians.

ART AND ARCHITECTURE

John Berger *The Success and Failure of Picasso*. Although most strongly associated with Provence, Picasso was also influenced by and influenced Roussillonais artists.

Kenneth J. Conant *Carolingian and Romanesque Architecture, 800–1200*. Good European study with a focus on Cluny and the St-Jacques pilgrim route, which includes strong coverage of the sections through Languedoc.

Julia Bloch Frey *Toulouse-Lautrec: A Life*. An intimate look at the life of the painter, with emphasis on his friends, family, and artistic contemporaries.

John Golding *Cubism: A History and an Analysis 1907–1914*. Excellent work on the formative stages of Cubism, particularly relevant for a journey to Céret.

Pamela Robertson *Charles Rennie Mackintosh in France: Landscape Watercolours*. The first book to explore this period in the artist's life includes extracts from his letters to friends and family.

Sarah Whitfield *Fauvism*. A survey of the movement emphasizing the major figure of Matisse, but with good material on Maillol and lesser-known artists.

REGIONAL LITERATURE

Michael Baigent, et al. *Holy Blood, Holy Grail*. Learn what happened to the Holy Grail, how Jesus didn't die on the cross, how the Knights Templar are a force to be reckoned with and how Rennes-le-Château is the key.

Rosemary Bailey *Love and War in the Pyrenees*. Vivid first-person accounts of life during the Occupation, engagingly told by this award-winning British travel writer who has a home near Prades. Her other two books, *Life in a Postcard* and *The Man Who Married a Mountain*, are also set in the area.

Alessandro Baricco *Silk*. Sensual love story set in the aftermath of the silk crisis of nineteenth-century Languedoc.

Natalie Zemon Davis *The Return of Martin Guerre*. A vivid account of peasant life in the sixteenth-century Pyrenean village of Artigat. The return of a long-lost villager sparks a sensational and gripping courtroom drama.

Lawrence Durrell *Spirit of Place: Letters and Essays on Travel*. A collection of letters to friends and contemporaries, including T.S. Eliot, written during Durrell's retirement in Sommières.

André Gide *If It Die...An Autobiography.* Gide's spiritual autobiography, sensual and introspective, including his time spent in Uzès.

Arthur Guirdham *The Cathars & Reincarnation.* In this non-fiction study an English schoolgirl is allegedly hypnotically induced to recall her past life as a Cathar.

Christopher Hope *Signs of the Heart: Love and Death in Languedoc.* Award-winning South African-born novelist writes about his life in Languedoc – a playground for effetely complacent if ill-at-ease expats.

Kate Mosse *Labyrinth.* Best-selling novel set between thirteenth-century Carcassonne and the modern-day French Pyrenees. Mosse's three follow-up novels – *Sepulchre, The Winter Ghosts* and *Citadel* – are also set in the South West.

Zoé Oldenbourg *Destiny of Fire.* Historical novel set in the age of the Albigensian Crusade, written by a respected French historian.

Antoine de Saint-Exupéry *Night Flight.* The aviator and author of *The Little Prince* recounts in novel format the dangers and exhilaration of flying the southern Atlantic route from Toulouse in the 1920s and 30s.

Adam Thorpe *The Standing Pool.* In this suspense novel two Cambridge academics take their young child on sabbatical for a year to Languedoc.

TRAVEL, FOOD AND WINE

Sabine Baring-Gould *In Troubadour-Land: A Ramble in Provence and Languedoc.* A very British, late nineteenth-century aristocratic ramble through the French south, offering an interesting perspective of the region under the Third Republic.

Derry Brabbs *The Roads to Santiago: The Medieval Pilgrim Routes Through France and Spain to Santiago de Compostela.* An excellent guide to the pilgrimage routes accompanied by inspiring colour photographs.

James Bromwich *The Roman Remains of Southern France.* The only comprehensive guide on the subject – detailed, well illustrated and approachable. In addition to accounts of the famous sites, it will lead you off the map to little-known discoveries.

Benjamin Lewin *Wines of Languedoc.* A good introduction to the wines of Languedoc and Roussillon, with details of leading domaines and vintages.

April Orcutt *Floating Through France: Life Between Locks on the Canal du Midi.* A collection of poems and essays inspired by the Canal du Midi; perfect reading as you float along.

Jeanne Strang *Goose Fat and Garlic.* More than two hundred recipes from the South West, interspersed with anecdotes from the author's fifty or so years of living in the region.

FILMS

Betty Blue *37°2 Le Matin* (Jean-Jacques Bineix, 1986). This cult film about a wannabe novelist and his crazy girlfriend (Béatrice Dalle) was partly shot at the stilt houses in Gruissan-Plage.

Breathe *Respire* (Mélanie Laurent, 2014). Filmed in and around Béziers, this movie about an intense and dangerous friendship between two teenage girls was nominated for Lumières and César awards.

Hell *L'Enfer* (Claude Chabrol, 1994). Filmed in Castelnaudary, Revel and Lac de St Ferréol, this film charts the descent into madness by a hotel manager who believes that his sexy young wife (Emmanuelle Béart) is cheating on him.

Lacombe, Lucien (Louis Malle, 1974). The third in Malle's coming-of-age trilogy reveals the tensions and dangers of Languedoc during the German occupation. Nominated for an Oscar for Best Foreign Language Film.

The Man Who Loved Women *L'homme qui aimait les femmes* (François Truffaut, 1976). This cult French comedy about a man obsessed by women, which eventually leads to his downfall, was filmed in Montpellier. In 1983 it was remade in Hollywood and starred Burt Reynolds.

The Secret of the Grain *La graine et le mulet* (Abdel Kechiche, 2007). In Sète, an ageing North African dockworker dreams of escaping drudgery and starting a restaurant in this subtle and tender family drama. The film won 18 awards, including a César for Best Picture (2008).

The Return of Martin Guerre *Le retour de Martin Guerre* (Daniel Vigne, 1982). Award-winning film that vividly recreates the world of the Pyrenees of the *ancien régime*. When Martin Guerre (Gérard Depardieu) returns to his wife after years away he is welcomed; however, when he begins to demand his wife's rights to the family wealth, suspicions arise.

Occitan and Catalan

By the time the Roman Empire in the west disintegrated, Latin had become the language of daily speech in nearly all of what is now France. Over the course of the following centuries, spoken Latin began to evolve into local variants and eventually into new Romance languages, from Spanish to Romanian. In the south of France (and in part of modern Italy) Occitan (pronounced ok-si-tán) or the Langue d'Oc developed – so called for its word for "yes", which set it apart from the northern French Langue d'Oïl ("oui").

Occitan itself had discrete **regional variants**, chief among them Provençal in the east (including Nîmes), Limousin in the north, Gascon in the west (including Ariège and the Vall d'Aran in Spain) and Languedocien, from the Corbières to the Camargue. In northeast Spain and across the present-day border into southern France emerged the Catalan language, which bears similarities to both Occitan and Castilian Spanish. Ironically, the name Catalan derives from the same root as the name of its chief rival language, Castilian, both terms referring to the castles which covered the landscapes of each region.

Occitan language and culture

Around the turn of the first millennium, a distinct Occitan literary language emerged, thanks to the wealth of the southern counts and their patronage of **troubadours**. These poets composed and performed works that were sung accompanied by music, for which they were also known as *trovadors* or *jongleurs*. The themes of their works varied from popular or religiously toned epics, like the *Chanson de Roland*, to portrayals of courtly love. Across these could be found recurring motifs, including righteous battle, unrequited love and, above all, the glorification of good manners, sophistication and virtues, such as knightly loyalty or pious chastity. Troubadours were not merely court entertainers – many were noblemen themselves, and the first is said to have been the powerful duke, William IX of Aquitaine, father of Eleanor of Aquitaine, later Queen of England. But the bulk of them were not wealthy, and they practised their art as a way of ingratiating themselves with a noble house.

The Albigensian Crusades of the thirteenth century brought about the end of many of the native ruling families in Languedoc and led to an influx of northern nobles. Naturally, these were French in cultural orientation rather than Occitan, and the literature declined as sources of patronage dried up. The decline of the language was met with some alarm, and in 1323 a group of poets from Toulouse determined to save the poetic tradition of the troubadours by instituting the **jocs florals** ("floral games") – a sort of poetic Olympics in which winners were awarded gilded flowers. The tradition has continued since that time, held annually on May 3, although in 1694, Louis XIV Frenchified it and established in Toulouse a society called the Académie des Jeux Floraux, which administers the games to this day. In 1539, on the eve of the Wars of Religion, François I declared at Villers-Cotterêts that French – the dialect of the **Langue d'Oïl** – was to be the only language of administration in his realms.

It was not until the mid-nineteenth century that Occitan was revived in literature, with the venerated Provençal poet **Frédéric Mistral** its most powerful champion. Born in 1830, Mistral spent a lifetime working to revive and modernize Provençal Occitan, producing countless works of literature and grammar, and campaigning in favour of

Occitan folk practices, such as *tauromachie*. His efforts were recognized on an international level when he received a Nobel Prize in 1904.

Nevertheless, reform was slow. Although it may have been the common language of the villages and fields through the middle of the twentieth century, the relentlessly centralist policies of the state and the greater diffusion of French-language education and literacy conspired against Occitan's revival. In Toulouse, the **Escola Occitana** (1919) and the **Institut d'Études Occitanes** (1945) were founded to promote and modernize the language, but it was not until 1951 that it was permitted to teach Occitan in schools, and only in 1969 that educational authorities officially ranked it as a language.

Since the 1920s the number of speakers has decreased from ten million to two million – an optimistic estimate which sets the proportion of Occitan speakers as fourteen percent of the whole of Languedoc. (By contrast, in Corsica some fifty percent of the populace speaks native Corse.) Nevertheless, there are many cultural festivals throughout the year, such as the Festival Occitania (🌐festivaloccitania.com), which holds events in Toulouse, Tarn and Ariège in September and October. Most importantly, in 2006, Occitan (and Catalan in Roussillon) became mandatory subjects in the region's schools, in a programme undertaken by the Montpellier Academy. As a visitor, you're unlikely to encounter Occitan either spoken or written, apart from Occitan street signs and Occitan announcements in the Toulouse metro system.

Although readership and audiences are limited, authors such as **Max Roqueta**, **Bernat Maciet** and **Marcèla Delpastre** have begun to publish novels in Occitan, theatre companies tour performing original and traditional works, and musical groups of the 1980s and 90s, like the **Fabulous Troubadours**, created the modern Occitan musical style called **nòva cançon**, which blends traditional melodies and instruments with modern styles. A recent addition to the regional music scene is **Lo Còr de la Plana**, who blend polyphonic singing in Occitan with hand-claps and percussion, with an energy and intensity uncharacteristic of *a capella* groups. For the most part, however, Occitan musicians have adopted other genres, from jazz, blues and folk, to rap and punk fusions (here known as *ragga-aïoli*).

Catalan language and culture

Most of the world's ten million Catalan speakers live in Spain, in a band of territory stretching south from the Pyrenees to Valencia, and in the Balearic Islands (though proponents of Valencian, Mallorquin and Menorquin hold these to be distinct languages). The 125,000 Catalan speakers of France live in the *département* of Pyrénées-Orientales, which incorporates the Catalan cultural regions of **La Cerdanya** and **Rosselló**, and has its capital at Perpignan (Perpinyà in Catalan). Here, they represent 37 percent of the population, although only half of that figure claims a high proficiency level.

The **Cerdagne** and **Roussillon**, traditionally part of the realms of the Counts of Barcelona, were long disputed in border wars waged with the French. The French Crown took permanent control of the territory in the 1620s under Richelieu, but the land was not formally ceded by Spain until the Treaty of the Pyrenees (1649), negotiated by Louis XIV. Curiously, a fine reading of the text of the treaty allowed

Spain to maintain control of the town of Llívia, a few kilometres inside the French border, which has remained a Spanish enclave to this day.

Catalan, like Occitan, was a language of troubadours of the Middle Ages, and had a healthy tradition of narrative literature before Spanish or English. One of the most famous early Catalan works is the autobiographical *Llibre del fets* (Book of Deeds), written in the thirteenth century by the great count-king, **Jaume I the Conqueror**, son of Pere the Catholic, who was killed by Simon de Montfort at Muret. Throughout the Middle Ages, Catalan culture flourished thanks to the powerful maritime dominion of Barcelona. The count-king Joan I the Hunter (1387–96) instituted a Catalan version of the **Jocs Florals**, in imitation of the Occitan contest. Winners were given a real, rather than a golden flower – an early reflection perhaps of the famous Catalan frugality. But as happened to Occitan, the domination of a powerful "foreign" administration – in this case, the Hapsburgs of Madrid – contributed to the marginalization of the language, and literary usage declined after the fifteenth century.

The wave of regional and national consciousness that swept through Europe in the mid-nineteenth century affected Catalonia as well. Here the linguistic renaissance was spearheaded by the philologist **Pompeu Fabra i Poch**, who set about standardizing the Catalan grammar, and writers, such as the poet **Manuel Milà i Fontanals**. With the victory of strongly Castile-centric Franco in the Spanish Civil War, a stream of Catalan refugees spilled over the border into France, giving the native language and culture an additional boost in Roussillon and the Cerdagne. Catalan was eventually admitted to the state school curriculum, with mandatory instruction beginning in autumn 2006.

Today, however, while there is a lively Catalan culture in Catalonia proper, in Roussillon it is almost nonexistent. Some folkloric customs have survived the centuries of French domination, though, such as the distinctive **Christmas customs** (see box, p.279), and the penitents' processions of **Setmana Santa** (Holy Week). A recent addition is the **sardana**, a dance brought to Roussillon by the refugees of 1939, and a symbol of Catalan nationalism. Participants, frequently wearing the traditional woven *espardinya* shoes, form a circle linking hands and do a slow hopping dance to the minor strains of an eleven-piece *colbla* (orchestra).

The sizeable independence movement in Spanish Catalonia advocates the unification of all of the *Països Catalans*, including Roussillon and the Cerdagne, as a separate state. Indeed, the most potent symbol of Catalan identity, **Canigó** (*Canigou* in French), sits in French territory, between Prades and the border. An imposing mountain casting its shadow over all of Roussillon, it had long been venerated by the region's inhabitants when a monastery was founded on its slopes by the grandson of Guifré the Hairy in 1001. Over the centuries its symbolism intensified, and for Catalans it became their sacred mountain, celebrated in literature such as Jacint Verdaguer's epic *Canigó* of the late nineteenth century. To this day it is the site of a yearly midsummer torch-lit pilgrimage on the evening of June 23 to celebrate the *día de Sant Joan* (St John's Day).

The traditional pagan solstice holiday, celebrated here, as in many societies, by raising a great fire, stands as a Catalan "national" holiday, celebrated in both Spanish and French Catalonia. But aside from annoying graffiti on buildings and road signs, there is little evidence of nationalist fervour on the French side of the border. Although Catalan speakers of Roussillon, and even many non-speakers, delight in the distinctiveness which the region's diluted Catalan identity gives them, they tend to recall the revolts against the French merely for their sense of rose-tinted nostalgia.

STUDYING CATALAN

Naturally, the best place to **study Catalan** is in Catalonia proper, but if you are determined to do so in Roussillon, your best option is to take a course at **Prades'** Catalan summer university (☎ 04 68 96 34 51 and (34) 933 172 411, ⊕ uce.cat), which takes place during the last two weeks in August.

French

French can be a deceptively familiar language because of the number of words and structures it shares with English. Despite this, it's far from easy, though the bare essentials are not difficult to learn and can make all the difference. Even just saying "Bonjour Madame/Monsieur" and then gesticulating will usually get you a smile and helpful service. People working in tourist offices, hotels and so on, almost always speak English and tend to use it when you're struggling to speak French – be grateful, not insulted.

Of the **phrasebooks** and **dictionaries** available, the *Rough Guide Audio Phrasebook and Dictionary – French* is a handy and comprehensive e-book, with both English–French and French–English sections, along with an audio download to help with pronunciation, travel tips and a menu reader.

French pronunciation

One easy rule to remember is that consonants at the ends of words are usually silent. *Pas plus tard* (not later) is thus pronounced "pa-plu-tarr". But when the following word begins with a vowel, you run the two together: *pas après* (not after) becomes "pazaprey".

Vowels are the hardest sounds to get right. Roughly:

a	as in hat	o	as in hot
e	as in get	o, au	as in over
é	as in gate	ou	as in food
è	as in get	u	as in a pursed-lip version
eu	like the **u** in hurt		of use
i	as in machine		

More awkward are the combinations *in/im, en/em, an/am, on/om, un/um* at the ends of words, or followed by consonants other than *n* or *m*. Again, roughly:

in/im	like the **an** in **an**xious	on/om	like the **don** in **Don**caster
an/am,	like the **don** in **Don**caster		said by someone with a
en/em	when said with a nasal		heavy cold
	accent	un/um	like the **u** in **u**nderstand

Consonants are much as in English, except that: *ch* is always "sh"; *c* is "s" if followed by *e* or *i*, or if it has a cedilla beneath it (ç); *h* is silent; *th* is the same as "t", *ll* is like the "y" in yes; *w* is "v"; and *r* is growled (or rolled).

FRENCH WORDS AND PHRASES

BASIC VOCABULARY

French nouns are divided into masculine and feminine. This causes difficulties with adjectives, whose endings have to change to suit the gender of the nouns they qualify. If you know some grammar, you will know what to do. If not, stick to the masculine form, which is the simplest – it's what we have done in this glossary.

today	aujourd'hui
yesterday	hier
tomorrow	demain
in the morning	le matin
in the afternoon	l'après-midi
in the evening	le soir
now	maintenant

later	plus tard	big	grand
at one o'clock	à une heure	small	petit
at three o'clock	à trois heures	more	plus
at ten-thirty	à dix heures et demie	less	moins
at midday	à midi	a little	un peu
man	un homme	a lot	beaucoup
woman	une femme	cheap	bon marché
here	ici	expensive	cher
there	là	good	bon
this one	ceci	bad	mauvais
that one	celà	hot	chaud
open	ouvert	cold	froid
closed	fermé	with	avec

NUMBERS

1	un	21	vingt-et-un
2	deux	22	vingt-deux
3	trois	30	trente
4	quatre	40	quarante
5	cinq	50	cinquante
6	six	60	soixante
7	sept	70	soixante-dix
8	huit	75	soixante-quinze
9	neuf	80	quatre-vingts
10	dix	90	quatre-vingt-dix
11	onze	95	quatre-vingt-quinze
12	douze	100	cent
13	treize	101	cent un
14	quatorze	200	deux cents
15	quinze	300	trois cents
16	seize	500	cinq cents
17	dix-sept	1000	mille
18	dix-huit	2000	deux mille
19	dix-neuf	5000	cinq mille
20	vingt	1,000,000	un million

DAYS AND DATES

January	janvier	Sunday	dimanche
February	février	Monday	lundi
March	mars	Tuesday	mardi
April	avril	Wednesday	mercredi
May	mai	Thursday	jeudi
June	juin	Friday	vendredi
July	juillet	Saturday	samedi
August	août	August 1	le premier août
September	septembre	March 2	le deux mars
October	octobre	July 14	le quatorze juillet
November	novembre	November 23 2002	le vingt-trois novembre
December	décembre		deux mille deux

TALKING TO PEOPLE

When addressing people, you should always use *Monsieur* for a man, *Madame* for a woman, *Mademoiselle* for a young woman or girl. Plain *bonjour* by itself is not enough. This isn't as formal as it seems, and it has its uses when you've forgotten someone's name or want to attract someone's attention.

Excuse me	Pardon	OK/agreed	d'accord
Do you speak English?	Parlez-vous anglais?	please	s'il vous plaît
How do you say in French?	Comment ça se dit en français?	thank you	merci
		hello	bonjour
Comment vous appelez-vous?	What's your name?	goodbye	au revoir
My name is…	Je m'appelle…	good morning/ afternoon	bonjour
I'm English	Je suis anglais[e]	good evening	bonsoir
Irish	irlandaise[e]	good night	bonne nuit
Scottish	écossais[e]	How are you?	Comment allez-vous?/Ça va?
Welsh	gallois[e]		
American	américain[e]	Fine, thanks	Très bien, merci
Australian	australien[ne]	I don't know	Je ne sais pas
Canadian	canadien[ne]	Let's go	Allons-y
a New Zealander	néo-zélandais[e]	See you tomorrow	À demain
yes	oui	See you soon	À bientôt
no	non	Sorry	Pardon/Je m'excuse
I understand	Je comprends	Leave me alone	Fichez-moi la paix! (aggressive)
I don't understand	Je ne comprends pas		
Can you speak more slowly?	S'il vous plaît, parlez moins vite	Please help me	Aidez-moi, s'il vous plaît

FINDING THE WAY

bus	autobus/bus/car	hitchhiking	autostop
bus station	gare routière	on foot	à pied
bus stop	arrêt	Where are you going?	Vous allez où?
car	voiture	I'm going to…	Je vais à…
train/taxi/ferry	train/taxi/ferry	I want to get off at…	Je voudrais descendre à…
boat	bâteau		
plane	avion	the road to…	la route pour…
train station	gare (SNCF)	near	près/pas loin
platform	quai	far	loin
What time does it leave?	Il part à quelle heure?	left	à gauche
		right	à droite
What time does it arrive?	Il arrive à quelle heure?	straight on	tout droit
		on the other side of	à l'autre côté de
a ticket to…	un billet pour…	on the corner of	à l'angle de
single ticket	aller simple	next to	à côté de
return ticket	aller-retour	behind	derrière
validate your ticket	compostez votre billet	in front of	devant
valid for	valable pour	before	avant
ticket office	billeterie/vente de billets	after	après
		under	sous
how many kilometres?	combien de kilomètres?	to cross	traverser
how many hours?	combien d'heures?	bridge	pont

QUESTIONS AND REQUESTS

The simplest way of asking a question or making requests is to start with *s'il vous plaît* (please), then name the thing you want in an interrogative tone of voice. For example:

| Where is there a bakery? | S'il vous plaît, la boulangerie? | Can we have a room for two? | S'il vous plaît, une chambre pour deux? |
| Which way is it to the Maison Carrée? | S'il vous plaît, pour aller à la Maison Carrée? | Can I have a kilo of oranges? | S'il vous plaît, un kilo d'oranges? |

Question words:		when?	quand?
where?	où?	why?	pourquoi?
how?	comment?	at what time?	à quelle heure?
how many/how much?	combien?	what is/which is?	quel est?

ACCOMMODATION

a room for one/two people	une chambre pour une/deux personnes	hairdryer	sèche-cheveux
a double bed	un grand lit	blankets	couvertures
a room with a shower	une chambre avec douche	quiet	calme
		noisy	bruyant
a room with a bath	une chambre avec salle de bain	hot water	eau chaude
		cold water	eau froide
for one/two/three	pour une/deux/trois nuits	Is breakfast included?	Est-ce que le petit déjeuner est compris?
Can I see it?	Je peux la voir?	I would like…	Je voudrais prendre
sheets	draps	breakfast	le petit déjeuner
to book	réserver	I don't want…	Je ne veux pas de…
a room on the courtyard	une chambre sur la cour	breakfast	petit déjeuner
first floor	premier étage	Can we camp here?	On peut camper ici?
second floor	deuxième étage	campsite	un camping/terrain de camping
with a view	avec vue	tent	tente
key	clé	tent pitch	emplacement
an iron	fer à repasser	youth hostel	auberge de Jeunesse
launderette	une laverie		

CARS

service station	station-service	put air in the tyres	gonfler les pneus
to park the car	garer la voiture	battery	batterie
car park	un parking	the battery is dead	la batterie est morte
no parking	défense de stationer/ stationnement interdit	spark-plugs	bougies
		to break down	tomber en panne
petrol station	station essence	petrol can	bidon
fuel	essence	insurance	assurance
(to) fill it up	faire le plein	green card	carte verte
oil	huile	traffic lights	feux
air line	ligne à air	red light	feu rouge
		green light	feu vert

HEALTH MATTERS

doctor	médecin	I have a headache	J'ai mal à la tête
I don't feel well	Je ne me sens pas bien	stomach ache	mal à l'estomac
		pain	douleur
medicines	médicaments	it hurts	ça fait mal
prescription	ordonnance	chemist	pharmacie
I feel sick	J'ai la nausée	hospital	hôpital

OTHER NEEDS

bakery	boulangerie	tobacconist	tabac
food shop	alimentation	stamps	timbres
supermarket	supermarché	bank	banque
to eat	manger	money	argent
to drink	boire	toilets	toilettes
camping gas	camping gaz		

MENU READER

BASIC FOOD TERMS

l'addition	bill/check
beurre	butter
bouteille	bottle
chauffé	heated
couteau	knife
cru	raw
cuillère	spoon
cuit	cooked
emballé	wrapped
à emporter	takeaway
fourchette	fork
fumé	smoked
huile	oil
lait	milk
moutarde	mustard
œuf	egg
pain	bread
poivre	pepper
salé	salted/spicy
sel	salt
sucre	sugar
sucré	sweet
table	table
verre	glass
vinaigre	vinegar

SNACKS

Un sandwich/une baguette	a sandwich
au jambon	with ham
au fromage	with cheese
au saucisson	with sausage
à l'ail	with garlic
au poivre	with pepper
au pâté	with pâté
croque-monsieur	grilled cheese and ham sandwich
croque-madame	grilled cheese and ham sandwich with a fried egg
pan bagnat	bread roll with egg, olives, salad, tuna, anchovies and olive oil
tartine	buttered bread or open sandwich
œufs	eggs
au plat	fried
à la coque	boiled
durs	hard-boiled
brouillés	scrambled
omelette	omelette
nature	plain
aux fines herbes	with herbs
au fromage	with cheese

PASTA (*PÂTES*), PANCAKES (*CRÊPES*) AND FLANS (*TARTES*)

nouilles	noodles
pâtes fraîches	fresh pasta
crêpe	sweet pancake
galette	savoury pancake made with buckwheat
socca	thin chickpea flour pancake
panisse	thick chickpea flour pancake
pissaladière	tart of fried onions with anchovies and black olives
tarte flambée	thin pizza-like pastry topped with onion, cream and bacon

SOUPS (*SOUPES*)

bisque	shellfish soup
bouillabaisse	soup/stew with chunks of assorted fish
bouillon	broth or stock
bourride	thick fish soup with vegetables
consommé	clear soup
pistou	parmesan, basil and garlic paste, added to soup
potage	thick vegetable soup
rouille	red pepper, garlic and saffron mayonnaise served with fish soup
soupe à l'oignon	onion soup with bread and cheese topping
velouté	light, velvety soup

STARTERS (*HORS D'ŒUVRES*)

assiette de charcuterie	plate of cold meats
crudités	raw vegetables with dressings
hors d'œuvres	appetizers

FISH (*POISSON*), SEAFOOD (*FRUITS DE MER*) AND SHELLFISH (*CRUSTACÉS* OR *COQUILLAGES*)

aiglefin	small haddock or fresh cod
anchois	anchovies
anguilles	eels
barbue	brill

baudroie (lotte)	monkfish
bigorneau	periwinkle
brème	bream
bulot	whelk
cabillaud	cod
calmar	squid
carrelet	plaice
colin	hake
congre	conger eel
coques	cockles
crabe	crab
crevettes grises	shrimp
crevettes roses	prawns
daurade	sea bream
éperlan	smelt or whitebait
escargots	snails
flétan	halibut
friture	assorted fried fish
gambas	king prawns
hareng	herring
homard	lobster
huîtres	oysters
langouste	spiny lobster
langoustine	saltwater crayfish
limande	lemon sole
lotte	monkfish
loup de mer	sea bass
maquereau	mackerel
merlan	whiting
moules (marinières)	mussels (with shallots in white wine sauce)
oursin	sea urchin
palourdes	clams
poissons de roche	fish from shore-line rocks
raie	skate
rouget	red mullet
saumon	salmon
sole	sole
St-Jacques	scallops
thon	tuna
truite	trout
turbot	turbot
violet	sea squirt

FISH DISHES AND TERMS

aïoli	garlic mayonnaise served with salt cod and other fish
anchoïade	anchovy paste or sauce
arête	fish bone
assiette du pêcheur	assorted fish
beignet	fritter
darne	fillet or steak
la douzaine	a dozen
frit	fried
friture	deep-fried small fish
fumé	smoked
grillé	grilled
hollandaise	sauce made with egg yolks, butter and lemon juice
à la meunière	in a butter, lemon and parsley sauce
mousse/mousseline	mousse
pané	breaded
poutargue	mullet roe paste
raïto	sauce of red wine, tomatos, olives and capers
quenelles	light dumplings
thermidor	lobster grilled in its shell with cream sauce

MEAT (*VIANDE*) AND POULTRY (*VOLAILLE*)

agneau (de pré-salé)	lamb (grazed on salt marshes)
andouille, andouillette	tripe sausage
bifteck	steak
bœuf	beef
boudin blanc	sausage made of various cuts of pork
boudin noir	black pudding
caille	quail
canard	duck
caneton	duckling
contrefilet	sirloin roast
coquelet	cockerel
dinde, dindon	turkey
entrecôte	rib steak
faux filet	sirloin steak
foie	liver
foie gras	(duck/goose) liver
gigot (d'agneau)	leg (of lamb)
grenouilles (cuisses de)	frogs (legs)
langue	tongue
lapin, lapereau	rabbit, young rabbit
lard, lardons	bacon, diced bacon
merguez	spicy, red sausage
mouton	mutton
museau de veau	calf's muzzle
oie	goose
onglet	prime cut of beef
os	bone
poitrine	breast
porc	pork
poulet	chicken
poussin	baby chicken
ris	sweetbreads
rognons	kidneys

rognons blancs	testicles	marmite	casserole
sanglier	wild boar	médaillon	round piece
steak	steak	mijoté	stewed
tête de veau	calf's head (in jelly)	ollada	pork-based soup from Roussillon
tournedos	thick slices of fillet		
tripes	tripe	pavé	thick slice
tripoux	mutton tripe	périgourdin	prunes, foie gras and truffles
veau	veal		
venaison	venison	pieds et paquets	mutton or pork tripe and trotters

MEAT AND POULTRY DISHES AND TERMS

aile	wing	poêlé	pan-fried
au feu de bois	cooked over wood fire	poulet de Bresse	chicken from Bresse – the best
au four	baked		
blanquette, daube, estouffade, hochepôt, navarin, ragoût	types of stew	rôti	roast
		sauté	lightly cooked in butter
		steak au poivre	steak with a black peppercorn sauce
blanquette de veau	veal in cream and mushroom sauce		
		steak tartare	raw chopped beef, topped with a raw egg yolk
bœuf bourguignon	beef stew with red wine, onions and mushrooms		
		tagine	North African casserole
botifarra	pork sausage from Roussillon	tournedos rossini	beef fillet with foie gras and truffles
brochette	skewer		
canard à l'orange	roast duck with an orange and wine sauce	viennoise	fried in egg and breadcrumbs
cargolada	dish of grilled land snails from Roussillon	**TERMS FOR STEAKS**	
		bleu	almost raw
carré	best end of neck, chop or cutlet	saignant	rare
		à point	medium
choucroute	pickled cabbage with peppercorns, sausages, bacon and salami	bien cuit	well done
		très bien cuit	very well done
civet	rabbit stew	**GARNISHES AND SAUCES**	
confit de canard	preserved duck	béarnaise	sauce of egg yolks, butter and tarragon
coq au vin	chicken cooked until it falls off the bone, with wine, onions and mush rooms		
		beurre blanc	sauce of white wine and shallots, with butter
		bonne femme	sauce with crème fraîche, fish stock, white wine, butter and shallots
côte	chop, cutlet or rib		
cou	neck	bordelaise	in a red wine, shallot and bone-marrow sauce
cuisse	thigh or leg		
embutit	pork sausage from Roussillon	chasseur	white wine, mushrooms and shallots
en croûte	in pastry	diable	strong mustard and tabasco seasoning
épaule	shoulder		
farci	stuffed	forestière	with bacon and mushrooms
garni	with vegetables		
gésier	gizzard	fricassée	rich, creamy sauce
grillade	grilled meat	mornay	cheese sauce
grillé	grilled	périgourdine	with foie gras and possibly truffles
hâchis	chopped meat or mince hamburger		
		piquante	gherkins or capers, vinegar and shallots
magret de canard	duck breast		

provençale	tomatoes, garlic, olives, oil and herbs

VEGETABLES (*LÉGUMES*), HERBS (*HERBES*) AND SPICES (*ÉPICES*)

ail	garlic
anis	aniseed
artichaut	artichoke
asperges	asparagus
avocat	avocado
basilic	basil
betterave	beetroot
blette/bette	Swiss chard
cannelle	cinnamon
câpre	caper
cardon	cardoon, closely related to artichoke
carotte	carrot
céleri	celery
champignon, cèpe, chanterelle	types of mushrooms
chou (rouge)	(red) cabbage
choufleur	cauliflower
concombre	cucumber
cornichon	gherkin
échalotes	shallots
endive	chicory
épinards	spinach
estragon	tarragon
fenouil	fennel
férigoule	thyme (in Provençal)
fèves	broad beans
flageolets	white beans
gingembre	ginger
haricots (verts, rouges, beurres)	beans (French/string, kidney, butter)
laurier	bay leaf
lentilles	lentils
maïs	corn
menthe	mint
moutarde	mustard
oignon	onion
panais	parsnip
persil	parsley
petits pois	peas
piment	pimento
pois chiche	chick peas
pois mange-tout	mangetout
pignons	pine nuts
poireau	leek
poivron (vert, rouge)	sweet pepper (green, red)
pommes de terre	potatoes

primeurs	spring vegetables
radis	radish
riz	rice
safran	saffron
salade verte	green salad
tomate	tomato
truffes	truffles

VEGETABLE DISHES AND TERMS

alicot	puréed potato with cheese
allumettes	very thin chips
à la vapeur	boiled
beignet	fritter
biologique	organic
boulangère	fine layers of potatoes and onion soaked in stock and baked
farci	stuffed
feuille	leaf
fines herbes	mixture of tarragon, parsley and chives
gratiné	browned with cheese or butter
gratin dauphinois	sliced potatoes in a cream and cheese sauce baked in the oven
à la grecque	cooked in oil and lemon
jardinière	with mixed diced vegetables
mousseline	mashed potato with cream and eggs
à la parisienne	sautéed in butter (potatoes); with white wine sauce and shallots
parmentier	pie topped with potato mash
petits farcis	stuffed tomatoes, aubergines, courgettes and peppers
pimenté	peppery hot
piquant	spicy
pistou	ground basil, olive oil, garlic and parmesan
râpée	grated or shredded

FRUIT (*FRUIT*) AND NUTS (*NOIX*)

abricot	apricot
noix de cajou	cashew nut
amande	almond
ananas	pineapple
banane	banana
nectarine	nectarine
cacahouète	peanut

cassis	blackcurrant
cerise	cherry
citron	lemon
citron vert	lime
datte	date
figue	fig
fraise (des bois)	strawberry (wild)
framboise	raspberry
fruit de la passion	passion fruit
grenade	pomegranate
groseille	redcurrant
mangue	mango
marron	chestnut
melon	melon
mirabelle	small yellow plum
myrtille	bilberry
noisette	hazelnut
noix	nuts
orange	orange
pamplemousse	grapefruit
pastèque	watermelon
pêche	peach
pistache	pistachio
poire	pear
pomme	apple
prune	plum
pruneau	prune
raisin	grape
reine-claude	greengage

FRUIT DISHES AND TERMS

agrumes	citrus fruits
beignet	fritter
compôte	stewed fruit
coulis	sauce of puréed fruit
crème de marrons	chestnut purée
flambé	set aflame in alcohol
fougasse	type of bread, can be savoury or sweet
frappé	iced

DESSERTS (*DESSERTS* OR *ENTREMETS*) AND PASTRIES (*PÂTISSERIE*)

barquette	small boat-shaped flan
bavarois	refers to the mould, could be a mousse or custard
bombe	rounded ice-cream dessert
brioche	sweet, light breakfast roll
calisson	almond sweet
charlotte	custard and fruit in lining of almond fingers
chichi	long, thin doughnut
clafoutis	tart with fruit (usually cherries) coverd in a heavy batter and baked
coupe	a serving of ice cream
crème Chantilly	vanilla-flavoured and sweetened whipped cream
crème fraîche	sour cream
crème pâtissière	thick, eggy pastry-filling
crêpe suzette	thin pancake with orange juice and liqueur
flan/crema catalana	thick custard dessert
fromage blanc	thick cheese, like yoghurt
gaufre	waffle
gênoise	rich sponge cake
glace	ice cream
île flottante/oeuf à la neige	soft meringues floating in custard
macaron	macaroon
madeleine	small sponge cake
Mont Blanc	chestnut purée and cream on a rum-soaked sponge cake
mousse au chocolat	chocolate mousse
omelette norvégienne	baked Alaska
palmier	caramelized puff pastry
parfait	frozen mousse, sometimes ice cream
pâte	pastry or dough
petits fours	bite-sized cakes/pastries
poires belle hélène	pears and ice cream in chocolate sauce
sablé	shortbread biscuit
savarin	a filled, ring-shaped cake
tarte	tart
tarte tatin	caramelized apple tart
tarte tropézienne	sponge cake filled with custard cream topped with nuts
tartelette	small tart
yaourt	yoghurt

Architectural glossary

ambulatory passage round the outer edge of a church's choir

apse semicircular termination at the east end of a church

Art Deco geometrical style of art and architecture popular in the 1920s and 30s

Art Nouveau ornamental style of art and architecture which developed in the late nineteenth century, emphasizing decorative detail

artesonado Spanish-style cabinet-work ceiling

Baroque High Renaissance period of art and architecture, distinguished by extreme ornateness

bas-relief stone carving with a shallow three-dimensional aspect ("high relief" sculpture has very pronounced depth)

Carolingian dynasty founded by Pepin the Short; mid-eighth to early tenth centuries, named after its finest king, Charles the Great (Charlemagne); also refers to art, sculpture, etc of the time

caryatid sculpted female figure used as a column

chapterhouse room in a monastery or church where the clergy met daily to discuss business

chevet east end of a church

Classical architectural style incorporating Greek and Roman elements (such as pillars, domes, and colonnades), at its height in France in the seventeenth century and revived in the nineteenth century as Neoclassicism

clerestory upper windowed storey of a church

crenellation battlements along a wall or tower

Cubism early twentieth-century art movement which used overlapping planes and geometric shapes in defiance of pictorial perception

curtain wall straight upright medieval defensive wall

dolmen Neolithic stone formation, frequently consisting of a henge

faïence porcelain and glazed earthenware decoration

Fauvism artistic school of early twentieth-century France, characterized by vivid colour

fin-de-siècle referring to the end of the nineteenth-century

folly overly ostentatious rural buildings of seventeenth- to nineteenth-century aristocracy

fresco wall painting applied to wet plaster

frieze sculpted decorative band, typically along the upper or lower limit of a wall, and usually in low relief

Gothic architectural style of the thirteenth to sixteenth centuries, characterized by pointed arches, rib vaulting, flying buttresses, broad windowed surfaces and a general emphasis on verticality

Impressionism late nineteenth-century French style of painting which emphasized the perception of objects through the effect of light, rather than shape

majesté Romanesque and early Gothic sculptures of Christ on the Cross (*majestat* in Catalan)

Merovingian dynasty ruling France and parts of Germany from the sixth to mid-eighth centuries; also refers to art, etc of the period

Mozarabic Arab- and North African-influenced art and architectural style from Spain, brought to France around 900–1100 by Christians

narthex entrance hall of a church

nave main body of a church

nymphaeum Roman or Greek shrine to a nymph, typically located at a fountainhead or spring

oppidum pre-Roman hill-top settlement

opus mixtum Roman building technique consisting of interspersed layers of stone and brick

Orientalism study of Eastern and, particularly, Middle Eastern peoples from a Western and usually imperialistic and heavily romanticized perspective

pantocrator depiction of Jesus as "Lord of all Creation"

polychrome painted in colour

refectory dining room of a monastery

relief the three-dimensional quality of a sculpture; its depth

Renaissance artistic/architectural movement developed in fifteenth-century Italy and imported to France in the sixteenth century

retable altarpiece

Romanesque early medieval architectural style distinguished by squat forms and naive sculpture

rood screen barrier set in some churches between the area of the altar and choir and the rest of the nave (where the main congregation gathers)

sarcophagus Latin for "coffin," referring to carved stone tombs

stucco plaster used to embellish ceilings, etc

Surrealism early twentieth-century art movement whose apparently irrational juxtaposition of contrasting images expressed subconscious thoughts

transept transverse arms of a church

tribune apse containing a bishop's throne; a gallery or raised area in a church

trompe l'oeil decorative technique popular in the Baroque period, wherein a 2-D painting gives the impression of being a 3-D object

tumulus Neolithic burial mound, frequently concealing a dolmen

tympanum a sculpted panel above a church door

vault an arched ceiling or roof

voussoir sculpted wedge-shaped stones in the arch over a church door

Small print and index

Rough Guide credits

Editor: Neil McQuillian
Layout: Anita Singh
Cartography: Richard Marchi
Picture editor: Marta Bescos
Proofreader: Stewart J. Wild
Managing editor: Monica Woods
Assistant editor: Payal Sharotri

Production: Jimmy Lao
Cover photo research: Roger Mapp
Editorial assistant: Aimee White
Senior DTP coordinator: Dan May
Programme manager: Gareth Lowe

Publishing information

This fifth edition published 2017

Distribution

UK, Ireland and Europe
Apa Publications (UK) Ltd; sales@roughguides.com
United States and Canada
Ingram Publisher Services; ips@ingramcontent.com
Australia and New Zealand
Woodslane; info@woodslane.com.au
Southeast Asia
Apa Publications (SN) Pte; sales@roughguides.com
Worldwide
Apa Publications (UK) Ltd; sales@roughguides.com
Special Sales, Content Licensing and CoPublishing
Rough Guides can be purchased in bulk quantities
at discounted prices. We can create special editions,
personalised jackets and corporate imprints tailored to
your needs. sales@roughguides.com.
roughguides.com
Printed in China
All rights reserved

© Brian Catlos, 2017
Maps © 2018 Apa Digital (CH) AG
License edition © Apa Publications Ltd UK
Foix weather statistics (p.11) © Ariège tourist office
All rights reserved. No part of this publication may be
reproduced, stored in or introduced into a retrieval system,
or transmitted in any form, or by any means (electronic,
mechanical, photocopying, recording or otherwise) without
the prior written permission of the copyright owner.
352pp includes index
A catalogue record for this book is available from the
British Library
ISBN: 978-0-24127-393-7
The publishers and authors have done their best to ensure
the accuracy and currency of all the information in **The
Rough Guide to Languedoc & Roussillon**, however,
they can accept no responsibility for any loss, injury, or
inconvenience sustained by any traveller as a result of
information or advice contained in the guide.

Help us update

We've gone to a lot of effort to ensure that the fifth edition
of **The Rough Guide to Languedoc & Roussillon** is
accurate and up-to-date. However, things change – places
get "discovered", opening hours are notoriously fickle,
restaurants and rooms raise prices or lower standards. If
you feel we've got it wrong or left something out, we'd like
to know, and if you can remember the address, the price,
the hours, the phone number, so much the better.

Please send your comments with the subject line
"Rough Guide Languedoc & Roussillon Update" to
mail@uk.roughguides.com. We'll credit all contributions
and send a copy of the next edition (or any other Rough
Guide if you prefer) for the very best emails.

A ROUGH GUIDE TO ROUGH GUIDES

Published in 1982, the first Rough Guide – to Greece – was a student scheme that became a
publishing phenomenon. Mark Ellingham, a recent graduate in English from Bristol University, had
been travelling in Greece the previous summer and couldn't find the right guidebook. With a
small group of friends he wrote his own guide, combining a contemporary, journalistic style with a
thoroughly practical approach to travellers' needs.

The immediate success of the book spawned a series that rapidly covered dozens of
destinations. And, in addition to impecunious backpackers, Rough Guides soon acquired a
much broader readership that relished the guides' wit and inquisitiveness as much as their
enthusiastic, critical approach and value-for-money ethos. These days, Rough Guides include
recommendations from budget to luxury and cover more than 120 destinations around the
globe, from Amsterdam to Zanzibar, all regularly updated by our team of roaming writers.

Browse all our latest guides, read inspirational features and book your trip at **roughguides.com**.

ABOUT THE AUTHORS

Brian Catlos spent years travelling across five continents, studying and working as – among other things – a coffee-shop runner in Amsterdam, a tree-planter in Canada and a motorbike courier in London. A professor of Religious Studies at the University of Colorado, he is the author of award-winning scholarly and popular history books. He now lives in Spain and the US. Brian has been writing on Languedoc and Roussillon since 1998.

Victoria Trott is a freelance travel and food writer who specializes in France. A graduate in French and Spanish from Leeds University, she has worked as an au pair in Annecy and the Camargue, taught English in Lyon, managed a chalet company in Courchevel and helped run the villa of an American billionaire on Cap Ferrat. She has written or updated guidebooks on Paris, Brittany, Burgundy and most of the south of France, and writes for a variety of national and international media.

Acknowledgements

Victoria Trott I would like to thank everyone who has assisted me with writing and researching this guide but in particular Mado Goncalves at ADT Ariège Pyrénées, Christian Rivière at Tarn Tourisme, Miriam Fillaquier at ADT Aude, Sabrina Lucchese at ADT Hérault, Valerie Crouineau at Gard Tourisme, Nathalie Lacomme at CDT Haute-Garonne, Sarah Seguy at Carcassonne tourist office, Emilie Pennings at Lunel tourist office and Amanda Monroe at Voyages SNCF. At Rough Guides, I would like to thank Rachel Fox for recommending me for the job, Monica Woods for hiring me, and Neil McQuillian, my editor, for being very easy to work with.

Readers' updates

Thanks to all the readers who have taken the time to write in with comments and suggestions (and apologies if we've inadvertently omitted or misspelt anyone's name):

Adam Barwell; Hugh Bennett; James Boulger; Valerie and Craig Charlesworth; Kenneth Collins; Peter Dorfman; Caroline Duff; David Dunn; Barbara Fitzgibbon; Karen Gething; Peter King; Claude Nurse; Collette O'Connor; Marian Smith; Anthony Spellman; Mike Starkey; James Thomas.

Photo credits

All photos © Rough Guides, except the following:
(Key: t-top; c-centre; b-bottom; l-left; r-right)

1 Alamy Stock Photo: Zoonar GmbH
2 Alamy Stock Photo: Hemis
4 Alamy Stock Photo: JAUBERT French Collection
5 Alamy Stock Photo: Hemis
8 Alamy Stock Photo: Christophe Boisvieux
9 Alamy Stock Photo: Didier ZYLBERYNG (c); Hemis (t). **Office de Tourisme de Sète** (b)
11 SuperStock: Jean-Marc Barrere
12 Alamy Stock Photo: robertharding
13 Alamy Stock Photo: Hemis (c, b). **Dreamstime.com:** Photoprofi30 (t)
14 Alamy Stock Photo: A Media Press (c). **Dreamstime.com:** Bjulien03 (b). **SuperStock:** Didier Zylberyng (t)
15 4Corners: SIME / Matteo Carassale (br). **Alamy Stock Photo:** Didier Zylberyng (t). **Dreamstime.com:** Richard Semik (bl)
16 Alamy Stock Photo: guichaoua (b). **Getty Images:** Print Collector (t)
17 Alamy Stock Photo: Hemis (b). **Dreamstime.com:** Surz01 (c). **Getty Images:** Print Collector (t)
18 Alamy Stock Photo: Ivoha (tl); Chris Lewington (tr)
20 Alamy Stock Photo: Radius Images
48–49 Alamy Stock Photo: Ian Dagnall
51 AWL Images: Hemis
63 Alamy Stock Photo: Arco Images GmbH (b); Hemis (t)
73 Alamy Stock Photo: Horizon Images / Motion (t). **Dreamstime.com:** Dulsita (b)
84–85 Dreamstime.com: Delstudio
87 Alamy Stock Photo: David Muscroft

99 Alamy Stock Photo: Hemis (b); Paul Quayle (t)
113 Alamy Stock Photo: Thierry Grun / Aero (t); Chris Lewington (b)
124–125 Alamy Stock Photo: Wim Wiskerke
127 Robert Harding Picture Library: Neil Emmerson
143 Alamy Stock Photo: age fotostock (b). **Dreamstime.com:** Claudio Giovanni Colombo (t)
162–163 Dreamstime.com: Stevanzz
165 Alamy Stock Photo: Ben Ramos
181 Alamy Stock Photo: Hemis (b). **Getty Images:** AFP (t)
191 Alamy Stock Photo: Lucas Vallecillos (t). **Dreamstime.com:** Richard Semik (b)
202–203 Alamy Stock Photo: David South
205 Dreamstime.com: Claudio Giovanni Colombo
223 Alamy Stock Photo: Hemis (t). **Dreamstime.com:** Photoprofi30 (b)
238–239 Dreamstime.com: Amoklv
241 Dreamstime.com: Grantotufo
247 Alamy Stock Photo: Hemis (t); Paul Quayle (b)
259 Alamy Stock Photo: Hemis
270–271 Dreamstime.com: Leonid Andronov
273 Dreamstime.com: David May
291 Alamy Stock Photo: Iain Frazer (t). **Dreamstime.com:** Thomas Dutour (b)
308 Getty Images: DeAgostini

Cover: Old town street, Collioure **AWL Images:** Stefano Politi Markovina

Index

Maps are marked in grey

Map symbols

The symbols below are used on maps throughout the book

– – – –	Chapter boundary	⌣	Mountain pass	🎿	Skiing
▬▬ ▪ ▪	International boundary	⌇	Gorge/cliff face	Ⓣ	Tram stop
▬▬ ▪ ▪	Regional boundary	⌒	Cave	Ⓜ	Metro station
⫿⫿⫿⫿⫿	Steps	∿	Spring	★	Bus stop
▬▬▬	Motorway	∴	Ruins	⊠–⊠	Gate
⋯⋯	Road	杂	Lighthouse	@	Internet café
▒▒▒	Pedestrianized street	⊙	Statue	P	Parking
▭▬▭	Railway	♔	Castle	✚	Hospital
⋉⋉⋉⋉	Tourist railway	🏛	Monument	ⓘ	Tourist office
– – – –	Footpath	▮	Tower	⊠	Post office
— —	Ferry route	▮	Fortress		Building
⋯⋯	River	♦	Museum		Church (town maps)
◆	Point of interest	⌂	Abbey		Park/forest
▲	Mountain peak	⌂	Monastery	✝✝	Cemetery
⌃⌃	Mountain range	✝	Church (regional maps)		Saltpan
⌂	Mountain refuge	✈	Airport		Beach

Listings key

▪	Accommodation
●	Eating
▪	Drinking/nightlife
●	Shopping

ESCAPE THE EVERYDAY

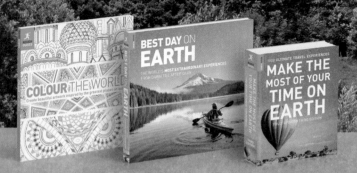

ADVENTURE BECKONS
YOU JUST NEED TO KNOW WHERE TO LOOK

roughguides.com